Third Edition

ADULT DEVELOPMENT
AND AGING
MYTHS AND EMERGING REALITIES

Richard Schulz
University of Pittsburgh

Timothy Salthouse
University of Michigan

Prentice Hall, Upper Saddle River, New Jersey 07458

Library of Congress Cataloging-in-Publication Data

Schulz, Richard
    Adult development and aging : myths and emerging realities /
Richard Schulz and Timothy Salthouse. — 3rd ed.
        p.   cm.
    Includes bibliographical references and index.
    ISBN   0-13-080766-4
    1. Adulthood—Psychological aspects.   2. Aging—Psychological
aspects.   I. Salthouse, Timothy.   II. Title.
BF724.5.S38   1999
155.6—dc21   98-30673
                                                              CIP

Acquisitions Editor: Jennifer Gilliland
Assistant Editor: Anita Castro
Senior Managing Editor: Bonnie Biller
Production Editor: Joan E. Foley
Copyeditor: Anne F. Lesser
Editorial Assistant: Kate Ramunda
Prepress and Manufacturing Buyer: Tricia Kenny
Cover Art Director: Jayne Conte
Cover Art: George Tooker (b. 1920), "Mirror II," 1963. Egg tempura on gesso panel, 20 in. X 20 in.
        1968.4. Gift of R. H. Donnelley Erdman (PA 1956). Copyright Addison Gallery of
        American Art, Phillips Academy, Andover, Massachusetts. (Photo by Greg Heins) All rights reserved.
Photo Researcher: Beth Boyd
Line Art Coordinator: Guy Ruggiero
Illustrator: Hadel Studio

For permission to use copyrighted material, grateful
acknowledgment is made to the copyright holders listed
on page 407, which is considered an extension of this
copyright page.

This book was set in 10/12 Usherwood by Pub-Set,
and was printed and bound by R. R. Donnelley & Sons Co.
The cover was printed by Phoenix Color Corp.

ISBN 0-13-080766-4

Prentice-Hall International (UK) Limited, *London*
Prentice-Hall of Australia Pty. Limited, *Sydney*
Prentice-Hall Canada Inc., *Toronto*
Prentice-Hall Hispanoamerica, S.A., *Mexico*
Prentice-Hall of India Private Limited, *New Delhi*
Prentice-Hall of Japan, Inc., *Tokyo*
Simon & Schuster Asia Pte. Ltd., *Singapore*
Editora Prentice-Hall do Brasil, Ltda., *Rio de Janeiro*

CONTENTS

PART II
PHYSICAL AND COGNITIVE DEVELOPMENT

3   Physical Aspects of Aging   43

4   Sensation and Perception   80

5 Memory 108

6 Intelligence and Cognition 134

PART III
PERSONALITY AND SOCIAL DEVELOPMENT

7 Personality and Theories of Life-Span Development 160

8   Relationships and Interpersonal Behavior   190

9   Work and Retirement   236

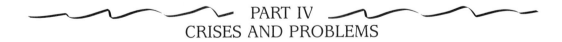

PART IV
CRISES AND PROBLEMS

10   Stress and Coping   270

PREFACE

The study of adult development and aging is a young but rapidly growing science. Although we know much more about this area today than we did a decade ago, many of us still subscribe to unfounded myths about adult development and aging. One of the major goals of this book is to contrast existing myths about adult development with the best available empirical data, in order to separate fiction from fact. To this end, we have summarized and synthesized the most current research literature available at the time of the writing of this third edition.

Much of what we know about adult development is emergent: We have some understanding of this complex process, but definitive answers are not always available. Indeed, we may never have definitive answers to some questions, because the answers change along with changes in the social and technological environments within which individuals develop. We thus identify many important questions for which the existing empirical data are still speculative. New information may quickly alter existing conceptions of the field.

Writing a book on adult development and aging inevitably raises the question, Should individual chapters be organized by chronological age or by topic?

We have opted for the latter strategy because age per se is not necessarily a good marker of adult development, and we believe the complexity and diversity of this material is easier to understand when organized by topic. Although our choice of topics is heavily influenced by our backgrounds in psychology and gerontology, we have not ignored important biological, sociological, and medical contributions to our understanding of adult development and aging. This book covers traditional psychological topics, such as sensation and perception, memory and learning, intelligence and creativity, and psychopathology; but it also includes separate chapters on stress and coping, social relationships, and work and retirement.

Our approach differs from existing topical treatments of adult development in that we provide the reader with a fundamental understanding of a particular topic and the most current age-related data. For example, in discussing memory and cognition, we offer sufficient background information on relevant theories and research methods to enable the reader to appreciate how research on age-related changes has evolved and to understand the significance of the most current findings.

For this third edition, all chapters have been extensively revised and updated. The chapters on memory, and intelligence and cognition, have been completely rewritten to reflect the perspective and expertise of the co-author, Timothy Salthouse. Although we must take responsibility for any errors in this book, we benefited immensely from the feedback and suggestions provided for this edition by reviewers Barbara R. Bjorkland, Florida Atlantic University, and Naomi Wentworth, Lake Forest College.

This book also includes several valuable aids designed to make this complex, interdisciplinary body of knowledge more accessible to the reader. Each chapter (except chapter 2, which discusses research methods) contains a feature called "Myths About Aging" that highlights key issues and contrasts old beliefs with current views. At the end of each chapter is a summary of major concepts and a list of terms to remember, which are clearly defined in the Glossary. This edition also features study questions at the end of each chapter, which are designed to promote critical thinking. A lengthy reference list enables students and instructors to pursue in-depth topics of special interest. Finally, the Instructor's Manual is available to all teachers who adopt the text. It includes an extensive list of multiple-choice and discussion questions for each chapter, cumulative exams, learning objectives, and suggested readings rated by level of difficulty.

In sum, this book is designed for those who value textbooks based on the best available current data and who appreciate that knowledge about adult development is in a state of flux, with new information becoming available almost daily. This book will especially appeal to instructors who want to encourage their students' critical thinking skills and ability to understand and use research-based knowledge, along with conventional wisdom, as the basis for thought and action.

Our knowledge of adult development and aging is advancing at an incredibly rapid pace. This is particularly true in the health, biological, and cognitive sciences. Although tracking and understanding these advances is a formidable challenge, it is an exciting time to be studying this topic. We have probably learned more about the nuts and bolts of adult development and aging in the last decade than we have in all of previous recorded history. We hope our enthusiasm for this topic is conveyed by this book and that new generations of students will follow the path we did and choose the study of aging as their life's work.

Richard Schulz

Timothy Salthouse

INTRODUCTION

At any given point in our lives we know a great deal about where we've been, and we have a pretty good idea about where we are headed. It may be impossible to predict with certainty how our lives will unfold, but we have a strong sense of the major milestones we will encounter and the life experiences that lie ahead of us. We know, for example, that we'll embark on our first important job sometime in our 20s, have children in our late 20s and 30s, perhaps become grandparents in our 50s and 60s, and we'll probably retire in our sixth or seventh decade of life.

We also know that our abilities, attitudes, and behaviors will change with time as well. Those of us who play tennis in our 20s will not be as quick on the court in our 50s; nor are we likely to hit a golf ball as far in our 60s as we did in our 30s. The type of car we drive and what we do for fun will all change in time. We may even become wiser, perhaps more mellow, to use a 1960s phrase, as we progress through our fifth, sixth, or seventh decade.

Most of us are fair experts on adult development and aging, in part because we've lived some of it, observed it in others, read about it, and we've experienced it through media, such as television and films. You may think, therefore, that a book such as this has little new and useful to offer, but we hope you feel differently after reading it. Much of what most people know about adult development and aging is out of date, lacking in sufficient detail, and sometimes just plain wrong. One of the important goals of this book is to enrich your knowledge about this topic and set the record straight on a variety of misconceptions about adult development, using the best available data. A second major goal is to help you develop useful critical thinking skills that should help you understand how important questions about development are scientifically investigated. These skills will help you winnow through the vast amounts of new information you will be exposed to in future years. Much of this information will be chaff and some of it will be wheat. Knowing which is which will be essential to planning your own future development.

This book is about adult development and aging. *Adult* implies we will not be concerned with such periods of life as infancy, childhood, and the early teens. Although the law specifies minimum ages for certain behaviors (driving an automobile, military service), there is no clearly identifiable age at which human beings leave adolescence and enter adulthood. As a general guideline, we will be dealing with events that occur after about age 20.

Development means we will be studying changes that occur over time. We will be particularly interested in those progressive and predictable changes that occur with increasing age. Adult humans are not static entities; they change as they grow older, often substantially. However, it is also important not to exaggerate the magnitude of these changes. Many common beliefs about the negative effects of aging have proved to be mere myths when investigated scientifically. In this book, therefore, we (1) *describe* important differences and similarities between younger and older adults, basing our observations on data derived from empirical research; (2) suggest likely *explanations* for those age-related differences that we discover; and (3) indicate how this information might help us improve adult life. In addition to describing various phenomena and identifying the underlying causes, behavioral scientists also strive to apply their findings in ways that will *modify* our environment for the better.

The developmental approach focuses on changes within the individual throughout adulthood (**intra-individual changes**), the extent to which such changes occur at different rates among different adults (**interindividual differences**), and how individuals adapt to those changes. (See Baltes & Baltes, 1990; Baltes, Reese, & Nesselroade, 1977.) If the typical adult shows a moderate loss of hearing between ages 40 and 70, this is a significant *intra*-individual change. Having described this phenomenon, we next face the task of explaining why such auditory declines occur. For example, a specific part of the auditory system might degenerate with increasing age. If we correctly identify the cause, we may then be in a position to devise appropriate corrective methods (e.g., a mechanical device that takes over the function of the impaired organ).

Alternatively, we might find significant *inter*individual differences in the amount of intra-individual change. That is, some adults may experience much greater auditory declines than others do. Further investigation might then reveal that these hearing losses are caused primarily by frequent exposure to extremely loud noise. This would suggest such corrective measures as protective earmuffs for those who work with loud machinery and greater caution by those who enjoy listening to loud music on personal headphones.

In sum, adult development and aging refers to the progressive, predictable processes that characterize the evolution and maturation of human beings from the age of about 20 on. Aging is inevitable, but the rate of aging varies greatly among individuals.

HUMAN AGING AND LIFE EXPECTANCY

Journey back for a moment to the dawn of civilization. During this chaotic era, primitive humanity tried desperately to survive with rudimentary knowledge and few tools. Not surprisingly, very few achieved the age of 40; in fact, the average life span during these prehistoric times was in all probability a mere 18 years! Those who did succeed in reaching their mid-20s or early 30s were regarded as unusually wise and capable because of this great accomplishment.

As civilizations grew and living conditions improved, however, longevity increased. There are now more than 30 million people in the United States age 65 and older, including more than 100,000 over 100 years of age—a phenomenon that has been referred to as "the graying of America."

Definitions

AGING. Human **aging** is defined as the process or group of processes occurring in living organisms that, with the passage of time, decrease the probability of survival (Spirduso, 1995). These changes are universal and inevitable. They cannot be avoided or reversed; no one can escape growing old, nor can a middle-aged or elderly person become young again (although some have tried, as we see in Chapter 3). Thus, aging differs from illnesses and diseases, which are avoidable, may have external causes, and may be cured or alleviated.

The distinction between aging and illness is very important. Although the chances of becoming ill, disabled, and even dying increase with age, especially in very old age, aging and illness are not necessarily tied together. (See, for example, Schaie, 1988.) Suppose a researcher finds that 70-year-olds have significantly poorer hearing than 40-year-olds. The researcher might be tempted to conclude this difference in hearing is caused by aging. If so, nothing can be done about it. Growing older is inevitable, so you would simply have to expect some noticeable (and annoying) hearing losses by about age 70.

However, let us now suppose that the researcher properly decides to investigate this issue more carefully. She finds that the hearing losses among the 70-year-olds are actually caused by a disease that attacks part of the inner ear.

This changes the conclusion dramatically! The real problem is that 70-year-olds are more susceptible to this disease than 40-year-olds are. These hearing losses can therefore be prevented by finding a cure for this disease (which is certainly more likely than finding a cure for growing older). Or, if you are fortunate enough not to contract this disease, you will avoid the associated decline in your hearing. By correctly attributing the research results to illness, and *not* to aging, a more optimistic conclusion is reached. We encounter numerous examples of this crucial distinction throughout this book.

LIFE EXPECTANCY.   **Life expectancy at birth** refers to the number of years that will probably be lived by the average person born in a particular year. In 1995, for example, the life expectancy at birth for women in the United States was 79.3 years. This means that if you had a daughter born this year, and if the course of her development proved to be neither more nor less favorable than the average for everyone born in 1995, she will live approximately 79 years. She might instead be more fortunate than the average woman born in 1995, and live to 90 or even 100. Or she might be less fortunate, and be struck down by an accident or illness at an early age. The life expectancy figure is an average: It represents the best guess as to an individual's life span, but it could easily be wrong in any one instance.

Alternatively, we may ascertain an individual's **life expectancy at a specific age.** In 1995, the life expectancy for American women age 65 was 19.2 years. That is, the average American woman who reached age 65 during 1995 could reasonably expect to live to about age 84. The *at birth* life expectancy figure,

In the United States, women live significantly longer than men. Among adults age 80 and older, women outnumber men by more than 2 to 1.

which was considerably lower, no longer applies to these women because they have demonstrated a favorable course of development: They avoided fatal illnesses or accidents during infancy, childhood, adolescence, and early adulthood.

MAXIMUM LIFE SPAN. The extreme upper limit of human life is known as the **maximum life span.** It is the theoretical, species-specific, longest duration of life. This figure is typically inferred from the greatest authenticated human age on record: Until recently a Japanese man, Shigechiyo Izumi, held the record for the longest life span. He died of pneumonia at age 120 on February 21, 1986. He was identified as 1-year old in the 1867 census carried out in Japan. This record was recently eclipsed by a French women who died at the age of 122. Some individuals claim to have lived considerably longer, but this has proved to be one of the many myths that pervade the field of adult development and aging[1] (Smith, 1993).

Life Expectancy, Past and Present

HISTORICAL TRENDS. It has been estimated that the average ancient Roman lived for only about 22 years, settlers in the 1620 Massachusetts Bay Colony survived for approximately 35 years, and the average resident of the United States born in 1900 lived for some 47 years. (See Table 1–1.) By 1995, however, U.S. life expectancy at birth reached a new high of 75.8 years, and this number is expected to increase to 82 by the year 2050 (Smith, 1993; U.S. Bureau of the Census, 1997).

Since 1900, the largest gains in life expectancy have been demonstrated by females of all ages, infants, children, and young adults. Conversely, life expectancy at birth tends to be somewhat lower for males. For example, a male

TABLE 1–1 Human Life Expectancy at Birth from Prehistoric to Contemporary Times

TIME PERIOD	AVERAGE LIFE SPAN (IN YEARS)
Prehistoric Times	18
Ancient Greece	20
Ancient Rome	22
Middle Ages, England	33
1620 (Massachusetts Bay Colony)	35
19th–century England, Wales	41
1900, USA	47.3
1915, USA	54.5
1954, USA	69.6
1967, USA	70.2
1971, USA	71.0
1983, USA	74.7
1990, USA	75.4
1995, USA	75.8

Source: U.S. Bureau of the Census (1997).

[1]Throughout this book, we highlight common myths and the corresponding empirical evidence in chapter boxes for ready reference.

born in 1995 had a life expectancy of 72.5 years, which is almost 7 years less than the corresponding value for females, 79.3 years. (See Table 1–2.)

Life expectancy at birth is also lower for some minority ethnic groups than for whites. For example, a black male born in the United States in 1995 had a life expectancy of 64.8 years, as compared to 73.6 years for a white male. (See Table 1–3.) Life expectancy has increased for all groups since 1900, but at somewhat different rates.

INTERPRETING INCREASES IN LIFE EXPECTANCY.   The data in Tables 1–1 and 1–2 appear to reflect an amazing increase in human longevity. But as we see throughout this book, appearances are often deceiving. Because of improved medical procedures (e.g., vaccinations that prevent infectious diseases) and better standards of public health (living conditions, nutrition, sanitation), the mortality rates for American infants and children have dropped sharply since 1900. More people are living into their 60s and 70s, so the average life expectancy at birth has increased accordingly.

To clarify this point, suppose we obtain one small sample of people born in 1900 and a second small sample of people born in 1915. We then ascertain the life span of each of these individuals:

GROUP 1—BORN 1900 (1900 COHORT)		GROUP 2—BORN 1915 (1915 COHORT)	
Person	Years Lived	Person	Years Lived
James	2	Robert	50
Mary	58	Jane	47
Ellen	60	Jeffrey	62
Steven	56	Alma	60
Thomas	61	Louise	64
Mean:	47.4	*Mean:*	56.6

(A sample of only five cases is far too small for any valid scientific conclusions to be drawn, but serves for purposes of illustration. Also, for convenience, we have rounded off years lived to whole numbers.) All members of group 1 were born in 1900; this group is therefore referred to as the 1900 **cohort**. Notice that James succumbed to an illness early in childhood, and lived for only 2 years. The members of the 1915 cohort had the good fortune to be born at a time when a method for preventing this illness had been discovered, resulting in a decrease in childhood mortality rates.

If we look only at the means for each cohort, we might incorrectly conclude that between 1900 and 1915, a way was found to increase everyone's life span by about 9 years. In actuality, however, those born in 1915 *who reached old age* did not survive a great deal longer than did members of the 1900 cohort *who reached old age*. Much of the difference between the group means is due to the fact that more people born in 1915 survived the perils of infant and childhood diseases, and reached old age. That is, the life expectancy *at birth* increased substantially.

To be sure, life expectancies at older ages have also increased significantly during the past century. To illustrate, consider the life expectancies at age 65 shown in Table 1–2. In 1900, the average 65-year-old man lived for an additional 11.3

TABLE 1–2   Life Expectancy at Birth and at Age 65
as a Function of Sex and Calendar Year (United States)

		LIFE EXPECTANCY AT BIRTH		LIFE EXPECTANCY AT AGE 65	
	Year	Male	Female	Male	Female
	1900	46.4	49.0	11.3	12.0
	1910	50.1	53.6	12.1	12.1
	1920	54.5	56.3	12.3	12.3
	1930	58.0	61.3	12.9	12.9
	1940	61.4	65.7	11.9	13.4
	1950	65.6	71.1	12.8	15.1
	1960	66.7	73.2	12.9	15.9
	1970	67.1	74.9	13.1	17.1
	1980	69.9	77.5	14.2	18.4
	1990	71.6	79.2	15.1	18.9
	1995	72.6	78.9	15.5	19.0
Net Gain	1900–1995	26.2	29.9	4.2	7.0

Source: U.S. Bureau of the Census (1997).

years. A man who reached age 65 in 1990 had a further life expectancy of 15.0 years, or 3.7 years longer. Although this increase is smaller than the corresponding gain in the life expectancy at birth (25.2 years), it is important; many people would willingly spend a considerable amount of money to add almost 4 years to their lives. The data for women reflect an even greater increase: The life expectancy at age 65 rose by 7 years between 1900 and 1990, and the life expectancy at birth gained 29.9 years. (The difference in life expectancy between men and women may be leveling off, however. Notice that between 1980 and 1990, the gains in life expectancy at birth and at age 65 were about the same for both sexes.)

Adults past age 70 are also living longer. The life expectancy at age 85 has increased by 24% since 1960, and an additional 44% increase is projected by the year 2040 (U.S. Bureau of the Census, 1997). On the popular morning television show *Today*, the names of persons who have reached their 100th birthday are often announced. If this were done for everyone in the United States, rather than just for those who elect to write in, some 35,000 names would have to be announced each year. The 1990 Census counted 35,808 centenarians (Suzman, Willis, & Manton, 1992)!

In sum, much of the apparent increase in human longevity is due to substantially greater life expectancies at birth and to the impact of public health measures adopted in the early part of this century. As a result, many more Amer-

TABLE 1–3   Life Expectancy as a Function of Sex
and Ethnic Group for the United States in 1995

	MALES	FEMALES
Whites	73.6	79.6
Blacks	64.8	74.0

Source: U.S. Bureau of the Census (1997).

Because of increased life expectancies worldwide, three- and even four-generation families are much more common.

icans are reaching old age than ever before, and this trend will continue well into the next century. (See Figure 1–1.) There have also been smaller but significant increases in life expectancies at older ages, indicating that those of us who do survive until old age are likely to live a few years longer than did our counterparts of a century ago.

DEMOGRAPHICS

GEOGRAPHICAL TRENDS.   A common misconception is that most elderly Americans live in the southern sunbelt states. In fact, as of 1986, California and New York had the largest number of persons age 65 and older (American Association of Retired Persons, 1997). The use of simple head counts is somewhat misleading, however: These large states have more people of all ages, and therefore more of the elderly.

A better measure can be obtained by dividing the number of elderly in a given state by the total number of people in that state. Using this index, Florida does have the highest concentration of the elderly; as of 1996, 18.5% of Floridians were 65 or older. But the large majority of the 19 states with the next highest concentration of the elderly are all in the North and Midwest, led by Pennsylvania, Rhode Island, Iowa, and West Virginia. (See Figure 1–2.)

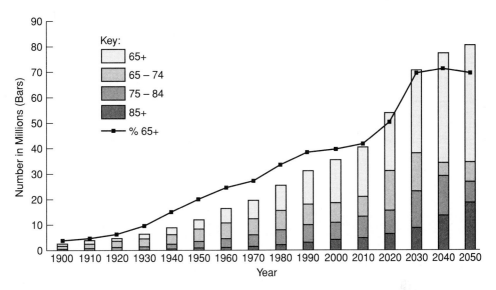

FIGURE 1–1 **Growth of the 65+ population, by age group: 1900 to 2050.**
(*Source:* U.S. Bureau of the Census (1997).)

FIGURE 1–2 **Persons 65+ as percentage of total population.**
(*Source:* U.S. Bureau of the Census (1997).)

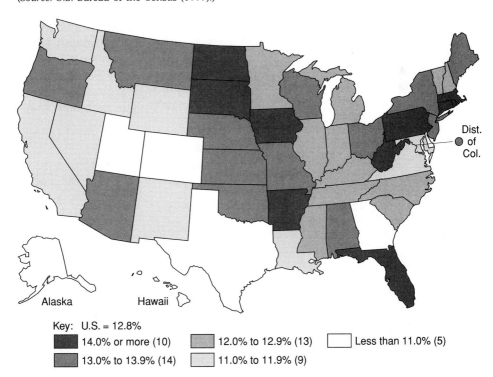

MYTHS ABOUT AGING

Demographics

Myth	Best Available Evidence
Some human beings have lived to be 130, 140, or even 170 years old.	Empirical evidence has failed to support these claims. A man from the Ukraine who supposedly was 130 years old had falsified his date of birth in order to escape military service during World War I; he actually was only 78 years old (Medvedev, 1974). A convenient fire destroyed the records of an Ecuadorian man who claimed to be 130 years old. Further investigation revealed that he died at age 93. And an American man who allegedly died in 1979 at age 137, and who was at one time noted in the *Guinness Book of World Records* for this reason, was later found to have died at age 104 (Meister, 1984). The notoriety that comes with extreme old age apparently offers a strong temptation to exaggerate the truth. The greatest authenticated human ages are 122 years for a French woman, 120 years (a Japanese man), 113 years and 273 days (a California woman), and 113 years and 124 days (a Canadian man).
Most elderly Americans live in the southern sunbelt states.	Florida does have the highest concentration of the elderly, but most of the states that rank second through twentieth are all in the North and Midwest.
The dramatic increase in the number of elderly persons is occurring only in a few developed countries, such as the United States, Canada, and in western Europe.	Because of worldwide advances in medical care and birth control, many nations face the prospect of an increasingly older population. This includes both developed countries (Japan, Canada, the United States) and developing countries (China, India, Mexico).

IMPLICATIONS FOR OUR PRESENT SOCIETY. By the year 2000, the population of the United States will be 276 million. The distribution by age is shown in Figure 1–3. Two important facts can be gleaned from this figure. The generation of baby boomers, those born between 1946 and 1964, will dominate the age distribution well into the next century. And the old-old, those age 85 or more, currently represent a relatively small proportion of the over-60 age group and of the population as a whole.

Since 1940, however, the percentage of elderly Americans has increased markedly. This is due only in part to the gains in life expectancy just mentioned. The annual birthrate in the United States rose significantly just prior to 1920, rose again after World War II, and declined dramatically after the mid-1960s. As a result, the proportion of Americans age 65 and older is now larger, and it will increase even more as the baby boom generation ages.

Barring some highly unexpected development, the number of elderly Americans will continue to increase for the next half century. (See Figure 1–1.) The gains will be greatest among those over 85, who constitute the most rapidly growing segment of the American population (Brody et al., 1983). By the year 2050, it is estimated that the proportion of Americans age 85 and older will jump from about 1% to over 5% of the total population, and approximately 1 of every 4 Americans over age 65 will be 85 or older.

Dramatic increases are also projected for the over-65 age group as a whole. During the past two decades, mortality rates have declined by 1% to 2% per

FIGURE 1–3 **U.S. population by age and sex (1996).**
(*Source:* U.S. Bureau of the Census (1997).)

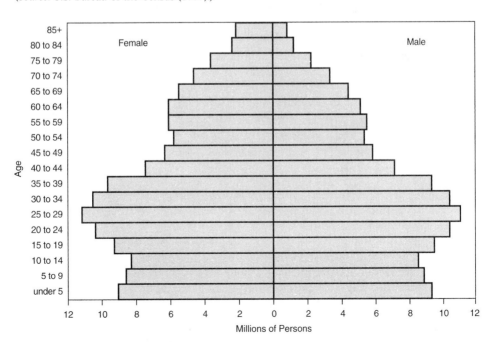

year. If these declines continue, almost two fifths of the American population will be above age 65 by the year 2080, with the number of centenarians approaching 19 million (Vaupel & Gowan, 1986). These demographic changes may portend major social changes as well:

> Will increased life expectancy be accompanied by increased healthy, productive, active life expectancy? . . . Who would wish to live to age 120 in, as Shakespeare wrote, "mere oblivion, sans teeth, sans eyes, sans taste, sans everything"? The evidence [pertaining to this issue] is weak. . . . In any case . . . it would seem to be prudent to place a very high priority on the development of ways of delaying or alleviating debilitating conditions [in the elderly].
>
> As the proportion of the population over age 65 begins to approach the proportion between ages 20 and 64, delayed retirement will almost certainly be required to save Social Security from bankruptcy. If more of the elderly hang on to their jobs, however, promotional opportunities will diminish for the young, and whatever gain there may be in wisdom and experience in an organization may be offset by a lack of fresh thinking and new blood. In addition, the increase in the proportion of the elderly might result in a further shift of political power, and even greater governmental focus on the needs of the elderly and inattention to the needs of the young. A major challenge to society will be to develop career patterns and societal norms that enable the elderly to contribute while simultaneously giving the young a chance.
>
> When lifespans reach or even exceed a century, the division of life into three successive stages of education, employment, and retirement will undoubtedly have to be rethought. Not only to contribute productively to society but simply to understand society, octogenarians will have to have learned about the advances and changes that have occurred since they finished high school or college. Delaying the age of retirement to age 80 or 85 might permit periodic leaves from work—a year, say, every decade, for ongoing education.
>
> In addition, a reduction in the hours worked per week and an increase in the number of weeks of vacation per year might facilitate part-time education on a more or less continuous basis. The 64,000 hours or so of lifetime work under the emerging system of 35 hours per week . . . from age 22 to 62, could alternatively be arranged so that a person works 28 hours a week, with two months' vacation per year and a year's leave every decade, from age 22 to 82. If [the] median lifespan approaches a century, that would still leave 18 years of retirement. (Vaupel & Gowan, 1986, p. 433)

INTERNATIONAL TRENDS.   The dramatic increase in the number of elderly adults is not unique to the United States. It is occurring throughout the world.

In terms of simple head counts, the United States has the world's third largest population of adults age 65 and older and the largest old-old population (age 85 and older). As of 1985, however, the highest *concentration* of adults age 65 and older was found in Sweden. The United Kingdom, Germany, Italy, and France also had a higher concentration of the elderly than did the United States. (See Figure 1–4.)

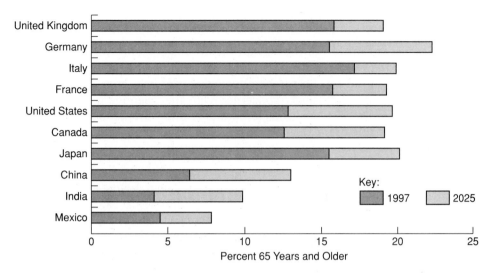

FIGURE 1–4 **Percentage of population 65+ in selected countries: 1997 and 2025 (projected).**
(*Source:* U.S. Bureau of the Census (1997).)

In 1995, the greatest life expectancy at birth occurred in Japan; it was approximately 3.4 years greater than that in the United States. This was due primarily to reductions in infant mortality. Life expectancy at age 65 was about the same in both countries, but the infant mortality rate in Japan was only one half that of the United States. As in this country, females worldwide live longer than males; India is perhaps the only exception.

Of greater importance, however, are projected future developments. Because of worldwide advances in medical care and birth control, many nations face the prospect of an increasingly older population. Among developed countries, Japan, most of Europe, the United States, and Canada are expected to experience the greatest increases in the concentration of elderly adults. In countries that are still developing, such as China, India, and Mexico, the elderly population will also increase substantially, and at a much faster rate. By the year 2025, the percentage of elderly adults in these countries will begin to approximate today's concentration in the developed countries.

This trend has potentially serious consequences. In many ways, the changes that are expected to occur in the United States will be mild by comparison to those that take place in developing nations. How can the world as a whole provide for the needs of a population that lives longer in retirement? How will countries that are lacking in technology cope with large elderly populations? How can developed countries best assist their less developed neighbors in caring for the elderly? If older adults throughout the world are to avoid deprivation and suffering, these important questions will have to be answered in the days to come.

The Scientific Study of Aging

Because so many more of us are living longer than ever before, the past few decades have seen a considerable growth of interest in the study of adult development and aging. Researchers, policymakers, educators, and laypersons alike have become increasingly concerned with the scientific study of aging and the special problems of the aged (**gerontology**), and with the medical study of the diseases, debilities, and care of aged persons (**geriatrics**). The following are among the problems and issues of current importance.

◆ Will our physiological, sensory, and cognitive processes sustain us as we grow toward old age? Or should we expect serious deterioration in our physical abilities, vision, audition, memory, and intellectual capacities? What aspects of aging might we be able to influence and change?

◆ Are most elderly adults so ill and helpless as to require extensive medical care or institutionalization, or do most remain self-sufficient and independent? As more and more individuals live to older ages, what can we expect the quality of life to be for the oldest old?

◆ Should we expect to undergo significant changes in personality during the lengthy course of adulthood? Or is personality most likely to remain relatively stable?

◆ Are social relationships typically satisfying after middle age? Or are most older adults ignored by their families and peers?

◆ Because life expectancies are greater for women than for men, the American population includes significantly more older women than older men. This discrepancy is particularly large in the upper age ranges. (See Figure 1–5.) What

FIGURE 1–5 **Number of men per 100 women by age group (1996).**
(*Source:* U.S. Bureau of the Census (1997).)

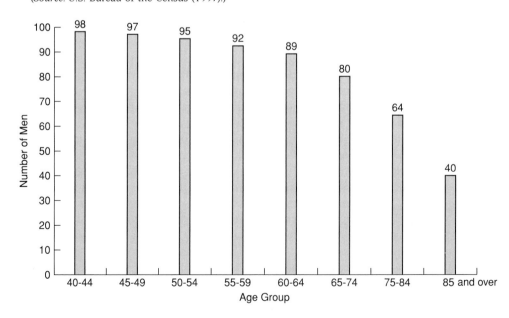

problems does this cause for older women who become divorced or widowed, and what can be done to improve matters?

◆ Should we expect retirement to be a rewarding or a traumatic experience? What, if anything, can be done to make the former outcome more likely?

◆ Will we have considerably more difficulty dealing with our stressful environment in middle and old age? Or will our greater experience in living make us more adept at coping with such problems?

◆ Are certain kinds of psychopathology more likely to afflict older adults? If so, what can be done to treat these disorders?

◆ For many individuals, dying has become a lengthy process, preceded by long periods of chronic disability. How may terminally ill patients and their loved ones be helped to cope with these traumatic months, or even years?

The purpose of this book is to present, discuss, and evaluate the empirical research evidence dealing with such issues.

SUMMARY

Adult development and aging deals with the description, explanation, and modification of changes that occur during the adult life course. The developmental approach focuses on changes within the individual over time (intra-individual changes) and on the extent to which such changes occur at different rates among different individuals (interindividual differences). It is also important to identify major similarities between younger and older adults, so as not to exaggerate the negative effects of aging.

In the chapters that follow, you will be able to compare common myths and preconceptions to the best information that is currently available. When you do this, we think you will agree that we have learned a great deal about development in adulthood and old age. Still, much remains to be discovered.

Human Aging and Life Expectancy

Human aging is caused by processes within the individual that significantly decrease the probability of survival. Unlike illnesses and diseases, these changes are universal, inevitable, and irreversible. We all grow old, and none of us can become young again.

Life expectancy at birth has increased dramatically during the past century. In 1900, the average man and woman could expect to live about 46 and 49 years; today, the corresponding figures are approximately 73.2 and 80.2 years. Much of these gains are due to sharp reductions in the number of premature deaths, such as accidents and illnesses during infancy and childhood. That is, many more Americans are reaching old age than ever before. There have also been smaller but important increases in life expectancies at older ages, indicating that those who do survive until old age are likely to live a few years longer than did their counterparts of a century ago.

The percentage of elderly Americans has increased markedly since 1940, a trend that is expected to continue for the next half century. In fact, the most rapidly growing segment of the American population is the old-old—those individuals aged 85 and older. The dramatic increase in the number of elderly adults is not unique to the United States; it is occurring throughout the world. Such demographic changes have focused attention on many important problems and issues and have caused a considerable growth of interest in the scientific study of adult development and aging.

STUDY QUESTIONS

1. When drawing conclusions about adult development, why is it important to distinguish between changes related to *aging* and changes caused by *illness*?
2. The life expectancy at birth in the United States has increased by more than 30 years since 1900, but the life expectancy at age 65 has increased by less than 15 years. Why is the increase in life expectancy at birth so much greater? What does this imply about the likelihood of your living to age 90 or older?
3. The old-old is the fastest growing age group in the United States. Ten years from now, what changes are likely to result with regard to (a) health care and costs? (b) Social Security? (c) the responsibilities of young and middle-aged adults to their parents? (d) voting and political power? (e) adult education?
4. Imagine a new therapeutic agent is discovered that can extend the healthy life expectancy of human beings for an additional 50 years. How might this affect our society? How might this affect education, work, personal outlooks on life, the economy, and institutions like marriage (imagine being married to someone for 75 or 100 years)? Now imagine that this therapy is very expensive so only the rich can afford to buy it. How would this change its impact on society?
5. Why might the increasing number of older adults be an even greater problem in some foreign countries than in the United States?

TERMS TO REMEMBER

Note: Important terms (emphasized in boldface type within each chapter) are defined in the Glossary.

Aging	Intra-individual changes
Cohort	Life expectancy at a specific age
Geriatrics	Life expectancy at birth
Gerontology	Maximum life span
Interindividual differences	

RESEARCH METHODS AND ISSUES

Many things that people once "knew" to be true have proved to be wholly incorrect. To cite just two famous examples, we are now well aware that the earth is not flat and that it is not at the center of our universe. This enlightenment was made possible by scientific research, which is superior to subjective opinion in one important respect: It relies on hard data that can be verified and reproduced. When research study after study points to a particular conclusion, only an unusually stubborn individual would continue to argue otherwise.

During the past few decades, gerontologists and geriatricians have taken a closer look at some popular beliefs about aging—for example, that the majority of adults age 65 and older are physically disabled and psychologically distressed, lonely, and poverty stricken. Researchers in various disciplines, including psychology, sociology, anthropology, social work, biology, economics, and medicine have investigated such important issues by obtaining appropriate empirical data.

Not infrequently, this research has shown that prevailing stereotypes about aging and the elderly have about as much validity as the flat-earth theory.

Although specific research methods vary from one discipline to another, a common underlying logic binds them together. There are also common problems: Tracing the course of important variables during adulthood, such as intelligence and personality, has proved to be far from an easy task. In this chapter, therefore, we discuss some of the ways in which researchers gather and interpret information about adult development and aging. We also examine some of the major methodological difficulties that pervade research in this area.

We realize your interest in this subject may be more practical than theoretical and you may have no plans ever to design and conduct a research study. Even so, there is good reason to be concerned with methodological issues. In your studies and throughout your life, you will surely be a consumer of research results. The behavioral sciences are relatively young, and can boast of few (if any) flawless research methods. Therefore, the procedures selected by an investigator may to some extent bias the results in a particular direction. *What* we know about adult development and aging is often inextricably linked with *how* this information has been obtained, and we must consider both of these aspects in order to avoid serious misinterpretations.

The discussion that follows reviews both basic principles of research as well as many of the specific research tools commonly used by gerontologists. Within the latter category, we include a discussion of sequential designs, which, although complex, were created to address some of the problems that plague the more traditional designs.

BASIC PRINCIPLES

Statistical Inference

VARIABLES.   Scientific research deals with relationships among **variables,** or characteristics that can take on different values. For example, an economist may be interested in the relationship between aging and level of income: Does the financial state of most adults improve, decline, or remain about the same as they grow toward old age? Or a cognitive psychologist may hypothesize that aging is related to significant declines in intelligence, memory, or the ability to learn.

In the preceding examples, age, income, learning, memory, and intelligence are variables; there are at least some people who score at different levels. If, instead, every adult had precisely the same degree of intelligence or ability to remember, these phenomena would *not* be variables. They would be constants, and researchers would find them to be of much less interest—albeit considerably easier to describe, because knowing the score of one individual would tell you everyone else's score as well. Variation is thus the raison d'être of the research scientist.

POPULATIONS AND SAMPLES.   Researchers in the behavioral sciences must contend with an extremely troublesome problem: They can never measure *all* of the cases in which they are interested. For example, a gerontologist cannot obtain data from all 30-year-olds and all 60-year-olds in the United States; a physiological psychologist cannot study the heart and lungs of all adults in the world; an experimental psychologist cannot observe the maze behavior of all rats. The behavioral scientist wants to know what is happening in a given **population**—the complete set of people, animals, objects, or responses that are alike in at least one respect. Yet it would be much too time consuming and expensive to measure such populations in their entirety. In fact, because the population of interest may well consist of millions of people (e.g., Americans over age 65, women, men, blacks, whites), even measuring a substantial proportion of cases is out of the question. What to do?

One reasonable procedure is to measure a relatively small number of cases drawn from the population (that is, a **sample**). A sample of, say, 100 people can readily be interviewed, given a written questionnaire, or recruited as subjects in a laboratory experiment. However, conclusions that apply only to the 100 people who happen to be included in the sample are unlikely to be of much interest. To advance our knowledge to any significant degree, a researcher must be able to draw much more general conclusions, such as, "The friendships and social relationships of 60-year-olds in the United States tend to be no less satisfying than those of 30-year-olds." A finding like this is typically obtained from a research study that included 100 or 200 individuals, yet it is stated in terms of the entire populations from which the samples were drawn—that is, all 60-year-olds and all 30-year-olds in the United States.

How is this possible? There are various mathematical procedures for drawing inferences about what is happening in a population, based on what is observed in a sample from that population (**inferential statistics**). (See Figure 2–1.) We do not discuss such procedures here because they are dealt with extensively in other texts and courses. For our purposes, the important point is that there is *no* way to ensure that a sample is in fact representative of the population from which it came. To be sure, a larger sample is more likely to be representative of the corresponding population, and larger samples are being used more often in current research. But no matter how carefully a researcher draws a sample, it is still possible that **statistics** computed from this sample (e.g., means, standard deviations, correlation coefficients) will differ to a substantial extent from the corresponding population values (**parameters**). The use of appropriate inferential statistics does make correct inferences about the population more likely, but not certain.

Therefore, no single study ever proves or disproves a theory or hypothesis; more substantial evidence must be collected before definitive conclusions can be attempted. For this reason, we must expect to meet with some ambiguity and controversy when we review the findings of research on adult development and aging.

Common Research Designs

EXPERIMENTAL DESIGNS. In **experimental designs,** the experimenter directly manipulates one or more variables (**independent variables**) and observes their effects on various other variables (**dependent variables**). For example, suppose a

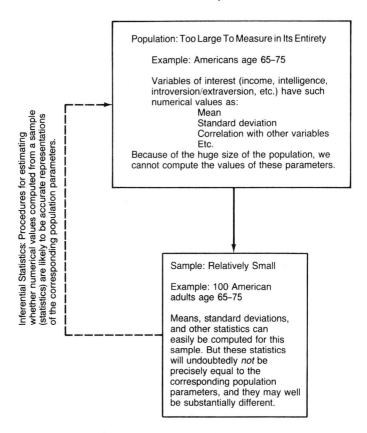

FIGURE 2–1 **Populations and samples.**

gerontologist wishes to ascertain whether a certain training program will enable middle-aged Americans to learn difficult verbal material more quickly. One way to test this hypothesis is by obtaining two groups of Americans age 45 to 60, one of which receives the new training program (the **experimental group**). The second group does *not* undergo training; this **control group** is used as a baseline for evaluating the performance of the experimental group. To control for the effects of irrelevant variables (such as intelligence), the decision as to which individuals receive the training program is made **randomly** (e.g., by flipping a coin), so each person has an equal chance of winding up in the experimental group or the control group. Learning may be indexed by testing the ability of individuals to recognize or recall the material after a specified period of time. (See Figure 2–2.)

In this experiment, receiving or not receiving training is the independent variable, and amount learned is the dependent variable. If the experimental group performs significantly better on the tests of recognition and recall than does the control group, this would support the hypothesis that the training program is beneficial. Because individuals were assigned randomly to treatments, it is unlikely that the observed differences between the two groups were due to some other reason—such as a disproportionate number of more intelligent peo-

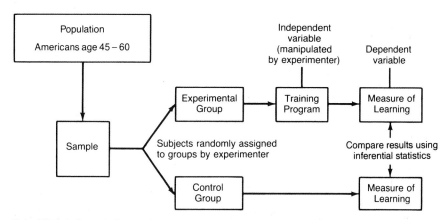

Note. Although the control group does *not* receive the training program, it would normally be given some unrelated activity that would take about the same amount of time. Otherwise the experimental group might perform better on the measure of learning solely because the experimenters spent more time with that group, causing a significant increase in motivation.

FIGURE 2–2 A simple experimental design.

ple in the experimental group or an unusually large number of adults with poor memories in the control group. Thus experimental designs typically permit cause-and-effect statements to be made, such as, "This training program caused improved performance on a verbal learning task."

One important advantage of the experimental design is that it puts the researcher in control; he or she can test hypotheses by stipulating precisely what the different experimental conditions will be. But this is also a disadvantage, because the resulting experiment may well be artificial and unrealistic. For example, some individuals in the learning experiment previously described may not be motivated to perform well because they regard the task as irrelevant to everyday lives.

QUASI-EXPERIMENTAL DESIGNS. Although **quasi-experimental designs** also utilize independent and dependent variables, individuals are *not* assigned randomly to treatments. Suppose a gerontologist wishes to test the hypothesis that repeated exposure to loud noise causes significant hearing losses. In theory, it might be desirable to assign individuals randomly to one of two groups: an experimental group that is subjected to very loud noise and a control group that does not receive this treatment. If the experimental group suffers significantly greater auditory declines than does the control group, the hypothesis would be supported. In practice, however, we obviously cannot risk inflicting significant auditory damage on study participants in order to obtain information.

One alternative is to use a quasi-experimental design. Exposure to loud noise would remain the independent variable, and amount of hearing loss would be the dependent variable. However, preexisting groups would be used instead of randomization. That is, we might compare the auditory ability of adults from three different backgrounds: relatively noisy American cities, less noisy rural American environments, and even less noisy primitive cultures that have no access to radio or television. If those who live in quieter environments demonstrate

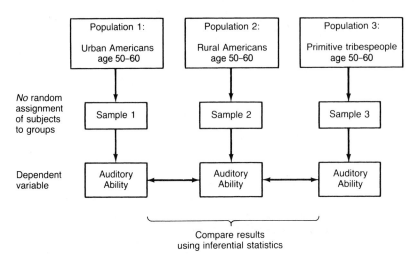

FIGURE 2–3   **A quasi-experimental design.**

significantly less hearing loss than those in noisier environments, this would provide some support for the hypothesis. (See Figure 2–3.)

Quasi-experimental designs have more drawbacks than experimental designs because the failure to assign individuals randomly to groups makes it harder
to rule out alternative explanations. Primitive cultures and large American cities
differ in many ways other than noise level, and some of these differences could
conceivably be responsible for any observed differences in hearing loss. However,
when interpreted cautiously, quasi-experimental designs do enable researchers to
gain useful information in situations where experimental designs are not feasible.

CORRELATIONAL DESIGNS.   In **correlational designs,** individuals are not assigned to
groups by the experimenter, nor are there specific independent and dependent
variables. Instead, two or more variables are measured in order to ascertain the
co-relationship between them.

To illustrate, suppose a gerontologist wishes to determine the relationship
between intelligence and age. One possible approach is to obtain a sample of adults
of various ages, measure the age and intelligence of each person, and compute
the correlation coefficient between these two variables. (See Figure 2–4.) If the
older adults are consistently lower in intelligence than the younger adults, a substantial negative correlation will be obtained. If the older individuals are considerably higher in intelligence, a large positive correlation will be obtained. And if
there is no consistent relationship, with some older individuals demonstrating
higher intelligence and some having lower intelligence, the correlation will tend
toward zero.

Correlational designs typically do *not* permit cause-and-effect statements to
be made. There are three possible reasons for a high correlation between two
variables (X and Y): X causes Y, Y causes X, or the co-relationship between X and
Y is caused by some third variable. For example, a high positive correlation was
once obtained between the number of storks in various European cities and the

number of births in each city. That is, cities with more storks had more births, and cities with fewer storks had fewer births. Taken at face value, these data might seem to support the fable that babies are brought by storks. In actuality, this correlation was caused by a third variable: size of city. Storks like to nest in chimneys. Larger cities have more houses and thus more chimneys, providing more nesting places for storks. And larger cities also have more births, because there are more people. Conversely, smaller cities have fewer people, births, houses, chimneys, and storks. Although this example may well be apocryphal, it does illustrate the difficulty of ascertaining cause and effect when the correlational design is used.

Although correlational and experimental designs differ in many important respects, they are by no means wholly unrelated. In fact, research in the applied behavioral sciences often begins with descriptive correlational studies, which are then followed by experimental studies. For example, researchers first observed that individuals who ate low-fat diets and who exercised more had lower rates of heart disease. If this association is truly causal then it should be possible to demonstrate experimentally that adopting a low-fat diet and exercising more causes heart disease to decrease. Many of the questions addressed by gerontologists followed this type of progression. The early research was descriptive and correlational, whereas much of the current research has adopted experimental designs.

FIGURE 2–4 **A correlational design.**

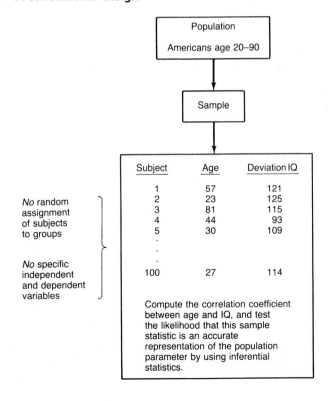

AFTERWORD: GERONTOLOGICAL RESEARCH AND THE MEASUREMENT OF CHANGE.   As we observed in Chapter 1, the study of adult development and aging involves the study of change or intra-individual differences over time. This poses another important methodological problem: How best to study change? Should we obtain a sample of, say, 20-year-olds, and continue to study them for many years? Or might we save considerable time and effort by obtaining samples of adults of various ages and comparing their performance on various tasks? Issues like these are vital to research on adult development and aging; yet they are by no means easy to resolve, as we see in the following section.

DEVELOPMENTAL RESEARCH METHODS

Researchers have devised various strategies for studying adult development and aging, each of which has its own distinct advantages and disadvantages.

Longitudinal Research

DEFINITION.   In a **longitudinal study**, the same individuals are observed over a period of time, often many years. (See Figure 2–5.) In 1955, for example, gerontologists at Duke University obtained a sample of 270 individuals whose ages varied from 59 to 94. On 11 different occasions during the next 21 years, the researchers administered measures of physiological functioning, intelligence, personality, reaction time, vision, audition, and attitudes toward retirement and other issues to those who remained in the study (Siegler, 1983).

ADVANTAGES.   The great advantage of longitudinal research is that it provides direct information about intra-individual change. If we wish to test the hypothesis that intelligence, memory, or any other variable declines or increases during adulthood, the most obvious (and theoretically best) procedure is to

In a longitudinal study, measurements are obtained from the same subjects over a period of time, often years.

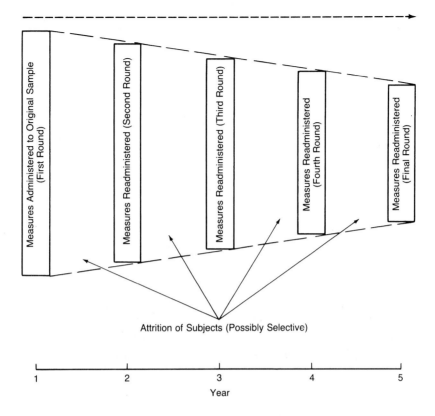

FIGURE 2–5   Longitudinal research: A five-year study with measurements obtained annually.

study a sample of adults for a number of years and trace the course taken by this variable.

To illustrate, suppose a sample of 100 30-year-olds is given a test of memory and obtains a mean score of 27.0. Thirty years later, all 100 individuals are rounded up and given the same test once more, and their mean score at age 60 is 18.0. If the difference between 27 and 18 is statistically significant (i.e., likely to be an accurate indication of what is happening in the corresponding populations), this finding would support the hypothesis that memory declines with increasing age. Because the same 100 individuals were studied over a period of 30 years, no critic could argue that the results were biased because the researcher inadvertently obtained a group of 60-year-olds with unusually poor memories (or an overly capable group of 30-year-olds).

DISADVANTAGES.   Considerable amounts of money and effort are required to study a sample of people for many years. Unfortunately, the resources of many researchers are so limited that longitudinal studies are simply out of the question.

Even when the longitudinal approach is feasible, the researcher usually finds that some individuals drop out before the study is completed. Some may move to faraway locations; others may die; still others may not be sufficiently motivated to continue participating. In the Duke study previously cited, only 44 of the original 270 individuals remained at the conclusion despite efforts like these:

> The issue of sample maintenance is important in any longitudinal study. In the . . . Duke study, tremendous care and attention were given to developing relationships with the study participants so that their cooperation over the length of the study would be maximized. As an inducement to participation, the results of the physical examination were communicated to study participants and to their personal physicians shortly after completion of a given round of the study. . . . Special attention was paid to keeping in contact with individuals by sending birthday and Christmas cards and to continuing to stay in touch by mail, even if the subjects had moved away from the Durham area. (Siegler, 1983, pp. 141–142)

The problem here is not simply that the number of study participants is reduced. If that were the only concern, longitudinal researchers would only have to oversample at the outset of the study in order to ensure that a sufficient number of participants remained at the end. However, a major problem arises if those who drop out are significantly different from those who remain, for this **selective attrition** may well produce misleading results. That is, instead of being representative of the population from which the sample was drawn, the study participants who complete the study will be atypical in some important respects.

This selective attrition is by no means unlikely. For example, individuals with relatively little education may see less value in scientific research and be more likely to drop out. So too may those who are low in ability and find the experimental task unpleasantly difficult. If so, measurements obtained toward the end of the longitudinal study will be based on a sample that is now unusually high in ability and educational level. If the variable being studied does decline with increasing age (e.g., intelligence during late adulthood), and if the sample becomes more and more capable as the study proceeds, these two effects will tend to cancel each other out. Thus, the longitudinal study will *underestimate* the amount of intra-individual change over time. That is, the study will show *less* change (and perhaps considerably less) than is actually the case.

Alternatively, a longitudinal study may *overestimate* the amount of intra-individual change over time. If the experimental task is an easy one, individuals who are high in ability may become bored and be more likely to drop out. If the variable being studied does decline with increasing age, and if the sample becomes less and less capable as the study proceeds, the study will show *more* change (and perhaps considerably more) than is actually the case. However, this form of selective attrition is not as common.

In addition to selective attrition, measurement problems may bias the results of a longitudinal study. What seems to be true change over time might actually represent nothing more than measurement error: Psychological research instruments are far from perfect, and we cannot expect study participants to obtain precisely the same scores on two different occasions, even if they have not changed at all.

As a second possibility, one measurement period might influence the following one. If study participants remember their previous answers to a psychological questionnaire, and repeat those answers because they erroneously believe it is desirable to be consistent, they will appear to have undergone less change than is actually the case.

A third measurement problem concerns longitudinal studies that continue for many years: Their procedures may become outmoded. Gerontologists are not solely concerned with questions about aging; they also try to improve their research methods. A researcher who begins a 20-year study in 1975 may find that substantially improved designs or instruments are available in 1985. There is no way for this researcher to go back in time, change the research design, and replace the data obtained between 1975 and 1985. Yet by current standards, the data obtained with the old and inferior methods may be too flawed to be useful. This problem is particularly important in medical research, in which technological advances in measuring physiological functions occur fairly often. For example, we now have much more sophisticated and accurate methods for measuring heart and lung functions than were available 10 to 20 years ago.

A fair amount of personnel turnover may occur during the life of a longitudinal study, which may introduce another source of measurement error. Newer staff members may administer or score subjective measures (e.g., the Rorschach) somewhat differently than did the original researchers, thereby producing score changes that have nothing to do with true intra-individual changes.

Some critics argue that even when the longitudinal method does detect significant intra-individual changes, it cannot guarantee that these changes are due to aging. Suppose the political attitudes of a sample of 20-year-olds are measured in 1965 and again when they reach middle age in 1995, and the latter measurement reveals a pronounced increase in liberalism. Taken at face value, these data might seem to indicate that young adults will become more liberal as they grow toward middle age. However, a more likely explanation is that the results were due primarily to cultural influences. There were many changes in American society between 1965 and 1995, such as the increasing emphasis on the rights of women and various minorities. Thus it may well be these trends, rather than aging, that caused the increase in liberalism. If so, and if there are no similar societal changes during the next 30 years, then we should *not* expect today's young adults to become markedly more liberal by the time they reach middle age. (One way to deal with this problem would be to measure the political attitudes of a sample of young adults in 1995. If this group proved to be about as liberal as the middle-aged group in the longitudinal study, this would suggest the results were indeed due to cultural influences rather than to aging.)

Finally, longitudinal studies require considerable patience. It can be quite frustrating to have to wait 10 or 20 years before the results can be published, nor does it do a researcher's career much good to have a lengthy period without any new publications.

AFTERWORD. In theory, longitudinal research is an effective way to study adult development and aging. This method enables the researcher to observe intra-individual change directly, and intra-individual change is what adult development is all about. Research practice, however, is another story. Of the disadvantages discussed previously, the most troublesome is the question of time and effort. A longitudinal study is a major undertaking, one that exceeds the resources of many researchers.

Are there any feasible alternatives? Some theorists contend that not all questions about adult development and aging require the longitudinal approach or are important enough to justify it. According to this argument, valuable information can be obtained in some instances by using a more convenient research design—the cross-sectional study.

Cross-Sectional Research

DEFINITION.   In a **cross-sectional** study, all measurements are performed at about the same time. (See Figure 2–6.) For example, a researcher may draw one sample of 20-year-olds and another sample of 60-year-olds and compare them on one or more variables, using any of the research designs discussed previously in this chapter (experimental, quasi-experimental, correlational).

FIGURE 2–6   Cross-sectional research: A comparison of 20-year-olds and 60-year-olds.

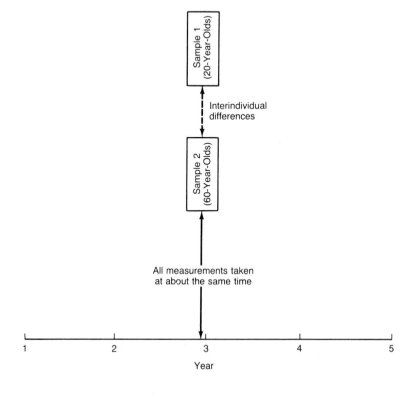

ADVANTAGES.   Cross-sectional studies are much easier and less costly to carry out than longitudinal studies. The process of gathering and analyzing the data typically takes a few months or a few years at most; many years of observation are not required. There is no long wait for results to analyze and publish, nor is it likely that the research procedures will become outmoded during the course of the study.

It has been argued that cross-sectional research is appropriate when our objectives are limited to description. If we wish only to describe how today's 60-year-olds and 20-year-olds differ on certain variables, it is not unreasonable to draw a sample from each population and compare the resulting statistics.

DISADVANTAGES.   Although the cross-sectional approach has achieved widespread popularity, it also suffers from significant methodological weaknesses. This method is not well suited for *explaining* age-related differences, primarily because it confounds the effects of aging and cohort.

To illustrate, suppose that in 1980 a researcher who is interested in the area of personality draws one sample of 20-year-old U.S. citizens and one sample of 60-year-old U.S. citizens. The researcher administers appropriate measures of personality to each group and finds some statistically significant differences between the two samples. These results may have nothing at all to do with aging! The environmental and social influences during the 1920s and 1930s (when the 60-year-olds were children and adolescents) differed markedly from those in the 1960s and 1970s (when the 20-year-olds were children and adolescents). For example, each group experienced different educational practices and expectations: A college education was much less common 50 years ago. Each group encountered different levels of technology: Television, personal computers, and jet planes did not exist 50 years ago. Social standards differed considerably, with

Just as these pictures illustrate the difference in dance styles between young and old persons, cross-sectional studies tend to exaggerate difference between generations on many dimensions.

the attitudes of the majority being considerably more conservative 50 years ago. And each group experienced different national and world events, such as the Depression and Prohibition versus the Vietnam War. Consequently, the personality differences discovered by this researcher might *not* be caused by growing from age 20 to age 60. They could easily result from the different influences on a child in the 1920s as opposed to a child in the 1960s (**cohort effects**). That is, two different possibilities have been **confounded** in this study:

1. Personality may change as a result of growing from age 20 to age 60.
2. The personality of adults born in 1920 (the 1920 cohort) may differ from the personality of adults born in 1960 (the 1960 cohort) because they experienced different social and historical influences during childhood and adolescence.

More specifically, suppose the researcher finds the 60-year-olds have more conservative attitudes about politics and sex than the 20-year-olds. This does *not* necessarily mean that people typically become more conservative about these matters as they grow older. Because the 1920s were more conservative than the 1960s, it is much more likely that the 60-year-olds were also quite conservative as young adults, and stayed much the same thereafter.

Thus a result that appears to be due to aging in a cross-sectional study may be due instead to cohort effects. That is, we cannot determine whether any observed interindividual differences are due to intra-individual changes or to some wholly different reason. Because one primary goal of the developmental researcher is to study and explain intra-individual change, this is a serious disadvantage.

AFTERWORD. Because cross-sectional studies are relatively easy to carry out, examples abound in the chapters that follow. But because such research confounds **aging effects** and **cohort effects**, the results must be interpreted with extreme caution. Admittedly, longitudinal studies are not exempt from cultural influences and other problems that affect the interpretation of data. But longitudinal research at least allows us to observe whether or not intra-individual change has occurred, whereas cross-sectional research does not. Ideally, questions about adult development and aging are best addressed by comparing the results of several studies that have investigated the same phenomenon using both methods.

Sequential Research

RATIONALE. As we have seen in the preceding pages, the scientific study of variables is seriously hindered when two or more sources of variation are confounded. The confounding of aging effects and cohort effects in cross-sectional research makes it extremely difficult to explain any differences that are obtained, however valuable the results may be for descriptive purposes.

A third source of confounded variation we have not yet discussed is **time of measurement.** According to one famous (and possibly apocryphal) story, a social psychologist once hypothesized that the attitudes of young American adults toward foreigners become more tolerant with increasing age. This researcher obtained a sample of 20-year-old U.S. citizens, measured their attitudes toward citizens of various other countries, and repeated these measurements annually during the following 10 years. In the last round of the study, a surprising development occurred: The study participants' attitudes toward the Japanese *declined* sharply. Before concluding this change was due to aging and that young adults in general become markedly more anti-Japanese on reaching age 30, we should note that this study began in the summer of 1933. The final measurements were obtained a few months after December 7, 1941, when the Japanese attacked Pearl Harbor. It was this event, rather than aging, that produced the dramatic change in attitudes. Had the study ended just 1 year earlier, no such change would have been detected.

Thus, there are three important sources of variation in studies of adult development and aging: aging, cohort, and time of measurement. To determine whether or not aging causes certain changes, researchers must somehow control for the effects of cohort and time of measurement. This is far from an easy task. Whereas cross-sectional studies confound aging effects and cohort effects, longitudinal studies confound aging effects and time of measurement effects. That is, because longitudinal research requires that individuals be measured at different times, any significant changes could be due either to aging or to the times at which the measurements were obtained. Even cross-sectional studies may be influenced to some extent by time of measurement effects, because the different samples may well be observed on different days.

In an attempt to resolve these problems, some theorists have created research designs that combine the cross-sectional and longitudinal methods. This approach, which strives to retain the advantages of each method while minimizing the disadvantages, is known as the **sequential research** strategy. (See, for example, Schaie, 1965, 1973, 1977; Schaie & Baltes, 1975.) We hinted at just such a possibility in a previous example: When we studied the political attitudes of a sample of young adults as they grew to middle age between 1965 and 1995, obtaining a second sample of 20-year-olds in 1995 helped us determine whether the observed increase in liberalism was due to aging or to cohort differences.

TYPES OF SEQUENTIAL RESEARCH. There are three major sequential research designs. In any one type, two of the possible sources of variation (aging, cohort, time of measurement) are treated as independent variables, and the third source remains uncontrolled. Although it would be preferable to treat all three sources of variation as independent variables, this is impossible because they are *not* independent of one another: Once the values of two of these sources are specified, the value of the remaining source is automatically determined.

To illustrate, suppose we wish to study adults at age 50 who are members of the 1910 cohort. The only possible way to do this would be to obtain the measurements in 1960. If we collect our measures at any other time, we will have study participants who are either the wrong age or members of the wrong cohort. In 1985, for example, the members of the 1910 cohort were 75 (not 50), and 50-year-olds were members of the 1935 cohort (not 1910).

Delegates to a political convention, although not randomly selected, are thought to be representative of their state membership.

The researchers must therefore decide which source of variation is least likely to bias the results of the study in question and choose the sequential design that treats this source as the uncontrolled variable. If, say, time of measurement is regarded as the least likely source of bias, the researcher would select the sequential design that leaves this source uncontrolled and treats aging and cohort as independent variables. (The dependent variable is the one whose relationship to aging the researcher is trying to ascertain, such as attitudes, intelligence, or memory.) Thus, the three types of sequential research are the following:

1. Treat age and cohort as independent variables; assume that time of measurement has no effect (*cohort-sequential strategy*).
2. Treat age and time of measurement as independent variables; assume that cohort has no effect (*time-sequential strategy*).
3. Treat cohort and time of measurement as independent variables; assume that aging has no effect (*cross-sequential strategy*).

An example of a *cohort-sequential study* is shown in Figure 2–7. The researcher has chosen to study the 1920 and 1930 cohorts and compare adults who are 40 and 50 years old. Thus, age and cohort are the independent variables because they are manipulated, chosen by the experimenter. Having made these decisions, there is no choice as to the time at which the measurements are taken. To study the 1920 cohort at age 40 and 50, the measurements must be made in 1960 and 1970; to study the 1930 cohort at age 40 and 50, the measurements must be made in 1970 and 1980. In this design, therefore, time of measurement is the uncontrolled variable.

A comparison of groups B and C alone (or groups D and E alone) would be a longitudinal study because the same individuals are observed over time. Here, aging effects and time of measurement effects are confounded. A comparison of groups B and E alone would be a cross-sectional study (aging effects and cohort effects are confounded) because two different samples are compared at about the same time. And a comparison of groups B and D alone (or groups C and E alone) would involve the confounding of cohort effects and time of measurement effects because different cohorts of the same age are measured at different times. (This is referred to as a time-lag comparison.) The cohort-sequential strategy strives for broader conclusions by including all of these groups in the statistical analysis. *If* it is correct to assume that time of measurement is not important, then this design makes it possible to compare the relative magnitude of aging effects and cohort effects. A good example of the application of this technique is the Seattle Longitudinal Study (Schaie & Hertzog, 1983).

An example of a *cross-sequential study* is shown in Figure 2–8. The 1920 and 1930 cohorts have been selected for inclusion by the researcher, and the times of measurement have been designated as 1960 and 1970. Thus cohort and time of measurement are the independent variables. Having made these decisions, there is no choice as to the ages of the individuals in this study. When the 1920 cohort is measured in 1960, the members must be 40 years old; the 1930 cohort will be 30 years old in 1960; and so on. In this design, therefore, age is the uncontrolled variable.

FIGURE 2–7   **A cohort-sequential study.**

Independent Variables: Age (40; 50)
                      Cohort (1920; 1930)

Uncontrolled Variable: Time of Measurement

Duration of Study: 20 Years (1960–1980)

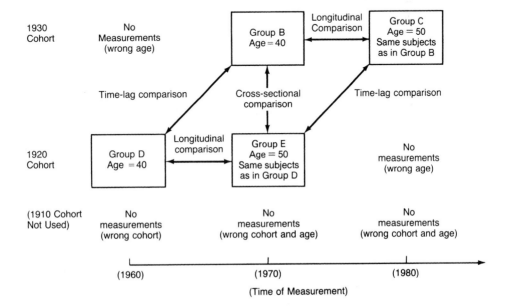

Independent Variables: Cohort (1920; 1930)
                     Time of Measurement (1960; 1970)

Uncontrolled Variable: Age

Duration of Study: 10 Years (1960–1970)

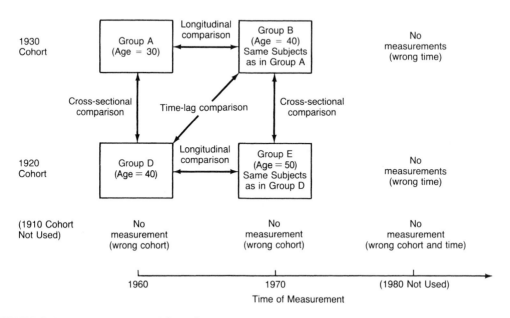

FIGURE 2–8 **A cross-sequential study.**

Here, a comparison of groups A and D alone (or groups B and E alone) would be a cross-sectional study; a comparison of groups A and B alone (or groups D and E alone) would be a longitudinal study; and a comparison of groups B and D alone would be a time-lag study. In contrast, the cross-sequential strategy includes all of these groups in the statistical analysis. *If* it is correct to assume that aging effects are unimportant, then this design makes it possible to compare the relative magnitude of cohort effects and time of measurement effects. An example of a time-sequential study is provided by Bee (1987, p. 18).

The third type of sequential design, the *time-sequential* strategy, can be represented in a similar fashion. (See Figure 2–9.) The Duke Longitudinal Study serves as a good example of this method (Palmore, 1981; Siegler, 1983). Because the preceding discussion should serve as a sufficient introduction to sequential research, we leave the details to the interested reader as an exercise.

EVALUATION.   Sequential research designs were devised because of dissatisfaction with the longitudinal and cross-sectional methods. When the underlying assumptions are justified, these strategies provide important information that cannot be obtained from the traditional methods. However, sequential designs also have serious drawbacks.

First of all, sequential designs cannot control for selective attrition. Such attrition is just as likely to occur in sequential research as in longitudinal research, and it is just as likely to create the kinds of problems discussed previously in this chapter.

Second, the assumptions that underlie sequential research may well be questionable in many instances. Aging, cohort, and time of measurement are all potentially significant influences, yet we are required to assume that one of these sources is not a problem in each sequential design. This is particularly troublesome in the case of the cross-sequential strategy, in which we must assume that aging itself is unimportant! Nor are matters much better with the time-sequential strategy, which assumes that cohort has little effect on the data. This

FIGURE 2–9 **A time-sequential study.**

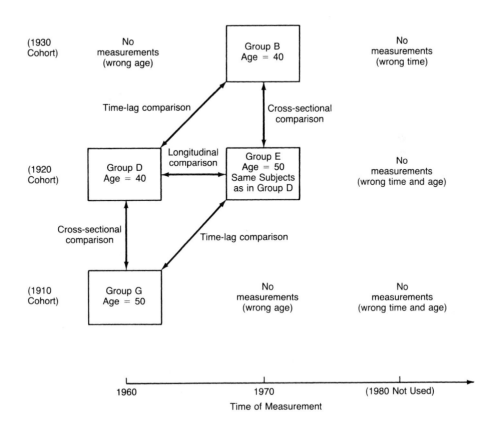

Independent Variables: Age (40; 50)
Time of Measurement (1960; 1970)

Uncontrolled Variable: Cohort

Duration of Study: 10 Years (1960–1970)

may be a viable assumption in some instances; for example, declines in visual acuity are more likely to be caused by age-related physiological changes than by cultural differences between cohorts. But it is highly questionable in many other cases, as we have seen throughout this chapter. Perhaps the assumption of the cohort-sequential strategy is most plausible, namely that time of measurement is relatively unimportant. Yet this source of bias can also be significant.

Finally, sequential designs can be extremely time consuming. The cohort-sequential study illustrated in Figure 2–7 requires some 20 years to complete (from 1960 to 1980). If we broaden the scope somewhat and include the 1940 cohort as well, the duration of the study increases to 30 years because this cohort did not reach age 50 until 1990. Obviously, sequential research can be just as major an undertaking as longitudinal research—especially because one suggested solution to the problem of questionable assumptions is to carry out all three sequential strategies at once! As one critic has observed,

> Collectively, sequential designs appear to offer ingenious solutions to methodological problems in research on aging. . . . However, completing an experimental aging study that adheres fully to the requirements of any one of these designs is not easy to accomplish. It requires the wisdom of a Solomon, the longevity of a Methuselah, the patience of a Job, and the backing of a Rockefeller. Moreover . . . the solutions arrived at through the use of a sequential design may be more illusory than real. (Kausler, 1982, p. 134)

AFTERWORD.   Sequential research is designed to separate sources of variation that are confounded in longitudinal and cross-sectional research. In theory, this approach should enable us to determine the extent to which any significant changes in the dependent variable are caused by aging effects, cohort effects, and/or time of measurement effects. In practice, sequential research is better suited to providing an accurate and thorough *description* about changes over time (as opposed to an explanation of why these changes occur). Nevertheless, the simultaneous study of cross-sectional and longitudinal sequences is always desirable because it affords the opportunity to cross-check results using different methodologies.

As investigators become more familiar with these methods, and as further improvements are made, the quantity of sequential research may well increase. For the present, however, the considerable time and effort required by sequential designs have limited their use in developmental research.

The empirical evidence discussed in the following chapters is therefore based primarily on cross-sectional and longitudinal research, with emphasis on the former. To interpret the results of this research correctly, you must ask yourself the following question: Could the findings be biased by confounded sources of variation? That is, in a cross-sectional study, are results attributed to aging more likely to be caused by cohort effects? In a longitudinal study, might results attributed to aging be biased by the times at which the measurements were taken? Until researchers develop more effective methods for answering such questions, common sense as well as statistical analyses must be used to interpret research results in adult development and aging.

OTHER METHODOLOGICAL ISSUES

Much more could be said about the methodological problems that confront developmental researchers. We conclude our discussion by examining some of the factors that threaten the internal and external validity of a research study and by taking a closer look at the meaning of chronological age.

Internal and External Validity

THREATS TO INTERNAL VALIDITY. The preceding pages illustrated the fact that scientific research deals with the relationships among variables. These relationships may involve cause and effect, as when a gerontologist wishes to ascertain whether aging causes declines in intelligence or memory, or they may be correlational. The extent to which a research study correctly identifies such relationships is referred to as **internal validity.**

Among the most serious threats to the internal validity of a research study are confounding, selective attrition, and the effects of practice. If, say, aging effects and cohort effects are confounded, we cannot tell whether any observed changes in the dependent variable are caused by aging or by cultural influences. If the individuals who drop out during the course of a longitudinal study tend to be low in ability, leaving us with an unusually capable group during the later rounds of measurements, we may erroneously conclude that aging does not cause declines in the dependent variable. Or the earlier testings in a longitudinal study might bias subsequent ones: Age-related declines in the dependent variable might be concealed because study participants benefit from the practice provided by the previous sessions, or because the procedures have become more familiar and less anxiety provoking. In each of these cases, the study is low in internal validity; it will *not* correctly identify cause-and-effect relationships among the variables of interest.

Various procedural factors may threaten the internal validity of a research study. Mechanical instruments may wear out over time, making it more (or less) difficult to obtain high scores during the latter part of a longitudinal study. Thus the researcher may attribute declining scores to aging when these changes are actually caused by switches that are harder to operate. Alternatively, if there is a significant amount of personnel turnover during the study, score changes that seem to be age related may occur because inexperienced staff members administer and evaluate the measures differently.

Comparing behaviors at different ages can also be a source of problems. Suppose we accept "aggressiveness" as an important aspect of human behavior, and we wish to determine if this variable changes in any significant way during adulthood. We might find a young adult is more likely to abuse someone physically or to deliver a stinging insult. An older adult may, instead, prefer to spread unflattering rumors or to engage in devious and subtle plots against another person. Should all of these behaviors be regarded as various forms of aggressiveness or as something quite different? This is by no means an easy question to answer, but unless we can do so, we may well reach incorrect conclusions about the relationship between aging and aggressiveness.

THREATS TO EXTERNAL VALIDITY.   Earlier in this chapter, we observed that research scientists usually cannot study all of the cases in which they are interested. Instead, they must deal with relatively small samples from the specified populations. **External validity** involves the extent to which the research findings can be generalized from the specific samples included in the study to the large populations in which the researcher is interested.

One particularly important threat to the external validity of a research study is the way in which the sample is obtained. To illustrate, let us suppose once again that we wish to measure the political attitudes of young adults as they grow to middle age. Because our goal is to draw conclusions about all young adults, it would be a poor idea to limit our sample to students at a particular university. College students differ in numerous respects from young adults in general, such as rating higher in intelligence and socioeconomic status. And students at any one university may well differ from those at other institutions because they may have been subjected to higher or lower enrollment standards. Therefore, it is unlikely that the results obtained from this sample will apply to the population of young adults in general. We should, instead, draw a sample that includes young adults from all walks of life, including those who have never attended college. (It is perfectly legitimate to define the population of interest as all college students at a given university. In this case, we would be justified in obtaining a sample of only these students. But the results of such a study could safely be generalized *only* to the specified population, namely the young adults at this one university.)

Ideally, a researcher should obtain a **random sample** from the specified population. That is, each element of the population should have an equal chance of being included in the sample. This can be difficult to achieve in practice, however, and it is often necessary to settle for approximations of random samples.

Other significant threats to external validity involve the setting and measures used in the study. If the study participants must engage in laboratory tasks that seem artificial and unrelated to their everyday lives, their performance may suffer from a lack of motivation. Therefore, it may be incorrect to generalize the results of such studies to real-life situations, even if the sample was (more or less) randomly drawn from the specified population. For example, the ability to remember lists of unrelated words in the experimental laboratory may not be an accurate index of older adults' ability to remember what they read in the morning newspaper. (See the discussion of ecological validity in Chapter 5.) Similarly, many psychological questionnaires were standardized using college students as study participants. These measures may not be appropriate for older populations, and the researcher must be careful to select instruments that have equivalent meanings for adults of different ages.

AFTERWORD.   The factors listed previously are not the only threats to the internal and external validity of a research study, but they are among the most important. A further discussion of such issues is beyond the scope of this book; the interested reader is referred to Cook and Campbell (1979), Nesselroade and Labouvie (1985), and Schaie (1983).

The Meaning of Chronological Age

CHRONOLOGICAL AGE AND PHYSICAL, PSYCHOLOGICAL, AND SOCIAL MATURITY.   Even the apparently simple variable of chronological age has been a source of controversy. Some adults of a particular chronological age may devote considerable effort to remaining physically fit, with the result that they have the physiology of a much younger person. Conversely, a serious illness or unfavorable hereditary influences may cause a relatively young adult to look and feel much older. Nor does a person's level of psychological or social maturity necessarily correspond to his or her chronological age: Some adults in their 40s and 50s are childishly dependent on their parents, whereas some young adults have the psychological maturity of a much older person.

In common with most gerontologists, we refer to the approximate midpoint of the human life span as *middle age* and to the latter portion as *old age*. We also refer to adults who have reached old age as *elderly* or *the aged*. But because chronological age can differ considerably from physiological, psychological, and social age, terms like these are rough approximations at best. As is the case with any chronological age group, the elderly differ from one another in many important respects. There is no sharp and universally recognized dividing line between old age and middle age, between late middle age and early middle age, or between middle age and young adulthood. Such terms refer only to what is true on the average; the limitations of chronological age as a measure of adulthood make numerous exceptions inevitable.

The remaining chapters in this book are therefore organized by topic, rather than by periods related to chronological age. Also, many of the findings we review are discussed in terms of general trends (e.g., how intelligence changes with increasing age).

CHRONOLOGICAL AGE AND CAUSATION.   It is also important to recognize that age itself actually does not "cause" anything. Time has no physical existence; it cannot impinge on our senses or alter our physiology.

When we say that aging causes a decline in the efficiency of the cardiovascular system, we mean this decline is caused by some factors yet to be determined that change with increasing age. That is, we are using age as a sort of proxy explanation until more specific information can be obtained. When researchers obtain the relevant data, we can make more definitive and useful statements. For example, older people have accumulated more damage due to smoking and cholesterol intake; smoking and high levels of cholesterol increase the probability of heart disease; thus quitting smoking and consuming less cholesterol will help preserve cardiovascular health. In the meantime, it is useful to know that certain changes are age related and important aspects of human life differ significantly for young, middle-aged, and elderly adults.

AFTERWORD.   Because of the methodological difficulties discussed in this chapter, firm conclusions are not available in some areas of interest. Nevertheless, important research has been and is currently being carried out. Quite a few common beliefs and stereotypes about adulthood have been shattered by appropriate empirical data, and significant discoveries have been made that are well worth your attention.

The social sciences are not exact sciences, and adult development and aging is no exception. If you are looking for a precise chart that will tell you exactly what to expect as you or your loved ones grow through adulthood, you are undoubtedly going to be disappointed. If instead you appreciate how difficult it is to understand and predict the behavior of those complicated organisms known as human beings, and if you are willing to be tolerant of the inevitable ambiguities and uncertainties that pervade this field, you will probably find the study of adult development and aging rewarding. Most of us will spend many years as an adult. The findings reviewed in this book represent the best scientific evidence as to what those years will be like.

SUMMARY

Because scientific research relies on hard data that can be verified and reproduced, it has shattered many incorrect beliefs and stereotypes. However, even the best developmental research methods have significant weaknesses. What we know about adult development and aging is often inextricably linked with how this information has been obtained, and we must consider both of these aspects in order to avoid serious misinterpretations.

Basic Principles

Scientific research deals with the relationships among variables, or characteristics that can take on different values. Social scientists can never measure all of the cases in which they are interested; these populations are much too large. The researcher must instead deal with relatively small samples and use appropriate statistical procedures to draw conclusions about what is happening in the corresponding populations.

Researchers in adult development and aging use three types of designs to study the relationships among variables. Experimental designs focus on cause-and-effect relationships: The researcher manipulates one or more independent variables and observes the effects on various dependent variables while assigning individuals randomly to experimental or control groups. Quasi-experimental designs enable the researcher to study independent and dependent variables when individuals cannot be randomly assigned to groups, but they make it more difficult to decide among possible causes. In correlational designs, two or more variables are measured in order to ascertain the co-relationship between them. There are no specific independent or dependent variables, individuals are not assigned randomly to groups by the experimenter, and cause-and-effect relationships are difficult to identify.

Developmental Research Methods

In a longitudinal study, the same individuals are observed over a period of time, often many years. In theory, longitudinal research is the most desirable way to study adult development and aging; it enables the researcher to observe intraindividual change directly. But this method requires considerable amounts of money and effort, and the results may be biased by such factors as selective attrition or practice effects. Thus many researchers have opted instead for cross-sectional studies that are much easier to carry out because individuals are observed at about the same time. However, the cross-sectional method suffers from a serious flaw: It confounds aging effects and cohort effects.

When sources of variation in a research study are confounded, the investigator cannot tell which is responsible for changes in the dependent variable. In cross-sectional research, in which aging effects and cohort effects are confounded, any observed changes in the dependent variable might be caused by either aging or the different social and historical influences experienced by each cohort. In longitudinal research, aging effects are confounded with time of measurement effects: Any observed changes in the dependent variable might be caused either by aging or by extraneous events that occur during the study and affect all cohorts living through that period of history.

Sequential research strategies are designed to separate sources of variation that are confounded in longitudinal and cross-sectional research. However, these strategies also have drawbacks. They are vulnerable to selective attrition; the underlying assumptions may well be questionable in some instances; and they require considerable amounts of time, money, and effort.

Other Methodological Issues

Internal validity involves the extent to which a research study correctly identifies relationships among the variables of interest. Threats to the internal validity of a study include confounding, selective attrition, practice effects, and deficiencies in the apparatus or the ways in which instruments are administered and scored. External validity involves the extent to which the research findings can be generalized from the specific samples included in the study to the large populations in which the researcher is interested. Threats to the external validity of a study include poorly drawn samples, and settings and measures that are too artificial for the results to be generalized to real-life situations.

Chronological age is not necessarily related to an individual's physical, psychological, or social maturity. Terms such as *middle age* and *old age* are, therefore, rough approximations at best; members of age groups such as the elderly differ from one another in many important respects. Nor does age itself actually cause anything: Time has no physical existence and cannot affect us directly.

When we say that aging causes a particular change, we mean this change is caused by some factors yet to be determined, and those factors change with increasing age. That is, age serves as a proxy explanation until more specific information can be obtained.

Because of the methodological difficulties discussed in this chapter, firm conclusions may not be available in some areas of interest. Nevertheless, important research has been and is currently being carried out. Most of us will spend many years as an adult. The findings reviewed in this book represent the best scientific evidence as to how those years will be.

STUDY QUESTIONS

1. Why is it important to obtain information about adult development and aging from empirical research, rather than relying on common opinions and beliefs?
2. What is the one most important reason why researchers obtain their data from samples (often fairly small samples)? What problems does this cause? What does this imply about the ability of any one research study to "prove" anything, or arrive at the "truth"?
3. What are the main strengths and weaknesses of experimental designs, quasi-experimental designs, and correlational designs? Of longitudinal studies, cross-sectional studies, and sequential research? What does this imply about our need to know *how* a study was conducted in order to interpret the results correctly?
4. Is there a specific age at which a person becomes an adult (a) legally? (b) physically or physiologically? (c) psychologically? (d) with regard to social and interpersonal skills? Might a person become an adult in these areas at quite different ages? What does this imply about using chronological age as a measure of adulthood?

TERMS TO REMEMBER

Aging effect
Cohort effect
Confounding
Control group
Correlational design
Cross-sectional research
Dependent variable
Experimental design
Experimental group
External validity
Independent variable
Inferential statistics
Internal validity

Longitudinal study
Parameter
Population
Quasi-experimental design
Random assignment of study
  participants to groups
Random sample
Sample
Selective attrition
Sequential research
Statistic
Time of measurement effect
Variable

PHYSICAL ASPECTS OF AGING

It is highly unlikely that a 60-year-old will establish a new world record for the 100-meter dash; nor would we expect a 10-year-old to accomplish this feat. Human beings, like many other organisms, follow a predictable pattern of physical development that determines what we can do and how well we can do it. Most of us are very familiar with how humans develop for the first two decades of life because we have experienced them ourselves, but what happens to our bodies during the subsequent decades? Some of us (e.g., the authors of this book) have intimate knowledge of at least several of those subsequent decades, but we must still ask this question: How representative is our experience compared to what happens to most people? This chapter tries to answer this question.

Most of our physical abilities reach their maximum capacity either before or during early adulthood, and then begin to wane. However, we tend not to notice the declines that occur during our 20s, 30s, and 40s. These changes are very gradual, and they are likely to be compensated for by our increased experience and knowledge. Thus we may be more competent behind the wheel of an automobile at age 35 than at age 20, even though our manual dexterity and perceptual response speed have declined slightly, because we have learned to anticipate potential danger and to drive defensively.

Eventually, however, the physical effects of aging become more pronounced. Are such declines likely to hinder us substantially later in life? Or do most adults find that their bodily processes sustain them fairly well as they grow toward old age?

In this chapter, we begin to examine the empirical evidence dealing with this issue. First we investigate the kinds of physical changes that occur as we grow from young to old adulthood, or *how* we age. (This topic is too extensive to be treated in a single chapter, so discussions of sensation and perception, sexuality, and stress are deferred until later in this book.) These changes do not occur according to a strict timetable. Some individuals may become prematurely gray haired during their late 20s or early 30s, but some may retain a youthful physique well past middle age. Adults age at different rates, and such groupings as "the middle aged" and "the elderly" are actually rather heterogeneous with regard to their physical capacities, amount of energy, and degree of mobility and independence. (Recall our previous discussion of the limitations of chronological age as an index of adulthood.) We therefore discuss general age-related trends, with the understanding that any specific adult may well differ significantly from this average picture.

A second important issue concerns *why* we age. Scientists have proposed various explanations for the unfailing tendency of human beings to grow older, and we review the evidence regarding these theories of aging.

Although we characterized aging in Chapter 1 as universal and inevitable, not all adults are willing, in the words of Dylan Thomas, to "go gentle into that good night." Some prefer to "rage against the dying of the light" by seeking ways to ward off the specter of death, and to inhibit or even to reverse the physiological declines associated with aging. We therefore conclude this chapter by reviewing such quests for the fountain of youth, which are as old as humanity itself. Included in our discussion is a method for estimating, *very approximately*, your own probable life span.

AGE-RELATED PHYSICAL CHANGES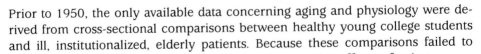

Prior to 1950, the only available data concerning aging and physiology were derived from cross-sectional comparisons between healthy young college students and ill, institutionalized, elderly patients. Because these comparisons failed to control for health, they grossly exaggerated the negative effects of aging.

More recent longitudinal studies, as well as experimental studies with animals, have provided more accurate data about normal physiological changes during adulthood—that is, those changes *not* associated with illness and injury.

These researchers have found that our bodies possess an enormous reserve capacity: We can survive the loss of one lung, one kidney, more than one half of the liver, and large amounts of the stomach and intestines if we are not subjected to severe emotional or physiological stressors.

Because of this redundancy, many of our bodily processes decline very gradually even after middle age. To be sure, growing old does have disadvantages. But we can afford much of what we lose, and the age-related physiological declines that occur among healthy adults are not nearly as severe as is commonly believed.

Observable Characteristics

The process of aging leaves clearly visible traces. Although individual differences prevail, elderly adults do tend to look significantly different from the middle aged, who typically appear different from young adults.

SKIN AND FACE.   The first facial indication of adult aging is the appearance of lines in the forehead, which usually occurs by age 30. Between ages 30 and 50, additional lines become evident elsewhere in the face. These include "crow's feet," lines caused by squinting; lines that link the nostrils to the sides of the mouth, which result from smiling; and furrowed brows, caused by frowning. Thus, during the first half of adulthood, repeated facial expressions produce some of the lines and wrinkles associated with aging. This implies that adults who frown less often, and those who avoid squinting by obtaining needed corrective lenses, will enjoy a smoother countenance.

Typical effects of aging of the skin include wrinkling, sagging, and leathery appearance of sun-exposed areas. However, for some individuals such as the woman in these pictures, changes in appearance are minor, even over several decades.

After age 50, however, more extensive facial wrinkling is likely to occur. There is a significant decrease in collagen, the fiber that makes the skin more resilient, and in the amount of water on the inside of the skin. This makes the skin stiffer and less elastic, resulting in more pronounced facial lines. These changes are hastened by frequent exposure to strong sunlight. The skin also becomes thinner and more spread out, somewhat like a piece of dough that has been stretched too far. This is evidenced in such ways as bags under the eyes and sagging skin on the cheeks. Because of these changes, and because of an increase in capillary fragility, the skin of older adults is more vulnerable to bruising. By age 70, the skin has become rougher and has lost its uniformity of color, with a variety of shades clearly evident (Kligman, Grove, & Balin, 1985).

Our facial features also undergo changes during adulthood. By the time you reach old age, accumulations of cartilage will make your nose a half inch wider and another half inch longer. Your earlobes will become somewhat fatter, and your ears will grow about a quarter of an inch longer. The circumference of the head increases by a quarter of an inch every 10 years, presumably because the skull thickens with increasing age. However, these changes are usually far less noticeable than the age-related changes in the skin.

Because these trends are only average tendencies, how might you predict the rate at which your own skin and face will age? The aging of the skin is determined by hereditary influences, so you can obtain some valuable clues simply by observing your parents' features. In fact, except for such remedial actions as cosmetic surgery, about all you can do to preserve a more youthful skin is to avoid excessive exposure to the sun's ultraviolet rays. Furthermore, if you are female, the aging of your skin during the second half of adulthood will probably be more noticeable than if you are male (although dryness can be inhibited by using lotions and protective creams). One reason is that the production of skin oil (sebum) declines significantly after menopause in women, but it remains virtually unchanged for men throughout adulthood.

HAIR.   Not too long ago scientific knowledge about age-related changes in the hair was not much greater than that possessed by the average hairdresser (Kligman, Grove, & Balin, 1985). Recent advances in the treatment of hair loss are beginning to advance our knowledge of hair growth and loss over the life course. Most adults over 40 experience some graying of scalp hair, which is caused by hereditary influences. Scalp hair also becomes thinner over the course of adulthood, especially after age 65. This thinning occurs in two ways: The rate of growth decreases, and individual strands of hair gradually decline in diameter. For example, in 20-year-old men, the diameter of a single hair is 101 microns (millionths of a meter). For 70-year-old men, this diameter is only 80 microns. The density of scalp hair varies greatly from one adult to another, however, although blondes generally have more hairs than brunettes.

Some men experience a loss of hair that begins at the temples, proceeds to the circle on the back of the head (the "monk's spot"), and continues until the entire top of the head is bare (**male pattern baldness**). This form of hair loss is due solely to hereditary influences, but it can be treated with products such as

Hair loss among men is a common feature of aging. Most people face this loss with equanimity.

Rogaine, which have proved to be effective for some men. Other men retain most of their cranial hair throughout adulthood. Even in these cases, some hair loss usually occurs around the temples, but there are exceptions. We can all think of examples such as former president Ronald Reagan who retained a full head of hair well beyond his 80th birthday.

Male pattern baldness also affects some 75% of all women, although rarely to the extent of becoming totally hairless. This pattern involves a thinning of the hair on the top and sides of the head, and it can become so pronounced that some women in their 70s and 80s opt to wear wigs. Contrary to a common belief, however, childbirth does *not* cause scalp hair loss in women.

In other areas of the body, an opposite trend is observed. As men grow older, hair becomes longer and more profuse in the ears, the nostrils, the eyebrows, and sometimes on the back. Most women past 65, especially those of Mediterranean origin, have an excessive growth of long, dark, and thick hair over the lip and chin. The reasons for such localized hirsutism are not yet known (Kligman et al., 1985).

HEIGHT. A man's height decreases by about half an inch between ages 30 and 50, and by another three quarters of an inch between ages 50 and 70. This is due to the effects of gravity, which causes the muscles to weaken and the bones of the spine to deteriorate and become compressed (Ryan & Elahi, 1996).

The height loss for women is slightly greater, and may total as much as 2 inches between ages 25 and 75. One reason is a higher incidence of metabolic bone disease among women following menopause. Another important cause is a loss of bone calcium with increasing age, a decline that can be slowed by regular exercise and an appropriate diet.

WEIGHT. As we grow from young adulthood to middle age, our weight tends to increase. (See Table 3–1.) Many of us become less active during this period, and there is a decrease in the rate at which the resting body converts food into energy (our **basal metabolism,** which slows down by about 3% every 10 years). Because less metabolizing tissue is available after age 20, the number of calories required each day to maintain our present weight declines by about 10% every 10 years (Ryan & Elahi, 1996; Spirduso, 1995).

If we were to reduce our food intake accordingly, our weight would remain about the same. But the typical pattern is to eat much the same amounts, or perhaps even more, as we grow from young adulthood to middle age. The result is an inability to burn up enough food; an accumulation of fat throughout the body; skin that becomes flabby in the waist and chest areas, which may increase in size by as much as 5 to 6 inches; and a gain in weight that may total 10% to 15% between age 20 and 50. For obvious reasons, these changes are commonly referred to as "middle-age spread." (See Figure 3–1.)

After middle age, however, our weight is likely to level off and begin a slow decline. During this period, we tend to lose more weight due to tissue and mus-

TABLE 3–1 Recommended Weight Ranges for Individuals of Varying Height and Age

HEIGHT (ft and in)	AGE-SPECIFIC WEIGHT RANGE FOR MEN AND WOMEN[a]				
	20–29 yr	29–39 yr	39–49 yr	50–59 yr	60–69 yr
4 10	84–111	92–119	99–127	107–135	115–142
4 11	87–115	95–123	103–131	111–139	119–147
5 0	90–119	98–127	106–135	114–143	123–152
5 1	93–123	101–131	110–140	118–148	127–157
5 2	96–127	105–136	113–144	122–153	131–163
5 3	99–131	108–140	117–149	126–158	135–168
5 4	102–135	112–145	121–154	130–163	140–173
5 5	106–140	115–149	125–159	134–168	144–179
5 6	109–144	119–154	129–164	138–174	148–184
5 7	112–148	122–159	133–169	143–179	153–190
5 8	116–153	126–163	137–174	147–184	158–196
5 9	119–157	130–168	141–179	151–190	162–201
5 10	122–162	134–173	145–184	156–195	167–207
5 11	126–167	137–178	149–190	160–201	172–213
6 0	129–171	141–183	153–195	165–207	177–219
6 1	133–176	145–188	157–200	169–213	182–225
6 2	137–181	149–194	162–206	174–219	187–232
6 3	141–186	153–199	166–212	179–225	192–238
6 4	144–191	157–205	171–218	184–231	197–244

[a]Values in this table are for height without shoes and weight without clothes.

Source: Modified from Ryan and Elahi (1996).

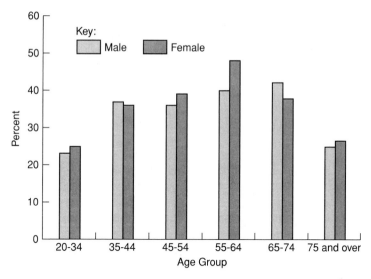

FIGURE 3–1 **Percentage of population overweight: 1988–1991.**
(*Source:* U.S. Bureau of the Census (1997).)

cle deterioration than we gain in fat. Although these rather unappealing changes characterize most individuals in developed countries around the world, it is important to appreciate that they are not inevitable. We can control our weight through diet and exercise.

VOICE. As we grow older, the vocal cords stiffen and vibrate at a higher frequency. By old age, therefore, the speaking voice increases in pitch by about two or three notes on the musical scale. The voice may also begin to quaver, presumably because there is some loss of control over the vocal cords.

AFTERWORD. Most of the changes previously discussed are so well known that they have become hallmarks of the aging process. These changes are primarily cosmetic; they have no direct effect on our vigor, daily functioning, or health. Nevertheless, their psychological effects can be considerable. Millions of middle-aged and elderly women (and some older men) suffer considerable damage to their self-esteem because of these changes, so much so that they spend substantial amounts of money on cosmetic products and/or surgery in an effort to appear younger. As Weg (1983, p. 251) observes, "Societal adoration of youth has placed a premium on looking young; . . . The young, unlined, and gently curvaceous body of the woman and the lithe but macho and powerful body of the man cannot be preserved forever. [Yet] . . . societal attitudes toward aging and the aged have helped to create the fearsome image of old age that can be likened to a punishment."

The desire to look young is understandable. Increasing age brings us closer to the specter of death (see Chapter 12), whereas youth is associated with vitality and the prospect of many years yet to live. Nevertheless, the preoccupation of our society with a young appearance seems excessive. Looking old is not an illness, nor is it necessarily indicative of any serious impairments in functioning. Rather, it is a normal consequence of the aging process.

Internal Changes

MUSCULATURE. With increasing age, our muscles decrease in strength, endurance, size, and weight relative to total body weight. Muscle fiber is replaced by connective tissue, which causes the muscles to become stiffer and to heal more slowly after an injury. And muscle is gradually replaced by fat, leading to an overall softening of the body. Thus the typical 175-pound man possesses 70 pounds of muscle at age 30, but he retains only about 60 pounds of muscle by old age. It is important to note, though, that these changes may not be due to aging but rather to inactivity, diet, or other long-standing conditions (Spirduso, 1995; Williams, 1995).

Muscle strength reaches its maximum during the 20s and 30s and declines thereafter, particularly after age 60. This has been observed in such areas as handgrip strength and knee extension strength, among others. In fact, there is a 20% reduction in muscle power at age 70 as compared with age 20. There is large variability in the extent to which muscle mass and strength are lost, and much of the loss appears to be related to disuse. (See Horvath & Davis, 1990; Schulz & Curnow, 1988; Spirduso, 1995.)

THE HEART AND CARDIOVASCULAR SYSTEM. The muscles of the heart also deteriorate as we grow older, decreasing their efficiency in transporting blood to the rest of the body. Age-related declines include a prolonged contraction time of the heart muscle, decreased response to various medications that ordinarily stimulate the heart, and increased resistance to electrical stimulation. The heart's electrical system that regulates the heartbeat also becomes less efficient with increasing age. If we go beyond the heart and examine blood vessels such as the arteries we would typically find that they become narrower and less flexible; accumulations of cholesterol collect on the artery walls, which are themselves growing thicker. The net effect is to clog the arteries, increasing the amount of resistance to the flow of blood from the heart. The stiffening of blood vessels has been linked to the increase in blood pressure often observed among elderly individuals, although it is not clear whether blood pressure increases are an inevitable consequence of aging. Because age-associated increases in blood pressure are not found in individuals who live in isolated, less technologically developed societies or in people who grow old in special environments such as mental institutions, it may be that increased blood pressure is a disease process as opposed to a normal aging process (Williams, 1995). (See Figure 3–2; Lakatta, 1990).

The rate of the heartbeat at rest remains about the same throughout adulthood, but there is a significant decline in the maximum heartbeat during exercise. The maximum heart rate changes in a linear fashion and can be estimated by simply subtracting one's age from 220. At age 30, for example, maximum

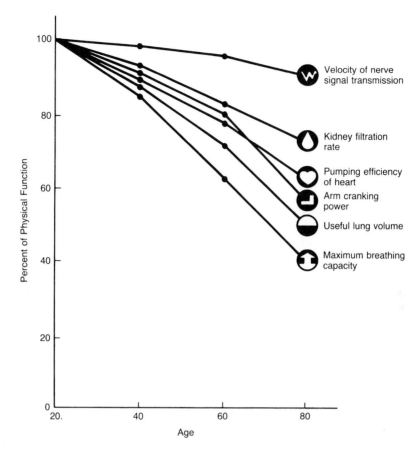

FIGURE 3–2 **Average declines in bodily processes with increasing age for sedentary individuals.**
(*Source:* Modified from Weg (1983, p. 253); Spirduso (1995).)

heart rate is about 190 beats per minute during intense activity; at age 50 it declines to 170 beats per minute. It also takes longer for the older heart to return to the resting rate.

Regular and appropriate exercise, as prescribed by one's personal physician, is generally regarded as an effective way to improve cardiovascular health and extend life (Blair, Kohl, Barlow, Paffenbarger, Gibbons, & Macera, 1995). Exercise lowers the rate of the heart at rest, increases the efficiency of the heart and blood vessels, lowers hypertension (high blood pressure), and reduces the amount of cholesterol in the blood. There is no evidence that exercise will prevent a heart attack, but it can make a satisfactory recovery more likely (Lakatta, 1990; Spirduso, 1995).

THE ENDOCRINE SYSTEM AND MENOPAUSE. One of the most significant changes in a woman's life is menopause, the point in adult development when menstruation stops permanently, signifying the end of her ability to have children. Menopause is the last stage of a gradual biological process in which the ovaries reduce their production of female sex hormones, estrogen and progesterone. This process begins about 3 to 5 years before the final menstrual period and ends on average at about age 50. One of the most common symptoms of menopause is hot flashes or flushes, a sudden sensation of intense heat in the upper part, or all, of the body. The face and neck may become flushed, with red blotches appearing on the chest, back, and arms. This may be followed by sweating and then cold shivering as the body temperature readjusts. Other signs include vaginal and urinary tract changes. The walls of the vagina become thinner, dryer, less elastic, and more vulnerable to infection. The urinary tract also becomes more susceptible to infection. The reduction of sex hormones is also linked to bone loss or osteoporosis in women and to an increased risk of cardiovascular disease. To combat the symptoms associated with declining estrogen levels, many women have turned to hormone replacement therapy (HRT). Although not appropriate for all women, HRT is thought to be an effective treatment for preventing bone loss and heart disease.

THE BRAIN.   At birth, the human brain consists of approximately *1 trillion* neurons. These neurons are the basic building blocks of the brain.

Over the entire life span, the weight of the brain decreases by 5% to 10%, indicating that some neurons have been lost. Losses are particularly marked in some areas such as the cerebellum and hippocampus. The decline in weight occurs more quickly after age 50, amounting to approximately 2% per decade. Ultimately, this weight loss results in smoothed-out ridges and enlarged fissures (Bondareff, 1996; Horvath & Davis, 1990).

Other significant changes that occur in the aging brain may have serious consequences. First of all, damaged and dying neurons may collect around a core of protein substances in the brain. The number of these **neuritic plaques** increases with age and is particularly large among adults age 90 and older. High concentrations of these plaques have been found in individuals suffering from Alzheimer's disease, one of the most destructive of all illnesses that afflict the elderly. (See Chapter 11.) This suggests that neuritic plaques may well interfere with the normal functioning of healthy neurons.

A second important change concerns threadlike structures found within the neurons of the brain. The number of these **neurofibrillary tangles** increases with age in selected areas of the brain, and their presence has also been associated with Alzheimer's disease and other serious disorders.

A less ominous change in the aging brain has to do with **lipofuscin,** a yellow pigment deposited in the neurons as we grow older. The amount of lipofuscin increases linearly with increasing age, but this does *not* appear to be related to serious brain disorders. A fourth change involves important chemical substances, called **neurotransmitters,** which facilitate both communication among the neurons in the brain and the normal functioning of the body. One such neurotransmitter, *dopamine*, is responsible for controlling the motor movements of the body. *Acetylcholine* is involved in memory processes, and *norepinephrine* is linked to memory and learning as well as to the body's response to stress. All of these substances show a decline with increasing age. (See Morgan & May, 1990.) Although these declines are usually not substantial enough to affect normal functioning, large reductions in the neurotransmitters are clearly related to pathology. For example, the severe movement disorders of those who suffer from Parkinsonism is due to insufficient levels of dopamine in the brain. Furthermore, modest decreases in these neurotransmitters may be related to other illnesses.

The news about the aging brain is by no means all bad. Changes in brain structure and biochemistry do not necessarily affect our thinking and behavior. Although our cognitive abilities do seem to decline somewhat with age (see Chapter 5), most older individuals retain high levels of cognitive and behavioral functioning. In addition, recent research suggests that the brain may be more flexible and adaptive than was previously believed (Cotman, 1990; Cotman & Neeper, 1995). Research carried out during the last decade has shown that the brain is capable of preserving, and even repairing, its own circuitry. For example, healthy neurons may grow new neuronal connections to replace ones that are defective or have been lost. At present, there is considerable research interest in identifying those factors that maintain the health of brain cells, stimulate their growth, and protect them against various metabolic insults (Cotman, 1990). Indeed, it appears that some behaviors such as exercise, which promote health in general, may also have beneficial effects on the health and functioning of the brain. Numerous studies with animals have shown that physical activity can influence both brain structure and chemistry in beneficial ways (Cotman & Neeper, 1995).

LUNGS AND THE PULMONARY SYSTEM.   All living cells in the body use oxygen and produce carbon dioxide as a by-product. In conjunction with the circulatory system, the pulmonary system delivers oxygen to the cells and removes carbon dioxide. Aging typically brings a measurable decline in the efficiency of the pulmonary system. The muscles that operate the lungs weaken, and the tissues in the chest cage stiffen, reducing the ability of the lungs to expand. At age 30, for example, we can take a maximum of 6 quarts of air into the lungs. By age 50, this figure may well decline to about 4.5 quarts. And by age 70, the maximum possible air intake for many people is only 3 quarts.

These declines are not inevitable, however. Adults who maintain a high level of physical activity lose much less of their pulmonary efficiency than sedentary persons do. In fact, many elderly adults who are in excellent physical condition have a maximum oxygen consumption that equals or even exceeds that of younger, sedentary individuals (Fleg & Lakatta, 1988; Spirduso, 1995; Williams, 1995). In sum, among healthy individuals the aged pulmonary system functions very well under resting and moderate exercise conditions. Even under extreme exercise conditions the limiting factor is typically not severe breathlessness but rather the inability of the heart to keep up with the demands of intense physical exertion (Spirduso, 1995). Smoking is very detrimental to the functioning of the lungs.

STAMINA.   Because of these changes in the heart, lungs, and muscles, our stamina declines as we grow older. There is less oxygen available to us, and the heart disperses it more slowly through the bloodstream to the muscles. A healthy 70-year-old can still run a marathon with proper training, but it will take him or her at least an hour longer than it would at age 30.

One index of stamina is to determine how many pounds can be turned with a weighted crank in 1 minute, yet still have the heartbeat return to normal after 2 minutes of rest. Using this measure, our stamina decreases by about 15% between ages 30 and 50 and by another 15% between ages 50 and 70.

The age at which our athletic abilities reach their peak depends not only on physiological factors, but also on the type of activity. For athletic events that require strength, speed, and explosive power, such as swimming and running short distances, peak performance is typically achieved during the early 20s. For tasks that involve endurance, acquired skills, and knowledge (long-distance running, golf), peak performance is usually reached during the late 20s and early 30s. (See Table 3–2.)

Despite the age-related declines in physical ability, well-trained competitive masters athletes are capable of very impressive athletic achievements (Spirduso, 1995). For example, a 65-year-old marathon runner of today could have won the marathon at the first Olympic games in 1896. (See Table 3–3.)

BONES AND JOINTS.   Throughout life, old bone is replaced by new bone. Beginning at about age 25 the rate of bone formation begins to fail to keep pace with the rate of bone resorption. As a result, bone loss occurs at the rate of about 1% per

TABLE 3–2   Age of Peak Performance by Type of Event

AGE	MEN	WOMEN
17		swimming
18		
19	swimming	
20		
21		
22		running short distance
23	running short distance	jumping
24	jumping	running medium distance
	running medium distance	tennis; baseball (most strikeouts per
	tennis	innings pitched)
25		
26	baseball (batting)	baseball (earned run average)
27	running long distance	running long distance
28		
29		
30		
31	golf	golf
32		
33		
34		

Source: Schulz and Curnow (1988); Schulz, Musa, Staszewski, and Siegler (1994).

TABLE 3-3 Peak Performance by Olympic Athletes in 1896 and by Masters Athletes in 1990

EVENT (measurement units)	BEST TIME IN OLYMPIC GAMES of 1896	AGE CATEGORY FOR MASTERS ATHLETES IN 1990			
		50–54	55–59	60–64	65–69
100 m (in s)	12.0	11.2			12.5
200 m (in s)	22.2	22.9			25.6
400 m (in s)	54.2	52.2	53.8	55.2	61.1
800 m (in min:s)	2:11.0	2:00.4	2:05.1	2:12.9	2:20.5
1,500 m (in min:s)	4:33.2	4:05.0	4:14.4	4:30.0	4:41.8
Marathon (in hr:min:s)	2:58.5				

Source: Spirduso (1995).

year. By the age of 90, some women may have lost 90% of their bone mass, whereas men may have lost 10% to 25% (Spirduso, 1995).

Among middle-aged and older adults, particularly women, mineral losses may cause the bones to become more brittle and less flexible. Severe bone degeneration can lead to a disease called **osteoporosis,** which most often afflicts women after menopause. Osteoporosis is characterized by a loss of bone mass and increased porosity, which significantly increases the probability of bone fractures and makes recovery slower and more difficult. Although osteoporosis is an illness, rather than a normal consequence of aging, it bears mentioning here because it is so common; more than 20 million Americans are affected by this condition (Meier, 1988; National Institute on Aging, 1998).

Diet and exercise may help prevent osteoporosis. We have learned from numerous space flights that the lack of mechanical stress on the bones experienced by astronauts living in a zero gravity environment accelerates bone loss. Physical exercise, and a diet rich in calcium and vitamin D, and exposure to sunlight can be very effective means for minimizing bone loss.

Women need to be particularly concerned about bone loss during perimenopause, the transitional phase when estrogen levels drop significantly. The most effective therapy against osteoporosis for postmenopausal women is estrogen, which saves more bone tissue than even very large daily doses of calcium. Although taking estrogen is good for the bones, it affects many other tissues and organs in the body and may not be the right choice for all women.

As we grow through adulthood, years of flexing wear down and loosen the cartilage around the joints. Cartilage is the substance that provides the lubricating surface of most joints. Thus our movements tend to be stiffer and slower after age 50, and we are more likely to experience some degree of pain in the joints (Spirduso, 1995).

REFLEXES AND REACTION TIME. A **reflex** is an automatic reaction to external stimulation such as light or mechanical force. The speed of some simple reflexes, such as the knee-jerk reflex, remains relatively constant during adulthood. However, other reflexes deteriorate with increasing age. Deep tendon reflexes undergo a severe decline, so much so that ankle jerks are absent in approximately one half of the elderly (Harridge & Saltin, 1996; Spirduso, 1995).

Many situations in life such as driving a car or playing a sport require rapid response if we are to avoid outcomes such as hitting a pedestrian or being hit on the head with a baseball. **Reaction time** is a measure of our ability to respond quickly. It is defined as the time between the onset of a stimulus and the subject's response, and is usually measured in hundredths of a second. Simple reaction time measures an individual's ability to respond to a single stimulus with a single prescribed response; choice reaction times typically involve several stimuli and the selection of one of several responses. Our ability to respond to a single stimulus depends largely on sensory and motor abilities. Choice reaction times require in addition some cognitive processing. In general, age-related declines in simple reaction time are smaller than declines in choice reaction times. Aging produces a significant decrease in our ability to react quickly to stimuli (such as a novel sound), especially after age 70 (Seidler & Stelmach, 1996). This is due primarily to changes in the brain, which takes longer to process the information and to respond appropriately. Older adults therefore tend to perform more poorly on tasks that are highly speeded or more complex, an issue we discuss further in Chapter 5 (Cerella, 1995).

DIGESTION.   Digestion involves many body organs, including the esophagus, stomach, pancreas, gallbladder, liver, small intestine, and colon. As we grow older, the muscles of the digestive system act more slowly, and the production of acid is reduced. The ability to digest fat, protein, and carbohydrates may therefore decrease slightly among the elderly, but this usually does not lead to significant problems (Ausman & Russell, 1990; Williams, 1995). In fact, when digestive problems do occur, they are usually attributable to other causes. Older adults are more likely to require laxatives and sedatives, and these drugs tend to reduce the efficiency of the digestive system. A loss of appetite may also be caused by depression, a common form of adult psychopathology. (See Chapter 11.)

EXCRETION.   During the course of adulthood, each kidney loses approximately one half of its nephrons (tubules). Because of this reduced reserve, the kidneys filter waste out of blood only one half as fast at age 70 as at age 30. Another consequence is that stress is more likely to precipitate kidney failure in older adults.

The bladder loses some 50% of its capacity by old age, and it becomes less elastic. As a result, urinary elimination is more frequent, more urgent, and less complete among older adults. Constipation is more likely, however, due to slower peristalsis and increased absorption of water from the large intestine (Lindeman, 1996; Williams, 1995).

AFTERWORD: AGING AND VULNERABILITY TO DISEASE.   The physiological changes just discussed are part of the normal process of aging. Most of these changes experienced as a part of the normal process of aging are not troublesome in any practical sense. Some involve a certain amount of inconvenience or discomfort but are not incapacitating or fatal, such as stiffness in the joints or declines in muscle strength. Thus most older people deal quite well with these changes. Of the approximately 95% of adults over age 65 who are able to remain in their communities, the large majority (77%) suffer no significant limitations in their mobility and cope more than adequately with the challenges of everyday living. Insofar as normal aging is concerned, then, there is no empirical support for the stereotype of the physically incapacitated and helpless older adult. (See Figure 3–3.)

However, aging does have one ominous physiological aspect. Because of the reduced efficiency of most bodily systems, older adults are more vulnerable to disease than are young adults, and they are twice as likely to be physically disabled and to require hospitalization. Some age-related ailments can cause severe pain, such as arthritis. Others are fatal. Cardiovascular disease, cancer, and cerebrovascular accidents (strokes), the three leading causes of death in the United States, have their greatest incidence among older persons. Therefore, to understand more fully the nature of age-related physiological changes, we must now consider the relationship between aging and pathology.

Aging and Pathology

Major Causes of Death.   The probability of dying from cardiovascular disease, cancer, or a stroke increases dramatically as we grow past middle age. Among adults age 25 to 44, only about 1 of every 4,000 suffers a fatal heart attack. This figure increases to approximately 1 in 300 for those age 45 to 64, whereas about 1 of every 25 adults past age 75 dies from heart disease. Similar age-related increases are found in the mortality rates for cancer and strokes. (See Table 3–4.)

FIGURE 3–3   Percentage of noninstitutionalized adults age 65 and older who have difficulty with various daily activities.
(*Source:* U.S. Bureau of the Census (1997).)

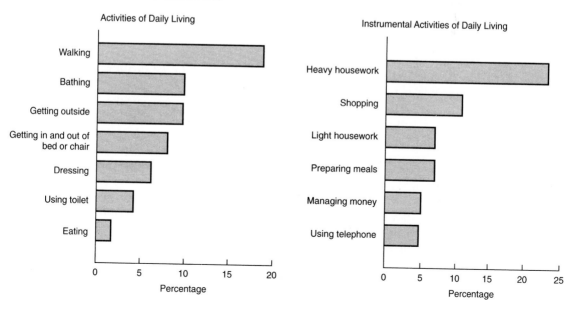

TABLE 3–4   Rank Order of Leading Causes of Death, by Age

	AGE GROUPS			
LEADING CAUSES OF DEATH	15–24	25–44	45–64	65+
Heart disease	5	3	2	1
Cancer	4	2	1	2
Accidents and adverse effects	1	1	3	7
Cerebrovascular diseases	6*	7	4	3
Chronic obstructive pulmonary diseases	6*	10	5	4
Pneumonia, flu	6*	9	9	5
Suicide	3	4	8	9
Chronic liver disease, cirrhosis	8	6	7	8
Diabetes mellitus	7	8	6	6
Homicide and legal intervention	2	5	10	10

*Tied ranks.

Source: U.S. Bureau of the Census (1997).

Cardiovascular disease, the leading cause of death in the United States, is defined as any problem of the heart or blood circulation. It is most often caused by a thickening and hardening of the arteries (atherosclerosis). As we grow older, some atherosclerosis is inevitable; it leads to cardiovascular disease only when it becomes so severe that the heart cannot get enough blood and oxygen to function normally. For example, a heart attack (myocardial infarction) occurs when part of the heart muscle dies because of an inadequate flow of blood. Chest pains (angina) are caused by an inadequate supply of blood and oxygen to the muscles of the heart. A stroke occurs when a blockage in the flow of blood and oxygen causes brain tissue to be destroyed (Kerson, 1985; Williams, 1995).

Each year, cardiovascular disease causes approximately 1 million deaths in the United States, or roughly one half of all the deaths in this country. It is the leading cause of death for both men and women. The next most frequent cause, cancer, is responsible for only about one half as many deaths as cardiovascular disease. Thus, even if someone were to find a cure for cancer, the average life span would be extended by less than 2 years because heart disease is so prevalent. To be sure, there has been a substantial decline in the death rate from heart attacks since 1950, especially among older adults. (See Figure 3–4.) But the United States still has the greatest number of fatal heart attacks in the world; Japan has the fewest. One reason why the frequency of fatal heart attacks has declined during the past two decades is the fact that we have become more knowledgeable. Research has shown that some of the most important causes are within our control, at least to some extent. These include cigarette smoking (which doubles the risk of a heart attack), high blood pressure, a high level of blood cholesterol, obesity, physical inactivity, and stress (American Heart Association, 1998). Some personality characteristics may also be related to heart disease, although this is more controversial. (See Chapter 7.)

Various demographic characteristics are also associated with a greater likelihood of cardiovascular disease. You are much more likely to suffer a heart attack if you are age 65 or older and if you are male. Heart disease is the leading

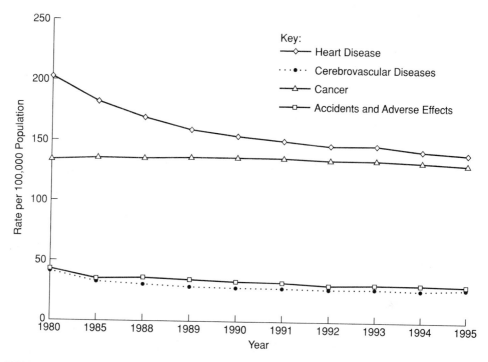

FIGURE 3–4 **Age-adjusted death rates, by selected causes: 1980–1995.**
(*Source:* U.S. Bureau of the Census (1997).)

cause of death among men age 40 and older, and 1 of every 5 men will develop coronary heart disease before reaching age 60. Conversely, it is only after age 60 that heart disease becomes the leading cause of death for women. Heart attacks are also more common among whites than among blacks. (See American Heart Association, 1998; Kerson, 1985.)

All **cancers** share a common definition: They are an uncontrolled growth of abnormal cells, which spread to other parts of the body through the blood or lymphatic systems. There are five common types of cancer cells, each of which tends to form in a different part of the body and grow at a different rate. *Carcinoma* arises in the surface layer of the skin, glands, or linings of body organs. *Melanoma* is a specific form of carcinoma that lodges in the cells which produce our skin pigment. *Sarcoma* emerges in connective or supporting tissues, such as bones, cartilage, and fat. *Lymphoma* originates in the lymph nodes, and *leukemia* results in transformations of white blood cells.

Cancer is the second greatest cause of death in the United States, accounting for approximately 3.5 million fatalities during the 1980s. One of every five Americans will experience cancer directly, and 75% will have a family member who contracts this illness (American Cancer Society, 1997). Although the number of cancer cases and resulting deaths has increased steadily during the past few decades, there is some good news: Today's cancer patients are more likely to survive for several years after the initial diagnosis than patients of 50 years ago.

Mortality rates are declining for younger people and for certain types of cancer that were formerly considered incurable (Hodgkin's disease, childhood leukemia, ovarian and testicular tumors). Nevertheless, a substantial proportion of all cancer patients still die within 5 years of diagnosis. (See American Cancer Society, 1997.) Most cancer is detected in middle age or later; approximately two thirds of those suffering from this disease are age 55 or older (American Cancer Society, 1997). Cancer is equally likely to strike men and women, although some types occur more often among members of one sex. There are, however, pronounced ethnic differences. During the past 30 years, the occurrence of cancer increased by 27% for blacks but only 12% for whites, whereas deaths from cancer increased by almost 50% for blacks but only 10% for whites (American Cancer Society, 1997).

Cancer is most often found in the lungs, colon or rectum, breast, and prostate. Lung cancer, the most common form for women as well as men, is the most frequent cause of death among the cancers. In theory, this variety should be the most easily preventable; cigarette smoking is linked to 83% of all lung cancer and to 30% of all deaths from cancer. One reason for the frequency of lung cancer fatalities is the fact that it stalks its victims silently: The symptoms typically become apparent only when the disease is in its advanced stages, making successful treatment less likely (American Cancer Society, 1997; Williams, 1995).

Strokes are characterized by brain damage, and by the often severe disabilities that result. Strokes most often occur when a cerebral artery becomes occluded, blocking the flow of blood to the cerebral hemispheres; or when a blood vessel ruptures, producing a brain hemorrhage. The likelihood of a stroke increases sharply with increasing age, making this one of the most common illnesses afflicting older adults. Eighty percent of first-time stroke patients are age 65 and older, and the median age for a first stroke is 71 years for men and 74 years for women. Blacks are much more likely than whites to die of strokes, in part because they more often suffer from high blood pressure. In all, the annual number of strokes in the United States ranges from 600,000 to 750,000, and about 150,000 of these strokes are fatal.

The frequency of strokes in the United States has declined steadily in recent years, and survival rates have increased. Although approximately 30% of stroke sufferers do not survive the first 30 days, many live for years. Survival, however, carries a price. Because strokes often cause severe physical, cognitive, and social disabilities, they are the third leading cause not only of death in older persons but also of chronic long-term disability. (See Biegel, Sales, & Schulz, 1991.)

ACCIDENTS.   From birth to age 44, you are more likely to die from an accident than from any other single cause. However, the odds against such an event are decidedly in your favor; the death rate due to accidents for this age group is only about 1 in 2,300.

Older adults have relatively low accident *rates*. For example, adults over age 65 suffer only about one half as many accidents as do children age 6 to 16. But because the middle aged and elderly have more brittle bones and less efficient bodily systems, the *consequences* of their accidents are more severe; healing is significantly slower, hospitalization is more often necessary, and death is more likely.

Thus, for adults past age 75, the death rate due to accidents is approximately 1 in 600. Among adults age 65 to 74, motor vehicle accidents are the most common cause of accidental death (U.S. Bureau of the Census, 1997; Williams, 1995).

CHRONIC HEALTH CONDITIONS.   **Chronic** conditions are characterized by a slow onset and a long duration. Although these **disorders** are rarely found among young adults, they account for the majority of disabilities after middle age. The most common are arthritis and hypertension.

Arthritis is a disease category that includes more than 100 different conditions, including inflammation of the joints (rheumatoid arthritis), degenerative joint disease (osteoarthritis), gout, connective tissue disease, and others. The primary symptom, pain in the joints, can be intense—so much so that arthritis is currently the major cause of limited activity among older adults. However, the severity of this disease varies greatly from person to person; one adult with arthritis may suffer only from occasional flare-ups, whereas another may be housebound. As many as 80% of all recently retired persons experience some degree of arthritis (Brock, Guralnik, & Brody, 1990; Williams, 1995), whereas approximately 25% of adults age 45 to 64 and almost one half of those 65 and older require treatment for this disorder. (See Figures 3–5 and 3–6.)

FIGURE 3–5 **Most prevalent chronic conditions as a function of age in females.** (*Source:* U.S. Bureau of the Census (1997).)

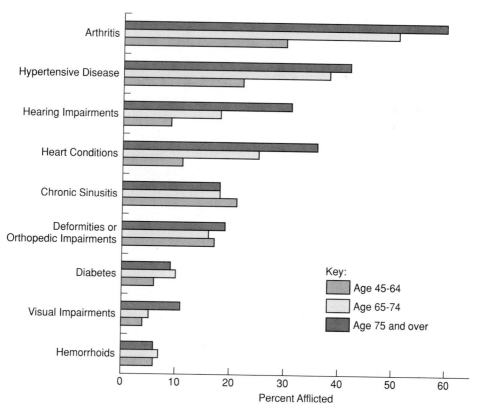

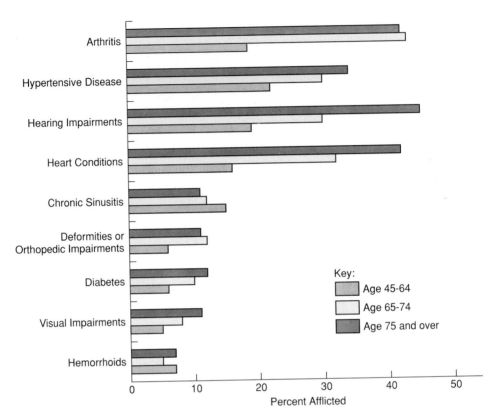

FIGURE 3–6 **Most prevalent chronic conditions as a function of age in males.**
(*Source:* U.S. Bureau of the Census (1997).)

The etiology of arthritis is still unclear, nor are there any known cures. Various forms of treatment may help alleviate pain and maintain the mobility and strength of the afflicted joints, including anti-inflammatory drugs (e.g., aspirin; cortisone derivatives), mild exercise, heat, and cold (Williams, 1995).

Hypertension involves a consistent pattern of elevated blood pressure. Among the probable causes are excessive weight, stress, smoking, and perhaps a high salt intake. In contrast to arthritis, hypertension does not produce noticeable pain. Yet it can have even more serious consequences because it increases the likelihood of strokes, congestive heart failure, and heart attacks and other coronary diseases (O'Brien & Bulpitt, 1995). Approximately 40% of strokes in elderly men and 70% of strokes in elderly women are directly related to high blood pressure.

Hypertension is significantly higher in blacks than in whites, especially for women. According to one estimate, hypertension afflicts 39% of black women, 25% of white women, 38% of black men, and 33% of white men. As a result, blacks are much more likely than whites to die of strokes. (See National Institute on Aging, 1989f.) About half of all older persons between the ages of 65 and 74 in the United States suffer from this disease.

Losing weight, eating less salt, engaging in moderate and regular exercise, and increasing relaxation may also be effective in lowering blood pressure, particularly for people with mild or borderline high blood pressure (Williams, 1995). If nondrug treatments are unsuccessful, various prescription drugs are commonly used to control high blood pressure. Because of concerns about the side effects of drug treatment for high blood pressure, some experts advise restraint in their use (Williams, 1995).

The adverse effects of arthritis, hypertension, and other chronic conditions are more widespread than may be apparent. Family members who help to care for their loved one may experience considerable emotional pain (Biegel, Sales, & Schulz, 1991; Schulz, O'Brien, Bookwala, & Fleissner, 1995), and society must explore alternative ways of providing the professional care that these patients need. (We have more to say about these issues in Chapter 9.) Furthermore, most chronic conditions affect the patient's sense of well-being, as well as the ability to function. For example, arthritis is not only extremely painful and often debilitating; it also causes a decline in the patient's mental health and perceived physical health. (See Table 3–5.) Thus, even though most chronic conditions are not life threatening, their consequences can be extremely serious.

AFTERWORD: AGING, ACTUAL HEALTH, AND SELF-PERCEIVED HEALTH. Although physical helplessness and dependency are *not* characteristic of old age, certain painful chronic disorders are more likely (e.g., arthritis). As a result, adults past age 75 experience about twice as many days per year of restricted activity and bed disability as do those age 45 to 54. Also, the probability of suffering a fatal illness or accident is much greater after middle age.

Nevertheless, the majority of older Americans assess their health favorably. Some 72% of adults age 65 and over described their health as good, very good, or excellent. Only 9% feel their health is poor. These percentages are only somewhat smaller than the corresponding figures for younger adults: Approximately 82% of the middle aged (age 45–54) and 92% of young adults (age

TABLE 3–5 Effects of Chronic Conditions on Functional Status and Well-Being

	FUNCTIONING			Mental Health	Perceived Health	Bodily Pain
Chronic Condition	Physical	Role	Social			
Angina	X	X	X	X	X	X
Arthritis	X	X	X	X	X	X
Back problems	X	X	0	0	X	X
Diabetes	X	X	X	0	X	0
Gastrointestinal disorders	X	X	X	X	X	X
Hypertension	0	0	0	0	X	X
Myocardial infarction	X	X	X	0	X	0

Key: 0: No significant difference between patients with chronic condition and adults with no chronic conditions.
X: Patients suffering from chronic condition report significant negative effects compared with adults with no chronic conditions.

Source: Adapted from Stewart et al. (1989), *JAMA*; 262 (7): 907–913. © 1989, American Medical Association.

25–34) rate their health as good or excellent (Schulz et al., 1994; U.S. Bureau of the Census, 1997).

Personal health status is a function of both actual and self-perceived health. Adults who believe themselves to be physically healthy are more likely to be active and independent, whereas those who regard their health as poor tend to behave accordingly and even die sooner (Idler & Angel, 1990; Idler, Kasl, & Lemke, 1990; Schulz et al., 1994). To be sure, the generally positive self-perceptions of older adults are due in part to more pessimistic expectations. It is well known that illness and disability are more common after middle age, so older adults may regard some degree of pain and inconvenience as normal for their age. Even so, we can conclude our discussion of aging and pathology on an optimistic note: Despite the greater likelihood of certain chronic disorders and potentially fatal illnesses, the substantial majority of older adults do *not* regard themselves as in poor health or as seriously disabled. It should not be surprising therefore that older persons rate the quality of their lives very highly.

THEORIES OF AGING

The physical changes described in the preceding pages have been affecting humankind for thousands of years. Human beings have been trying to understand why these changes occur for just as long, partly out of curiosity but also because we would like to discover ways in which aging might be stopped, slowed, postponed, or even reversed. Theories of aging have been around for more than 2,000 years. For example, Galen (A.D. 129–c. 199) thought aging was due to changes in body humors that began early in life and these changes gradually caused a slow increase in dryness and coldness of the body. Roger Bacon (c. 1220–1292) was one of the first to suggest a "wear and tear" theory of aging (e.g., aging is the result of abuses of and insults to the body system) and that good hygiene might slow the aging process. Even Charles Darwin (1809–1882) had a theory of aging, attributing it to the loss of irritability in nervous and muscular tissue. Scientists still do not know *why* we age. Various biological theories of aging have been proposed, some of which appear to be quite promising. However, no one theory has as yet achieved general acceptance. Modern theories of aging are extremely complex and beyond the scope of this book. Accordingly, the discussion that follows only provides a general overview of three types of theories: genetic cellular theories, nongenetic cellular theories, and physiological system theories.

Genetic Cellular Theories

The maximum life span varies greatly among different species. As we observed in Chapter 1, the greatest recorded human age is 120 years. In contrast, the maximum life span for horses is 46 years; cats, 28 years; dogs, 20 years; black rats, 5 years; and the mayfly, only 1 day. (See Table 3–6; Comfort, 1964; Kirkwood,

MYTHS ABOUT AGING

Physiological Aspects

Myth	*Best Available Evidence*
Our physiological processes remain at a fairly constant level of efficiency until we approach old age, at which time they undergo a drastic decline.	Most of our bodily functions reach their maximum capacity prior to or during early adulthood and begin a gradual decline thereafter.
Most adults proceed at much the same rate through a series of similar physical stages.	Age-related physical changes do *not* occur according to a strict time-table. Adults age at different rates, and such groupings as "the elderly" are more heterogeneous than is commonly believed.
Most adults past age 65 are so physically incapacitated that they must depend to a great extent on other people.	Helplessness and dependency are *not* characteristic of old age. Some 87% of adults over 65 are able to cope more than adequately with the demands of everyday living.
Taking large doses of antioxidants (or ginseng, or selenium, or pantothenic acid, or vitamin C) will extend the length of your life.	There are *no* drugs, pills, powders, vitamins, dietary supplements, or diets with proven anti-aging capacities.

1985.) Furthermore, humans with long-lived parents and grandparents live an average of 6 years longer than those whose parents die before the age of 50 (National Institute on Aging, 1993). It has also been observed that human body cells grown in tissue cultures (in vitro) are able to divide only about 50 times, after which they age and die (Hayflick, 1986). The reproductive capacity of cells taken from old animals is even more limited; these cells can undergo only about one half as many divisions as those obtained from young animals.

Findings such as these imply that cellular aging is programmed by our genes. According to this view, life span, as well as other age-related events such as puberty and menopause, are controlled by one or more specific genes that dictate cellular aging and ultimately the longevity of the organism. Some kind of

TABLE 3–6   Maximum Recorded Life Spans
for Various Species

COMMON NAME	MAXIMUM LIFE SPAN (YEARS)
Human	120
Galapagos tortoise	100 +
Indian elephant	70
Eagle owl	68
Snapping turtle	58 +
Chinese alligator	52
Horse	46
Golden eagle	46
Chimpanzee	44
Gorilla	39
Brown bear	36
Common toad	36
Domestic dove	30
Anaconda	29
Domestic cat	28
Swine	27
Porcupine	27
Domestic dog	20
Sheep	20
Gray squirrel	15
Vampire bat	13
Black rat	5
House mouse	3

Source: Modified from Kirkwood (1985, p. 34).

clock mechanism exists in normal cells, and this mechanism controls the capacity of the cells to function and to replicate (Hayflick, 1986; National Institute on Aging, 1993). Because a direct relationship exists between the life span of a species and the capacity of its cells to divide, this suggests in turn that age-related changes are programmed into the genes of each species. Thus **genetic cellular theories** attribute aging to changes in two complicated kinds of molecules: **deoxyribonucleic acid (DNA),** which controls the formation of proteins required by the cell to maintain life (Watson, 1969), and **ribonucleic acid (RNA),** which transfers information from the DNA molecules to another location in the cell where the proteins are assembled.

DNA DAMAGE THEORIES.   Some genetic cellular theories posit that damage to the DNA molecules is responsible for human aging. This damage may be caused by exposure to radiation, or it may consist of harmful cellular mutations (e.g., Martin & Baker, 1993; National Institute on Aging, 1993; Yates, 1996).

Although some early studies appeared to support DNA damage theory, more recent research has unearthed some important contradictions. Mutations and radiation affect dividing cells, whereas the physiological effects of aging are due primarily to cells that are no longer able to divide. Mutations occur too slowly to account for the pronounced physiological changes that occur with increasing age. Furthermore, in marked contrast to aging, damage to the DNA molecules is usually reversible because most cells contain appropriate repair mechanisms. (See Martin, 1977; Tice & Setlow, 1985; Wheeler & Lett, 1974.) For these reasons, it is extremely doubtful that damage to the DNA molecule itself plays much of a role in aging (Vijg, 1996).

ERROR THEORIES.   An alternative model focuses on the transmission of genetic information from the DNA molecules to the place where proteins are assembled (ribosome). This transfer is accomplished with the aid of the RNA molecules. Errors are more likely insofar as the RNA molecules are concerned because these molecules are relatively unstable and are formed continuously, whereas DNA molecules are highly stable and are maintained throughout the life span of a cell. According to this model, errors in transmission produce a protein or enzyme that is *not* an exact copy of the original and which therefore cannot carry out its function of maintaining life. As a result, the cells grow older and die, and so do we. (See Martin, 1977; Martin & Baker, 1992; Reff, 1985.)

To date, error theorists have not been able to specify the precise nature of the hypothesized errors in transmission. In fact, the details of the transfer process itself have not yet been clearly fully identified. However, recent advances in technology have enabled researchers to improve their ability to measure accurately the rate of mutation. Some recent findings suggest possible relationships between somatic mutations and age-related illnesses such as certain types of cancer (Vijg, 1996). *In sum*, the error hypothesis remains a promising one, likely to be a source of active controversy and research in the future.

Nongenetic Cellular Theories

Some researchers argue that in vitro experiments with culture tissue are not applicable to aging as it occurs in living tissue (in vivo) and that the concept of an innate biological clock is therefore incorrect. Instead, these theorists contend that aging involves a gradual deterioration of bodily cells that is *not* internally programmed. Consider an automobile that ages over a period of years: The engine becomes less efficient, the battery dies, rust invades the exterior, and so on. These changes are more or less predictable but do not follow any specific timetable, internal or otherwise. Rather, wear and tear plays a major role: A car sheltered in a garage and rarely driven will last far longer than one driven 20,000 miles per year and parked in the street.

Unlike machines, the human body has mechanisms for self-repair. New cells are continually formed to replace old ones, and molecules may undergo replacement within a single cell. Nevertheless, various factors might conceivably cause cells to wear out faster than the repairs can take place. Thus **nongenetic cellular (wear and tear) theories** assume that with the passage of time, changes occur in the cells that impair their effectiveness. That is, aging is due to progressive damage to the organism from its internal and external environment.

ACCUMULATION THEORIES.   According to some theorists, aging is caused by the accumulation of various harmful substances in the cells of the organism. All older cells contain a dark-colored, insoluble substance (lipofuscin), with the amount of this material increasing at a constant rate over time. (See National Institute on Aging, 1993.) It is logical to assume that this "cellular garbage" interferes with cellular functioning because it takes up space and serves no useful purpose and might even ultimately result in the death of the cell. But although this hypothesis is a tenable one, there is as yet no conclusive evidence in its favor.

CROSS-LINKAGE THEORIES.   A second possibility is that with the passage of time, harmful cross-linkages (bonds) develop between component parts of the same molecule or between two different molecules. Extracellular proteins (e.g., collagen) develop an increasing number of cross-linkages with increasing age, and collagen is related to the aging of the skin (as we have seen). This model posits that cross-linkages ultimately lead to severe oxygen deficiency and to other biochemical failures (National Institute on Aging, 1993; Sprott & Austad, 1995). However, the available empirical evidence concerning cross-linkages and aging is also inconclusive.

FREE RADICAL THEORY.   A third nongenetic cellular theory attributes aging to the operation of specific cross-linking agents called *free radicals*. These chemical compounds contain one or more unpaired electrons in the outer orbitals and thus are able to link to tissue and cause damage. Free radicals oxidize and attack other cellular components, causing alterations and malfunctions that accumulate throughout life (see Balin & Vilenchik, 1996; National Institute on Aging, 1993; Scoggins, 1981). The resulting damage associated with the accumulation of free radicals is thought to be a cause of aging and has been linked to a number of aging-related diseases. It has been suggested that free radicals in the body can be reduced by consuming supplementary doses of vitamin C and E and beta-carotenes. Although this hypothesis is currently being studied seriously, at present no clear evidence supports the use of vitamin supplements as anti-aging agents.

Physiological System Theories

A third group of theories attributes aging to the gradual failure of certain physiological systems and to the resulting inability of these systems to coordinate important bodily functions. According to this view, in order for the body to function properly both cellular functions and organ systems have to be carefully integrated and coordinated. When one or more of the regulatory systems of the body breaks down, the organism eventually dies. A great deal of evidence suggests that regulatory processes are particularly vulnerable to aging. To date, a great deal of research has focused on the **immune system** and the **neuroendocrine system**.

IMMUNOLOGICAL THEORIES.   The immune system protects the body against invading microorganisms and against atypical mutant cells that may form within the body (e.g., cancer). It does so in two ways: by generating antibodies that react with the proteins of foreign organisms, and by forming special cells that engulf and digest the foreign cells.

Aging has a pronounced negative effect on the capabilities of the immune system. The production of antibodies peaks during adolescence and declines thereafter, and the ability to recognize mutated cells also declines with increasing age. Thus the increase in cancer rates among older adults, discussed previously, may well be due to failures of the immune system. In fact, some theorists define aging as a disease of the immune system. For example, one interesting hypothesis—autoimmunity theory—relates aging to the development of antibodies that act against normal and necessary bodily cells. (See Miller, 1995; Weksler, 1981.) This theory proposes that with age the immune system loses its capacity to distinguish foreign antigens from normal body materials. As a result, antibodies are formed that attack and destroy normal cells or fail to recognize and destroy small detrimental mutations that occur in cells. Thus the development of autoimmunity may be doubly lethal; the immune system not only becomes less protective against foreign objects, but it actively begins to destroy its host (Spirduso, 1995). Although we are still in the early stages of testing hypotheses derived from immune function theories, this approach has great potential in helping us understand the aging of the organism.

NEUROENDOCRINE THEORIES.   The neuroendocrine system is a complicated interactive system that includes a number of glands (e.g., pituitary, thyroid, pancreas, adrenal, ovaries, and testes) and the hypothalamus. Proper function of this system requires both the central nervous system (e.g., the hypothalamus) and the endocrine system to be in good working condition. Its function is to regulate various important bodily processes, such as metabolic rate, glucose and water level, and temperature. This system is critical in helping the body adapt to real or perceived environmental challenges, such as increases or decreases in temperature, increases in physical work, or psychological threats. (See Mobbs, 1995.)

The functioning of the endocrine system declines significantly with increasing age. For example, when blood sugar rises, the pancreas of older adults does not release sufficient insulin as quickly. (See Mobbs, 1995; Williams, 1995.) This is one reason why diabetes is more prevalent among the middle aged and elderly (see Figures 3–5 and 3–6).

Researchers have been particularly interested in the functioning of the hypothalamus and pituitary gland (i.e., the hypothalamus-pituitary axis), which regulates the thyroid, the adrenal gland, and the release of sex hormones, estrogen and testosterone. For example, adequate levels of estrogen in females seem to protect them against some symptoms of aging such as cardiovascular disease. After menopause, when estrogen levels decline, biological aging appears to accelerate in women, and estrogen replacement therapy seems to slow down this process. This type of evidence has caused some researchers to speculate that some sort of biological clock resides in the hypothalamus and controls the rate of aging. These are provocative and important ideas worthy of future research efforts.

AFTERWORD.   Do we possess a built-in biological clock that governs the rate of aging and perhaps even the time of our death? Or do our cells undergo a gradual breakdown over time that is *not* genetically programmed, with aging due primarily to cellular wear and tear? Or is aging caused by the failure of certain physiological coordinating systems, such as the immune or endocrine systems?

As the preceding survey indicates, we do not yet know the answers to these questions. The theories we discussed represent only a sampling of those that have received research attention during the last few decades. Conceivably, there may be some truth in all of them. Because each one of these theories focuses on a different aspect of the aging process, they are not necessarily incompatible. Indeed, aging may occur because of an interaction among genetic, damage, and system mechanisms. Research into the causes of aging is still at an early stage, hence the large number of competing theories. But interest in this area is flourishing, so we may reasonably expect more conclusive findings to emerge in the not too distant future.

LENGTHENING LIFE

The quest for perpetual youth is as old as recorded history. People of various eras have tried to reverse the process of aging with magic, potions, sorcery, rituals, unusual diets, vitamins, and chemicals of various kinds.

Many of these procedures appear ludicrous by modern standards. The ancient Babylonians and Australian aborigines sought to prolong life by administering semen potions, or aphrodisiacs made from tigers' testes, to the feeble or dying. When the biblical King David was old and ill, his doctors prescribed close contact with a young female virgin, trusting that this would enable him to absorb her youth. The Taoists of 300 B.C. believed that men could achieve greater longevity by failing to reach sexual climax, thereby preserving their life essence, or semen. And the 16th-century explorer Ponce de León heard tales of a fountain in the Bahamas whose waters rejuvenated the aged, and he set out to find it. Navigation techniques not being very advanced in those days, he never did locate the fountain of youth. Instead, he accidentally discovered Florida, which ironically is now a major retirement area for the elderly.

Despite centuries of efforts like these, there are as yet *no* scientifically accepted elixirs, drugs, or dietary supplements that will extend the length of human life. There *are* ways to improve your chances of staying healthy and living longer, but these methods involve the more difficult course of changing your behavior.

Modern Quests for the Fountain of Youth

People today are of course much more realistic about the possibility of lengthening human life—or are we? Americans spend *billions of dollars each year* on unproven anti-aging remedies (Meister, 1984). Some of these popular prescriptions are based on misrepresentations or overgeneralizations of gerontological research findings; others are pure quackery.

ANTI-AGING HEALTH FRAUDS. "Moon dust," promoted as a cure for arthritis and other afflictions, cost $100 for 3 ounces—and turned out to be just plain sand. The "miracle spike," a tube containing about a penny's worth of barium chloride (a chemical used in rat poison), was supposed to be worn around the neck as a cure for cancer and diabetes. It cost $300. The "Congo Kit," billed as a cure for arthritis, was actually two hemp mittens. Promoters have also advised arthritics to bury themselves in the earth, sit in an abandoned mine, or stand naked under a 1,000-watt bulb at the time of the full moon. These are just a few of the several hundred worthless, unproven, and sometimes harmful ways that entrepreneurs have sold hope to the desperate.

The telltale signs of dishonest promoters include the following:

◆ Promising a quick or painless cure
◆ Promoting a product made from a "special" or "secret" formula, usually available through the mail and from only one sponsor
◆ Presenting testimonials or case histories from satisfied patients
◆ Advertising a product as effective for a wide variety of ailments
◆ Claiming to have the cure for a disease (such as arthritis or cancer) that is not yet understood by medical science. (National Institute on Aging, 1998)

A good rule of thumb is that if it seems too good to be true, it probably is.

Not all anti-aging treatments are as bizarre as these examples. In this section, we discuss some of the more plausible approaches.

ANTIOXIDANTS. Some advertisements and popular best-sellers contend that life can be extended by taking large doses of **antioxidants,** compounds that block much of the damage to bodily proteins caused by free radicals. Although some laboratory experiments have obtained significant positive results with specially bred mice, there is as yet no convincing evidence that antioxidants will extend human life.

As we have seen, free radical theory remains controversial. Even if this theory is correct, the body's need for antioxidants can be met simply by eating a variety of nutritious foods, and there is no indication that surplus amounts will do a better job of fighting free radicals. Some antioxidant supplements are actually useless because they are digested before body cells can use them (e.g., superoxide dismutase, or SOD), and large doses of certain other antioxidants can be harmful (National Institute on Aging, 1998). Some very recent findings suggest that antioxidant supplements may improve the cognitive functioning of Alzheimer's patients, but this hypothesis needs further verification.

DNA AND RNA. Some proponents of DNA damage theory argue that supplements containing DNA and RNA will slow aging, cure senility, and treat skin and hair changes. Here again, no scientific evidence supports these claims (National Institute on Aging, 1998). When DNA and RNA are taken by mouth, they are broken down into other substances and cannot get to individual cells or do any good.

OTHER DIETARY SUPPLEMENTS. Various other dietary supplements have been promoted as anti-aging remedies. These include selenium, ginseng, paraaminobenzoic acid (PABA), pantothenic acid, and vitamins C and E, and a variety of different hormones.

Although selenium is an essential nutrient, there is no evidence that it reverses or retards the aging process, and excess amounts are toxic. Ginseng is notorious as an aphrodisiac and rejuvenator, yet no convincing empirical data support these claims. Large doses of ginseng may well produce such side effects as nervousness, insomnia, gastrointestinal disorders, and elevated blood pressure. Huge doses of PABA do appear to darken gray hair, but also tend to cause nausea, vomiting, and blood disorders. Pantothenic acid is a component of Royal Jelly, the substance that turns female bees into long-lived fertile queens instead of short-lived sterile workers. This useful vitamin is present in so many foods that deficiencies are virtually impossible, making supplemental doses unnecessary. Nor is there scientific reason to believe that dietary supplements of vitamin C, or of any other vitamin, have any effects on the aging process (National Institute on Aging, 1996).

DHEA, or dehydroepiandrosterone, is a hormone that has turned back some signs of aging in animals. When given to mice, it has boosted their immune system and helped prevent some kinds of cancer. Substances labeled DHEA are being sold as a way to extend life, although no one knows whether they are effective.

Growth hormone (GH) is another substance claimed to slow down aging and extend life (Wolfe, 1998). Growth hormone declines in humans after their fourth decade and is hypothesized to be responsible for some of the physical, psychological, and immunological declines associated with late life. For more than 13 years researchers have been testing the idea that keeping GH secretion at its youthful level in old age should help maintain the individual's youthful physical characteristics such as muscle and bone strength. At this point in time, this idea still stands as a hypothesis as opposed to known fact (Wolfe, 1998). A note of caution is also appropriate. Hormone therapies of various types are currently available, some with proven effectiveness such as estrogen therapy. However, the side effects of some hormones can be very serious; high amounts of some hormones have been linked to cancer.

RESTRICTED DIETS. Yet another proposed method for extending life is to eat fewer calories while maintaining a nutritionally sound diet ("undernutrition without malnutrition"). Unlike other diets, this regimen is *not* discontinued when the dieter achieves the weight generally accepted as ideal, but is continued indefinitely.

Insofar as laboratory animals are concerned, the preponderance of research evidence does support this hypothesis. Food restriction is one strategy that appears to alter the rate of aging. In a typical study of this type, rats are fed a diet that is nutritionally adequate but only two thirds as much as they would normally eat. Animals treated in this way had much longer average and maximum life spans than did control animals who were allowed to eat all they wanted. Milder caloric restrictions, begun early in life, have been found to produce moderate life extension with only slight reductions in growth. Although some scientists are strong advocates of food restriction for humans (Dr. Roy Walford, a biochemist who has been a strong proponent of this theory once tried it himself, eating only every other day), this idea also evoked some highly negative reactions among the scientific community. Critics of this perspective have pointed out that important differences between rats and humans make generalization from animals problematic. A specific problem noted by some critics is that the diet fed to rats is extremely high in protein and was developed to encourage rapid and artificial growth.

Recent research in this area has focused on monkeys (National Institute on Aging, 1998). Investigators have found that reducing caloric intake by 30% lowers body temperature in monkeys, which is thought to be the result of lowered metabolic rate. Lowered body temperature might enhance longevity as a result of its impact on various cellular processes such as DNA damage and repair and the development of certain tumors. Because of the similarity of primates to humans these studies may be more relevant to understanding the effects of caloric restriction in humans. In any case, the critical experiment in humans has not been done and perhaps never will be. It is interesting to note, though, that among humans, the heaviest and thinnest members of a given cohort have the shortest longevity, and those slightly over their ideal body weight live the longest. (See National Institute on Aging, 1996; Spirduso, 1995.)

AFTERWORD. The vast sums of money spent on purported anti-aging remedies attest to the desperation with which some people regard the prospect of aging and death. At present, there are no liquids, pills, powders, or any other substances with proven anti-aging capacities. But some valid steps can be taken to help ensure a longer life, as we see in the following section.

Life-Lengthening Behaviors

Psychological and social factors are now almost universally recognized as important determinants of human longevity. These include stress, personality variables, marital status, social relationships, and such psychological disorders as depression. These issues are discussed in the chapters dealing with stress, interpersonal relationships, and adult psychopathology. Insofar as physiological factors are concerned, empirical evidence indicates that your chances of remaining healthy and living longer depend to a considerable extent on your own behavior.

NOT SMOKING. Smoking has been clearly related to oral and lung cancer, other pulmonary diseases, and cardiovascular disease. Conversely, ceasing or reducing the amount of smoking decreases the likelihood of premature death. Quitting smoking is desirable even for older adults: When a person stops smoking, benefits to the heart and circulatory system begin immediately, and the risk of heart attacks, strokes, and other circulatory diseases starts to decline. Quitting smoking will not reverse chronic lung damage, but it may slow this disease and help prevent any further decline.

Recent evidence has shown that nonsmokers who breathe the smoke of others are more likely to develop smoking-related diseases, such as lung cancer and heart disease. For this reason, the option of smoking has been eliminated or curtailed in virtually all enclosed public spaces in the United States (e.g., airlines and restaurants). In addition, there is increasing good evidence that smoke in the home is a health hazard for babies and young children, as well as for those who suffer from asthma or heart disease.

A BALANCED DIET. Eating a balanced diet and maintaining a desirable weight will also increase your longevity. Obesity is related to diabetes, osteoarthritis, cardio-vascular disease, and hypertension, and the effects of stress are greater among individuals who suffer from nutritional deficiencies. Food and vitamins are *not* elixirs of youth, but appropriate nutrition will help reduce the likelihood of harmful and fatal illnesses.

REGULAR EXERCISE. Exercise is extremely important throughout life for both men and women. Appropriate regular exercise helps maintain cardiovascular health, strong muscles and bones, and flexible joints, and it helps reduce hypertension and the amount of body fat. It may also enhance cognitive and motor performance. Exercise also improves mood by causing the release of "feel good" hormones called endorphins. Conversely, the absence of even minimal exercise is related to reduced cardiovascular efficiency, a loss of bone calcium, and gastrointestinal problems. Sedentary persons also suffer more from chronic back pain, stiffness, insomnia, and irregularity (National Institute on Aging, 1998).

OTHER FACTORS. Those who have *regular health checkups* tend to live longer; even serious illnesses can often be readily treated if caught in the early stages. *Practicing safety habits* to prevent falls and fractures in the home and using seat belts when riding in an automobile are also recommended by most authorities. Although there are occasional cases where seat belts have proved disadvantageous in an accident, the odds are much greater that they will help to avoid serious injury and even death. *Alcoholic beverages when taken in moderation* may be beneficial to survival, but alcohol should never be used when driving. The effects of alcohol on the brain change with increasing age, so a single drink will impair the cognitive functioning of an older adult more than it will a young person. Practicing *safe sex* such as using condoms can also prevent many health problems, some of which are life threatening. *Avoiding exposure to the sun and the cold* can also extend life. Skin cancer has been linked to exposure to the sun. Older persons are less able to adapt to the extreme cold temperatures and may place themselves at risk during extreme temperature shifts. Sufficient time for sleep, rest, and relaxation is also conducive to longer life and will help promote *a positive attitude toward life*. Finally, *maintaining one's network of family and friends and staying active through work and play* are also important. Research has repeatedly shown that being in a supportive environment and remaining active are linked to greater longevity (see National Institute on Aging, 1996).

AFTERWORD. These recommendations may seem trite or even sermonic. But they are effective, whereas the same cannot be said of the various anti-aging

TABLE 3–7 Percent Engaging in Personal Health Practices, by Selected Characteristics, 1990 (18 Years of Age and Over)

Characteristics	Eats Breakfast	Rarely Snacks	Exercises Regularly	Has Two or More Drinks on Any Day	Current Smoker	20% or More Above Weight
Male	54.6	25.6	44.0	9.7	28.4	29.6
Female	58.0	25.4	37.7	1.7	22.8	25.6
White	57.8	25.8	41.5	5.8	25.6	26.7
Black	46.9	22.7	34.3	4.3	26.2	38.0
Hispanic	52.5	29.3	34.9	4.6	23.0	27.6
Non-Hispanic	56.7	25.2	41.2	5.6	25.7	27.5

Source: U.S. Bureau of the Census (1997).

remedies currently being sold on the open market. However, considerably more effort is required: Rather than merely consuming some magical anti-aging substance, you must engage in and/or change various important behaviors. As shown in Table 3–7, there is considerable room for improvement in our health-related behaviors.

How long will *you* live? Even if we omit the possibility of accidents, there is no scientific way to answer this question with any great degree of accuracy. However, some of the more important physiological, psychological, and social contributors to longevity have been incorporated into the questionnaire shown in Table 3–8. By answering these questions, you can obtain a *very approximate* guide to your personal longevity. More importantly, this questionnaire will help improve your understanding of the factors that play a significant role in lengthening human life.

TABLE 3–8 Estimating Your Personal Longevity

1. **Basic Life Expectancy**
   If you were born in 1970, your basic life expectancy is 67 years if you are male and 75 years if you are female. Write down your basic life expectancy in the space at the right. (If you were born considerably before or after 1970 and wish to enter a more precise estimate, consult Table 1–2, Chapter 1, under the heading "Life Expectancy at Birth.") _____

   For each item that follows, decide how it applies to you, and add or subtract the appropriate number of years from your basic life expectancy.
2. **Current Longevity**
   a. If you are now in your 50s or 60s, add 10 years because you have already proven yourself to be quite durable. _____
   b. If you are now over age 60 and active, add another 2 years. _____
3. **Family History**
   a. If two or more of your grandparents lived to age 80 or beyond, add 5 years. _____
   b. If any parent, grandparent, sister, or brother died of a heart attack or stroke before age 50, subtract 4 years. If instead any one of these relatives died from these diseases prior to age 60, subtract only 2 years. _____
   c. Subtract 3 years of each case of diabetes, thyroid disorders, breast cancer, cancer of the digestive system, asthma, or chronic bronchitis among your parents or grandparents. _____

(Continued)

TABLE 3-8   *(Continued)*

4. **Marital Status**
   a. If you are married, add 4 years. _____
   b. If you are over 25 and not married, subtract 1 year for every unwedded decade. _____
5. **Economic Status**
   a. Subtract 3 years if you have been poor for the greater part of your life. _____
6. **Physique**
   a. Subtract 1 year for every 10 pounds you are overweight. _____
   b. For each inch that your waist measurement exceeds your chest measurement, deduct 2 years. _____
   c. If you are over 40 and *not* overweight, add 3 years. _____
7. **Exercise**
   a. If your exercise is regular and moderate (e.g., jogging three times a week), add 3 years. But if your exercise is regular and vigorous (e.g., long-distance running 3 times a week), add 5 years instead of 3 years. _____
   b. If your job is sedentary, subtract 3 years. But if it is active, add 3 years. _____
8. **Alcohol**
   a. If you are a light drinker (one to three drinks a day), add 2 years. If instead you are a teetotaler, subtract 1 year. And if instead you are a heavy drinker (more than four drinks per day), subtract 7.5 years. _____
9. **Smoking**
   a. If you smoke cigarettes: less than one pack per day, subtract 2 years; one to two packs per day, subtract 4 years; two or more packs per day, subtract 8 years. _____
   b. Subtract 2 years if you regularly smoke a pipe or cigars. _____
10. **Disposition**
    a. Add 2 years if you are a reasoned, practical person. _____
    b. Subtract 2 years if you are aggressive, intense, and competitive. _____
    c. Add 3 years if you are basically happy and content with life. If instead you are often unhappy, worried, and plagued by feelings of guilt, subtract 3 years. _____
11. **Education**
    a. If you failed to complete high school, subtract 2 years. If instead you had 4 additional years of school after high school, add 1 year. _____
    b. For a fifth year of school after high school, add 2 more years. _____
12. **Environment**
    a. If you have lived most of your life in a rural environment, add 4 years. But if you have lived most of your life in an urban environment, subtract 2 years. _____
13. **Sleep**
    a. If you typically sleep more than 9 hours per night, subtract 5 years. _____
14. **Temperature**
    a. If the thermostat in your home is set no higher than 68°F, add 2 years. _____
15. **Health Care**
    a. If you have regular medical and dental checkups, add 3 years. _____
    b. If you are frequently ill, subtract 2 years. _____

The final figure entered above is the estimate of your personal longevity. Please note that this is only a rough approximation. Although this questionnaire is based on factors known to be correlated with longevity, these correlations are far from perfect, and the number of years lived by any one individual may differ significantly from the estimated longevity.

SUMMARY

Age-Related Physical Changes

Age-related physical changes do not occur according to a strict timetable. Adults age at different rates, and such groupings as "the middle aged" and "the elderly" are actually rather heterogeneous with regard to their physical characteristics and capacities. Nevertheless, some important general trends can be identified.

The process of aging leaves clearly visible traces. Lines form in the forehead and elsewhere in the face. The skin becomes stiffer, less elastic, more spread out, and eventually loses its uniformity of color. Cranial hair becomes thinner and more gray or white. Height decreases by an inch or two, due primarily to years of coping with the effects of gravity. Weight increases from young adulthood to middle age, but tends to decline somewhat thereafter. These changes are primarily cosmetic; they have no direct effect on our vigor, daily functioning, or health.

With increasing age, muscle tissue slowly declines in strength, tone, and flexibility. The cardiovascular, pulmonary, and excretory systems become less efficient. Our stamina decreases. The joints become more brittle and less flexible. Our ability to react quickly to stimuli declines significantly. These changes may cause some inconvenience or discomfort, but they are *not* incapacitating. The vast majority of older adults remain in their communities, suffer no significant limitations in their mobility, and cope more than adequately with the challenges of everyday living.

Aging does have one ominous physiological aspect: Because of the reduced efficiency of most bodily systems, older adults are more vulnerable to chronic disorders, diseases, and fatal illnesses and accidents. The most common chronic disorder is arthritis, which may take various forms. The primary symptom, pain in the joints, varies from mild to debilitating. A second major chronic disorder, hypertension, involves a consistent pattern of elevated blood pressure. Hypertension increases the likelihood of strokes and coronary heart disease. Older adults have relatively low accident rates, but their consequences tend to be more severe. The probability of dying from cardiovascular disease, cancer, or a stroke increases dramatically after middle age. Despite these age-related problems, the majority of older Americans assess their health favorably.

Theories of Aging

Although age-related physiological changes have been affecting humankind for thousands of years, scientists still do not know *why* we age. Various biological theories of aging have been proposed, no one of which has as yet achieved widespread acceptance.

Genetic cellular theories posit that age-related changes are programmed into the genetic structure of each species, much like a built-in biological clock. Some researchers contend that aging is caused by damage to DNA molecules, which control the formation of essential bodily proteins. Other theories focus on errors in the transmission of genetic information from the DNA molecules to the place where proteins are assembled, which is accomplished with the aid of RNA molecules.

Nongenetic cellular theorists reject the concept of an innate biological clock. Instead, they contend that aging is due to progressive cell damage from the internal and external environment (wear and tear). Such damage has been attributed to the accumulation of waste materials within the cells, to the formation of harmful cross-linkages between parts of the same molecule or between two different molecules, and to the operation of protein-destroying chemical compounds (free radicals).

According to a third group of theories, aging is caused by the failure of certain physiological systems to coordinate important bodily functions. Some researchers define aging as a disease of the immune system, which protects the body against harmful microorganisms and mutant cells. Other theorists relate aging to changes in the endocrine system.

At present, the available empirical evidence does not strongly support any of these theories of aging. Indeed, we may find that all of them play some role in the aging process. Research into the causes of aging is still at an early stage, but the great interest in this area suggests that more conclusive findings may well emerge in the not too distant future.

Lengthening Life

The quest for perpetual youth is as old as recorded history. People in ancient times tried to reverse or retard the aging process by resorting to magic, rituals, and potions; today, people spend billions of dollars on unproven anti-aging treatments and dietary supplements. Despite centuries of effort (and some claims to the contrary), there are as yet *no* scientifically accepted drugs, liquids, pills, powders, chemicals, or vitamins that will extend human life. Empirical evidence does indicate that you can stay healthy and live longer by not smoking and avoiding the smoke of others, eating a balanced diet and maintaining a desirable weight, obtaining appropriate regular exercise, having regular health checkups, using seat belts when riding in an automobile, using alcoholic beverages in moderation (and never when driving), and allowing sufficient time for sleep, rest, and relaxation, maintaining a positive attitude toward life, staying in contact with family and friends, and staying active through work, play, and community activities.

STUDY QUESTIONS

1.   "Societal attitudes toward aging and the aged have helped to create the fearsome image of old age that can be likened to punishment." To which observable

external changes does this statement refer? How debilitating to the individual are these changes? What changes in societal attitudes toward aging would you recommend? Do movies and television programs generally encourage or discourage positive societal attitudes toward aging?

2. Based on current research, at about what age is a person most likely to develop cardiovascular disease such as hypertension? Cancer? Arthritis? When is a person most likely to have a stroke? What does this imply about how the increasing number of older adults will affect (a) the health care professions, (b) society in general?

3. You decide to write a science fiction story in which someone finally discovers why human beings grow older, and then the character develops a method to retard the aging process and prolong life. Which of the theories of aging discussed in this chapter would you use as your point of departure? Why?

4. A friend wants to know what can be done in order to live longer. Based on the results of empirical research, what behaviors would you recommend? What behaviors would you strongly argue against? What aspects of your advice do you think would be most difficult for your friend to follow?

5. Pick an issue of some popular magazine and examine the advertisements in them. How many can you identify that are designed to reverse or halt aging processes? How valid are the claims they make?

TERMS TO REMEMBER

Antioxidants	Male pattern baldness
Arthritis	Neuritic plaques
Basal metabolism	Neuroendocrine system
Cancer	Neurofibrillary tangles
Cardiovascular disease	Neurotransmitters
Chronic disorder	Nongenetic cellular (wear and tear) theories of aging
Deoxyribonucleic acid (DNA)	Osteoporosis
Genetic cellular theories of aging	Physiological theories of aging
Growth hormone	Reaction time
Hypertension	Reflex
Immune system	Ribonucleic acid (RNA)
Lipofuscin	Strokes

4

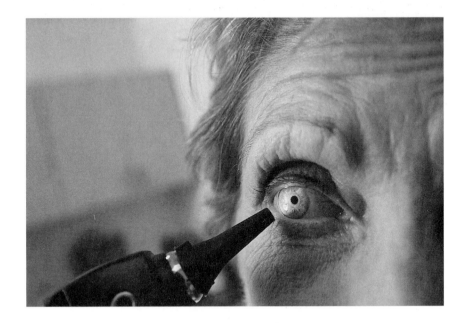

SENSATION AND PERCEPTION

All information about our environment and many pleasurable (and painful) experiences come to us through our senses: perceiving and avoiding various obstacles while walking or driving, reading an interesting book, watching a favorite television program, observing if the weather is fair or foul, listening to some good music, engaging in friendly conversation, enjoying a tempting meal, or caressing a loved one, to cite just a few examples. We are so used to relying on our sight, hearing, and other senses that we typically take them for granted. Yet our physical capacities do tend to decline as we grow older, as we observed in Chapter 3.

How do our sensory and perceptual abilities change with increasing age? Should you expect to suffer serious sensory losses on reaching old age or only minor impairments that will have little effect on your daily functioning? Are some kinds of tasks more seriously affected by sensory losses than others, so that older adults should be advised to avoid certain activities or jobs?

This chapter deals with these issues: how we take in, organize, and experience the world around us and what important age-related changes occur in these processes. We concentrate primarily on vision and audition, the two most widely researched senses. We also discuss smell, taste, touch, and proprioception (the sense of position and movement, which can be a serious problem for some elderly individuals).

VISION

Declines in visual ability may well have important practical consequences for older adults. Gradually changing vision may be the reason for gradually decreasing mobility and independence, increased isolation, the occurrence of frightening visual impressions, and significant reductions in income (Kline & Scialfa, 1996; Yurick, Spier, Robb, Ebert, & Magnussen, 1984). As with other aspects of aging, however, the magnitude of age-related visual changes varies considerably from one individual to another.

The Anatomy of the Visual System

THE LENS. Most visual sensations originate in some external object, which emits or (more often) reflects certain amounts and wavelengths of light. The **lens** of the eye bends the light rays that pass through it in order to project a suitably sharp, inverted image on the retina. The eye is able to focus on different objects because a set of muscles makes appropriate changes in the shape of the lens: It is flattened when the object is at a distance and thickened when the object is closer. These adjustments are known as **accommodation.** (See Figure 4–1.)

With age, the lens yellows, becomes thicker, less flexible, and more opaque, although some of these changes may be related to exposure to sunlight. One important consequence of these changes is that by age 60, the ability of the lens to adjust focus, or accommodate, is substantially impaired (Kline & Scialfa, 1996). Interestingly, recent research suggests that the lens continues to grow and develop throughout the adult life span. New fibers continually cover older ones, similar to the growth rings found in tree trunks. Thus the lens contains cells derived from all age periods (Stefansson, 1990).

THE IRIS AND PUPIL. The **iris,** a muscle that surrounds the pupillary opening, controls the amount of light that enters the eye. It contracts when there is a significant increase in light and dilates when the illumination decreases, with the pupil changing size accordingly (the **pupillary reflex**). Pupil size declines during adulthood and old age, making it more difficult to see under low light conditions.

THE RETINA. The **retina** serves a particularly important function: It transforms the incoming light energy into nerve impulses that can be communicated to the brain. There are two kinds of photoreceptor cells in the retina, cones and rods. (See Figure 4–2.) **Cones** are most plentiful in the **fovea,** a small circular region

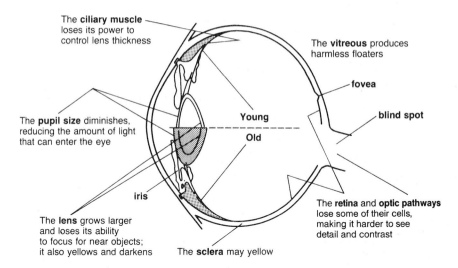

FIGURE 4–1   **Anatomy of the eye: Major structures and anatomical differences between young and old.**
(*Source:* Reproduced, with permission, from Weale, R., (1985) "What Is Normal Aging? Part XI: The Eyes of the Elderly." *Geriatric Medicine Today, 4* (3): 29. Copyright 1985 by Med Publishing, Inc.)

FIGURE 4–2   **Anatomy of the eye: Cones and rods.**
(*Sources:* Adapted from Gleitman (1983, p. 123); Coren et al. (1978).)

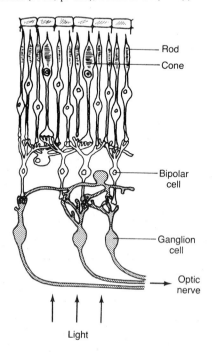

located at the center of the retina, and more sparse toward the periphery. The cones make daytime vision possible because they respond to high levels of illumination, and they are also responsible for all sensations of color. **Rods** are completely absent from the fovea and more plentiful in the periphery of the retina. The rods make night vision possible because they operate at low levels of illumination. However, they convey only colorless sensations. When your eyes take some time to adjust to a dark room after having been exposed to bright light, the size of your pupils increases and you shift from cone vision to rod vision, a process known as **dark adaptation.** We need both kinds of receptors because the range of light to which we are exposed is enormous: The brilliant midday sun is *100 billion* times brighter than our absolute threshold, or the dimmest stimulus that the eye is capable of detecting. In all, the eye contains some 6 million cones and 120 million rods.

THE OPTIC NERVE AND BLIND SPOT. The cones and rods report to the brain indirectly, through two intermediaries: bipolar cells and ganglion cells. The ganglion cells extend throughout the retina at one end and converge into a bundle of fibers at the other. This bundle leaves the eyeball as the **optic nerve.** The point where the optic nerve intersects the retina is known as the **blind spot** because it contains no receptors of any kind and cannot produce any visual sensations at all.

VISUAL ACUITY. Our visual system enables us to distinguish one object from another, an ability known as **visual acuity.** In daylight, visual acuity is the greatest in the fovea, where the cones are most densely bunched. Therefore, to see a particular object most clearly, you must move your eyes so the object's image falls on both foveas. At night, however, you cannot see a faint star by looking at it directly. Rods are responsible for night vision, and there are none in the fovea. Under these conditions, you must look off at an angle and let the image of the star fall on the periphery of the retina—as experienced sailors know well.

Age-Related Changes in the Visual System

Long before old age, our eyes begin to undergo significant change. For example, the pupillary reflex responds more slowly after age 50, and the pupils do not dilate as completely. The lens becomes larger, more yellow, and less flexible after age 40. And the cornea, the transparent covering of the iris, decreases in luster by age 40 and increases in curvature and thickness past age 50 (Kline & Scialfa, 1996; Williams, 1995). Some of these anatomical changes have important functional consequences.

DARK ADAPTATION. As we grow older, our eyes adapt to the dark less rapidly and less effectively. (See Figure 4–3; *lower* threshold intensities indicate a *better* ability to see in the dark.) Middle-aged and elderly adults have considerably more difficulty dealing with sudden and pronounced decreases in illumination, for example going from bright sunlight into a darkened movie theater. Sudden increases in illumination are also troublesome, such as encountering the headlights

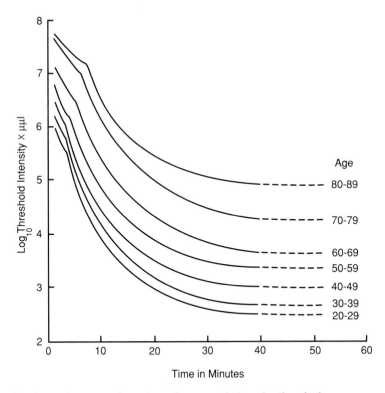

FIGURE 4–3 Dark adaptation as a function of age and time in the dark.
(*Source:* Adapted from Hunt & Hertzog (1981).)

of an oncoming car while driving at night. When designing environments for older adults, therefore, it is important to avoid abrupt transitions in light intensity, shadows, and glare (as might result from shiny floors or the chrome on wheelchairs).

In general, the middle aged and elderly need a higher level of illumination in order to perceive visual stimuli as well as young adults. Thus older adults are less efficient at tasks that must be performed under low illumination, such as detecting dimly lit signals or patrolling dark areas at night.

ACCOMMODATION. The process of accommodation also deteriorates with increasing age, particularly between ages 40 and 55. This reduced ability to focus on nearby objects (**presbyopia**) may well necessitate corrective measures, such as reading glasses or bifocals. Tasks like driving an automobile will also be more difficult because we must often shift our focus back and forth from points far down the road to the gauges directly in front of us.

VISUAL ACUITY. Our ability to identify stationary objects (**static visual acuity**) shows a decided drop with age; the percentage of adults with 20/20 vision declines markedly after age 45. (See Figure 4–4.) Our ability to identify moving objects (**dynamic visual acuity**), such as credits on TV or road signs while driving, also decreases appreciably as we grow older, although not necessarily at

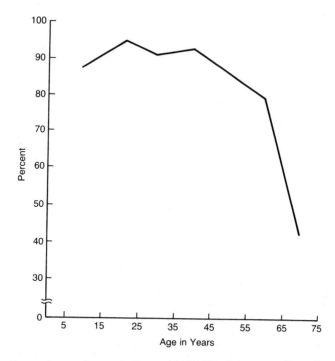

FIGURE 4–4   Percentage of population with 20/20 vision as a function of age.
(*Sources:* Hunt & Hertzog (1981); Department of Health, Education, and Welfare (1977).)

the same rate as static visual acuity (Gilmore, 1996; Kosnik, Winslow, Kline, Rasinski, & Sekuler, 1988).

In one study, a group of young adults (mean age 33 years) and a group of elderly adults (mean age 66 years) were asked to identify a small road sign while in a moving automobile at night. Although the two groups were matched on static visual acuity, they performed very differently: The younger adults were able to read the sign at distances some 25% greater than the elderly subjects (Sivak, Olson, & Pastalan, 1981). This implies that older drivers will react more slowly to road warning signs and to other external stimuli because this task depends on dynamic visual acuity, an ability that has declined. The frequency of driving accidents has also been shown to be positively correlated with dynamic visual acuity, especially for older subjects (Hills, 1980). These findings suggest the common eye chart is *not* sufficient to predict the performance of middle-aged and elderly adults on tasks like driving an automobile because it measures only static visual acuity.

In some instances, degenerative changes in the retina may cause such severe difficulties that large-print books, magnifiers, and other visual aids are needed. However, these changes normally do not occur until extreme old age (Welford, 1980).

COLOR SENSITIVITY.   The yellowing of the lens after age 40 affects our ability to see certain colors, notably those at the blue-green end of the spectrum. The effect is somewhat like viewing the world through yellow sunglasses: Older adults can discern yellows, oranges, and reds more easily than violets, blues, and greens. This is not a serious defect, but it can cause problems under some conditions (e.g., a tennis court illuminated at night with bluish light, or a white soup bowl on a white place mat). For this reason, the color controls on television sets in homes for the elderly must often be set at atypical values in order to make the hues appear more realistic.

THE QUALITY OF VISUAL INFORMATION PROCESSING. The elderly have somewhat more difficulty recognizing shapes, numbers, letters, and words (Kline & Scialfa, 1996). As a result, reading a sign or locating someone in a crowd may be more troublesome. The differences between younger and older adults are rather small, however, indicating that age is a relatively minor factor insofar as these visual abilities are concerned.

THE SPEED OF VISUAL INFORMATION PROCESSING. Numerous studies indicate that we process visual information more slowly as we grow older. In studies of critical flicker frequency, for example, subjects are typically shown a rapidly flashing light. Older adults require a significantly longer interval between the flashes in order to perceive that the light is not on continuously, indicating that the sensitivity of the visual system declines with age. A related experimental procedure is to show subjects a stimulus object, followed shortly thereafter by a masking stimulus that blocks it from view. Here again, the elderly require a significantly longer exposure time in order to identify the original stimulus. This implies that certain important activities, such as reading, will be done more slowly by older adults (Kosnik et al., 1988; Scialfa & Kline, 1996).

Some studies require the subject to locate a target object in a field of distracting stimuli as quickly as possible, a task that depends on both sensory processes and decision-making ability. (See Figure 4–5.) Adults age 60 and older

As we grow older, it becomes more difficult to process visual information quickly. This is especially true when we must concentrate on two or more tasks simultaneously, such as trying to glean information from a lengthy road sign while maintaining a safe distance from the car in front.

```
Z   N   O   R   E   X   V

L   A   I   Q   B   D   W

S   M   K   E   O   P   Y

E   L   A   X   R   V   Q

N   A   W   O   M   D   C

V   L   O   A   Y   K   J

B   Q   N   S   H   R   U
```

Task: To mark each horizontal line that contains a "Q" under severe time pressure (e.g., there are 500 lines in all and a one-minute time limit).

FIGURE 4–5 **Sample visual scanning task.**

perform such visual scanning tasks significantly more slowly than young adults (e.g., Rabbitt, 1977, 1979). This is especially true if the subject must concentrate on other tasks simultaneously, for example, when the driver of an automobile must pick out the relevant information from a lengthy road sign while continuing to guide the car. However, there appears to be relatively little decline in visual scanning ability between ages 20 and 50 (Scialfa & Kline, 1996). Thus, if an employer is seeking someone to proofread a manuscript in a brightly lit room, there would be little reason (insofar as this visual ability is concerned) to prefer a 20-year-old to a 40-year-old.

Alternatively, subjects may be asked to detect a target letter flashed on a display screen. Here again, elderly adults perform more poorly if the letter may appear anywhere on the screen, forcing them to divide their attention. But if the target letter always appears at the center of the screen, allowing subjects to focus their attention on a single spot, no significant age differences in performance are obtained. (See Plude & Hoyer, 1985, 1986.)

WHAT OLDER PERSONS SAY ABOUT THEIR VISION. When older persons are asked about situations that are visually challenging to them, they often identify driving at twilight, circumstances where there is high contrast between shadowed and brightly lit areas, entering and leaving dark areas, and situations requiring visual search. Self-reported vision loss has been found to be related to both physical and emotional disabilities in the elderly (Kline & Scialfa, 1996).

AFTERWORD. As we grow older, changes in the eye reduce the quality or intensity of the light that enters the retina. These changes imply that older people are in effect operating under poorer lighting conditions than young adults, a decline that can be mitigated but not eliminated by increased illumination (Kline & Schieber, 1985; Welford, 1980).

Although the visual system changes considerably during adulthood, our eyes remain our most reliable sense. The deterioration that occurs is not drastic enough to incapacitate older adults, but it can make some visual tasks considerably more difficult. For example, if rapidly moving targets must be detected under conditions of low illumination, young adults will perform this task far better than the middle aged or elderly. If instead the task requires rapid identification of single, motionless stimuli, young adults may be somewhat superior. But if the task is one of visual scanning, young adults will have little or no advantage over the middle aged, although the elderly will be at a disadvantage. Thus the negative effects of aging on your visual system tend to be greater for tasks that are more complicated. However, appropriate training can improve the visual performance of older adults on some complicated tasks (Ball & Sekuler, 1986).

Disorders of the Visual System

Although our visual system fares rather well with increasing age, a significant number of older adults do report that their ability to see is impaired (Stefansson, 1990; Williams, 1995). (See Table 4-1.)

COMMON EYE COMPLAINTS. As we observed in the preceding section, there is a gradual decline in our ability to focus on nearby objects after age 40. Presbyopia cannot be prevented, but it is easily compensated for with eyeglasses or contact lenses.

In bright light, you may observe tiny spots or flecks floating across your field of vision. These floaters are normal and usually harmless, although a sudden change in the type or number of spots may indicate a significant problem.

Sometimes the tear glands produce too few tears, resulting in itching and burning sensations or even reduced vision. Such dry eyes can be safely and effectively treated with prescription eyedrops ("artificial tears"). Conversely, excessive tears may result from an increased sensitivity to light, wind, or temperature, or from an eye infection or blocked tear duct. These problems are also readily treated and corrected (National Institute on Aging, 1998).

MAJOR EYE DISEASES. Cloudy or opaque areas may develop in part or all of the lens, inhibiting the passage of light and causing a significant decline in vision. (See Figure 4–6.) These **cataracts** usually form gradually, without pain, redness of the eye, or excessive tears; they are most common after age 60. Some recent research evidence suggests that cataract formation may be linked to enzyme modifications or to changes in the characteristics of lens protein (Hoenders & Bloemendal, 1983; Lerman, 1983; Ohrloff & Hockwin, 1983). Some cataracts remain small enough to be safely ignored. Those large enough to cause significant problems can be surgically removed, a safe procedure that is almost always successful.

Glaucoma occurs when the fluid pressure in the eye becomes excessive, causing internal damage and gradually destroying one's vision. If glaucoma is de-

TABLE 4–1 Percentage of Noninstitutionalized
Population with Vision Impairments, by Age and Sex

	UNDER 45	45–64	65–74	75 AND OVER
Male	2.9	5.3	7.8	11.4
Female	1.3	3.8	4.8	11.1

Source: U.S. Bureau of the Census (1997).

Most adults maintain good eyesight into their eighties and beyond, although corrective lenses may well be necessary.

tected in its early stages, however, it can usually be controlled well enough to prevent blindness. Common methods for this purpose include prescription eyedrops, oral medication, laser treatments, or perhaps surgery. As with cataracts, the initial stages of glaucoma seldom involve any pain or discomfort, so routine eye examinations of adults over 35 typically include a test for eye pressure (National Institute on Aging, 1998).

Most serious of all are the **retinal disorders,** the leading causes of blindness in the United States. In **senile macular degeneration,** a specialized part of the retina responsible for sharp central and reading vision (the macula) loses its ability to function effectively. Warning signs include blurred vision when reading, a dark spot in the center of one's field of vision, and distortion when viewing vertical lines. If detected early enough, senile macular degeneration may be amenable to laser treatments. **Diabetic retinopathy** occurs when small blood vessels that normally nourish the retina fail to function properly. As the name implies, this disease is one of the possible complications resulting from diabetes. The early stages of diabetic retinopathy are denoted by distorted vision, the later stages by serious visual losses. **Retinal detachment,** a separation between the inner and outer layers of the retina, has a more favorable prognosis: Detached retinas can usually be surgically reattached well enough to restore good, or at least partial, vision. This is probably the best known of the retinal disorders, due to media coverage of cases involving famous athletes (e.g., champion boxer Sugar Ray Leonard).

AFTERWORD. It is desirable to have a complete eye examination every 2 to 3 years, to permit the early detection of diseases like cataracts and glaucoma. This is especially true for those who have diabetes or a family history of eye disease.

NORMAL VISION—A person with normal vision or vision corrected to 20/20 with glasses sees this street scene. The area of the photographs is the field of vision for the right eye.

CATARACT—An opacity of the lens results in diminished acuity but does not affect the field of vision. There is no scotoma, but the person's vision is hazy overall, particularly in glaring light.

With cataracts, print appears hazy or lacking in contrast.

MACULAR DEGENERATION—The deterioration of the macula, the central area of the retina, is the most prevalent eye disease. This picture shows the area of a decreased central vision called a central scotoma. The peripheral or side vision remains unaffected so mobility need not be impaired.

With macular degeneration, print appears distorted and segments of words may be missing.

GLAUCOMA—Chronic elevated eye pressure in susceptible individuals may cause optic nerve atrophy and loss of peripheral vision. Early detection and close medical monitoring can help reduce complications.

In advanced glaucoma, print may appear faded and words may be difficult to read.

FIGURE 4–6 **Effects of some major visual disorders.**
(*Source:* Courtesy of Lighthouse Low Vision Service, © 1985, The New York Association for the Blind.)

However, visual disorders are by no means inevitable with increasing age. Most of us maintain good eyesight into our 80s and beyond, albeit with the aid of corrective lenses in many cases. Furthermore, we also have the option of adapting the environment in ways that will maximize the visual competence of older adults. For example, most people with vision problems find low-vision aids very helpful. These are special devices that are stronger than regular eyeglasses and might include telescopic glasses, lenses that filter light, and magnifying glasses.

AUDITION

The Anatomy of the Auditory System

THE EARDRUM. Auditory sensations are caused by physical movements in the external world, which disturb the surrounding air particles. These particles push other air particles in front of them, ultimately creating a chain reaction of sound waves that travel in all directions—much like the ripples that spread when a stone is thrown into a lake. Some of these sound waves are collected by the outer ear and funneled toward a taut membrane, the **eardrum,** which responds by vibrating. (See Figure 4–7.)

THE OSSICLES AND OVAL WINDOW. The eardrum transmits its vibrations across an air-filled cavity, the middle ear, by way of a mechanical bridge. This connecting link consists of three small bones (**ossicles**), which respond to the vibrations of the eardrum by moving in sequence. The third ossicle imparts the initial vibratory pattern to a membrane that separates the middle ear from the inner ear (the **oval window**).

FIGURE 4–7 **Anatomy of the ear: Major structures.**
(*Sources:* Adapted from Gleitman (1983, p. 119); Lindsay & Norman (1977).)

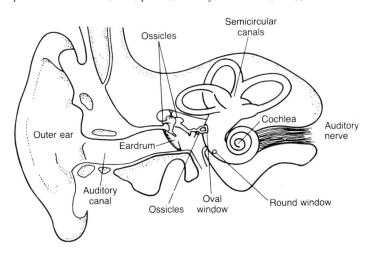

THE COCHLEA AND AUDITORY NERVE.   The movement of the oval window creates waves in the fluid that fills the **cochlea,** a coiled tube in the inner ear. The pressure resulting from these waves causes deformations in the **basilar membrane,** which bisects the cochlea throughout most of its length. (See Figure 4–8.)

The anatomical structures described thus far are merely accessories, which conduct and amplify the sound waves so they can affect the true auditory receptors—**hair cells** lodged near the basilar membrane. The deformations of this membrane stimulate the hair cells by bending them, whereupon the cells communicate appropriate sound impulses to the brain via the **auditory nerve.** Thus our sense of hearing depends on mechanical pressures within the ear, yet it is capable of detecting stimuli that are far away. As a result, the auditory sense has been likened to feeling at a distance (Gleitman, 1983).

LOUDNESS AND PITCH.   The brain transforms physical sensations of sound into two psychological dimensions, **loudness** and **pitch.** Sounds are louder when the original movements in the environment are more intense, increasing the height (amplitude) of the resulting sound waves. Higher pitches are heard when the frequency of the sound waves is greater (i.e., when there are more waves per second). At higher frequencies, the sensation of pitch is determined by the place on the basilar membrane where the peak deformation occurs: The closer this maximum point is to one end of the membrane, the higher (lower) the pitch that we experience. At low frequencies, however, deformation is equal throughout the basilar membrane. Here, pitch is determined instead by the firing frequency of the auditory nerve. Finally, for moderate frequencies, pitch is probably related to both the place and firing frequency mechanisms.

The **intensity** of a sound, which we perceive as loudness, is measured in **decibels.** Zero decibels corresponds to our threshold of hearing; a whisper is about 20 decibels; normal conversation is approximately 60 decibels; shouting is about 100 decibels; and the loudest rock band on record registered some 160 decibels (which is about 20 decibels *higher* than the threshold of pain!). The

FIGURE 4–8   Anatomy of the ear: The middle ear and cochlea.
(*Sources:* Adapted from Gleitman (1983, p. 120); Lindsay & Norman (1977); Coren et al. (1978).)

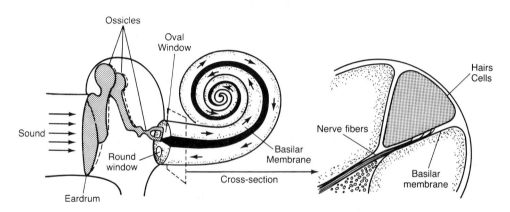

frequency of a sound, which we perceive as pitch, is usually measured in **hertz** (or kilohertz; one kHz = 1,000 hertz). The piano ranges from 27.5 hertz at its lowest note through 261.6 hertz (middle C) to 4,180 hertz at its highest note. Young adults can hear tones from 20 to 20,000 hertz, with the greatest sensitivity occurring at the middle of this region.

Age-Related Changes in the Auditory System

SENSITIVITY TO TONES AND PITCH.   Most often, methods for measuring our hearing use pure tones as the test stimuli. Losses in our ability to detect these tones begin to occur by about age 40, although pronounced changes are not evident until some time later (Fozard, 1990).

For example, the typical 30-year-old male can detect a 6 kHz tone (6,000 hertz) at a volume of about 4 decibels, which is softer than the rustling of leaves. Yet the same tone must be presented to the average 65-year-old man at approximately 40 decibels, the level of normal conversation, in order to be heard. (Average tone sensitivities for men in Western industrial society, as a function of age, are shown in Figure 4–9.) The greatest declines occur at frequencies above 2.5 kHz, due primarily to atrophy and degeneration of the hair cells and supporting mechanisms in the cochlea. Men experience greater hearing loss with age than women. This difference has been attributed to both differential noise

Performers such as Eubie Blake serve as strong testament that high levels of sensory, motor, cognitive, and creative functioning can be maintained into very old age.

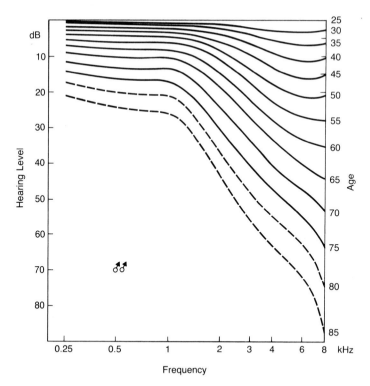

FIGURE 4-9   Ability to detect pure tones as a function of age and frequency (data for men only).
(*Source:* Adapted from Hunt & Hertzog (1981).)

exposure and to gender differences in the normal aging of the auditory system (Kline & Scialfa, 1996).

To the extent that a job requires the detection and/or discrimination of middle- to high-frequency tones, many middle-aged and elderly adults may well be at a significant disadvantage. Older adults may also have more difficulty understanding words that are shouted because this often increases the pitch of the voice as well as the loudness.

SPEECH PERCEPTION.   Our ability to perceive and understand speech also declines with increasing age, although the magnitude of this loss depends to a considerable extent on prevailing listening conditions as well as other cognitive demands placed on the individual (Pichora-Fuller, Schneider, & Daneman, 1995). In one study (Bergman et al., 1976), speech perception was studied under three markedly different conditions:

◆   *Normal speech:* no background noise or interference.
◆   *Selective listening:* trying to understand one person's speech with competing voices in the background.

◆ *Interrupted speech:* trying to understand speech that is interrupted electronically several times per second, as might happen if a radio program were afflicted with intermittent static.

As shown in Figure 4–10, little decline was found in normal speech perception until after age 60. A somewhat greater decrement occurred in selective

FIGURE 4–10 **Ability to perceive speech under different listening conditions: Percentage decrement from age 20 years.**
(*Source:* Bergman et al. (1976), "Age-Related Decrements in Hearing for Speech: Sampling and Longitudinal Studies," *Journal of Gerontology, 31*, pp. 533–538. Reprinted by permission of the *Journal of Gerontology.*)

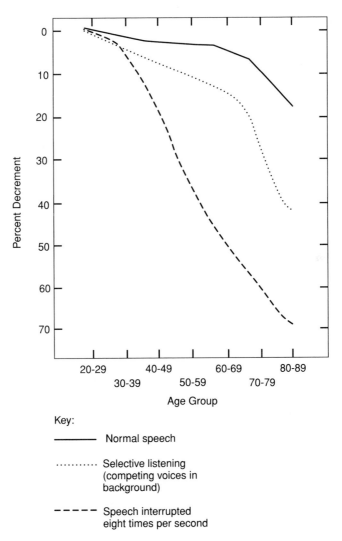

listening, amounting to about 10% between ages 20 and 50 and almost 20% by age 70. The greatest impairment was found in our ability to perceive interrupted speech: This loss was approximately 35% between ages 20 and 50, and it reached 60% by age 70. These decrements are generally attributed to an increase in the time required by the auditory cortex to process the incoming information and to changes in the peripheral nervous sensory system. Such findings indicate the importance of securing good listening conditions and improving the acoustic properties of buildings, where older adults are concerned. It may also be helpful to maximize visual communication cues, as by seating nursing home residents face to face in dining rooms and lounges so they can observe one another's lip movements and facial expressions.

Because the ability to perceive and understand speech differs from the ability to perceive pure tones, standard audiological evaluations now include tests of speech discrimination as well as tone discrimination. Where indicated by the subjects' symptoms, tests of more complex central auditory functions are also conducted. In view of these complications, hearing tests should be performed by a qualified audiologist, rather than by a hearing aid dealer or layperson. The trained audiologist is also able to assess the extent to which an individual is handicapped by the degree of hearing loss indicated by the test scores. This assessment requires an understanding of the subject's living and working environment.

WHAT OLDER PERSONS SAY ABOUT THEIR HEARING.   A variety of self-report hearing measures such as the Hearing Handicap Inventory or the Your Hearing instrument have been used to assess older persons' evaluation of their own hearing (Slawinski, Hartel, & Kline, 1993). In one study both the degree and variability of self-reported hearing problems were found to increase significantly with age, including those associated with listening to speech under conditions of background noise, the perception of normal and distorted speech, and the perception of short segments of speech and the perception of high-pitched sounds. Experienced hearing problems were greater for respondents who judged their hearing as being of poor quality (Slawinski et al., 1993). Self-report assessments of hearing tend to be moderately correlated with objective measures of hearing, suggesting that people have a fairly good sense about their hearing impairments.

AFTERWORD: AGING VERSUS ENVIRONMENT.   Compared to vision, our hearing suffers considerably more of a decline as we grow older. However, not all changes in the auditory system are due to increasing age. Certain environmental events can produce marked impairments in hearing, notably the exposure to intense high-frequency noise for a long period of time.

For example, significant noise-related hearing losses and even deafness are common among rock musicians. When a large sample of Wisconsin residents was compared with members of a less technological (and less noisy) culture, Sudanese tribesmen, the latter showed much smaller losses in hearing with increasing age (Bergman, 1980). Cordless telephones, which have the ringer in the earpiece, and personal stereos, which deliver intense sound more directly to the eardrum through earphones, are currently being evaluated as potentially serious sources of hearing loss. In fact, it appears that the U.S. population as a whole is becoming increasingly hard of hearing: From 1940 to 1980, the incidence rate of deafness increased from under 200 per 10,000 to approximately 300 per 10,000 (Hunt & Hertzog, 1981). Currently, more than 40% of men and 30% of women aged 75 or older have hearing impairments (U.S. Bureau of the Census, 1997).

If we were to consider only our own culture, we might erroneously conclude that substantial declines in hearing with increasing age are an inescapable part of the human condition. In actuality, however, both aging and our environment contribute to the hearing losses commonly found among middle-aged and elderly Americans. The atrophy of our auditory system is one price that we pay for living in a noise-ridden, industrialized society. To be sure, our society does pay some attention to preventing such losses: Employees who operate noisy machinery and adults who practice with handguns or rifles at firing ranges may well be required to wear industrial earmuffs or earplugs. Yet given the prevalence of noise we encounter, it is by no means unlikely that tomorrow's adult Americans will also experience significant hearing troubles, perhaps even more than we do today.

Disorders of the Auditory System

A substantial number of older Americans report that they suffer from hearing impairments, men more so than women. (See Table 4–2.)

PRESBYCUSIS. Some 13% of Americans over the age of 65 show advanced signs of **presbycusis**. This disorder involves a progressive loss of hearing in both ears for high-frequency tones, which is often accompanied by severe difficulty in understanding speech (Matlin, 1984). Presbycusis results from the deterioration of mechanisms in the inner ear; this may be caused by aging, long-term exposure to loud noises, certain drugs, an improper diet, or genetic factors. The onset of this disorder is gradual, and it typically becomes pronounced after age 50.

Hearing aids alone are unlikely to resolve this problem. They serve to amplify sounds in the external world, yet speech will remain distorted because of the inner ear degeneration. Speech reading, informational counseling, and hearing aid orientation are important aspects of comprehensive aural rehabilitation with patients suffering from presbycusis (Rees & Duckert, 1990).

CONDUCTIVE HEARING LOSS. **Conductive hearing loss** occurs when sound waves are unable to travel properly through the outer and middle ear. This disorder is caused by impediments in the ear, such as dense wax, excessive fluid, an

TABLE 4–2 Percentage of Noninstitutionalized
Population with Hearing Impairments, by Age and Sex

	UNDER 45	**45–64**	**65–74**	**75 AND OVER**
Male	4.3	19.2	29.9	44.7
Female	3.0	8.7	18.3	30.8

Source: U.S. Bureau of the Census (1997).

abnormal bone growth, or an infection. Sufferers experience external sounds and other people's voices as muffled, but their own voices appear louder than normal. This disorder is less common than presbycusis and can usually be resolved through flushing of the ear, medication, or surgery (Rees & Duckert, 1990).

CENTRAL AUDITORY IMPAIRMENT.   Those who suffer from **central auditory impairment** have great difficulty understanding language. However, the ability to detect external sounds is not affected. This rare disorder is caused by damage to the nerve centers within the brain, which typically results from an extended illness with a high fever, lengthy exposure to loud noises, the use of certain drugs, head injuries, vascular problems, or tumors. Unlike presbycusis, central auditory impairment may occur at any age; it may also interact with presbycusis in older adults. There is no cure for central auditory impairment, although rehabilitation by an audiologist or speech-language pathologist may be helpful in some instances (National Institute on Aging, 1998).

AFTERWORD.   It has been estimated that 30% of all adults between the ages of 65 and 74, and 50% of those between 75 and 79, suffer some degree of hearing loss. In the United States alone, the total amounts to more than 10 million older people (National Institute on Aging, 1983b). In fact, hearing impairments rank second only to arthritis among the leading health problems of those over the age of 75 (Brock, Guralnik, & Brody, 1990).

Hearing disorders have significant practical consequences: failing to understand what other people are saying, which may significantly affect relationships with family and friends; letting a ringing telephone or doorbell go unanswered, and missing an important call; being unable to enjoy movies, plays, concerts, and television programs without closed captions; having to give up driving an automobile because the warning signal of an ambulance or fire engine cannot be heard. In addition, stimuli such as the plumbing sounds from another room provide an important auditory background that helps us to keep in touch with our surroundings. When hearing-impaired persons cannot detect these background stimuli, they may well become afraid to venture out into all but the most familiar environments. As a result, hearing losses have caused elderly people to be incorrectly diagnosed as confused, unresponsive, uncooperative, or even pathologically depressed, thereby denying them help that would have been readily available. Hearing impairments may even lead to true depression, with sufferers becoming so frustrated at their inability to communicate with other people (or so suspicious because others always seem to mumble incoherently) that they withdraw from social interactions (Williams, 1995).

Despite these serious consequences, all too many adults steadfastly refuse to admit that they have a hearing problem. Whether this defensive behavior is due to fear, vanity, or misinformation, it is clearly unwise. Most hearing impairments are amenable to treatment, at least to some extent; so the best course is to face the issue squarely and seek appropriate medical assistance. The most common method for improving the hearing of elderly patients is through the amplification provided by an appropriate hearing aid (Rees & Duckert, 1990; Williams, 1995). Hearing aids may take various forms, such as an instrument that hooks behind the ear, an amplifier built into the temple of a pair of eyeglasses, a device worn inside the ear, or a larger receiver carried in a shirt pocket. One or two hearing aids may be worn, depending on the extent and nature of the hearing loss.

Hearing aids do not restore hearing to normal, and the quality of sound obtained through a hearing aid is much different from what the healthy individual hears without one. So older adults may well show some resistance to such aids or have difficulty adjusting to them. It may therefore be desirable to have the patient's spouse, or other close relative or friend, participate in the sessions with the audiologist and provide encouragement and support. Nevertheless, the benefits provided by the hearing aid are likely to be well worth the initial difficulties.

In addition to hearing aids, other helpful **assistive listening devices (ALDs)** are available. ALDs include a wide array of amplifications systems that are tailored to specific listening situations such as movie theaters, concert halls, churches, or even one's living room. These systems use infrared, FM radio, or other transmission methods to enhance the clarity and volume of the signal. The listener wears a special device such as earphones that enable them to pick up these signals. Many other additional devices (e.g., amplified telephones, low-frequency doorbells, closed-captioned TV decoders, flashing alarm clocks and smoke detectors, alarm bed vibrators, etc.) have been designed for the hearing impaired for everyday use, and many more will undoubtedly become available as the technology in this area advances (Rees & Duckert, 1990). Taking advantage of these resources can significantly improve the quality of life of hearing-impaired persons.

TASTE AND SMELL

The chemical senses of smell and taste are essential to survival and our ability to enjoy life. They help us select food, get the right nutrients, and they help protect us from toxins that might be fatal. Our senses of taste and smell are closely interrelated. For example, both of these senses play an essential role in determining the desirability of various foods. It is therefore difficult to study these senses separately, although some researchers have sought to do so.

Taste (Gustation)

TASTE SENSITIVITY AND AGING.   Sensory researchers have identified four primary qualities of taste: sweet, bitter, sour, and salty. Taste sensitivity experiments typically present the subject with a solution based on one primary quality (e.g., a sucrose solution in the case of sweetness) and a separate quantity of water. The keener the subject's sensitivity to, say, sweetness, the smaller the concentration of sucrose that can be differentiated from plain water.

Several studies suggest that adults past age 50 have more difficulty detecting all four primary taste sensations (Schiffman, 1996), although the declines in sensitivity are relatively small (Bartoshuk & Weiffenbach, 1990). In one study, researchers found that even centenarians could reliably discriminate the four primary tastes, although they were not quite as good at doing this as younger persons (Receputo et al., 1996). Like our sense of hearing, the ability to taste is affected by both normal aging processes as well as other factors such as medications, medical conditions, and possibly environmental pollutants. Thus it is difficult to know the extent to which observed changes within any one person are due to normal aging or health-related conditions.

TASTE PREFERENCES AND AGING.   Our senses of taste and smell discriminate more effectively among different substances (qualitatively) than among different concentrations of the same substance (quantitatively). Nevertheless, very little research has been conducted on age-related taste preferences. In one study, such different foods as corned beef and apples were liquefied in a blender to remove all textural cues; the results suggested that older adults dislike bitter stimuli more than younger subjects do (Engen, 1977).

Smell (Olfaction)

OLFACTORY SENSITIVITY AND AGING.   Several studies have found that our ability to detect various odors declines with age (Schiffman, 1996). In one large study, 1,955 volunteers ranging in age from 5 to 99 were tested with 40 chemically simulated scents that included cinnamon, cherry, pizza, gasoline, tobacco, mint, soap, grass, lemon, motor oil, and root beer. The results suggested that olfactory ability is usually at its best between the ages of 20 and 40, begins to diminish slightly by age 50, and declines rapidly after age 70. Among subjects aged 65 to 80, some 60% suffered severe losses in olfactory sensitivity, and about 25% lost all ability to smell. For those over 80, the proportion with severe olfactory losses was 80%, and nearly one half could not smell anything (*Miami Herald*, December 14, 1984).

One of the most extraordinary of all olfactory studies was conducted with the cooperation of *National Geographic* magazine. The September 1986 issue contained an insert with six "scratch-and-sniff" samples, and a series of questions including "What is your age?" About 1.5 million readers took this test and sent in their answers, which may well be the largest sample on record. The results indicated that after age 70, the ability to smell the odorants declined with increasing age. Subjects in their 50s and 60s were just as likely as younger adults to detect that some odor was present, but they perceived it as less intense than it actually was and were less likely to name the odor correctly. Furthermore, the noxious odorants added to natural gas as a warning signal (mercaptans) were more difficult for older adults to detect and were perceived as less unpleasant. This implies that the elderly are significantly less likely to respond to dangerous gas leaks in their homes. Therefore, some theorists recommend that a different odor, to which older people are more sensitive (e.g., rose), be added to natural gas. (See Bartoshuk & Weiffenbach, 1990, pp. 438–439.)

Like vision and hearing, there are methods available that help compensate for chemosensory losses in the elderly. In one study (Schiffman, 1996), researchers added flavors such as simulated bacon and beef to meals provided in a retirement home. They showed that elderly persons will eat more food when it is flavor enhanced, the consumption of flavor-enhanced food appears to enhance immune function that is not attributable to altered nutrient intake, and they had improved grip strength.

As with taste, illness and injury can cause olfactory sensitivity to decline. If you have ever suffered from a severe respiratory infection or sinus disease, you probably experienced a temporary lapse in your ability to smell (and to taste). These lapses are more common among older adults because the frequency of such illnesses increases with age. Alzheimer's disease, Parkinson's disease, and even mild head trauma can cause a permanent loss in olfactory sensitivity (Bartoshuk & Weiffenbach, 1990; Nordin, Monsch, & Murphy, 1995).

AFTERWORD. The available research evidence indicates that both senses—taste and smell—decline with age, although the sense of taste may be less affected than smell. These findings have important implications has important implications for the health and safety of the elderly, as we have seen.

SOMESTHESIS:
THE SKIN AND KINESTHETIC SENSES

The Skin Senses

Data concerning the skin senses are sparse, often dated, and frequently contradictory. Furthermore, any decrements in somesthetic sensitivity among the elderly may well be due to the more frequent occurrence of disease and injury, rather than to aging per se.

TOUCH AND VIBRATION. The importance of our sense of touch is easily taken for granted. Nevertheless, this sense is involved in many important behaviors: judging the smoothness of a piece of wood or the closeness of a shave, identifying a switch on the automobile console without taking one's eyes off the road, caressing a loved one. Although studies examining age-related changes in touch and vibratory sensitivity are still relatively rare, existing evidence suggests that our sensitivity to touch and pressure decrease with age, our ability to discriminate small distances between two points exerting pressure on the skin declines, as does our ability to identify objects through touch alone (Desrosiers, Hebert, Bravo, & Dutil, 1996; Stevens & Patterson, 1995).

Changes in vibratory sensitivity are helpful in diagnosing and assessing disorders of the nervous system. Older adults are significantly less sensitive than young adults to vibratory stimuli, particularly in the lower extremities (Perret & Regli, 1970). Age-related declines are most apparent after the age of 65 and are typically greater among men than women (Gescheider, Bolanowski, Hall, & Hoffman, 1994). However, such decrements have not been shown to have any notable practical consequences for those individuals who do experience them.

∼⌣ MYTHS ABOUT AGING ⌣∼

Sensation and Perception

Myth	Best Available Evidence
The effects of aging are much the same for all visual tasks.	Some visual abilities decline significantly more with increasing age than do others. Tasks that involve perceiving objects that are dimly lit, moving, or masked by other stimuli become considerably more difficult after middle age, and locating a target object in a field of distracting stimuli becomes more difficult after about age 60. In general, the effects of aging are more pronounced on visual tasks that are more complicated.
The majority of elderly adults suffer such serious auditory deterioration that they have considerable difficulty perceiving speech and loud sounds.	Hearing is the sense most affected by aging, and there is some indication that the population of the United States is becoming increasingly hard of hearing in part because of long-term exposure to intense noise such as loud industrial machinery. But serious hearing impairments are the exception rather than the rule, especially among those who obtain regular hearing checkups after middle age.
Because of age-related changes in our sensory system, older persons are likely to experience more pain than younger persons.	There is no strong evidence that age itself affects pain sensitivity or that age affects the qualitative properties of pain. However, the frequency and intensity of chronic pain is higher among older persons because of chronic health conditions associated with aging.

TEMPERATURE.   The temperature sensitivities and preferences of older adults do not appear to differ in any significant way from those of younger subjects. But the ability to cope with cold temperatures and maintain bodily warmth, and the ability to cope with hot environments, decline with increasing age (Finch, 1977; Young, 1991). This may explain in part why mortality rates increase among the elderly when there are sudden and extreme changes in ambient temperature.

Seasonal variation in mortality has been shown to occur in all American states, even those with temperate climates. (See Table 4–3.) This suggests that factors other than the acute effect of low absolute temperature contribute to these variations, such as abrupt temperature changes. The magnitude of the seasonal effect on mortality is large: During the coldest month of 1979 (January), there were approximately 20,000 more deaths from all causes and 12,000 more deaths from heart disease than for the warmest month (August). (See Anderson & Rochard, 1979; Collins et al., 1977.)

PAIN.   Pain is defined as an unpleasant sensory and emotional experience associated with actual or potential tissue damage (Harkins & Scott, 1996). Given the increased likelihood of pathology among the elderly, any age-related changes in pain sensitivity would have important practical consequences. Perhaps for this reason, pain is the skin sense most often subjected to age-related studies. Unfortunately, these data are highly contradictory: Many studies report a marked decline in pain sensitivity with increasing age, but numerous others find no such decrements (e.g., Corso, 1987; Harkins, Price, & Martelli, 1986; Harkins & Scott, 1996), and a few even report increased pain sensitivity among older adults (Kenshalo, 1977). The best conclusion we can draw at this point in time is that there is no strong evidence that age itself reduces pain sensitivity or that age affects the qualitative properties of pain. We can, however, be confident in concluding that the frequency and intensity of chronic pain is higher among older persons when compared to younger persons. Moreover, chronic pain is likely to be an important source of depression in the elderly (Harkins & Scott, 1996).

Proprioception and Kinesthesia

One important and distressing problem faced by the elderly is their susceptibility to falls and the sometimes fatal complications that result. Such falls may be caused by dizziness, by muscular weakness, or by decreased input from the proprioceptive and **kinesthetic** receptors that detect movements or strain in the muscles, tendons, and joints. **Proprioception** refers to the sensations generated by the body that let you know the location of your limbs in space, and kinesthesia refers to one's sense of location while moving through space. It is well known that older persons exhibit increased postural sway and have an increased tendency to lose their balance. But it is not clear to what extent these problems are due to aging of the proprioceptive system as opposed to factors such as

TABLE 4–3 Average Number of Deaths per Day, by Age and Month, in the United States (1979)

| AGE | Total | MONTH | | | | | | | | | | | |
		January	February	March	April	May	June	July	August	September	October	November	December
All ages[a]	5,251	5,576	5,465	5,286	5,270	5,201	5,091	5,030	4,940	5,007	5,254	5,335	5,573
Under 45 years	603	576	580	590	588	610	625	634	614	619	602	599	603
45–64 years	1,159	1,237	1,211	1,173	1,173	1,156	1,134	1,123	1,105	1,093	1,153	1,158	1,196
65–74 years	1,233	1,304	1,290	1,249	1,245	1,224	1,192	1,178	1,164	1,165	1,233	1,252	1,302
75 years and over	2,254	2,457	2,382	2,273	2,262	2,209	2,138	2,093	2,056	2,128	2,265	2,324	2,472

[a]Includes figures for age not stated.

Source: Feinleib (1984).

deconditioning of muscles or illness. Nevertheless, current thinking holds that there are some declines in proprioception and kinesthetic function. An important functional consequence of these declines is that it affects the ability to maintain posture (Weisenberger, 1996).

AFTERWORD. Some older adults may experience some declines in somesthetic sensitivity. However, the great majority probably need not be concerned about the possibility of serious deterioration.

In comparison with vision, audition, taste, and smell, much less is known about the relationship between aging and the skin and kinesthetic proprioceptive senses. One reason research has been relatively sparse in this area is that it has been difficult to carry out. Recent advances in computer technology have greatly facilitated research in this area, and it is likely that future knowledge will accumulate at much faster rates than before.

SUMMARY

Vision

The lens bends the light rays passing through it in order to project a suitably sharp image on the retina, and the iris controls the amount of light that enters the eye. The retina transforms light energy into nerve impulses with the aid of two kinds of photoreceptor cells: Cones are responsible for day vision and sensations of color, and rods are responsible for night vision. The shift from cone to rod vision is known as dark adaptation.

As we grow older, dark adaptation becomes less rapid and less effective. It becomes increasingly more difficult to focus on nearby objects and to shift back and forth rapidly between far and near objects. The ability to identify both stationary and moving objects declines, with some older individuals experiencing greater losses in dynamic visual acuity. It becomes more difficult to discern colors at the blue-green end of the spectrum, and visual information processing takes place more slowly. These changes are not debilitating, but they do make certain tasks considerably more difficult to perform.

Common eye complaints include presbyopia, floaters, dry eyes, and excessive tearing. These problems are usually readily amenable to treatment. Major eye diseases include cataracts, glaucoma, and the retinal disorders, the last of these representing the leading causes of blindness in the United States. Although eye ailments are common enough to warrant complete examinations every few years, most older adults maintain good eyesight into their 80s and beyond, albeit with the aid of corrective lenses in many instances.

Audition

External sound waves are collected by the outer ear and funneled toward the eardrum, which responds by vibrating. These vibrations are then transmitted via the ossicles, oval window, cochlear fluid, and basilar membrane to the auditory receptors, the cochlear hair cells. The brain transforms physical sensations of sound into two psychological dimensions. The intensity of a sound, which we perceive as loudness, is measured in decibels. The frequency of a sound, which we perceive as pitch, is measured in hertz or kilohertz.

Losses in our ability to detect pure tones begin by about age 40, but do not become pronounced until some time later. The greatest declines occur at frequencies above 2.5 kHz. Declines in our ability to understand speech normally do not become pronounced until after age 50; the extent of these losses depends in large part on prevailing listening conditions. Hearing tests include tests of tone discrimination and speech discrimination and should be conducted by a trained audiologist. Auditory losses may result from aging, from such environmental conditions as prolonged exposure to intense noise, and from various ear diseases.

Major auditory disorders include presbycusis, conductive hearing loss, and central auditory impairment. Audition is the sense most affected by aging: About 30% of all adults between ages 65 and 74, and 50% of those between 75 and 79, suffer some degree of hearing loss. Yet all too many older adults refuse to admit that they have a hearing problem, with the result that some have been incorrectly diagnosed as unresponsive, uncooperative, or even pathologically depressed.

Taste and Smell

Several early studies suggested that adults past age 50 have more difficulty detecting all of the four primary taste sensations. Very few studies have dealt with age-related taste preferences; one experiment suggests that older adults have a stronger dislike for bitter stimuli than younger subjects do.

Several recent studies indicate a reduced sensitivity to a number of different odors with increasing age, especially after age 70. For example, older adults are less likely to detect a gas leak because of their reduced olfactory abilities. Changes in odor preference are unlikely to occur after age 30. For both taste and smell, losses in sensitivity may also be caused by illnesses, such as upper respiratory infections and Alzheimer's disease.

Somesthesis:
The Skin and Kinesthetic Senses

Data concerning the skin senses are sparse, often dated, and frequently equivocal: Some declines with increasing age have been observed in touch and vibratory sensitivity, and in the ability to cope with cold temperatures. Some studies report a marked decline in pain sensitivity with increasing age; others do not. Here again, decrements in sensitivity are probably due more to the increased likelihood of disease and injury at older ages than to aging per se. One important problem faced by the elderly is their susceptibility to potentially fatal falls, which may be due in part to decreased input from the various kinesthetic receptors.

Little is known about the relationship between aging and the skin and kinesthetic senses as compared to vision, audition, taste, and smell. However, the growing research interest in these topics suggests that important new information may well become available in the not-too-distant future.

STUDY QUESTIONS

1. Based on the empirical evidence presented in this chapter, are middle-aged and elderly adults less competent at driving an automobile than younger adults? Which should take precedence: the need of older adults to engage in an activity (such as driving, so they can be independent and transport themselves) or the needs of society (to improve safety on the road, even if only slightly)?
2. How might a hearing disorder give the false impression of being a psychological disorder, or even result in a true psychological disorder? How might this information be useful when counseling an older adult to correct declines in hearing with an appropriate mechanical aid?
3. Make a list of all of the technological devices currently available to help older persons compensate with sensory loss.
4. How have cross-cultural studies helped us understand the reasons for declines in hearing with increasing age in the United States?
5. Why do some theorists recommend that a special odor be added to natural gas that is delivered to homes where elderly adults live?

TERMS TO REMEMBER

Accommodation
Assistive Listening Devices (ALDs)
Auditory nerve
Basilar membrane
Blind spot
Cataracts
Central auditory impairment
Cochlea
Conductive hearing loss
Cones
Dark adaptation
Decibel
Diabetic retinopathy
Dynamic visual acuity
Eardrum
Fovea
Frequency
Glaucoma
Gustation
Hair cells of the ear
Hertz
Intensity
Iris
Kinesthesis
Lens
Loudness
Olfaction
Optic nerve
Ossicles
Oval window
Pitch
Presbycusis
Presbyopia
Proprioception
Pupillary reflex
Retina
Retinal detachment
Retinal disorder
Rods
Senile macular degeneration
Somesthesis
Static visual acuity
Visual acuity

5

MEMORY

Memory is one of the most fundamental cognitive abilities, and at the same time perhaps the cognitive ability most closely linked with aging in our culture. Furthermore, because memory failure is one of the earliest indicators of dementia, it is important in the diagnosis of mental disorders such as Alzheimer's disease. For all of these reasons, researchers have been interested in determining what is responsible for adult age differences in memory.

Salthouse (1993) studied the relations between age and memory in normal healthy adults in which 305 adults between 19 and 84 years of age attempted to remember two different lists of 12 unrelated words. The words were spoken by the examiner at a normal reading rate, and then the research participants were immediately asked to write as many words as they could remember in any order. The average number of words correctly recalled across the two lists serves as the measure of memory performance. Figure 5–1 displays the relation between this measure and the age of the research participants.

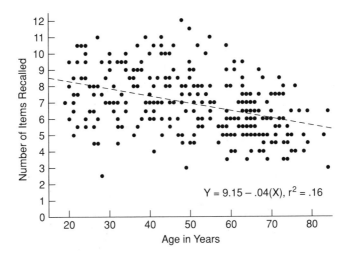

FIGURE 5–1 **Average recall performance as a function of age.**
(*Source:* Salthouse (1993).)

The magnitude of the age relations in these data can be expressed in several ways. For example, the regression equation indicates that about one less word is remembered for every 25 additional years of age, and the correlation coefficient of –0.40 indicates that about 16% of the variance (i.e., the square of the correlation) in the scores is associated with age. Additional analyses reveal that over 85% of the participants under the age of 40 correctly recalled 6 or more items compared to less than 52% of those over the age of 60, and 46% and 11%, respectively, of the two groups recalled 9 or more words.

Two characteristics of the data in Figure 5–1 are typical of results with many different types of memory tests. First, there is considerable variability in the level of performance at all ages. Not only was the lowest score in this sample achieved by someone in his or her 20s and the highest score achieved by an individual in the late 40s, but there are numerous people in their 60s and 70s who perform above the average level (corresponding to the position of the dotted line at each age) of people in their 20s and 30s. However, the second point to note from Figure 5–1 is that the average trend is clearly negative. That is, although it is quite true that there are many exceptions to the rule, the average level of performance does decrease with increased age. Because the decrease is both statistically significant and corresponds to a fairly substantial reduction in memory performance over a period of 50 years, researchers interested in memory and aging would like to explain this phenomenon.

Two major approaches have been used to investigate age-related differences in memory and other cognitive processes. The *process-oriented approach* attempts to specify the detailed nature of the age differences observed in measures of memory. This is usually done by manipulating conditions to try to isolate the critical aspect(s) responsible for the age differences in a particular task. This analytical strategy is somewhat analogous to a mechanic trying to diagnose a problem with an automobile in which he or she attempts to determine which part is defective by devising and administering tests that will emphasize the functioning of particular parts or systems. Researchers trained in experimental psychology, and particularly the information processing tradition within cognitive psychology, are the most frequent users of this approach.

The *correlational approach* focuses on the patterns of relations among variables to determine whether the levels of performance on different variables are related to each other, as well as to age. This strategy might be considered roughly analogous to a stock market analyst who is trying to determine whether a systematic pattern underlies the changes in stock prices or to a weather forecaster who is trying to predict the weather. A key characteristic of situations such as these is that it is recognized that the systems are very complex, and consequently that it may be valuable to consider broad patterns of influence rather than focusing exclusively on a single potential determinant. The correlational approach is often associated with the psychometric tradition within psychology.

Both of these approaches have strengths and weaknesses, and we consider results from each perspective in this chapter. That is, rather than taking only an experimental or only a correlational approach, results from both types of studies are discussed.

MEMORY PHENOMENA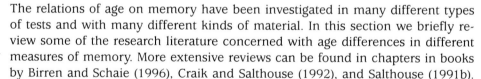

The relations of age on memory have been investigated in many different types of tests and with many different kinds of material. In this section we briefly review some of the research literature concerned with age differences in different measures of memory. More extensive reviews can be found in chapters in books by Birren and Schaie (1996), Craik and Salthouse (1992), and Salthouse (1991b).

By far the vast majority of memory research has been conducted with verbal material. The most common type of to-be-remembered information in memory studies has been lists of unrelated words because with these materials it is possible to control characteristics such as the familiarity of the words, relations among words, the ordinal position in which the items occur, and so on. The data in Figure 5–1 were obtained from a study involving the presentation of unrelated words. A similar test of word recall is included in the latest version of one of the most popular standardized memory test batteries, the Wechsler Memory Scale III (or WMS-III; Wechsler, 1997). In the WMS-III the same list of 12 words is repeated four times with a recall attempt after every presentation, with the sum of the correct responses across the four recall attempts serving as one of the scores. The line labeled Word Recall in Figure 5–2 portrays the average age relations on this measure in the normative sample of 1,150 adults between 16 and over 85 years of age.

Another type of verbal stimulus material that has been used in a number of research projects is meaningful paragraphs or discourse. Some researchers have hypothesized that memory tests with unrelated items may not accurately

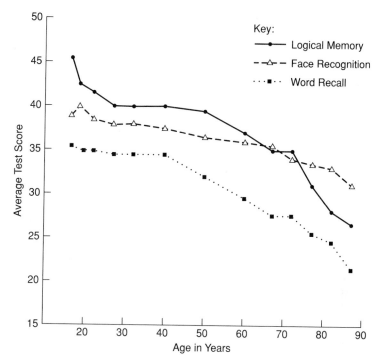

FIGURE 5–2 Wechsler Memory Scale III word recall.
(*Source:* Salthouse (1993).)

reflect true age relations in memory because the material is not meaningful, and hence is unlike what people normally encounter in their daily lives. Several studies have therefore investigated memory for short paragraphs, with the recall evaluated either with verbatim (exact wording) or thematic (gist) criteria. Because connected discourse was presumed to be more ecologically valid than unrelated words, memory for this type of information was predicted to exhibit smaller age-related differences than that for less meaningful material.

Comparisons of recall of unrelated words and meaningful prose can be complicated because although there is a clear criterion for determining whether a list of words is correctly recalled, special scoring procedures are needed to evaluate the degree to which the theme or gist of a paragraph is correctly re-called. Nevertheless, age differences in prose recall are often found that are similar to that observed with unrelated words. One illustration of the similarity in patterns is evident in the WMS-III because the **Logical Memory** subtest involves participants listening to a story and then attempting to recall as much as they can remember. For purposes of scoring, the story is divided into discrete units and the accuracy of recall is evaluated in terms of the total number of units mentioned in the recall attempt. The line labeled Logical Memory in Figure 5–2 portrays the age relations for this test in the WMS-III standardization sample. Notice that although the absolute levels of the scores are higher than those for the measure of memory for unrelated words (which is not easily interpretable because the maximum was 75 in Logical Memory and only 48 in Word Recall), the two types of memory have similar relations with age.

Age differences in memory have also been investigated with several other types of verbal material. For example, one of the earliest studies reporting age differences in memory involved recall of details from a movie (Conrad & Jones, 1929). Lower levels of recall with increased age have also been found for information presented in a simulated news broadcast (Stine, Wingfield, & Myers, 1990) and for information presented in the form of cooking recipes (Hastroudi, Johnson, & Chrosniak, 1990).

Because of the possibility that age-related memory differences might be related to processes of verbal rehearsal, researchers have also investigated age differences with a variety of nonverbal stimuli. Of particular interest in some of the initial studies was whether the age-related differences might be smaller, or possibly even completely absent, with material that was not easily verbally coded and subject to verbal rehearsal. However, the answer to this question is a definite *no* because similar age-related trends have been found in memory for a variety of nonverbal stimulus materials.

A particularly clear example of the similarity of age relations for different types of stimulus material is apparent in measures of recall performance from a matrix memory task. In this task the stimulus pattern consists of a display of a 5 × 5 matrix of letters, with 7 of the letters highlighted to serve as targets. On different trials in the task, the research participant is instructed to remember either the identities of the target letters or the spatial locations of the target positions. The target letters are recalled by writing them on 7 blank lines, and the target positions are recalled by marking Xs in 7 cells of a blank 5 × 5 matrix. (See panels A and B of Figure 5–3 for an illustration.) One of the unique features about this task is that exactly the same stimulus material is presented in both cases, but merely by changing the instructions the participant can be asked to remember either verbal (i.e., identities of the target letters) or spatial (i.e., locations of the target positions) information.

Several studies have used this task in comparing adults of different ages. The data in panel C of Figure 5–3 illustrate the results from a study by Salthouse, Kausler, and Saults (1988) involving a total of 363 adults between 18 and 80 years of age. Notice that on the average people tend to remember fewer spatial positions than letter identities, but the relation of age is very similar for both verbal information and spatial information. Other studies have reported very similar findings with slightly different versions of these tasks (e.g., Salthouse, 1995).

Memory has also been tested when the participants were instructed to remember musical melodies that were either presented visually, in the form of a musical score, or auditorily, in the form of the sounds from one or more instruments. With both types of presentation, older adults have been found to be less accurate at recognizing or reproducing the musical information. An interesting feature of some of this research is that the magnitude of the age-related declines in memory for music has been found to be similar regardless of the amount of

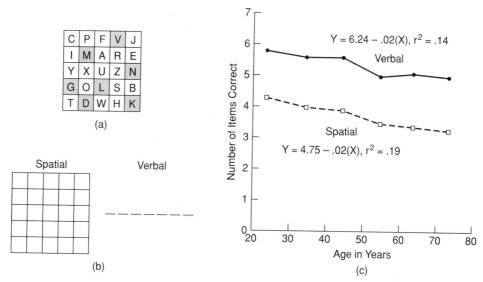

FIGURE 5–3 Recall performance tests.
(*Source:* Salthouse, Kausler, & Saults (1988).)

experience the individuals have had with music. For example, in the Meinz and Salthouse (1998) study, the age differences in accuracy of reproducing short melodies was nearly the same for experienced musicians as for people with little or no familiarity with music. Charness (1979, 1981) has also found age differences in memory for mid-game chess positions by chess players and in memory for bridge hands by bridge players. Results of this nature suggest that age-related effects on memory seem to be at least somewhat independent of the amount of experience the individuals have had with the material, but more research is needed before definitive conclusions can be reached about the joint effects of age and experience on memory.

Age differences have also been investigated for memory of faces and other kinds of photographs. A typical procedure with this type of material involves presenting a series of photographs and then asking the respondent to select the previously presented photographs from among a set of old and new photographs. The face memory subtest in the WMS-III is an example of this type of test because 24 faces are initially presented, and then the respondent is asked to identify the previously presented faces when they are randomly intermixed with 24 new faces. The line labeled Face Recognition in Figure 5–2 illustrates the age relations for this form of memory. Notice that it appears the relation of age to performance is somewhat weaker than that evident in the Logical Memory and Word Recall tests. Although this might be interpreted as indicating that memory for faces does not exhibit age differences as large as those for memory for verbal material, such a conclusion would be premature on the basis of the WMS-III results because the subtests in this test battery differed not only in the type of information remembered but also in the nature of the memory test. That is, the verbal information was assessed with a recall response and the face information was assessed with a recognition response, and we see later in the chapter that age differences are generally smaller with tests of recognition than with tests of recall even when the same kind of information is involved.

Other types of nonverbal information in which age differences in memory have been reported are spatial layouts or routes (e.g., Arbuckle, Cooney, Milne, & Melchior, 1994; Lipman & Caplan, 1992), and details of eyewitnessed events (e.g., Cohen & Faulkner, 1989; Yarmey & Kent, 1980). One particularly interesting study, conducted in an actual science museum, consisted of asking visitors to recall the positions of different exhibits at the end of their tour through the museum (Loftus, Levidow, & Duensing, 1992). As with other kinds of memory tests, accuracy in recalling this kind of spatial information was lower as the age of the individual increased.

In the last 10 years or so researchers have investigated several new types of memory that seem particularly relevant to everyday situations. For example, a number of studies have examined memory for previously performed activities that are thought to resemble naturally occurring events such as remembering whether you turned off the stove before you left the house or remembering where you placed your keys. One manner in which memory for activities has been investigated has involved asking the participants in a project in which several different tasks were performed to recall the identities of those tasks at the end of the session. Accuracy of the recall of previously performed activities is consistently lower among older individuals than among younger ones (e.g., Salthouse, Kausler, & Saults, 1988). Furthermore, the same general pattern has been reported when memory for the tasks performed during the session was assessed in a telephone interview conducted several months after participation in the study (Earles & Coon, 1994).

A particularly interesting variant of the memory for activities paradigm consisted of asking golfers in a miniature golf competition about their own shots earlier in the course of play (Backman & Molander, 1986). As with the other types of memory, age differences favoring young adults were found even with this personally salient information.

Another form of memory that has been investigated in recent years is what is known as *prospective memory*, or remembering to perform actions at some time in the future. This is the kind of memory presumed to be involved when you are told to remember to buy milk on your way home from work or to give a message to another individual the next time you see her. A number of studies have compared young and old adults in measures of prospective memory, but when interpreting the results of these studies it is important to distinguish between prospective memory with and without external reminders. That is, if the individual is relying on external aids, such as notes on a calendar, then various organizational skills or personality traits such as compulsiveness may be contributing to performance as much or more than actual prospective memory. Rigorous control over the use of external aids is generally only possible with specially designated targets and actions performed in the laboratory where the

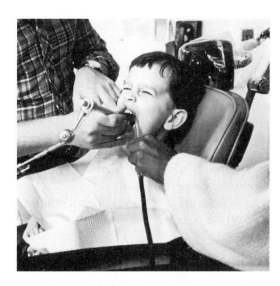

Some fears are due to classical conditioning, for example, when the stimulus of the dentist's chair has been repeatedly associated with the pain and discomfort of having one's teeth drilled.

researcher can monitor exactly what the individual is doing. As an example, the research participant might be asked to study a set of photographs of faces for a subsequent memory test, but also to make a special response whenever the person in the photograph is wearing glasses (e.g., Maylor, 1996a). Most studies such as this have found adult age differences favoring young adults in measures of prospective memory, although there is some controversy whether these differences are larger with event-based (i.e., perform the action whenever a particular event occurs) or time-based (i.e., perform the action after a specific time interval has elapsed) conditions (see Maylor, 1996b, for a review).

Another type of memory that has only been investigated fairly recently is known as *source memory* because it refers to memory for where, when, or from whom the relevant information was acquired. This is considered analogous to the situation in which someone knows a particular fact, but can't remember where the fact was learned. Laboratory studies of this phenomenon have been carried out by presenting information in several different ways, such as visually or auditorily, at different locations, from different individuals, and so on, and then later testing for both the content of the information and the source (or mode of presentation) of the information. The typical results from these types of studies are that age differences are evident in both content and source information (e.g., McIntyre & Craik, 1987; Schacter et al., 1991, 1994).

A related phenomenon is known as **reality monitoring** because in this situation the research participant is asked to distinguish between events that actually occurred and those that were merely imagined. Reality monitoring accuracy has been investigated in the laboratory by a two-step procedure. In an initial condition some actions are performed by the research participant, and others are just imagined to have been performed. In a second phase of the study the individual is later asked to remember both the actions that were previously described, and also whether they were performed or imagined. Older adults have been found to perform at lower levels than young adults in several studies of this type (e.g., Hashtroudi et al., 1990).

This brief review indicates that age differences have been found in many different types of tasks and materials, including some explicitly designed to resemble familiar situations. However, results such as these should not be considered surprising because there are numerous reports that complaints about memory increase with age. Perhaps the most common method of acquiring information about self-perceived memory problems is with various kinds of questionnaires asking about concerns with memory that are administered to relatively large samples of adults across wide ranges of age. There are now quite a few studies involving the administration of questionnaires that indicate the frequency and severity of self-reported memory lapses increase with age (e.g., Hertzog, Dixon, & Hultsch, 1990; Zelinski et al., 1990).

How can the age differences in many types of memory be explained? What theoretical conceptualizations could account for the observed differences in memory performance between young and old adults? The next section reviews some of the major theoretical conceptualizations that have been proposed to answer these questions.

MODELS OF MEMORY

Memory was one of the first higher-order cognitive abilities investigated by early experimental psychologists, most notably by the German psychologist Ebbinghaus in the late 1880s, and it has continued to be a very active area of investigation in contemporary cognitive psychology. This extensive body of research has resulted in a number of alternative conceptualizations of memory, and many of these models have been used to try to help understand age differences in memory. Next we briefly examine some of the various ways in which memory has been conceptualized and discuss the results of age-comparative research relevant to the major distinctions within each conceptual model. (See Salthouse, 1991, for more extensive discussion of the models and citations to the relevant articles.)

Interference Interpretations

One of the oldest hypotheses concerning adult age differences in learning and memory attributes those differences to an increase with age in the susceptibility to various kinds of interference. The essence of this interpretation is apparent in an anecdote of unknown origin. According to the story, a professor of ichthyology became a dean of students, and subsequently complained that every time he learned the name of a new student, he forgot the name of another fish. This tale is probably apocryphal, but it nevertheless illustrates the basic idea of *interference theory*: Humans have a limited capacity for remembering (or perhaps merely for storing and accessing what is remembered), and because older adults have remembered so much more information over their lifetimes than have young adults, they are operating closer to their capacity limits than are young adults. In other words, the interference interpretation postulates that memory is less effective with increased age because the extensive amount of remembering in the past degrades or disrupts the ability to remember at the current time.

At least two different types of interference can be identified. **Proactive interference** is interference due to activity that occurs prior to the presentation of the to-be-remembered material. In contrast, **retroactive interference** is interference due to activity that occurs subsequent to the presentation of the to-be-remembered material. Both types of interference have been extensively investigated in psychological laboratories.

Interference from prior activity has typically been investigated by manipulating the amount of material presented before the critical, to-be-learned, material. For example, several lists of unrelated words might be presented, and then the degree to which memory performance decreases with each successive list could be determined for people of different ages. If the residual memory capacity was smaller among older adults, or if they were less able to remember additional information for whatever reason, then we would expect them to exhibit greater decrements in recall across successive lists than young adults.

Although this type of experiment obviously represents an abstract and somewhat artificial situation, the results from experiments such as this should nonetheless be informative if the interference interpretation is valid. That is, effectiveness of new learning and memory could be impaired if the years of past learning and remembering have filled the storage system closer to capacity, or if the large amount of prior learning involving similar materials means the new items that are to be remembered are no longer very distinctive and consequently easily confused with one another.

Unfortunately, results from studies investigating proactive interference in adults of different ages have been inconsistent, with some reports of greater interference among older adults but other reports of no differences in interference, or even greater interference among young adults. Although this interpretation is intuitively appealing, the lack of convincing evidence thus means no definitive conclusion can be reached at the current time concerning age differences in sensitivity to interference due to prior activity.

Interference from subsequent activity has typically been investigated by manipulating the amount of material occurring between the initial presentation and test of the critical to-be-remembered material. For example, a list of words could be presented, followed by one or more lists of other words, and then the research participant asked to recall the words from the original list. The general finding in studies of this kind has been that, as we might expect if some type of interference were operating, performance decreases with more intervening material. If the memory systems of older adults are more fragile and more susceptible to disruption or displacement from intervening material, then the magnitude of this retroactive interference effect might be expected to be larger with increased age. However, as was the case with proactive interference, research with these procedures has yielded mixed results. Some studies have found that the amount of retroactive interference is greater with increased age, but others have found nearly the same amount of decrease in performance with interpolated material for young adults as for old adults. In general, interference interpretations have not been very successful in accounting for adult age differences in memory. One of the reasons may be that it is very difficult to assess the exact nature, or amount, of remembering that takes place outside of the laboratory. (For example, try to estimate how much you have used your memory in the last 24 hours.) Another reason why some researchers are skeptical of the interference interpretation is that the assumption of a limited or finite capacity for memory has been questioned. As we see later, recent research suggests that a great deal of information is apparently preserved in memory even though the individual may have little or no conscious awareness of its existence.

Memory Stores

Another popular conceptualization of memory is based on a distinction among types of memory varying with respect to the presumed duration of the stored information. For example, the sensory store system is assumed to last up to a few seconds, short-term or primary memory is assumed to last up to about 30 seconds, long-term or secondary memory is assumed to last from minutes to years, and information preserved for decades is assumed to be stored in tertiary or remote memory. (See Table 5–1 for a summary of major properties of the first three types of memory.)

TABLE 5–1   A Comparison of Sensory Memory, Primary Memory, and Secondary Memory

CHARACTERISTIC	SENSORY MEMORY	PRIMARY MEMORY	SECONDARY MEMORY
How information is entered	Without effort	Paying attention	Encoding (e.g., rehearsal)
How information is maintained	Not possible	Continued attention	Continued rehearsal, organization of the information
Form of information	Literal copy of input	Acoustic, visual, or semantic codes	Abstract symbols and their relationships (e.g., meanings)
Capacity	Large	Small (3–7 items)	Enormous
Duration of information	About one-quarter second (iconic memory); one-quarter to 5 or 6 seconds (echoic memory)	From 1 to 2 seconds to about half a minute	From 1 to 2 minutes to many years
Function	To preserve information until it can be consciously processed	To maintain active control of cognitive activity	To store information for later use
How information is forgotten	Decay	Decay and interference	Decay, interference, poor retrieval strategies
Computer analog	Input (buffer) memory	Working memory registers	Core memory; peripheral storage (e.g., disks, tapes)

The sensory store is postulated to consist of an unprocessed trace of the sensory stimulation, which may last for between 0.1 and 2 seconds in the visual modality, depending on characteristics of the stimulus and of the poststimulus illumination. Adult age differences in sensory storage have been investigated in numerous studies, but because there is little evidence relating the sensory store to other memory systems, it is of limited interest in the present context and not discussed further.

Primary memory, also known as short-term memory, refers to retention of information over relatively short intervals and is sometimes assumed to consist of the information currently in conscious awareness. One of the simplest ways of measuring primary memory capacity is with immediate **memory span** tests. That is, a series of unrelated items is presented and then the largest number of items that the individual can repeat back in the order of presentation is used as his or her memory span for that material. Many different kinds of material have been used in memory span assessments, including digits, letters, words, colors, geometric patterns, and pictures of familiar objects.

Age-related differences in memory span measures are often small, but sometimes statistically significant. For example, Salthouse and Babcock (1991) tested a total of 460 adults between 18 and 87 years of age with between 2 and 9 randomly selected digits or unrelated words in memory span procedures. Mean spans for both digits and words decreased with age, and the correlations with age were −0.27 for digit span and −0.39 for word span. Recent meta-analyses in which the results of many studies are integrated quantitatively with one another also indicate small to moderate age-related declines in memory span measures (e.g., Verhaeghen, Marcoen, & Goossens, 1993; Verhaeghen & Salthouse, 1997). Although memory span tasks were initially assumed to assess primary memory, this assumption has been challenged because of the possibility that some of the information recalled in memory span tasks may be retrieved from secondary memory rather than only from primary memory. The basis for this claim is that memory span performance is frequently much higher when the material can be organized into meaningful units based on information in long-term or secondary memory, as with familiar letter strings such as IBM, CBS, and FBI.

Another procedure that has been used to estimate the capacity of primary memory, independent of the contributions of secondary memory, is based on the **serial position function** in free recall. That is, when unrelated items are recalled they typically lead to a U-shaped function relating recall performance to serial position, with a high probability of recall for items at the beginning and end of the list, but a much lower probability of recall for items in the middle of the list.

The higher level of performance in the initial segment, known as the **primacy segment,** has been attributed to greater opportunities for attending to, or rehearsing, the first items to be remembered. The higher level of recall in the final segment, known as the **recency segment,** has been postulated to reflect the additional benefit of primary memory because the last few items are assumed to still be in primary memory. Performance in the middle segment is hypothesized to represent the contribution of secondary memory. Figure 5–4 illustrates

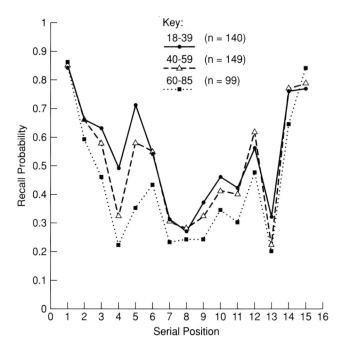

FIGURE 5–4   **Serial position functions.**

serial position functions from a recent sample of 388 adults who attempted to remember a single list of 15 unrelated words. Because only a single list was used, some of the fluctuations across serial positions (e.g., positions 4 and 12) may be due to idiosyncratic characteristics of the words in those positions, but the typical serial position function is still apparent. Notice that adults younger than 40 years of age remembered more words at most of the serial positions than adults between 40 and 59, or over 60 years of age. However, of particular interest here is that the age differences were somewhat smaller in the recency segment of the function (i.e., the probability of recall from the last 1 or 2 items in the list) postulated to reflect primary memory.

   Secondary memory, sometimes known as long-term memory, has been investigated in numerous memory experiments involving the presentation of various kinds of material followed by a recognition or recall test after intervals ranging from several seconds to hours. Among the procedures that have been used to investigate secondary memory are *paired associate memory*, in which pairs of words are presented and later the first member of the pair is presented with the individual asked to recall the second member; *free recall memory*, in which a list of unrelated words is presented and later the individual is asked to recall as many of the items as possible in any order; and *prose memory*, in which the individual reads or hears a meaningful paragraph and is later asked to recall as much as he or she can remember, with the scoring based on either a gist or a verbatim criterion. In all of these types of tests a consistent pattern of poorer performance with increased age, similar to the functions portrayed in Figure 5–2, has been reported. Results of this nature have led to a widespread consensus that adult age differences are pronounced in measures of secondary memory.

Tertiary, or remote, **memory** refers to memory for information or events from a very long time in the past. It is commonly believed among the general public that this type of memory is not as affected by increased age as secondary or primary memory. For example, people are often impressed with the amount of detail reported by grandparents in recalling events from their childhood, which is assumed to reflect the functioning of remote memory.

However, memory researchers are frequently skeptical about this kind of evidence because of two major methodological problems. First, it is difficult to verify the accuracy of the information when it is very old, particularly when it is idiosyncratic to the individual, as is the case for nearly all personal or autobiographical information. And second, it is often impossible to control the number of times that the material has been previously recalled or rehearsed, and therefore the memory may only be as old as the interval since the last time it was rehearsed. For both these reasons, anecdotal reports are often of dubious value to memory researchers.

Some attempts have been made to test memory for objectively verifiable events, such as asking questions about news events, names or faces of famous people, song titles, or television programs from different periods in the past. The results of these studies have been mixed with respect to age-related effects, perhaps in part because of the difficulty of controlling previous exposure to the material. For example, it is unlikely that the only opportunity to have acquired the relevant information was when it was personally experienced, and if it could have been acquired at different times then it also could have been rehearsed for varying amounts. One way of evaluating the general accessibility of information is in terms of the performance of people who weren't even born at the time of the event or during the period of prominence of the person, song, or television program. If performance is above a chance level of accuracy among people who didn't personally experience the events (e.g., knowledge about World War II among people born after the war was over), then the scores of all respondents would presumably have to be adjusted by this value to remove the contribution of later opportunities to acquire the information. However, few of the studies concerned with age differences in remote memory have employed adjustments of this type, and consequently the extent to which the tests truly assess remote memory has been questioned.

Some of the most intriguing research on very long-term memory has been conducted by Harry Bahrick, a psychologist at Ohio Wesleyan University. His research has focused on verifiable information such as names of high school classmates, locations of campus landmarks, and knowledge of foreign languages or mathematics acquired in school (e.g., Bahrick, Bahrick, & Wittlinger, 1975; Bahrick & Hall, 1991). Furthermore, by asking the respondents about their subsequent exposure to the relevant information (e.g., in the form of class reunions, campus visits, travel to foreign countries, etc.), Bahrick was able to assess the degree to which the critical information may have been rehearsed after the initial acquisition. An interesting finding from Bahrick's research is that although accuracy of memory was found to decrease across the first few years after the initial exposure, there was little additional loss for the next 50 years! This suggests that there may be relatively stable retention of certain types of information for decades, and lends some credibility to the anecdotal reports of impressive memory for very old information by older adults.

The conceptualization of memory based on separate storage systems has proven useful in research on aging because age-related effects tend to be larger in measures of secondary memory than in measures of either primary or tertiary memory. There is still some concern that the relatively small age differences in measures of primary and tertiary memory may reflect methodological problems as much as, or more than, genuine age-related invariance, but there is little doubt that most measures of secondary memory exhibit moderate to large age-related differences.

Memory Stages

Another conceptualization of memory is based on the assumption that successful performance in a memory task involves three stages or processes: registration or encoding of information, retention or storage of information, and recall or retrieval of information. A substantial amount of research has therefore been conducted to determine which of these processes is or are most affected by increased age. These localization efforts have been complicated because of the inevitable interdependence of the processes. For example, material cannot be retrieved if it was never stored, and it cannot be stored if it was never encoded. Despite the logical interconnections, there has been considerable interest in determining whether one of these stages is more affected by increased age than the others.

Encoding refers broadly to the registration of information or to the formation of an internal representation that outlasts the physical stimulus. Memory could obviously fail if the relevant information was never adequately acquired. One way in which encoding processes have been investigated is by determining the effectiveness of different kinds of instructions concerned with how the to-be-remembered information should be processed. For example, research participants have been asked to try to form an integrative image relating to-be-remembered words or to find unique associations for the target items. A general finding is that memory is better if the to-be-remembered material is elaborated or if associations are formed to link the new information with existing knowledge. Unfortunately, the research results involving adult age comparisons have not been very consistent because some researchers have found greater benefit for older adults, some have found no differential benefit, and some have found a greater benefit of manipulations designed to affect encoding for young adults than for older adults.

Despite these ambiguous results, many memory researchers believe that one of the reasons for poor memory performance on the part of older adults is deficient encoding. That is, it is assumed that reductions in the effectiveness of registration is one of the factors contributing to lower levels of performance in many memory tasks with increased age.

Storage refers to the preservation of information from the time of presentation to the time of test. This is a possible source of adult age differences in memory because people might differ in the ability to retain information over time, even if there were little or no differences in encoding or retrieval. Effectiveness of storage has typically been investigated by examining forgetting functions, which relate performance on tests of memory to the length of the interval between presentation and test. As we would expect, the accuracy of memory generally declines as the interval between presentation and test increases. Research with adult age comparisons has revealed somewhat different patterns of results with short and long intervals. With short intervals, up to a few minutes, it is generally found that after the initial one or two items the forgetting functions are nearly parallel for adults of different ages. This pattern suggests that the rate of forgetting is similar across age groups and short-term storage ability is not compromised with increased age.

The picture is somewhat more complicated with longer intervals, particularly of 24 hours and more, because there are some reports that older adults forget information at a faster rate than young adults across periods of weeks and months. This is not always found, however, and it is not yet clear what is responsible for the different patterns of results with retention intervals ranging from days to months. No strong conclusion is therefore possible at the current time regarding the effect of age on rate of forgetting over intervals of more than a few hours.

Retrieval refers to the processes by which previously encoded and stored information is accessed or made available for current processing. This is also a possible source of individual differences in memory because even if people possess the same amount of information, they could differ in performance on memory tests if they vary in the ability to retrieve or access that information.

The primary method by which retrieval processes have been investigated consists of comparing the magnitude of age differences in tests presumed to vary in their retrieval requirements. For example, tests of recognition, such as multiple-choice exams, are hypothesized to have lower demands for retrieval because the information is already accessible, and the correct answer merely needs to be discriminated from the incorrect alternatives. In contrast, tests of recall, such as open-ended exam questions, are hypothesized to require much more retrieval of the information.

Because age differences on recognition tests are frequently smaller than those on recall tests, it is often claimed that aging is associated with an impairment in the effectiveness of retrieval processes. However, this is not the only possible inference from this pattern of results because recognition and recall tests almost certainly differ in other respects besides the requirement for retrieval. For example, performance on recognition tests can be based on partial information, and thus scores might be higher on tests of recognition because less information may be needed to produce a correct answer than on tests of recall. The two types of tests may also differ in the number of hypothesized processes required for successful performance, with only two—encoding and storage—required in recognition tests, whereas three—encoding, storage, and retrieval—are required in recall tests. Age differences might therefore be smaller in tests of recognition not because of the absence of retrieval processes, per se, but either because less information is needed to achieve a respectable level of performance or because fewer processes are involved and there may be some type of limit on the number of processes that can be efficiently executed within a limited period of time.

Although there is still some controversy on this issue, it is probably fair to say that most researchers on memory and aging believe that both encoding and retrieval processes are negatively affected by increased age, but that at least short-term storage processes seem to be fairly well preserved.

Levels of Processing

The basic idea in the **levels-of-processing** conceptualization is that memory is the product of a series of processing operations, and the strength or durability of the memory trace is determined by the quality—as reflected by the depth or extent—of the processing carried out at the time of presentation. (See Figure 5–5.) Initial research within this perspective involving young adults revealed that memory performance could be dramatically altered by varying the nature of the instructions about the type of processing to be carried out at the time of presentation. For example, the research participants could be instructed to perform

FIGURE 5–5 **A depth-of-processing model of learning and memory.**

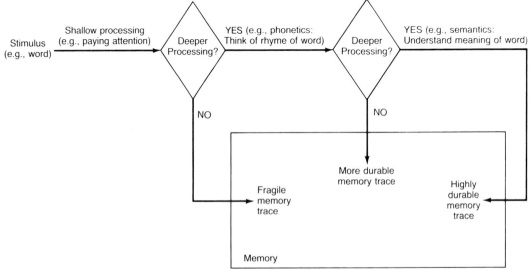

very superficial or shallow processing such as determining whether the words contained a specific letter. Alternatively, they could be instructed to provide a synonym for each word, which is assumed to require much deeper, semantic, processing of the material. Although these manipulations are relatively simple, they are postulated to be analogous to the difference when studying for an exam between merely reading the material versus attempting to elaborate and integrate it with one's existing knowledge.

A very consistent finding in many studies is that performance on memory tests is better for individuals who engaged in the deep processing task than for those who engaged in the shallow processing task. Because other aspects of the memory situation remained constant, these results have been interpreted as evidence for the importance of level, or depth, of processing in memory. One of the predictions from the levels-of-processing framework with respect to age differences was that older adults might be less capable of engaging in deep processing, and therefore their poorer performance in memory tasks may be a consequence of a deep processing deficit. However, this hypothesis has not been supported by the research results because adults of all ages have been found to benefit from deep processing instructions. Moreover, although some studies have found that the age differences in memory performance are reduced when everyone is instructed to engage in deep processing, others have found that older adults still perform at lower levels than young adults under these conditions.

The idea that performance on memory tests can be influenced by the type of processing carried out at the time of presentation is now well accepted, but based on the available evidence it does not appear that the quality or depth of processing is the major factor contributing to adult age differences in memory.

Episodic and Semantic Memory

In the early 1970s, a memory researcher named Endel Tulving pointed out different kinds of information in memory. In particular, he emphasized a distinction between information that is generic with respect to time and place of origin, which comprises nearly all of the factual knowledge one possesses, and information that is episodic in the sense it is associated with a particular temporal or spatial acquisition context. Tulving further noted that most memory experiments have studied episodic information because the task for the research participant is typically to try to remember information presented earlier in the experimental session. In contrast, most of the information we use in daily life can be considered to be generic or semantic in nature because it is part of our long-term knowledge system.

The distinction between **episodic** and **semantic memory** has been influential in research on aging because it is frequently claimed that age-related effects are much more pronounced in measures of episodic memory than in measures of semantic memory. For example, young and old adults in many studies tend to have very similar levels of performance in tests of vocabulary or general information that can be considered to reflect semantic or generic memory, but older adults usually perform at lower levels than young adults in tests of episodic memory for words or other material presented earlier in the experimental session.

Although this general pattern is undeniable, it is still not clear what is responsible for these different age trends. One possibility is that different neuroanatomical systems are responsible for different types of memory, and for some reason one system is more affected by age-related processes than the other. Another possibility is that semantic information is highly overlearned and with increased age there are many more opportunities for learning. According to this interpretation, the critical variable influencing the size of the age differences in tests of memory may not be the type of information, but instead the amount of previous exposure with the material. Until the reasons for the different age relations with semantic and episodic memory are clarified, the distinction between the two types of memory may be more useful for descriptive rather than explanatory purposes.

Explicit and Implicit Assessments

Most research on memory has involved the presentation of some material and then asking the individual at a later time to demonstrate his or her knowledge of that material by means of performance on a recognition or recall test of memory. These types of tests are referred to as explicit tests of memory because the research participant is deliberately instructed to consciously recollect the information. In the last 10 to 15 years there has been considerable interest in tests of memory that do not involve deliberate recollection. That is, instead of asking people to remember the information, the effects of prior experience are assessed indirectly or implicitly, and presumably without any conscious recollection (see Howard, 1996, for a review).

One of the most dramatic examples of the distinction between explicit and implicit assessments of memory comes from research on severe amnesics. In some studies exactly the same tests are administered in multiple sessions, and yet the individual exhibits no memory of ever having performed the tasks before. This failure is a reflection of explicit memory based on deliberate recollection. However, the same individuals frequently exhibit as much improvement from one session to the next as people with normal memories. The fact that they benefit from prior experience is evidence that the information is still available, or implicit, in their memory systems.

A variety of procedures have been used to investigate **implicit memory** in comparisons of normal adults of different ages. For example, in one procedure two groups of research participants might be shown a list of words with instructions to rate them on some dimension, such as number of letters, likability, or semantic category. The purpose of these instructions is to minimize deliberate attempts to remember the material. Some time later all research participants would be shown a set of word stems, consisting of the first three letters of words. One group of participants would be told that these word stems should be treated as cues for the words that were presented earlier, and that they should attempt to recall as many of those words as possible. The other group would simply be told to write the first word that comes to mind when viewing each word stem. For purposes of comparison, a third group of research participants would receive the same instructions as the second group but would not have received the earlier presentation of the words. (See Table 5–2 for an illustration of these procedures.)

Performance in the first group can be assumed to be based on deliberate recollection and explicit memory processes because the individuals are trying to recall the words presented earlier. Memory in the second group could be inferred from the extent to which those individuals wrote more words from the earlier list than the individuals in the third group, who were never exposed to the earlier list. That is, the only reason why people in the second group would write more of the relevant words than those in the third group is because they retained some memory of the previously presented words. The difference between their performance and the group that did not receive the earlier presentation can therefore be used as an indirect or implicit assessment of memory.

Results from comparisons of adults of different ages have generally revealed much smaller age-related differences with implicit assessments of memory than with explicit assessments. This is an extremely interesting finding because it implies that much of the information to which we have been exposed may still be available within our memory system, but that it is merely more difficult to gain access to that information as we grow older. In part because of this intriguing implication, and in part because the implicit assessment perspective is still fairly recent, the distinction between implicit and explicit assessments of memory is currently a very active research area in the field of aging and cognition.

TABLE 5–2   Assessment of Implicit Memory

	GROUP 1	**GROUP 2**	**GROUP 3**
	Rate Words for Pleasantness		Perform Unrelated Activity
	famous	famous	
	doctor	doctor	
	library	library	
	pilfer	pilfer	
	.	.	
	.	.	
	.	.	
	Recall the word that began with these letters	Complete the stem with the first word that comes to mind	
fam_ _ _	famous	family	family
lib_ _ _ _	library	library	liberty
pil_ _ _	pilfer	pilfer	pillow
doc_ _ _	doctor	docile	docile
Percentage items from prior list	100	50	0

Working Memory

Another active topic in contemporary memory research concerns **working memory,** which resembles short-term or primary memory but differs in that it incorporates aspects of processing as well as storage. That is, this type of memory is not simply a passive repository of information as is typically assumed with short-term memory, but instead is postulated to incorporate active processing as well as storage.

Working memory is hypothesized to be analogous to random-access memory (RAM) in a computer, which is where computations are carried out and temporary products are stored. In the human memory system, working memory is assumed to be where instructions are interpreted and executed, strategies are devised, external input is processed, temporary products are stored, and solutions are generated. Because it is required in all of these important functions, many aspects of cognition could be impaired if the size or efficiency of working memory decreases with increased age.

Because working memory is defined as simultaneous storage and processing, it has been measured with tasks that require aspects of both storage and processing. Several modified memory span tasks have been developed in which the individual is required to carry out a specified type of processing while also remembering a series of items. For example, a modification of the word span task known as the reading span task involves the research participant reading a series of sentences and answering questions about each sentence. After a series of sentences and questions, he or she then attempts to recall the last word in each sentence. The number of sentences and questions increases until the individual is incorrect on either the processing (answering the questions) or the storage (remembering the last word of the sentence) component on two of three trials. Other working memory tasks have involved different types of materials, such as arithmetic problems, with the research participant instructed to remember the last digit in the problem while also selecting the correct answer to the arithmetic problem.

A common finding in comparisons of adults of different ages on working memory tasks is that adults in their 60s average about two items less than adults in their 20s in these tasks. Results such as these have been interpreted as indicating that working memory decreases in efficiency or effectiveness with increased age. In addition, evidence from statistical control procedures indicates that working memory is an important factor in the age differences in higher-order cognition, such as reasoning. Working memory therefore appears to be an important link between memory and cognition or intelligence.

AFTERWORD. The functioning of memory is extremely complicated and apparently more complex than any of the existing memory models because none can account for all of the available results. For this reason, no definitive answer is yet possible about the source of age differences in memory. Interesting variations have been found to exist in the magnitude of the age differences across different

MYTHS ABOUT AGING

Memory

Myth	Best Available Evidence
Most old persons suffer from severe memory impairments and cannot remember such basic information as the names of their loved ones and where they live.	Secondary memory does decline significantly with increasing age, but usually not to this extent. Memory impairments of this magnitude typically result from severe illnesses, such as Alzheimer's disease or other dementias (Chapter 11). Memory declines in healthy middle-aged and elderly adults are likely to take the form of absent-mindedness, such as forgetting what one said an hour ago and repeating it to the same listener or deciding to do something 10 minutes from now and then forgetting to do so.
Most middle-aged and elderly adults conform to the maxim, "You can't teach an old dog new tricks."	Although it is true that the rate of learning is often slower with advancing age, most of the research suggests that people of all ages can learn and remember information if allowed enough time. Because memory problems may contribute to difficulty in learning, specialized methods of instruction may be particularly helpful to older learners.
Because of age-related declines in memory and learning, most older people should not be given complicated and challenging jobs.	Although older adults frequently perform more poorly on difficult memory tests, most jobs probably do not have high demands to remember novel information. Furthermore, as people gain experience in a job they are likely to increase their level of performance regardless of any memory limitations they might be experiencing.

kinds of memory assessments, but many questions still remain about why increased age is associated with lower performance on many tests of memory.

PATHOLOGY

When are memory problems serious? If an elderly relative begins complaining of memory problems should you conclude that he or she is developing Alzheimer's disease? Although problems associated with memory is one of the first signs of dementias such as Alzheimer's disease, the prevalence of dementia is infrequent even among adults in their 70s and 80s. It is therefore unlikely that a 60- or 70-year-old who appears to be in good health is suffering from a disease such as Alzheimer's merely because he or she reports difficulties in remembering.

Memory and other cognitive problems are usually considered serious when the scores on several different types of tests are low for one's age (typically defined as the 5th percentile or lower), when the change from a previous higher-functioning state has been fairly rapid, and when the problems begin to interfere with independent living. If all of these conditions exist then it is clearly advisable to seek medical attention. However, even under these circumstances the diagnosis will not necessarily be irreversible dementia because depression and metabolic disorders caused by malnutrition and drug interactions can also affect memory. In fact, it is even more important to consult with a physician if one of these conditions is suspected because unlike Alzheimer's disease, they can be successfully treated if they are diagnosed sufficiently early.

MEMORY INTERVENTIONS

We often hear of remarkable memory improvement programs and of demonstrations of very impressive performance in different forms of memory. These experiences naturally lead to the question of whether different kinds of memory improvement programs might be effective in preventing, or reversing, age-related declines in memory. Two major types of interventions have been investigated in research attempting to improve memory. These involve training various specific skills or trying to change the individuals' attitudes and beliefs about memory.

Techniques designed to train specific skills, or what are known as **mnemonics,** usually involve procedures based on associations, rhyming, or various kinds of encoding procedures. All of these techniques are designed to improve memory by capitalizing on known features of memory function. For example, if the goal is to increase your ability to remember faces, you might be asked to try to associate a distinctive feature of a person with something unusual about him or her that can be easily remembered. A large number of mnemonic procedures also emphasize careful attention to encoding because information can never be successfully retrieved if it was not effectively encoded.

The other major type of memory training program focuses on attitudes and beliefs. For example, self-efficacy is something that may affect memory because

Research evidence clearly indicates that the secondary memory of older adults is inferior to that of younger adults. One good way to combat the effects of such declines, and to deal more effectively with daily activities, is by using such external aids as memoranda and shopping lists.

if we believe memory loss is inevitable, and nothing can be done about it, this may become a self-fulfilling prophecy if we invest less effort, or give up after the first experience at failure. Intervention strategies designed to alter attitudes and beliefs consist of attempting to restructure our attitudes and beliefs about memory to break out of this vicious circle.

There are two major goals of most memory interventions in research on aging. One goal is to improve the functioning of older adults and is essentially concerned with determining whether the level of memory performance of older adults can be increased. The second goal is to try to reduce or eliminate age differences in memory, and research in this area focuses on the issue of whether older adults can be trained to perform at the level of younger adults. These are quite different questions because the first concerns whether the absolute level of memory function can be altered, and the second has to do with whether the relative differences in the memory performance of young and older adults can be eliminated.

The research literature suggests that the answer to the first question is a qualified *yes*. Several studies have found that the memory performance of most people can be improved, even people of very advanced age. However, there are still major questions about the generalizability and durability of the acquired skills. That is, although it may be possible to improve an individual's memory for items on a shopping list, this improvement may not generalize to memory of names or faces of people, remembering plots of stories, or directions to unfamiliar locations. Furthermore, although the intervention may be effective immediately after training, it might not persist over a period of months or years.

Most of the research results at the current time suggest that the answer to the second question concerning memory intervention appears to be *no*. That is, little evidence indicates that age differences in memory can be substantially reduced by any of the short-term interventions that have been investigated thus far because in most of the studies young adults have been found to benefit as much or more than older adults.

One of the most impressive projects of this type consisted of a series of studies carried out by Kliegl, Smith, and Baltes (1989, 1990) at the Max Planck Institute for Education and Human Development in Berlin, Germany. In their largest study, young and old residents of Berlin were trained to remember a sequence of Berlin landmarks and also how to link those landmarks to words that were to be remembered using a technique known as the **method of loci**. After 20 sessions of training, nearly all of the participants were able to repeat more than 30 of 40 unrelated words in their original order of presentation. There were still age differences in efficiency of this performance, however, because the older adults were not as effective as young adults when the rate of presentation of the words was controlled by the examiner instead of the participant.

One of the results from the Kliegl et al. project (1989, 1990) which is particularly relevant to the current discussion is that the researchers found that instead of being reduced, the age differences were actually magnified after training. In other words, the difference between the performance of young adults and the performance of older adults was actually larger after the memory training than before the training. This was interpreted as evidence for age-related decreases in latent reserve potential that could only be assessed by providing training to ensure that everyone was using the same optimal strategy, and testing people at the limits of their functioning. Regardless whether this interpretation is valid, the results are clearly inconsistent with the idea that age differences in memory could be eliminated after training with mnemonic procedures.

SUMMARY

Although there is a great deal of variability in memory at all ages, increased age is often associated with lower levels of performance in tests of memory. Furthermore, the age differences are not limited to a particular type of material because older adults have been found to remember fewer items than young adults with unrelated words, meaningful paragraphs and new stories, faces, displays of spatial information, and activities performed in the past.

A variety of different models have been used to try to understand the nature and causes of age differences in memory. Some of the theoretical distinctions have been found to correspond to variations in the magnitude of the age differences, whereas others do not. For example, age differences are often larger for secondary memory than for either primary or tertiary memory, for encoding and retrieval processes than for storage processes, for episodic memory than for semantic memory, and in explicit tests of memory than in implicit tests of memory.

Occasional memory lapses are normal, and merely because someone is concerned about his or her memory does not necessarily mean a pathological condition exists.

Finally, several types of interventions have been found to be effective in improving certain aspects of memory, but there currently do not appear to be any techniques that reverse or prevent age-related declines in memory.

STUDY QUESTIONS

1. The data portrayed in Figure 5–1 are fairly typical of research in aging and memory in that less than 25% of the score variance across people is associated with age. What are some of the other factors that might be responsible for the rest of the variance?

2. Which of the models of memory would be most consistent with the view that age-related declines might be minimized among people who keep mentally active?

3. What are some of the practical consequences of age-related declines in memory? Can you think of any practices (e.g., minimizing the demands on memory by always placing items in the same locations) that might reduce their impact?

4. Think of a situation when you had to remember some fairly complicated information. Do you think that the techniques you followed were effective, and if so, could they form the basis of an intervention that might improve memory or prevent age-related decline?

TERMS TO REMEMBER

Activity memory	Proactive interference
Encoding	Reality monitoring
Episodic memory	Recency segment
Implicit memory	Retrieval
Levels of processing	Retroactive interference
Logical Memory	Secondary memory
Memory span	Semantic memory
Method of loci	Serial position function
Mnemonics	Storage
Primacy segment	Tertiary memory
Primary memory	Working memory

INTELLIGENCE AND COGNITION

This chapter is concerned with higher-order processes of thinking, reasoning, and decision making. These processes are considered somewhat more complex than memory because in addition to getting information into the nervous system and then out again, the information is transformed or rearranged in some way.

The most common method of assessing higher-order cognition is with standardized tests of intelligence. These are often referred to as psychometric intelligence tests because they rely on objective, standardized procedures for determining the level of intelligence (i.e., the term **psychometric** is derived from *psyche* referring to mind, and *metric* referring to measurement). There are both advantages and disadvantages to these types of tests. One major disadvantage is the considerable controversy with respect to whether tests of this type actually measure important and interesting aspects of behavior. For example, even the strongest proponents of intelligence tests acknowledge that they do not measure characteristics such as wisdom, judgment, and insight, which are likely to be important in many life situations. Another disadvantage of psychometric tests is that even though standardized intelligence testing has been around for almost 100 years, there is still little consensus as to what intelligence really means. This, in turn, has led to vigorous debates about whether intelligence can be meaningfully measured, and whether any measurement of it is necessarily biased toward or against particular ethnic groups.

In this chapter we largely bypass these debates about whether psychometric tests of intelligence really measure intelligence. Instead, we rely on data from standardized intelligence tests primarily as a source of information about the nature of relations between age and various types of cognitive performance. It is in this respect that there are several advantages of standardized intelligence tests. First, standardized intelligence tests have been developed and refined to have very high levels of reliability. That is, the scores of the same people across different test occasions are generally quite similar, indicating the tests are measuring something about the individual that is consistent and stable. Second, standardized intelligence tests have also been established to have moderately good validity in the sense that the scores have been found to correlate significantly with other tests of intelligence and with external criteria such as performance in academic settings and level of occupational status. And third, the major intelligence tests have been standardized with relatively large representative samples of adults from a wide range of ages. This latter feature is particularly important because most of the research in the field of aging has been based on convenience or availability samples in which the participants were recruited in the easiest manner possible. However, with psychometric intelligence tests great efforts have been taken to ensure that the sample used to establish the norms was representative of the U.S. population. Not only does this mean the samples are much larger than those in most laboratory-based research studies, but they have been selected to be similar to the relevant population in terms of socioeconomic class, ethnic background, gender, amount of education, geographical region, and so on.

Although intelligence tests have become quite controversial, the combination of reliability, validity, and moderately large representative samples make them ideal for determining the relationship between age and different types of cognitive performance. Even if one disputes the assumption that the tests measure aspects of intelligence, they are valuable as a source of information about how certain types of cognitive performance vary as a function of age.

HISTORY AND BACKGROUND

The first large-scale group-administered intelligence test designed for adults was developed shortly after the United States declared its entry into World War I in April 1917. A group of psychologists, meeting at their annual convention, decided they wanted to make a contribution to the war effort and one way they could do so was to develop and administer intelligence tests which could be used for selection and placement of personnel in the military. A committee of psychologists therefore modified several existing tests to create two new intelligence test batteries. The battery designed for people who could read was known as the **Army Alpha** test, and the other, designed for people who could not read, was known as the Army Beta test.

A total of over 1.7 million men were administered one or the other of these two tests during World War I. Of course, most of the people entering the military were under the age of 30, but a wider age range was available among the men selected to serve as officers in the military. The Army Alpha battery consisted of eight short tests designed to assess general information, vocabulary, abstract reasoning, comprehension, and arithmetic word problems. For most of the analyses the scores on the tests were summed to provide a single overall composite score. In the largest sample spanning a wide age range, consisting of 15,000 officers between 20 and 55 years of age, the composite score decreased systematically with increased age such that the men in their 50s had scores only about 80% as high as the men in their 20s.

Although these results seemed to suggest an age-related decline in cognitive ability, the researchers who summarized the results of the Army Alpha and Army Beta testing were reluctant to accept that interpretation. Instead, they made the very plausible suggestion that although there was a good representation of young adults, the sample was biased in favor of less select older adults. Their argument was that many of the brightest and most competent older adults were likely to have been engaged in essential occupations and hence were exempt from military service, but because very few young adults had already established themselves in careers and essential occupations, they were not differentially represented in the military sample.

The differential representation interpretation of the age-related declines in measures of cognitive functioning remained plausible until 1933 when two researchers, Jones and Conrad, administered the same Army Alpha test to nearly the entire population of several rural New England communities. Ingenious efforts, such as offering free movies and enlisting the cooperation of community leaders, were successful in obtaining nearly complete participation of the residents of these communities. Note that although the resulting sample may not have been representative of the overall population, the researchers argued it was less subject to criticisms of differential selectivity than the World War I military sample because nearly all members of the targeted communities participated. The major finding from the Jones and Conrad study was that the age trends in the composite Army Alpha score decreased with increased age in a manner very similar to that in the military sample, thereby suggesting that differential selectivity was probably not the primary factor contributing to the age-related declines in measures of cognitive and intellectual ability.

Another intelligence test developed in the late 1920s and early 1930s is the predecessor to what is currently the most commonly used intelligence test for adults. This test was developed by David Wechsler, and resembled a combination of the Army Alpha and Army Beta batteries because the **WAIS Verbal Scale** consisted of tests based on language comprehension, and the **WAIS Performance Scale** consisted of nonverbal tests. (See Table 6–1 and Figure 6–1.) Unlike the

TABLE 6-1 Test Items Similar to WAIS Verbal Subtests

Information
1. Who wrote *Huckleberry Finn*?
2. Where is Finland?
3. At what temperature does paper burn?
4. What is entomology?

Arithmetic
1. How many 32 cent stamps can you buy for two dollars?
2. If two oranges cost 67 cents, what will a dozen oranges cost?
3. How many hours will it take a cyclist to travel 60 miles at a rate of 12 miles per hour?

Digit Span
1. Repeat these numbers in the same order: 7—1—6—2—2—8—3.
2. Repeat these numbers backward: 9—4—1—5.

Comprehension
1. Why should we obey traffic laws and speed limits?
2. Why are antitrust laws necessary?
3. Why should we lock the doors and take the keys when leaving a parked car?
4. What does this saying mean: "Kill two birds with one stone"?

Similarities
1. In what way are a hammer and a screwdriver alike?
2. In what way are a dog and a plant alike?
3. In what way are coal and gasoline alike?

Vocabulary
1. What does "careful" mean?
2. What does "tantamount" mean?

Source: Modified from Gleitman (1983, p. 393).

earlier tests, however, examinees taking the Wechsler battery were administered both types of tests. Because Wechsler's definition of intelligence incorporated both verbal and performance tests, the two scores are usually combined to provide an estimate of an individual's overall intellectual level. However, Wechsler believed that comparisons of intellectual level were meaningful only with respect to people of a similar age, and therefore an individual's intelligence quotient was determined relative to people his or her age. In other words, the IQ scores derived from Wechsler's tests are adjusted so they reflect an individual's intellectual level relative to people of roughly the same age, not relative to the entire population. Wechsler made this adjustment because of an assumption that age-related declines were normal and should be taken into account when evaluating an individual's intellectual level. Although we can debate the merits of this argument, it is important to recognize that one consequence of this adjustment is to complicate comparisons of adults of different ages because the IQ scores do not represent the same absolute levels of performance at different ages.

However, it is possible to use the information in the manuals for the Wechsler tests to determine the relations of the various subtests to age. This can be valuable because although scores on the verbal and performance scales have been found to be highly correlated for most people, there are much stronger relations of age to the performance scores than to the verbal scores. That is, scores on the performance tests tend to be lower with increased age, whereas the pattern with the verbal tests is largely one of stability across the adult years. This pattern is illustrated in Figure 6-2, which is based on the normative data from the most recent version of the Wechsler cognitive battery, the Wechsler Adult Intelligence Scale-III (WAIS-III). The figure was prepared by converting the mean

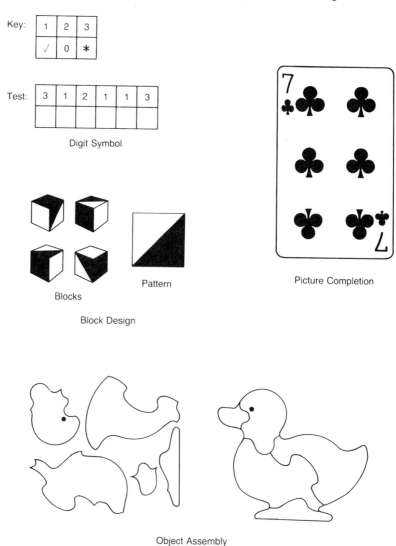

FIGURE 6–1   Test items similar to WAIS performance subtests.
(*Source:* Modified from Gleitman (1983, p. 393).)

raw scores at each age to scaled scores relative to a reference group between 20 and 34 years of age, summing the scaled scores for the subtests comprising the verbal and performance portions of the battery, and then using a conversion table to determine the verbal and performance IQs corresponding to the summed scale scores. The resulting values therefore reflect the scores representing age-adjusted IQs of 100 expressed in terms of a common reference distribution. When the results are portrayed in this way, the verbal scores increase slightly up to about age 50 and then decrease somewhat in the late 70s, whereas the performance scores appear to decrease continuously after about age 30.

In the WAIS Block Design Performance Scale, the subject is asked to assemble the blocks so that the pattern on top matches the design on the printed card. This subtest is timed; bonus points are awarded if the solution is reached with extraordinary speed.
(*Source:* Copyright © 1981 from The Psychological Corporation. All rights reserved.)

   Although the Wechsler test battery has been widely used for over 60 years, it has been criticized because the individual tests appear to assess a mixture of different cognitive abilities. This has been considered undesirable because it is difficult, if not impossible, to specify exactly what a particular test is evaluating. An alternative approach, initiated by Thurstone and Thurstone, attempted to identify relatively pure tests of different mental abilities, and then combined a

FIGURE 6–2   WAIS Verbal and Performance Scale scores as a function of age.
(*Source:* WAIS III.)

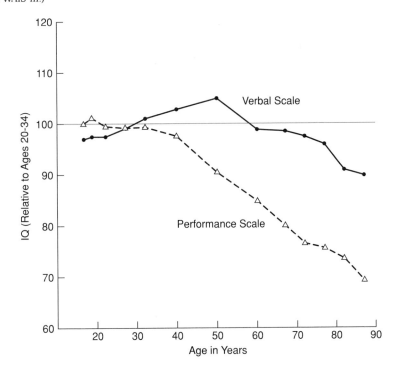

set of those tests to form a test battery known as the **Primary Mental Abilities.** A version of this test battery has been used in Schaie's Seattle Longitudinal Study (Schaie, 1996), which many researchers consider the most important study of the relation between age and psychometric aspects of cognitive functioning.

The five tests used in Schaie's version of the Primary Mental Abilities Test are vocabulary, figural rotation, series completion reasoning, arithmetic, and word fluency (i.e., writing as many words that begin with a particular letter in a limited period of time). Because the individual tests were selected to represent distinct abilities, the scores from the Primary Mental Abilities Test Battery are often reported for each test separately. In several different cross-sectional samples, the scores have been found to decrease with increased age for the figural rotation spatial ability test and the series completion reasoning test, but to remain relatively stable or increase with advancing age for the vocabulary, arithmetic, and word fluency tests. This pattern is roughly comparable to that portrayed in Figure 6–2, with the first two tests corresponding to the Performance Scale, and the latter three tests corresponding to the Verbal Scale.

GENERALIZATIONS ABOUT AGE DIFFERENCES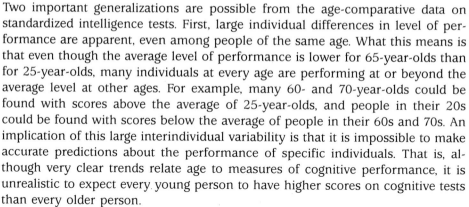

Two important generalizations are possible from the age-comparative data on standardized intelligence tests. First, large individual differences in level of performance are apparent, even among people of the same age. What this means is that even though the average level of performance is lower for 65-year-olds than for 25-year-olds, many individuals at every age are performing at or beyond the average level at other ages. For example, many 60- and 70-year-olds could be found with scores above the average of 25-year-olds, and people in their 20s could be found with scores below the average of people in their 60s and 70s. An implication of this large interindividual variability is that it is impossible to make accurate predictions about the performance of specific individuals. That is, although very clear trends relate age to measures of cognitive performance, it is unrealistic to expect every young person to have higher scores on cognitive tests than every older person.

A second generalization from the results of standardized tests is that the age trends vary across different kinds of tests. This is especially apparent in the Wechsler tests where there is little or no age-related decline for the tests comprising the Verbal Scale, but moderately large age-related declines for the tests comprising the Performance Scale. Different age trends are also evident in various tests from the Primary Mental Abilities test battery.

In part because of these differential age trends, a distinction has been made between two types of cognitive ability or intelligence. One type of intelligence, which primarily reflects the knowledge or information one has acquired in the past, is sometimes known as **crystallized intelligence.** The other type of intelligence, which corresponds to the efficiency or effectiveness of processing at the time of assessment, is known as **fluid intelligence.** In contrast to crystallized intelligence, which can be considered to represent the accumulated products of processing carried out in the past, fluid intelligence refers to one's current ability to solve novel or unfamiliar problems (Cattell, 1987; Horn & Hofer, 1992).

Because the distinction between the Verbal and Performance scales in the Wechsler tests is roughly analogous to the distinction between crystallized and fluid intelligence, it can be concluded that although there are declines in fluid intelligence with increased age, crystallized intelligence remains constant or increases slightly throughout most of the adult years. The stability or modest increases in crystallized intelligence with increasing age can perhaps be understood in terms of a greater accumulation of products of past processing when there have been more opportunities to acquire knowledge. That is, when people have had more experience learning the meaning of words and miscellaneous information about their culture, it is reasonable that their storehouse of knowledge would expand.

Although the absence of declines in crystallized intelligence with increasing age seems to be readily explained, the reasons for age-related declines in fluid intelligence have been difficult to determine. Later in this chapter we consider several interpretations that have been proposed to account for the well-documented declines in fluid intelligence.

Longitudinal versus Cross-Sectional Comparisons

Some of the early studies comparing results from longitudinal and cross-sectional designs revealed that the age-related differences in measures of cognitive functioning were often smaller with longitudinal comparisons than with cross-sectional comparisons. However, the results of some of those studies are difficult to interpret because the longitudinal studies involved measures that predominantly reflected crystallized types of cognition, whereas the cross-sectional studies involved mixtures of both crystallized and fluid measures of cognition. Because we have seen that the age-related differences are generally larger with fluid measures of cognition than with crystallized measures, we would naturally expect larger age-related differences in the comparisons involving fluid measures than in those involving crystallized measures. Because of this confounding of the type of comparison (i.e., longitudinal vs. cross-sectional) with the type of cognitive measure (i.e., fluid vs. crystallized), several of the early comparisons were somewhat misleading.

Some of the most impressive results with both cross-sectional and longitudinal data are those from Schaie's Seattle Longitudinal Study (Schaie, 1996). This project is unique in that the same tests were used in both cross-sectional and longitudinal comparisons. The Seattle Longitudinal Study started in 1956 with 500 people who ranged from 25 to 67 years of age. Every 7 years since 1956 the project has continued with testing of participants from the previous years, as well as recruiting and testing of new participants from the same wide age range. In each of the test sessions after the first, the data have been analyzed with respect to age-related trends in both cross-sectional and longitudinal comparisons. In most of the comparisons the age-related differences have been found to be smaller in the longitudinal contrasts than in the cross-sectional contrasts.

However, even though scores on exactly the same tests are being compared, many of these comparisons are also somewhat misleading because the interval between the ages has been much shorter for the longitudinal contrasts than for the cross-sectional contrasts. For example, although the project has continued from 1956 through 1991, only a total of 71 people, or 14.2%, of the original participants continued to participate and contribute data across the entire 35-year interval. Most of the longitudinal comparisons are therefore based on retest intervals, or age ranges, of 7 to 14 years, whereas the cross-sectional comparisons involve age ranges of nearly 60 years (i.e., from about 20 to 80 years of age). Because age-related effects are likely to be cumulative, we would naturally expect them to be much larger across an age range of 40 to 50 years, as in most cross-sectional comparisons, than across an age range of less than 20 years, as in most longitudinal comparisons.

For the reasons just described, the most meaningful type of comparison between cross-sectional and longitudinal data is probably that expressed in terms of magnitude of cognitive performance change per year of age. When both types of data are converted to this annual change scale, the results can be more directly compared because now the differences or changes refer to the same age interval. Examination of the results expressed in this manner reveals that the age-related differences may not be very different for cross-sectional and longitudinal comparisons. That is, estimates of the annual cross-sectional differences and the annual longitudinal changes are often between about 0.02 and 0.04 standard deviation units per year (see Salthouse [1991b] and Zelinski & Burnight [1997]).

Actually, because of the complications of selective attrition and repeated practice in longitudinal studies, but not in cross-sectional studies, we might expect there to be smaller age-related change estimates in longitudinal studies. That is, longitudinal comparisons might underestimate true age-related change because the lowest functioning individuals might be less likely to continue to participate in longitudinal studies, and because each testing occasion provides another opportunity for practice that may minimize any age-related cognitive declines that could be occurring. Indeed, Salthouse (1991) found evidence for these types of effects in a reanalysis of Schaie's data.

Because there is still relatively little data from longitudinal comparisons of cognitive variables extending for 30 or more years, conclusions about age relations from cross-sectional and longitudinal designs must be considered tentative. Nevertheless, we have seen that recent analyses, which take into consideration the type of cognitive variable and the range of ages, suggest that results from cross-sectional and longitudinal comparisons may not be as discrepant as sometimes believed.

SPECIALIZED COGNITIVE ABILITIES

In this section we briefly review research on the relation of age to different types of cognitive abilities. Not all cognitive abilities are discussed, but the ones described represent most of the major dimensions of cognition that have been subjected to empirical investigation.

Reasoning

Several different types of reasoning have been investigated in age-comparative research. One type is known as deductive reasoning because in this case the task for the individual is to deduce what necessarily follows, given a certain set of information. For example, some tests of deductive reasoning ask the respondent to evaluate the truth or falsity of different kinds of syllogisms. A **syllogism** is a simple argument composed of several premises and a conclusion. Research based on syllogisms can either require the individual to determine whether a conclusion necessarily follows from the premises or to indicate what conclusion is implied from the premises. An example of the latter type of problem is as follows:

> R and S do the OPPOSITE;
> Q and R do the SAME;
> If Q INCREASES, what will happen to S?

In this particular example, if Q increases then so will R (from the second premise), and if R increases then S will decrease (from the first premise), and therefore the answer to what will happen to Q is that it will decrease.

Several studies have been conducted with this type of task, and in all of them increased age has been associated with lower levels of accuracy. To illustrate, Salthouse and colleagues (1989) found that accuracy in these decisions decreased by approximately 4.3% for every 10-year increase in age. Other types of deductive reasoning tests have asked participants to evaluate arguments of the kind that might appear in an editorial page of a newspaper or in political advertisements. Even with this less abstract type of material, people in their 60s and 70s have been found to perform at lower average levels than people in their 20s.

A second type of reasoning is known as **inductive reasoning** because in this case the task is to attempt to determine what new conclusions can be inferred from the available information. Examples of inductive reasoning are various series completion tests in which a sequence of items is presented and the respondent is asked to select the best continuation of the sequence from among a set of alternatives. Here is an example of a numeric series completion problem:

> 3 5 8 12 _____ {13, 15, 17, 19}

Age relations on series completion tests such as those used in the Army Alpha Test and the Primary Mental Abilities test battery used by Schaie in the Seattle Longitudinal Study are generally in the moderate to large range, with people in their 60s and 70s performing quite a bit lower on the average than people in their 20s.

Another type of inductive reasoning test is known as the matrix reasoning test. Versions of this test are used in the Raven's Matrix Reasoning Test, and as one of the subtests in the new version of the WAIS–III. The exact format varies across different tests, but in most of them a matrix of patterns is displayed with one missing cell, and the task for the examinee is to select the best completion of the missing cell from among a set of alternatives. Figure 6–3 contains sample

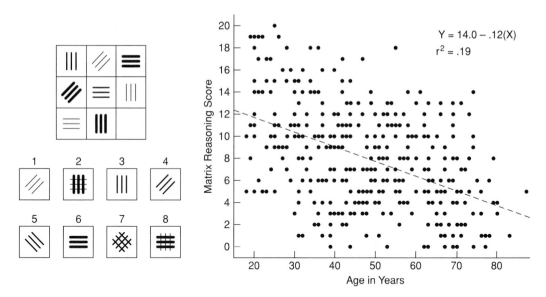

FIGURE 6–3 **Matrix reasoning test and relation of age to performance.**
(*Source:* Salthouse (1993).)

items for this type of test and the relations of age to average performance on the test from a recent study. Notice that although there is a great deal of variability at all ages, the average level of performance, represented by the dashed line, clearly decreases with increased age.

Still another form of inductive reasoning test is known as **concept formation**. A variety of concept formation tasks have been widely studied in experimental psychology, and versions of concept formation tests have also been used in neuropsychological assessments. One of the most interesting studies of concept formation involving adults of different ages was published by Arenberg (1968). An innovative feature of Arenberg's research was that rather than using the stimuli traditionally used for a concept formation task, which usually consist of shapes varying in number, size, and color, the stimuli in his version of the task were meals in which one of the foods was poisoned. The task faced by the individual was therefore to consider the meals eaten by several people when dining at a restaurant and then to determine which particular food was responsible for poisoning one of the diners. Although this situation was assumed to be more meaningful to the research participants than the task with more abstract stimuli, Arenberg found large age-related differences in performance on this task favoring younger adults. Several experimentally oriented studies have also been conducted with concept formation tasks. For example, research has been conducted to determine whether adults of different ages vary in the likelihood of using particular strategies in concept formation tasks. One strategy that has been identified is for the individual to stay with the same hypothesis about the critical dimensions or attribute when positive feedback is provided and to change the hypothesis or guess when negative feedback is provided. The strategy is known as the win stay–lose shift strategy because the optimal use of this strategy involves staying with a hypothesis that is winning and shifting from a hypothesis that has lost. At least two studies (Fristoe, Salthouse, & Woodard, 1997; Offenbach, 1974) have found that older adults are less likely to follow this type of win stay–lose shift strategy in concept formation tasks. These results imply that one of the reasons older adults perform at lower levels than young adults in concept formation tasks is that they may not recognize the value of the feedback information to the same degree as young adults.

Decision Making

Relatively few studies have investigated age differences in decision making. One task that has been investigated by a number of researchers is based on the familiar 20 Questions game in which the individual is supposed to select the target item from among an array of items by asking only yes or no questions and trying to make the identification with the fewest possible number of questions. Several studies have found that younger adults perform more efficiently than older adults in this type of task, as though they are better able to remember the answers to previously asked questions or to remember the efficient strategy of asking questions that reduce the remaining number of possibilities by the maximum amount.

A more complex type of decision involves **multiattribute decision making**. This type of decision making is presumably involved in most everyday situations in which people have to reach a decision that involves many different kinds of information. For example, decisions about which house to buy, which type of medical benefits plan to adopt, and whether to switch to a new job all involve a number of different dimensions or attributes that need to be considered in order to reach an optimum decision. Among the questions that could be asked with age-comparative research on this kind of decision making are whether there are age differences in the ability to evaluate information, in the amount of information (i.e., the number of attributes) that can be simultaneously considered when making a decision, and in the quality of the resulting decision. Unfortunately, there have apparently been no studies of this type involving comparisons of people of different ages. This is a topic area that would be very valuable to pursue because decision making is obviously an important aspect of everyday life, and there is currently very little information on whether, and if so how, it is related to age.

A few studies have compared people of different ages in terms of the styles or strategies used in decision making. For example, one study based on interviews of middle managers of different ages found that many of these individuals reported they had changed their style of decision making as they got older (Birren, 1969). Among the reports of changes were claims that as they grew older and more experienced the managers delegated more responsibility to others and concentrated on only the most important aspects of the situation.

Creativity

There have been two quite different approaches to investigating the relations between age and creativity. One approach has examined measures of creative or professional productivity as a function of the age of the individual when the achievement occurred. Research of this type has a long history dating back at least several centuries, but two researchers who have reported tremendous amounts of data of this type are Harvey Lehman in the 1950s (e.g., Lehman, 1953) and Dean Simonton in the 1980s and 1990s (e.g., Simonton, 1996). Both researchers found that measures of productivity for a wide variety of fields tend

 MYTHS ABOUT AGING

Intelligence and Cognition

Myth	*Best Available Evidence*
There is a universal decline in intelligence with increasing age. Thus, you are very likely to suffer serious and widespread deterioration in intellectual ability during your old age.	Some intellectual abilities do show significant decrements as we grow older, especially after middle age. But the declines in other abilities are small and do not appear to have much effect on our daily functioning. Age-related changes in intelligence test scores may not accurately reflect true changes in intelligence because of cohort effects, extraneous variables, selective attrition, and/or other methodological problems. The majority of elderly adults do *not* suffer extreme deterioration in intelligence, although some losses may be expected in such areas as perceptual integration, response speed, and certain aspects of memory.
If you have not made any creative contributions by about age 40, you probably never will.	Creativity does tend to peak prior to middle age, but numerous important creative works have been produced during the latter part of the creator's life.

Some studies suggest that creativity declines after age 40, but there are many famous exceptions. For example, painter Claude Monet did not begin his noted *Water Lily* series until age seventy-three.

to peak around age 40. Similar patterns have been reported for artists, musicians, inventors, and even military leaders. There are now so many comparisons of this type that the basic phenomenon seems fairly well established. That is, for a surprisingly large number of fields, the highest level of productivity seems to occur when the person is around age 40, although the peak occurs slightly earlier for certain fields, such as mathematics and theoretical physics, and somewhat later for other fields, such as philosophy and history. What is still not clear from this kind of research is whether the observed relations are primarily determined by the chronological age of the individual or by his or her career age. Simonton has suggested that the critical variable may not be the age of the individual, but rather the number of years he or she has worked within a particular career. His hypothesis is that there are a finite number of ideas or potential contributions a person can make within a particular field, and if he or she were to switch to a different field then a new pool of potential creative ideas might come into play with a return of the function relating age to productivity to the original starting point. Simonton's hypothesis is largely speculative at the current time, but it may be possible to examine its validity in the future if large enough numbers of people can be studied who have made major career shifts in midlife.

Another way in which creativity has been studied is with measures of **divergent thinking.** There are a number of tests of divergent thinking (see Table 6–2), but most require the individual to try to generate many different answers to

TABLE 6–2   Tests of Divergent Thinking Devised by Guilford

- *Word Fluency:* Write as many words as possible containing a specified letter. The letter may appear anywhere in the word.
- *Expressional Fluency:* Write a meaningful four-word sentence, where each word must begin with a specified letter (e.g., W _____ A _____ M _____ S _____).
- *Alternate Uses:* List as many uses as possible for a specified object (e.g., a newspaper), other than the most obvious one.
- *Ideational Fluency:* Given a specified category (e.g., "things that will burn"), name as many things as possible that belong in that category.
- *Plot Titles:* Given a one-paragraph description of a short story plot, write a brief, interesting, and relevant title for that story.
- *Consequences:* Given a hypothetical event (e.g., people no longer need or want sleep), list as many consequences of this event as possible (e.g., no more alarm clocks).
- *Making Objects:* Using only a given set of figures (e.g., circle, triangle), draw a specified object (e.g., a face, a lamp).
- *Match Problems:* Given a set of matchsticks that form a pattern (e.g., two rows of three square boxes), remove a certain number of matchsticks so as to produce a specified result (e.g., remove three matchsticks to reduce the number of boxes from six to four).

Source: Guilford (1967).

a potential problem. Among the divergent thinking tests that have been used in studies of aging are the unusual usages test in which the respondent is supposed to generate as many different ways to use a familiar object as possible, and a variety of block arrangement tests in which the respondent is supposed to create as many different arrangements of a set of blocks as possible. Nearly all of the research of this type has revealed moderately large age-related declines in the number of "creative" responses produced in these types of divergent thinking tests (e.g., McCrae, Arenberg, & Costa, 1987). Although the empirical results are fairly clear, there are still debates about whether divergent thinking is a reasonable method of assessing creativity. In particular, some critics have suggested that creativity is specific to particular domains in the sense that a person may be highly creative within one field but not in other fields. To the extent this is true, general or domain-independent tests of creativity may have little or no validity for predicting the likelihood that someone will make an important discovery or produce an artistic, literary, or musical masterpiece.

Wisdom

Wisdom has been a topic of great interest among researchers focusing on aging because it is often assumed to be a quality that increases with age. There are few good definitions of wisdom, but it is presumably related to good judgment about fundamental aspects of human experience. (See Table 6–3.) In light of the lack of adequate definitions, it is probably not surprising that few research studies have investigated relations between age and wisdom.

   Wisdom has also been difficult to investigate because unlike intelligence or other cognitive abilities, there is no generally accepted criterion against which

Historically, wisdom has been viewed as an ability that is passed from one generation to the next through social interaction.

the validity of the wisdom tests could be evaluated. Furthermore we cannot simply rely on the existence of age-related increases as evidence that wisdom is being measured because the speculations about the relation of age to wisdom may be incorrect. That is, although it is often assumed that wisdom increases with age, this attribution may have no foundation, or it may simply be that wisdom is a characteristic of a very small number of older adults, but it is not a characteristic of old people in general. Furthermore, because many measures of knowledge have been found to increase with age, it is important to have some means of distinguishing wisdom from other forms of knowledge.

Various tests requiring the interpretation of proverbs are sometimes considered to assess a form of wisdom because proverbs are often assumed to capture basic truths about human existence. In this respect an individual who is better able to select or generate appropriate interpretations of proverbs might be postulated to possess certain attributes of wisdom. Whether or not this is true is not easily determined, but a number of studies have reported that accuracy of proverb interpretation tends to be lower with increased age (Albert, Duffy, & Naeser, 1987; Bromley, 1957).

A different approach to the investigation of wisdom has been carried out by Paul Baltes and his colleagues at the Max Planck Institute in Berlin (e.g., Baltes & Staudinger, 1993). Those researchers have proposed several criteria to be used in evaluating the wisdom of responses provided by individuals to life problem situations. For example, one life problem used in their research involves offering

TABLE 6–3   Facets of Wisdom: Views Suggested by Various Researchers

HOW WISDOM DEVELOPS	CHARACTERISTICS OF A WISE PERSON
Through extensive experience and the acquisition of knowledge.	Intelligent, emphatic.
By integrating conflicting types of information in a growth-oriented way.	Has exceptional insight, gives good advice.
By developing logical reasoning and shrewdness.	Realizes that knowing is uncertain, that he or she may err, and that all questions cannot be answered.
By learning to integrate cognitive and emotional matters, an ability that increases with increasing age.	Is generally competent, has good judgment and good communication skills.
By developing the ability to synthesize opposing views with what one already knows, rather than ignoring them—an ability that increases with increasing age.	Probes for knowledge, seeks truth, is not dismayed by ambiguous information that lacks a clear-cut right answer.
By striving for a balance between knowing and doubting, an ability acquired primarily through supportive interpersonal relationships rather than aging.	Understands self and others; is intuitive. Solves own problems effectively, advises others; may manage social institutions.

Source: Modified from Birren & Fisher (1990).

advice to a young couple who were deciding whether or not to move so the husband could take a new job in a different city. Baltes and his colleagues tried to identify people who may have a higher likelihood of being wise according to their criteria by seeking nominations of wise people from members of the community and also by studying people in helping professions such as certain types of judges and clinical psychologists. Even with these special samples, however, they have not found strong evidence that increased age is associated with higher scores on their wisdom measures.

POTENTIAL EXPLANATORY FACTORS

Health

Perhaps the first factor that most people think of when trying to explain age-related declines in cognitive abilities is health status. Many types of diseases or health-related problems increase in prevalence with age, and it is plausible to suspect that problems affecting either the central nervous system or the cardiovascular system may impair intellectual performance. Although the argument appears reasonable, it has been surprisingly difficult to obtain convincing evidence for this interpretation. What would probably be the strongest evidence in support of the health-based interpretation would be a discovery that there were little or no age-related declines in measures of fluid intelligence for people established to be in very good health, but moderate to large declines for people in poorer health. However, the difficulty has been in obtaining accurate assessments of an individual's health status.

One of the simplest ways to evaluate someone's health is by asking the person to rate his or her own health on a scale ranging from poor to excellent. Because this is a very easy method of assessment, it has been used in many studies, including some with moderately large samples of adults across a wide age range.

The results of those studies have typically revealed that the age-related declines were nearly identical for the entire sample, and for the subsample of people who rated their health to be excellent. Figure 6–4 illustrates this pattern with data from several studies described in Salthouse (1991b). Because very similar declines with increased age were evident among people who are apparently not experiencing any health problems, these results are inconsistent with the view that declines in health are responsible for the declines in fluid intelligence.

However, numerous questions have been raised regarding the validity of self-report assessments of health, and it is possible that they do not reflect the individual's true health status. In addition to biases associated with personality characteristics, such as optimism or hypochondriasis, people may not be fully aware of all their health problems. A more desirable procedure would be to base the evaluations of health on a thorough physical examination carried out by one or more trained medical professionals. The problem with this alternative is that

FIGURE 6–4   Self-assessment of health factors related to fluid intelligence.
(*Source:* Salthouse (1991b).)

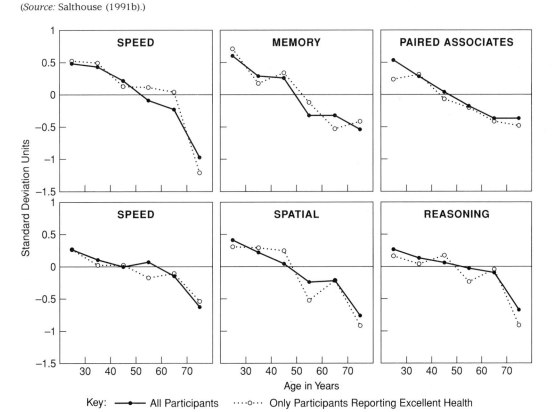

comprehensive examinations of this type are typically very expensive, and consequently, samples in which all participants have undergone rigorous health screening are usually quite small. Nevertheless, it is noteworthy that the results from at least several studies with what might be termed superhealthy adults, as determined by rigorous medical examinations, have been similar to those from studies relying on self-report assessments in that the age trends in measures of fluid intelligence have been similar for the healthiest individuals and for samples of unselected adults (Albert, Duffy, & Naeser, 1987; Botwinick & Birren, 1963). It is still possible that the physical exams may have failed to detect health-related problems that contribute to lower levels of performance on tests of fluid intelligence, but currently little evidence suggests that much of the age-related declines in cognition are attributable to greater prevalence of health problems among older adults.

Education

Another factor often mentioned as a potential contributor to age-related declines in fluid intelligence is the historical change in the amount of education the average adult has received. Because the average number of years of education has been increasing over the last 50 years in the United States, it is possible that at least some of the lower scores on tests of fluid intelligence among older adults are attributable to them having fewer years of education than the younger adults with whom they are being compared.

Although it might seem simple to test this differential education hypothesis, perhaps by comparing people with exactly the same amount of education, a number of factors complicate the interpretation of any results that might be obtained. First, even though it may not be easy to evaluate, we cannot be certain that changes have not occurred in the quality of education, independent of any changes that might have occurred in the quantity of education the average person has received. Second, along with the changes in the average amount of education have been changes in the opportunity to acquire a higher education. That is, 30 to 50 years ago it was much more likely that the people who went to college were from higher socioeconomic groups than those who did not go to college, but this is probably less true at the current time. If factors related to socioeconomic status, such as income, occupation, and perhaps parental intelligence, are associated with an individual's level of fluid intelligence, then comparisons of young and old adults with the same level of education may actually involve a select group of older adults being contrasted with a less select group of young adults. (Note that to the extent this type of bias exists, comparisons of education-matched groups of young and old adults may actually result in underestimates of the true magnitude of age-related decline in cognitive ability.)

A third complication in research attempting to investigate the role of education on adult age differences in fluid intelligence is that even if people of different ages are matched in terms of the amount of education they received, they will almost certainly differ in terms of the time that has elapsed since the completion of their education. In other words, because most people complete their formal education by their mid-20s, a 30-year-old college graduate will have only 5 to 10 years for any forgetting to occur, whereas a 60-year-old college graduate would have had 35 to 40 years of "opportunities" to have forgotten the information acquired during the period of formal education.

A final complication has to do with whether education is assumed to be a cause or a consequence of higher levels of fluid intelligence. Although it is plausible to think of more education as leading to increases in crystallized, or knowledge-based, intelligence, it is not obvious that it is also responsible for increases in the fluid, or processing efficiency, type of intelligence. In fact, a reasonable argument could be made that fluid intelligence is more of a cause, rather than a consequence, of the amount of education an individual acquires because high levels of fluid intelligence are often a prerequisite for admission into colleges and other institutions of higher learning. Unless the individual has a high level of certain types of intellectual or cognitive ability, therefore, he or she may not have the opportunity to acquire advanced levels of education.

Although the interpretations have been controversial, the pattern of results from comparisons involving people with the same amounts of education have been remarkably consistent. In almost all of the comparisons, the age-related trends have been nearly parallel for people with different amounts of education, and similar in overall shape to those obtained from unselected samples. As we would expect, people with greater amounts of education perform at higher levels than people with less education, but the relations of the scores on tests of fluid intelligence to age have been very similar regardless of educational level. It therefore appears that shifting educational patterns are probably not responsible for much of the age-related declines that have been reported in measures of fluid intelligence.

Unspecified Environmental or Cultural Changes

Patterns of education are not the only thing that has changed over the last 50 years or so, and it is possible that changes in a variety of other factors might have contributed to some of the cross-sectional age differences in measures of fluid intelligence. One intriguing version of this argument is that people may not change much in their intellectual or cognitive abilities after they reach maturity, and almost all of the age differences observed in cross-sectional comparisons might be attributable to successive generations performing at higher levels of functioning in cognitive tests. The key feature of this view is that people do not deteriorate relative to their earlier levels, but rather that they essentially become obsolete because more recent generations of people perform at progressively higher levels. A relevant analogy might be that of computers because older computers may still be functioning at the same level as when they were new, but they are less powerful than the latest computers because of the increase in speed and memory in newer generations of computers.

One research design that is relevant to the possibility that **environmental change factors** are contributing to the age differences observed in cross-sectional studies is a time-lag design. In this design comparisons are made of people of the same ages, but at different points in time. For example, 20-year-olds could be compared in 1950, 1970, and 1990. The reasoning is that if changes in the physical or cultural environment, rather than changes occurring within the individual, are responsible for the different levels of performance observed across people of varying ages, then similar differences should be evident when everyone is compared at the same age but at different periods in time. That is, just as comparisons of the performance of new computers from 1988 and 1998 would reveal large differences, comparisons of 20-year-olds in 1950 and 20-year-olds in 1990 might reveal large differences if it really is the case that successive generations are achieving at higher levels in cognitive tests.

Some of the best data on **time-lag effects** come from European countries where various types of intelligence tests have been administered to all males registering for the draft when they reach the age of 18 (Flynn, 1987). What is particularly impressive about this project is that in many of the countries data were available from over 90% of the 18-year-old males across a period of almost 50 years. Analyses of the data from several countries revealed a very similar pattern of substantially higher performance on the same standardized test for more recent generations. In fact, the magnitude of this generational difference over a period of 30 years was nearly as large as the average performance difference between 20- and 50-year-olds in cross-sectional comparisons.

Similar, although often somewhat smaller, time-lag improvements have been reported with other standardized tests. For example, one study found that soldiers in World War II performed at an average level on the Army Alpha test that would have corresponded to the 83rd percentile of the distribution of scores for World War I soldiers (Tuddenham, 1948). Most of the tests used to evaluate scholastic achievement also exhibit this phenomenon because the norms become obsolete over time and need to be updated every several years.

One of the surprising aspects of the time-lag improvements is that they are not restricted to crystallized or knowledge-based types of intelligence. In fact, there are some reports that the generational improvements have been larger on measures of fluid intelligence than on measures of crystallized intelligence. This suggests it is not simply the case that successive generations are acquiring more knowledge than earlier generations because the fluid intelligence measures reflect abstract or novel problem-solving ability.

Although time-lag improvements in cognitive or intellectual performance have been well documented, neither the reasons for these improvements nor their implications for interpreting age differences are yet very well understood. One factor that can almost certainly be ruled out is genetic improvements in the species because evolutionary changes require much longer than one or two generations to occur. Educational changes are another possibility, but the fact that the time-lag improvements have been about the same magnitude for 6-year-olds as for 18-year-olds suggests that it is not the major factor because most 6-year-old children have not yet been exposed to formal education. Among the other factors that are still considered plausible as determinants of the time-lag improvements are historical changes in prenatal care, public health practices, nutritional habits, general cultural stimulation through many kinds of media, and increased test sophistication.

Now consider the implications of these time-lag improvements for the interpretation of cross-sectional age differences in intellectual abilities. One possibility is that those differences are completely spurious as indications of true age-related changes because they may merely reflect the phenomenon of progressively higher scores in successive generations. In other words, this interpretation would be consistent with the obsolescence view in which people do not decline after reaching maturity, but instead they perform at lower levels than younger people because more recent generations reach higher levels of intellectual functioning before stabilizing. However, another possibility is that the factors responsible for the time-lag improvements affect people of all ages throughout their lives. As an example, think of the impact of inflation on salaries. Time-lag comparisons across a 40-year period of the entry-level salaries for a particular occupation would undoubtedly reveal dramatic increases over historical time, and yet sizable relations could still exist within that occupation between age and average salary. Because the effects of cumulative inflation would severely distort the relations of age in longitudinal comparisons, the most appropriate method for detecting age relations under these circumstances would probably be with cross-sectional contrasts.

Another method of investigating the role of environmental change factors on age differences in cognitive functioning is with comparisons among individuals whose environment has not changed appreciably across their lifetimes. This may be very difficult to do with humans because we still do not know which particular aspects of the environment might be important for cognitive functioning, and could be changing over time. However, it is much more feasible with animals because of their shorter life spans and the possibility of exerting rigorous control over the environment across their entire lives. Although no versions of the Army Alpha or the Wechsler tests exist for rats and monkeys, their cognitive abilities can be investigated in a number of ways.

For example, one procedure that has been used to assess memory in rats involves a **radial maze** in which food is placed at the end of each of the arms of the maze. For a given series of tests the rat is placed in the center of the maze and is allowed to wander freely and consume any food that is found. As soon as the food is consumed in one of the arms, the rat is removed and placed in the center of the maze again without replacing the consumed food. Because the food in that arm of the maze has already been consumed, the rat should gradually learn to avoid entering any of the paths of the maze it had already entered in that series of tests. One measure of memory performance in this test is the number of arms of the maze that are entered after the food in that arm had already been consumed. Higher scores therefore represent poorer memory because if the rat had an accurate memory of past responses it would learn to avoid the arms of the maze that had already been entered. The major finding with respect to age differences in this situation is that older rats tend to have higher scores, indicative of poorer memory, than do younger rats (e.g., Gallagher & Rapp, 1997). Because this pattern of age differences occurs under circumstances where it is very unlikely that the environment could have changed in significant ways, and because the pattern is very similar to that observed in studies with humans, the results are inconsistent with the view that unspecified changes in the environment are responsible for a large proportion of the age differences found in measures of fluid intelligence.

Disuse

The final category of explanation for age differences in fluid intelligence that we consider attributes those differences to lack of recent practice with the relevant abilities. This **disuse** perspective is aptly characterized by the cliché "Use it or lose it" because the basic idea is that knowledge is forgotten and skills become rusty if they are not continuously used. It is not surprising that this perspective is popular among both researchers and the general public because it implies that people have some control over their own destiny as far as their cognitive status is concerned. In other words, if this perspective is correct, then declines will occur only for those abilities that, for one reason or another, are not used frequently. This is clearly an optimistic view of the relation between age and intellectual ability, and it is important to consider the type of evidence pertaining to its validity.

One category of research relevant to the disuse interpretation involves comparisons of the performance of people of different ages on activities that can be presumed to be familiar to almost everyone. The reasoning is that if age-related declines are attributable to disuse, then there should be little or no age-related declines on highly familiar or frequently performed activities. Actually this argument is somewhat more complicated than it initially appears because if an activity is frequently performed by people of all ages, then the amount of cumulative practice or experience with that activity will almost certainly be much greater for older adults than for young adults. To the extent that there are benefits of extensive experience, performance thus might be expected to increase rather than decrease with increasing age. It turns out that this potential complication is not a problem for interpretation, however, because the age relations on familiar or everyday types of activities that appear to involve fluid intelligence are very similar to those observed in abstract unfamiliar laboratory tasks. To illustrate, older adults have been found to perform at lower levels than young adults on measures of comprehension and memory of prescription drug information (Park, Morrell, Frieske, & Kincaid, 1992), comprehension of bus schedules and fares (Neale, Toye, & Belbin, 1968), and effectiveness of following instructions for the assembly of objects (Morrell & Park, 1993).

Many of these activities were deliberately selected because of their frequency of occurrence in everyday life, and thus they can probably be assumed to have minimal amounts of disuse. The discovery of moderate to large age-related differences favoring young adults in these measures is therefore inconsistent with the interpretation that declines in measures of cognitive functioning are attributable to lack of recent experience with the relevant abilities.

Another type of evidence relevant to the disuse interpretation of age-related cognitive decline is based on comparisons of the age trends in people with different amounts of relevant experience. That is, instead of selecting activities which might be familiar to everyone, the focus in this type of research has been on groups of people who have extensive amounts of experience within a particular domain. The assumption in this case is that if disuse is responsible for the cognitive decline, there should be little or no decline among people for whom the relevant abilities have been in continuous use. However, most of the research with these types of special populations has found that even highly experienced people tend to exhibit age-related declines in measures of fluid intelligence. This has been reported in studies of English teachers and measures of word memory (Klein & Shaffer, 1986), in studies of architects and measures of spatial visualization (Salthouse, Babcock, Mitchell, Skovronek, & Palmon, 1990), and in studies of college professors with measures of reasoning (e.g., Christensen & Henderson, 1991; Sward, 1945). There are some exceptions to this pattern, but it is clearly not the case that age differences are never found when comparisons are made of people who have extensive amounts of experience with a particular activity.

The third category of evidence relevant to the disuse perspective concerns the effects of added experience on the pattern of age differences. If the age-related declines in cognitive functioning are due to lack of use, then we would expect that providing people with additional experience would eliminate the disuse and perhaps also eliminate the age differences. Even if the age differences did not completely disappear, this perspective would lead to an expectation of greater benefits of the added experience for the older adults who were presumably the initially most disadvantaged due to disuse. However, this is not what the results typically reveal. The general pattern has been that everyone improves in measures of fluid intelligence with additional experience or training, but that younger adults tend to maintain a higher level of performance than older adults (see Table 4–5 in Salthouse, 1991). In some cases the benefits of experience have been similar in young and old adults, whereas in other cases younger adults appeared to benefit more than older adults. Only when there were upper limits on the level of performance and younger adults were closer to those limits than older adults has there been convincing evidence of greater improvement with additional practice or training for older adults. The results with added experience are therefore not consistent with at least some expectations from the disuse perspective.

Although the disuse interpretation remains popular, surprisingly little empirical evidence provides support for it. Not only are age differences found in activities that can be presumed to be highly familiar to most people, but people with extensive experience in a particular area still exhibit age-related declines in relevant measures of performance, and contrary to expectation, older adults do not benefit more than young adults by additional experience that should have eliminated any disuse.

SUMMARY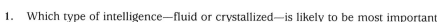

Adult age differences in cognitive and intellectual abilities have been well documented in large standardized mental ability tests since World War I. However, not all types of intelligence decline with increasing age because measures of acquired information and knowledge, sometimes known as crystallized intelligence, tend to remain stable across most of the adult years, whereas measures of the efficiency of solving novel problems, sometimes known as fluid intelligence, gradually declines beginning as early as the late 20s. Even with the fluid intelligence measures, however, there is a great deal of variability at every age, and consequently it is difficult to make accurate predictions on the basis of one's age. Many of the comparisons in the past have revealed smaller age-related effects in longitudinal contrasts than in cross-sectional contrasts, but the results may not be as discrepant as sometimes believed when factors such as type of cognitive ability, range of age or retest interval, effects of practice, and selective attrition are taken into account.

Age differences are evident in specialized types of cognition such as deductive and inductive reasoning, decision making and creativity, and possibly even in some aspects of wisdom. The reasons for age-related decline in measures of fluid intelligence are still not understood, and the existing evidence is not completely consistent with expectations based on health, education, general environmental change, or disuse. For example, although impressive increases in scores on standardized intelligence tests have been reported over historical time by people of the same age, the reasons for these increases are not yet known, nor are their implications for understanding relations between age and cognition. Also, the "use it or lose it" view in which declines are attributed to disuse remains popular despite a surprisingly small amount of positive evidence.

STUDY QUESTIONS

1. Which type of intelligence—fluid or crystallized—is likely to be most important during the working years, and why?
2. The age-comparative research on reasoning seems to suggest that with increasing age adults are less effective at several types of abstract reasoning. However, the most important decision makers in many societies are often older adults. How might this apparent paradox be explained?
3. Although the disuse theory of cognitive aging is intuitively appealing, it has been difficult to find convincing evidence in its support. Can you think of how you might be able to provide a strong test of its plausibility?
4. Most people probably believe that intelligence, creativity, and wisdom are not the same, but currently little evidence from age comparisons supports a distinction among the three concepts. What type of research might be helpful in clarifying the differences among these concepts?

TERMS TO REMEMBER

Army Alpha
Concept formation
Crystallized intelligence
Disuse
Divergent thinking
Environmental change factors
Fluid intelligence
Inductive reasoning

Multiattribute decision making
Primary Mental Abilities
Psychometric tests
Radial maze tests
Syllogism
Time-lag effects on intelligence
WAIS Performance Scale
WAIS Verbal Scale

PERSONALITY AND THEORIES
OF LIFE-SPAN DEVELOPMENT

Understanding how human personality develops and then changes over the life course has been a major preoccupation of psychologists for more than a century. Gerontologists have been particularly interested in answering the question, What happens to the personality of an adult as he or she grows older? In this chapter we examine both traditional approaches to answering this question as well as a new breed of life-span theories that attempts to describe more dynamic and integrative approaches to human development.

If you speculate about this question, you will probably conclude there are a variety of possible (and interesting) answers. First of all, the personalities of most adults may change in certain ways. The precise nature of these changes may be a controversial issue: Some adults might learn from their experiences, alter their patterns of behavior appropriately, and cope more and more effectively with the demands of living as they grow older. Some adults might become enmeshed in self-defeating behavior patterns and deal less and less effectively with their environment and their problems. Or the personality development of some adults might be only partially constructive and fall somewhere between these two extremes. Thus, we might find that personality often follows the old maxim of "two steps forward and one step backward," with a given adult showing positive growth at some times and negative changes on other occasions. But whatever the specific details might be, one important possibility to be considered is that the adult personality does change significantly with increasing age.

Alternatively, personality may be largely determined by an early age and remain stable throughout adulthood. The precise age at which personality development ceases may be a controversial issue: perhaps as early as age 5 or 6 years (as in Sigmund Freud's theory), perhaps during adolescence. Nevertheless, if this hypothesis is correct, we would expect to find that the personality of each and every adult shows little or no change over the years—not to mention extremely short textbook chapters on the subject of personality and aging.

Although the issue of stability versus change is of primary importance, we could list many more possible relationships between age and personality. For example, the adult personality might change if sufficiently strong stimulation is experienced (i.e., strong enough to affect an older and less impressionable individual), but not otherwise. If the change hypothesis is supported, we might find that most adults follow much the same pattern or stages of personality development. Or we might discover that the personalities of different adults develop in quite different ways, depending on each individual's previous life history and current situation.

The preceding speculations are intended to suggest the potentially intriguing and important nature of this area. However, psychology strives to be the science of human behavior; and a science relies on empirical data rather than on speculation or anecdotal information. Thus, our goal in this chapter (as elsewhere in this book) is to seek out scientifically acceptable evidence.

SUBSTANTIVE AND METHODOLOGICAL ISSUES

The preceding questions about personality and aging might seem to be easily answered. Appearances are often deceptive, however, and the study of personality and aging has been hindered by various methodological difficulties. Therefore, before we survey the relevant research findings, let us first consider some of the problems encountered by those who seek to investigate this challenging area.

The Meaning of Personality

One important substantive issue concerns the term *personality*. You will not find any unanimity among psychologists as to the meaning of personality (let alone any one accepted definition), nor any firm consensus regarding those aspects of human behavior to which it refers.

Although this husband and wife have aged physically, their personalities probably have not changed nearly as much.

To be sure, psychologists do tend to agree on certain general considerations. **Personality** is most often conceptualized as the organized, distinctive pattern of behavior that characterizes a particular individual. Typically then, the concept of personality is a comprehensive one: It includes the individual's physical, mental, emotional, and social characteristics. It also incorporates such specific areas as motivation, normality and psychopathology, interpersonal behaviors, thoughts, dreams, defensive behaviors and mechanisms, beliefs, and values, among others.

In addition, personality is generally considered to be relatively stable and enduring. It may change over a long period of time (e.g., the many years that constitute adulthood), and a person may well behave differently in different situations. But personality involves long-lasting and important characteristics of an individual, ones that continue to exert a strong influence on behavior. Some aspects of personality are unobservable, such as thoughts, memories, and dreams, whereas others are observable (overt actions, "body language"). And virtually all theories agree that at least some vital aspects of personality are concealed from oneself (unconscious), although the extent and importance of such unconscious materials and processes vary from theory to theory. (See, for example, Darley et al., 1981, p. 397; Ewen, 1988.)

Because personality encompasses so much of our behavior, its study is extremely important. Yet because it is difficult to measure unobservable and unconscious processes with any accuracy, the study of personality is also highly challenging. Furthermore, from a historical perspective, it is only quite recently that personality has become a widely used concept in describing and understanding human behavior. Thus, it should not be surprising that the field of personality is rife with controversy and disagreement. When we examine the evidence concerning personality and aging, therefore, we of necessity acknowledge these important substantive issues by discussing separately some of the different approaches to (and conceptions of) personality.

Methodological Issues

As we observed in Chapter 2, various methodological problems and issues must be faced by those who wish to conduct research on adult development and aging. These include the limitations of cross-sectional studies; the difficulty of doing longitudinal studies (which also have their limitations); the problem of determining which effects are truly due to aging, as opposed to cohort or to major life experiences; the weaknesses of chronological age as a measure of aging; trying to understand the meaning of different behaviors at different ages; and procedural and mathematical difficulties that hinder the accurate measurement of psychological change. (You may wish to review our earlier discussion of these issues before proceeding further.)

LABORATORY RESEARCH, CLINICAL INSIGHT, AND PSYCHOMETRIC STUDIES.   Insofar as personality is concerned, another important methodological controversy must be considered: How should this variable be studied?

Some psychologists prefer to derive their information about personality solely from their observations of patients in psychotherapy (e.g., Freud). They point out that psychopathology differs from healthy behavior in degree, rather than in kind, so the more extreme behaviors of these patients reveal principles that are universal (and that would be much harder to detect in relatively well-adjusted people). They argue that the intense misery of psychopathology may well be the only reason why a person would submit to prolonged study by a psychologist and reveal important but deeply personal issues. And they contend that laboratory research on personality all too often involves unrealistic tasks that bear little resemblance to real-life activities, samples that are small and/or atypical (such as college students or volunteers), and experimental procedures that are too insensitive to measure the deeper aspects of personality with any accuracy. (See, for example, Ewen, 1988; Neugarten, 1977; Sechrest, 1976; Starrat & Peterson, 1997; Wachtel, 1980.)

Other psychologists argue that if psychology is to be a science, it must generate predictions that can be tested under the controlled conditions of the research laboratory. They contend that clinical observation is too subjective and the power of suggestion may influence patients to behave in ways that support the therapist's theories. Or the therapist may more readily perceive evidence that supports his or her conception of personality, and disregard or misinterpret contradictory data.

A third method for studying personality involves the administration of questionnaires to adults in various locales (e.g., institutions for the aged; their homes). Such psychometric studies tend to be less artificial than laboratory research, but are also less amenable to experimental controls. Thus, they possess some of the strengths and weaknesses of both of the approaches previously discussed.

There is merit to all of these procedures for studying the human personality. We therefore consider all of these sources in our quest for scientifically acceptable evidence concerning personality and aging.

TRADITIONAL APPROACHES TO UNDERSTANDING PERSONALITY DEVELOPMENT

Stage Theories

Some investigators have opted for a comprehensive, and ambitious, strategy. They believe there are qualitative shifts, or distinct **stages** in the development of the individual over the life course. As a result, they have divided most or all of adulthood into a series of stages, ones that are supposedly experienced by most or all adults (Hampson, 1995; Pervin, 1990).

STAGES DEVISED BY NOTED PERSONALITY THEORISTS.   Sigmund Freud's clinical observations led him to conclude that personality is firmly established by about age 5 to 6 years, so his well-known psychosexual stages (e.g., oral, anal, phallic) end well before adulthood. This is currently regarded as one of Freud's significant errors, because most modern psychologists have concluded that personality continues to develop through older childhood and adolescence. But Freud is also widely praised for calling our attention to infancy and childhood, which are indeed the most important periods for personality development. Also, as we see later in this chapter, his hypothesis that personality does not change during adulthood remains tenable. (See, for example, Freud, 1905/1965a, 1933/1965b, 1916–1917/1966. For a discussion of Freudian and other theories of personality, see Ewen, 1988.)

One of the few other personality theorists who have devised formal developmental stages is Harry Stack Sullivan, a noted American psychiatrist who rejected Freud's version of psychoanalysis. Sullivan posits seven specific epochs through which personality may develop, six of which occur prior to adulthood. One reason why Sullivan has little to say about adulthood is that he defines it psychologically, rather than chronologically, and he doubts that very many people in our society will ever attain this degree of maturity. "I believe that for the great majority of our people, preadolescence [the psychological stage that normally corresponds to a chronological age of about 8½ to 10 years] is the nearest that they come . . . that from then on, the stresses of life distort them to inferior caricatures of what they might have been" (Sullivan, 1947/1953, p. 56; see also Sullivan, 1953/1968).

Carl Jung, the Swiss psychiatrist who once was a psychoanalyst but who split with Freud in order to devise his own theory of personality, does not posit a formal series of developmental stages. However, Jung does draw a sharp distinction between youth and middle age. During adolescence and early adulthood, the individual is most concerned with materialism and sexuality. But the period from about age 35 to 40 serves as the gateway to the latter half of life, which is a time of considerable importance. "A human being would certainly not grow to be seventy or eighty years old if this longevity had no meaning for the species. The afternoon of human life must also have a significance of its own, and cannot be merely a pitiful appendage to life's morning" (Jung, 1930–1931/1971, p. 17; see also Jung, 1933; 1917, 1928/1972). According to Jung, middle age is highlighted by a shift to more spiritual and cultural values; by drastic reversals in one's strongest convictions and emotions, often leading to changes of profession, religion, and/or spouse; and perhaps by at last becoming one's own self and realizing one's true potentials, although this ideal is rarely if ever achieved to the fullest.

Erik Erikson, a clinician trained in psychoanalysis by Freud's daughter, Anna, sought to remedy some of the major deficiencies of Freudian theory while retaining its strengths. Most importantly for our purposes, Erikson posits a series of eight stages that extend from infancy through old age. Just as the development of our physical organs unfolds according to a predetermined genetic schedule, all eight Eriksonian stages are present in some elementary form at birth and unfold according to an innate plan. However, the course of healthy personality development can easily be disrupted. Every Eriksonian stage is characterized by a specific psychosocial problem, or "crisis" (in the medical sense of a crucial turning point for better or worse, rather than in the political sense of imminent catastrophe). Each crisis is brought on by the resulting greater demands made by the parents and society, and each one must be resolved during the appropriate stage for personality development to proceed successfully. Furthermore, the outcome of any stage need not be permanent. A severe later crisis may well revive earlier ones and nullify prior accomplishments, and subsequent favorable conditions may facilitate the resolution of previous failures. (See, for example, Erikson, 1963, 1968.) Only the last three of Erikson's stages deal with adulthood:

> **Stage 6: Young Adulthood.** The crisis of this stage is intimacy versus isolation. To resolve it successfully, the young adult must learn to sacrifice some of his or her own wishes in order to form close relationships with other people.
>
> **Stage 7: Adulthood.** The crisis of this stage is generativity versus stagnation. Successful resolution is denoted by an interest in procreation and the next generation, and a widening interest in and concern for other people.

Stage 8: Maturity. The crisis of this stage is ego integrity versus despair. Successful resolution is indicated by feelings of satisfaction and affirmation about the life one has lived, and relatively little fear of death.

Erikson's theory has had a major impact on our thinking about personality development. It has been criticized as unclear, poorly defined, and difficult to test using rigorous scientific methods, yet it has generated considerable interest among researchers, writers, and the lay public. (See Logan, 1986; Ruth, 1996; van Geert, 1987; Viney, 1987.)

Loevinger (1976), for example, sought to extend Erikson's theory by focusing on the ego as the chief organizer of personality. That is, the ego integrates our morals, values, goals, and thought processes. Loevinger proposes eight stages of ego development, beginning in infancy, with the last six stages occurring during adulthood. At each stage, Loevinger identifies four areas that are important to personality development:

1. **Character development:** A person's standards and goals.
2. **Interpersonal style:** A person's pattern of relationships with other people.
3. **Conscious preoccupations:** The most important things on a person's mind.
4. **Cognitive style:** The characteristic way in which a person thinks.

Because Loevinger's theory is more empirically based than Erikson's, its impact on adult developmental research is increasing. For example, several studies have examined the relationship between ego development and cognitive development. Greater ego development has been found to be related to more effective coping strategies at all ages, as with such social dilemmas as what to do about an unwanted pregnancy (Blanchard-Fields, 1986; Labouvie-Vief, Hakim-Larson, & Hobart, 1987).

STAGES BASED ON LIFE SITUATIONS.   Several theorists have defined adult stages in terms of situations or events that are expected to occur during specified periods in one's life.

Levinson (1978; Levinson et al., 1974) posits six stages that focus primarily on early and middle adulthood. He based his conclusions on interviews with 40 men from four occupational groups, including blue-collar and white-collar workers, business executives, and academicians. Therefore, these stages apply to men only:

1. **Age 20–24:** Leaving the Family. This is a transitional period from adolescence to early adulthood. During this time, the young man moves out of his family's home and establishes psychological distance from them.
2. **Early 20s to Late 20s:** Entering the Adult World. This is a time of exploration, with the young man trying out various occupational and interpersonal adult roles.
3. **Early 30s to Early 40s:** Settling Down. During this period, the man deepens his commitment to his chosen occupational and social roles.

4. **Age 35–39:** Becoming One's Own Man. This is the high point of early adulthood, a time when the man's adult roles become well established.
5. **Early 40s:** The Midlife Transition. The man now begins to experience a feeling of bodily decline and a clear recognition of his own mortality.
6. **Middle 40s:** Restabilization and the Beginning of Middle Adulthood. Some men make new creative strides during this period; others lose their vitality.

According to Levinson, adult personality development consists of alternating periods of stability and transition. During the more stable periods, we build our values, beliefs, and priorities; during periods of transition, we change them. Everyone undergoes some transitions, which do not necessarily cause significant turmoil for the individual. This is somewhat similar to Erikson's view that crisis is the basis for personality development.

Levinson places special emphasis on the midlife transition, which he believes occurs among men during their early 40s. Men face four important issues at this time. They fluctuate between attachment and separateness, wanting both intimate relationships with others and time for introspection and self-study. They struggle with the issue of personal change, realizing they have the capacity to destroy previous aspects of their lives and create new ones. They allow both masculine and feminine traits to emerge. And they must come to grips with their own aging. (See Levinson, 1986, 1987.)

The simplicity of Levinson's model makes it appealing to nonprofessional readers, and some popular books and articles have been based on it (e.g., Gail Sheehy's *Passages*, 1976). A somewhat different set of situational stages, derived from clinical observation and from a cross-sectional study of 524 white middle-class men and women ranging in age from 16 to 60, has been suggested by Gould (1972, 1978). Gould believes that an internal clock defines the tasks to be accomplished at each of seven periods; our primary task is to achieve adult maturity by growing out of our basic biological helplessness and abandoning the major false assumptions of childhood and adolescence. The following are the stages posited by Gould:

1. **Age 16–18.** This is a time of conflict between autonomy (wishing to get away from one's parents) and dependency (wishing to remain protected and guided by them).
2. **Age 18–22.** The young adult now feels more autonomous and somewhat removed from the family, but worries about being recaptured and made dependent by them. The peer group is used as an ally to help cut family ties.
3. **Age 22–28.** This is a time of autonomy, feeling separate from one's family and concentrating on building one's life. Peers are still important, but self-reliance is even more so.
4. **Age 28–34.** The adult now questions his or her life choices and grows tired of fulfilling these roles, but continues to do so.
5. **Age 34–43.** Time appears to be growing short for shaping the behaviors of one's adolescent children or for succeeding in life. The adult's parents renew

previous requests for help with their problems and conflicts, possibly in an indirect way.

6. **Age 43–53.** This is a time of bitterness, and feeling that the course of one's life can no longer be changed. Also typical of this period are blaming one's parents for a lack of fulfillment in life, finding fault with one's children, and seeking sympathy from one's spouse.

7. **Age 53–60.** Feelings during this period are more positive than during one's 40s. Relationships with one's spouse, parents, children, friends, and self become warmer and more satisfying.

A third set of stages is based partly on situations and partly on human physiology. Bühler (1968; see also Kimmel, 1980, pp. 8–12) observed that there appear to be five major biological phases during one's life. She and her students examined some 400 autobiographies collected during the 1930s in Vienna, and proposed five life stages to correspond to these biological phases, as outlined in the following:

Age 0–15 Progressive growth. Remaining at home; goals in life are not yet chosen.

Age 15–25 Continued growth, combined with the ability to reproduce sexually. Experimenting with self-chosen life goals, including various temporary professional and social roles.

Age 25–45 Stability. Specific life goals are chosen, and a sense of direction is firmly established. Vitality is high.

Age 45–65 Loss of sexual reproductive ability. Abandonment of some activities owing to a loss of physical ability. Considerable interest in assessing one's success or failure in achieving self-determined life goals.

Age 65 on Biological decline. Feelings of fulfillment or failure in life. Speculations about death. Often, a preoccupation with religious questions. Previous activities continue, possibly combined with new short-term goals that are intended to satisfy immediate life needs.

EVALUATION OF STAGE THEORIES.   Stage theories have a certain appeal: They cover a broad range of people and ages, and they are simple enough for the general public to comprehend and use as a developmental yardstick. They are also attractive because they appear to reflect basic truths about human development, and because they propose that we continue to grow and develop throughout our lives (which provides hope for those whose current lives are far from satisfactory). However, it is important to keep in mind that stage theories also suffer from some basic flaws.

For example, both Levinson's and Gould's models include a stage that represents a midlife crisis. (For Levinson, it is the early 40s; for Gould, age 43–53.) But when Costa and McCrae (1978) examined this empirically, using self-reports, they found no evidence for a general crisis at midlife. Instead, they discovered that those who suffer such personal crises tend to experience them across the whole range of adulthood, and tend to be more neurotic.

Even the sample used in Costa and McCrae's longitudinal study can be criticized as being unrepresentative because it consisted of volunteers. Accordingly, Farrell and Rosenberg (1981) undertook a major midlife study to address this issue. They obtained a sample of 500 men, ranging in age from 25 to 30 and from 38 to 48. A battery of measures was administered to both groups, including one instrument specifically designed to assess the existence of a midlife crisis. No significant age differences were obtained on the midlife-crisis scale.

Tamir (1989) examined the proposition that men at middle age leave (or at least want to leave) their wives for young blond women, and drive off in fancy sports cars wearing trendy clothes and shiny jewelry. The fact that few middle-aged men actually divorce their wives argues against this stereotype.

These research findings imply that the midlife crisis may well occur less frequently, or not at all, in relatively healthy people. Currently, the evidence that adults pass through universal, unidirectional stages is weak. (See also Shanan & Jacobowitz, 1982, pp. 151–152, 155–156; Thomae, 1980, pp. 285–286.)

Conceptually, stage theories fail to deal with individual differences in the timing of major life transitions. As we have noted, adults of the same chronological age may well differ significantly from one another with regard to their physiological, psychological, and/or social development. Even though the stage theorists undoubtedly intend their age ranges as general guidelines, rather than as inflexible boundaries, it still seems highly unlikely that all (or even many) adults will encounter the same stage at similar ages. Even when specific ages are not emphasized (as in Erikson's theory), differences among adults are probably too great for a stage model to have widespread applicability. (The belief that adults become increasingly alike as they grow older is one of the many myths about aging; see, for example, Kausler, 1982, p. 2.) The problem of obtaining adequate and representative samples has also been a particularly difficult one for the stage theorists because they are attempting to draw conclusions about such a wide range of ages and behaviors. Thus, it is hardly surprising that the various stage theorists have produced inconsistent and contradictory models.

Some of the specific ideas proposed by the stage theorists may ultimately prove to be worthwhile. For now, however, existing stage theories are best viewed as beginning steps in understanding adult personality development.

Trait Theories

A popular conceptual alternative is to define personality in terms of **traits,** or specific components that initiate and guide consistent forms of behavior. (See, for example, Allport, 1937, 1955, 1961; Ruth, 1996.) To illustrate, a person with the trait of "friendliness" is usually motivated to seek out other people, start a conversation, and express an interest in their activities. Conversely, an individual with the trait of "shyness" tends to avoid others, show little concern for them, and remain silent. Other traits include ambitiousness, cleanliness, enthusiasm, punctuality, talkativeness, dominance, submissiveness, generosity, penuriousness,

 **MYTHS ABOUT AGING**

Personality Development

Myth	*Best Available Evidence*
During adulthood, your personality will develop through a series of specific stages that is much the same for all individuals.	There is no single set of stages that accurately describes the course of adult personality development.
During your 40s (or thereabouts), you will experience a "midlife crisis"—a time of considerable psychological turmoil, worry, and despair.	Most adults do not experience an unusually severe crisis at midlife. Those who do tend to have suffered similar crises throughout their adulthood.
The elderly are much more likely to view themselves as powerless pawns, influenced primarily by external events they cannot control.	General expectations about control change little with increasing age, although the elderly do perceive themselves as having less control over their lives in such specific areas as intellectual functioning, health, and personal development.
Anyone can achieve anything they want to achieve as long as they set their mind to it and work hard at it.	Although humans have great capacity to shape their own development, their ability to achieve certain outcomes is limited by their genetic potential, societal constraints, and the sequential nature of human development.
Developing highly specialized skills as early in life as possible will yield big payoffs throughout life.	Not necessarily. Investing time and energy to develop one skill may deprive you of the opportunity to develop other needed skills that contribute to functioning later in life.

and so forth (with emphasis on the "and so forth," because Allport estimates there are some 4,000 to 5,000 traits!).

As is often the case with psychological theory, the exact nature of traits is a matter of some controversy. Allport concludes that every adult personality is unique and composed of numerous "personal traits" that differ (often in rather

Personalities, like physical appearances, come in many different varieties.

(*Source:* Eibel-Eibesfeldt, Irenaus. *Human Ethology* (New York: Aldine de Gruyter) © 1989 Eibel-Eibesfeldt. Reprinted with permission.)

subtle ways) from those of anyone else. Because a particular culture does tend to evoke roughly similar modes of adjustment, he concedes there are some general aspects of personality ("common traits") that can be used to compare most adults. Other trait theorists contend instead there is some degree of genuine, fundamental commonality among adults.

In this section, we examine the evidence concerning aging and some particularly important traits. Although a wide variety of traits has been studied over the last few decades, including characteristics such as rigidity, cautiousness, and field independence/field dependence, we focus here on those traits that have generated the most interest and debate in recent years.

MULTITRAIT PERSONALITY INVENTORIES.   One of the most popular methods for assessing personality consists of written multiple-choice or true-false questionnaires. The one most often used with older adults is the Minnesota Multiphasic Personality Inventory (MMPI), which contains 550 items and is intended primarily for the diagnosis and measurement of psychopathology. Also quite popular, but designed to tap more normal characteristics, is the Sixteen Personality Factor Questionnaire (Cattell, Eber, & Tatsuoka, 1970). The 16 PF yields scores on 16 traits, such as reserved versus outgoing, humble versus assertive, serious versus happy-go-lucky, and shy versus venturesome. One instrument currently in use for measuring personality throughout adulthood is the "NEO Inventory," which assesses five distinct traits: Neuroticism (N), Extraversion (E), Openness (O), Agreeableness (A), and Conscientiousness (C). Some of the difficulties and results of this approach are examined next.

Collecting personality data from older respondents may be more difficult than it is for younger persons. Some older adults may be unable to give appropriate answers because of impairments in memory and/or abstract thinking. And because the elderly grew up in an era when psychology was far less popular than it is now, they may well regard measures of personality as meaningless and refuse to take them seriously. Analyzing the results obtained from personality measures is not an easy task. Just as it can be difficult to separate aging effects from cohort effects, some measures of personality (e.g., the Rorschach) are affected by such potentially confounding variables as cognitive ability and socioeconomic status. (See Lawton, Whelihan, & Belsky, 1980.)

As a result, the evidence dealing with aging and measures of personality is limited. Studies using the 16 PF indicate that the elderly are more reserved, serious, conscientious, shy, socially aware, self-reproaching, conservative, and self-reliant than younger adults, but lower in intelligence. However, these findings may well be due to cohort effects rather than to aging (except for intelligence, some aspects of which decline somewhat with increasing age). With regard to the MMPI, older adults tend to score higher (i.e., more pathological) on hypochondria and depression, but lower on psychotically oriented scales like schizophrenia and paranoia. There is also some evidence in support of the stability hypothesis: One longitudinal study of physically and emotionally healthy men reported considerable stability in MMPI scores over a 30-year period (Leon et al., 1979).

An important new psychometric approach is that of McCrae and Costa (1984, 1987; Costa & McCrae, 1988, 1997; Costa, Somerfield, & McCrae, 1996), who have devised a measure of personality based on the mathematical procedure of factor analysis. Their "NEO Inventory" taps five major traits, each of which includes a number of subordinate traits:

Neuroticism: A lack of self-control, an inability to deal adequately with stress, and an unusual proneness to anxiety, anger, depression, and fears of shame and ridicule.
Extraversion: Warmth and friendliness, a desire to be with other people, assertiveness, keeping busy and behaving energetically, seeking excitement and taking risks, and frequent positive emotions (e.g., happiness).
Openness to Experience: A willingness to experience one's own feelings strongly and without defensive distortions, a vivid imagination and a tendency to develop elaborate daydreams, a sensitivity to art and beauty, a willingness to try something new, actively seeking out new ideas, and an open-mindedness to values that differ from one's own.
Agreeableness: Tender-mindedness and compliance.
Conscientiousness: Orderliness, self-discipline, and need for achievement.

The NEO inventory has been extensively used in both cross-sectional and longitudinal studies of adults. In one very large cross-sectional study of 10,000 persons aged 35 to 84, the investigators found small age-related declines in Neuroticism, Extraversion, and Openness and small increases in Agreeableness and Conscientiousness. However, longitudinal studies indicate very modest change or none at all over relatively long time spans. Using this measure, Costa and McCrae found that personality remains remarkably stable during adulthood; over a 12-year period, very little change was observed on any of the NEO dimensions. This finding is consistent with the 30-year MMPI study previously mentioned (Leon et al., 1979) and with other longitudinal trait studies (e.g., Siegler, George, & Okun, 1979).

As is often the case with psychological theory, the exact nature of traits is a matter of some controversy. Allport concludes that every adult personality is unique, and is composed of numerous "personal traits" that differ (often in rather subtle ways) from those of anyone else. But since a particular culture does tend to evoke roughly similar modes of adjustment, he concedes that there are some general aspects of personality ("common traits") that can be used to compare most adults. Other trait theorists contend instead that there is some degree of genuine, fundamental commonality among adults.

In this section, we will examine the evidence concerning aging and some particularly important traits.

LOCUS OF CONTROL. This trait was first conceptualized by Rotter (1966). Locus of control refers to a consistent belief about obtaining rewards and avoiding punishments: Some people believe this depends primarily on their own actions and behaviors (**internal locus of control**), but others expect their good and bad experiences are caused largely by mere chance and the actions of other people (**external locus of control**). Like virtually all traits, locus of control is a continuous variable; an individual may fall anywhere along the scale from strongly internal to strongly external. More internally oriented adults are likely to try to run their own lives in their own way, whereas those who are more externally oriented tend to see little point in such efforts.

The available evidence strongly indicates that for both younger and older adults, internals are superior to externals in psychological adjustment. In particular, internals are more likely to cope well with personal crises, to be satisfied with their lives, and to enjoy a positive self-concept (e.g., Lefcourt, 1976; Palmore & Luikart, 1972; Reid, Haas, & Hawkings, 1977; Wolk & Kurtz, 1975).

One possible exception to this general rule concerns internals who have been institutionalized and live in an environment that features high constraints and firm rules imposed by others (e.g., a nursing home). Will these internals also demonstrate superior adjustment, or will they become frustrated and disappointed because they cannot control their own destinies in such a setting? Much of the evidence bearing on this issue is mixed, with some findings favoring internals (Reid et al., 1977), some favoring externals (Felton & Kahana, 1974), and some indicating no relationship between locus of control and adjustment (Wolk, 1976).

Although locus of control is clearly an important aspect of the adult personality, our fundamental question remains: Does this trait change as one grows older? Many of the studies that have dealt with this issue have produced conflicting results. For example, some cross-sectional and longitudinal studies suggest that adults become more external over the years (e.g., Bradley & Webb, 1976; Lachman, 1983; Siegler & Gatz, 1985); one 4-year cross-sequential study found that the elderly are more internal than the middle aged (Lachman, 1985); and some cross-sectional research indicates that older adults are more internal than young adults (e.g., Gatz & Siegler, 1981; Staats, 1974). In fact, two reviews of studies carried out before 1986 found support for all of the three possibilities: that perceived internal control increases, decreases, and remains relatively stable with increasing age (Lachman, 1986; Skinner & Connell, 1986).

One possible explanation for these conflicting results is that locus of control appears to involve a number of different dimensions (Levenson, 1974; Paulhus, 1983). That is, how much internal (or external) control you perceive depends on the specific area of your life: intelligence, health, work, social relationships, and so on. Older adults might well be more external than college students with regard to intelligence and health because these variables are commonly believed to decline in late adulthood. But older adults might be more internal with regard to social competence because they have had more experience dealing with people.

More recent research has supported some of these hypotheses. Several cross-sectional and longitudinal studies have found that insofar as intelligence is concerned, perceived internal control does decline with increasing age. That is, as adults grow older, they are more likely to believe that other people are better able to solve intellectual problems. There is also some indication that older adults are more external with regard to physical health; they more often believe that aging is associated with an increased susceptibility to disease and a lower likelihood of being cured, factors beyond their control. Thus, older adults in these studies visited their doctors more often and were more likely to abide by the doctor's decision. (See Beisecker, 1988; Keller et al., 1989; Lachman, 1986; Lachman & Leff, 1989; Reker, 1987; Smith et al., 1988.) Longitudinal and cross-sectional studies have also found that older adults are more external about their personal development: They perceive themselves as having less control over their future and as being less likely to make desired changes in their lives (Brandtstadter, 1984, 1986; 1989; Brandtstadter & Renner, 1990; Fisseni, 1985). Note that in these studies, no significant relationship was found between age and a general, unidimensional measure of internal versus external control. It was only in certain specific areas, such as intelligence, physical health, and personal development, that older adults perceived themselves as having less control over their own lives.

In sum: Recent studies consistently show that increasing age is related to increased externality (less personal control) in the areas of intellectual functioning, health, and personal development, but not to an increase in general externality. The extent to which these results are influenced by cohort effects, as opposed to aging effects, remains unclear at this time. Nevertheless, recognizing the **multidimensional** nature of locus of control has helped to clarify its relationship to aging.

EXTRAVERSION-INTROVERSION.   This well known and important trait was originated by Jung (1921/1976); some subsequent conceptual modifications have been suggested by Eysenck (e.g., 1967; Eysenck & Eysenck, 1969; Starrat & Peterson, 1997). People who are primarily **extraverted** are consistently outgoing, venture forth with careless confidence into the unknown, and are particularly influenced by other people and by events in the external world. Conversely, those who are more **introverted** are shy, inscrutable, and keenly interested in the inner world of their own psyche. According to Jung, we inherit a predisposition to be more introverted or more extraverted, but both tendencies are present in every personality. Consequently, even extraverts (introverts) must allow free expression to their introverted (extraverted) aspects in order to be psychologically healthy.

There has been a sharp controversy concerning the course of this trait during adulthood. Some investigators contend that adults become more introverted as they grow older (e.g., Botwinick, 1973; Neugarten, 1977, pp. 636–637; Neugarten & Associates, 1964). Others regard this as yet another of the many myths about aging, and argue instead that introversion–extraversion tends to remain relatively stable during adulthood (e.g., Costa & McCrae, 1976, 1978, 1980; Kausler, 1982, p. 602; Shanan & Jacobowitz, 1982, pp. 151–152). The studies reporting stability may perhaps be somewhat more compelling because they are more recent and make greater use of longitudinal designs, but it is difficult at present to reach any firm conclusions about the course of extraversion–introversion during adulthood.

EVALUATION OF TRAIT THEORIES.   One criticism of trait theories concerns the issue of circularity. For example, if we characterize people who avoid others and tend to remain silent as "shy," can we then turn the same definition around and conclude that these individuals engage in these behaviors because they are shy? Clearly, we cannot; such circular reasoning would explain nothing at all about the causes of shyness. This lack of explanatory power is particularly evident in a statement made by Allport himself: "[A man] likes blue because he likes blue" (Evans, 1970, p. 37).

It has also been argued that human behavior is not consistent enough to be analyzed in terms of traits alone. These critics contend that people may well be shy (or aggressive, or serious, or whatever) on some occasions but not others, and psychologists must therefore concentrate on the complicated interactions between traits and specific situations. In addition, the occurrence or nonoccurrence of a given trait may well be influenced by the individual's chronological age, biological age, sex, mental and physical health, and by prevailing social conditions. (See Diener, Larsen, & Emmons, 1984; Mischel, 1968, 1973, 1977; Thomae, 1980.) Even Allport himself expressed a similar concern (1968, p. 63).

Trait theory also has staunch advocates, however, and has stimulated a considerable amount of research. (See, for example, Bem & Allen, 1974; Costa & McCrae, 1976, 1978, 1980, 1995; McCrae & Costa, 1984; Wiggins, 1974.) Furthermore, as we have seen, gerontological trait research has added significantly to our knowledge. Stereotypes of the elderly as more rigid and inflexible, more likely to view themselves as powerless pawns, and less active than younger adults have been shattered by appropriate hard data. The popular beliefs that older adults are more introverted and more cautious have also been strongly challenged, although here the evidence is more equivocal.

These strengths and weaknesses notwithstanding, trait theory research has yielded consistent findings: Personality, measured in terms of traits, remains remarkably stable during adulthood. This is clearly at odds with stage theory (and the related research), which posits that personality changes significantly during adulthood—so much so, in fact, that numerous stages must be used to define the changes. How can this disparity be explained?

Because of the conceptual difficulties that hinder stage theory (discussed previously), trait research may more accurately depict the course of personality during adulthood. However, the stability found in so many trait studies may instead be due at least in part to methodological bias, namely the way in which trait data are collected (Heckhausen & Baltes, in press). In these studies, subjects are asked to indicate the extent to which various statements describe their behavior. How subjects decide on their answers is not known, but they may well compare themselves to other adults of the same age (Harris & Associates, 1975, 1981; Schulz & Fritz, 1988). If so, and if the personality of the reference group changes over time, subjects may fail to report personality changes that have actually occurred. For example, consider a young adult who is shy. As he grows older, he becomes more socially adept and less shy, but so do other adults of the same age. Years later, therefore, he is still more shy than most of his peers. So he reports on the trait measure that he is just as shy as in years past, even though he has become less shy and more outgoing, because his position relative to the reference group by which he judges himself is about the same. Although this hypothesis is an interesting one, there is as yet insufficient research evidence for any firm conclusions to be drawn.

NEW APPROACHES: SYNTHETIC MODELS
OF LIFE-SPAN DEVELOPMENT

One of the most important developments in social gerontology in the last decade is the emergence of new theoretical perspectives on development throughout the life course. Some of the common characteristics of these approaches is that they focus on development from infancy to old age, they consider the interactive nature of development within multiple domains such as physical, social and cognitive functioning, and they place equal emphasis on how society broadly shapes the development of the individual and how individuals selectively shape their own development. Examples of this approach include Laura Carstensen's socioemotional selectivity theory (in press; 1998), Paul and Margret Baltes's (1990) selective optimization with compensation model, the work on successful aging and well-being of Carol Ryff (1991), and the life-span theory of control of Heckhausen and Schulz (1995). It is beyond the scope of this chapter to examine each of these approaches in detail; however, we briefly describe the work of Schulz and Heckhausen as an example of this approach.

GENERAL PRINCIPLES REGULATING
DEVELOPMENT ACROSS THE LIFE COURSE

Human beings have a vast potential for what they can become and accomplish in a lifetime. To some extent, this potential is constrained by the genetic makeup of the individual. In extreme cases involving congenital illnesses, the constraints may be severe enough to make a typical life course difficult to achieve. For most individuals, the genetic potential is not a major constraint and is, in any case, relatively unknown. Although much of infancy and childhood is characterized by generalized skill acquisition and cognitive development, one of the initial challenges faced by socializing agents, such as parents, is to provide opportunities for children to sample diverse domains so there is some convergence between the inherent abilities of the child and the investment of time and effort. Identifying such a convergence and subsequently investing large amounts of training resources in a specific domain is often characteristic of children who ultimately develop world-class expertise in areas such as playing a musical instrument or becoming a professional athlete (Ericsson et al., 1993). On the whole, though, social systems are designed to maximize the acquisition of broad generalizable skills throughout infancy, childhood, and adolescence. During late adolescence and young adulthood, there is increasing pressure for specialization as individuals embark on individualized career paths. How much time and energy and what specific domains one should invest in are some of the challenges faced by individuals in this stage of development. Because of biological limits on the length of life, the age-graded structure of the life course, and the fact that skill acquisition takes a relatively long period of time, the individual has few opportunities to make mistakes in choosing domains for expertise development. To the extent that individuals invest in the development of domains that are highly generalizable (e.g. traditional academic skills), the number of alternative career paths remains relatively high. But investing in highly specialized domains (e.g., athletic performance in a specific sport) is much riskier because failure to achieve professionally competitive levels of performance leaves one with few alternative domains to pursue. This is the classic dilemma of high school or college athletes who invest great energy in developing expertise in their chosen sport but who are not good enough to become professional athletes. *In sum*, desirable features for early life course development are exposure to diversity followed by selective investment in highly generalizable domains.

Taken together, this characterization of development suggests four general principles for maximizing development across the life course. First, there must be diversity in the opportunity to sample different performance domains. Second, there has to be selectivity in pursuing and allocating resources to developmental paths that are consistent with genetic and sociocultural opportunities. Third, the individual must compensate for and cope with failure encountered as different action-goals are pursued and with declines associated with late life development. And fourth, the individual must manage trade-offs across domains and sequential life phases and recognize that the allocation of resources to one domain may compromise the opportunity to develop others.

Diversity in functioning is important for optimal development for several reasons. Maintaining diversity reduces the risk and vulnerability associated with narrow specialization. More important, however, diversity provides the raw material or basis for future developmental advances. In this way, diversity in human development is analogous to the role of variability in evolutionary change (Scarr, 1993). Variability provides the options that selection as the basic evolutionary process can work on. The principle of diversity has important implications for socializing agents responsible for childhood development. Early in their development, children should be exposed to a variety of domains of functioning, so that they are challenged, develop diverse skills, and have the opportunity to test their genetic potential.

A second principle regulating development is **selectivity**. In order to realize their developmental potential, individuals must selectively invest time and energy resources. Because the repertoire of human behaviors is so vast and time is limited, the organism relatively early must identify which options to pursue and which to give up. Selectivity must work hand in hand with diversity so the potential for high levels of functioning in some domains is maintained while at the same time broad, generalizable skills are developed. Such general-purpose skills and abilities are likely to exhibit positive transfer to many different domains, avoiding the problems associated with selection that is narrowly focused.

A third hallmark of human development is **compensating** for and coping with failure and decline. Three types of failures or developmental challenges are identified in our model: (1) normative developmental failure experiences encountered when individuals attempt to enlarge their competencies, (2) developmental declines characteristic of late life, and (3) non-normative negative events.

Human beings are unique even among mammals in that little of their behavior is prewired. Almost all competence must be acquired through learning. The acquisition of new skills and knowledge is maximized when engaging challenges that are of intermediate levels of difficulty, at which failure occurs at least some of the time. This level of challenge engages individual capacities that are not yet fully realized but well within reach. Indeed, humans show a strong preference for tasks of intermediate levels of difficulty when compared to tasks they can easily accomplish or are out of their reach (Lewin, Demobo, Festinger, & Sears, 1944). One consequences of this it that they have to cope with regular and frequent failures in attaining the action goals they set for themselves.

A second type of challenge occurs during middle and old age when individuals reach the downward slope of the inverted U function and experience declines in their ability to do things that they once were able to do.

The third type of challenge involves the myriad of negative and often random events that befall humans in their everyday lives. This might involve a physical assault such as a severe illness or other stressful life event such as job loss. Taken together, these experiences elicit multiple responses: frustration of goal attainment and negative perceptions of the self. Compensation for frustration is important because without it the individual would not persist in the face of failure. It fosters commitment to a goal even in the face of obstacles. Failure experience may also undermine individuals' sense of themselves, their level of self-ascribed competencies, and their general self-esteem. All of these consequences can undermine future motivational resources for development. As a result, the organism needs specifically adapted strategies to compensate for failure experiences that may undermine the self-concept.

The fourth principle concerns the **management of trade-offs** between domains and life-span phases. Selective investment in a given functional domain at a certain point in the life course often has important implications for alternative domains that compete for resource investment. These implications may be positive or negative. In general, investing in broad skills and abilities is likely to have positive trade-offs to other domains of functioning pursued in subsequent life-span phases, whereas narrowly focused investments are likely to be more limited in their applicability to alternative or subsequent developmental paths. Thus, one of the major challenges faced by individuals throughout the life course is assessing what the trade-offs are for a given investment of time and effort and making decisions about whether or not to continue within a given domain or switch to another.

These principles apply to development throughout the life course, including adulthood and old age. Because of age-related changes in the physical capacity of individuals and constraints imposed by society, it is important that individuals avail themselves of a diverse range of performance domains available to them. Diversity is important throughout the life course for optimal development (Adelman, 1994). The choice of domains to be sampled and developed should be consistent with the capacity of the individual, and trade-offs between selected and nonselected options must continue to be managed. Managing trade-offs among alternative domains becomes a major challenge during adulthood when individuals must regulate multiple domains both sequentially and in parallel. Finally, the process of life course development is necessarily punctuated by failure. The individual must develop resilience to cope effectively with these failures.

The importance of these principles is perhaps best understood if we apply them to some specific examples. Consider the life course of a world-class professional athlete. The genetic potential of such individuals is typically recognized early in life either because the child exhibits extraordinary athletic performance or because one or both parents were themselves professional athletes and therefore the potential is assumed to be there. This in turn results in the allocation of resources (e.g., time, energy, money) to the development of skills in the chosen sport. In extreme cases, the allocation of resources may be so focused on a particular activity that the development of more generalizable skills is neglected. Because professional athletics is highly competitive, the timing of training and skill acquisition must be carefully orchestrated to converge with the biological development of the individual. In most sports, peak levels of performance are achieved between the ages of 20 and 30, and the individual requires about 10 years of intensive training in order to be professionally competitive. Thus, many children begin intensive training programs at about age 10 so they are prepared to become professionals in their late teens or early 20s. If the individual overcomes the failure experiences along the way and succeeds in making it into the professional ranks, the rewards can be great in terms of financial resources and recognition. However, athletic careers tend to be short lived, as the effects of biological declines, wear and tear, and injuries take their toll on the individual's ability to remain competitive.

In terms of the principles articulated here, the life course of professional athletes is characterized by low levels of diversity in their exposure to multiple performance domains and selective allocation of resources into one or few domains very early in life. It is also characterized by high levels of resilience, but of a type likely to be very domain specific. We consider this a high-risk life course trajectory because (1) the probability of achieving the primary goal is low, (2) it leaves the individual with few alternative options if the primary goal is not achieved, (3) it may lead to resilience in very limited domains, and (4) it is aimed at only half of the normative life course (e.g., the first 30 to 40 years). Even if individuals reach their primary goal of becoming professional athletes, they must still develop and implement life course plans for the postprofessional period of their lives.

A similar analysis could be applied to the development of performing artists such as musicians and dancers. However, there are some differences between these domains and professional sports. First, there are a variety of fallback positions available if the individual doesn't attain world-class levels of performance. For example, a musician who doesn't succeed as a soloist can join an orchestra or become a teacher. Second, the careers of performing artists tend to be longer than those of professional athletes. Thus, individuals who do achieve their primary goal can anticipate spending most of their adult lives working in their chosen domains.

Professional athletes and world-class performance artists represent unique life course trajectories in that the development of the individual is focused on achieving optimal performance in a specific domain. This analysis could be extended and applied to peak performance in virtually any domain that is measurable. Indeed, a number of researchers have argued that the age-performance functions described in the peak performance literature provide fundamental insights into the biological and cognitive developmental potential of the human organism (Schulz & Curnow, 1988; Schulz, Musa, Staszewski, & Siegler, 1994). It could be argued that few individuals aspire toward world-class performance, or even that the costs of aspiring to such levels of performance are too high in terms of time and energy invested, and as a result such individuals do not serve as good models for characterizing the lives of most people. Most individuals invest their early years developing highly generalizable skills while at the same time sampling more specialized domains such as athletics and the performing arts. Exclusive investment in any one domain is avoided; instead, trade-offs across multiple domains are managed such that options for future developmental paths remain numerous. Educational systems in the United States and many other countries emphasize the development of generalized skills prior to specialization.

A Model of Developmental Regulation Across the Life Course

As we noted, the fundamental requirements of developmental regulation across the life span are managing diversity and selectivity and developing the capacity to compensate for failure. How is this to be achieved? A general model of successful development is presented in Figure 7–1. Key elements of this model are the processes of selection and compensation.

Selection mechanisms direct the person/environment interactions and provide both diversity and focus in the choice of domains pursued. Selection

FIGURE 7–1 **A general model of development.**

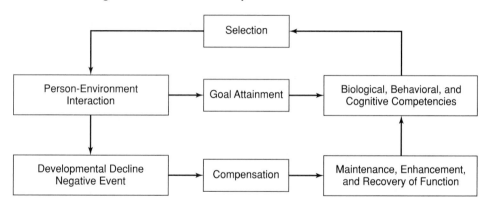

processes are guided by a consideration of interdomain and temporal trade-offs. Person-environment interactions primarily yield two types of outcomes: success and failure experiences. Successes help maintain existing levels of competence as well as develop new ones. Failure experiences, however, have the potential of undermining existing competencies. As a result, compensation mechanisms are needed to protect the individual from these threats. Such compensating mechanisms promote the maintenance, recovery, and enhancement of functioning.

Most existing theories of successful aging focus on compensating for failure and decline. Investigators interested in this area have focused on a variety of mechanisms aimed at maintaining or recovering functions that normatively decline in late life. For example, Rowe and Kahn (1987, 1998), in their influential article on usual and successful aging, describe ways in which elderly individuals can prevent, maintain, remediate, or compensate for declines in carbohydrate metabolism, bone density, and cognitive function. Similarly, Salthouse (1991a) focuses on accommodation, remediation, and compensation as mechanisms for **coping** with cognitive declines in late life. Backman and Dixon (1992) provide a fine-grained analysis of these processes in their description of compensatory mechanisms. Brandtstadter and colleagues (Brandtstadter & Ware, 1994) and P. Baltes and M. Baltes and colleagues (Marsiske et al., 1995) identify mechanisms similar to those of Rowe and Kahn, and Salthouse, although they develop a more elaborate framework that emphasizes both compensation and selection processes.

Accommodative strategies include activities such as rearranging personal goals, values, and aspirations. Prevention and maintenance involves focused activity aimed at forestalling or eliminating normative declines and might include specific activities such as changing one's diet. **Remediation** is achieved when a prior level of ability or functioning is restored through an intervention. A common example would be the restoration of atrophied muscle through exercise. **Compensation** includes a broad array of activities in which functioning is maintained or enhanced or a goal is achieved through alternative means such as assistive devices like glasses or the help of others (Backman & Dixon, 1992). The broad consensus among these divergent theoretical positions suggests that any theory of successful aging must incorporate similar mechanisms.

Models of successful aging have been useful in focusing our attention on developmental phenomena in the second half of the life course, but they also have a number of limitations. Because they were designed to address issues of decline in middle and old age, they contribute little to our understanding of developmental regulation during early stages of development where the emphasis is on the expansion and growth of functional abilities. Theories of child development, in contrast, have focused on the maturation and acquisition of skills, and say little about developmental decline common in late life.

Although theories of child and adult development overlap in some areas and are complementary in others, they leave a number of key questions unanswered. For example, what is the relative importance of selection and compensation processes at different stages in the life course? What motivates selection and compensation mechanisms? How are they regulated and managed to optimize development over the life course? What does it mean to develop successfully over the life course as opposed to developing successfully during childhood or old age?

In order to address these questions, Schulz and Heckhausen (1996) articulated a life course theory of control that provides a bases for the derivation of a life-span model of developmental regulation (Heckhausen & Schulz, 1995). The life-span theory of control proposes the construct of control as the central theme for characterizing human development from infancy to old age. The underlying assumption of this position is that humans desire to produce behavior-event contingencies and thus exert primary control over the environment around them throughout their life span. We further distinguish between primary control and secondary control. **Primary control** targets the external world and attempts to achieve effects in the immediate environment external to the individual, whereas **secondary control** targets the self and attempts to achieve changes directly within the individual. Both primary and secondary control may involve cognition and action, although primary control is almost always characterized in terms of behavior engaging the external world, and secondary control is predominantly characterized in terms of cognitive processes localized within the individual.

Heckhausen and Schulz (1995) further emphasize the functional primacy of primary over secondary control. Because primary control is directed outward, it enables individuals to explore and shape their environment to fit their particular needs and optimize their developmental potential. Without engaging the external world, the developmental potential of the organism cannot be realized. As a result, it is both preferred and has greater adaptive value to the individual.

Extensive empirical research suggests that striving for primary control is inherently part of the motivational systems of mammals. The developmental origin of activities directed at controlling external events and acquiring generalized expectations about control can be traced to the very beginning of life. Even neonates are able to detect behavior-event contingencies (Janos & Papousek, 1977), and mammals of all types prefer behavior-event contingencies to even-event contingencies even in the absence of consummatory behavior (Singh, 1970). The striving for primary control assures development within specific domains as well as the sampling of diverse domains over time (cf. White, 1959). Primary control provides the foundation for diversity and selectivity throughout the life course.

Early development is characterized by an increased ability to exert primary control over the environment. The action-outcome experiences of the child provide the basis for the development of self-competence, including generalized and exaggerated expectancies of control and perceptions of self-efficacy. Children between the ages of 3 and 4 are able to experience appropriate emotional reactions to failure (Geppert & H. Heckhausen, 1990; H. Heckhausen, 1984) and therefore require compensating mechanisms to counteract this threat to their motivational resources. During childhood and adolescence a broad range of secondary control strategies develop, including changing aspiration levels, denial, egotistic attributions, and reinterpretation of action goals (see review in Heckhausen & Schulz, 1995a). Perceptions of control are highly exaggerated early in life (Weisz, 1983), showing little correspondence to actual primary or secondary control. This delusional sense of control is adaptive in that it provides the motivation to engage the environment at a time when the organism is rapidly developing.

Early adulthood is characterized by increasing levels of primary and secondary control as well as increased selectivity with respect to the domain specificity of control. Selectivity continues to increase throughout adulthood while diversity gradually decreases. Because of the limited capacity of the individual and external constraints, the increased selectivity at older ages has to be compensated for with decreased diversity. This trade-off between diversity and selectivity is a hallmark of development in late middle and old age.

During late middle age and old age, the strategy of choice leans more toward the elaboration and increased use of secondary control strategies. Increasing age-related biological and social challenges to primary control put a premium on secondary control strategies as means for maintaining the potential for primary control. As the ratio of gains to losses in primary control becomes less and less favorable, the individual increasingly resorts to secondary control processes.

Throughout the life course, primary and secondary control work together to optimize development of the organism through selection processes and compensation of failure. As shown in Figure 7–2, motivation for primary control is a central driving force in our model, although we acknowledge that other motivational forces not shown in our model (e.g., need for autonomy and relatedness, Deci & Ryan, 1985) also drive human behavior. This model shows how the

FIGURE 7–2 **The role of primary control in a life-span model of successful development.**

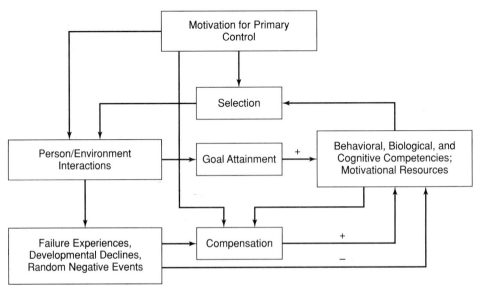

motivation for primary control provides both the impetus for and regulation of the individual's interactions with the environment. Viewed sequentially, our model indicates that person/environment interactions are motivated by the motivation for primary control and guided by selection processes. Selection processes are in turn regulated by the competencies and motivational resources of the individual. A given interaction will result in either positive outcomes, such as goal attainment, or negative outcomes, such as failure. Goal attainment leads to the maintenance or enhancement of competencies and motivational resources.

In contrast to other models of successful aging, we identify three types of potential failure experiences: normative developmental failure experiences encountered when individuals attempt to enlarge their competencies, developmental declines characteristic of late life, and non-normative or random negative events. These failure experiences have the potential of undermining competencies and motivational resources and therefore require some form of compensation. Compensation mechanisms serve to maintain, enhance, and remediate competencies and motivational resources. The other central mechanisms identified in our model is selection. Selection processes regulate the choice of action goals so that diversity is maintained and positive and negative trade-offs between domains and life stages are taken into account. Moreover, selection processes manage the allocation of motivational and behavioral resources to goals that have been selected. Both compensation and selection processes are motivated by desires for primary control and can be characterized in terms of primary and secondary control processes.

Four control-related processes characterize selection and compensation (Heckhausen & Schulz, 1993). Selective primary control refers to the focused investment of resources such as effort, time, abilities, and skills required for a chosen goal. Development of skills and abilities through processes of acquisition and practice are also examples of selective primary control. Selective secondary control targets internal representations that are motivationally relevant to goal pursuit. Relevant representations include the value ascribed to the chosen goal, the values associated with alternative goals, the perceived personal control of goal attainment, and the anticipated effects or consequences of goal attainment. Thus, selective secondary control effectively enhances the value of a chosen goal while devaluing nonchosen alternatives.

Compensatory primary control is required whenever the physical or cognitive capacities of the individual are insufficient to attain a chosen goal. This may happen in older adults due to aging-related declines, but also in infants, children, or inexperienced individuals in general due to immaturity or insufficient skill. Compensatory primary control refers to the use of external resources such as assistance from others or technical aids such as wheelchairs or hearing aids. Compensatory secondary control serves to buffer the negative effects of failure or losses on the individual's motivation for primary control. Baltes and colleagues refer to similar phenomena as "resilience of the self" (Baltes & Baltes, 1990; Baltes, Smith, & Staudinger, 1992; Staudinger, Marsiske, & Baltes, 1993). Compensatory secondary control strategies include disengagement from prior goals (e.g., sour grapes, Elster, 1983); engagement with new alternative goals; self-protective patterns of causal attribution (Snyder, Stephan, & Rosenfeld, 1978); strategic social comparison with others (Wood, 1989); and strategic intra-individual comparisons (Ryff, 1991; Suls & Mullen, 1982). Although we have emphasized the functional or adaptive aspects of each of these strategies, it is important to note that each has a dysfunctional counterpart (see Heckhausen and Schulz, 1995, for a discussion of dysfunctional primary and secondary control strategies). In general, these strategies become dysfunctional when they undermine the long-term primary control potential of the individual.

To the extent that individuals are able to use these strategies in ways that maximize their long-term primary control potential, we would judge them to be optimizing development throughout the life course. Implicit in our view of developmental regulation is the idea that successful aging includes the development and maintenance of primary control throughout the life course. Put another way, individuals able to engage and impact the environments around them for the longest period of time would be judged to be most successful. Although this definition implies an absolute definition of success—the more primary control the better—it is important to note that at the individual level, the potential for primary control is limited by the genetic makeup of the individual and the available sociocultural opportunities. Thus, evaluations of success must be tempered by the biological and sociocultural resources of the individual.

EVALUATION OF LIFE COURSE THEORIES.   One of the strengths of life course theories of development is that they attempt to articulate a set of general principles that can be applied to development from infancy to old age. Another strength is they recognize that the development of the individual is equally determined by the social or cultural context in which the individual lives and the individual him or herself. Thus, development is subject to both constraints and opportunities. Although intuitively appealing and logically compelling, the value of this approach will ultimately depend on its ability to generate new empirical research that substantially enhances our understanding of development. To date, the empirical track record for this approach is promising. Numerous studies have been reported in the literature in recent years to support elements of this theoretical perspective, although we are still in the early stages of generating research ideas and data based on this approach.

AFTERWORD.   Many adults believe their personalities change, usually for the better, as they grow older (Woodruff & Birren, 1972). However, the evidence dealing with this issue is contradictory. Stage theory and research supports the belief that personality changes significantly during adulthood, but trait research has consistently shown that personality remains remarkably stable during adulthood. It has been suggested that the results of trait research are due at least in part to methodological bias, but there is as yet insufficient research evidence to support this hypothesis. Life-span theories of development have been focused on articulating the general mechanisms that regulate change and stability over the life course. As such, they help us understand why some characteristics of individuals are likely to change while others remain the same.

Although we have stressed the importance of various methodological problems, this by no means implies a bleak outlook for future research in this area. There is renewed interest in the scientific study of personality and aging, and increased sophistication in the design of more recent research. Moreover, the emergence of life-span theories of development has helped articulate new questions that should keep researchers busy for many years to come. The next decade may well provide us with even more valuable insights concerning personality, adulthood, and life-span development.

SUMMARY

Substantive and Methodological Issues

The study of personality and aging is complicated by methodological problems. Some of these were discussed in Chapter 2: the considerable time, effort, and money required to conduct longitudinal studies, and their vulnerability to selective attrition; the inability of cross-sectional research to distinguish between aging effects and cohort effects; the weakness of chronological age as a measure of aging; the problem of understanding the meaning of different behaviors at different ages. Also, the three most common ways to study personality—laboratory research, clinical insight, and psychometric studies—all have significant strengths and weaknesses.

With regard to substantive issues, there is no unanimity among psychologists as to the meaning of personality. However, personality is most often conceptualized as the organized, distinctive pattern of behavior that characterizes a particular individual. This comprehensive definition includes an individual's physical, mental, emotional, and social characteristics. Personality is extremely important because it encompasses and influences so much of our behavior. Yet its study is also highly challenging because a significant portion of personality involves processes that are unobservable or even unconscious.

Personality and Theories of Life-Span Development

Some investigators have chosen to divide most or all of adulthood into a series of stages that are supposedly experienced by most or all adults. Stage theories are appealing because they are simple and straightforward, cover a broad range of people and ages, and propose that we continue to grow and develop throughout our lives. However, they have proved to be of limited value in understanding adult personality development. It is doubtful whether most adults are sufficiently alike to pass through the same stages at similar ages, although these theories may highlight major life transitions experienced by many people.

A popular conceptual alternative is to define personality in terms of traits or specific components that initiate and guide consistent forms of behavior. Some investigators have sought to measure the traits of older adults with standardized personality inventories, and this research also indicates that traits remain stable during adulthood. Trait theory has been criticized for circular definitions that lack explanatory power and for presenting an unrealistically consistent picture of human behavior. But this approach has devoted advocates as well and has provided useful and important information.

Yet another possible approach is to synthesize multiple views of development and articulate general rules regulating how individuals develop from infancy to old age. This approach is embodied in several theories of life-span development and has led to important new questions and studies of how and when people change.

Stage theory and research supports the belief that personality changes significantly during adulthood, but trait research has consistently shown that personality remains remarkably stable during adulthood. Life-span theories of development may be able to reconcile these contrasting views in that they predict both change and stability depending on which segment of the life course is being examined, the domains that are being studied, and the social and cultural context of the individual.

There is renewed interest in the scientific study of personality, aging, and life-span development, and increased sophistication in the questions being asked and in the design of more recent research. Therefore, the next decade may well provide us with even more valuable insights concerning personality and adulthood.

STUDY QUESTIONS

1. What important information about personality can be gleaned from clinical observation that would be difficult to obtain in the research laboratory? What important information about personality can be obtained from empirical research that would be difficult to derive from clinical observation? What does this imply about how personality should be studied?

2. According to current research evidence, are you likely to (a) experience a "midlife crisis"? (b) pass through particular stages of development at the same chronological age as do other adults? Why have these ideas become so popular with the general public?

3. Based on current research evidence, should you expect to become more neurotic and introverted as you grow past middle age? Why might the stereotype of the rigid older adult be supported by observing one or two such persons, even though they may be quite atypical of older adults in general?

4. According to current research evidence, is your personality likely to change drastically during adulthood or remain relatively stable? What does this imply about how to change those aspects of your personality that lead to harmful and self-defeating behavior?

5. A popular expression suggests that "you can be anything you want to be." Based on models of life-span development, is this true? What constraints might limit your ability to become anything you want to be?

6. Apply the concepts of selectivity and compensation to your own development up to now. Would you say your early development is characterized by concentrating on few or many domains?

TERMS TO REMEMBER

Compensation
Coping styles
Diversity
External locus of control
Extraversion
Internal locus of control
Introversion
Multidimensional variable

Neuroticism
Personality
Primary control
Secondary control
Selectivity
Stage
Trait

RELATIONSHIPS
AND INTERPERSONAL BEHAVIOR

Interpersonal relationships are vital to our existence. Most of us need and want to spend time with interesting acquaintances, with warm and supportive close friends, and with loved ones who occupy a unique and special place in our lives. Also, sooner or later, many adults opt for that singular and intimate form of relationship known as marriage.

In our quest to understand the course of adult development, therefore, we must deal with yet another crucial question: Does aging affect interpersonal behavior? For example, do adults tend to have more, fewer, or about the same number of friends as they grow toward old age? Does the frequency and enjoyment of sexual behavior decline markedly after middle age? Are marriage and relationships with one's children significantly more or less satisfying for the elderly? More generally, is old age a time of marked social isolation?

Various stereotypes suggest that older is not better. Examples include elderly parents who supposedly lament that their children no longer visit them, and aged individuals who presumably live alone and ignored in impoverished circumstances. As noted throughout this book, however, such stereotypes often prove to be mere myths when held up to the light of empirical evidence. Therefore, let us once again reserve judgment until we have examined appropriate research data.

In this chapter, we investigate the course of interpersonal relationships during adulthood. First, we present a conceptual system for organizing important events in the adult life course. We then discuss the characteristics of adult friendships and the nature and dynamics of such intimate relationships as love, marriage, parenting, and grandparenting. We conclude with a survey of currently popular psychological theories about the interpersonal behavior of the elderly.

CLASSIFYING MAJOR LIFE TRANSITIONS: TEMPORAL AND STATISTICAL NORMATIVITY

Definitions

Most of us experience many major life transitions between birth and death, such as going to college, choosing a job, getting married, and having children. Furthermore, many of these experiences are commonly expected to occur at fairly specific ages (Hareven, 1996). Individuals make transitions into and out of various roles in relation to social time clocks set by biological development of the organism and by the culture and the historical times in which one lives. In one early study, for example, middle-class and middle-aged adults concluded that men and women should complete their education and get married in their early 20s, and should become grandparents by age 45 to 50 (Neugarten et al., 1968).

Of course, not all adults adhere to such social norms. Some marry considerably later in life, some devote more years to their education, and so on. Thus one useful way to classify life events is according to the age at which they occur. More specifically, an event is **temporally normative** if it occurs at an age that is typical for most people in that culture. Examples include Americans who become widowed or suffer a stroke at age 65 to 70 or who get married for the first time at age 25. Conversely, an event is temporally non-normative if it occurs at an atypical age. In our society, becoming widowed or suffering a stroke at age 35 or getting married for the first time at age 45 are **temporally non-normative life events.**

A second good way to classify life transitions is according to their frequency, regardless of age. Thus an event is **statistically normative** if it happens to the majority of individuals in a given culture. Most people in this country experience marriage and retirement at some point in their lives, so these life events are statistically normative. In contrast, few Americans of any age suffer from strokes or spinal cord injuries or are lucky enough to win a state lottery. Therefore, these life events are **statistically non-normative.**

If we combine these dimensions, the result may be depicted as a two-by-two table. (See Table 8–1.) Note that whether an event is temporally normative or non-normative depends solely on the age at which it occurs. Conversely,

TABLE 8–1   Classifying Major Life Events According to Temporal and Statistical
Normativity

	TEMPORALLY NORMATIVE	TEMPORALLY NON-NORMATIVE
Statistically Normative	Getting married for the first time at age 25 Becoming widowed at age 65 Retiring at age 65 Having first child during late 20s	Getting married for the first time at age 45 Becoming widowed at age 35 Retiring at age 40 Having first child at age 45
Statistically Non-normative	Suffering stroke at age 65 Spinal cord injury at age 18–30	Suffering stroke at age 35 Spinal cord injury at age 55 Winning state lottery (any age)

Source: Schulz & Rau (1985, modified).

whether an event is statistically normative or non-normative depends solely on how many people in that culture experience that event at some point in their lives. (See Schulz & Rau, 1985.)

Implications

Virtually all of us experience some life events from each of the four cells in Table 8–1. By definition, however, most of us spend most of our time dealing with statistically and temporally normative events. These events are the most common, so they are also the ones for which friends, loved ones, and society are best prepared to offer any necessary assistance. For example, experienced college counselors and professors are likely to understand and help resolve the scholastic and emotional problems of the 20-year-old student, and widowhood support groups are generally effective for those over 60.

What of those relatively few adults who experience an unusually large number of non-normative life events? Because these events are by definition rare and unpredictable (albeit perhaps more interesting), friends, relatives, and society are less likely to know how to provide appropriate help. Thus a woman who is widowed at age 25 may have no friends who can give her appropriate emotional support because they are all too young to have undergone a similar experience. A 45-year-old man who enters college for the first time may prove to be somewhat of a puzzle to his counselor and professors. An adult who marries and has children late in life may have some difficulty dealing with teachers and other parents, who do not expect a 6-year-old child to have a 50-year-old father and a 45-year-old mother. Or a person who suffers a spinal cord injury at any age may find that this rare event leaves friends feeling helpless and confused and unable to respond effectively. In fact, adults who must deal with many non-normative life events (and the corresponding stress) may well be more likely to suffer physical illness, psychopathology, or even premature death.

We defer a further discussion of stress and non-normative life events until Chapter 10. The remainder of this chapter concentrates on those life events that are statistically normative, including marriage and parenting.

ADULT FRIENDSHIPS

Some social scientists prefer to explain the behavior of friends, lovers, spouses, and families in roughly similar terms. But although friendships may vary from casual to loving, even the best and closest of these would seem to differ in many significant respects from an intimate relationship with one special person. In accordance with those theorists who support the latter view, we treat friendship and marriage in separate sections.

Definition

What characteristics define a friend? How does a friend differ from a casual acquaintance, or from someone you know well but who does not seem to belong in this desirable category? In order to be a friendship, a relationship between two people must be characterized by the following:

◆ *Voluntary*. The relationship is entered into freely and without coercion.
◆ *Mutual*. Both persons contribute to the relationship, and both derive benefits from it.
◆ *Flexible*. Behaviors change to meet the needs of the persons. For example, one person may be supportive at some times and in need of support at other times.
◆ *Terminable*. The relationship may be ended at any time.
◆ *Equal and reciprocal*. Neither person consistently adopts a superior role, as by trying to manipulate the relationship or refusing to share important information.
◆ *Emotional*. Both parties contribute their feelings to the relationship. These feelings represent an involvement in the total personality of the other person.

Adult friendships take many different forms and are a central feature of adult lives.

(See Brown, 1981; Matthews, 1986.) By these standards, a person who consciously keeps secrets from another individual would not be considered a friend. Consider the following example:

A Friendship Betrayed

> A magazine editor told . . . how upset he was when his closest friend, a man he had gone to high school with, withheld from him the fact that he had cancer "until he was practically on his deathbed. I tried to respect that; I know he was suffering and had his own reasons for not telling me, but—it sounds terrible, I know— I was hurt . . . like he'd let me down." (Brenton, 1974; Matthews, 1986, p. 26)

No maliciousness was involved; in fact, the terminal patient may well have been trying to spare the editor's feelings. Yet concealing this vital information violated the elements of reciprocity and total personal involvement, so it proved harmful to the friendship.

Styles of Adult Friendships

Even when a friendship satisfies these criteria, it may be expressed in different types of behavior (Adams & Blieszner, 1995; Blieszner, 1995; Matthews, 1986). Matthews (1986) describes three basic friendship styles: independent, discerning (or discriminative), and gregarious (or acquisitive).

THE INDEPENDENT STYLE.   Adults who develop the **independent style of friendship** do not regard anyone else as a best friend, or even as a close friend. Although they do share good times with other people, they emphasize their self-sufficiency and maintain a certain psychological distance from others.

The Independent Style of Friendship

> [A woman] I am a very private person. I always lived by the rule "no explain, no complain." When you say too much you are revealing too much about yourself. You should retain a little bit of your privacy and thereby you get pride and you get self-discipline. The very private things you keep to yourself.
> [A man] Oh, I consider all of [the people in my retirement complex] to be friends. There are some that I wouldn't give you a dime a dozen for them. But still you participate in the stuff that we do here. You have to go along with them, but I wouldn't call them friends.
> [A man] I love friends. I love people. But I've been stung by friends, and I could never place myself in the position where I'd say, "Well, he or she is a very good friend of mine." I won't let myself get hurt anymore. (Matthews, 1986, pp. 35, 39)

These adults do not want or expect their friendships to be intimate. They give the impression of being surrounded by a sea of people, none of whom are closer emotionally than the others.

THE DISCERNING STYLE.   Adults who develop the **discerning style of friendship** have a small number of friends to whom they feel close and regard as very important.

The Discerning Style of Friendship

> [A woman] I formed a very close friendship in high school within a group of girls . . . and there was a really close friendship with one of these girls. . . . Another friend was a close friend in college and I married her brother, so that friendship was maintained. . . . We have a lot of more casual friends, for instance, that we play bridge with and that sort of thing, but not the type of friends that you are totally unreserved or honest with, that you can . . . say how you really feel about something. I'm pretty on guard most of the time with most people.
>
> [A man] [My best friend and I] had a lot of what we considered very serious discussions, you know, about our lives and the future and what our goals might be and that sort of thing. . . . We had a lot of interesting times together, had a lot of fun together. He had a good sense of humor as well as a rather keen mind and we had a very enjoyable time. We were very close. . . .
>
> [A man] There's one couple . . . we've known each other a long time, but I don't consider [the man] a friend. I guess there'd be lots of people you'd put in that category. Yes, you are glad to see each other and they know you, but you wouldn't just on the spur of the moment call them up or they call you. . . . (Matthews, 1986, pp. 45–47)

These adults draw a clear distinction between close, trusted, long-term friends and more casual, impersonal acquaintances.

THE GREGARIOUS STYLE. Adults who develop the **gregarious style of friendship** feel close to a fairly large number of people. There may be a core of half a dozen friends whom they describe as very special and another group of several dozen people whose company they enjoy.

The Gregarious Style of Friendship

> [A man] Sometimes it's hard to draw the line between acquaintances and friends, but there must have been, I'd say, fifty or so of them anyway, that I considered good friends, played cards with, just a lot of companionship.
>
> [A woman] In the past three or four years we've met several couples that we see fairly often. Otherwise you become isolated. And the ones that die and the ones who move out of town, unless you make friends you're isolated. You have to make a conscious effort to make friends. (Matthews, 1986, pp. 53, 55)

These adults are also optimistic about the prospect of acquiring new friends in the future.

The Purposes of Adult Friendships: Whom Do We Choose and Why?

Why do adults have friends? What sort of people are we likely to choose as our friends? The answers to these questions are by no means simple ones because friendships can serve various important purposes.

INTERPERSONAL SIMILARITY. The popular notion that opposites attract one another may hold true in rare instances, but it is not generally supported by empirical evidence. Instead, we are usually attracted to those who have similar beliefs, values, and personalities. A man who engages in the discerning style of friendship put it this way:

> A friend in my opinion is somebody who has similar ideas. For me it means he would have to love classical music. He would have to have an interest in art, not in artists, but like to go to museums. Read good books, love nature, somebody you could have a serious talk [with], not just, "How is your car?" (Matthews, 1986, p. 48)

People who resemble us may be easier to communicate with and relate to because they tend to perceive events in similar ways. Or it may be reassuring to see our own characteristics and opinions reflected, and thereby implicitly endorsed, by someone else.

PSYCHOLOGICAL SUPPORT. Not all studies support the importance of interpersonal similarity. Some findings suggest that although we may at first be drawn to those who resemble ourselves, long-term friendships actually depend far more on psychological support: A good friend is one who makes you feel good, and is there when needed. In the words of one woman,

> [My friends] always called me when [my son] was [terminally] ill. They never asked me because they knew if I wanted to talk about it, I'd talk. But they never questioned me. Because at the time I wasn't always able to talk about it. And they knew if they asked me at the wrong time, they didn't know what they were going to get back. But they knew enough so if I talked about it, they listened. And they're still my friends today. (Matthews, 1986, p. 78; see also Adams & Blieszner, 1995; Bailey, Finney, & Heim, 1975; Troll & Smith, 1976)

Thus mutual trust, and feeling comfortable with one another, may ultimately prove to be more important determinants of friendship than similarity. As we have seen, however, even close friends may find it difficult to offer effective psychological support in the case of non-normative life events.

SELF-DISCLOSURE. One vital aspect of a close and trusting friendship is **self-disclosure,** or revealing information about ourselves that we would normally keep secret. As we observed in the case of the cancer patient and magazine editor, the refusal to make such self-disclosures can seriously jeopardize a friendship.

Most of us seem to need at least one confidant with whom we can safely share our innermost thoughts and feelings, especially those which seem particularly vulnerable to criticism by other people (e.g., Candy, 1977). The loss of this important confidant may even lead to depression, whereas maintaining this relationship makes it easier to survive other crises and personal disasters.

PHYSICAL ATTRACTIVENESS. To many psychologists, an individual's inner personality is much more important than mere physical characteristics. Yet even in our psychologically enlightened era, physical attractiveness remains an attribute of prime importance. It is a major determinant of success in our society (Berscheid

& Walster, 1974; Hatfield & Sprecher, 1986), and it significantly affects most people's perception of the ideal friend. A man who is seen with a good-looking friend, especially a female, is likely to enjoy increased stature in the eyes of his friends and associates (Sigall & Landy, 1973). Apparently, then, many of us still assume that what is beautiful is good and worthwhile. Indeed, recent studies suggest that attractive persons are mistakenly rated as healthier than their less attractive peers (Kalick, Zebrowitz, Langlois, & Johnson, 1998).

However, those of us who are less than beautiful need not despair. Research has shown that for both same-sex and cross-sex friendships, people tend to choose those who are approximately similar in physical attractiveness (e.g., Cash & Derlaga, 1978; Murstein & Christy, 1976; Shanteau & Nagy, 1979). That is, most adults normally do not pursue friendships with the most physically attractive candidates. Instead, we select those similar enough to ourselves so that our overtures are less likely to be rejected.

INTELLIGENCE AND COMPETENCE. We tend to prefer friendships with people who are intelligent and competent, perhaps because such individuals are more likely to provide us with effective support and assistance. In fact, in the long run, intelligence may be an even more important component of personal attractiveness than physical characteristics (Gross & Crofton, 1977; Solomon & Saxe, 1977).

OTHER FACTORS. We value friends who are psychologically and emotionally stimulating and introduce us to enjoyable new experiences. We are also likely to choose friends who are usually pleasant and agreeable; who clearly like and approve of us; and who live close to us, making them more accessible on those occasions when we need a friend (Kaplan & Anderson, 1973; McCormick, 1982).

Less is known about the choice of cross-sex versus same-sex friendships. Traditionally, cross-sex friendships have been viewed with marked suspicion: Can they really be platonic, or must a sexual element inevitably intrude? At present, relatively little research deals with this issue. Married couples appear to resolve this problem by associating primarily with other couples, with the presence of the other spouse presumably allaying any fears of infidelity (Hess, 1972).

Friendships and Aging

Most of the available information about friendships and aging has been obtained from cross-sectional studies. Therefore, these data must be interpreted with caution.

NUMBER OF FRIENDSHIPS. The number of friends one has, especially close friends, appears to remain relatively stable throughout adulthood (e.g., Antonucci, 1984; Babchuck, 1978–1979; Lowenthal et al., 1975). One of the rare longitudinal studies in this area, which focused on a sample of men from age 50 to age 64, also found no significant decline in the number of friendships during these years (Costa, Zonderman, & McCrae, 1983). However, there is some indication that casual friendships may become less common with increasing age. We also appear to change our best friends frequently during young adulthood, but only rarely after middle age. (See Fischer, 1982; Fischer et al., 1977; Stueve & Gerson, 1977.) Women appear to be better at maintaining friendships over long periods of time than men. In one study more than half the older women who reported having a close friend in childhood or adolescence indicated they were still friends; older men, in contrast, reported that the majority of their close friendships developed during midlife or later (Antonucci, Sherman, & Akiyama, 1996). Women also have more friends on average than men in later life, and their friends are more likely to be close confidants; men are more likely to rely on their wives to fill this role. In general, women develop better relationship skills early in life and this serves them well when they get older, making them more adaptable to changed circumstances such as widowhood (Arber, 1996).

Even individuals over the age of 85 are able to maintain friendships. They also report making new friends after age 85, although the criteria for those friends differ somewhat. Respondents reported that their expectations for intimacy and shared history are somewhat lower.

How do adults manage to maintain about the same number of friends as they grow older? Some friendships last for years because the participants are highly committed to the relationship, and go to great lengths to ensure its continuation (e.g., traveling hundreds of miles to visit a friend who has moved away; frequent telephone calls or letters). Other friendships endure without much effort because of favorable circumstances, as when the individuals live very near one another. Furthermore, even when an adult friendship does end, this may not be a permanent loss. Most often, such friendships end by quietly fading away, rather than by being actively terminated. (For example, one person may move to a distant city.) These passive endings are usually regarded as no one's fault, so there is no residue of hard feelings, and the friendship may well be reactivated at a later date. Finally, even when a friendship is irrevocably lost, an older adult is likely to have formed numerous acquaintances over the years. This provides a pool of prospects from which a new friend can be developed. (See Matthews, 1986.)

These findings indicate that as we grow through adulthood, we do not suffer an increasing shortage of good friends. We do sift through our various interpersonal relationships and retain those that we value the most. Moreover, there is a tendency with age to substitute friendship networks with family networks (Adams & Blieszner, 1989).

PURPOSES AND BENEFITS.   Some data indicate that adults past middle age interact with their friends less often, increasing the amount of time spent with relatives (Antonucci, Sherman, & Akiyama, 1996; Stueve & Fischer, 1978). Yet other studies report that for adults age 55 and over, the frequency of contact with close friends is significantly related to satisfaction with life in general, whereas the frequency of contact with family members is not (e.g., Arking, 1976; Blau, 1981; Graney, 1975; Larson, 1978; Newsom & Schulz, 1996; Palmore, 1981; Spakes, 1979; Wood & Robertson, 1978).

Why should close friendships be so beneficial for older adults? Although relatively little research attention has been devoted to this issue, it would seem

that psychological support is particularly important. Adults of all ages who receive such support from their friends cope better with various adverse life
events, including physical disabilities, losing a job, and widowhood. Asking a
close friend for help may be easier than calling on one's adult children, which
appears to involve a greater loss of independence (Lee, 1985). And it is likely to
succeed. The amount of psychological support provided by close friends does
not appear to decline appreciably with increasing age, at least insofar as normative life events are concerned. (See Antonucci, 1984; Cobb & Kasl, 1977; Kasl &
Berkman, 1981; Schulz & Decker, 1983.) There is even some indication that close
friends can give effective support in the case of some non-normative life events,
such as rape and cancer (Burgess & Holmstrum, 1978; Vachon et al., 1977). Although these specific events are rare ones, they are not wholly dissimilar from
illnesses or injuries in general, which most friends have some experience in
dealing with.

Some studies also suggest that adults of all ages who have more friends,
and social contacts, and higher levels of social support enjoy lower mortality
rates and better mental health (Berkman, 1995; Berkman, Leo-Summers, &
Horowitz, 1992; Berkman & Syme, 1979; Hirsch, 1981; House, Robbins, & Metzner, 1982; McKinlay, 1981; Mitchell & Trickett, 1980; Penninx, van Tilburg,
Kriegsman, Deeg, Boeke, & van Eijk, 1997). Similar findings have also been obtained for older white males with numerous social ties (Blazer, 1982; Schoenbach et al., 1986). Overall, the evidence strongly indicates that having friends
and social relationships is important for physical and mental health, even
though a few investigators have obtained no significant relationship between
the number of friends and psychological well-being (Lieberman, 1982; Schaefer
et al., 1981).

AFTERWORD. All in all, research evidence provides little support for the stereotype of the friendless and lonely older adult. Although this unfortunate picture
is undoubtedly accurate in some instances, it represents the exception rather
than the rule. To be sure, the number of casual friends that one has may well
decrease to some extent with increasing age, particularly at very old ages. But
most adults do not suffer any appreciable decline in the number of close friends
as they grow through adulthood or in the amount of psychological support received from these friends.

LOVE, MARRIAGE, AND DIVORCE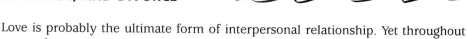

Love is probably the ultimate form of interpersonal relationship. Yet throughout
most of recorded history, the meaning of love has been shrouded in mystery.
Until recently, most social scientists regarded love as too intangible, complicated,
and unscientific (and much too personal and controversial) to study empirically
(Berscheid & Walster, 1978; Reis, 1995; Wrightsman & Deaux, 1981). The subject
of love is no longer shackled with these taboos and doubts, and researchers have
begun to take a serious interest in this most important phenomenon.

Conceptions of Love

As might be expected of an area that has only recently been subjected to empirical research, as yet no single definition of love is widely accepted by social
scientists, although most people would agree that love is a multifaceted experience with psychological, physiological, and behavioral components.

PASSIONATE AND COMPANIONATE LOVE.   According to Walster and Walster (1978),
there are two kinds of love. **Passionate love** is characterized by total absorption
in another person, intense physiological arousal, and moments of ecstasy and
complete fulfillment. In contrast, **companionate love** is highlighted by trust,
affection, and respect for those who are closely involved in our lives. Companionate love tends to be more common than passionate love and more typical of
long-term relationships.

D-LOVE AND B-LOVE.   Abraham Maslow, a noted personality theorist, has posited
a different dichotomy of love. **D-love** ("deficiency love") takes the form of a selfish need to receive love from other people and is often accompanied by anxious
and manipulative efforts to win the loved one's affection. Nevertheless, D-love is
not wholly undesirable. This need must be satisfied in order for us to develop
unselfish **B-love** ("being love"), which is nonpossessive, giving, honest, and richer
and more enjoyable than D-love. That is, if we do not receive sufficient love at
some periods in our lives, we will be unable to give genuine love to other people (Maslow, 1968, 1970).

THE ART OF LOVING.   Other personality theorists regard love as a phenomenon
that transcends mere one-to-one relationships. To Erich Fromm, the "art of loving" involves four main aspects: a genuine caring for and giving to other people,
an accurate knowledge of their true feelings and wishes, a respect for their right
to develop in their own way, and a sense of responsibility toward all humanity:

> Love is not primarily a relationship to a specific person; it is . . . an orienta-
> tion of character which determines the relatedness of a person to the world as a
> whole. . . . If I truly love one person I love all persons, I love the world, I love life.
> (Fromm, 1956/1974, pp. 38–39)

According to Fromm, everyone has the capacity for genuine love. However,
fulfilling this potential is very difficult. We all begin life as wholly self-centered
(narcissistic) infants, and pathogenic experiences in later life can cause us to re-
vert to this immature state. Authoritarian parents who use the child to fulfill their
own frustrated ambition for social or professional success, or parents who are
overly pessimistic, joyless, narcissistic, or physically abusive, may well cause the
child's healthy ability to love to be replaced by narcissistic tendencies (Fromm,
1941, 1947, 1956/1974).

PSYCHOMETRIC CONCEPTIONS.   How can we determine empirically if someone is in
love with a given person? Simply asking this individual if he or she is in love, and
receiving a yes or no answer, would seem to be a rather inaccurate and unscien-

tific approach. A more detailed alternative has been developed by Rubin (1970), who constructed two 9-item scales. One of these is designed to measure romantic love, the other to tap how much the other person is liked:

SAMPLE LOVE-SCALE ITEMS	SAMPLE LIKING-SCALE ITEMS
"I would forgive _____ for practically anything."	"I think that _____ is unusually well adjusted."
"If I could never be with _____ , I would feel miserable	"_____ is the sort of person who I myself would like to be."
"I feel that I can confide in _____ about virtually everything."	"Most people would react very favorably to _____ after a brief acquaintance."

Subjects are asked to indicate the extent of their agreement with each item, using a scale ranging from 1 (most negative) to 9 (most positive). In one study, 158 college couples who were dating but not engaged were asked to complete these scales twice: once with respect to their dating partner and once with respect to a close friend of the same sex. The results indicated a conceptual distinction between romantic love and liking. The data also revealed significant differences in the nature of the relationships formed by men and women: Women included more liking in their love relationships, and more loving in their liking (friendly) relationships. That is, women liked their love partners and loved their same-sex friends more than men did (Rubin, 1970; see also Booth, 1972).

Love and Marriage

THE DEVELOPMENT OF LOVE. Many relationships that end in marriage proceed through a fairly standard sequence: casual dating, more frequent dating, going steady, informal engagement (being "engaged to be engaged"), and—ultimately— formal engagement. As the relationship progresses, the initial, idealized image of the loved one yields to a more realistic appraisal of the other's strengths and weaknesses (Pollis, 1969). Apparently, "love is blind" only at the outset.

In any loving relationship, different factors tend to be important during different stages. The early attraction is typically based on superficial aspects, such as physical attractiveness. In later stages, however, we are more likely to value opportunities for self-disclosure, similar beliefs, and similar levels of emotional maturity. When a relationship is relatively new, self-disclosure is usually limited; few deeply personal matters are shared with one's partner. Only gradually do we become willing to confide our innermost thoughts and feelings to the one we love (Adams, 1979; Altman & Taylor, 1973; Levinger, 1974, 1978).

There also appears to be an inverse relationship between attraction and attachment. Attraction is high during the early stages, due to novelty and intrigue; but attachment is low, because there has not yet been sufficient time to develop firm emotional bonds. If the relationship should end at this time, the couple will normally experience only temporary unhappiness and disappointment. As the relationship continues, the novelty and corresponding attraction decreases, and the attachment becomes much more powerful. Thus a breakup during this later period can cause emotional pain that is never completely overcome.

ENDURING LOVE: MARRIAGES THAT LAST.   Why do some loving relationships survive for many years? A recent study focused on 351 couples who remained married for 15 years or more, 300 of whom reported that they were happily married. The most frequently cited reason for the enduring relationship was stated, "My spouse is my best friend" (Lauer & Lauer, 1985; Lauer, Lauer, & Kerr, 1995; see Table 8–2). Liking one's spouse as a person, meaningful communication and self-disclosure, openness, trustworthiness, caring, and giving were considerably more important to a lasting marriage than passionate love. Other factors that were typical of lengthy marriages included recognizing and accepting the spouse's faults, believing that marriage is a long-term commitment, and avoiding displays of intensely expressed anger. The following quotes were typical.

A Man Married for 24 Years:

> "[My wife] isn't perfect. But I don't worry about her weak points, which are very few. Her strong points overcome them too much." (p. 24)

A Man Married for 20 Years:

> "Commitment means a willingness to be unhappy for a while. I wouldn't go on for years and years being wretched in my marriage. But you can't avoid troubled times. You're not going to be happy with each other all the time. That's when commitment is really important." (p. 25)

A Man Married for 36 Years:

> "Discuss your problems in a normal voice. If a voice is raised, stop. Return after a short period of time. Start again. After a period of time both parties will be

TABLE 8–2   Why Marriages Endure: Reasons Most Often Given by a Sample of 351 Couples Married for at Least 15 Years, in Order of Frequency

MEN	WOMEN
1. "My spouse is my best friend."	1. "My spouse is my best friend."
2. "I like my spouse as a person."	2. "I like my spouse as a person."
3. "Marriage is a long-term commitment."	3. "Marriage is a long-term commitment."
4. "Marriage is sacred."	4. "Marriage is sacred."
5. "We agree on aims and goals."	5. "We agree on aims and goals."
6. "My spouse has grown more interesting."	6. "My spouse has grown more interesting."
7. "I want the relationship to succeed."	7. "I want the relationship to succeed."
8. "An enduring marriage is important to social stability."	8. "We laugh together."
9. "We laugh together."	9. "We agree on a philosophy of life."
10. "I am proud of my spouse's achievements."	10. "We agree on how and how often to show affection."

Source: Lauer & Lauer (1985, abridged).

able to deal with their problems and not say things that they will be sorry about later." (p. 26)

Virtually all of these couples preferred peaceful interactions; only one couple reported that they often yelled at each other. Interestingly, sex was far down the list of reasons for a happy marriage. Although sexual relations were important to these couples, fewer than 10% regarded sex as one of the primary factors keeping the marriage together. However, the men and women in this study placed considerable emphasis on sexual fidelity. One wife who had been married 27 years stated that she could resolve almost any problem with her husband given enough time, but infidelity "would probably not be something I could forget and forgive" (p. 26).

A follow-up study of older persons who had been married for at least 45 years yielded similar results (Lauer, Lauer, & Kerr, 1995). Respondents reported they always or almost always agreed on matters such as family finances, recreation, demonstrations of affection, friends, sexual relations, proper behavior, philosophy of life, ways of dealing with in-laws, and so on. More than 70% of couples indicated they confided in their mates all or most of the time, kiss their spouse every day, and laugh together once a day or more.

Paradoxically, then, a relationship that may have originated primarily because of passionate love is likely to require strong elements of friendship and companionate love in order to endure. As these investigators concluded, "The redemption of difficult people through selfless devotion may make good fiction, but the happily married people in our sample expressed no such sense of mission. Rather, they said, they are grateful to have married someone who is basically appealing and likable" (Lauer & Lauer, 1985, p. 24).

Role Factors in Marriage. More than a decade ago, a *Newsweek* cover story emphasized the increasing prevalence of "househusbands." According to empirical research during the late 1970s, however, the demise of the traditional housewife role has been greatly exaggerated.

Many couples do tend to share household duties while they are childless. But this egalitarianism usually does not continue after the first child is born, even if both spouses are working. Instead, the need to earn more money and the generally higher income potential for men drives the husband to concentrate on his career, leaving the wife to assume primary responsibility for the home and family. As a result, couples with children are likely to adopt traditional roles: The wife does most of the housework, prepares the meals, and takes care of the children in addition to taking on a part-time or full-time job; the husband may make minor house repairs, shovel snow, mow the lawn, and take out the garbage (Campbell, Converse, & Rodgers, 1976; Hoffman & Manis, 1978; Keith, Schafer, & Wacker, 1995; Pleck, 1977). Conversely, shared duties and role equality are most often found in childless marriages.

Marriage and the Empty Nest. The time a married couple spends together after the last child leaves home, up until the death of one spouse, is known as the **empty nest.** According to folklore and popular literature, this is a painful time for most parents—particularly women, who supposedly lament that their all-important role of mother is all but gone. How much truth is there to this common belief?

During this decade, the duration of the empty nest period has increased considerably. In 1900, it lasted for only about 2 years and often occurred during the couple's old age. Due to such recent trends as smaller families, the closer spacing of children, and a longer life span, the empty nest now lasts for an average of 13 years. Nevertheless, recent data do not support the prevailing stereotype. Couples are likely to view the departure of their children in mostly favorable terms. True, there is some sense of loss. But there is also relief from the relentless responsibility of daily child rearing, more opportunities to indulge personal interests, and increased freedom and privacy, which result in markedly improved marital relationships and individual well-being (Barber, 1989; Hagestad, 1980). Although exceptions undoubtedly exist, the "pain of the empty nest" must be regarded as yet another of the myths that pervade the field of adult development and aging.

CARING FOR A SERIOUSLY ILL SPOUSE.   When an older parent becomes seriously ill (e.g., from cancer, heart disease, or Alzheimer's disease), care is most often provided by the adult offspring. We discuss this issue later in this chapter, in the section dealing with intergenerational relationships.

As married couples grow old, it is not uncommon to find that one spouse becomes chronically ill or disabled. As a result, one spouse becomes the caregiver for the other. The spouse who most often has to provide such care is the wife; the husband is usually older, and men have shorter life expectancies. Caregiving for a major illness goes far beyond the bounds of normal care and can be extremely burdensome. The wife's personal life suffers greatly; because she lives with the patient, her privacy and leisure activities are severely restricted. Her emotional involvement with the patient tends to be even greater than that of the children because of her longer personal relationship with him. As a result, the negative impact of a major illness is even often greater on caregiving wives than on grown children who serve as caregivers. There are also some positive effects, however: increased self-esteem because of her patience, compassion, courage, and strength in such difficult circumstances, and feeling appreciated by her husband and closer to him. Interestingly, the few husbands who care for seriously ill wives appear to function quite well; they are better able to put limits on the amount of care they provide by relying more on supportive family members and professional services. (See Biegel, Sales, & Schulz, 1991; Schulz, O'Brien, Bookwala, & Fleissner, K., 1995; Schulz, Newsom, Mittelmark, Burton, Hirsch, & Jackson, 1997; Schulz et al., in press; Williamson & Schulz, 1995.)

Divorce

DEMOGRAPHICS.   The preceding sections have emphasized the more pleasant aspects of marital relationships: being attracted to another person, learning to share our innermost feelings, liking as well as loving one's spouse. However, marriage is not without a certain degree of risk. Each year, the blissful expectations of approximately 1.2 million American couples are shattered by divorce. The U.S. divorce rate has increased consistently during the past three decades and doubled between 1968 and 1978, with the result that the average median duration of a marriage is currently 9.47 years (U.S. Bureau of the Census, 1997). In fact, divorce has become statistically normative (more or less); it terminates one of every two marriages (Glick, 1979; Lauer & Lauer, 1985).

Divorce is most common among adults aged 30 to 45 and among black females. The median age at the time of divorce is 36 years for men and 33 for women (U.S. Bureau of the Census, 1997). (See Figure 8–1.) Youthful marriages, in which both the man and woman are younger than age 21, are significantly more likely to end in divorce than marriages after the age of 30. Nevertheless, the elderly are far from immune. Among Americans age 65 and older, more than half a million are divorced, and approximately 10,000 new cases are registered each year. As we see in Chapter 10, divorce among the elderly may well be even more stressful and pathogenic than widowhood.

CAUSES OF DIVORCE. As we have seen, couples with happy marriages tend to regard one another as best friends. In contrast, those headed for divorce are likely to have arguments that become increasingly severe. Instead of one spouse backing off when the other is upset and initiating peacemaking overtures, anger and rejection are met with greater anger and rejection. This causes the conflict to escalate and increases the likelihood of leaving permanent emotional scars. (See Raush et al., 1974.)

FIGURE 8–1 Divorce rate as a function of age and ethnic group.
(*Source:* U.S. Bureau of the Census (1997).)

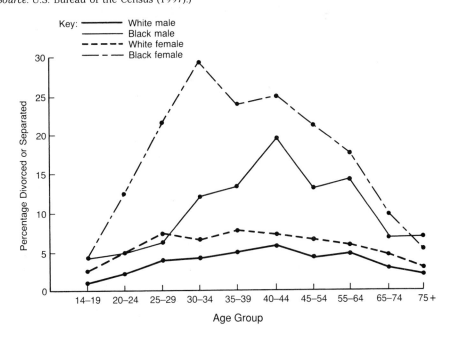

Other common causes of divorce include alcoholism, desertion, brutality, adultery, jealousy, moodiness, irritating habits, spending money foolishly, and using drugs (Amato & Rogers, 1997; Bennett, 1984; see also Table 8–3). The personality of each spouse is also an important consideration, for those with a strong commitment to maintaining the marriage are more likely to do so even in the face of serious obstacles (as we have seen). Other factors come into play as well. For example, persons with a strong religious commitment or whose parents are not divorced are less likely to become divorced themselves.

The increasing U.S. divorce rate may also be due in part to the easing of divorce laws and the establishment of "no fault" divorces, for which incompatibility and breakdown of the relationship are accepted as sufficient grounds. Also, because women have made greater inroads into the workplace during the last half century (Chapter 9), their financial status has improved. Thus not as many women must remain mired in an unhappy marriage in order to survive economically. For these reasons, the increased divorce rate is not entirely negative; it may well indicate that more people can now extricate themselves from relationships that have become unbearable.

STAGES OF DIVORCE.   Divorced people tend to proceed through several behavioral stages, much like a rite of passage (Chiriboga, 1979). At first, they prefer to nurse their psychological wounds in isolation, so they segregate themselves from other people. Next, they experience a period with no clear social identity; they are no longer married, but not yet truly single. During the first few months after the divorce is granted, many men who were fed and cared for by their wives must now learn to prepare their own meals and keep the house clean. Conversely, many women must learn those tasks that were formerly performed by their husbands, such as having the car repaired or balancing the checkbook. The ex-spouses spend much of this time in dealings with one another, often arguing bitterly over financial matters. However, not all of these interactions are negative. One study found that some 12% of divorced couples had sexual relations with one another during the first 2 months following the divorce, and most stated that they would turn first to their ex-spouses if they needed help handling a crisis (Hetherington, Cox, & Cox, 1976). Ultimately, divorced individuals do begin to seek out other people and reestablish themselves socially.

TABLE 8–3   Social-Structural Characteristics and Reported Behaviors of Self or Spouse That Predict Divorce

SOCIAL-STRUCTURAL CHARACTERISTICS	REPORTED BEHAVIORS OF SELF OR SPOUSE
Young age at marriage	Jealousy
Few years married	Moodiness
Low or no church attendance	Infidelity
Remarriage for one or both partners	Irritating habits
Both spouses' parents divorced	Spending money foolishly
	Drinking or using drugs

Source: Amato & Rogers (1997).

THE EFFECTS OF DIVORCE. Divorce is usually a traumatic experience. There is some indication that when one spouse favors and initiates the divorce, this individual is more likely to establish a satisfactory life in the future, whereas the other spouse tends to suffer long-lasting emotional scars. On the whole, however, divorce would seem to affect women more deeply than men. Only 14% of divorced American women are awarded alimony, and fewer than half of these receive it regularly; 44% are awarded child support, with fewer than half receiving it regularly, although changes in federal and state laws will likely increase the percent of males making support payments. Thus, despite the improving financial status of U.S. women, numerous divorcees must either find ways to support themselves (and their children, if any) or else accept a markedly reduced standard of living. Older women are likely to have particular difficulty in this regard because their generation was not as tolerant of women in the workplace, making it less likely that they ever developed any income-producing skills. In contrast, divorced men are usually employed, so they can continue to derive income and satisfaction from their work.

Furthermore, establishing a satisfying heterosexual relationship may well be particularly difficult for divorced older women. There are more single women than single men, so divorced women are less often asked by friends to serve as blind dates or unattached party guests. The woman is most likely to gain custody of the children and to become anxious about their reactions to and possible jealousy of any dates and sexual relationships that she may have. Thus it is hardly surprising that divorced women (and single men) show the most symptoms of stress in our society.

The effect of divorce on children varies with their age and with the parents' ability to cope with the resulting problems. Young children tend to blame themselves for the divorce, to worry about being abandoned, and to have fantasies that their parents will reconcile. Adolescents are likely to experience initial anger and turmoil, but are generally better able to cope with the divorce. There is also some evidence that after a divorce, parents are less affectionate with their children, adolescent girls become more promiscuous, and boys are more feminized. (See Anthony, 1974; Hetherington, 1972; Hetherington, Cox, & Cox, 1977; Hetherington & Duer, 1972; Kelly & Wallerstein, 1976; Wallerstein & Kelly, 1974, 1975, 1976.) However, children in single-parent families appear to function better than children in families with two parents where there is frequent conflict (Rutter, 1979).

Divorce can be a shattering experience for the husband as well. It has been argued that divorce laws and decrees are often unfair not only to women, but also to men. Some fathers report that their efforts to gain joint custody of the children involved years of expensive legal wrangling and caused so much hard feeling that the relationship with the children was seriously impaired. Others contend that they are denied proper visitation by their ex-wives, presumably due to the latter's anger and bitterness. As one fathers'-rights activist put it, "I've seen some men sobbing away, so overcome by the system. . . . The system is so stacked against men that they don't fight" (*Time*, November 24, 1986).

Nevertheless, if a marriage is truly unbearable and if the couple's religious and personal beliefs permit, the least of evils may well be to end it and give each spouse the opportunity to find happiness elsewhere. In any case, it appears that divorce will remain a common phenomenon for the foreseeable future.

REMARRIAGE.   The emotional pain caused by a broken marriage does not prevent many adults from trying again. More than 20% of the current marriages in this country include at least one spouse who has been married previously (Bowers & Bahr, 1989).

The probability of remarrying decreases with increasing age for both men and women. (See Figure 8–2.) However, remarriage rates are much lower for older women than for older men. As we observed in Chapter 1, there are many more unmarried older women than unmarried older men (see Figure 1–5). Also, older men have more latitude in their choice of spouse: Social custom looks with disfavor on women who marry much younger men, but not the reverse. Thus re-married men tend to be more satisfied with their marriages than are remarried women, who have a smaller pool from which to select and are more likely to settle for less desirable partners.

In general, those who remarry later in life have more stable and satisfying marriages than do those who remarry as young adults. One reason is that older adults can draw on greater experience as to what makes a relationship successful, by combining practical with romantic considerations. (See Bahr & Peterson, 1989.)

AFTERWORD: INTIMATE RELATIONSHIPS AND AGING.   Empirical data indicate that it is disadvantageous to marry too early; youthful marriages are more likely to end in divorce. Also, divorces are most common between the ages of 30 and 45. For the most part, however, it is difficult to draw any age-related conclusions with regard to marriage and divorce. Some adults find marriage to be an increasing source of love and fulfillment as they grow older, but others experience increasing conflicts that make continuation of the marriage virtually impossible. Some useful clues as to why marriages endure or fail have been unearthed by social scientists; but these factors involve the personality, motivation, and interpersonal behavior of the spouses, rather than age per se.

The relationship between love and aging is also far from clear, partly because adults pursue many diverse courses insofar as intimate relationships are concerned. Some marry young; some do so later in life. Some marry once, for better or worse; some marry numerous times. Some eschew marriage altogether and remain single throughout their lives, possibly engaging in a number of loving relationships along the way. And some find fulfillment from homosexual relationships, rather than heterosexual ones. We can only conclude that the love adults derive from intimate relationships does not necessarily decline in quantity or quality with increasing age, at least not until old age makes the death of the loved one more likely. The negative relationship between age and the capacity for sexual expressions of love has also been exaggerated, as we see in the following section.

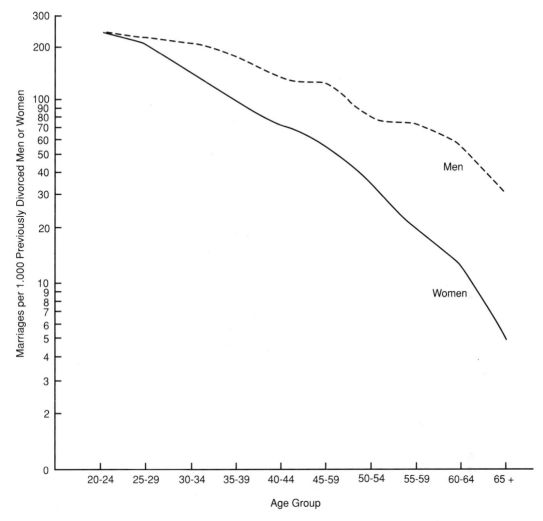

FIGURE 8–2 **Remarriage rates of previously divorced men and women, by age.**
(*Source:* U.S. Bureau of the Census (1997).)

SEXUALITY AND AGING

Heterosexual Relationships

RESEARCH PROBLEMS AND PREVAILING STEREOTYPES. As was the case with love, human sexuality has only recently been subjected to much empirical research. This is also an extremely personal and sensitive area, and it is one that poses significant conceptual and methodological problems. For example, should researchers define heterosexuality solely in terms of intercourse? If so, should sexual behavior be measured in terms of frequency (number of coital acts per week or month), percentages (how many adults of a given age still participate in sexual intercourse), or level of intensity (degree of physical arousal and excitement)? Or perhaps a sound definition of human heterosexual behavior should also include less overt behaviors, such as thoughts, fantasies, wishes, and affectionate touching. But is behavior that does not end in orgasm truly sexual? When does friendly caressing turn into sexual foreplay?

To complicate matters further, it has been argued that we engage in sex for many reasons. The most obvious motives are sexual desire and the need to satisfy biological and reproductive drives. But sex may also be used to obtain affection and intimacy, to exert power over another person, to escape boredom, to make up with a loved one after a fight, to gratify feelings of pride and self-esteem, and to confirm one's masculinity or femininity.

Until recently, very little was known about the relationship between sexuality and aging. Because no one knew much about the sexual desires and behaviors of the middle-aged and elderly, it was widely assumed that there was nothing to know—that is, older adults did not and should not have any interest in sex. In one early study that used a sentence completion task, a sample of college students most often stated that "sex for most old people is negligible, unimportant, and past" (Golde & Kogan, 1959). The majority of a sample of 646 college students concluded that their parents had sexual intercourse no more than once a month, and some 25% of this sample believed their parents had abandoned sex completely (Pocs et al., 1977). These views are so incorrect as to be ludicrous, yet they are by no means limited to laypeople. When middle-aged and elderly patients complain of sexual difficulties or disinterest, some physicians respond with supposedly humorous statements like "Well, what can you expect at your age?" or "Maybe you've had as much [sex] as you're going to get!" (Labby, 1984). This smug and insensitive attitude is likely to feed the patient's loss of sexual self-confidence, thereby creating a self-fulfilling prophecy: Sex in later adulthood becomes impossible because the individual believes it is abnormal and impossible. All too many older adults accept this erroneous stereotype, abandon any efforts to engage in sex, and miss out on some of the major interpersonal satisfactions and rewards that their lives still have to offer.

During the last few decades, however, we have become increasingly aware that there is indeed sexual life after middle age. To be sure, some adults have ambivalent feelings about sex and welcome advancing age as an excuse to abandon it. More often, however, the fear of losing the capacity to obtain sexual pleasure and intimacy is a very powerful one. As an anonymous sage once observed, "Sex doesn't make you live longer, it only makes you want to!" Thus insofar as many middle-aged and older adults are concerned, it is fortunate that empirical data about sexuality and aging have begun to allay such fears (Seidman & Reider, 1994).

YOUNG ADULTHOOD.   Most researchers define sexual behavior as that which results in or is intended to result in orgasm, notably coitus. By this definition, young men tend to be more sexually active than young women. More American males have intercourse by 16 to 17 years of age, and females do so by 17 to 18 years of age. Most young adults between the ages of 18 and 24 have multiple, serial sex partners. Between the ages of 25 and 29 monogamy appears to be the norm. The large majority of heterosexually active men and women report having had only one sex partner in the preceding year. The average frequency of intercourse among monogamous individuals is one to three times per week. Up to 20% of adult men report they have had a homosexual experience, but only 1% to 6% report such an experience during the preceding year (Seidman & Rieder, 1994). Some 44% of men and 30% of women report having had sexual intercourse by age 16, with these figures increasing to 95% for men and 81% for women by age 24.

There is some indication that the frequency of sexual behavior has increased during the past few decades, especially among younger adults and younger women. This increase is a cohort effect. Social standards have changed considerably during the last half century; sexual behavior is now more accepted (and expected). As a result, younger generations are undoubtedly more willing to report (or even to exaggerate) their sexual activity. As psychologist Rollo May has observed, "[Whereas] the Victorian nice man or woman was guilty if he or she did experience sex, now we are guilty if we don't (1969, p. 40). Conversely, couples who grew up during the more conservative 1940s are more likely to favor modesty and to understate the extent of their sexual behavior. It has also become more acceptable for women to state openly that they have sexual desires and interests, due in part to the efforts of female advocacy groups.

Figure 8–3 indicates that the frequency of sexual behavior among married couples such as intercourse does decrease from young adulthood to middle age.

FIGURE 8–3 **Average number of times Americans had intercourse per year, by age.** (*Source:* Seidman and Rieder (1994).)

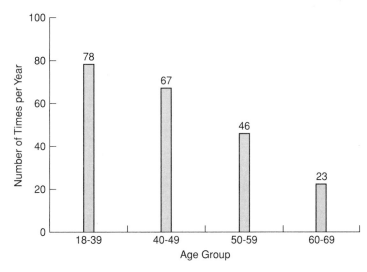

This is due in part to environmental constraints: Many couples have children during this period, and the rigors of night feedings or the presence of an active child or teenager may well make some reduction in sexual activity more convenient. Aging is also partly responsible for this decrease, particularly insofar as men are concerned.

MALE SEXUALITY AND AGING. Numerous studies have found that male sexual activity declines with increasing age. The peak of male potency occurs during the late teens, although the first substantial drop in interest and desire is not usually not experienced until about age 50 (Pfeiffer, Verwoerdt, & Davis, 1972). A second significant drop in the number of men who remain sexually active has been reported to occur at about age 70 to 80. However, there is some disagreement as to the extent of this decline. In various studies, some of which were longitudinal, the percentage of men who remain sexually active at older ages has been estimated as follows:

> At age 60: 53–60%*; 95%
> At age 70: 45%*; 70%*; 70%
> At age 78: 25%*
> * = longitudinal study

(See Hegeler, 1976; Kinsey, Pomeroy, & Martin, 1948; Pfeiffer, 1974; Pfeiffer, Verwoerdt, & Wang, 1968, 1969; Seidman & Rieder, 1994; Verwoerdt, Pfeiffer, & Wang, 1969.)

The results of a cross-sectional study of men age 45 to 69, all of whom were members of a medical group insurance plan, are shown in Table 8–4. Although older men were less sexually active, 76% of the oldest group continued to have sexual intercourse one or more times per month (Pfeiffer, Verwoerdt, & Davis, 1974). Some more recent studies suggest that levels of male sexual activity after middle age remain even more stable (George & Weiler, 1981). An estimated 60% of married couples where both spouses are between ages 60 and 70 have intercourse at least occasionally (Busse & Blazer, 1980), as do 25% to 30% of couples past age 75 (McCary, 1978). Few researchers have focused on men over 80, but some instances of sexual intercourse by men age 90 or even older have been reported (*National Geographic*, 1973).

These data point to two significant conclusions. As age increases, fewer men are sexually active, and those who are active are less so than younger men. Nevertheless, a substantial number of men continue to engage in sex throughout much or even all of their adult lives. Although aging does appear to be partly responsible for declines in sexual capacity and interest among men, an important question remains: Why are some older men still sexually active, whereas others are not?

FACTORS AFFECTING MALE SEXUAL ACTIVITY. Although men do not experience the dramatic shift in sex hormone levels experienced by women when they go through menopause, their level of testosterone does decline gradually with age.

TABLE 8-4 Frequency of Sexual Intercourse Reported by Men and Women in a Medical Group Insurance Plan

	PERCENTAGE REPORTING INTERCOURSE					
GROUP	Not at All	Once a Month	Once a Week	2–3 Times a Week	More than 2–3 Times a Week	Percent Still Sexually Active
Men, Age						
46–50	00	05	62	26	07	100
51–55	05	29	49	17	00	95
56–60	07	38	44	11	00	93
61–65	20	43	30	07	00	80
66–70	24	48	26	02	00	76
Women, Age						
46–50	14	26	39	21	00	86
51–55	20	41	32	05	02	80
56–60	42	27	25	04	02	58
61–65	61	29	05	05	00	39
66–70	73	16	11	00	00	27

Note: For men, $N = 261$; for women, $N = 231$. There were at least 41 subjects in each subgroup.
Source: Pfeiffer, Verwoerdt, & Davis (1972).

Most men go through a stage similar to menopause, referred to as the male climacteric. This shift may be accompanied by changes such as a slightly higher pitched voice, facial hair growing more slowly, and muscles becoming more flabby. As a man grows older, several physiological changes begin to occur in response to overt sexual stimulation. As a man grows older it takes two to three times longer to achieve full penile erection, and direct physical stimulation by the partner may well be necessary. Ejaculation is significantly less forceful. The volume of seminal fluid decreases. And more time is required following orgasm before another erection is possible (Burt & Meeks, 1985; Masters & Johnson, 1966, 1970).

If a partner fails to understand the nature of these changes, the couple's sex life may be adversely affected. For example, instead of attributing the man's desire to have sex without ejaculation to the effects of aging, the woman may erroneously conclude he does not find her attractive or he is having an affair with someone else. On purely physiological grounds, however, there is no reason why these changes should have a profound effect on the man's sexual activity, nor is there any scientific support to date for the idea of a male menopause (Kolodny, Masters, & Johnson, 1979).

More importantly, men who have had more sexual experiences early in life tend to remain more sexually active during middle and old age. This has been referred to as the "use it or lose it" syndrome (Solnick & Corby, 1983; see also Pfeiffer & Davis, 1972). As Masters and Johnson put it, "The most important factor in the maintenance of effective sexuality for the aging male is consistency of active sexual expression. . . . For the male geriatric sample . . . those men currently interested in relatively high levels of sexual expression report similar activity levels from their formative years. It does not appear to matter what manner of sexual expression has been employed, as long as high levels of activity were maintained" (1966, pp. 262–263). Conversely, extended periods of abstinence pose a serious risk to the sexual functioning of the older male. Therefore, if the man's partner becomes unavailable (as through hospitalization), masturbation may be a valuable way of maintaining sexual capacity and interest.

A second determinant of sexual activity among older men is physical health. Men who are (or who believe they are) in poor health are significantly less likely to engage in sexual intercourse (Pfeiffer & Davis, 1972). Sex is unappealing when one does not feel well, and ill health is more common at older ages. However, the general belief that intercourse is likely to precipitate fatal heart attacks in older men is not supported by empirical data. Although sexual activity is somewhat stressful, deaths during intercourse are rare and account for only 1% of sudden coronary fatalities. It has also been argued that some 7 out of 10 such deaths occur during extramarital affairs and are due largely to the accompanying guilt and anxiety (Butler & Lewis, 1976). And other investigators have concluded that the oxygen cost during sexual intercourse is no greater than when climbing a flight of stairs, walking briskly, or performing ordinary tasks (Hellerstein & Friedman, 1970). Even adults who have had heart attacks can usually resume sexual activity upon recovery, possibly with the aid of nitroglycerin (or other coronary dilator) 10 minutes prior to intercourse if angina is unusually likely (Labby, 1984).

Third, the sexual desires of older men may be inhibited by negative attitudes. As we observed at the outset of this section, all too many men accept the stereotype of the sexless older adult and erroneously conclude that they can no longer function effectively in this area. One or two failures to sustain an erection may therefore lead to a vicious circle: The resulting performance anxiety makes it progressively more difficult to enjoy sex, and the ensuing failures produce still more performance anxiety. Other attitudes that may lead to a decline in sexual activity include possible monotony resulting from many years of sex with the same partner and worries about work and career problems (Masters & Johnson, 1970).

In sum: Men are more likely to remain interested in sex through middle and old age if they enjoyed sex more often during young adulthood (or even if they merely had sexual experiences more often), if they are in good health, and if they believe they can indeed maintain effective sexual behavior as they grow older.

FEMALE SEXUALITY AND AGING.   In marked contrast to men, women reach their sexual peak in their mid-30s and suffer relatively little loss in capacity thereafter. To be sure, middle age does bring some physiological changes: Lubrication of the vagina decreases, the vaginal walls lose elasticity, more precoital stimulation may be required, orgasmic experiences may be somewhat slowed, and menstrual periods eventually cease (Burt & Meeks, 1985). However, no evidence indicates that these changes cause any significant decline in female sexual capacity. For example, although menopause may inhibit sexual desire if the woman (erroneously) believes it must, the resulting freedom from the possibility of unwanted pregnancy may produce a reduction in anxiety and greater sexual satisfaction.

Also, although the duration and intensity of orgasmic episodes may be reduced, the subjective levels of sensual pleasure appear to continue unabated. As Kinsey et al. (1953) put it, "[There is] no evidence that the female ages in her sexual capacities;" Masters and Johnson (1966) concluded, "there is no time limit drawn by the advancing years to female sexuality." Orgasmic response has been observed in women age 70 to 80 and older (Kleegman, 1959; Solnick & Corby, 1983).

Nevertheless, the number of women who remain sexually active and the frequency of these activities decrease substantially with increasing age. In the study reported in Table 8–5, for example, the percentage of women who engaged in sexual intercourse declined from 86% at age 46 to 50 to 27% at age 66 to 70. And fewer women than men in each age group remained sexually active, with the greatest differences occurring in the oldest groups. Similarly, other studies have found that only 20% to 40% of 60-year-old women and 15% to 30% of 70-year-old women engage in sex (Newman & Nichols, 1960; Verwoerdt, Pfeiffer, & Wang, 1969). Thus, although the sexual capacity of women declines relatively little with increasing age, their sexual activity decreases markedly and is significantly lower than that of men of similar ages. How can this apparent paradox be explained?

FACTORS AFFECTING FEMALE SEXUAL ACTIVITY.   Numerous studies have found that female sexual activity depends to a large extent on the presence of a socially acceptable and sexually capable partner, such as a healthy spouse. Thus marital status is an important predictor of sexual activity among older women, but not among men (e.g., Kinsey et al., 1953; Pfeiffer & Davis, 1972; Pfeiffer, Verwoerdt, & Davis, 1972; Pfeiffer, Verwoerdt, & Wang, 1968, 1969).

American women marry men who average 4 years older, and who are therefore likely to become ill and/or lose interest in sex before the woman does. Furthermore, women in our society live longer than men, so there are many more widows than widowers. (See Table 1–2; Figure 1–5.) For these reasons, middle-aged and elderly women are much more likely to be without an appropriate sexual partner than are older men. In fact, some 53% of women past age 65 are widows, and there are approximately 30 single men for every 100 single women over 65. Thus the woman's superior sexual capacity at older ages proves to be a dubious benefit, because her sexual activity is likely to be limited by the declining health or death of her (usually older) male partner. According to Kinsey et al. (1953), "[The decrease in sexual activity among women is] controlled by the male's desires, and it is primarily his age rather than the female's loss of interest or capacity which is reflected in this decline."

Women who enjoy sex more during young adulthood, and those who experience more coital orgasms, are more likely to remain sexually active in later life. However, mere frequency of intercourse during early adulthood is not significantly related to female sexual interest and activity after middle age. Also, in contrast to men, physical health appears to have little influence on the sexual functioning of older women (Solnick & Corby, 1983).

PROBLEMS OF THE INSTITUTIONALIZED ELDERLY.   Negative stereotypes and the loss of sexual interest are particularly common among institutionalized men and women.

All too many men and women in nursing homes are denied this couple's opportunity for love and affection because of the misguided belief that the aged should not be interested in intimacy.

In one nursing home, 49% of the residents agreed that "sex over 65 is ridiculous" (Kahana, 1976).

Although this decline in sexual activity is due to ill health in some instances, it is furthered by the attitudes and actions of many nursing home personnel. Few institutions provide sufficient privacy for sexual intercourse, and many ignore the desires of nonmarried residents by segregating men and women and/or ridiculing any expressions of sexual interest (Solnick & Corby, 1983; see also Burnside, 1975; Schlessinger & Miller, 1973). Conversely, ending the isolation of male and female residents tends to produce better social adjustment, a richer social life, reduced anxiety, and at least some increases in pleasurable sexual activity (Silverstone & Wynter, 1975; Wasow, 1977). At present, however, the sexual rights of the institutionalized elderly remain an essentially unresolved issue.

AFTERWORD.   Elsewhere in this chapter (and in this book), we have had to conclude that the relationship between aging and important aspects of human behavior is ambiguous. Here, the evidence is clear. Male sexual capacity and interest decline to some extent with increasing age, especially after about age 70, but this decrement is not nearly as great as has been widely believed. The sexual capacity of women decreases relatively little as they grow through adulthood, but the frequency of their sexual activity declines even more than that of men. Women tend to marry men who are older and who are therefore likely to become ill and/or die before the woman does. So women are much more often without a socially acceptable and sexually capable partner.

Nevertheless, many men and women remain sexually active throughout much or all of adulthood. According to Comfort (1974, p. 442), "Most people can and should expect to have sex long after they no longer wish to ride a bicycle." The findings discussed here have led to profound changes in our conception of sexual behavior among older adults. Even more importantly, these discoveries should enable many older adults to liberate themselves from the shackles of negative stereotypes and self-defeating doubts and to enjoy the pleasures of this most intimate form of interpersonal relationship.

Homosexual Relationships

Less is known about the relationship between aging and homosexual activity, possibly because homosexuality has long been regarded as a form of mental illness. In 1973, however, the American Psychiatric Association removed homosexuality from the official list of mental disorders. Currently, homosexuality is considered a mental disorder only if the individual is distressed about his or her homosexuality and would prefer to be more heterosexual (American Psychiatric Association, 1987).

Whatever the reasons, the status of this area resembles that of research on heterosexuality and aging some 50 years ago. According to one common stereotype, homosexual males supposedly find aging to be particularly stressful, lonely, and depressing.

The Myth of the Aging Male Homosexual

One popular myth about the older male homosexual is that he "no longer goes to bars, having lost his physical attractiveness and his sexual appeal to the young men he craves. He is over-sexed, but his sex life is very unsatisfactory. He has been unable to form a lasting relationship with a sexual partner, and he is seldom sexually active anymore. When he does have sex, it is usually in a 'tearoom' (public toilet). He has disengaged from the gay world and his acquaintances in it. He is retreating further and further into the "closet." . . . He is labeled "an old queen," as he has become quite effeminate. (Kelly, 1977, p. 329)

Few empirical studies deal with such issues, however, and the minimal data that do exist offer little support for the prevailing stereotypes. Older homosexual males tend to report that they are still sexually active and their sexual relationships are quite satisfactory (Adelman, 1990; Kelly, 1977; Kimmel, 1977; Pope & Schulz, 1990). Some of these subjects stated that sex became less important as they grew older, but others indicated that their sex lives were now more satisfying than in young adulthood. Virtually all preferred contacts with men of similar ages, rather than with young men. There was also some indication that aging was not overly depressing for these homosexual men because they had previously learned how to cope with living alone, and because they had developed a network of friends on whom to rely for social and sexual companionship.

Data concerning homosexual women are even more sparse, although one study suggests that gay females tend to discontinue sexual activity at an early age (Christenson & Johnson, 1973). If homosexuality continues to be regarded with increasing tolerance, future research may well shed more light on the relationship between this form of interpersonal behavior and aging.

INTERGENERATIONAL RELATIONSHIPS

Parents and Adult Children

As we observed in Chapter 1, more people are living to an older age than ever before. Many of these aging individuals are parents; some 81% of middle-aged and elderly adults have living children (Atchley & Miller, 1980). Because it is statistically normative to have children prior to age 35, most of the children of older Americans are also adults. During the past few decades, therefore, the relationship between parents who are past middle age and their adult children has become increasingly important.

There are two major issues for us to explore in this area. First, are adult children likely to ignore their aging parents in order to put their own interests and children first? That is, does parenthood become significantly less satisfying as one grows past middle age? Second, ill health is more common at older ages. Elderly parents may therefore become partly or wholly dependent on their adult children because of health problems ranging from gradually increasing arthritic disability to a sudden fall that fractures a hip or the ravages of Alzheimer's disease (Chapter 11). How well do those in an intergenerational relationship cope with the demands posed by an elderly parent who requires considerable care?

MYTHS ABOUT AGING

Interpersonal Relations

Myth	Best Available Evidence
Middle-aged and elderly adults have significantly fewer friends than do young adults.	The number of casual friendships does decline to some extent with increasing age. But older adults have as many close friends as do young adults, and these relationships contribute significantly to their overall life satisfaction.

Myth	*Best Available Evidence*
The years after the last child leaves home (the "empty nest") is a time of considerable emotional pain, particularly for women.	The relief from the responsibility of daily child rearing, greater opportunities to indulge personal interests, and increased freedom and privacy most often lead to improved personal well-being.
Few middle-aged adults, and virtually no elderly adults, have any interest in sex.	Many adults remain sexually active throughout much or all of adulthood. The sexual capacity of men does decline with increasing age, but not as much as has been widely believed. There is no evidence that aging has any important effects on the sexual capacity of women.
Adult children caring for an elderly parent with disabilities is the exception rather than the rule because Medicare provides all of the needed health care for older adults.	Family members, including children, provide the majority of support and day-to-day care needed by disabled older adults.
A century ago, elderly parents and their children lived together more often because families were more caring. The modern family is much more isolated, both geographically and emotionally.	There has been no significant change in the mutual caring shown by the American family. A century ago, elderly parents did live with their children more often, but this was due primarily to financial necessity; there was no social security system or variety of private pension plans. Today, more elderly parents live alone because they want to and can afford to do so, but most live no more than a half hour away from at least one adult child.
Most parents age 65 and older are neglected by their adult children who never visit them, or who callously place them in nursing homes at the slightest provocation.	Approximately 80% of parents over age 65 see at least one of their adult children every 1 to 2 weeks. Most families place elderly parents in nursing homes only as a last resort, and with the utmost reluctance.

FREQUENCY OF CONTACT.   According to popular belief, elderly parents are grossly neglected by their children—or, even worse, are callously placed in nursing homes at the slightest provocation and promptly forgotten. This notion is supported by two of the most pervasive cultural myths in the United States, which live on even though they are fallacious. The first of these myths holds that at some unspecified point in the past (perhaps c. 1900), the American family was far more devoted to one another than is the case today.

The Myth of the Classical Devoted Family

> This myth portrays the family of some 100 years ago as "a pretty picture of life down on grandma's farm. There are lots of happy children, and many kinfolk live together in a large rambling house. Everyone works hard. . . . All boys and girls marry, and marry young. Young people, especially girls, are likely to be virginal at marriage and faithful afterward. Though the parents do not arrange their children's marriages, the elders do have the right to reject a suitor and have a strong hand in the final decision. After marriage, the couple lives harmoniously, either near the boy's parents or with them, for the couple is slated to inherit the farm." (Goode, 1963, p. 6)

The second, related myth is that the modern American family has become isolated, and today's children take much worse care of their parents than was the case in the "good old days."

The Myth of the Modern Isolated Nuclear Family

> According to this myth, today's family has "fewer children, and they are economic liabilities rather than assets. They leave the nest at a relatively early age, marry without parental approval or guidance, receive training (at parental expense of course) for occupational advantage in a direction that takes them away from their parents. Contact is limited to occasional letters and obligatory telephone calls on holidays; exceptions to these patterns occur only when the children need money. As the parents experience the inevitable decrements of advancing age, such as widowhood and failing health with the attendant economic exigencies, the children are concerned but not motivated to do anything about it because they are too wrapped up in their own problems; too busy with their own careers, children, and mortgages to spare the time or resources their parents need. . . . [This implies that] if middle-aged children paid more attention to their elderly parents, the parents would be less lonely, better adjusted, happier, and more satisfied with their lives." (Lee, 1985, pp. 22, 26)

Another version of this view characterizes Americans today as "less willing than ever before to invest time, money, and energy in family life," and as turning more to "other groups and activities in this age of the 'me-generation' " (Bengtson, Rosenthal, & Burton, 1996, p. 254).

These myths have been soundly contradicted by empirical data. It is true that since 1900, the proportion of adults past age 65 who live with their children has declined from about 60% to approximately 10%. (Smith, 1979; White House

Conference on Aging, 1981). And many more elderly adults now live alone, especially women (Kobrin, 1976; Michael, Fuchs, & Scott, 1980; Soldo, Sharma, & Campbell, 1984). However, this does not mean that modern elderly parents are more often neglected by their children. The financial status of the aged has improved dramatically during the last 50 years (Chapter 9), so today's older adults can better afford to maintain their independence and live by themselves. Although it was much more common for parents to live with their children circa 1900, there is no evidence that they wanted to; they may well have had little choice in an era that had no social security system or private pension plans (Lee, 1985). Supporting this position is the fact that parents who currently live with their children tend to have extremely low incomes, indicating that they have chosen this course primarily because they cannot afford anything else (Lawton, 1980; Soldo, 1979).

Even though fewer parents now live with their children, the number who reside near at least one adult child has increased. As of 1975, more than half of all older Americans with children lived within 10 minutes' distance of at least one child, and some 75% were no more than a half hour away (Shanas, 1979). Thus the frequency of contact between today's older parents and their adult children is quite high. In one study of subjects in the United States, Britain, and Denmark, over 80% of all elderly parents saw at least one of their adult children during the preceding week (Shanas et al., 1968). More recent findings are similar: Some 55% of older parents saw one adult child within the previous 24 hours, and approximately 80% did so during the past 1 to 2 weeks.

Even when elderly parents become seriously ill, their children maintain frequent contact. About twice as many aged parents are cared for by relatives as are placed in nursing homes and other institutions. Most residents of nursing homes either have no close relatives to call on because they never married or have outlived their children or are so ill that they cannot be cared for at home. Rather than relegating their elderly parents to nursing homes at the slightest excuse, today's adult children typically regard institutionalization with the utmost reluctance and take this step only as a last resort.

QUALITY OF CONTACT. Frequent contact does not in and of itself ensure a rewarding interpersonal relationship. However, research data have also shown that most older parents and adult children have highly positive feelings for one another. In fact, many of these parents feel close enough to their children to use them as confidants (e.g., Atchley & Miller, 1980; Harris & Associates, 1975; Rossi, & Rossi, 1990).

These relationships are motivated by a sense of duty and likely involve the provision of mutual aid. This may take the form of housework, advice, moral support, babysitting, or financial assistance, with the last two of these more often provided by the parents. Thus it appears that many elderly parents continue to provide for their children whatever they can, for as long as they can (normally, at least through age 75). In turn, adult children support their parents when the latter's health or financial condition deteriorates (Soldo & Hill, 1995).

CARING FOR AN ELDERLY PARENT. It is becoming increasingly likely that adult children will have to care for an elderly, infirm parent. The old-old are the most rapidly growing segment of the American population, and the lingering geriatric and terminal illnesses are now the rule rather than the exception (Chapters 11 and 12). To be sure, a lucky few have parents who retain much of their health and independence even in old age.

An Autonomous Elderly Couple

Mr. R., age 98, is troubled by arthritis and some hearing loss, but he still cooks for himself in his New Jersey home. His wife, age 96, can no longer see well and has grown forgetful, but she still does her own shopping. Their 69-year-old married daughter lives a half mile away, and finds it a simple matter to care for her parents. "There are just some little things to worry about," she says, "like whether he locked the back door at night, or has he checked the windows in case of a storm." (*Newsweek*, May 6, 1985)

More often, however, caring for an elderly parent is far more difficult. The demands made on adult children in such situations can be extremely severe, as the following case histories indicate (*Newsweek*, May 6, 1985):

Intergenerational Conflict

Mr. J.'s ailing mother stayed at his home for two months. She had a falling out with his wife during this time, and also expressed displeasure with him. Even though he is 55 years old, "to her I'm still a child," he says. "Of course I try to resist that, but she doesn't think I have enough sense to turn out the lights. She thinks

Adult children are often the primary care providers to their disabled parents.

I'm irresponsible. When I go to light the stove, she gives me hell until I've properly disposed of the match."

A Blind, Paralyzed Widow

Mrs. L., a 79-year-old widow, is blind and paralyzed on one side of her body. Her two adult daughters have to put her to bed and get her up each day, dress her, move her to the dining room, and feed her. On weekends they take her to the park to sit in the sun, or to visit their married sister. The daughters have no time for any private life; neither has married.

A Partly Paralyzed, Incontinent Man

Mr. B. is 85 years old, partly paralyzed, and incontinent. His 60-year-old son hired a home attendant to care for his father, but the attendant found the task far too rigorous and quit in a week. Reluctantly, the son decided on a nursing home. "I had to either make that decision or keep changing his diapers myself," he says. He visits his father two to three times a week, but comes away depressed. "It would be good if Dad died," he says bluntly. "I don't see anything in him that shows me that he's comfortable."

How well does the modern family respond to such challenges? Numerous studies show that today's adult children (primarily daughters) are expending considerable effort and incurring substantial costs to help their elderly parents in time of need. For example, 87% of one sample of 700 elderly persons received at least half of the help they needed from their children or other relatives (Morris & Sherwood, 1984). According to some estimates, the average American woman spends 17 years raising children and 18 years helping aged parents. In fact, the care provided by children (and other kin) has helped to prevent or at least postpone the institutionalization of many elderly parents.

Nevertheless, such kin networks are not without serious problems. Caring for an ill elderly parent can be so demanding that even the most loving, considerate child suffers considerable resentment and guilt. Young parents who have only recently begun to recover from the financial and emotional strain of rearing their own child, or who must still contend with these burdens, may well find it difficult to cope with a parent who is now almost as helpless as an infant. Furthermore, seeing one's formerly authoritative and powerful parent become childishly dependent can prove to be psychologically disturbing. Those children who live far from their parents may be spared this daily anguish, but they must contend with the tactical problems of trying to help from a distance and with the guilt evoked by not being present. As a result, caregivers are three to four times more likely than non-caregivers to report symptoms of depression and anger (Schulz, O'Brien, Bookwala, & Fleissner, 1995; Schulz, Visintainer, & Williamson, 1990). Women are particularly vulnerable in this regard because it is the daughter who most often assumes primary responsibility for the elderly parent. If she is also working and a mother, she may well find this trio of responsibilities leaves her with so little time for leisure and recreation that her health and well-being decline.

Secondly, elderly parents may be less willing to receive help from their children than the children are to provide it. Independence and autonomy are highly valued in our society, and the elderly are no exception. In one study, for example, the majority of elderly adults differed significantly from young adults by stating that they would rather pay a professional for assistance than ask a family member (Brody et al., 1983). Elderly parents know their adult children have their own lives to live and that caring for an invalid is demanding and disruptive. Therefore, they may regard it as demeaning and distasteful to become dependent on their children. Those who take this course may well do so because they have (or believe they have) no other choice, and at considerable cost to their self-esteem and desire for independence (Lee, 1985). Also, parents may find it less pleasant to live with their children because they have much more in common with people of their own age.

These problems are likely to become even more severe in the not-too-distant future. It has been estimated that by the year 2040, the number of Americans over age 85 will increase from the present 2.2 million to nearly 13 million and the number over 65 will grow from 26 million to 66.6 million (see Chapter 1). In about 50 years, then, we may find a large number of old-old adults being cared for by old relatives, which may well be too great a strain for all concerned.

AFTERWORD.   Because family caregivers are likely to need help coping with ill parents and elderly parents are likely to fare better psychologically if they are not forced to depend on their adult children, formal support would seem to be desirable. Virtually every part of the United States does have an agency on aging, which provides basic information and assistance with regard to home health services and other problems. But once a family member assumes in-home responsibility for an elderly parent, the U.S. government takes a hands-off approach. Medicare does not provide for respite care, where a qualified professional fills in for the family caregiver for a few days. Nor does Medicare cover chronic long-term nursing home care, which can easily cost over $40,000 per year (Wiener & Illston, 1996). Caring for the ill elderly is at present a prominent issue among U.S. health policy planners, so some form of federal assistance may perhaps be forthcoming in the foreseeable future.

Empirical data clearly show that today's adult children are doing an outstanding job of caring for their elderly parents. But demographic data indicate that this problem may soon become so widespread as to make outside support essential.

Grandparenting

The increasing human life span has also produced more modern families that span three, or even four, generations. Becoming a grandparent in the United States occurs normatively during middle age (e.g., 40s and 50s). As a result, today's children and young adults are likely to have considerable overlap and at least some contact with one or more grandparents. It has been estimated that

94% of all elderly with children are grandparents and almost 50% are great-grandparents (Kivnick & Sinclair, 1996).

Grandparents are often pictured as having warm and close relationships with their grandchildren, partly because they can enjoy the pleasures of these interactions without having to shoulder parental responsibilities. We have all heard stories of grandfathers who go fishing with their grandsons on a regular basis, grandmothers who spend part of each day teaching their granddaughters to sew or bake cookies, and grandchildren who tenderly care for an aging or ill grandparent. Although some researchers have focused on issues like these, there are still few empirical data dealing with grandparenting (see Hendricks, 1995).

FREQUENCY OF CONTACT. There is no indication that modern grandparents are being neglected by their grandchildren. Among Americans over age 65 who have living grandchildren, about 75% see their grandchildren at least once every week or two, and some 50% do so every few days (Harris & Associates, 1975). Contact tends to be greater with grandmothers than grandfathers, and grandmothers typically report greater satisfaction with these relationships (Thomas, 1995).

Although grandparent-grandchild interactions are frequent, they are usually peripheral in the lives of both parties. As with elderly parents and adult children, grandparents most often live apart from their grandchildren (Atchley, 1977; Roberto & Stroes, 1995). Interactions between grandparents and grandchildren typically take the form of special events, such as an outing or a telephone call, rather than occurring routinely within the household. "The rocking-chair grandparent is no longer an appropriate image; neither is the child carer, cookie baker, or fishing companion" (Troll, 1980, p. 476; see also Hagestad, 1985).

QUALITY OF CONTACT. Some researchers have sought to determine the typical ways in which grandparents behave toward their grandchildren. In one classic study (Neugarten & Weinstein, 1964), interviews of 70 middle-class sets of grandparents revealed five specific styles of behavior:

1. **Formal:** Maintaining a clear distinction between parent and grandparent. Although these grandparents were interested in their grandchildren, they limited their assistance to occasional gifts or babysitting. This style was more common among grandparents past age 65.
2. **Fun-seeker:** Enjoying mutually pleasurable activities with the grandchildren; being informal and playful.
3. **Surrogate Parent:** Assuming the mother's parental responsibilities because she worked outside the home, or was otherwise unable to care for her children. This style was determined by necessity rather than by choice; grandparents preferred not to become surrogate parents unless there was no good alternative. The surrogate parent was almost always the grandmother, rather than the grandfather.
4. **Reservoir of Family Wisdom:** Assuming an authoritarian position and dispensing information, advice, and resources to the grandchildren. A relatively rare style that was more often adopted by grandfathers than by grandmothers.

Grandparenthood provides a rewarding opportunity to indulge one's grandchildren without the responsibilities that burden a parent.
(*Source:* UN/DPI Photo.)

5. **Distant Figure:** Maintaining little contact with the grandchildren, except for such occasions as birthdays or holidays.

Kivnick (1982) investigated the ways in which being a grandparent are meaningful and rewarding. Some 286 grandparents completed a lengthy questionnaire, and the responses were subjected to the mathematical procedure of factor analysis. The results indicated that grandparenthood is rewarding for several reasons. There is the opportunity to spoil and indulge one's grandchildren because grandparents are usually not burdened by the same responsibilities as parents. Grandparenthood provides a form of immortality through clan: The grandparent leaves behind not only children but also grandchildren. Grandparents enjoy receiving the grandchild's respect as a wise, helpful valued elder. Grandparenthood also facilitates a reinvolvement with one's personal past, by recalling relationships with one's own grandparents. However, grandparenthood is more central in the lives of some grandparents than others.

Other researchers have focused on the ways in which grandparents and grandchildren seek to influence one another's attitudes and styles of life. Many grandparents pass along recommended religious, social, and vocational values to their grandchildren (Cherlin & Furstenberg, 1985; Roberto & Stroes, 1995; Troll & Bengtson, 1979). This may be done through such methods as storytelling, giving friendly advice during an outing or visit, or working together on special projects. In turn, grandchildren may introduce their grandparents to such recent cultural innovations as new toys or styles of dress, thereby helping the grandparents to reduce their feelings of alienation from an ever-changing world. However, there is usually an unspoken agreement to protect the relationship by

avoiding topics likely to cause conflict. For example, during the 1960s, grandparents and radical student grandchildren were unlikely to discuss such volatile
issues as hair length and clothing preferences. These mutually avoided, sensitive
areas have been referred to as "demilitarized zones" (Hagestad, 1978).

Despite efforts like these, social scientists have been unable to agree on
standard styles of grandparenting. One possible reason is that grandparents may
vary in age from 40 to 100 or more, and grandchildren may vary from newborn
infants to age 60 or older. There may well be little common ground between
the way a 50-year-old adult treats a 2-year-old child and the behavior of an 80-
year-old adult toward a 16-year-old adolescent, even though both cases involve
interactions between a grandparent and a grandchild. For example, some data
indicate that grandparents age 50 to 70 show more positive emotions about
their grandchildren than do grandparents in their 40s and 80s (Troll, 1980). Thus
grandparent-grandchild interactions may be too idiosyncratic to be described in
terms of generally applicable styles. (See Bengtson & Robertson, 1985.)

THEORIES OF INTERPERSONAL BEHAVIOR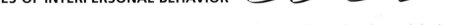

In the preceding pages, we have concentrated primarily on the what and the how
of adult interpersonal relationships: what happens to the number of friendships
with increasing age, how grandparents behave toward their grandchildren,
whether older parents and their adult children interact frequently, and so on. In
addition, social scientists are keenly interested in explaining why adults behave
as they do toward other people (Marshall, 1995).

For example, we have seen that elderly parents are considerably more reluctant to seek help from their adult children than the children are to provide it.
Why should this be so? The fear of disrupting the children's lives is a sensible
explanation, but a very specific one. A more general theoretical argument might
be that people are uncomfortable with relationships in which power is markedly
unequal. Few individuals enjoy receiving a great deal from a loved one or close
friend if they are unable to give anything in return. According to this theory,
then, adults who are unable to maintain a fairly equal amount of give-and-take
in an interpersonal relationship will dislike this relationship and tend to avoid it.
(See Lee, 1985.) Theories like this one have the potential advantage of explaining a wide range of adult interpersonal behavior, rather than dealing only with a
specific example.

During the past three decades, social scientists have proposed several such
theories to explain the interpersonal behavior of older adults. Devising a useful
theory is not an easy task, and no one of these theories is as yet regarded as
clearly superior to all of the others.

Role Theory

DEFINITION.   At any given point in the life course we occupy a number of different roles, many of which are related to the age and gender of the individual. A

person might be student, a mother, a retired person, or a widow. Each of these roles carries with it specific expectations about the behavior of the individual occupying that role. Additionally, roles confer a certain status to individuals within society. According to some theorist the combination of age and gender are powerful determinants of people's social roles and their interpersonal behavior (Moen, 1995).

Another way of thinking about roles is in terms of social integration, the degree to which individuals have formal attachments to society (George, 1995). Examples of attachments might include church membership or participation in voluntary organizations. Being socially integrated can be beneficial to the individual in a number of ways. It can give meaning to life; it can be a source of support, and it may provide access to important resources and knowledge about how to deal with life stresses. It should be no surprise therefore that individuals who are highly socially integrated typically enjoy better mental and physical well-being.

CONCEPTUAL DIFFICULTIES.　　Role theory continues to be a useful framework for describing and understanding the interpersonal behavior of individuals. It provides a means for connecting individual behaviors and feelings to the broad social structure of society and it encourages us to think about the interconnectedness of one stage in life with subsequent stages that follow. However, like many theories in the social sciences role theory is better at description than prediction and explanation. It helps us make sense of what we observe, but its value is more limited in helping us predict the behavior of individuals or societies.

Exchange Theory

DEFINITION.　　Our relationships with other people may bring us material or non-material rewards. For example, we may receive compliments that increase our self-esteem, entertainment, attention and affection, a valued gift, or obedience. We may also incur various costs, such as having to endure boredom or irritation, suffering anxiety (as on a first date), spending money, or investing time (which might otherwise be devoted to useful solitary activities). That is, interpersonal relationships can be viewed as processes wherein the people involved try to maximize the rewards and minimize the costs.

According to **exchange theory,** interpersonal interactions will be initiated and continued so long as they are sufficiently rewarding for both parties—that is, if the rewards exceed the costs. At any given moment in an interpersonal relationship, the rewards enjoyed by each party are unlikely to be precisely equal. However, the person who is currently gaining more from the relationship is obligated to try and restore a more equal balance in the future. If, instead, one individual is consistently unable to provide sufficient rewards, the other is likely to terminate the relationship because the costs are too great. An interpersonal relationship involves give-and-take, and it will not survive if one individual gives or receives too little (that is, if the relationship is imbalanced).

EXCHANGE THEORY AND AGING.　　Because the elderly tend to have less power and fewer resources than younger adults, their interpersonal relationships are particularly likely to be imbalanced. The only apparent recourse is to use compliance as a reward and to yield consistently to the wishes of the other person. This ultimately results in a serious loss of self-respect, however, whereupon the elderly are likely to withdraw from social activity. According to exchange theory, then, the aged presumably engage in fewer interpersonal relationships because of their inability to reward other people and maintain balanced interactions.

CONCEPTUAL DIFFICULTIES. There are several conceptual difficulties with the exchange approach. First of all, intrinsic, self-determined rewards can compensate for the absence of any specific returns from another person. Some individuals continue to interact with the elderly on the grounds of duty, charity, or a genuine interest in the aged, even though they obtain no extrinsic rewards at all. This implies that interactions that are imbalanced in terms of extrinsic rewards may continue to exist, rather than terminating as exchange theory predicts. (See Schulz & Manson, 1984.)

In addition, the effective reward and cost value of any interpersonal interaction is deceptively difficult to calculate. Our satisfaction with an interaction depends to a great extent on how the associated rewards and costs compare to our prior expectations, rather than on their absolute value. If, for example, we receive moderate rewards from an interpersonal interaction, we will tend to be happy if we expected very little but rather unhappy if we expected a great deal, even though the amount of the reward is the same in both cases.

Exchange theory has raised some interesting issues. However, these conceptual difficulties indicate that it cannot be accepted as a definitive explanation of the interpersonal behavior of the aged.

Disengagement, Activity, and Continuity Theories

DEFINITION. According to disengagement theory, there is a process of mutual withdrawal between the aged and society (Cumming & Henry, 1961). Elderly individuals withdraw from society because they realize their capacities have diminished, and they wish to protect themselves as much as possible from failure and rejection. Society withdraws from the elderly because it needs to replace them with younger, more capable persons in order to remain vibrant and viable. This mutual disengagement takes the form of a decrease in the number and diversity of contacts between the aged and society, and it is assumed to be universal, inevitable, and mutually satisfying.

Almost from its inception, **disengagement theory** sparked a controversy that has persisted for more than a decade. The major opposition has come from proponents of **activity theory,** which posits that the social activity of the elderly is positively correlated with their satisfaction with life. Activity theory does agree with disengagement theory in one respect: As we grow older, our social activity is assumed to decrease. But activity theory states that this decrease is dissatisfying and those older adults who are exceptions to this rule are happier. In contrast, disengagement theory predicts that reduced social activity is satisfying to the aged.

A third perspective, referred to as **continuity theory,** has been proposed by Atchley (1989). The basic idea of this theory is that over time individuals develop a strong sense of who they are, and they attempt to maintain this sense of self over time. Thus individuals will seek out social situations that support the view of themselves, thereby enabling a sense of continuity over time.

CONCEPTUAL DIFFICULTIES.   Choosing between these divergent theories would seem to be an easy task, but this is not the case. All three views are supported by a sizable amount of research evidence, and the same data has, at different times, been interpreted as favorable to different theories. Because one test of a good theory is that it can be effectively disconfirmed (and discarded), and this does not appear to be true for activity theory, disengagement theory, and continuity theory, we may reasonably conclude that all of these theories are at least somewhat flawed (Marshall, 1995; Schulz & Manson, 1984). It has been argued that these theories are not stated precisely enough for them to be convincingly disconfirmed even if they are incorrect, and they fail to take into account the complicated nature of the interactions between the elderly and society. At the same time, these theories play an important role in helping us to organize, describe, and think about the nature of interpersonal behavior throughout the adult life course.

AFTERWORD.   Because theories are by definition tentative explanations about reality, they often appear to be frustratingly inaccurate. However, they serve an important purpose. Established facts are often lacking in scientific work, and a theory offers guidelines that will serve us in the absence of more precise information. Although some of the theories previously discussed appear to be marred by conceptual flaws, all have points of interest and importance. Furthermore, these theories tend to be more complicated than our overview might indicate. Therefore, we encourage you to obtain more information by consulting the original sources cited in the preceding pages.

SUMMARY

Classifying Major Life Transitions

Most of us experience many major life transitions between birth and death. One useful way to classify these events is according to the age at which they occur: An event is temporally normative if it occurs at an age that is typical for most people in that culture and temporally non-normative if it occurs at an atypical age. A second good way to classify life events is according to their frequency, regardless of age: An event is statistically normative if it happens to the majority of individuals in a given culture, and statistically non-normative if it is experienced by relatively few people. Non-normative events are likely to be quite stressful, and adults who must deal with many such events are more vulnerable to physical and psychological illnesses or even premature death.

Adult Friendships

Adult friendships have been defined as voluntary, mutual, flexible, terminable, equal, reciprocal, and emotional. Three basic styles of friendship have been identified. The independent style involves a lack of best or close friends, personal self-sufficiency, and maintaining psychological distance from other people. The discerning style involves drawing a clear distinction between a small number of close, trusted friends and casual acquaintances. The gregarious style involves psychological closeness with a fairly large number of people and optimism about the prospects of making new friends.

Friendships can serve a variety of important purposes. They provide opportunities for self-disclosure and furnish us with psychological support. We tend to choose friends who have similar beliefs and personalities; who are physically attractive, intelligent and competent, pleasant and agreeable, and emotionally stimulating; who like and approve of us; and who live close to us.

Although casual friendships tend to become less frequent with increasing age, the number of close friends that one has remains relatively stable throughout the adult life span. Apparently, as we grow older, we sift through our interpersonal relationships and retain those that we value the most. Close friendships contribute significantly to the well-being and overall life satisfaction of older adults. Because of the well-known generation gap, the elderly are likely to have more in common with people of similar ages than with their children.

Love, Marriage, and Divorce

Various conceptions of love have been proposed by social scientists. These include such distinctions as passionate love versus companionate love, D-love versus B-love, and narcissism versus genuine love. Efforts have also been made to measure love psychometrically, using written questionnaires.

Many relationships that end in marriage proceed through a fairly standard sequence which begins with casual dating and ends with formal engagement. In any loving relationship, different factors tend to be important during different stages. It also appears that there is an inverse relationship between attraction and attachment, with many long-term loving relationships becoming more placid over the years. Among couples married for many years, the most commonly cited reason for the enduring relationship is "My spouse is my best friend." Other factors typical of lengthy marriages include meaningful communication and self-disclosure, openness, trustworthiness, caring, believing that marriage is a long-term commitment, and avoiding displays of intensely expressed anger. Families with children tend to follow traditional marital roles, with the wife doing the housework; role equality is most often found in childless marriages. The years after the last child leaves home (the "empty nest") most often lead to improved personal well-being and marital relationships because of the relief from the responsibility of daily child rearing, greater opportunities to follow personal interests, and increased freedom and privacy. When the husband becomes seriously ill, the negative impact is even greater on caregiving wives than on grown children who serve as caregivers.

Marriage entails some risk; approximately one of every two marriages ends in divorce. Divorce is most common among adults age 30 to 45, black females, and those who married prior to age 21. Yet more than half a million Americans age 65 or more are divorced, with many new cases registered each year. Common causes of divorce include jealousy, moodiness, infidelity, irritating habits, spending money foolishly, and drinking or using drugs. Divorced people tend to proceed through several behavioral stages, ranging from isolation to reestablishing social contact. Divorce is typically a traumatic experience for all concerned, most notably women and the spouse who did not initiate the divorce. But it may be argued that if a marriage is truly unbearable, the least of evils may well be to end it and give each spouse the opportunity to find happiness elsewhere. The emotional pain caused by a broken marriage does not prevent many adults from remarrying; more than 20% of the current marriages in the United States include at least one spouse who has been previously married.

Sexuality and Aging

Until recently, very little was known about the relationship between sexuality and aging. As a result, it was widely assumed there was nothing to know—that is, older adults had no interest in sex. During the past few decades, however, we have become increasingly aware that there is, indeed, sexual life after middle age.

Insofar as young adults are concerned, men tend to be more sexually active than women. There is some indication that the frequency of sexual behavior has increased during the last few decades, especially among younger adults and young women, although these data are inflated by cohort effects. The frequency of sexual behavior among married couples does tend to decrease from young adulthood to middle age, but this may be due largely to such environmental constraints as the presence of young children.

Male sexual capacity has been found to decline with increasing age, but not nearly as much as had been widely believed. There is likely to be a significant drop in sexual ability and interest at about age 50, and again at about age 70 to 80. As age increases, fewer men are sexually active, and those who are active are less so than younger men. Nevertheless, a substantial number of men continue to engage in sex throughout much or even all of their adult lives. Men are more likely to remain interested in sex through middle and old age if they engaged in sex more often during young adulthood, if they are in good health, and if they believe they can maintain effective sexual behavior as they grow older.

There is no evidence that aging causes any significant declines in female sexual capacity. However, sexual activity among women does decrease markedly with increasing age. Because women tend to marry men who are older, and men tend to die at a younger age, women are more likely to be without a socially acceptable and sexually capable partner. Women who enjoy sex more during young adulthood are more likely to remain sexually active in later life, provided an appropriate partner is available.

At present, the sexual rights of the institutionalized elderly remains an essentially unresolved issue. Nor is much known about the relationship between aging and homosexual behavior.

Intergenerational Relationships

Contrary to popular belief, modern American families are no less caring than were families of some 100 years ago. It is true that since 1900, the number of elderly parents who live with their children has declined markedly. But the financial status of the aged has improved dramatically during the past 50 years, so today's older adults can better afford to maintain their independence and live by themselves. In fact, the number of older parents who reside near at least one adult child has increased over the years. Thus today's adult children see their elderly parents often and expend considerable effort and money to help their parents in time of need. Children typically regard the institutionalization of an aged parent as a last resort, and the caregiving they provide has helped to prevent or at least postpone it in many instances.

Nevertheless, the demands of caring for an ill parent can cause even the most loving and dedicated child to become resentful and guilty. There is also some indication that elderly parents are less willing to receive help from their children than the children are to give it, primarily because this loss of independence is demeaning. Because the number of old-old and old adults is expected to increase dramatically during the next 50 years, the problem of caring for the ill elderly is likely to become particularly acute in the not-too-distant future.

There is no indication that grandparents are being neglected by their grandchildren; contact is frequent, albeit typically peripheral in the lives of both. Although some researchers have tried to establish the ways in which grandparents behave toward their grandchildren, it appears that such interactions are too idiosyncratic to be described in terms of generally applicable styles.

Theories of Interpersonal Behavior

Social scientists are also interested in explaining why adults behave as they do toward other people, and various theories have been devised for this purpose. Role theory argues that we occupy social roles often determined by our age and gender and these roles carry with them structured sets of expectations for how we behave. Exchange theory views interpersonal relationships as processes wherein the people involved seek to maximize their rewards and minimize their costs. This theory posits that the elderly engage in fewer interpersonal relationships because they are unable to reward other people and maintain balanced interactions. However, this theory suffers from important conceptual difficulties.

Disengagement theory posits a process of mutual and satisfying withdrawal between the aged and society. In contrast, activity theory holds that any substantial decrease in interpersonal activity among the elderly is dissatisfying to them. Although both of these theories have stimulated important research, neither one appears valid enough to stand alone as an explanation of adult interpersonal behavior. Continuity theory argues that we develop a sense of who we are in early adulthood and work to maintain that sense of self throughout our adult life course.

Because theories are, by definition, tentative explanations about reality, they often appear to be frustratingly inaccurate. But established facts are often lacking in scientific work, and theories offer guidelines that will serve us in the absence of more precise information. All of these theories have points of interest and importance and have contributed to our understanding of aging and interpersonal behavior.

STUDY QUESTIONS

1. Why is an event likely to be more stressful if it is temporally non-normative, such as beginning college at age 50 or becoming widowed at age 35? Is a statistically non-normative event, such as having a stroke, likely to be even more stressful if it is also temporally non-normative? Why or why not? Have you ever experienced an event that was temporally or statistically non-normative? How stressful was this event?

2. Of the purposes of adult friendships discussed in this chapter, which ones are most important to you when forming a friendship? Are all of these purposes satisfied by one close friend, or do different friends satisfy different purposes? Which style of friendship do you prefer from a friend? Which style (if any) best describes your behavior? Which of your current friends is most likely to be your friend 20 years from now? Why?

3. Of the various reasons why marriages endure (as presented in this chapter), which would be most important to you when deciding whether or not to marry someone? What advice would you give to a friend who is seeking a marriage partner and wants to significantly reduce the probability of divorce?

4. Based on the empirical evidence presented in this chapter, what advice would you give to a middle-aged person who wants to maintain a satisfying sexual relationship with his or her spouse? Would your recommendations differ for males and females?

5. According to current research data, are families of today more isolated and less devoted to one another than families of 100 years ago? What changes in our society might have created a false impression in this regard?

TERMS TO REMEMBER

Activity theory
B-love
Companionate love
Continuity theory
Discerning style of friendship
Disengagement theory
D-love
Empty nest
Exchange theory

Gregarious style of friendship
Independent style of friendship
Passionate love
Self-disclosure
Statistically non-normative life event
Statistically normative life event
Temporally non-normative life event
Temporally normative life event

WORK AND RETIREMENT

People work for many reasons. The most obvious of these is financial: Work enables us to support ourselves and our families. In addition, work may be interesting for its own sake. A writer, a carpenter, or a mechanic may derive considerable satisfaction from creating an innovative book, a well-crafted piece of furniture, or a finely tuned automobile engine. For many people, work supports their self-esteem and sense of identity. Society expects men in particular to hold a job and accords greater respect to certain types of workers (e.g., physicians and judges). In fact, when a person is asked, "Who are you?", occupation is one of the most frequently given answers. Work also offers important social rewards and punishments because it involves interactions with co-workers, supervisors, subordinates, and/or clients. If you are male, you are likely to work during half of your life; if you are female, for approximately two to three decades. Modern men and women spend more years at work than did their counterparts in 1900, particularly women. (See Figure 9–1.)

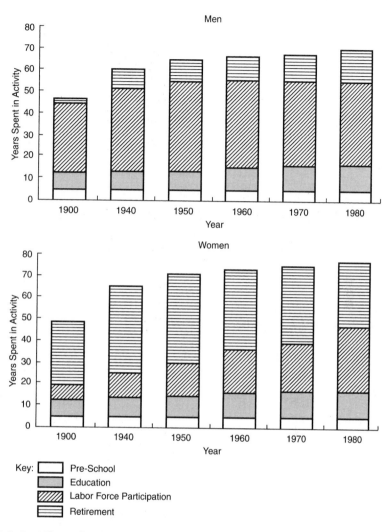

FIGURE 9–1   Life cycle distribution of education, labor force participation, retirement, and work in the home: 1900–1980.
(*Source:* U.S. Senate Special Committee on Aging (1987–1988).)

Because work is such a major aspect of human endeavor, the relationship between work and aging is of considerable importance, and there are various interesting and provocative issues for us to consider. With so many more of us living to old age, there may well be an increase in the number of middle-aged and older adults who wish to work. Are these older adults employment risks? That is, are they likely to perform more poorly, to develop negative attitudes that will interfere with organizational goals, or to become injured or ill? Or are older adults as competent as younger employees, but more likely to be the targets of unfair stereotypes and prejudice? Are more women of various ages seeking employment instead of motherhood? How does this affect their satisfaction with their adult years?

Most people expect they will someday retire from the world of work. Is this likely to be a painful experience? Are retirees more likely to suffer major psychological and physical disorders, or even death, because they are no longer needed at work? Does retirement cause such a severe drop in income that the retiree's standard of living declines substantially? Should retirees expect an increase in marital difficulties now that they must spend day and night with their spouses? As these questions indicate, our discussion of work and aging must also include the issue of retirement.

This chapter focuses on three major areas: first, work and its relationship to age and gender; second, retirement, its dynamics, and its likely effects on retirees and their families; and third, the economic future of the elderly in the United States, including the role of Social Security, Medicare, and Medicaid.

WORK AND ADULT DEVELOPMENT

Intrinsic and Extrinsic Aspects of Work

Work affects the quality of our lives in two important ways. One is direct, or **intrinsic,** and involves our satisfaction and dissatisfaction with the events that take place on the job. The other is indirect, or **extrinsic,** which refers to the influence of work on such nonwork areas as home and family life (Kahn, 1981; Rice, 1984).

Intrinsically, work may be engrossing and self-fulfilling or tedious and unpleasant. Extrinsically, work may or may not provide good housing, food, clothing, education for one's children, and recreation. Some individuals value the intrinsic aspects of work more highly; some are more concerned with the extrinsic aspects. Nevertheless, work has a pronounced effect on our overall well-being. (See Figure 9–2.)

Low-level and low-income jobs may compel an employee to live in meager surroundings, subsist on bare necessities, and endure a boring and tedious workday. Higher-level positions tend to provide a better standard of living and more interesting work, but are not always extrinsically advantageous; such jobs may have an adverse effect on an employee's family relationships because they are so stressful and time consuming. In one study (Evans & Bartolomé, 1980), some 40% of the wives of managers reported that their husbands' stress at work spilled over into their home lives.

> The Relationship Between the Quality of Work Life
> and the Quality of Nonwork Life
>
> "What annoys me is when he comes home tense and exhausted," observed the wife of one manager who was in her early thirties and had been married for eleven years. "He flops into a chair and turns on the TV. Or else he worries and it

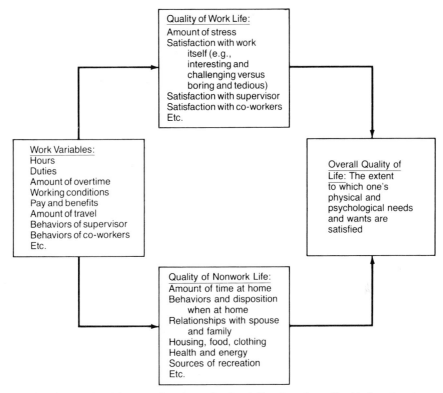

Note. Any single work variable may affect the quality of work life only or the quality of both work and nonwork life. Also any single work variable may have effects that are positive, negative, or both. For example, more overtime may lead to better housing (through greater income), but also to less time at home and poorer health. A change to more challenging and interesting duties may improve both the quality of work and nonwork life (because the employee is happier), or it may improve the quality of work life but have an adverse effect on the quality of nonwork life (because the employee neglects the family to spend more time at work, resulting in more marital strife).

FIGURE 9–2 Relationships among work variables, quality of life at work, quality of life away from work, and overall quality of life.
(*Source:* Modified from Rice (1984).)

drives me up the wall. If he's happy, that's OK. But three years ago he had a very tough job. He was always at the office, even weekends. We had no holidays at all and he was always tense at home—when he was home, that is. . . . I think he should get out of the commercial U.S.A.-type rat race." Another manager had been dissatisfied with his job for many years. His fifty-year-old wife commented: "I think that his work has an enormous effect on our family life, but he doesn't. We've often had violent arguments about it. He considers himself as one of those men who doesn't rant and rave and destroy his family, even when he is having problems at his work. And there I agree. . . . Instead, he closes up like a shell. Total closure. . . . He just doesn't exist. He's completely absent. It's quite clear that you can't reproach him for being disagreeable or aggressive, but it's just as bad in its way. . . . It's a big burden for a wife to bear."

If the employee's job satisfaction is high, there may instead be a positive spillover into the home and family life. According to one wife, "[My husband] really enjoys his work. . . . It's so much easier to live with someone who is happy." However, an intense interest in the job may provoke marital strife because the employee spends too little time with the spouse. "My wife feels that I should work less hard, travel less, and be content with a smaller salary," said one manager. "Sure, we don't need the money that much, but that isn't the point. What she doesn't realize is that I work for the satisfaction that it gives me. If I didn't work as hard, I'd be much less satisfied. I'd be miserable when I'm at home, and things would be even worse than now."

Thus the relationship between work and aging is important not only because we spend so much of our lives at work, but also because work significantly affects our satisfaction with life in general (Rowe & Kahn, 1998).

Work and Aging

JOB PERFORMANCE.   As we observed in Chapter 4, some sensory, motor, cognitive, and physiological capacities decline significantly with increasing age. Thus in laboratory studies it has been shown that older persons may be particularly disadvantaged when performing complex, demanding tasks that require monitoring and responding to multiple sources and types of information. For jobs that require these abilities, corresponding age-related decrements in performance may also be expected. To illustrate, airline pilots who reach age 60 are legally prohibited from flying commercial airplanes because of declines in sensory and processing abilities.

However, these types of jobs are not very representative of the vast majority of jobs that people hold. For most occupations it is appropriate to apply more practical criteria to assess performance, such as supervisory ratings, productivity indices (e.g., sales volume) turnover, absenteeism, and accident rates. Using records of productivity, researchers in Britain and the United States found higher rates of productivity among workers in their 50s than in their teens or 20s. Peak productivity occurred in the 40s and 50s and then declined between 2% and 16% thereafter (Cleveland & Shore, 1996).

Findings on age and turnover rates also suggest that older workers are more likely to stay on the job and are likely to have fewer avoidable absences from work. But there is an important exception to this trend: Those who suffer from chronic ill health have higher rates of absenteeism because they require more time to convalesce. These findings imply that, rather than rejecting older job applicants out of hand, organizations can obtain valuable employees by ascertaining the health of these applicants relative to the requirements of the job. Finally, although research results are mixed, the most common finding regarding age and accident rates is that they are lower among older workers (aged 55 and over) when compared to workers age 24 and younger and about the same when compared to workers aged 25 to 44 (Cleveland & Shore, 1996). However, when older workers do sustain an injury, they are more likely to be disabled and to require more time to recover (Doering, Rhodes, & Schuster, 1983).

Aging appears to have little detrimental effect in some professional and artistic fields, and may even be related to improved performance. As we observed in Chapter 6, people who are highly creative in early adulthood tend to remain so as they grow older. In fact, artists and musicians often do their best work late in life: Dali, Monet, Picasso, and Arthur Rubinstein made outstanding contributions during their 60s, 70s, and 80s. Conversely, deteriorating physical skills force most professional athletes to retire by age 35 or 40. The most productive years for mathematicians occur during their 20s and 30s, and their performance declines markedly with each decade. Therefore, even the greatest mathematicians must spend most of their lives burdened with the knowledge that they have passed their prime. Age-related decrements in job performance are also found in other physical sciences. When Nobel laureate I. I. Rabi was asked about the age at which physicists tend to run down, he replied,

> It very much depends on the individual.... I've seen people run down at thirty, at forty, at fifty. I think it must be basically neurological or physiological. The mind ceases to operate with the same richness and association. The information retrieval part sort of goes, along with the interconnections. I know that when I was in my late teens and early twenties, the world was just a Roman candle—rockets all the time.... You lose that sort of thing as time goes on.... Physics is an otherworld thing; it requires a taste for the unseen, even unheard of.... These faculties die off somehow when you grow up.... Profound curiosity happens when children are young.... Once you are sophisticated, you know too much—far too much. (Gardner, 1983, p. 154)

The most justified conclusion appears to be that age often bears little or no relationship to job performance, but some exceptions may be expected in certain jobs and professions.

AGE AND JOB TRAINING.   Is there truth to the old maxim that "you can't teach an old dog new tricks"? Findings from laboratory studies reported in Chapter 5 would suggest that when the content to be learned is very novel and the criterion for success is speed in completing training, then older workers might have more difficulty than younger workers. Research on the effectiveness of training interventions indicate that older workers do learn less quickly than their younger counterparts. However, this difference is small and typically inconsequential in most applied work settings. In those occupations that "require frequent training in new work methods, older workers may be more costly to the employer and less productive than younger workers" (Cleveland & Shore, 1996, pp. 632–633).

JOB SATISFACTION.   Throughout much of history, work was regarded as a necessary evil: arduous and demanding, valued for the extrinsic benefits that it provided, and rarely (if ever) gratifying for its own sake. To cite one famous example, a major attraction of the biblical Garden of Eden was the lack of any need to work; Adam was punished for eating the forbidden fruit by being told by God, "In the sweat of thy face shalt thou eat bread."

In most occupations, work performance does not decrease with age.

This gloomy conception of work has changed considerably during the last half century, facilitated in part by the discoveries of industrial social psychology. Research has shown that if an organization takes the trouble to make the workplace more conducive to the needs and wants of its employees, it may well reap such benefits as reduced absenteeism and turnover—and perhaps improved production as well, although the relationship between job satisfaction and productivity has proved to be considerably more complicated than might be expected. Also, as our society has become more concerned with humanitarian issues, we are less willing to accept the belief that an activity which occupies so much of our time and energy should cause extensive dissatisfaction. Although there are more than a few employers who still retain the traditional concept of work, the importance of intrinsic job variables has achieved widespread acceptance (as we have seen). Thus the concept of job satisfaction currently encompasses such aspects as the work itself (e.g., interesting versus boring), opportunities for autonomy and control (such as the freedom to decide how to do your work), chances for advancement, and relationships with the supervisor and co-workers, as well as such traditional aspects as pay, fringe benefits, working conditions, and job security.

The importance of some of these work variables appears to vary from early to late adulthood. One study found that young adults were more concerned with such intrinsic factors as chances for advancement, recognition and approval, and enjoyment of their work. Older employees tended to be more concerned with pay, working conditions, and company policy regarding such issues as coffee breaks and absenteeism. In another study dealing with engineers age 20 to 69, younger adults once again proved to be more interested in opportunities for promotion and for professional and personal development, whereas older workers were less willing to move to a new city. However, such aspects of the job as pay increases, feeling a sense of accomplishment, working on challenging projects, and having good relations with one's supervisors were important to young and old workers alike (Breaugh & DiMarco, 1979). Although the findings in this area are somewhat equivocal, opportunities for promotion and developing one's skills appear to be more important to young adults than to middle-aged and older workers.

In general, however, the relationship between aging and job satisfaction is far from clear (Cleveland & Shore, 1996). Some theorists have suggested that this relationship is U-shaped: Satisfaction is initially high for the new employee because of a honeymoon effect, declines as time goes by and reality sets in, and then increases because the worker forms more accurate expectations of the rewards that can be derived from the job. Other investigators have reported a more or less linear relationship between age and job satisfaction, with older employees tending to be more satisfied. The data are too equivocal to permit any firm conclusions, but there is no convincing evidence that older workers tend to be less satisfied with their jobs than younger adults or are more likely to develop morale problems (Doering, Rhodes, & Schuster, 1983). If anything, the reverse appears more likely to be true: Very dissatisfied younger adults may well quit and find jobs more to their liking before they reach more advanced ages, but middle-aged and older workers are likely to have so much difficulty finding new jobs that they learn to be satisfied with what they have.

PROBLEMS OF THE OLDER WORKER. The Older American Act defines an "older" worker as one at or past the age of 55. In many respects, these older workers face significantly greater problems than do young adults.

Older employees are less likely to lose their jobs than are younger workers, due in part to their seniority. However, they find it much more difficult to obtain a job if they do become unemployed. To be sure, the Age Discrimination in Employment Act of 1967 prohibited the denial of employment to applicants over 40 because of their age. And in 1986, the act was amended to prohibit job termination on the basis of age, at any age. Furthermore, many older adults are highly competent, have positive attitudes, and are less likely to be injured or absent than are young employees. Nevertheless, severe **age discrimination** still exists in the world of work.

Between 1979 and 1983, the number of age discrimination complaints increased by some 300%, and more than $24.6 million was awarded by the courts to over 5,000 individuals because of violations of the ADEA (Atchley, 1985). By 1993, the number of age discrimination complaints reached 15,000 (Atchley, 1996). Furthermore, there is good reason to believe that these figures seriously understate the actual extent of job-related age discrimination. Many people undoubtedly fail to file for damages because they are unaware of the protection offered by the ADEA, because they erroneously believe it is extremely difficult to file a complaint, or because they despair of ever proving their rejections were due to age. Case histories like the following are far from uncommon.

A 59-Year-Old Master Printer

A large printing company that published several popular magazines ceased operations and closed its plant. Seniority thus offered no protection to Mr. H., a master printer with 42 years of experience. Mr. H. had very strong ties to his present community; he had been born there, many of his relatives and all of his friends lived there, and he was active in his church and in local politics. To remain there, he was willing to change professions and to accept significantly less money than he had made as a printer. Jobs were available in local manufacturing companies, and his skills would have made it easy for him to adapt to their machinery. Nevertheless, he could not secure employment. Understandably bitter, he reluctantly opted for early retirement at age 62. (Atchley, 1985, pp. 189–190)

Such age discrimination appears to be due in part to negative stereotypes about older workers. In one study, a sample of 42 business students was asked how they would deal with various job problems:

◆ A recently hired shipping room employee who seemed unresponsive to customer calls for service.
◆ Whether to terminate or retain a computer programmer whose skills had become obsolete.
◆ Whether to transfer an employee to a higher-paying but more demanding job.
◆ Whether to hire someone for a position that required not only knowledge of the field, but also the capacity to make quick judgments.
◆ Whether to honor a request from a production staff employee to attend a conference dealing with new theories and research relevant to production systems.
◆ Whether to promote an employee to a marketing job that required fresh solutions to challenging problems and a high degree of creative and innovative behavior.

When the employees in these situations were described as "older," they were more likely to be fired or turned down for the job or promotion than when they were characterized as "younger." Because the work-related qualifications of these hypothetical employees were otherwise identical, the adverse treatment could only have been due to age. Although this study dealt only with students, research evidence also indicates that managers unfairly stereotype older workers as resistant to change, uncreative, slow to make decisions, and untrainable.

Age discrimination is also caused by the nature of organizational fringe benefits. Pensions for older workers are more costly to employers because contributions must be spread over a shorter period. Health insurance costs are also considerably higher for those age 45 to 65 than for young adults. Employers may therefore reject older applicants or try to phase out older workers so as not to incur these greater expenses, even though the ADEA prohibits justifying such decisions on the grounds of high pension costs.

In sum: Despite legal safeguards, age discrimination is still a problem in the world of work. All too many older workers are unfairly denied the opportunity to earn needed income, fulfill their potentials, satisfy their need for self-respect, and enjoy the other rewards that the workplace has to offer. And all too many short-sighted organizations fail to improve their production and profits because they refuse to employ these potentially competent, valuable workers.

MIDLIFE CAREER CHANGES.   If changing jobs is so difficult for those over 40, midlife career changes would seem to pose even greater problems. Some popular periodicals and scientific researchers contend that midlife career changes are fairly common. However, little statistical evidence supports this conclusion (Atchley, 1985).

According to one study, which focused on men in their 30s and 40s, midlife career changes are most often due to three factors: failing to realize one's potential in the first career, finding a new career that is potentially more satisfying, or changing one's life goals due to such events as divorce, widowhood, or sudden unemployment. But another study of managerial and professional men age 34 to 54 indicated that such career changes are more often due to external causes, such as losing one's old job, rather than to the employee's wishes and intentions. Some 34% of this sample changed careers solely because of external circumstances; another 26% experienced external pressures and also wanted to change careers. Only 17% changed their careers just because they wanted to (Thomas, 1977). Given the prevalence of age discrimination in the workplace, it would seem that midlife career changes may not be as feasible as some theorists believe.

AFTERWORD.   The study of work and aging is more problematic than might be apparent. Job satisfaction is a multidimensional variable, and there is some indication that aging is more closely related to some facets than to others (e.g., the importance of chances for advancement). Job productivity is also a multidimensional variable: The quality of an individual's work is not necessarily related to the quantity that he or she produces, and many jobs lack any obvious or easily obtainable quantitative measure of performance (e.g., teaching, clinical psychology, politics). In fact, the problem of determining satisfactory criteria of job performance has often proved to be a major stumbling block in industrial psychology research. When we also recall the limitations of chronological age as an index of human capacities, it is hardly surprising that relatively few clear relationships between aging and work variables have emerged from the research literature. Instead, such variables as job level and job complexity appear to be more important than age per se. Older workers are likely to be more experienced, to have reached higher-level positions, and to have more challenging and demanding jobs, and it is these aspects that are more closely related to their job performance and satisfaction.

Insofar as age discrimination at work is concerned, more definitive conclusions are justified. It is eminently fair to exclude older workers from jobs that they can no longer perform adequately because of cognitive or physical deterioration. Some would also argue that providing more jobs for older workers would reduce the number of openings available to young adults, who are more likely to need the income from work to support their families. Our economic society is a complicated one, and justifiable attempts to reduce unfairness to one group may inadvertently cause other groups to suffer. Nevertheless, adults in their 50s and early 60s still have much of their work lives ahead of them. Many of these individuals have a strong desire to work and are as or more competent than young adults. To discriminate against these employees solely because of age is not only illegal and harmful to the individual, but also likely to cost the organization valuable and productive workers.

Gender Differences

DEMOGRAPHY. The labor force consists of all people who are employed, plus those who are unemployed but are looking for work. Because our society has long regarded men as the primary breadwinners and women as the primary child rearers, it is not surprising to find considerably more men in the labor force. In 1996, for example, the labor force included 82.5% of men between the ages of 20 and 24, and from 93.2% of men between 25 and 54. The corresponding figures for women ranged from 71% to 75%. (See Figure 9–3.)

FIGURE 9–3 **Civilian labor force participation rates.**
(*Source:* U.S. Bureau of the Census (1997).)

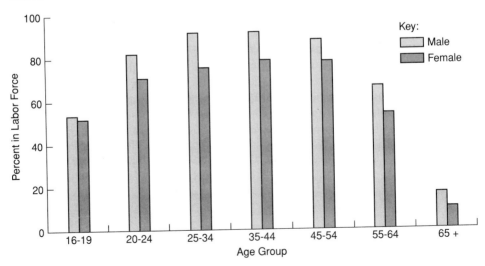

As with men, women work for many reasons. Historically, the most important of these is economic: Many women must work to support themselves (and perhaps their children as well), including the divorced (Chapter 8) and the poor. Because nonwhites are more likely to be economically disadvantaged than whites, the **work force** has traditionally included many more nonwhite women than white women, although these rates have tended to converge during the last three decades (see Table 9–1).

More recently, the increasing emphasis on individual rights has been reflected in pressures for more equal job opportunities for women. Our society has to some extent relinquished the stereotype that, except in cases of dire financial need, the woman's place is in the home. Women have felt increasingly free and sometimes compelled to join the work force in order to provide the primary or secondary family income, to express their independence, or to fulfill their potentials and need for achievement. Because of recent changes in the federal welfare system, many women with young children have had to join the work force. Thus there has been an increase in the percentage of working women during the last half century, although this trend has leveled off to some extent in recent years. Whereas only 25% of those at work in 1940 were women, this figure increased to 33% by 1958, to 44% by 1984, and 59% in 1996. Women have made considerable gains in some occupations once dominated by men: Between 1983 and 1996, the proportion of accountants who were women rose from 39% to 56%, and executive, administrative, and managerial positions from 32 to 43%. However, women still have a long way to go with respect to some occupations such as lawyers and judges (29% in 1996) and mathematical and computer scientists (31% in 1996). Also, women working full time in 1996 earned only 75% of what men did (U.S. Bureau of the Census, 1997).

THE COMPARABLE WORTH CONTROVERSY. To some theorists, the lower pay typically received by women is a clear sign of **sex discrimination**. They argue that employers are paying men significantly more for much the same work and/or are

TABLE 9–1   Civilian Labor Force Participation Rates, 1980–2005

Race and Sex	PARTICIPATION RATE (PERCENT)					
	1980	1990	1995	1996	2000 (projected)	2005 (projected)
Total	63.8	66.5	66.6	66.8	67.1	67.1
White	64.1	66.9	67.1	67.2	67.8	68.1
Male	78.2	77.1	75.7	75.8	74.9	73.9
Female	51.2	57.4	59.0	59.1	61.6	62.6
Black	61.0	64.0	63.7	64.1	62.7	61.9
Male	70.3	71.0	69.0	68.7	67.4	65.8
Female	53.1	58.3	59.5	60.4	59.0	58.8
Hispanic	64.0	67.4	65.8	66.5	65.4	64.7
Male	81.4	81.4	79.1	79.6	77.6	76.1
Female	47.4	53.1	52.6	53.4	53.3	53.6

Source: U.S. Bureau of the Census (1997).

Women have made considerable gains in some occupations once dominated by men and have achieved some important positions. But they have made less progress in other areas and may well be paid less than men for the same type of work.

denying women access to higher level and more lucrative positions. It has therefore been suggested that the demands and difficulty of various jobs be rated numerically, so that pay can be determined solely according to this criterion and men and women will receive comparable pay for comparable work.

Other theorists have taken strong exception to this proposal. They point out that women are much more likely than men to discontinue their work in order to bear and raise children, which has a negative effect on their seniority and chances for advancement. Statistical data indicate that women as a group have fewer years of experience and less seniority than men do. Also, if the mother chooses to return to work after the child is born, she may prefer a lower-level and less demanding job so she can spend more time at home. These critics generally agree there is sex discrimination in the workplace, but they contend the best way to alleviate this problem is by allowing pay to fluctuate freely in accordance with the supply and demand for the jobs in question.

The issue is likely to remain a controversial one. Because of the difficulty of evaluating the demands made by different jobs, as well as the opposition to such programs, it seems unlikely that an effective system for determining comparable worth will be forthcoming in the near future.

CAREER AND/OR MOTHERHOOD. As Figure 9–3 indicates, the majority of young women seek some form of employment. More than 50% of women age 16 to 19, and approximately 71% of women age 20 to 24, were part of the labor force in 1996. Some of these women opt for full-time careers, and some leave the labor force permanently in order to raise a family. Various studies have shown that women who elect to work full time are no less (or more) satisfied with their adult years than are those who opt for motherhood (e.g., Baruch & Barnett, 1980). As Carl Jung, the noted psychiatrist, once observed, "The shoe that fits one person pinches another; there is no universal recipe for living" (1931, p. 41).

Still other women choose to combine work and family roles, either for financial reasons or because they enjoy their jobs and do not wish to abandon them. Research evidence indicates that married women who work enjoy better mental health than those who do not, but they also experience greater inter-role conflicts than do male workers. This is apparently due to the fact that the woman's multiple roles tend to be salient simultaneously, whereas the man's multiple roles are more likely to operate sequentially. That is, the woman's family responsibilities normally continue throughout the day, so she is more likely to encounter situations where she must be at work yet take care of home and children at the same time. Conversely, the man can more often concentrate solely on work during the day and pursue family activities during the evening. (As we observed earlier, the role of the "househusband" has been greatly exaggerated. After the first child is born, the husband typically seeks to earn more income, and the wife assumes primary responsibility for family matters.) Thus married women who work perceive the home as more of a burden and are more likely to cite scheduling conflicts as a source of problems, whereas working men more often view their home environment as a support system (Kessler & McCrae, 1981; Sekaran, 1983; Staines & Pleck, 1983). The working married woman is particularly likely to experience inter-role conflicts if she has young children, if her decision to work is not supported by her husband, if she works for many hours during the week, and if she has a higher level of career aspiration (Gore & Mangione, 1983).

The generally positive picture we have painted of work and motherhood requires one important caveat. Recent changes in welfare laws in the United States are forcing many mothers of young children into the labor force. For example, only 19% of married women with children under 6 years of age were in the labor force in 1960. This number rose to 63% in 1996. Many welfare mothers have to accept jobs with low wages and limited or no benefits. It is too early to tell how welfare mothers cope with the added stress of taking on a job, but this topic will be heavily researched in the years ahead.

Afterword.   The stereotype that the woman's place is in the home has been shattered by empirical data: Women who choose to work are no less satisfied with their adult lives than are women who opt to raise a family, nor is there any indication that they are, in general, less competent employees than men. However, women who elect to combine work and family roles may find it difficult to meet their obligations in both areas. Although sex discrimination is still a significant problem in the workplace, the influence of women at work has increased considerably during the past four decades—and is likely to continue to do so in the future.

RETIREMENT

Leaving the world of full-time work involves financial, psychological, and physical changes. For most people, **retirement** brings a reduction in annual income. Work can no longer be used to gratify the retiree's self-esteem and need for achievement. The opportunity for social interactions with co-workers, supervisors, and subordinates is no longer available. And instead of spending some 8 hours per day in the work environment, the retiree must now either remain at home or find other activities to fill the day.

Thus it is not uncommon to hear about people who retire and then die unexpectedly within weeks or even days, presumably because they cannot cope

Myths About Aging

Work and Retirement

Myth	*Best Available Evidence*
Most middle-aged and older adults are poor employment risks. Compared to young adults, they do inferior work, have poorer attitudes because they are more set in their ways ("you can't teach an old dog new tricks"), and more often become injured or ill.	There are some jobs where age-related decrements in performance are found, such as those requiring certain perceptual and memory tasks skills (Chapters 4 and 5). In general, however, there is no indication that older workers perform more poorly on most jobs, or that they are more likely to suffer from low morale. Older workers are less likely than young adults to be injured on the job, although they are more likely to become disabled and to take longer to recover when an injury or illness does occur.

Myth	*Best Available Evidence*
A woman's primary role is to have children, so those who choose instead to pursue full-time careers will find their adult lives to be significantly less fulfilling.	Women who pursue full-time careers are no less (or more) happy with their adult years than are those who opt for motherhood.
Since work is so important to us, retirement is likely to cause severe psychological trauma or even an early death.	Most people adjust reasonably well to retirement, and do not experience serious psychological or physical trauma because they have left the world of full-time work.
Most elderly retirees live in near-poverty, reside in drab apartments, and have great difficulty acquiring even the bare necessities of living.	Although there are important exceptions, the majority of retirees live in homes that are paid for and have enough money to enjoy themselves during retirement.
Because retirement causes husband and wife to spend so much more time together, it produces a substantial increase in marital strife.	There is no indication that retirement causes significantly more marital problems for most retired couples.
Most retirees relocate to such places as Florida and Arizona.	Only a small percentage of retirees change their residences because of retirement.
One major advantage of reaching retirement age is that all of one's health-care costs are paid for by the government.	The government pays only a portion of the health-care costs of the elderly. Some services, such as long-term care, are not covered at all until the individual uses up all resources and qualifies as being poor.

with this major life change. Less extreme but equally prevalent are anecdotes about retirees who become demoralized, suffer low self-esteem and feel useless, become isolated and lonely, and sometimes require psychiatric help because they feel depressed or because they cannot tolerate having to spend both day and night with their spouses. Nevertheless, these stories do not necessarily indicate that retirement causes these problems. Retirement may instead result from an existing physical or psychological disorder. Most people do not retire until age

60 or later, and health tends to decline toward the end of the adult life span. If some adults choose to retire because poor health makes it too difficult for them to function at work, and if their disorders become considerably more serious or even terminal in subsequent months, it is clearly erroneous to conclude that an otherwise healthy individual was made ill by retirement. (Compare with the discussion of stressful life events in Chapter 10.)

Also, as we have seen, work may be valued more for its extrinsic than its intrinsic aspects. It may be boring and stressful, rather than interesting and enjoyable, yet serve as an essential source of income. For some, or even many jobs, then, retirement may represent more of a relief than a deprivation. In this section, we seek to determine whether the supposedly adverse effects of retirement are supported by research evidence or whether these beliefs are merely more of the myths that pervade the field of adult development and aging.

Overview

DEFINITION.   Retirement can be defined in various ways. Some theorists regard any person who performs no gainful employment during a given year as retired. Others apply this definition only to those who are currently receiving retirement pension benefits. And still others consider anyone who is not employed full time, year round, as retired.

For purposes of the present discussion, a **retired person** is someone with a lengthy history of work who is not employed at a full-time paying job and who receives at least some income from a pension due to prior employment. Thus retirement is an earned reward, one that results from having previously been a member of the labor force. Also, retirement does not necessarily mean a total separation from the world of work. Some retirees opt for part-time jobs or choose to do some work on a self-employed basis, as we see later in this chapter.

DEMOGRAPHIC CONSIDERATIONS: MANDATORY VERSUS VOLUNTARY RETIREMENT.   The proportion of older people who retire has increased dramatically since the turn of the century. In 1900, approximately 60% of men over 65 were actively employed. By 1990, however, this figure dropped to 16% and has remained there ever since then (U.S. Bureau of the Census, 1997).

Some might attribute this decline primarily to mandatory retirement policies, which require an employee to retire at a specific age (e.g., 65 or 70). However, the empirical evidence indicates otherwise. In 1978 the Age Discrimination in Employment Act was amended to prohibit mandatory retirement before age 70 in most sectors of the economy. Subsequent amendments eliminated mandatory retirement altogether with the exception of a few occupations where the public safety is at risk (e.g., law enforcement, firefighting, combat, piloting aircraft). Surprisingly, however, this did not produce a substantial increase in the number of older workers. In fact, between 1970 and 1986, the percentage of men age 65 to 69 in the labor force decreased from 39% to 25%. A decline also occurred for men 60 to 64 years old, from 73% to 55%. Thus, even though adults are now able to work for more years than ever before, more and more are opting for early retirement. Only about 4% to 7% of those who retire are compelled to do so against their will because of age (Binstock & George, 1996).

Another recent trend involves part-time work and the elderly. Many people like the option of part-time employment after age 65, and empirical data indicate that such an option is increasingly available. (See Table 9–2.)

Apparently, then, mandatory retirement does not force many well-qualified and willing employees to leave work prematurely. We must therefore look elsewhere to ascertain the reasons for the increasing popularity of **early retirement.**

The Preretirement Years

ATTITUDES TOWARD RETIREMENT. Almost all working adults expect to retire someday, usually before age 65. The majority of young and middle-aged workers probably do not think about retirement to any great extent. However, most employees past age 45 who do speculate about retirement view it as positive and desirable.

Some cross-sectional studies suggest a significant negative relationship between age and attitudes toward retirement. However, this finding is due to cohort effects rather than to aging: More recent generations are more accepting of retirement. In 1951, for example, the majority of steelworkers believed that retirement was justified only if an employee was physically unable to continue working. But by 1960, the same majority concluded that retirement is a benefit that they deserve for having worked for so many years. Of considerably more importance than age is the worker's financial status: The higher the income that one expects to receive during retirement, the more favorable are the attitudes toward this life event transition (Binstock & George, 1996).

How prevalent are optimistic views of retirement? Approximately 67% of employed adults do not anticipate financial problems during retirement, even though they also expect retirement to reduce their incomes by up to 50% from preretirement levels (Atchley, 1985). Few employees take concrete action to ensure that their retirement income will be adequate; only about 4% to 8% of men age 60 and older participate in formal retirement preparation programs (Beck,

TABLE 9–2 Median Income of Families and Unrelated Individuals by Age (U.S.)

AGE	ALL FAMILIES	UNRELATED INDIVIDUALS
55 and over	$30,565	$10,527
60 and over	27,445	9,956
65 and over	24,795	9,525
75 and over	20,912	8,769

Note: For families, age group is determined by the age of the family's householder.

Source: U.S. Bureau of the Census, Special Tabulation on Aging (1990); Schulz & Kerchis (1996).

1984; Harris & Associates, 1975, 1981). However, there is no indication that this lack of formal preretirement planning has any substantial impact on postretirement well-being.

FACTORS AFFECTING THE DECISION TO RETIRE.   Because mandatory retirement policies affect only a very small number of employees, the decision to retire must often be due to other reasons. These include the employee's job level and **job satisfaction,** age discrimination and employer pressures to retire, actual and self-perceived health, the expectation of a more enjoyable life, and the influence of one's family, friends, and co-workers.

Those who hold higher-level jobs tend to regard retirement more favorably because of their sound financial position, but they are also more likely to postpone retiring because they find their work to be too enjoyable. As Dr. Charles B. Huggins, 81-year-old Nobel Prize winner in physiology and medicine, put it, "Why should I retire as long as I love my work and can still do it well? I'm not a furniture mover, you know. . . . Research has always been my pleasure as well as my job. There is nothing that matches the thrill of discovery" (*Wall Street Journal*, March 10, 1983). Employees with low-level jobs are also likely to put off retirement, but for reasons that are primarily financial. These workers favor retirement in theory, because their jobs are typically dull and routine, but they often cannot afford it because of their low income and poor pension plans. Consequently, middle-level employees are the ones most likely to choose early retirement. They tend to have adequate retirement programs and don't enjoy their jobs enough to want to continue working past the minimum retirement age. A common expectation of these workers is that life will be more satisfying if they retire.

Age discrimination is also a factor in the decision to retire early, as we have seen. Employers may well refuse to hire qualified job applicants who are past middle age; or they may find various ways to let older workers know that their continued presence on the job is no longer desired, by transferring them to less attractive positions or treating them with less respect and consideration. As a result, older employees and job applicants may reluctantly decide that early retirement is their only feasible option.

Because older workers do suffer declines in certain physical and physiological capacities, and they are more likely to become disabled when they do sustain injuries on or off the job, some may be compelled to retire because they find the job has become too demanding. Most men who opt for early retirement under Social Security cite health as their reason for doing so. However, this finding probably cannot be accepted at face value: To some employees, health is undoubtedly a more socially acceptable reason for retiring early than admitting they just don't want to work anymore (J. H. Schulz, 1988). For those who reach the normal retirement age of 65 or 70, health issues appear to have little effect on the decision to retire.

Family and peer pressures may also influence the decision to retire. Some spouses and children may want the employee to retire at an earlier age, but others may not. An adult who lives in a leisure community populated primarily by retirees may experience peer pressure to conform, whereas another employee who lives among full-time workers may face precisely the opposite pressures.

AFTERWORD.   Some workers do choose early retirement because they sincerely believe their health is inadequate, or because of employer, family, or peer pressures. A few are forced to retire because they have reached a specific age. We do not mean to minimize the plight of those who find their work to be psychologically or financially rewarding, yet who are compelled against their wishes to retire. Nevertheless, research evidence clearly indicates that retirement is most often a welcome, desired event. The majority of employees retire voluntarily because they expect to enjoy life more as a result and because they anticipate few financial problems. In fact, more and more adults are choosing early retirement for these reasons. Let us now ascertain whether these positive expectations are likely to be realized.

Retirement and Its Effects

PHASES OF RETIREMENT.   Some theorists have suggested that retirees tend to proceed through a series of distinct psychological and emotional stages (Atchley, 1982, 1985, 1996). Retirement may well begin with a euphoric and busy honeymoon phase, during which the individual eagerly tries to do many of the things that were ruled out by full-time work (such as extended travel). This intense activity may be followed by a period of letdown or disenchantment, especially if the individual's prior expectations of retirement were unrealistically positive.

Disenchanted with Retirement

Mr. A., a 64-year-old former data technician for the U.S. Postal Service, found that retirement was not the paradise he had expected. "I spent the first eight months [of retirement] fixing up my lawn and house," he observed. "Then I ran out of things to do." Similarly, Mr. D., a 68-year-old retiree, found that "three years of loafing were all I could take."

These retirees must now take stock of themselves and their life situation, adjust to the realities of retirement, and seek out appropriate new activities. If this reorientation phase is successful, the retiree then settles into a predictable and generally satisfying retirement routine. Such retirees accept the limitation brought on by advanced age, keep busy to at least some extent, are self-sufficient, and manage their own affairs. Very few choose to isolate themselves from other people; most want to retain at least some social contacts, especially with their families (Chapter 8). But there are retirees who cannot resolve the reorientation phase successfully and who remain in a state of disenchantment even after some years have passed. Finally, some elderly adults become so ill that they can no longer function independently; they are more properly described as sick or disabled rather than retired (the termination phase). A few may instead terminate retirement by returning to full-time work.

These **phases of retirement** are not intended to represent an inevitable sequence. Some retirees may not experience some phases, or they may encounter them in a different order. For example, death may claim a retiree before the termination phase is reached. Some retirees may not have enough money for the activities involved in a honeymoon period and may therefore omit this phase. Several cross-sectional studies suggest that many retirees proceed directly from the honeymoon phase to the retirement routine, without suffering a period of disenchantment (e.g., Atchley, 1982). Other retirees may prefer to indulge in a period of rest and relaxation either immediately after retirement or following the honeymoon period. This inactivity typically gives way to boredom and restlessness, however, whereupon the retiree enters the reorientation phase and must face the challenge of establishing a satisfactory daily routine.

Research evidence concerning this phase model is sparse and somewhat equivocal. Some tentative findings indicate that enthusiasm does tend to be high immediately after retirement, and some degree of emotional letdown or reassessment is likely during the second or third year of retirement (Adams & Lefebvre, 1981; Ekerdt, Bossé, & Levkoff, 1985). Other studies have failed to find any evidence of a honeymoon effect (Beck, 1982). Perhaps the most important inference to be drawn from the phase model is the fact that although some retirees ultimately experience strong and prolonged feelings of disenchantment, many others do not. That is, some adults find it considerably easier to adjust to retirement than others do. Why is this so? How do successful retirees make this period more satisfying and rewarding? The answer appears to involve several important aspects of the individual's lifestyle prior to retirement: financial status, degree of social and recreational activity, and health.

FINANCIAL EFFECTS. Some early cross-sectional studies have suggested that retirement produces a substantial drop in income, so much so that the retiree's standard of living and satisfaction with life are adversely affected. However, this conclusion has now been shown to not apply to the majority of current retirees (Atchley, 1996). One longitudinal, multivariate, and large-sample study analyzed data obtained from six extensive research programs, which spanned from 2 to 10 years and comprised a total of more than 23,000 men and women age 45 to 70 and older. The results indicated that financial differences between retirees and those who are still working are due in large part to differences in the amount of preretirement income, rather than to retirement per se. Early retirement does have more of an adverse financial effect than later retirement because the individual must usually accept a smaller income in order to begin collecting benefits sooner. But when preretirement level of income is statistically controlled, most of the purported negative financial consequences of retirement turn out to be small or insignificant (Palmore, Fillenbaum, & George, 1984). Although there is a drop in income at retirement, the typical retired household is no more likely than the employed household to feel economically strapped or to draw upon savings.

A similar conclusion has been reached by the President's Council of Economic Advisers, which recently reported that the financial status of retirees has improved markedly during the last 30 years. Most elderly people today live in homes that are paid for, with enough money to enjoy their leisure years. In fact, due in part to the automatic cost-of-living increases in Social Security payments that began in 1974, America's senior citizens have received greater percentage increases in their average annual incomes during the past decade than did those below age 65.

Finances and Retirement: A Typical Example

"I hear all these retired folks complaining that they don't have this and they don't have that," says Mr. H., a 74-year-old retired shipping clerk. "I'm not pinched. . . . My house is paid for. My car is paid for. Both my sons are grown up. I don't need many new clothes. Every time I go out and eat somewhere, I get a senior citizen's discount. This is the happiest period of my life. These are my golden years." (*Wall Street Journal*, February 21, 1983)

The picture is by no means entirely bright, however. Those with lower-level jobs and poor fringe benefits may well find themselves in serious financial difficulty during retirement. This is particularly true for those who are low in education and/or have been the object of prejudice in the workplace, such as blacks and women.

An Economically Disadvantaged Retiree

Mrs. B. is a black 72-year-old widow who lives in a senior citizen's housing project in Washington, D.C. She once worked as a janitor, a job that provided minimal retirement benefits. Now she barely scrapes by on her annual Social Security income and her late husband's veteran's pension. "It's just terrible," she says. "Social Security payments are so low that they don't even want you to have enough money to eat or to buy medicine. . . . Social Security benefits may go up $15, but the cost of everything I need has already gone up $15 or $20." (*Wall Street Journal*, February 21, 1983)

Here again, however, preretirement characteristics rather than retirement per se were primarily responsible for Mrs. B.'s financial difficulties. In fact, many low-level and minority group employees earn so little income that retirement has virtually no financial effect; their pay is essentially replaced by food stamps and other age-related income supports. As the authors of one longitudinal study concluded, "the presence of these supports, and the finding that retirement had no adverse effects on the [incomes of black men], forcibly indicates how low their work-related income must have been" (Fillenbaum, George, & Palmore, 1985).

In sum: Although the aged were indeed an economically disadvantaged group some 40 years ago, this is no longer true. For this reason, some observers have become critical of Social Security. As some policy makers have observed, today's workers are paying for benefits to retirees that far exceed contributions the retirees made during their working years. An individual who goes on Social Security today will recoup their entire lifetime contributions in less than 10 years.

TABLE 9-3   Percentage Below Poverty Level
of Persons by Age and Sex (U.S.)

AGE	MALE	FEMALE
Under 18	18.0	18.5
18 to 64	9.2	12.8
65 to 74	7.1	12.9
75 and over	10.8	19.8

Source: U.S. Bureau of the Census, STF3A, STF3C (1990).

However, there is another side to the story. Even as recently as 1984, older Americans had a lower economic status than other adults in our society. (See Table 9–3.) Furthermore, the economic status of the elderly is far more varied than that of any other age group. Although some older adults have substantial financial resources, a surprising number have practically none. (See Table 9–4.) Comparisons of average figures may therefore be misleading, with the high values for some retirees obscuring the fact that quite a few elderly adults are below or just barely above the poverty level (U.S. Bureau of the Census, 1997). Thus a significant number of elderly individuals suffer serious financial problems during retirement.

Whether the younger generation is supporting the elderly to an unfair extent is a highly controversial issue. The economic status of the aged is likely to remain a source of keen political debate. However, the stereotype of the elderly retiree who lives from hand to mouth on a meager fixed income, resides in a drab and dingy apartment, and struggles desperately to secure the bare necessities of life must be emphatically rejected in light of the available research evidence.

ACTIVITY VERSUS BOREDOM.   Here again, the general picture is an optimistic one: The majority find retirement to be a busy and satisfying period. In particular, those individuals who developed enjoyable hobbies and recreational activities prior to retirement are most likely to enjoy their years away from full-time work. However, those who had few avocations during their working years may well find that retirement is disenchanting and depressing. Thus a county coordinator of adult and community education in Florida observes, "Our biggest battle is loneliness. A lot of people dream about paradise. They sell their homes and move here. After the drapes are up and the carpets are down, paradise can turn into a living hell if they don't find something to do" (*Wall Street Journal*, March 2, 1992).

TABLE 9-4   Percentage Below Poverty Level
of Persons by Age and Race (U.S.)

AGE	WHITE	BLACK
Under 18	12.5	39.8
18 to 64	8.5	23.4
65 to 74	8.4	28.6
75 and over	14.6	37.3

Source: U.S. Bureau of the Census, STF3A, STF3C (1990).

Those who develop satisfying hobbies prior to retirement are more likely to enjoy their years away from work, as with this retiree's interest in Bonsai gardening.

Those retirees who do become bored and disenchanted may seek to resolve their problems by joining a senior center and developing new interests. Or part-time work may prove to be an effective and rewarding way to keep busy. One Florida retirement community is filled with elderly gas station attendants, grocery store baggers, retail clerks, and owners of small businesses. Most of these older adults are paid at or near the federal minimum wage, yet they value this opportunity to be active.

We may conclude that there is a close relationship between an individual's preretirement and retirement lifestyles. Those who begin retirement with many avocational (or vocational) activities that they want to pursue are likely to find this time of life to be full and rewarding. Conversely, those with few hobbies and nonjob social activities during their working years may well find they have far too much time on their hands during retirement. (Compare with the discussion of the stability of personality during adulthood in Chapter 7 and the social lifestyles of the elderly in Chapter 8.)

HEALTH. Early cross-sectional studies also suggested that health is likely to be adversely affected by retirement. Here again, however, these findings have been contradicted by more recent longitudinal studies. As discussed previously, poor health after retirement may well be caused by deteriorating health before retirement. Some workers exaggerate their health problems in order to have a more socially acceptable reason for seeking early retirement. And declines in health may be due simply to advancing age, rather than to retirement; ill health is one of the stressful life events that we are more likely to encounter as we grow older (Chapter 10). In actuality, retired people are no more likely to be sick than are people of the same age who are still working (Atchley, 1996; see also Ekerdt, Baden, Bossé, & Dibbs, 1983).

There are individuals who do retire in reasonably good health, only to deteriorate thereafter. Yet such cases tend to be balanced by those whose health improved after retirement because they are no longer subjected to stressful, unhealthy, or dangerous working conditions. In fact, in one longitudinal study, some 38% of a sample of 263 men claimed that retirement had a positive effect on their health (Palmore, Fillenbaum, & George, 1984).

All in all, the evidence does not indicate that retirement exerts a significant negative effect on the physical and mental health of the retiree. In particular, there is no justification whatsoever for the stereotype of retirees who suffer severe psychological breakdowns, or even an early death, because they are no longer needed at a full-time job.

MARITAL DIFFICULTIES.   Another myth about retirement is expressed in the saying, "I married you for better or for worse, but not for lunch." That is, the extensive contact between husband and wife during retirement is believed by some to bring a substantial increase in marital tension and strife. For example, the director of a Florida mental health clinic concluded that marriages sometimes develop strains under the pressure of the enforced togetherness that retirement brings. "For the first time in their lives," he noted, "they have to eyeball each other 24 hours a day."

In many instances, however, the relationship between husband and wife improves after retirement. The spouses are now able to enjoy mutual recreational activities, and they have time for caring and communication that may not have existed during the working years. This appears to be more true for middle-class and upper-middle-class couples, where the wife is likely to welcome her husband's retirement and increased involvement in household tasks. But in working-class marriages, the wife is more likely to expect and to value exclusive control over the household. When her husband uses some of the extensive free time created by retirement to participate in household chores, she may well become irritated because her domain has been invaded.

Alternatively, preretirement factors may play a significant role. An increase in marital strife may occur after retirement only because the marriage was an unhappy one to begin with, and neither spouse enjoys the idea of having to spend more time with the other. *In sum:* There is no strong evidence that retirement has an adverse effect on the marriages of most elderly couples.

CHANGES IN RESIDENCE.   Another common belief is that most adults change their residence soon after retirement. In actuality, migration rates decline substantially from age 25 onward and rise only slightly at retirement. Retirement meccas such as those in Florida and Arizona would seem to command a disproportionate amount of media attention, perhaps because of their extremely high densities of older adults. Yet only a very small proportion of retirees move to such communities; the overwhelming majority do not relocate (Atchley, 1985).

AFTERWORD. Some studies purport to show that retirement has a severe adverse effect on income, physical and mental health, life satisfaction, self-esteem, and marital harmony. However, these studies all too often overlook the possibility that the people in question had such problems even before they retired. More carefully controlled longitudinal studies indicate that the effects of retirement are considerably more positive. Retirement does bring a drop in income, but this often involves little or no change in the retiree's standard of living. Although there are exceptions, retirement does not in general cause ill physical or psychological health, feelings of uselessness and depression, dissatisfaction with life in general, declines in self-esteem, or increased marital strife. Some jobs are not intrinsically satisfying, and some employees do not mind retirement because they value the extrinsic aspects of work more highly. Or some employees who do enjoy the intrinsic aspects of their jobs may decide that 40 years of work is quite enough, and it is time for a new lifestyle. Although there are those who continue to work into their 70s and beyond, retirement has become a respected and desirable life event in our society. The majority of adults welcome it as an earned reward for their many years of work and retire voluntarily in order to pursue other activities.

The plight of those individuals who do suffer severe financial and emotional problems during retirement is a painful one, and their problems should not be underestimated. Future research in this area may profitably focus on identifying and assisting those who are likely to experience such difficulties. But the empirical evidence clearly indicates that the lot of most retirees has improved dramatically during the last four decades; few lead impoverished lives, either financially or socially. Retirement is most often a positive and welcome event, one that opens the way to a rewarding and busy twilight of the human life span.

THE ECONOMIC FUTURE OF THE ELDERLY: CAN AMERICA AFFORD TO GROW OLD?

Projected Trends

Although the majority of retirees are financially comfortable, there are troublesome signs regarding the economic future of the elderly in the United States. We have noted some of these trends previously in this book.

First of all, the number and proportion of elderly persons are expected to increase dramatically during the next 50 years. (See Chapter 1.) This is particularly true for the very old (persons above the age of 85), many of whom will suffer from chronic health problems that require extensive and expensive health care.

A second trend involves the changing ratio between the number of persons in the work force and those who are not. As shown in Table 9–5, the ratio of

TABLE 9-5   Ratio of Nonworkers to Workers and Dependency Ratios, 1960–2030 (projected)

	1960	1970	1980	1990	2010	2030
Ratio of nonworkers to workers	1.26	1.14	.94	.85	.78	.92
Total age dependency ratio	.72	.67	.55	.56	.55	.70

Note: The ratio of nonworkers to workers is the ratio of all nonworkers in the population to all workers in the population, regardless of age. The total age dependency ratio is defined as the ratio of the population age 65 and older and below age 16 to the population between ages 16 and 64.

Source: Zedlewski et al. (1989).

nonworkers to workers is expected to increase substantially by the year 2010. At that time, there will be less than one worker for every nonworking person—a sizable group that will require some form of financial support.

To be sure, the gains in income among the elderly that have occurred during the last decade are expected to continue for the next 40 years. This is due in part to increased Social Security benefits and to the greater availability of private pension funds. In fact, one study (Zedlewski et al., 1989) suggests the income of adults age 65 and older will increase by approximately 50% between 1990 and 2030. (See Table 9-6.) But if much of this increase is to come from Social Security, the resources of this program may well be strained beyond the breaking point.

Taken together, then, these trends raise an important question: Will we be able to support the elderly in the style to which they have become accustomed? To answer this question, we must examine the major federal government support programs and how they work.

Federal Government Programs

SOCIAL SECURITY.   Currently, about 92% of all civilian workers must make Social Security payments. These workers are therefore eligible to receive benefits when

TABLE 9-6   Projected Real Median Income by Marital Status, Age, and Sex: 1990–2030

| | 1990 | 2010 | 2030 | PERCENTAGE CHANGE | |
				1990–2010	2010–2030
Married Couples	$15,530	$24,390	$36,660	+57	+50
Age: 65–69	17,260	28,180	40,100	+63	+42
70–79	14,956	23,920	36,830	+60	+54
80+	12,620	16,180	29,080	+28	+80
Unmarried Men	$7,200	$10,850	$16,860	+51	+55
Age: 65–69	8,360	14,680	18,240	+76	+24
70–79	7,600	11,750	17,880	+55	+52
80+	6,321	8,490	14,350	+34	+69
Unmarried Women	$6,000	$8,090	$12,900	+35	+59
Age: 65–69	6,320	10,070	14,950	+59	+48
70–79	6,200	8,440	13,740	+36	+63
80+	5,620	7,280	11,520	+30	+58

Source: Zedlewski et al. (1989).

they retire or if they become disabled before they retire. **Social Security** is the primary source of income for retired individuals. (See Table 9–7.)

The large majority of Social Security benefits are paid to retirees in the form of a monthly pension, or—in the case of health care—through Medicare. A retiree's exact monthly pension depends on many factors: the age when benefits begin, the number of eligible family members, and current earnings. In 1995, a retired married couple received an average of $1221 per month. The benefit formula is weighted to provide retired workers who had lower earnings a relatively larger return on their contributions.

Both employers and employees pay equal amounts into Social Security. In 1997, each worker paid 6.20% of their earnings up to $65,400, plus an additional 1.45 percent of all income for the Hospital Insurance portion of Medicare. Recent legislation has already slightly increased this rate, and it is likely to increase further in the years ahead. A large surplus of funds must be accumulated to support the large number of elderly persons who will become eligible for Social Security and to keep future workers from having to bear this entire burden (Myer, 1995). Yet as we observed earlier in this chapter, young adults may well object to having substantial contributions to Social Security deducted from their paychecks.

One way to reduce the amount needed by Social Security is to delay the age of retirement beyond 65, which is exactly what Congress did in the 1983 Social Security amendments. Beginning in the year 2000 and continuing until 2022, the retirement age will increase by 2 months each year. Full Social Security benefits will therefore be delayed until age 67. However, it remains to be seen whether this strategy (along with increased payments) will resolve the problems that face Social Security.

The future of Social Security remains murky. Currently, contributions to the fund exceed benefits paid out and are projected to continue to do so until about 2012 when the baby boom generation enters retirement. Trust fund assets are then projected to decline and will be completely depleted by the year 2031. How to deal with this problem has triggered a national debate that will likely continue into the next century (J. H. Schulz, 1995).

MEDICARE.   The second major expenditure of Social Security dollars is the **Medicare** program. In 1984, Medicare spent an average of $2,051 per person over the age of 65. (See Table 9–8.)

TABLE 9–7   Sources of Income as a Percentage of Total Reported Income by Age (U.S.)

AGE	EARNINGS	SOCIAL SECURITY	PUBLIC ASSISTANCE	RETIREMENT	INTEREST, DIVIDENDS, RENTAL	OTHER
55 to 59	82.2	1.4	0.5	5.8	8.9	1.1
60 to 64	64.3	8.2	0.8	11.5	13.9	1.3
65 to 74	26.2	30.1	1.4	17.4	23.2	1.6
75 to 84	11.1	39.7	2.0	14.2	31.8	1.2
85 and over	7.0	40.3	2.6	10.6	38.2	1.3

Source: U.S. Bureau of the Census, Special Tabulation on Aging (1990).

TABLE 9–8   Estimated Federal Spending for Persons
Age 65 or Older, 1990 and 1995

PROGRAM	1990 (BILLIONS)	1995
Social Security	$193	$260
Medicare	96	181
Federal civilian retirement	21	26
Medicaid	14	32
Military retirement	7	10
Veterans' pensions	7	9
Housing assistance	6	8
Supplemental Security Income	4	6
Railroad retirement	4	3
Benefits for coal miners	1	1
Food stamps	1	1
Total	354	537

Source: U.S. Bureau of the Census (1997).

Medicare consists of two parts: Hospital Insurance (also called Part A), and Medical Insurance (Part B). Medicare's Hospital Insurance helps pay for four basic health care services: inpatient hospital care, care in a skilled nursing facility, home health care, and hospice care (health care for the terminally ill). However, there are limits on the amounts that Hospital Insurance pays for each type of care. For example, care in a skilled nursing facility is provided for only a limited period of time after an individual is first hospitalized. In addition, the individual has to qualify as needing skilled nursing care rather than just custodial care. Medical Insurance helps pay for doctor's services (e.g., visiting a doctor's office for an illness), hospital outpatient services, and some additional services and supplies not covered by Part A.

The large majority of people are automatically enrolled in Medicare when they become eligible for Social Security benefits. All eligible individuals automatically receive Hospital Insurance coverage (Part A). To receive Medical Insurance coverage (Part B), however, individuals must pay a small monthly premium. Like most other health insurance plans, both parts of Medicare have deductibles and coinsurance—costs that must be either paid by the individual or covered through a private supplemental insurance plan. Users of Medicare services readily agree that dealing with this system is often complicated and frustrating.

As was the case with Social Security, the future of Medicare is also bleak. Because the number of beneficiaries and the use and cost of medical services have increased considerably, the growth in Medicare spending has been rapid: It increased by more than 11% per year from 1973 to 1984 (Aaron, Bosworth, & Burtless, 1989). From 1985 to 1995 expenditures continued to increase at a rapid rate; total expenditures on Medicare were $72 billion in 1985 and $181 billion in 1995. To address the increasing costs of Medicare, Congress recently passed legislation that increased the taxes paid by workers into the Hospital Insurance fund, placed limits on the amounts paid to hospitals and doctors for services provided to the elderly, and increased the amount paid by elderly persons who use Medicare services. Yet here again, these actions alone will not resolve the financial problems of Medicare in the future.

MEDICAID. Medicaid is a combined federal and state program that pays for health care for certain very poor people: individuals who are pregnant, aged, disabled or blind, and families with dependent children. To be eligible for Medicaid, an individual must have both a low income and few assets that can be converted into income. Each state sets its own criteria of eligibility for Medicaid and determines what services will be covered under this program. Medicaid is designed to assist the poor regardless of age, but about 37% ($36.5 billion in 1995) of its resources are spent on services for the elderly. Medicaid is the principal source of public financing for nursing home care. Like Medicare, the cost of Medicaid has increased dramatically since 1980, growing from $21 billion in 1980 to $121 billion in 1995 (U.S. Bureau of the Census, 1997).

Medicare pays very little for nursing home care, so disabled elderly persons who cannot live independently often must pay for years of such care out of their own pockets. Because one year in a nursing home costs an average of $40,000, even those elderly people who have considerable resources can quickly use up their life savings, as well as their pensions. Once this happens, and if their pension incomes are low enough, they finally become eligible for Medicaid.

Many policymakers object to a health care system that forces people to become paupers. To address this problem, some individuals have proposed private and government insurance plans that would pay for long-term health care for the elderly. Currently, however, few people are willing to spend private funds to pay for such a plan, and the government is very reluctant to institute yet another health care service that will become extremely expensive as the population ages. At present, therefore, this important and troublesome issue remains unresolved.

AFTERWORD. Ultimately, the economic well-being of the elderly is closely tied to the economic well-being of the United States as a whole. All of the projections presented in the preceding section are based on the assumption of continued economic growth and a reduction in the federal deficit. To the extent that we fail to achieve these goals, the elderly (along with everyone else) are likely to suffer economic hardships. The recent economic boom in the United States is reason to be optimistic about our ability to successfully confront these challenges.

Even if our economy remains relatively sound, the increasing number of elderly Americans may well place a severe strain on Social Security and other resources. Dealing with such problems will require insightful political leadership and quite possibly some sacrifices for all of us.

SUMMARY

Work and Adult Development

For most of us, work provides the income necessary to support ourselves and our families. Work may also be interesting for its own sake, contribute to our self-esteem and sense of identity, and provide important social rewards and punishments. Thus work exerts a significant effect on the quality of our lives and overall well-being in two major ways: intrinsically and extrinsically.

Measuring job performance is a difficult task. One approach has been to use practical criteria such as supervisory ratings, productivity, turnover, absenteeism, and accident rates. By these indicators older workers do at least as well and sometimes better than younger workers. Older workers reach peak productivity in their 40s and 50s and decline by small amounts thereafter; they have lower turnover and avoidable absenteeism rates than younger workers, and they tend to have fewer on-the-job accidents. Aging appears to have little detrimental effect on job performance in some professional and artistic fields. For example, artists and musicians often do their best work late in life. Conversely, the most productive years for mathematicians and professional athletes occur during their 20s and 30s. However, the research evidence in this area is equivocal. The most justified conclusion appears to be that age often bears little or no relationship to job performance, but that some exceptions may be expected in certain jobs and professions.

There is some indication that young adults are more concerned with chances for advancement and for professional and personal development than are middle-aged and older workers. In general, however, the relationship between aging and job satisfaction is far from clear. Although the data are too equivocal to permit any firm conclusions, there is no convincing evidence that older workers tend to be less satisfied with their jobs than young adults.

Older workers are less likely than young adults to be injured on the job or to be absent. But when they do sustain an injury, they are more likely to be disabled and to require more time to recover.

Even though many older adults are as competent and as satisfied as young employees, and even though federal legislation prohibits the denial of employment to those over 40 because of their age, age discrimination still exists in the workplace. This is due in part to negative stereotypes about older workers, who are more likely to be incorrectly perceived as resistant to change, slow to make decisions, and untrainable. Also, pensions and other fringe benefits for older workers are more costly to the employer.

Some theorists have argued that midlife career changes are becoming increasingly common, but little statistical evidence supports this conclusion. When such career changes do occur, they are most often caused by such external pressures as losing one's old job.

The study of work and aging is more problematical than might be expected. Job satisfaction and productivity are multidimensional variables, and chronological age provides only limited information about human capacities. Such age-related variables as job level and job complexity appear to be more closely related to job satisfaction and performance than age per se. To discriminate against employees over 40 solely because of age is not only illegal and harmful to the individual, but is also likely to cost the organization valuable and productive workers.

There are significantly more men than women in the labor force, but the percentage of women has increased substantially during the last half century. Women have made considerable inroads into some occupations once dominated by men. However, women still have a long way to go with respect to some occupations such as lawyers and judges (29% in 1996) and mathematical and computer scientists (31% in 1996). Also, women working full time in 1996 earned only 75% of what men did.

Some theorists have argued that the difficulty of various jobs should be rated numerically, so men and women can be assured of comparable pay for comparable work. Other theorists point out that although there is still sex discrimination in the workplace, women have hurt their own chances for advancement and higher pay by willingly discontinuing their work in order to bear and raise children. They conclude that the fairest course is to allow pay to fluctuate freely in accordance with supply and demand. With the difficulty of evaluating the demands made by different jobs, it appears unlikely that an effective system for determining comparable worth will be forthcoming in the near future.

Women who elect to pursue full-time careers are no less (or more) satisfied with their adult years than are women who opt for motherhood and raising a family. Married women who work enjoy better mental health than those who do not, but they are also more likely to experience inter-role conflicts. In the majority of couples, women still have primary responsibility for family matters, so those who elect to combine work and family roles may find it difficult to meet their obligations in both areas. Sex discrimination remains a significant problem in the world of work, but the influence of women has increased considerably during the past four decades and is likely to continue to do so in the future.

Retirement

A retired person is one who is not employed at a full-time paying job and who receives at least some income from a pension earned through prior employment. The proportion of older people who retire has increased dramatically since the turn of the century. Although it is often assumed that mandatory retirement policies compel many people to leave work sooner than they would like, this belief is not supported by the empirical evidence. In fact, more and more people are opting for early retirement.

Most employees past age 45 who speculate about retirement view it as positive and desirable, a reward they deserve for having worked for so many years. Nor do most adults anticipate financial problems during retirement. Those who hold higher-level positions tend to regard retirement more favorably because their financial position is sound, but they are also more likely to postpone retiring because they find their work to be too enjoyable. Employees with low-level jobs are likely to favor retirement in theory because their jobs tend to be dull and routine, but they often cannot afford to retire early because of their low income and poor pension plans. Thus middle-level employees are the ones most likely to opt for early retirement because they tend to have adequate retirement programs but do not enjoy their jobs enough to want to continue past working age. It is a common expectation of these workers that life will be more satisfying if they retire. Age discrimination, family and peer pressures, and health are also factors in the decision to retire early. However, the importance of health may well be exaggerated: To many employees, health is undoubtedly a more socially acceptable reason for retiring early than admitting that they just don't want to work anymore.

Some theorists have suggested that retirees tend to proceed through a series of distinct psychological and emotional stages, such as a honeymoon effect, disenchantment, rest and relaxation, reorientation, the retirement routine, and termination. However, the research evidence concerning this model is sparse and somewhat equivocal. Perhaps the most important conclusion is that some retirees ultimately experience strong and prolonged feelings of disenchantment, although many others do not. This appears to depend in large part on the individual's lifestyle prior to retirement. Those who tended to have adequate finances, numerous satisfying hobbies and recreational activities, good health, and happy marriages prior to retiring are likely to find it considerably easier to adjust to retirement and to enjoy these years. Those with poor finances, few avocations, ill health, and unhappy marriages before retiring may well find retirement disenchanting and depressing.

In general, the majority of elderly adults find retirement to be a satisfying and busy period. The financial status of retirees has improved markedly during the last 40 years, and the stereotype of the elderly retiree who lives from hand to mouth on a meager income and who resides in a drab and dingy apartment must be rejected in the light of the available research evidence. Many retirees find that leaving the world of full-time work gives them time not previously available to pursue desired activities, although some find it necessary to accept low-level, part-time jobs in order to keep busy. There is no indication that retirement per se exerts a significant negative effect on the physical and mental health of the retiree or that it has an adverse effect on the marriages of most couples.

The plight of those who do suffer severe financial and emotional problems during retirement should not be underestimated. But retirement is most often a positive and welcome event, one that opens the way to a rewarding and busy twilight of the human life span.

The Economic Future of the Elderly

Although the majority of retirees are financially comfortable, there are troublesome signs regarding the economic future of the elderly in the United States. The number of elderly persons, particularly the very old, is expected to increase dramatically during the next 50 years. Furthermore, there will be less than one worker for every nonworking person by the year 2030. Whether Social Security, Medicare, and Medicaid can cope with so many older adults and nonworkers remains to be seen.

One currently unresolved problem involves nursing home care. Medicare pays very little for this, and one must be virtually poor in order to qualify for Medicaid. Yet new long-term health care plans for the elderly are unlikely to be approved because they will become extremely expensive as the population ages.

If we fail to achieve continued economic growth and to reduce the federal deficit, the elderly (along with everyone else) are likely to suffer economic hardships. In any case, continuing to provide good support for the elderly is likely to become a major challenge in the years ahead.

STUDY QUESTIONS

1. What is the relationship between job satisfaction and satisfaction with life in general? Why might a person who is very satisfied with his or her job be dissatisfied with life in general? Why might a person who is satisfied with life in general be very dissatisfied with his or her job? Are these likely possibilities? If so, can you give examples from your own life or from the life of someone you know? Clarify.
2. Although illegal, age and sex discrimination are still prevalent in the workplace. Why do employers continue to engage in these activities? What harm does this do? Other than litigation, can anything be done to reduce the amount of age and sex discrimination?
3. What can you do to make your retirement more satisfying (a) now? (b) on reaching middle age? (c) when you retire? What factors are likely to make retirement dissatisfying? Which is more common in the United States, retirement that is satisfying or dissatisfying?
4. Is our current Social Security system unfair to young adults because they must contribute too much to support too many older adults who do not need financial aid? Is the Social Security system unfair to retirees? Or is the Social Security system generally fair to both young adults and retirees?
5. Is the Social Security system equally fair to high and low wage earners? What proposals have you recently heard about that are aimed at changing the Social Security system? Would you be in favor of making small adjustments or a major revamping of the Social Security system? Why?
6. How will the increasing number of older adults affect such federal programs as Social Security, Medicare, and Medicaid in this next decade? What changes in these programs are likely to be necessary?

TERMS TO REMEMBER

Age discrimination
Early retirement
Extrinsic benefits of work
Intrinsic benefits of work
Job satisfaction
Medicaid
Medicare

Phases of retirement
Retired person
Retirement
Sex discrimination
Social Security
Work force

10

STRESS AND COPING

A capable college student becomes so tense during an important examination that she cannot recall even the simplest facts and turns in a blank paper. A college football team needs to win its final game to earn a bowl invitation, trails by two points late in the game, and fights its way down to the opponent's goal line, only to have its normally reliable field goal specialist kick the ball so low that the defense blocks it easily. An employee who must deal every day with irascible customers and a demanding supervisor, but who cannot find another job or afford to quit, develops intense stomach pains.

Stories about the adverse effects of **stress** on human beings appear frequently in the news media. We hear about major traumatic events that result in serious physical or mental disorders; we read about certain types of work that are considered stressful enough to cause physical illnesses; we find that some athlete's performance was subpar because he or she experienced too much stress. However, stress is not always disadvantageous. A student who is too nonchalant about a forthcoming exam may fail to prepare adequately and receive a poor grade. Or members of a top-rated football team may be so relaxed for a game with an inferior opponent that they suffer an ignominious defeat. Too much stress may well be injurious, but too little may result in lackluster and inferior performance.

Nevertheless, the debilitating effects of excessive stress are of primary concern in today's society. Numerous programs have been designed to teach people how to cope with stress. Many self-help books claim that heart attacks, depression, anxiety, hypertension, and other health problems can be avoided by changing our lifestyles in ways that will reduce stress. And a thriving pharmaceutical industry dispenses vast quantities of anti-anxiety medications, such as Valium and Librium. Thus stress is widely regarded as a major disrupting force in the lives of individuals of all ages, and concern with this problem appears to have reached epidemic proportions.

What might this imply about the course of adult development? Conceivably, life may become more stressful with increasing age. Adults must typically contend with such new and demanding situations as work, marriage, raising children, divorce, the death of a loved one, and, eventually, retirement and old age. However, the opposite hypothesis is also a reasonable one. That is, we may well become more sure of ourselves as we grow older and more established in work and family roles. The security provided by this firmer foundation in life, and increased maturity, may render us less vulnerable to those sources of stress that we encounter.

In this chapter, we examine empirical data dealing with stress and coping during adulthood. We begin with a brief historical tour of the development of scientific interest in stress research, which illustrates the diverse approaches used by various theorists. We then define the concept of stress by presenting and discussing a general theoretical model. We conclude by examining the relationship between aging and stress, with emphasis on those sources of stress typically encountered during the adult life course and ways of coping with them.

INTUITIVE PERSPECTIVES ON STRESS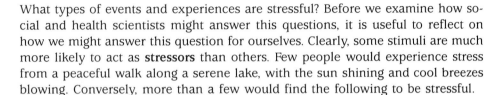

What types of events and experiences are stressful? Before we examine how social and health scientists might answer this questions, it is useful to reflect on how we might answer this question for ourselves. Clearly, some stimuli are much more likely to act as **stressors** than others. Few people would experience stress from a peaceful walk along a serene lake, with the sun shining and cool breezes blowing. Conversely, more than a few would find the following to be stressful.

EXTERNAL PRESSURES AND OVERSTIMULATION. If you are required to achieve a level of performance that is very difficult for you or to behave in ways that run counter to your strongest convictions, you may well experience considerable stress. This is particularly true if the pressures continue for a substantial period of time. Common examples include an unusually demanding job, college course, parent, or army drill sergeant. However, such pressures are not always from the outside. Some people create considerable stress for themselves by establishing goals that they think are reasonable, but which are actually far too demanding and perfectionistic.

BOREDOM AND UNDERSTIMULATION.   External pressures are among the best known sources of stress. Although we all welcome some opportunity to relax and take life easy, having nothing to do for too long can also be stressful. Some people enjoy facing a challenge, improving their skills, and achieving difficult goals and cannot tolerate a succession of tasks that are too easy. Others welcome the excitement of risky vocations or avocations, such as tightrope walkers, test pilots, parachute jumpers, automobile racers, and those who like to take rides on roller coasters. Thus stress and frustration can be caused by external demands and pressures that are too low, as well as those that are too high.

CONFLICTS.   Stress may result from having to make difficult and painful decisions. For example, young men during the 1960s who opposed the Vietnam War had to choose between two very unpalatable alternatives. They could submit to the draft and possibly risk their lives in what they regarded as a bad cause, in order to remain in good social standing; or they could avoid combat by going to prison. (Some sought to escape from this "avoidance-avoidance conflict" by emigrating to other countries, thereby incurring the pain of leaving their homes and loved ones.) Or a conflict may arise because the same object or goal has both positive and negative qualities (an "approach-avoidance conflict"). Thus a shy person may want to approach an attractive stranger and ask for a date, yet fear the possibility of rejection and ridicule. A military commander may have to send troops on a mission that is extremely important but likely to result in a very high casualty rate. Or a hungry laboratory rat may have to run through an electrified grid and receive a moderately painful shock in order to reach a food reward. Either approaching or avoiding the goal is both desirable and undesirable, so some discomfort is inevitable. The greater the strength of the conflicting alternatives, the greater the stress that is likely to result.

FRUSTRATION AND DISAPPOINTMENT.   Stress may also occur when our needs and wishes are frustrated, either by obstacles in the external world or by our own limitations. Examples include being turned down for a job or promotion because another applicant is superior or because one lacks the necessary skills; losing a loved one or a valued possession; and suffering extended periods of hunger, which are far from uncommon in various parts of the world. The greater the disappointment, or the longer the period of deprivation, the more stress one is likely to experience.

NOXIOUS STIMULI.   Stress can also be caused by exposure to such noxious stimuli as cold, heat, pain, and infectious agents. Alternatively, a noxious stimulus may be psychological rather than physical. For example, in marked contrast to tightrope walkers and test pilots, some people break out in a cold sweat when standing on a balcony that is only a few stories high. The more intense the stimulus, the greater the probable stress.

"A MARTYRDOM OF PINPRICKS." Numerous minor stressors that occur during the same period of time may have a cumulative effect and produce considerable stress. An individual who accidentally rips a button off a shirt while hurrying to dress for work in the morning, finds an unexpected small dent in the family car, gets caught in moderate rush-hour traffic, and discovers that the coffee machine is out of order on arriving at work may react to this series of relatively trivial aggravations by becoming extremely upset. If we must deal with several major stressors at about the same time, such as losing our job, the death of a loved one, and a serious illness, the effects may well be devastating.

Some of the more common stressors are summarized in Table 10–1. Once again, it is important to remember that these stimuli are only potential sources of stress. As we see when we review the scientific literature on stress, their effect on a given individual depends in part on the other components of the model: responses, consequences, and mediators on both the context and the person.

TABLE 10–1 Stressors Commonly Used in Animal and Human Research

| | HUMAN RESEARCH | |
Animal Research	Experimental Stimuli	Natural Events
Approach-approach conflicts (having to choose between two positive objects)	Approach-approach conflicts	Bereavement
	Approach-avoidance conflicts	Changes in status (e.g., job, salary, marriage)
Approach-avoidance conflicts (being presented with an object that has both positive and negative qualities)	Avoidance-avoidance conflicts	Conflicts
	Electric shock	Daily "hassles"
	Loss of prestige	Frustration
Avoidance-avoidance conflicts (having to choose between two negative objects)	Noise	Migration
	Overstimulation	Physical illness (including surgery and hospitalization)
	Sleep deprivation	Pressure to perform or achieve
Competition	Threatening, unpleasant films	Retirement
Electric shock	Uncontrollable situations	Social isolation
Exposure to cold	Understimation	Threats to self-esteem
Exposure to heat		Traumatic experiences
Exposure to novel stimuli		
Food deprivation		
Handling		
Immersion in ice water		
Immobilization		
Maternal deprivation		
Prolonged, forced swimming		
Sensory deprivation		
Sleep deprivation		
Social crowding		
Social isolation		

Source: Modified from Elliott & Eisdorfer (1982, pp. 14, 16).

THE SCIENTIFIC STUDY OF STRESS

Historical Background

FIGHT OR FLIGHT.   The scientific study of stress is a relatively recent phenomenon. Early in the 20th century, Walter Cannon observed that animals must respond quickly to life-threatening challenges in the environment in order to survive. Depending on the specific circumstances, the appropriate reaction might be to fight (as when faced with a weaker opponent) or to flee (if menaced by a superior enemy). Accordingly, Cannon characterized the standard response to danger as the **fight-or-flight reaction.** He showed that it is associated with the activation of specific aspects of the central nervous system, which results in increased cardiac output, heart rate, and arterial pressure (Cannon, 1929). Thus Cannon was among the first to investigate the effects of threatening external stimuli on an organism's behavior.

THE GENERAL ADAPTATION SYNDROME.   Undoubtedly the most prominent researcher in the field of stress and coping is Hans Selye. He dates the origin of the concept of stress to an experience he had in 1936, as a student of medicine at the University of Prague. Selye attended an introductory lecture on diagnosis presented by a famous hematologist, von Jaksch, who questioned five patients suffering from unrelated maladies. Without using any complicated instruments or chemical examinations, von Jaksch correctly diagnosed each of the patients. Selye was impressed by this demonstration, but he was also puzzled by the fact that von Jaksch

> [had not] said a word about all those signs and symptoms of disease which were perfectly obvious even to me, without previous knowledge of practical medicine. . . . All five patients, whatever their disease (one suffered from cancer of the stomach, another from tuberculosis, yet another from intense burns) had something in common: they all looked and felt sick. This may seem ridiculously childish and self-evident, but it was because I wondered about the obvious that the concept of stress was born. (Selye, 1983, p. 3)

Later, while attempting to discover a new sex hormone, Selye observed that laboratory rats given multiple doses of a crude ovarian extract developed such symptoms as gastric ulcers and enlargement of the adrenal gland. On investigating further, he found that crude extracts from other organs, extreme cold or heat, pain, and infectious agents all produced similar results. He therefore concluded that organisms exposed to a noxious stimulus of any kind exhibit the same pattern of responses. To Selye, this **general adaptation syndrome** consists of three stages:

1.   **The Alarm Reaction.** When an organism is confronted with a stressful situation, the immediate reaction is alarm. This represents a general call to arms of the body's defenses and is accompanied by such typical symptoms of injury as excessively rapid heartbeat (tachycardia), loss of muscle tone, decreased temperature, and decreased blood pressure.

2. **The Stage of Resistance.** During this stage, the body tries to limit the effects of the stressful situation. The symptoms evidenced during the first stage diminish or disappear, and the organism is prepared for either fight or flight.

3. **The Stage of Exhaustion.** If the choice between fight or flight proves to be unsuccessful in reducing stress, the organism loses its ability to adapt to the situation and enters the stage of exhaustion. This can result in tissue breakdown or even in death.

Each of these stages is accompanied by specific physiological changes. During the alarm reaction, for example, the cells of the adrenal cortex discharge secretory granules into the bloodstream. Conversely, during the stage of resistance, the cortex becomes rich in secretory granules. According to Selye, if these physiological changes do not occur, the organism is not experiencing stress.

In his later work, Selye (e.g., 1974) made two important additional contributions. He pointed out that not all stress is bad; in fact, too little stress can also have negative effects. Thus the moderate stress that may help a student or athlete to perform well must be distinguished from excessive stress, which is damaging because the organism cannot cope with the situation and enters the stage of exhaustion.

Selye also observed that stressful situations affect different individuals differently, depending on their biological makeup, age, training, dietary deficiencies, and other factors. For example, some athletes seem unusually able to rise to the occasion and perform well when the game hangs in the balance; others are more likely to "choke" under pressure and commit grave errors. Or a job that drives one employee to stomach ulcers may be handled with relative calm by another worker.

Although Selye's work represents a landmark in the study of stress, it does suffer from some significant shortcomings. (See, for example, Elliott & Eisdorfer, 1982; Stotland, 1984.) One of these concerns his definition of stress, which suffers from circularity: A stressful event is defined as whatever evokes the general adaptation syndrome, and the occurrence of this syndrome is what tells us that an event is stressful. In fact, arriving at an acceptable definition of stress is far from an easy task—as we see in the following section.

Modern Research Traditions

As was the case with intelligence (Chapter 6) and personality (Chapter 7), no single definition of stress is widely accepted by researchers in this field. Nevertheless, most definitions of stress share the common view that stress involves situations in which "environmental demands tax or exceed the adaptive capacity of an organism, resulting in psychological and biological changes that may place persons at risk for disease" (Cohen, Kessler, & Gordon, 1995, p. 3). Within this general framework researchers have pursued three general approaches to the study of stress. One tradition focuses on **environmental** events that are normatively thought to be adaptive challenges. A second tradition focuses on the

psychological or subjective perception of potential threats posed by environmental events. And the third, or **biological,** tradition focuses on the physiological systems that are activated in response to physical and psychological demands.

ENVIRONMENTAL TRADITION.   The underlying assumption of this approach is that there are a variety of life events that most people would agree are stressful. Thus having someone close to us become ill or die, losing a favorite pet, or having an accident are all events that challenge our adaptive capacities, and they are therefore defined as stressful. A representative study within this tradition might involve having individuals complete a stressful life events checklist and assessing the extent to which experiencing certain stressful events are associated with psychiatric or physical illness. Because this type of research is relatively easy to carry out and because early findings suggested strong links between being exposed to stressors and becoming ill, this approach has spawned a vast scientific literature. Although this approach is appealingly simple, it fails to recognize the importance of the organism's behavior. A demanding supervisor may be regarded as a mere annoyance by one employee, yet be perceived by a second worker as exerting enormous pressure. A forthcoming examination may cause one student considerable anxiety, whereas another student reacts with relative calm. Some people exhibit marked signs of stress when they travel by plane, but others do not. In each of these examples, the stimulus object or situation is the same, yet it is considerably more stressful for some individuals than for others. As we see later in this chapter when we explore some of this literature in greater detail, interpreting findings from this research tradition is considerably more problematic than was once thought.

PSYCHOLOGICAL TRADITION.   This approach places strong emphasis on the individual's perception and evaluation of the potential harm posed by a particular environmental event. Thus whether an event is experienced as stressful depends not only on the event itself but also on the individual's assessment of his or her ability to cope with that event. The most influential advocates of the appraisal process approach are Lazarus and Folkman (1984). Stimulus characteristics that affect the appraisal process include whether or not it has the potential to be harmful, its intensity, duration, and controllability. Characteristics of individuals that affect the appraisal process include beliefs about themselves, their values and commitments, and their personality. If individuals feel they possess effective coping responses when confronted with a threat, the stress response is short circuited. But if individuals are unsure about their ability to cope with a threatening situation, then stress is experienced. This research tradition has also generated a vast literature on how people assess stressors as well as cope with them.

BIOLOGICAL TRADITION.   This tradition is most closely linked to the early work of Cannon and Selye. It focuses on the activation of specific physiological systems that are responsive to physical or psychological demands. Prolonged or repeated activation of these systems is thought to increase the risk of developing a wide range of psychiatric or physical disorders. The two systems thought to be the primary indicators of the stress response are the sympathetic-adrenal medullary system (SAM) and the hypothalamic-pituitary-adrenocortical axis (HPA). Although a detailed discussion of these physiological systems and how they operate is beyond the scope of this book, it is useful to know the types of responses regulated by these systems. For example, SAM responses elicited by stressors include increased blood pressure, heart rate, sweating, and constriction of peripheral blood vessels. Stress-related disregulation of HPA has been linked to the occurrence of depression. Together, these two physiologic systems may be implicated in a variety of psychiatric and/or physical illnesses that are caused by suppression of cellular immune function, neurochemical imbalances, and cardiovascular irregularities.

AFTERWORD. Each of the approaches has made valuable contributions to our understanding of stress and disease. In many ways they complement each other, focusing on different stages of the stress-disease process. The environmental perspective focuses on the stimulus conditions that might elicit stress, the psychological tradition emphasizes the role of subjective appraisals in response to threatening situations, and the biological perspective shows how the experience of stress can result in bodily changes that increase the risk of illness. Next, we incorporate these perspectives in a general model of stress.

A General Model of Stress

A model integrating these approaches is presented in Figure 10–1. When confronted with a challenging life event or environmental demand, individuals

FIGURE 10–1   A general model of stress-health process.
(*Source:* Adapted from Cohen, Kessler, and Gordon (1995).)

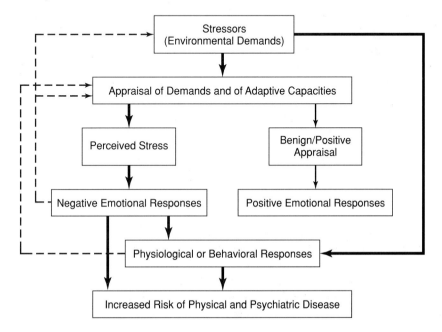

Major disasters are not the only causes of stress. Numerous minor stressors, such as one's car breaking down, may have a cumulative effect that results in considerable stress.

determine whether these demands pose a potential threat. At the same time, they assess their ability to cope with these demands. Stress is experienced when individuals feel their coping resources cannot meet the challenge posed by environmental demands. This in turn results in negative emotional states. If extreme enough, these emotional responses may directly result in psychiatric illness such as anxiety or depression. Negative emotional responses may also trigger behavioral or physiological responses that increase the risk of physical or psychiatric disease. Two additional characteristics of this model are important to point out. First, the model allows for the possibility that some environmental demands result in negative physiological or behavior responses even though they may not be appraised as stressful. For example, the workaholic may in fact enjoy putting in long hours to fulfill extreme demands put on him or her, and suffer negative health effects as a result. The second feature of this model is that although it is presented as a sequential, unidirectional model, real life is likely to be much more complicated than our illustration. We have included as dashed lines a few of the many possible feedback loops that might be included in such a model.

AN ILLUSTRATIVE EXAMPLE: FAMILY CAREGIVING.   We noted in Chapter 8 that one of the most challenging life stressors confronted by middle-aged and older individuals is having to care for a relative who is physically or cognitively impaired. Perhaps the most challenging of all caregiving situations is having to care for a relative who suffers from Alzheimer's disease or other dementing illnesses. Approximately 2 million Americans are estimated to be afflicted with Alzheimer's disease and related disorders (ADRD). Caregivers of persons with ADRD often face a "triple jeopardy"; they experience significant emotional stress, extreme physical and financial burdens, and in some cases, also have to deal with apathy or even hostility from the ADRD person they care for. These burdens often make caregivers "hidden patients" who require outside assistance and support to maintain their own health and functioning. How would the experience of caregivers be characterized in terms of our general stress-coping model?

An adaptation of this model applied to caregiving is presented in Figure 10–2. The sequential relations between components of this model can be described as follows. The primary stressors or environmental demands include the functional limitations and problem behaviors of the dementia patient and related social and environmental stressors. When confronted with these stressors, people evaluate whether the demands pose a potential threat and whether sufficient adaptive capacities are available to cope with them. If they perceive the environmental demands as threatening, and at the same time view their coping resources as inadequate, they perceive themselves as under stress. The appraisal of stress is presumed to result in negative affect such as depression and anxiety. Under extreme conditions, emotional responses may directly contribute to the onset of affective psychiatric disorders such as clinical depression. Negative emotional responses may also trigger behavioral or physiological responses, such as not getting enough sleep, not eating well, or failing to go to the doctor to take

FIGURE 10–2   A general model of the stress-health process applied to caregiving. (*Source:* Adapted from Cohen, Kessler, and Gordon (1995).)

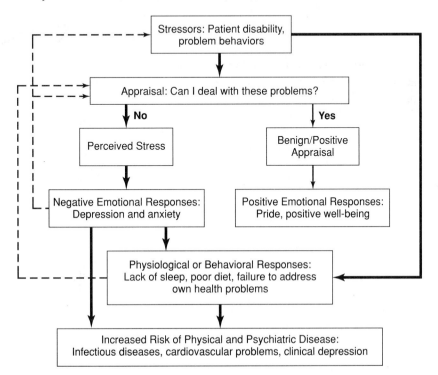

care of one's own illnesses, which place the individual at increased risk for psychiatric or physical illness.

It is also conceivable, although less likely when applied to dementia caregiving, that stressors are appraised as benign and/or that individuals feel they have the capacity to deal with the stressors. This in turn may lead to positive emotional responses such as feeling proud or experiencing general positive affect. Whether feeling good necessarily leads to salutary physiological and behavioral responses is still debated. Although this pathway is theoretically possible and has been demonstrated empirically in some instances, it is important to note that this pathway is both less common and, on the whole, has less empirical support.

Two other features of this model are important to point out. One critical feature is that environmental stressors can place the individual at risk for negative health outcomes even when the appraisal of the stressor does not result in perceptions of stress or negative emotional responses. This is illustrated by the arrow linking stressors to physiological and behavioral responses. For example, caregivers may take pride in doing an excellent job of caring for demented relatives without realizing they are neglecting their own needs such as eating regularly or seeing a doctor to attend to their own health problems. The second feature of this model concerns the existence of many possible feedback loops, a few of which are illustrated with dashed lines. Although the model is primarily unidirectional, we recognize that dealing with stressors is a complex, dynamic process in which responses at one stage of the model may subsequently feed back to earlier stages. One example of this process is represented by the dashed line linking emotional responses to the stressor and the appraisal process. A negative emotional response to a stressor might subsequently increase the stressor itself or impact negatively on the appraisal of the stressor. This might happen, for example, when a caregiver becomes distressed in response to the disruptive behavior of a care recipient, who then becomes more disruptive because of the caregiver's response, and so on.

STRESS AND AGING

The Effects of Major Life Events

METHODOLOGICAL ISSUES.   To reduce the study of stress to manageable proportions, some researchers representing the environmental tradition prefer to focus on the effects of major life events. It is reasonable to hypothesize that events like marriage and divorce are at least somewhat stressful, even though different individuals may well respond in different ways, and that some of these events are more stressful than others. Accordingly, some investigators have sought to quantify the amount of stress caused by various life events (McLeod, 1996; Turner & Wheaton, 1995).

Using this approach, the most stressful of all events, the death of a spouse, is arbitrarily assigned a rating of 100. The degree of stress associated with other events is then estimated relative to this standard, based on responses obtained from test populations. For example, divorce is accorded an intensity rating of 73; marriage, 50; and trouble with one's boss, 23. (See Table 10–2.) If you have been exposed in recent months to events that sum to 300 or more, it is estimated that the probability of your developing a major illness within the next 2 years is as high as 0.80.

The numerical scale shown in Table 10–2 is commonly cited in textbooks and articles. Yet it is controversial and has been strongly attacked on methodological grounds. This scale implies that stressful life events, notably those with high intensity ratings, cause such undesirable consequences as major illnesses. However, some of these life events may well result from existing disorders. (Recall once again that in the general model of stress, the relationships among potential stressors, emotional and behavioral responses, consequences, and mediators can be bidirectional.) Having sexual difficulties or more arguments with one's spouse, or being fired at work, could be due to an underlying psychological or physical illness. If this disorder then becomes more evident in subsequent months, it is clearly erroneous to conclude that an otherwise healthy individual was laid low by stress. (See Elliott & Eisdorfer, 1982; Siegler, 1980.)

 **MYTHS ABOUT AGING**

Stress and Coping

Myth	*Best Available Evidence*
Stress is always disadvantageous and debilitating and should be avoided whenever possible.	Extreme stress can have debilitating effects. But too little stress can inhibit your motivation and lead to lackluster and inferior performance. Some people enjoy facing a challenge, improving their skills, and achieving difficult goals; some willingly seek out risky and stressful vocations or avocations. Stress may also facilitate personal growth and development, as when we learn to deal with disappointment and frustration.
The intensity of a stressor can be assessed by assigning it a single score that applies in all instances. For example, the death of a spouse is always more stressful than divorce.	A life event is likely to be more stressful if it is temporally non-normative. For example, the elderly are likely to find divorce even more painful than widowhood. Thus the intensity of a given stressor may well vary as a function of the age at which it occurs.

Myth	*Best Available Evidence*
You will experience much more stress during the second half of your life than during the first half.	There is some truth to this idea, because some extremely stressful life events are more likely to occur during old age (e.g., widowhood, terminal illnesses). But the relationship between aging and stress is more complicated than this. Some traumatic life events are more common at older ages, but are more intense when they occur at younger ages. Other potential stressors are more common at younger ages and more intense at older ages.
As you grow older, your ability to cope with those stressful life events that you do face decreases markedly.	If your health, economic resources, and social resources decline as you grow toward old age, your ability to cope with stress may be compromised. But if these capacities remain more or less intact, there is no reason to expect your ability to cope with stressful life events to decline with increasing age.

This scale also focuses on events that require us to make significant readjustments in our lives: learning to live without a spouse, moving to a new location or a new school, changing jobs, and so on. Yet stress can be caused by chronic conditions that do not necessitate personal change. For example, an employee may face a consistent overload or underload at work. No daily or monthly readjustment is involved because the situation remains essentially the same, yet considerable stress may result. Or apparently minor daily hassles can accumulate to produce serious effects, as we have seen. These important sources of stress are not tapped by the readjustment scale.

Furthermore, this scale contains an overabundance of events that are more likely to befall young adults. The elderly are much less likely to get married or divorced, take out a mortgage, change their schools, be confined to jail, or switch to a different line of work. Suppose, then, that researchers find that these life events occur much less frequently with increasing age. Although this might mean the elderly lead relatively stress-free lives, it more probably reflects the youth-oriented emphasis of this particular set of events (Goldberg & Comstock, 1980; Kasl, 1983; Rabkin & Struening, 1976). Some researchers have tried to re-

TABLE 10–2   Stressful Life Events: The Social Readjustment Rating Scale

LIFE EVENT	SCALE OF IMPACT	LIFE EVENT	SCALE OF IMPACT
Death of spouse	100	Trouble with in-laws	29
Divorce	73	Outstanding personal achievement	28
Marital separation	65	Wife begins or stops work	26
Jail term	63	Beginning or ending school	26
Death of close family member	63	Change in living conditions	25
Personal injury or illness	53	Revision of personal habits	24
Marriage	50	Trouble with boss	23
Fired at work	47	Change in work hours or conditions	20
Marital reconciliation	45	Change in residence	20
Retirement	45	Change in schools	20
Change in health of family member	44	Change in recreation	19
Pregnancy	40	Change in church activities	19
Sex difficulties	39	Change in social activities	18
Gain of new family member	39	Small mortgage or loan	17
Business readjustment	39	Change in sleeping habits	16
Change in financial state	38	Change in number of family get-togethers	15
Death of close friend	37	Change in eating habits	15
Change to different line of work	36	Vacation	13
Change in number of arguments with spouse	35	Christmas	12
High mortgage	31	Minor violations of the law	11
Foreclosure of mortgage or loan	30		
Change in responsibilities at work	29		
Son or daughter leaving home	29		

Source: Holmes and Rahe (1967).

solve this problem by developing scales based on life events that are more appropriate for middle-aged and elderly adults (e.g., Kiyak, Liang, & Kahana, 1976; Plomin et al., 1990), one example of which is shown in Table 10–3.

Finally, the social readjustment rating scale may well sacrifice accuracy in order to gain simplicity. For example, the degree of stress caused by trouble with your boss is influenced by various other factors. If your skills are in great demand, and you have many possible job opportunities, this life event will probably be much less stressful than if you cannot afford to quit or be fired. Or pregnancy, and the gain of a new family member, may be much more stressful to an unmarried teenager than to a happily married 30-year-old woman. Therefore, expecting these potential stressors to have intensities of 23 and 39 in all instances may well be a serious oversimplification.

One possible alternative is to collapse the various life events into four major categories: changes in personal relationships, changes in financial resources, changes in environment and location, and changes in health. Then, separate scores may be obtained for each category (Wilson & Schulz, 1983; see also Schulz, 1985). Conceivably, we might find that changes within each category are more extreme for the elderly. For example, a relationship change for a

TABLE 10-3 Stressful Life Events Appropriate for Middle-Aged and Elderly Adults (mean age of sample, 58.6 years)

LIFE EVENT	MEAN RATED IMPORTANCE (3 = GREAT IMPORTANCE, 1 = LITTLE IMPORTANCE)	PERCENTAGE OF SUBJECTS IN THIS STUDY WHO EXPERIENCED THIS EVENT
Death of spouse	2.96	15.6
Death of child	2.96	5.1
Nursing home care for spouse	2.91	2.3
Serious illness of child	2.88	8.9
Divorce	2.85	12.3
Serious conflicts with child	2.83	6.4
Mental illness of spouse	2.81	3.2
Deterioration in married life	2.80	10.6
Mental illness of self	2.79	3.3
Home care for spouse	2.78	5.9
Can't manage to look after self	2.77	2.6
Getting married	2.76	92.7
Death of siblings or friends	2.75	28.4
Improvement in married life	2.67	16.8
Changes in relations with grandchildren	2.67	6.5
Home care for self	2.64	8.8
Forced change in residence with reduced contacts	2.59	5.6
Somatic illness of spouse	2.56	23.6
Somatic illness of self	2.41	29.0
Making a new acquaintance	2.22	38.9
Major improvement in financial status	2.20	36.1
Retirement	2.19	40.7
Major deterioration in financial status	2.13	18.9
Loss of sexual ability or interest	2.10	19.0
Paying fine for minor violation of law	1.93	13.2

Source: Plomin et al., "Genetic Influence of Life Events During Last Half of Life Span" (1990). *Journal of Psychology and Aging, 5,* pp. 24–30. Copyright 1990 by the American Psychological Association. Reprinted by permission.

young adult might involve breaking up with a boy- or girlfriend, whereas an aged individual might more often have to face the death of a loved one. Or we might hypothesize that the elderly are more likely to experience threats from several categories, such as suffering financial losses and having to relocate to a nursing home.

Another intriguing alternative is to focus on those frustrating daily hassles that we all must contend with. (Recall our previous discussion of "a martyrdom of pinpricks.") A scale to measure this stressor has been developed by Richard Lazarus and his associates (Delongis et al., 1982). They found that daily hassles predicted the outbreak of psychosomatic diseases significantly better than did life events scores, possibly because they occurred closer in time to these consequences. High levels of daily stress have also been found to often precede the occurrence of migraine headaches (Köhler & Haimerl, 1990).

Despite the controversy that surrounds the use of numerical scales, both life events and daily hassles can be useful tools for assessing stress. Consider, for example, the death of a spouse from cancer or an automobile accident. Here, it is not very likely that some response or consequence of the surviving spouse caused this unfortunate event. Rather, it is more logical to assume the stressful event caused various undesirable consequences. We may therefore ask, Does the likelihood that we will encounter stressful life events and daily hassles change markedly as we grow older?

LIFE EVENTS AND AGING. Growing old is widely believed to be quite stressful. Events such as retirement, widowhood, having all of one's children leave home, and failing health are more likely to occur during the second half of life. However, numerous other stressful life events are more likely to befall young adults (as we have seen). If the elderly expect certain events to be a natural aspect of old age (e.g., ill health), they may suffer relatively little stress. Also, as we grow older, increased experience in living may make it easier to deal with stress. Finally, it is useful to remember that individuals who survive to old age may be more resilient and are therefore better able to cope with stress.

What has empirical research evidence to say about this issue? Studies comparing the effects of life events on individuals of different ages are relatively rare. However, one study assessing the effects of disaster experiences on persons of different ages found that older persons experienced less distress. As suggested, these differences could be due to many reasons including the selection of non-adaptive elders out of the sample by death, age differences in maturity or resilience, a lowering of aspirations with age, or differences in the experienced stressfulness of older versus younger adults (McLeod, 1996). In one study, young newlyweds showed more emotional stress than adults age 50 and 60 (Lowenthal et al., 1975). Another study reported a relatively low incidence of stressful life events for 375 subjects, whose ages ranged from 45 to 70: in an 8-year period, 80% had not retired, 75% had no major illnesses, 94% had not been widowed, and 85% did not experience the last child leaving home (Palmore et al., 1979; see also Shanan & Jacobowitz, 1982). No comparison data were obtained from young adults, however.

Even joyful events, such as marriage, may be significant sources of stress. Some investigators regard marriage as more stressful than being fired from a job, although this is a complicated issue that also depends on such personal factors as age and competence.

Various research findings have associated changes in residence with negative consequences among the aged. In one study, patients were matched on such factors as age, sex, race, health, length of hospitalization, and ability to ambulate. Those transferred from one California institution to another had a significantly higher death rate than a control group that was not relocated. When patients who relocated from their homes to an institution were compared with patients transferred from another institution, the former group lived for an average of about 1 month less, presumably because they experienced a more severe environmental change (Schulz & Aderman, 1974; see also Schulz, 1978). Here again, however, a life event like relocation may instead be caused by an existing physical or psychological illness—hence the need to control for level of health when trying to ascertain the effects of stress.

The relationship between expectations and stressfulness is supported once again by the research evidence on the effects of bereavement. As we observed in Chapter 8, life events are more likely to be stressful if they are temporally non-normative (i.e., if they occur at an atypical age). Not surprisingly, mortality rates for the widowed are significantly higher than for married controls matched on age and sex. However, there is a markedly lower rate of illnesses and death when widowhood occurs at older ages. This event is more easily anticipated when one is old, and may therefore be less stressful. An elderly widow is also more likely to have at least some friends who are widows, who are willing and able to provide needed emotional support. Conversely, young widows tend to find themselves in so atypical a position that their friends do not know how to provide effective help. (See Kraus & Lilienfeld, 1959; Morgan, 1976; Stroebe et al., 1982.)

In contrast to widowhood, divorce is less common among the elderly. Therefore, when the aged do have to go through a divorce, they typically experience more extreme suffering and illnesses than do young adults (Chiriboga, 1982). In fact, one extensive study of the widowed found that older men suffered much more following a divorce or separation than did those who lost a spouse through death (Hyman, 1983). Thus the stressfulness of a life event is significantly influenced by its temporal normativity.

Age-related differences have also been observed with regard to daily hassles. Middle-aged men tend to worry more about economic problems, such as rising prices and taxes, whereas young adults express more concern with social and academic difficulties (Delongis et al., 1982).

In sum: Certain stressful life events are more likely to occur at different ages. (See Table 10–4.) Also, a life event is likely to cause considerably more stress if it occurs at an atypical age. Thus the relationship between aging and stress is not a simple one. Potential stressors like widowhood, ill health, and having to care for a disabled relative are more intense when they occur at younger ages but are more common at older ages. Conversely, such potential stressors as divorce and one's first job are more common at younger ages and more intense at older ages.

POSITIVE LIFE EVENTS AND STRESS. Stress is not due only to negative life events, such as widowhood and divorce. As indicated in Table 10–2, such happy occasions as marriage, pregnancy, and a good new job are also common sources of stress. This has been attributed to the resulting dramatic changes in one's self-image and style of living.

Stressed by Success

Mrs. J. was most embarrassed to be seeking the help of her university counselor. In the past few months, everything in her life had gone beautifully. She had just finished her doctoral dissertation, which her advisor regarded as outstanding. She had received an award as the best teacher-scholar at her university, and had lined up a publisher for the book she was writing. Though jobs were scarce, she had secured a position at an excellent Eastern university. Yet she felt very strange, like everything was unreal. She questioned whether she deserved this success, and wondered if she would wake up one day to find that it had all disappeared.

TABLE 10–4   Aging and the Likelihood of Specific Stressful Life Events

SOME EVENTS MORE LIKELY TO OCCUR DURING THE FIRST HALF OF LIFE	SOME EVENTS MORE LIKELY TO OCCUR DURING THE SECOND HALF OF LIFE
Beginning or ending school	Having to care for a disabled relative
Beginning to work (first job)	Ill health
Divorce	Last child leaving home
Jail term	Relocation to a nursing home
Marriage	Retirement
Pregnancy	Widowhood and the death of friends
Taking out a mortgage	Birth of a grandchild

The counselor helped Mrs. J. to understand the reasons for her stress. Because of her new job, she would soon be moving to a new area, thereby losing the respect and support she received in her present community. Her previous self-image as "just a nice, average person" had been greatly exceeded by her successes, and it was frightening to abandon this old, comfortable, and predictable view of herself. Her success also meant a change in the relationship with her husband: Previously she had moved because of his job changes, but now he was going to have to move because of hers. When she realized her grief and anxiety about losing her familiar roles was natural and understandable, she was able to face her new situation with considerable pleasure. (Schneider, 1984. See also Berglas, 1986.)

Stress, Disease, and Mortality

It is not uncommon to hear or read about individuals who apparently became ill or even died because of exposure to extreme stress. Heart attacks, suicides, and even homicides frequently are attributed to stress. The scientific basis for these beliefs has been debated for several decades, and this topic continues to be studied in both laboratory and real-world settings.

STRESS AND DISEASE.   Early studies on stress and health found weak to moderate relationships between life change stressors and physical health, mental health, and immune functioning (McLeod, 1996). Medical, psychological, and sociological researchers have found a significant relationship between stress and heart disease, with sudden cardiac death often preceded by several months of increased stress. There is some indication that such potential stressors as rejection by a loved one, a setback or continued emotional strain at work, or a loss of prestige increase the likelihood of coronary diseases (Cohen, Kessler, & Gordon, 1995). As noted, relocation has been linked with higher death rates among the elderly. Also, stressful life events have been related to the occurrence of suicide attempts (Dohrenwend & Dohrenwend, 1974).

Suppose that adults who experience considerable stress are more likely to die at a fairly young age. Studies of the elderly will fail to reveal an abnormal number of negative consequences because many of the adults who would show such symptoms have been weeded out by death. That is, the aged may represent a relatively select, stress-resistant group. Therefore, it is important to determine whether high levels of stress are associated with a shorter life span.

MORTALITY AND TYPE A AND TYPE B INDIVIDUALS.   It has long been believed that individual behavioral styles mediate the levels of stress that we experience. The so-called **Type A individual** is characterized by intense ambition, competitiveness, aggressiveness, restlessness, and perfectionism in many areas. These are the people who make business calls while waiting in the dentist's office, rather than waste a single moment of time; frequently battle against self-imposed deadlines; are perceived by their spouses as driving themselves much too hard; prefer respect to affection; and treat life as a deadly serious game that they are out to win. **Type B individuals** may be equally serious, and just as successful. But these people are more easygoing, are seldom impatient, do not feel compelled by time pressures, are less competitive and preoccupied with achievement, and tend to do one thing well. (See Wright, 1988.)

Although type theories may well oversimplify the human personality (Chapter 7), behavioral scientists have taken considerable interest in the Type A–Type B distinction. The early research in this area indicated that the incidence of coronary heart disease was two to three times greater among Type A individuals and as much as six times greater for Type A men between the ages of 39 and 49 (Friedman & Rosen, 1959, 1974; Jenkins, 1974, 1975; Suinn, 1977). As a result, stern warnings against following the Type A behavior pattern were often found in both the professional literature and the popular media.

More recent research has painted a somewhat different picture. First of all, the relationship between Type A behavior and coronary heart disease appears to be much weaker than the early evidence suggested (Booth-Kewley & Friedman, 1987). Second, Type A behavior may be an important precipitating factor only for a person's first heart attack (Matthews, 1988). Third, only some aspects of Type A behavior may be related to the increased probability of heart disease. To date, the best evidence suggests that hostility may be the culprit: People who are generally more hostile and display anger more frequently are more likely to have heart attacks (Friedman & Booth-Kewley, 1987; Matthews, 1988). Thus it may well be anger (rather than the overall behavior pattern) that makes Type A individuals more vulnerable to potential stressors and more likely to suffer such negative consequences as heart disease and an early death.

Until future research clarifies these important issues, probably the most advisable course is to follow this caution recommended by Wright (1988): Type A individuals are notorious for denying that they behave in this way, at least until they suffer their first heart attack. They (and all of us) would do better to run the race of life like a marathon, rather than as a series of intense 100-yard dashes.

AFTERWORD. The best available evidence indicates that stress is associated with decreased life expectancy, particularly for middle-aged men who fit at least some aspects of the Type A description. Therefore, the selective attrition caused by death may be another reason why the consequences of stress have not been found to be more severe among the aged.

Coping With Stress

Coping with stress refers to a particular class of responses: those thoughts (conscious and unconscious) and/or actions that we use to eliminate or alleviate the demands made by a stressor.

AGING AND COPING ABILITY. Does our ability to cope with stress decline as we grow older? If so, we should expect to find that negative consequences often occur for the first time at relatively advanced ages. However, this does not appear to be the case. For relatively normal older adults (i.e., those who do not have a history of serious physical or physiological disorders), stressful but temporally normative life events have not been found to cause significant personality changes or increases in maladjustment (Chiriboga, 1981; Costa & McCrae, 1980).

For those older adults who suffer from ill health or from a significant decline in economic and social resources, the ability to cope with stress may be compromised. But there is no indication that more normal elderly individuals suffer any appreciable decrement in their ability to cope with stress.

AGING AND COPING PROCESSES. When you are faced with a stressful life event, one possible course is to take action designed to resolve the troublesome situation **(problem-focused coping)**. For example, if you discover you have the symptoms of a potentially serious illness, you might seek out expert medical advice. If, instead, you must contend with a demanding parent or boss, you might choose among such task-oriented tactics as fight, flight, or compromise. That is, you may regard the stressful situation as a problem that can be solved by appropriate action.

Alternatively, you might try to achieve an emotional acceptance of the existing situation **(emotion-focused coping)**. Faced with the possibility of a major illness, you might concentrate on maintaining a positive and optimistic attitude. Or you might prefer to put this issue out of your mind, perhaps with the aid of one or more defense mechanisms. The differences between the problem-focused and emotion-focused methods for coping with stress are further illustrated by the following self-report items and statements (Folkman & Lazarus, 1980; Schmitz-Scherzer & Thomae, 1983).

Relaxation and distraction are effective ways of dealing with some stressors.

Problem-Focused Coping

"I got the person responsible to change his or her mind."

"I made a plan of action and followed it."

"I stood my ground and fought for what I wanted."

Emotion-Focused Coping

"I looked for the 'silver lining.' "

"I accepted sympathy and understanding from another person."

"I tried to forget the whole thing."

"Well, maybe I am not too well off, but what can you expect for someone my age?"

"Even if I am bad off, there are many whose health is worse."

Is there a relationship between aging and the choice of coping strategy? Early research in this area found that older adults are more likely to use emotion-focused coping, primarily because they more often must deal with life events that cannot be successfully resolved by problem-focused coping. For example, there is no way to eliminate the pain caused by certain arthritic conditions or incurable illnesses by direct action on the environment. So older adults opt instead to regulate their emotions by developing greater tolerance and acceptance of their situation. Thus it is the nature of the problems encountered by the elderly, rather than aging per se, that causes the preference for emotion-focused coping (Schulz et al., 1991; see also Folkman & Lazarus, 1980; Folkman et al., 1987; Koenig, George, & Siegler, 1988; Stephens, Crowther, Hobfoll, & Tennenbaum, 1990).

Additional evidence supporting this conclusion has been reported by Schmitz-Scherzer and Thomae (1983). They conducted a longitudinal study of some 222 German men and women, primarily from what was formerly West Germany. The older cohort was born between 1890 and 1895, and the younger cohort was born between 1900 and 1905. The subjects were assessed on six separate occasions between 1965 and 1977, so the ages at the times of assessment varied from 60 to over 80. Among other measures, subjects were asked the extent to which they perceived various problem areas to be stressful. Over the 12-year period, health problems became considerably more prominent with increasing age; family, economic, and housing problems either remained at about the same level or declined markedly. The younger adults in this study were also more likely to use problem-focused coping (finding the best doctor or treatment; getting the most out of their health insurance), whereas the older adults relied more on emotion-focused coping (learning to accept their disabilities; revising their expectations of life accordingly).

More recent research has produced similar findings. Folkman et al. (1987) found that younger adults were more likely to identify their problems as falling in the areas of finances and work, and to rely on problem-focused coping. Conversely, older adults more often identified their problems as involving health and home issues, and they preferred to use emotion-focused coping. In a cross-sectional study of 890 adults age 34 to 63, Brandtstadter and Renner (1990) found a gradual increase in the use of emotion-focused coping with increasing age. Felton and Revenson (1987) controlled for diagnosis, physical limitations caused by an illness, and perceived seriousness of an illness, and they still found a small but significant relationship: Older people were less likely to use problem-focused coping.

In sum: Both problem-focused and emotion-focused coping are commonly used to deal with stress, and both can effectively improve life satisfaction and reduce depression. However, emotion-focused coping is more common among the elderly. This is an adaptive and sensible solution in view of the kinds of stressors that they most often face.

AFTERWORD.   Stress is a significant problem in our society. It is experienced by adults of all ages, and it is associated with higher illness and mortality rates.

The relationship between aging and stress is a complicated one, and it involves various important issues. What potential stressors are most likely to be salient during young adulthood, middle age, and old age? What mediators factors cause different people to respond to stressors in different ways? How do adults of different ages cope with stress? How can we best deal with potential stressors, so as to minimize the probability of negative consequences?

As we have seen throughout this chapter, gerontological researchers and social scientists have discovered many important answers to these questions. Given the current interest in the scientific study of stress, we may expect further valuable findings to be forthcoming within the next decade.

SUMMARY

The Scientific Study of Stress

Walter Cannon was among the first to investigate the effects of threatening external stimuli on an organism's behavior. He characterized the standard response to danger as the fight-or-flight reaction. Modern investigators have added a third alternative to Cannon's dichotomy, namely compromise or surrender.

Undoubtedly, the most prominent name in the field of stress research is that of Hans Selye. He concluded that organisms exposed to noxious stimuli of any kind exhibit a three-stage pattern of responses, which he called the general adaptation syndrome. He also argued that stress occurs if and only if each stage is accompanied by specific physiological changes, a contention that has been challenged by modern researchers. Selye pointed out that too little stress can also have negative effects, and individual differences play an important role in the response to stressful situations.

Selye's definition of stress suffers from circularity: A stressful event is whatever evokes the general adaptation syndrome, and the occurrence of this syndrome is what tells us an event is stressful. However, it is not easy to arrive at an acceptable definition of stress. Some theorists have defined stress solely in terms of the external situation, or solely in terms of the organism's responses, but these approaches overlook important considerations. Accordingly, some investigators prefer to define stress in terms of the entire complex of stressors, responses, mediators, and consequences. This approach more readily enables us to understand why different individuals react differently to the same stressor. It also emphasizes that the relationships among the various components of stress are primarily bidirectional: Stress operates in a circular and dynamic fashion, with each of the components continuously modifying and being modified by the other elements.

Most modern scientific definitions of stress share the common view that stress involves situations in which environmental demands exceed the adaptive capacity of an organism, resulting in psychological and biological changes that may place persons at risk for disease. Within this general framework, researchers have pursued three general approaches to the study of stress. One tradition focuses on environmental events that are normatively thought to be adaptive challenges. A second tradition focuses on the psychological or subjective perception of potential threats posed by environmental events. And the third or biological tradition focuses on the physiological systems that are activated in response to physical and psychological demands.

Among the more common stressors are external pressures and overstimulation, boredom and understimulation, conflicts, frustration and disappointment, and noxious physical and psychological stimuli. Important responses include physiological changes, emotional changes, expectations, cognitions, perceptions, fight, flight, compromise, and the psychological defense mechanisms. The possible negative consequences of stress include such physical and psychological disorders as anxiety, depression, stomach ulcers, colitis, headaches, and coronary diseases. Or, if the level of stress is neither too high nor too low, good health and performance may result. Common mediators include personal competence, physical and psychological health, the physical setting, and the social milieu. For example, personal competence mediates the relationship between the stressfulness of one's environment, responses, and consequences.

Stress is not a simple phenomenon. It is virtually impossible to make simple statements that are also accurate, like "situation X is always stressful" or "stressor A invariably leads to response B." Of necessity, therefore, stress researchers typically simplify matters by studying one aspect of this phenomenon at a time.

Stress and Aging

It is reasonable to hypothesize that certain life events are stressful to varying degrees, even though different individuals may well respond in different ways. Some investigators have sought to quantify the amount of stress caused by various life events, but such scales have been strongly attacked on methodological grounds. The relationship between aging and stress is complicated, and it is affected by the temporal normativity of the life event. Some stressful events are more common at advanced ages but more intense when they occur at younger ages; others are more common at younger ages and more intense at older ages.

Stress is associated with coronary heart disease and other diseases, and with a decreased life expectancy. The likelihood of suffering a stress-related illness that leads to death is greater for middle-aged men who fit at least some characteristics of the Type A description. Thus the selective attrition caused by death may be another reason why the consequences of stress have not been found to be more severe among the aged.

For those adults whose health, economic resources, and social resources remain reasonably intact, there is no indication that the ability to cope with stress declines with increasing age. Both problem-focused coping and emotion-focused coping are typically used in stressful situations. The elderly rely more on emotion-focused coping because they must more often contend with situations that are not amenable to the problem-focused approach (e.g., incurable illnesses or injuries).

Gerontological researchers have investigated various important issues: determining those stressors most likely to be salient at different ages, identifying important contextual and individual difference factors, and ascertaining how adults of different ages cope with stress. The scientific study of stress has produced much valuable information in these areas and is likely to continue to do so in the future.

STUDY QUESTIONS

1. What are some of the harmful consequences of too much stress? What are some of the harmful consequences of too little stress? Why can it be difficult to determine how much stress is the right amount (that is, neither too much nor too little)? Hint: Why must we consider mediating factors such as personal competence when deciding how much stress a person is encountering?

2. In the general model of stress presented in this chapter, why is the relationship between appraisals of stressors and responses treated as bidirectional? Why is the relationship between responses and consequences treated as bidirectional? What does this imply about the definition of "stress"? Why is (only) the relationship between consequences and stressors treated as unidirectional? Under what circumstances might an environmental stressor result in illness even though the individual does not appraise the event as stressful?

3. How do the various psychological mechanisms help reduce stress? Have you ever used any of these strategies? Why is it difficult to reach firm conclusions about the differential effects of stressors on older and younger persons?

4. Why are the stressful life events listed in Table 10–3 more suitable for use with middle-aged and elderly adults than the stressful life events listed in Table 10–2? What does this imply about the different kinds of stressors typically encountered by older and younger adults?

5. In what situations would you use problem-focused coping to reduce stress? In what situations might you prefer emotion-focused coping? Or does the choice depend more on personal preferences than on situational factors?

TERMS TO REMEMBER

Biological tradition
Consequences of stress
Coping with stress
Defense mechanism
Emotion-focused coping
Environmental tradition
Fight-or-flight reaction
General adaptation syndrome
Mediator

Personal competence
Problem-focused coping
Psychological tradition
Responses to stress
Stress
Stressor
Type A individual
Type B individual

11

ADULT PSYCHOPATHOLOGY

A 68-year-old writer, once celebrated for his ability to remember complicated details, cannot sustain a simple thought or find basic words with which to express himself. A former supervisor cannot recall the plot of a television program she watched 10 minutes ago. A woman who has led a pleasant life becomes obsessed with the idea that she is a failure and only her suicide will enable her family to draw closer together. An elderly man experiences attacks of apprehension, fear, and even terror for no apparent reason.

Throughout this book, we have seen that the probability of contracting certain physical illnesses and injuries increases with increasing age. Yet these are by no means the only health problems that afflict older adults; as the preceding examples indicate, much pain and anguish can also be caused by mental disorders. In this chapter, we examine the empirical evidence dealing with adult **psychopathology.** Among the issues we discuss are the forms of psychopathology most common among older adults, including Alzheimer's disease, depression, and anxiety disorders; how mental health professionals diagnose and assess these disorders; how likely you are to suffer such disorders as you grow through adulthood; and appropriate methods of treatment.

SUBSTANTIVE
AND METHODOLOGICAL ISSUES

Defining Mental Health and Psychopathology

Before we can examine the various types of psychopathology that afflict middle-aged and elderly adults, we must first ask an important question: What defines a mentally healthy individual? That is, how do we distinguish between mental health and psychopathology? As elsewhere in this book (e.g., the sections on intelligence, personality, stress), arriving at a satisfactory definition is far from an easy task.

SITUATIONAL FACTORS. Whether behavior is pathological often depends on the specific situation. For example, suppose an older man spends much of each day crying, feeling sad, and refusing to leave the house to go to the movies or enjoy any other form of recreation. Your first thought might be that he is suffering from one form of psychopathology, namely depression. But suppose you are informed that his spouse died suddenly a few days ago. Now you would surely conclude he is going through the normal process of bereavement and not suffering from any psychological disorder at all!

As this example illustrates, we cannot judge whether an adult is pathological based solely on his or her behavior; the behavior must be evaluated in the context in which it occurs. As Williams (1972) observes,

> There is a danger in confusing the mental disorders with suffering, and mental health with happiness. A person who is clinically depressed is unhappy and suffers. But one can be unhappy and suffer without being clinically depressed, and, indeed, without any impairment in the capacity to act within the confines of one's natural abilities. (p. 4)

The death of a parent, spouse, or friend becomes temporally normative as we grow old (as we have seen); and the pain of bereavement is a natural emotion, one that may or may not result in such forms of psychopathology as clinical depression.

OTHER FACTORS. Behavior that is readily accepted in one culture may be regarded as pathological in another part of the world. For example, certain religious practices or beliefs such as hearing or seeing a deceased relative during bereavement might be normal in some settings but judged to be an indication of a psychotic episode in other settings. Judgments cannot be made about mental health without taking into account the cultural background and current environment of the individual. Age may also be a factor: Talking in nonsense syllables is normal for a baby, but likely to indicate pathology for an adult.

DEFINITION OF MENTAL HEALTH.   In spite of these difficulties, clinicians and researchers have identified some of the key components that distinguish mental health from psychopathology. **Mental health** reflects the ability of an individual to deal with the issues of life in an effective way. It involves the capacity to achieve a reasonably satisfactory integration of one's instinctual drives with goals, achievements, and interpersonal relationships in ways that are socially acceptable, personally satisfying, and appropriately flexible. In contrast, a mental disorder is conceptualized as a clinically significant behavioral or psychological syndrome or pattern associated with distress or impairment in one or more important areas of functioning or with a significantly increased risk of suffering death, pain, disability or an important loss of freedom. In addition, the syndrome or pattern must not be a culturally appropriate response to a particular event (American Psychiatric Association, 1994).

Diagnosis and Assessment

CAUSES OF PSYCHOPATHOLOGY.   During the 19th century, such pioneering clinical investigators as Sigmund Freud attributed psychopathology entirely to experiences during childhood, most often involving the parents. Examples include a lack of physical affection, excessive indulgence or frustration of the child's needs, overly severe parental standards, observing the parents' sexual intercourse, being seduced by an adult, or (in the case of the boy) being threatened with castration. Subsequent theorists rejected Freud's emphasis on sexuality while maintaining the focus on parental pathogenic behaviors, such as pampering, neglect, domination, overprotectiveness, overpermissiveness, ridicule and derision, perfectionism, blind adoration, partiality to other siblings, physical abuse, excessive anxiety, a lack of love and tenderness, inconsistent punishment, and dissuading the child from fulfilling his or her true innate potentials.

Modern clinicians agree that childhood causes of psychopathology are extremely important, but they have identified numerous others as well. (See Tables 11–1 and 11–2.) For example, such biological factors as endocrine disorders, infections, metabolic disorders, and even dietary deficiencies can contribute to depression and other forms of psychopathology. Insofar as psychosocial factors are concerned, exposure to a variety of stressors during adulthood has been linked to psychopathology (as we observed in the preceding chapter). Conversely, regular religious participation and being married are associated with a lower occurrence of psychiatric illness.

A detailed discussion of these causes of psychopathology is beyond the scope of this book; the interested reader is referred to the most recent edition of any of the major textbooks on abnormal psychology. The important point for our purposes is that because there are so many possible causes of psychopathology, diagnosing the disorder that afflicts a particular adult (and selecting an appropriate treatment) is an extremely difficult task. This is particularly true for elderly

Early clinical investigators such as Sigmund Freud felt that most psychopathologies had their roots in early childhood experiences.

adults, who are more likely to suffer from a variety of medical conditions (and take medications) that may contribute (directly or indirectly) to a psychological disorder. As a result, the diagnosis and assessment of older adults typically involves professionals from several disciplines (e.g., biomedical areas, psychology, psychiatry, social work, nursing), a variety of measures, and a formal classification system.

CLASSIFYING MENTAL DISORDERS: *DSM-IV.* Classification is an important aspect of any science, including psychology. Before we can arrive at meaningful explanations of human behavior, we must first organize what would otherwise be an overwhelming amount of data into a convenient framework.

One popular system for classifying the various forms of psychopathology is *DSM-IV,* the 1994 revision of the *Diagnostic and Statistical Manual of Mental Disorders* prepared by the American Psychiatric Association. *DSM-IV* is a revision of a system first used by the U.S. Army during World War II. The first edition of the *DSM* was published in 1952, with later editions (*DSM-II, III,* and *III-R*) appearing in the 1960s and 1980s.

Earlier versions of *DSM* had to be revised for several reasons. Most importantly, too many patients had symptoms that did *not* fall within one specific category. For example, obsessive-compulsive behavior is characterized by persistent thoughts and/or actions that a person cannot seem to stop. Thus the individual

TABLE 11-1   Psychosocial Risk Factors Associated with Psychiatric Illness

GENERAL CATEGORY	SPECIFIC EXAMPLES	RESEARCH FINDINGS
Demographic variables	Age	Lower prevalence of psychiatric disorders among older adults
	Sex	Affective and somatic disorders are more prevalent among women. Alcohol and substance abuse disorders are more common among men.
	Race/ethnicity	Increased rates of alcohol and drug abuse among nonwhites
Early events and achievements	Education	Low education increases risk of psychiatric illness. Some types of illness (e.g., major depression) may be more common among the highly educated.
	Childhood traumas	Increased risk of psychiatric illness
Later events and achievements	Occupation/income	Low socioeconomic status related to increased psychiatric illness
	Marital status	Married people are slightly less likely to have psychiatric illness.
Social integration	Personal attachments to social organizations (e.g., religious groups, community)	Religious participation and attendance is associated with fewer psychiatric illnesses.
	Environmental contexts	Higher rates of psychiatric symptoms among urban residents (as compared with rural residents)
Vulnerabilty and protective factors	Job stress, chronic financial strain, chronic physical illness, caregiving stress	All of these stressors are related to higher rates of psychiatric illness.
	Social support	High levels of social support are related to less psychiatric illness.
Provoking agents and coping efforts	Life events	Negative life events are related to increased illness, especially depression, alcohol abuse, and anxiety.
	Coping strategies	Effectiveness varies with type of stressor.

Source: Based on George (1989).

may feel compelled to check the alarm clock 15 or 20 times at night to be sure it is set properly. In contrast, anxiety involves extremely unpleasant feelings that are similar to intense nervousness. In the second version of *DSM*, obsessive-compulsive neurosis and anxiety neurosis were separate and distinct categories. Yet many patients were found to suffer from both obsessive-compulsive symptoms and anxiety, making it difficult to use this classification system. In *DSM-III-R*, and *DSM-IV*, however, obsessive-compulsive disorder is classified as one of the anxiety disorders, making it clear that these symptoms often occur together.

   DSM-IV evaluates people on five dimensions, or axes, including specific maladaptive or psychiatric symptoms (Axis I), any long-standing personality or developmental problems (Axis II), medical or physical disorders that may also be

TABLE 11-2 Biological Factors Associated with Psychiatric Illness

GENERAL CATEGORY	SPECIFIC EXAMPLES	POSSIBLE EFFECTS
Heredity		May be related to some types of dementia and schizophrenia
Drugs and medication	Alcohol, amphetamines, sedatives	May cause depression, treatable dementia, anxiety disorder
Endocrine disorders	Hyper- and hypothyroidism	May cause depression, treatable dementia
Infections	Encephalitis, neurosyphilis	May cause depression, dementia
Malignant disease	Metastases, tumors	May cause depression, dementia, treatable dementia
Metabolic disorders	Electrolyte imbalance, uremia	May cause depression, treatable dementia
Trauma	Postconcussion, subdural	May cause depression, dementia, treatable dementia
Nutritional disorders	Vitamin B12 deficiency, folate deficiency, caffeine	May cause treatable dementia, anxiety disorder

Source: Based on Jenike (1989).

present (Axis III), psychosocial and environmental problems (Axis IV), and global assessment of functioning (Axis V). A synopsis of Axis I is shown in Table 11-3. A good clinician would collect information in all five domains and develop a treatment plan accordingly.

A common misconception is that classifying a mental disorder is the same as classifying people. What is actually being classified when we use a system such as *DSM-IV* are disorders that people have. For this reason we try to avoid saying a person is a "schizophrenic," an "alcoholic," or a "depressive." Instead, it is more appropriate to say that a person "has schizophrenia," or an individual is "alcohol dependent" or "depressed."

DIAGNOSIS AND ASSESSMENT: I. INTERVIEWS. Even with the aid of *DSM-IV*, it is no simple task to decide which classification applies to a given adult. To answer this important question, clinicians typically rely on such formal **assessment** techniques as the interview.

You have undoubtedly encountered the interview at some point in your life, as when you applied for a job or for admission to college. The clinical interviewer pays close attention not only to *what* the respondent says, but also to *how* he or she answers. In particular, the emotions that accompany the interviewee's statements often provide the clinician with valuable clues regarding any mental disorders that may be present.

The specific information elicited during a clinical interview depends in part on the theoretical orientation of the interviewer. Some clinicians prefer to devote many of their questions to childhood causes, whereas others stress current behaviors and problems. Also, some clinicians like to operate from vague outlines and compose specific questions as the interview proceeds; others are more comfortable with a structured format that lists all of the questions to be asked. Two of the most widely used semistructured interviews for making psychiatric diagnoses are the Schedule for Affective Disorders and Schizophrenia (SADS,

TABLE 11–3   A Synopsis of *DSM-IV*, Axis I

---

1. **Delirium, Dementia, and Amnestic and other Cognitive Disorders.** The predominant disturbances are clinically significant deficits in cognition or memory that represent a significant change from a previous level of functioning. The cause of the deficit is either a general medical condition or a substance (i.e., drug abuse, medication, or toxin) or a combination of these factors.
2. **Schizophrenia and Other Psychotic Disorders.** Characterized by a gross distortion of reality; disorganization and fragmentation of thought, perception, and emotion.
3. **Mood Disorders.** Characterized by disturbances of emotion and mood. Includes bipolar disorder, major depression.
4. **Anxiety Disorders.** Characterized by unusually high anxiety and efforts to defend against it. Includes phobic disorder, anxiety states, obsessive-compulsive disorder.
5. **Somatoform Disorders.** Characterized by complaints of bodily symptoms for which there are no physical causes. Includes conversion disorder, hypochondriasis.
6. **Sleep Disorders.** Can be caused by a variety of factors such as a medical condition, the use, or recent discontinuation of use, of a substance, or another mental disorder.
7. **Adjustment Disorders.** Clinically significant emotional or behavioral symptoms in response to identifiable psychosocial stressor or stressors.

Note: For purposes of convenience, this table presents primarily the major categories of Axis I delineated by *DSM-IV*. Categories not relevant to the present chapter have been deemphasized, and many subcategories have been omitted.

Endicott & Spitzer, 1978) and the Structured Clinical Interview for *DSM-IV* (SCID, Spitzer et al., 1992). However, these interviews are lengthy and require considerable skill to administer.

An example of a structured procedure for conducting clinical interviews with older adults is outlined in Table 11–4. The first step is to obtain information about the patient's present symptoms (when they began, how long they have lasted, if they have become more severe over time), and about any previous occurrences of these or other symptoms. The interviewer must be careful not to accept the patient's reassurances at face value (e.g., "I guess I'm just getting old, and most people slow down when they get to be my age"), lest a treatable psychiatric disorder be overlooked. Common symptoms that should be investigated carefully include excessive weakness or lethargy, a depressed mood or "the blues," memory problems, difficulty in concentrating, feelings of helplessness and hopelessness, suspicion of other people, anxiety and agitation, sleep problems, and appetite problems (Blazer, 1989c). Any psychiatric symptoms and illnesses within the family should also be ascertained; for example, dementia sufferers may have a family history of this disorder.

As would be expected from our previous discussion, the interviewer also inquires about biological and psychosocial factors that may contribute to the patient's mental disorder. These include medical problems (assessed by a physical examination), medications that may produce or exacerbate psychological symptoms, and such potential stressors as the patient's family. Thus the interviewer tries to ascertain how the family interacts with the patient, the type and amount of support given to the patient by the family, and how family members are coping with the stress caused by the patient's illness. Finally, the interviewer may

TABLE 11–4   One Procedure for Conducting Psychiatric Interviews
with Geriatric Patients

I. **History**
   1. Symptoms
   2. Present episode, including onset, duration, and change in symptoms over time
   3. Past history of medical and psychiatric disorders
   4. Family history of depression, alcohol abuse/dependence, psychoses, and suicide
II. **Physical Examination**
   1. Evaluation of neurologic deficits, possible endocrine disorders, occult malignancy, cardiac dysfunction, and occult infections
III. **Mental Status Examination**
   1. Disturbance of consciousness
   2. Disturbance of mood and affect
   3. Disturbance of motor behavior
   4. Disturbance of perception (hallucinations, illusions)
   5. Disturbance of cognition (delusions)
   6. Disturbance of self-esteem and guilt
   7. Suicidal ideation
   8. Disturbance of memory and intelligence (memory, abstraction, calculation, aphasia, and knowledge)

Source: Blazer (1989c), "The Psychiatric Interview of the Geriatric Patient," *Geriatric Psychiatry,* p. 264. Edited by E. W. Busse and D. G. Blazer. Copyright 1989, American Psychiatric Press, Inc.

learn about the specific nature of the patient's disorder by directly observing the presence of specific symptoms, such as delusions, hallucinations, and suicidal wishes. (See Blazer, 1989c.)

Whatever the specific format may be, interviewing older adults requires considerable skill and sensitivity. Psychological assessment procedures may be frightening to the elderly, who are more likely to regard any illnesses they may have as incurable. Thus the interviewer must be careful to avoid such behaviors as irritability, impatience, and boredom, which are likely to increase the patient's fears and feelings of rejection. (See Gurland, 1982.) The pace of the interview should be unhurried, even if the patient takes considerable time to respond. The interviewer should be sensitive to such problems as hearing and vision impairments, by speaking slowly and clearly in a low-pitched voice and bringing up important points more than once. The interviewer should *not* shy away from such potentially sensitive areas as suicidal feelings, sexual problems, and feelings about growing old and dying, lest vital information be overlooked; but distressing topics should be avoided at the close of the interview, and a clear statement of the next step in the assessment process should be given, so the patient leaves with reduced anxiety.

DIAGNOSIS AND ASSESSMENT: II. PSYCHOMETRIC INSTRUMENTS.   A second important assessment procedure is the psychometric approach, which includes standardized questionnaires, tests, and projective devices. Such well-known measures of personality as the MMPI, Rorschach, and TAT, discussed in Chapter 7, are commonly used for diagnostic purposes.

One problem with these measures (and with interviews) is that they are time consuming. Suppose a clinician wishes to determine if an older adult enjoys reasonable mental health or needs treatment. What is needed here is not a lengthy measure that probes deeply into the patient's personality, but rather a quickly administered screening test that will indicate if a problem is likely to exist. If the subject scores well (healthy), no further action is taken, and considerable time is saved. If, instead, the subject scores relatively poorly (pathological), the clinician knows that longer and more detailed assessment procedures are needed. No diagnoses are made from the screening test, which provides only a rough indication of mental health.

One screening test that helps to detect cognitive dysfunction and dementia is the Mini-Mental State Examination (Folstein et al., 1975; see Figure 11–1). This instrument requires only 5 to 10 minutes to administer; it assesses recall, attention and calculation, language, and orientation. Seven to 12 errors suggest mild to moderate cognitive impairment; 13 or more errors suggest severe impairment.

A screening test widely used to help detect depression is the Center for Epidemiologic Studies Depression Scale, or CES-D (Radloff, 1977). Twenty questions are read to the subject, dealing with his or her feelings during the preceding week. (See Table 11–5.) The maximum possible score on each item (most depressed) is 3, and a total score of 16 or higher suggests the person is at risk for clinical depression. An earlier brief measure of depression, the Zung Self-Rating Depression Scale, uses somewhat similar items (e.g., "I am more irritable than usual," "My life is pretty full," "I'd do better if I felt better," "I feel downhearted, blue, and sad," "I feel that others would be better off if I am dead," "I don't have much to look forward to"). (See Okimoto et al., 1982; Zung, 1965, 1967.) However, the popularity of this instrument has declined in recent years because of a lack of normative data (Blazer, 1989c). A newer scale, the Geriatric Depression Rating Scale (GDS), was designed specifically with the elderly in mind. The GDS consists of 30 yes-or-no questions regarding symptoms of depression that are more relevant to the elderly (Carstensen, Edelstein, & Dornbrand, 1996).

AFTERWORD.   When *DSM-IV* is used in combination with appropriate assessment procedures, it is possible to arrive at very detailed diagnoses. Yet because of the methodological and substantive problems mentioned here, such diagnoses are not always as accurate as we would wish.

Furthermore, this practice is far from universal. A quite different picture is evidenced by actual doctors' notes concerning elderly patients in long-term care institutions who suffer primarily from physical and/or cognitive problems. These patients are frequently diagnosed in such simple terms as "depressed" or "senile," with no indication as to the procedure used to arrive at this conclusion. More often than not, these diagnoses seem to have been made casually during the course of a physical examination. Thus the problem of diagnosis and assessment may be exacerbated by the failure to use the best available procedures.

1 I would like to ask you a few questions dealing with concentration and memory. Some are a little bit more difficult than others.

	correct	error	not attempted refused	Record answers in error:
a. What is the year?	1	0	9	year: _____
b. What season of the year is it?	1	0	9	season: _____
c. What is the date?	1	0	9	date: _____
d. What is the day of the week?	1	0	9	day: _____
e. What is the month?	1	0	9	month: _____
f. What state are we in?	1	0	9	state: _____
g. What county are we in?	1	0	9	county: _____
h. What (city/town) are we in?	1	0	9	city: _____
i. What floor of the building are we on?	1	0	9	floor: _____
j. What is this address? (If institutionalized: What is the name of this place?)	1	0	9	address/name: _____

2 I am going to name 3 objects. After I have said them, I want you to repeat them. Remember what they are because I am going to ask you to name them again in a few minutes:

APPLE TABLE PENNY

Could you repeat the 3 items for me?

Do not repeat the items for the participant until after the first trial. The participant may give the items in any order. If there are errors on the first trial, repeat the items up to six times until they are learned.

first trial only

	correct	error	not attempted refused
a. apple	1	0	9
b. table	1	0	9
c. penny	1	0	9

3 Can you subtract 7 from 100, and then subtract 7 from the answer you get and keep subtracting 7 until I tell you to stop? Please do the subtraction out loud.

Count only 1 error if participant makes subtraction error, but subsequent answers are 7 less than the error.

Record Response:	correct	error	can't do	not attempted refused
a. 93 _____	1	0	7	9
b. 86 _____	1	0	7	9
c. 79 _____	1	0	7	9
d. 72 _____	1	0	7	9
e. 65 _____	1	0	7	9

4 I am going to spell a word forwards and I want you to spell it backwards. The word is *world*. W-O-R-L-D. Spell *world* backwards.

Repeat spelling if necessary.

Record Response:	correct	error	can't do	not attempted refused
a. D _____	1	0	7	9
b. L _____	1	0	7	9
c. R _____	1	0	7	9
d. O _____	1	0	7	9
e. W _____	1	0	7	9

5 Now what were the 3 objects I asked you to remember?

Objects may be repeated in any order.

	correct	error	not attempted refused
a. apple	1	0	9
b. table	1	0	9
c. penny	1	0	9

6 (Show wrist watch.) What is this called? 1 0 9

7 (Show pencil.) What is this called? 1 0 9

8 I'd like you to repeat a phrase after me: No if's, and's, or but's.

Allow only 1 trial. Code 1—Correct required an accurately articulated repetition.

correct error refused
1 0 9

9 Read the words on this card and then do what it says.

Hand card 11. Code 1—Correct required the participant to close his or her eyes. Card says: Close your eyes

correct error refused
1 0 9

10 *Read the full statement below and then hand participant a blank piece of paper. Do not repeat instructions or coach.*

I am going to give you a piece of paper. When I do, take the paper in your right hand, fold the paper in half with both hands, and put the paper down on your lap.

	correct	error	refused
a. takes paper in right	1	0	9
b. folds paper in half	1	0	9
c. puts paper down on lap	1	0	9

11 Write any complete sentence on that piece of paper for me. 1 0 9

Must have a subject and verb and make sense. Spelling and grammatical errors are OK. Repeat the instructions, if necessary.

12 Here's a drawing. Please copy the drawing on the same paper. 1 0 9

Hand participant card 12. Correct if 2 convex 5-sided figures and intersection makes a 4-sided figure.

Drawing

FIGURE 11–1 Items from the Mini-Mental State Examination.
(*Source:* Folstein et al. (1975).)

TABLE 11–5   The Center for Epidemiologic Studies Depression Scale (CES-D)

The following questions are read to the subject:
In the *last week,* how often would you say you
1.   were bothered by things that usually don't bother you?
2.   did not feel like eating; your appetite was poor?
3.   felt that you could not shake off the blues even with help from your family or friends?
4.   felt that you were just as good as other people?
5.   had trouble keeping your mind on what you were doing?
6.   felt depressed?
7.   felt that everything you did was an effort?
8.   felt hopeful about the future?
9.   thought your life had been a failure?
10.   felt fearful?
11.   found that your sleep was restless?
12.   were happy?
13.   talked less than usual?
14.   felt lonely?
15.   thought people were unfriendly?
16.   enjoyed life?
17.   had crying spells?
18.   felt sad?
19.   felt that people disliked you?
20.   could not get "going"?
The subject is given a card with these responses to choose from:
0 = Rarely or none of the time (less than one day in the last week)
1 = Some or a little of the time (1 or 2 days in the last week)
2 = Occasionally or a moderate amount of the time (3 or 4 days in the last week)
3 = Most or all of the time (5-7 days in the last week)

Note: The instructions read to the subject state, "The next few questions are about your feelings and attitudes. I am going to read a list of statements. For each statement, please tell me the category which best describes how often you felt or behaved this way. You can use this card to tell me your answers." Questions 4, 8, 12, and 16 are scored in the reverse direction ("rarely or none of the time" = 3, and so on). Thus the maximum possible score (most depressed) is 60 (3 × 20).

Source: Radloff (1977).

EPIDEMIOLOGY AND TREATMENT OF ADULT PSYCHOPATHOLOGY

Introduction

Now that we have established *what* the various kinds of psychopathology are, we must ascertain *how often* and *where* these disorders occur. The greater the frequency of a particular illness, the more people will benefit if we diagnose and treat it correctly. The study of the distribution of illnesses in time and place, and of the factors that influence this distribution, is known as **epidemiology** (see Last, 1995).

METHODS OF STUDY.   One way to obtain epidemiological data is by examining hospital records or **case registers** and counting how often each disorder occurs. Unfortunately, this straightforward procedure may well produce misleading results. Many individuals who suffer from certain disorders, such as depression, never go to a hospital or visit a psychotherapist. Using this method, therefore, allows numerous cases of pathology to remain undetected.

Instead, the epidemiologist may resort to a potentially more accurate method: assessing the mental health of every person in a specified geographical area, either directly or indirectly. However, such **field surveys** are expensive and difficult to conduct. They are most feasible in geographically isolated communities (e.g., islands such as Iceland), where the number of people to be assessed is relatively small and there is little movement of the population to other areas. To date, the majority of field surveys have been conducted in northern Europe and Japan.

INCIDENCE AND PREVALENCE RATES. Whatever the method, the results of epidemiological studies are typically expressed in two different ways. **Incidence rates** refer to the number of *new* cases of disease that occur within a specified period of time among a specified population. This includes those who contract the given illness for the first time and those who suffer a recurrent episode after having experienced a period of health:

Incidence Rate = Number of New Cases/Population at Risk

The denominator of this fraction, the **population at risk,** consists of all adults in the specified geographical area who might conceivably contract this illness. (Appropriate census or other demographic data may be used to determine this figure.) For example, suppose 50 new cases of depression occur each day among those age 65 and over in Baltimore, Maryland. Because approximately 100,000 people age 65 and above live in Baltimore, the daily incidence rate would be 50/100,000, or 0.0005 (or 0.05%). Alternatively, incidence rates may be based on a monthly or yearly period.

In contrast, **prevalence rates** refer to the *total number* of people in a given community who suffer from the illness in question:

Prevalence Rate = Total Number of Cases/Population at Risk

This figure may be based on a single point in time ("point prevalence") or on a specified period of time ("period prevalence"). Thus a 7% point prevalence rate of depression among adults in Baltimore would mean that at the specified point in time, 7% of the adults in this city were found to suffer from depression. Prevalence rates may instead be reported as rates per thousand; in the preceding example, this would be expressed as 70 per 1,000.

When the frequency of an illness changes markedly at different ages, or when we are primarily interested in the relationship between aging and psychopathology, epidemiological results are best reported in terms of age-specific incidence and prevalence rates. To illustrate, we might find that the incidence rate for depression in Baltimore is 35 per 1,000 for people age 60 to 69 but only 10 per 1,000 for those age 50 to 59. Or, we might discover that the incidence rate for this disorder remains much the same throughout adulthood.

AFTERWORD. Age-specific incidence and prevalence rates help us ascertain which disorders first occur in middle and old age. If a mental disorder that originates in childhood or adolescence persists into old age, we will find high prevalence rates and low incidence rates among the elderly. If, instead, a disorder typically occurs for the first time at an advanced age, the incidence rates will be markedly higher at older ages.

Age-specific incidence and prevalence rates are readily available for most major mental disorders. Before we turn to these findings, however, a note of caution must be sounded. As previously mentioned, field surveys and case registers may well yield significantly different figures for the same disorder. There is also some question as to the reliability of psychiatric diagnosis with elderly patients, even when attempts are made to be detailed and precise. Various investigators have used different methods of diagnosis and assessment, making it difficult to compare the results of different studies. Thus the data to be discussed in the following sections should be taken as a general indication of the extent of these disorders, rather than as a mathematically exact determination.

Alzheimer's Disease and Other Dementias

DEFINITION OF DEMENTIA. The term **dementia** (or **dementing illness**) refers to a disease that leads initially to the loss of cognitive functioning and, in later stages, to the loss of motor and physical functioning. In particular, the symptoms of dementia include the following (Biegel, Sales, & Schulz, 1991):

>   A decline in intellectual ability severe enough to interfere with the sufferer's work and social life
>   Impairments in memory, judgment, and abstract thinking
>   Language problems due to brain damage (aphasia)
>   An inability to carry out a requested action, even though the sufferer understands the request and is physically able to perform it (apraxia)
>   A failure to recognize or identify familiar objects despite good vision and sense of touch (agnosia).

Several different types of dementia are classified by *DSM-IV* depending on the etiology or cause of the symptoms. Dementia of the Alzheimer's type is probably the most prevalent of the dementias, followed by dementias due to vascular disease or stroke, dementia due to HIV disease, dementia due to head trauma, and so on. More than 70 different conditions can cause dementia. Of these, the two most common among elderly persons are Alzheimer's disease and vascular dementia. As a group, these are the most prevalent psychiatric disorders of later life. The criteria used by clinicians to diagnose dementia of the Alzheimer's type are shown in Table 11–6.

INCIDENCE AND PREVALENCE OF ALZHEIMER'S DISEASE. Considerable attention is currently being devoted to **Alzheimer's disease**, which has been singled out as a

TABLE 11-6   Diagnostic Criteria for Dementia of the Alzheimer's Type

A. The development of multiple cognitive deficits manifested by both
   1. memory impairment (impaired ability to learn new information or to recall previously learned information)
   2. one (or more) of the following cognitive disturbances:
      a. aphasia (language disturbance)
      b. apraxia (impaired ability to carry out motor acitivities despite intact motor function)
      c. agnosia (failure to recognize or identify objects despite intact sensory function)
      d. disturbance in executive functioning (i.e., planning, organizaing, sequencing, abstracting)
B. The cognitive deficits in Criteria A1 and A2 each cause significant impairment in social or occupational functioning and represent a signficant decline from a previous level of functioning.
C. The course is characterized by gradual onset and continuing cognitive decline.
D. The cognitive deficits in Criteria A1 and A2 are not due to any of the following:
   1. other central nervous system conditions that cause progressive deficits in memory and cognition (e.g., cerebrovascular disease, Parkinson's disease, Huntington's disease, subdural hematoma, normal-pressure hydrocephalus, brain tumor)
   2. systemic conditions that are known to cause dementia (e.g., hypothyroidism, vitamin B12 or folic acid deficiency, niacin deficiency, hypercalcemia, neurosyphilis, HIV infection)
   3. substance-induced conditions
E. The deficits do not occur exclusively during the course of a delirium.
F. The disturbance is not better accounted for by another Axis I disorder (e.g., Major Depressive Disorder, Schizophrenia).

"disease of catastrophic proportions" by the U.S. Department of Health and Human Services. The reported prevalence of dementia varies considerably among epidemiologic studies, depending on the ages of the subjects sampled, methods of determining the presence, severity, and type of cognitive impairment, and the regions of the country studied (Schulz & O'Brien, 1994). It has been estimated that the prevalence of mild dementia among adults age 65 and over may be as high as 12% and the prevalence of moderate to severe dementia probably ranges between 3% and 6% (American Psychiatric Association, 1994; Mortimer, 1988; Schulz and O'Brien, 1994); the majority of these dementias are thought to be caused by Alzheimer's disease. The prevalence of dementia, especially dementia of the Alzheimer's type and vascular dementia, increases with age, particularly after age 75, with a prevalence of 20% or more over age 85 years. If these percentages are converted into head counts, the implications are indeed alarming: There are approximately 1.5 to 2 million cases of probable Alzheimer's disease in the United States.

Incidence rates for Alzheimer's disease are more difficult to obtain, partly because few large-scale population studies have been carried out. One longitudinal study found an incidence rate of 0.083% at age 60, 0.333% at age 70, 1.337% at age 80, and 5.371% at age 90 (Sayetta, 1986). According to this study, you are 16 times more likely to contract Alzheimer's disease at age 80 than at age 60, and 65 times more likely to do so at age 90 than at age 60. A similar pattern of increasing rates with increasing age has been reported by other investigators, although the specific numerical values vary considerably (e.g., Akesson, 1969; Hagnell et al., 1983). Although more accurate incidence rates are needed, the available data do indicate that the likelihood of contracting Alzheimer's disease for the first time increases sharply as an adult grows from age 60 to age 90.

CAUSES OF ALZHEIMER'S DISEASE.   The causes of Alzheimer's disease are not yet known. Some researchers believe the cholinergic system of the brain may be responsible because the brains of Alzheimer's victims exhibit a significant decrease in an enzyme called choline acetyltransferase (Perry et al., 1978). Acetylcholine is a neurotransmitter involved in learning and memory. Other neurotransmitter systems have also been shown to be affected by AD, including the serotonergic system and the dopaninergic system (Youngjohn and Crook, 1996). Another area of investigation concerns the possibility of genetic determinants of Alzheimer's disease. The risk of senile dementia, Down syndrome, leukemia, and Hodgkin's disease have been found to be significantly higher among relatives of patients suffering from Alzheimer's disease than that in the general population (Heston & Mastri, 1977). More recent findings indicate that a genetic component to AD, with the risk of developing the disorder in first-degree relatives of AD victims being six times greater than the healthy elderly populations. Molecular genetics studies have identified AD loci on chromosomes 14, 19, and 21 (Clark and Goate, 1993).

Whatever the causes, Alzheimer's disease is associated with various physiological changes in the brain. These include a loss of neurons, widened fissures, narrower and flatter ridges, senile plaques scattered throughout the cortex, and the replacement of normal nerve cells in the basal ganglia with tangled thread-like structures.

ONSET AND COURSE OF ALZHEIMER'S DISEASE.   The age of onset for Alzheimer's disease can be either early (ages 40 to 65) or late (age 66 and over). The onset of Alzheimer's disease is deceptively mild, and its course is one of steady deterioration. In the first stage, patients may exhibit minor symptoms and mood changes. They may also have less energy and drive, be less spontaneous, be slower to learn to react, and forget some basic words. Patients may also lose their temper more easily than they did before. Because these symptoms are so subtle, they often go undetected or are regarded as temporary and unimportant changes in the individual.

In the second stage, patients may still be able to perform familiar activities, but they are likely to need help with complicated tasks. The ability to speak and to understand are noticeably impaired, and patients may be insensitive to the feelings of others.

The third stage is characterized by profound memory losses, particularly of the recent past. Patients may forget the time, the date, the season, and where they are, and they may fail to recognize familiar people. Psychotic symptoms may occur, including delusions, hallucinations, paranoid thoughts, and severe agitation.

Memory continues to deteriorate in the fourth stage, and patients are likely to need help with all of their activities. They are often completely disoriented and unable to recognize loved ones and close friends, and they often lose control of bowel and bladder. Patients may become completely mute and inattentive and be totally unable to care for themselves. The process of deterioration ultimately leads to the final stage, death, although this may take anywhere from 1 to 10 years; there is currently no cure for Alzheimer's disease, although its course may be slowed with some medications currently available.

Alzheimer's has been called the cruelest of all diseases because it kills its victims twice. First there is the living death of being unable to remember the simplest fact or perform the most basic daily function; then the body gradually sinks into coma and death. The ravages of Alzheimer's disease are graphically illustrated by the following case histories.

A Former Writer

He had been a successful writer for more than 40 years, celebrated for his ability to remember the details of a complex and important story virtually without using notes. But soon after his retirement at age 68, he began to experience difficulty in finding the right words to express himself, and he frequently appeared to lose the thread of his thoughts. Within months, he couldn't remember his schedule for the day. In a few years he could not remember if he had just eaten.

It became necessary to give the man sedatives and sleeping pills, otherwise he would wander around the entire night. When not sedated, he became irritable and sometimes violent. Eventually, he had to be placed in a nursing home, where he continued to decline until he was unable to perform even the simplest functions for himself. He could not remember the names of those close to him. (Fischman, 1984, p. 27)

A 46-Year-Old Supervisor

She immediately forgets the plot of the last television show she watched, and she has trouble reading newspaper articles because she loses the gist of the story after two or three sentences. She has long since forgotten the names and phone numbers of relatives, and no longer cooks or drives because she can't remember how. "Can you imagine the embarrassment of an educated woman not knowing who the president is, or having to ask where the bathroom is in your own house?" she asks in frustration. (*Newsweek*, December 3, 1984, p. 60)

A Harvard Graduate

This 57-year-old was diagnosed as having Alzheimer's disease three years ago. Now he stays home, while his wife holds down a part-time job. She must leave handwritten notes around the house so that he will remember to turn off the gas, or not go out until she comes back. He often speaks in cryptic, broken sentences. He sometimes can't remember the names of his stepchildren, or even his wife. One night he brought her a can of beer, and she reminded him that she prefers it in a glass. He went back and forth to the kitchen four or five times, always forgetting to bring the glass. She yelled at him, then felt guilty. Yet despite the stress, she clings to every moment because she knows her time with him is limited. (*Newsweek*, December 3, 1984, pp. 58–59)

A Noted Actress

Toward the end of her life, every move had to be plotted out for her, as if life had become a script she couldn't learn. "We are going to the dining-room table, we are going to have lunch," the nurses would say. And when she had to negotiate the tiny step to the bathroom: "Now we are coming to the step, lift up your left foot." Sometimes she missed it on the first try. "But quite often," her daughter reported, "she'll be able to do it."

This was not a towering achievement for the woman who had once effortlessly swirled across movie dance floors, matching Fred Astaire step for dazzling step. But it did represent a last, faint flicker of awareness. Three years later, bedridden and speechless, Rita Hayworth died. (*Newsweek*, December 18, 1989, p. 54)

COPING WITH ALZHEIMER'S DISEASE. Receiving a diagnosis of Alzheimer's disease has been likened to receiving a death sentence. Patients respond with a variety of strong emotions, including shock, anger, fear, despair, and disbelief; some deny or refuse to acknowledge their condition altogether. Most want to talk about it, however, and wish to be included in family plans regarding their future. Yet they are sad and fearful because they know that as the dementia progresses, they

Former President Ronald Reagan is one noted victim of Alzheimer's disease, currently regarded as a disease of catastrophic proportions by the United States Department of Health and Human Services.

will be unable to relate to their family with dignity and respect. Perhaps the most distressing aspect of Alzheimer's disease is the awareness of having profound cognitive deficits that will only get worse. Observing the unraveling of a self-identity that one has spent a lifetime creating is a load that virtually no one can bear with equanimity. (See Biegel, Sales, & Schulz, 1991; Cohen & Eisdorfer, 1986.)

As the number of individuals suffering from Alzheimer's disease has increased, so too has the quantity and diversity of available services. Diagnostic and treatment centers, located at many major universities throughout the United States, carry out research on Alzheimer's disease and offer experimental treatments as they become available. Formal support groups provide emotional aid to patients in the early stages of the disease. Adult day-care centers offer a safe and caring environment for patients in the middle stages. And for those in the later stages of Alzheimer's disease, some long-term care facilities provide special low-stimulus environments (Biegel, Sales, & Schulz, 1991). There are drawbacks, however. Such services are relatively few compared to the need, can be expensive, and may refuse to accept "difficult" patients who must be constantly watched or restrained. It has been said that each case of Alzheimer's disease claims not one but two victims, because caregiving involves considerable emotional and physical stress (Schulz et al., 1995). Approximately 70% of Alzheimer's patients remain at home and are cared for by a family member. One man, whose wife is in her 10th year of Alzheimer's and cannot speak or recognize anyone, put it this way: "You go through episodes of wanting to be relieved of it, the horror that goes on day after day, night after night. You often feel a desire that the person die—and then you feel like a monster for entertaining such thoughts."

A number of national organizations have responded to the extreme challenge associated with caring for an Alzheimer's patient at home. Foremost among these is the Alzheimer's Disease and Related Disorders Association (ADRDA), which coordinates a national network of support groups for caregivers and supports research on Alzheimer's disease. Some state government units have also developed services for caregivers of Alzheimer's patients, such as respite programs that provide temporary relief from the burden of caregiving.

DRUG TREATMENT OF AD. In 1993, the U.S. Food and Drug Administration approved the first drug (tacrine, trade name Cognex) intended to alleviate some of the cognitive deficits of AD. Although the availability of this drug generated a great deal of interest and hope in the general public, recent findings indicate it has few positive therapeutic effects when compared to placebo controls. Nevertheless, the search continues for pharmacological agents that might improve the memory and behavior problems of AD patients. The number of new treatments for this disease will likely increase dramatically in the years ahead.

VASCULAR DEMENTIA. A second form of dementia common among the elderly is **vascular dementia.** As the name suggests, this form of dementia is caused by vascular disease such as stroke. It is important to distinguish between this disorder and Alzheimer's disease in order to provide appropriate treatment,

although differentiation is difficult without special training and the use of sophisticated equipment.

Vascular dementia has an abrupt onset, progresses in stages, and is more
prevalent among men. It is caused by an inadequate flow of blood to the brain,
which results in the destruction of localized areas of brain tissue ("infarcts").
The symptoms of vascular dementia include impairments in memory, judgment, abstract thinking, and impulse control. There may also be a significant
change in personality, depending on the location of the infarcts. Vascular dementia follows a stepwise course with clearly differentiated levels of severity
at different times, whereas the development of Alzheimer's disease is more
gradual and progressive. Physical impairments are more common with vascular dementia.

AFTERWORD. Our discussion of dementia and Alzheimer's disease has been far
from pleasant. The symptoms are extremely distressing, both for patient and
caregiver. It has been suggested that almost 20% of those over age 85 have probable Alzheimer's disease. Dementia is currently the fourth leading cause of death
in the United States, accounting for 100,000 to 120,000 deaths annually. And the
prevalence rates are increasing; it is estimated that by the year 2050, the number of Alzheimer's patients may exceed 5 million. Thus the cost of this disorder,
in both suffering and dollars, is likely to increase substantially in the years to
come. This will prove to be a major challenge to our already burdened health
care and economic system, and to patients and families affected by this illness.

Most forms of adult psychopathology do not follow this pattern. The incidence and prevalence rates for most psychological disorders decline with increasing age, so it would *not* be correct to conclude that the likelihood of
contracting any psychological disorder increases in middle and old age; in fact,
the reverse is true (see Table 11–1). Dementias such as Alzheimer's disease are the
exception to the rule—unfortunately, a most painful and troublesome exception.

Depression

DEFINITION. Most of us experience periods of **depression** from time to time, but
this is not necessarily indicative of psychopathology. Clinical depression is characterized by negative changes in mood that are powerful and pervasive: The
sufferer experiences unusually strong and frequent feelings of dejection, worthlessness, gloom and dismay about the past, hopelessness about the future, and
often apprehension. Other features of clinical depression include loss of interest
or pleasure, appetite may be reduced, the individual may have trouble sleeping,
be agitated, and have feelings of decreased energy, tiredness, and fatigue. (See
Table 11–7.) Consider the following examples:

A 64-Year-Old Retired Travel Agent

Mrs. H. and her husband have two sons who live in another section of the country;
she hears from them only when they need financial assistance. She has led a pleas-

TABLE 11-7 Diagnostic Critieria for Major Depressive Episode

A. Five (or more) of the following symptoms have been present during the same 2-week period and represent a change from previous functioning; at least one of the symptoms is either (1) depressed mood, or (2) loss of interest or pleasure.
Note: Do not include symptoms that are clearly due to a general medical condition, or mood-incongruent delusions or hallucinations.
  1. depressed mood most of the day, nearly every day, as indicated by either subjective report (e.g., feels sad or empty) or observation made by others (e.g, appears tearful). *Note:* In children and adolescents, can be irritable mood
  2. markedly diminished interest or pleasure in all, or almost all, activities most of the day, nearly every day (as indicated either by subjective account or observations by others)
  3. significant weight loss when not dieting or weight gain (e.g., a change of more than 5% of body weight in a month), or decrease or increase in appetite nearly every day. *Note:* In children, consider failure to make expected weight gains)
  4. insomnia or hypersomnia nearly every day
  5. psychomotor agitation or retardation nearly every day (observable by others, not merely subjective feelings of restlessness or being slowed down)
  6. fatigue or loss of energy nearly every day
  7. feelings of worthlessness or excessive or inappropriate guilt (which may be delusional) nearly every day (not merely self-reproach or guilt about being sick)
  8. diminished ability to think or concentrate, or indecisiveness, nearly every day (either by subjective account or as observed by others)
  9. recurrent thoughts of death (not just fear of dying), recurrent suicidal ideation without a specific plan, or a suicide attempt or a specific plan for committing suicide
B. The symptoms do not meet criteria for a Mixed Episode.
C. The symptoms cause clinically significant distress or impairment in social, occupational, or other important areas of functioning.
D. The symptoms are not due to the direct physiological effects of a substance (e.g., a drug of abuse, a medication) or a general medical condition (e.g., hypothyroidism).
E. The symptoms are not better accounted for by Bereavement, i.e., after the loss of a loved one, the symptoms persist for longer than 2 months or are characterized by marked functional impairment, morbid preoccupation with worthlessness, suicidal ideation, psychotic symptoms, or psychomotor retardation.

ant and even exciting life, including extensive travel and active participation in community affairs. She believes that she has been a failure in life, however, and that she has not treated her husband or her sons properly. She has also become obsessed with the idea that if she were to kill herself, this drastic act would enable her family to draw closer together. Her physical health is excellent, and she is not subjected to unusual life stresses; yet she has a strong tendency for negative thinking about herself. (Gallagher & Thompson, 1983, pp. 27–28)

A 73-Year-Old Widower

Three years ago neighbors found Mr. B., a widower for 10 years, collapsed in his apartment. He was unkempt, unshaven, confused, and disoriented as to place and time. His only response to questions was, "I just want to die." The little food in his apartment apparently had not been touched for days. There was no evidence of alcohol or drug use, but lab tests did reveal a kidney infection and dehydration. He refused to eat, and complained that he was miserable. He viewed treatment as worthless because it was "only" extending his life. His speech and thinking were markedly slowed, his emotions were dulled, and he saw no hope for the future. (Gallagher & Thompson, 1983, p. 25)

It is not easy to distinguish depression from the dementias. Approximately 50% of all depressed patients demonstrate some degree of cognitive impairment, with 15% exhibiting severe, dementia-like symptoms. Conversely, about 25% of all patients suffering from dementia are also depressed. Thus it is not surprising that some curable cases of depression have been mistaken for Alzheimer's disease (Wolinsky, 1983). One way to differentiate true dementia from the dementia syndrome caused by depression is that the latter is reversible, whereas the former is not.

Some theorists distinguish between depression and related functional disorders, such as the demoralization that results from membership in a low-status group or from the loss of health and power. In contrast to depression, demoralization is *not* accompanied either by physiological symptoms or by perceptual and thought distortions (Gurland, 1982; Gurland & Toner, 1982).

INCIDENCE AND PREVALENCE RATES.   Although it is not uncommon to find elderly persons who have symptoms of depression, these symptoms are seldom severe enough to warrant a diagnosis of psychopathology. As shown in Table 11–8, about 15% of the elderly have psychiatric symptoms of depression. But as Table 11–9 indicates, only 0.5% to 1.6% actually suffer from major depression (Blazer, 1989; Koenig & Blazer, 1996). These rates of clinical depression are considerably lower than rates observed among young (2% to 5%) and middle-aged persons (2.5%). Despite the relatively low rates of major clinical depression in the elderly, it has been estimated that as many as 25% of the elderly experience mild but significant depressive symptomatology that affects their social and occupational functioning. Such individuals may benefit from treatment from health professionals. For all types of depression and at all ages, women are more likely to become depressed than men.

CAUSES OF DEPRESSION.   A wide variety of biological and psychosocial factors contribute to the emergence of depression in adulthood and old age. Genetic factors,

TABLE 11–8   Prevalence of Psychiatric Symptoms in Community Populations of Older Adults

SITE	NUMBER OF CASES	AGE	ASSESSMENT STRATEGY	DISORDER/ SYMPTOMS	PREVALENCE (PERCENT)
Durham County	997	65+	Depression scale	Depression	15
New Haven	2,811	65+	CES-D	Depression	15
Iowa	3,217	65+	Selected questions	Trouble falling asleep	14

Source: Blazer (1989, p. 245).

TABLE 11-9 Prevalence of Selected Psychiatric Disorders in Community Populations of Older Adults

New Haven Epidemiologic Catchment Area	3,058	65+	Interview	Major depression	male = 0.5 female = 1.6
				Alcohol abuse	male = 3.0 female = 0
				Schizophrenia	male = 0 female = 0.9
England	297	65+	Interview	Anxiety disorder	5–10
North Carolina	1,297	65+	Interview	Anxiety disorder	5.5

Source: Blazer (1989, p. 246).

which contribute to the formation of certain personality types, may increase the risk of depression in some persons. Early relationships and maladaptive patterns of coping with external stressors may also make some persons more vulnerable to depression. In middle and old age, problems with physical health and the ability to care for oneself have been linked to depression.

In addition, some factors have been found to *decrease* middle-aged and older adults' vulnerability to depression. For example, persons who have a supportive social environment and adequate economic resources are less likely to become depressed than those who have a poor support system or few economic resources. Recent findings suggest that religion may be another resource that protects older persons against depression (Koenig, 1995). Religion has been found to be particularly effective in enabling women and African Americans to cope with and adapt to interpersonal and physical health problems.

One of the major challenges of middle and old age is coping with medical illness and disability. Researchers have consistently found a strong relationship between depression and physical health, particularly when a physical illness results in chronic disability. Recent estimates suggest that at least 6% of older persons with medical illness also suffer from major depression (Hendrie et al., 1995).

Multiple mechanisms are likely to account for the relationship between depression and ill health, including neurochemical and neuroanatomical changes associated with specific illnesses. However, the most consistent and strongest correlate of depression in this population is the functional disability associated with medical illness. Level of disability measured in terms of limitations in instrumental or basic activities of daily living or in terms of restrictions in normal activities is strongly linked to the emergence of depression among medically ill populations (Alexopoulos et al., 1996; Kennedy et al., 1990; Williamson & Schulz, 1992). Indeed, some investigators have found that functional limitations account wholly for the association between ill health and depressed affect in old age (Parmelee, Katz, & Lawton, 1992a; Williamson & Schulz, 1992).

Our perspective on late life depression is derived from a broader life span theory of control, an integrative model characterizing human development from infancy to old age (see Heckhausen & Schulz, 1995; Schulz & Heckhausen, 1996). The underlying assumption of this position is that humans desire to exert primary control over the environment around them throughout their life span. Because medical illness and disability are more prevalent in late life and frequently impact critical functional domains, they represent major threats to control and are thought to be a major cause of affective disorders in late life (Backman & Dixon, 1992; Heckhausen & Schulz, 1995; Schulz & Heckhausen, 1996; Schulz, Heckhausen, & O'Brien, 1994).

When confronted with major medical illnesses and disability, most individuals effectively use a wide array of coping strategies available to them (e.g., disengagement from unattainable goals, self-protective causal attributions, strategic social and intra-individual comparisons, use of external resources and technical aids, etc.). The goal of these strategies is to maintain and expand existing levels of control in important life domains. When these strategies fail to redress the threatened loss of control, the individual experiences negative affect (Schulz, Heckhausen, & O'Brien, 1994; Schulz & Heckhausen, 1996) and associated disturbances in cognition, behavior, motivation, and somatic functioning.

Because the causes and manifestations of depression are so varied, a variety of treatment strategies have emerged to deal with this problem. The most common approaches currently in use are discussed next.

TREATMENT.   In marked contrast to the dementias, the anguish of depression can be eased by appropriate treatment. Currently popular methods include drug therapy, electroconvulsive therapy, cognitive therapy, behavior therapy, and family therapy.

Drug therapy is widely used to treat elderly patients suffering from depression, and the drugs most often used are **antidepressants.** Of the various antidepressants, tricyclics (e.g., nortriptyline, desipramine, doxepin) and selective serotonin reuptake inhibitors (SSRIs; e.g., fluoxetine, sertraline, paroxetine) are

Although controversial, electroconvulsive shock therapy may be the treatment of choice in some instances.

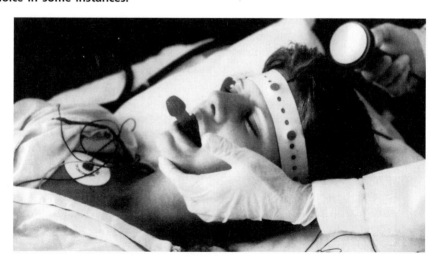

typically used with older adults; they tend to be effective yet relatively free of side effects (Blazer, 1989; Koenig & Blazer, 1996). SSRIs such as paroxetine are beginning to replace tricyclics as the first treatment of choice because they are easy to take and have fewer side effects.

The use of **electroconvulsive therapy (ECT)** (or "shock therapy") may be indicated when medications fail to relieve depression, or cannot be tolerated, or when an immediate effect is desired. Although this treatment method has been controversial, the induction of a seizure can reverse a major depression. Modern methods for administering ECT (e.g., administering the electric shocks to only one side of the brain, rather than to both cerebral hemispheres) have substantially reduced any negative side effects such as memory loss. ECT may work with 60% to 80% of patients who have failed to respond to other treatment modalities. These improvements end in relapses as often as 50% of the time, however, and memory losses do occur even when only one cerebral hemisphere receives shocks, so ECT should be prescribed only when other methods have proved ineffective. Yet in such instances, especially when the patient engages in self-destructive behavior (suicide attempts, refusing to eat), ECT may well be the treatment of choice.

Cognitive-behavioral therapy (CBT) differs from drug therapy and ECT in virtually every respect. It is based on the assumption that, in many instances, people behave in self-defeating and pathological ways because they are not aware of their true motives, beliefs, and feelings. Thus the goal of cognitive therapy is to help patients understand the causes and dynamics of their disorders and to change their self-defeating modes of thought and behavior. Individuals are trained to identify negative thinking, challenge maladaptive assumptions, avoid negative thoughts, and change dysfunctional attitudes and behaviors. This is done by means of verbal communication and by giving various assignments (e.g., keeping a daily or weekly log of behaviors and thoughts), rather than such physical methods as drugs or electric shocks. Although some theorists (including Freud and others) contend that patients over the age of 45 are too inflexible to profit from cognitive therapy, it is being used successfully with older adults suffering from depression. The success rate for CBT is comparable to rates obtained from drug treatment. The case of Mrs. H. is a good example:

The Treatment of Mrs. H

Because of Mrs. H.'s strong tendency to think negatively about herself, cognitive therapy was selected as the treatment of choice. . . . Mrs. H. was asked to keep a daily record of her negative thoughts, and to bring this to each therapy session for discussion. For example, she became unreasonably angry when her husband forgot to pick up some clothes from the cleaners, and grew intensely sad at night when she thought about her sons. Her view of life reflected an "all-or-none" philosophy: "either I'm a great success and completely happy, or a total failure and miserably unhappy." And she dwelt on the past in such terms as "if only I had . . ." and "I can't be happy unless things are the way they used to be."

With the aid of the therapist, Mrs. H. soon realized that such thoughts served to fuel her depression. She learned to recognize them as distorted and fallacious, and to reassess her situation from a more realistic perspective. Thus she learned that she could find new sources of happiness to replace the pleasures which she had enjoyed in the past, but which were no longer possible: "things change in life all the time, and this can open new paths to satisfaction." She also traced the roots of her negative thinking to her guilt about having been a working mother long before this was socially acceptable, and to the corresponding belief that she had seriously neglected her husband and children in order to pursue her own career. By learning to monitor her thoughts, and to replace her overly negative cognitions with more realistic appraisals, Mrs. H. was able to achieve a marked decrease in depression. (Gallagher & Thompson, 1983, pp. 27–29)

Instead of focusing primarily on enhancing the client's understanding of or cognitions about factors that lead to depression, the therapist may in addition prescribe behaviors aimed at reducing depression. In contrast to cognitive therapy, **behavior therapy** strives to change pathological behaviors and alleviate troublesome symptoms, using the principles and procedures devised by experimental psychologists in their study of normal behavior. Thus the behavior therapist may provide training in relaxation or assertiveness, model desired behavior, role-play troublesome situations with the client in order to help the client discover more effective behaviors, or use a variety of other techniques.

The Treatment of Mr. B

Mr. B. first received a series of 10 ECT treatments over a six-week period, and was released from the hospital as markedly improved. He functioned reasonably well for about eight weeks, when he again began to experience severe mood shifts.

Unlike Mrs. H., Mr. B. had few negative thoughts about himself. He was intensely lonely, however, and had had no meaningful interpersonal relationships since the death of his wife ten years ago. He also found few activities to be pleasant, and many to be unpleasant. Accordingly, behavior therapy was selected as the treatment of choice.

Relaxation training helped to decrease the aversiveness of Mr. B.'s interpersonal encounters, while role-playing and other techniques enabled him to improve his communication skills and develop more positive interactions with other people. He was encouraged to leave his apartment to have lunch, and then visit the park or his neighbors, so as to use his newly developed skills. Eventually he started to take the initiative to plan social activities, such as attending the local senior center and joining a card club. By the end of therapy, Mr. B. had significantly increased his social relationships. His depression was markedly reduced, and remained so during a one-year follow-up period. (Gallagher & Thompson, 1983, pp. 25–26)

Family support can help a depressed patient achieve a successful outcome, but family stress and dysfunction can exacerbate the depressive symptoms. Therefore, some clinicians prefer to meet with both the depressed patient and family members at the same time, a procedure known as **family therapy.** With the permission of the patient, the family is instructed as to the nature of the depressive disorder and the potential risks that may occur late in life (especially suicide). Family members can help advise the therapist about important changes in the patient's behavior, such as increased withdrawal from people or a preoccupation with medication or weapons, and they can remove potential suicide implements if necessary. The family can also be taught how to respond effectively to the patient's expressions of low self-esteem and pessimism, for example by paraphrasing what the patient says and expressing understanding without trying to intervene (e.g., "I hear what you are saying, and I understand"). Finally, if the symptoms of depression become severe enough to require hospitalization, the clinician can explain this to the family and secure their cooperation. (See Blazer, 1989.)

AFTERWORD. The preceding discussion supports a point made previously in this chapter: Most psychological disorders do *not* become more prevalent with increasing age. Clinical depression afflicts only a small percentage of older adults, and treatment methods are available for those who do contract this disorder. *In sum:* The normal course of aging is not necessarily, or even usually, accompanied by increases in depression.

Anxiety Disorders

DEFINITION. One of Freud's most valuable contributions was his discovery that psychological pain can be just as troublesome as physical pain, if not more so. He called such psychic pain **anxiety,** which is a highly unpleasant emotion similar to intense nervousness. (See, for example, Freud, 1926/1959.)

All of us experience anxiety at one time or another, and this is in no way indicative of psychopathology. When anxiety becomes so pervasive and intense as to cause serious interference with an individual's normal functioning, however, professional intervention is warranted.

There are several varieties of **anxiety disorder.** In *generalized anxiety*, severe anxiety occurs without any apparent cause. *Phobic disorders* involve an intense but irrational fear of a specific object or situation that is actually not dangerous, as with agoraphobia (the fear of being in public places from which escape might be difficult) and claustrophobia (the fear of closed places). In *obsessive-compulsive disorders*, thoughts or actions are repeatedly performed for no apparent reason except to reduce anxiety. For example, the sufferer may feel compelled to check that the front door is locked not once, but 10 or 15 times, before leaving the house. Anxiety disorders are typically accompanied by physical changes, including perspiring, dizziness, nausea, dry mouth, and an upset stomach. (See Table 11–10.)

INCIDENCE AND PREVALENCE RATES. Anxiety symptoms are more prevalent in elderly people than in younger age groups. The prevalence of clinical anxiety disorders among older adults is fairly high, and has been estimated at approximately 5%

MYTHS ABOUT AGING

Adult Psychopathology

Myth	Best Available Evidence
If you live into your 80s or beyond, you are very likely to suffer such severe mental deterioration that you become mindless or "senile."	Dementias do afflict a significant proportion of the elderly and are more likely to occur with increasing age. But even if you live to be 80 or older, the chances of your contracting a dementia are considerably less than 50%.
You are more likely to become more clinically depressed as you grow toward old age.	The incidence and prevalence of clinical depression do *not* increase with increasing age, although depressive symptoms are quite common among the elderly.
You are more likely to contract a serious mental illness as you grow older.	Although Alzheimer's disease is an important and troublesome exception, the incidence rates for most forms of psychopathology decline with increasing age.
Middle-aged and elderly adults are not amenable to treatment by cognitive and behavior therapy.	Successful cognitive and behavior therapy has been and is being done with the middle aged and elderly.

to 10% (Blazer, 1989b; see Table 11–9). Older adults may become anxious for various reasons, including failing health, the loss of loved ones and friends, intellectual declines, feelings of helplessness and worthlessness, and loss of control over the immediate environment. Phobic anxiety may be difficult to diagnose among the elderly, however, because they may well be embarrassed by these symptoms and conceal them behind protestations of physical illness (Jenike, 1989). As is true of most forms of psychopathology, incidence rates for anxiety disorders decline with increasing age (Brickman & Eisdorfer, 1989); you are less likely to contract such a disorder for the first time as you grow through adulthood.

TREATMENT.   Drug therapy is the most common form of treatment for symptoms of anxiety, despite the increasing evidence that the use of drugs such as benzodiazepines (e.g., Valium, Librium, Serax) is associated with increased risk of cog-

TABLE 11–10 Diagnostic Criteria for Generalized Anxiety Disorder

A. Excessive anxiety and worry (apprehensive expectation), occurring more days than not for at least 6 months, about a number of events or activities (such as work or school performance).
B. The person finds it difficult to control the worry.
C. The anxiety and worry are associated with three (or more) of the following six symptoms (with at least some symptoms present for more days than not for the past 6 months). *Note:* Only one item is required in children.
   1. restlessness or feeling keyed up or on edge
   2. being easily fatigued
   3. difficulty concentrating or mind going blank
   4. irritability
   5. muscle tension
   6. sleep disturbance (difficulty falling or staying aleep, or restless unsatisfying sleep)
D. The focus of the anxiety and worry is not confined to features of an Axis 1 disorder, e.g., the anxiety or worry is not about having a Panic Attack (as in Panic Disorder), being embarrassed in public (as in Social Phobia), being contaminated (as in Obsessive-Compulsive Disorder), being away from home or close relatives (as in Separation Anxiety Disorder), gaining weight (as in Anorexia Nervosa), having multiple physical complaints (as in Somatization Disorder), or having a serious illness (as in Hypochondriasis), and the anxiety and worry do not occur exclusively during Posttraumatic Stress Disorder.
E. The anxiety, worry, or physical symptoms cause clinically significant distress or impairment in social, occupational, or other important areas of functioning.
F. The disturbance is not due to the direct physiological effects of a substance (e.g., a drug of abuse, a medication) or a general medical condition (e.g., hyperthyroidism) and does not occur exclusivley during a Mood Disorder, a Psychotic Disorder, or a Pervasive Developmental Disorder.

nitive impairment, falls, and other illnesses (DeVries, 1996). Various forms of **psychotherapy** such as psychoanalysis and cognitive behavior therapy are also used to treat anxiety disorders. For example, in *systematic desensitization, a type of behavior therapy*, phobic anxiety is reduced by having the client list the feared stimuli in hierarchical order (e.g., "being in a public place," "approaching the public place," and ending with "thinking of going outside"). The client then imagines being in these situations, starting with the lowest one in the hierarchy (least anxiety-provoking) while practicing previously taught techniques of muscular relaxation. In some instances, the client may be asked to use the relaxation techniques while actually in the anxiety-provoking situation. Relaxation procedures have also been found to be effective in helping clients learn to control feelings of anxiety before they get out of hand.

Middle-aged and older persons may experience considerable anxiety in relation to physical symptoms they experience (e.g., "I must have cancer") or because they are concerned about being a burden to family members. Cognitive therapy can be an effective method for teaching anxious individuals to substitute negative anxiety-provoking thoughts with more realistic and reassuring ones (e.g., "I shouldn't jump to conclusions without first getting the problem evaluated"). Many older adults respond favorably to this form of treatment, and in many cases it may be preferable to medication.

AFTERWORD.   Our review of adult psychopathology has been both disturbing and reassuring. We have seen that Alzheimer's disease is extremely painful, incurable, and increasing in prevalence. The torment undergone by these patients, and by those who must care for them, can only be imagined by those of us fortunate enough to avoid this experience. This is truly a disease of catastrophic proportions, and it is a problem likely to become even worse in the next few decades.

Yet we have also observed that the incidence and prevalence of most forms of psychopathology decline with increasing age. (Thus we have chosen not to discuss certain disorders, such as schizophrenia and some forms of what used to be called neurosis. Although important, these disorders often originate in childhood or young adulthood; they are less likely to occur for the first time during late adulthood and are less common among older adults.) We have also seen that there are useful forms of treatment for older adults who do become clinically depressed or suffer from an anxiety disorder. The quality of differential diagnosis is improving, when one wishes to take the necessary time and effort, and an increasing number of therapeutic procedures are being offered for various geriatric disorders.

Although many effective treatment methods are currently available, many elderly persons are not receiving needed treatment for their disorders. There is a shortage of properly trained personnel; some professionals are biased against treating the elderly; and some elderly individuals are reluctant to seek treatment from mental health professionals. These are problems that must be resolved, so that more people can make the latter part of their lives as meaningful and fulfilling as possible.

SUMMARY

Substantive and Methodological Issues

It is not always easy to distinguish between mental health and psychopathology. Whether or not behavior is pathological may depend on the specific situation, cultural factors, and the age of the individual. In general, mental health reflects the ability to deal with the issues of life in an effective way, as by satisfying instinctual drives in ways that are socially acceptable and appropriately flexible.

Psychopathology may be caused by various factors. Such pioneering clinical investigators as Sigmund Freud attributed psychopathology entirely to experiences during childhood, notably those involving the parents. Modern clinicians agree that childhood causes are important but have identified numerous other factors related to psychopathology, some of which are psychosocial (e.g., age, sex, race, education, income, marital status, religious participation, stress) and some biological (such as medication, endocrine disorders, infections, tumors, metabolic disorders, concussions, and nutrition disorders).

Because there are so many possible causes of psychopathology, diagnosis and assessment can be a difficult task. One popular system for classifying the various forms of psychopathology is *DSM-IV*, the 1994 revision of the *Diagnostic and Statistical Manual* prepared by the American Psychiatric Association. Among the common assessment procedures are clinical interviews and psychometric instruments. The latter include measures that probe deeply into the patient's personality and rough, quickly administered screening tests.

Epidemiology and Treatment of Adult Psychopathology

The greater the frequency of a particular disorder, the more people who will benefit if we diagnose and treat it correctly. Field surveys and the case register method are commonly used to obtain epidemiological data, which are typically expressed in terms of incidence rates and prevalence rates.

Dementias lead initially to the loss of cognitive functioning and in later stages to the loss of motor and physical functioning. Of the more than 70 different conditions that can cause dementia, the two most common among elderly persons are Alzheimer's disease and vascular dementia. Alzheimer's has become a disease of catastrophic proportions; it may afflict as many as 6% of adults over age 65, and 20% of adults over 85. Alzheimer's disease is currently not curable. It has been called the cruelest of all diseases because it kills its victims twice: First there is the living death of being unable to remember the simplest fact, perform the most basic daily function, or even recognize loved ones and recall one's own identity; then, the body gradually sinks into coma and death. The course of Alzheimer's disease is gradual and progressive. The causes of the disease are not yet known. Various services exist to help Alzheimer's patients and their caregivers, who also experience considerable emotional and physical stress. In contrast to Alzheimer's disease, vascular dementia has an abrupt onset, progresses in stages, is more prevalent among men, more often involves physical impairments, and is caused by an inadequate flow of blood to the brain. The symptoms of vascular dementia include impairments in memory, judgment, abstract thinking, and impulse control and possible changes in personality.

Clinical depression is characterized by negative changes in mood that are powerful and pervasive. The sufferer experiences unusually strong and frequent feelings of dejection, apprehension, worthlessness, gloom and dismay about the past, and hopelessness about the future. Although it is not uncommon to find elderly persons who have elevated symptoms of depression, these are rarely severe enough to warrant a diagnosis of clinical depression; the prevalence of clinical depression among older adults is low, and the incidence declines with increasing age. Various forms of treatment are available to those who do contract clinical depression, including antidepressant medications, electroconvulsive therapy, cognitive behavior therapy, and family therapy.

Anxiety is a universal experience and considered pathological only when it becomes so pervasive and intense as to interfere seriously with an individual's normal functioning. Varieties of anxiety disorder include generalized anxiety, phobic disorders, and obsessive-compulsive disorders. The prevalence of anxiety disorders among older adults is fairly high, but various forms of psychotherapy and (if necessary) chemotherapy have proved effective in treating this disorder.

Although many effective treatment methods are currently available, many elderly persons are not receiving needed treatment for their disorders. This problem must be resolved, so that more people can make the latter part of their lives more meaningful and fulfilling.

STUDY QUESTIONS

1. How do definitions of what is considered pathological or abnormal vary by culture and by age? Can you provide specific examples of behaviors that might be considered pathological in one culture but not another?
2. What are the most important causes of adult psychopathology? What does the variety of causes imply about our ability to diagnose the disorder that afflicts a particular individual?
3. Why is it important to classify the various kinds of mental disorders? Why has it proved necessary to revise the standard classification system several times? What does this imply about our ability to diagnose the disorder that afflicts a particular individual?
4. Why has Alzheimer's disease been called the cruelest of all diseases?
5. Of the disorders discussed in this chapter, which are you significantly more likely to contract as you grow past middle age? What does this imply about the general level of mental health among older adults?
6. How do methods for treating depression differ from methods for treating anxiety disorders? Have these methods proved successful with older adults, or is their effectiveness limited to young adults?

TERMS TO REMEMBER

Alzheimer's disease	Electroconvulsive therapy (ECT)
Antidepressant	Epidemiology
Anxiety	Family therapy
Anxiety disorder	Field survey
Assessment	Incidence rate
Behavior therapy	Mental health
Case register method	Organic mental disorder
Cognitive-behavior therapy (CBT)	Population at risk
Dementia (dementing illness)	Prevalence rate
Depression	Psychopathology
Drug therapy	Psychotherapy
DSM-IV	Vascular dementia

DEATH AND DYING

In Chapter 1, we observed that many more of us are living to old age than ever before. There has also been a significant change in our manner of dying: Illnesses that are of long duration (**chronic**) have replaced those that are brief and severe (**acute**) as the major causes of death. This means that dying will be a fairly drawn-out process for many of us. Furthermore, this process is likely to place considerable demands on those family members and friends who are with us during this difficult time. As a result, death and dying has become an important aspect of adult development and aging.

Partly for this reason, recent years have seen a remarkable crescendo of discussion about death and dying. Library shelves are now filled with volumes concerning the philosophical, religious, sociological, anthropological, psychological, and medical views of death. It is not unusual for more than 700 books to be published on these topics in a single year. Entire journals are now devoted to the inspection, dissection, and analysis of every imaginable aspect of death and dying.

This fascination with death is hardly new. Noted philosophers from Epicurus to Bertrand Russell, playwrights, poets, novelists, and many others have written incisively about death for more than 2,000 years. During the past two decades, however, our quest for knowledge has taken a significant turn: For the first time, investigators in a variety of disciplines have sought to collect systematic empirical data about death and dying. Much of this data gathering has been stimulated and carried out by psychologists; but sociologists, anthropologists, and physicians have participated as well. This area is also prone to methodological problems, and some researchers have drawn intriguing but overly speculative conclusions that go far beyond the actual evidence. Yet we can now answer some important questions about death and dying and make educated guesses in various areas where firm conclusions are not yet possible.

This chapter addresses four major issues. First we examine the demography of death, including leading causes and mortality rates. Next we survey the evidence dealing with the fear of death, which some psychologists and philosophers believe to be a major determinant of human behavior. Our third topic concerns the experiences of the terminally ill and the effects on their families and friends. For example, do all of the dying proceed through a series of similar psychological stages? Or are their experiences with the specter of death primarily different? The final section deals with the grief and bereavement that result from the death of someone close to us and describes how these intense and painful feelings may be alleviated.

THE DEMOGRAPHY OF DEATH

Although the course of human history has been highlighted by astonishing scientific advances, methods for preventing death exist only in the realm of science fiction. In 1995, for example, the number of deaths in the United States totaled 1,926,000 (U.S. Bureau of the Census, 1997). However, important changes have occurred in the most common causes and places of death.

Causes of Death

In Chapter 11, we observed that classification is an important aspect of any science. This also applies to the study of mortality rates: Causes of death are classified according to formal criteria established by the World Health Organization, aided by such standardized instruments as the death certificate. This useful form records such information as immediate and other causes of death; whether death was due to an accident, suicide, or homicide; the time and place of death; and biographical data, such as the deceased's name, sex, age, birthplace, and immediate family.

LEADING CAUSES OF DEATH.   As noted at the outset of this chapter, deaths in our society are more often due to chronic than to acute illnesses. Deaths from communicable diseases have decreased markedly since 1900; for example, pneumonia and influenza caused only 4% of all deaths in 1988. Conversely, more than half of all current deaths are caused by such degenerative diseases as heart ailments, cancer, and strokes. Of course, the most likely cause of death varies somewhat by age and gender. Young adults are more likely to die from causes such as accidents, homicides, and suicides, and older persons are more likely to die from chronic health conditions such as heart disease and cancer.

As noted in Chapter 3, we have become more knowledgeable about the dangers of cigarette smoking, high blood pressure, high blood levels of LDL cholesterol, obesity, physical inactivity, and stress. Partly for this reason, there has been a decline in deaths from heart disease and strokes since 1950. In addition, the number of accidental deaths declined from 105,700 in 1980 to 89,700 in 1995. And the age-adjusted death rate for cancer decreased slightly between 1991 and 1995. Unfortunately, however, a new killer threatens many: **acquired immunodeficiency syndrome (AIDS)**. AIDS was the 15th leading cause of death in 1988, producing 16,602 fatalities. By 1994, AIDS deaths had increased to 43,975 in the United States. More recently, the availability of new treatments for AIDS has had a significant impact on the number of deaths. After 7 consecutive years of increasing mortality due to AIDS, 1995 was the first year in which mortality rates decreased significantly (U.S. Bureau of the Census, 1997).

THE DEMOGRAPHICS OF SUICIDE.   The total number of recorded suicides per year in the United States is about 30,000 persons. This translates to about 83 suicides per day, and about 17 of these suicides are committed by elderly persons. Thus the rate of suicide among the elderly is disproportionately high. Although suicides increase with age, this is mostly due to white males, especially those over age 65. Conversely, suicide rates for females tend to remain fairly constant with increasing age. For nonwhites, there is a slight tendency for suicide rates to peak at about age 20 and again at about age 80, but the rates remain significantly lower at all ages than the corresponding figures for whites. (See Figures 12–1 and 12–2.) The risk of suicide is highest among while males who are socially isolated, depressed, and/or physically ill or disabled and who have lost significant relationships. Elderly persons who attempt suicide are also more likely to succeed. About 1 in 20 suicide attempts among young adults result in death, whereas 1 in 4 attempts among the elderly result in death. The preferred mode of death for both elderly men and women is firearms (Kastenbaum, 1995).

Places of Death

Relatively little research attention has been paid to the locations where Americans are most likely to die, even though this information can be readily obtained from death certificates. In the 1940s and 1950s, people were much more likely to die at home than they are today. (See Table 12–1.) Recent data indicate that 21% of persons die at home and another 4.4% die while enrolled in a hospice program. About half of the individuals enrolled in hospice programs also die at home (Mor & Hiris, 1983; Morris et al., 1984). Older men are more likely to die

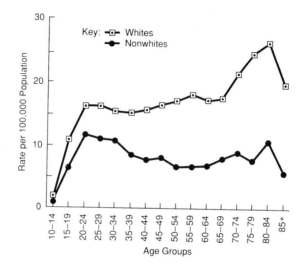

FIGURE 12–1 **Suicide by age and race, United States, 1985.**
(*Source:* McIntosh (1988–1989), "Official U.S. elderly suicide data bases: Levels, availability, omissions." *Omega: Journal of Death and Dying, 19,* pp. 337–350.)

in hospitals than women, and the reverse is true for deaths in nursing homes (Matcha & Hutshinson, 1997). Because women typically outlive their husbands, they are more likely to spend the last years of their lives in a long-term care facility.

Regardless of whether one dies at home or in an institution, various medical personnel play an important role in the process of dying. Many terminal pa-

FIGURE 12–2 **Suicide by age and sex, United States, 1985.**
(*Source:* McIntosh (1988–1989), "Official U.S. elderly suicide data bases: Levels, availability, omissions." *Omega: Journal of Death and Dying, 19,* pp. 337–350.)

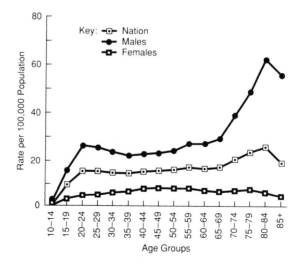

TABLE 12-1 Percentage of Deaths at Home and in Institutions
in the United States, 1949, 1958, 1994–1995

LOCATION OF DEATH	1949	1958	1994–1995	
			Male	Female
Home	50.5	39.1	20.8	20.9
Hospice	—	—	4.4	4.4
In an institution	49.5	60.9	74.8	74.6
General hospitals	39.5	46.6	61.9	47.6
Convalescent and nursing homes, homes for the aged, etc.	1.6	6.0	12.3	23.4
Nervous and mental hospitals	3.2	3.5	—	—
Chronic disease and other special hospitals	0.9	1.5	—	—
Tuberculosis hospitals	0.9	0.6	—	—
Maternity hospitals	0.2	0.1	—	—
Other	3.2	2.6	0.6	3.6

Source: Adapted from Lerner (1976); Matcha & Hutchinson (1997).

tients come to rely on these professionals not only for medical care, but also for social and emotional support. This is likely to cause problems for both the staff and the patient, as we see in a subsequent section.

THE FEAR OF DEATH

Some theorists believe the **fear of death (death anxiety)**, conscious and unconscious, is the prime mover for all human behavior.[1] In his Pulitzer Prize–winning book, *The Denial of Death*, Ernest Becker (1973) argues that

> *Of all things that move man, one of the principal ones is his terror of death.* . . . The idea of death, the fear of it, haunts the human animal like nothing else; it is a mainspring of human activity—activity designed largely to avoid the fatality of death, to overcome it by denying in some way that it is the final destiny for man.

The overriding importance of death anxiety as a motivator is characteristic of the school known as existential psychology, typified by Rollo May:

> To grasp what it means to exist, one needs to grasp the fact that he might not exist, that he treads at every moment on the sharp edge of possible annihilation and can never escape the fact that death will arrive at some unknown moment in the future. . . . Without this awareness of nonbeing . . . existence is vapid [and] unreal. . . . [But] with the confrontation of nonbeing, existence takes on vitality and immediacy, and the individual experiences a heightened consciousness of himself, his

---

[1]Some writers use the term *fear* when the cause is known and readily available to consciousness, and they reserve the term *anxiety* for causes that are vague or unconscious. Others use the two terms more or less interchangeably, as do we in this book.

world, and others around him. . . . [Thus] the confronting of death gives the most positive reality to life itself. (May 1958/1967, pp. 47–49)

As these theorists suggest, the fear of death can be both a destructive and a creative force. This universal fear may lead to neurosis, or even to psychosis; but it is also responsible for the pleasures of existence and for many of humanity's most outstanding achievements. Because of death anxiety, some people are motivated to transcend their physical mortality through their productions: Artists and writers may hope their works will live forever, scientists may seek major discoveries that will have lasting benefits for all of humankind, politicians may strive to have their accomplishments permanently recorded on the pages of history, and so on. Or, for many people, having children may be a form of immortality.

Although existentialist theory is important and provocative, it is by no means universally accepted. Others have argued that most of us experience little anxiety over the prospect of dying because it looms far in the future (e.g., Schulz, 1978). In fact, many different conceptions of death have been proposed by philosophers, religious leaders, psychologists, and others, some of which date back to ancient Greece. Nevertheless, there does appear to be general agreement on at least one point: Death is an experience that few people eagerly seek out. What is it about death that makes it so undesirable to most of us?

Reasons for Fearing Death

There are two general reasons why death is unattractive: It involves physical suffering and psychological suffering. These two categories are not mutually exclusive; neither one exists in isolation, and each can intensify the other.

THE FEAR OF PHYSICAL SUFFERING.   As noted previously, deaths from chronic degenerative diseases (e.g., cancer) have increased significantly since 1900. We are all aware that patients with terminal cancer may experience months or even years of pain, undergo forms of therapy that have distressing side effects, or suffer the removal of limbs or breasts. To many people, the possibility of such extreme pain, deterioration, and sometimes disfigurement is frightening indeed. So, too, are the dependency and loss of control that may accompany physical deterioration.

THE FEAR OF ISOLATION AND LONELINESS.   Being identified as a dying person often results in profound life changes. The terminal patient is often isolated and may well be treated differently by family, friends, and health professionals, who are likely to consider death a taboo subject. Thus the prospect of a lingering terminal illness may evoke fears of being lonely or of being unable to talk about the issues that are most important to the patient.

THE FEAR OF NONBEING.   Human beings are the only creatures on earth who must live with the constant awareness that they will someday cease to exist. As we have seen, this knowledge of our ultimate nonbeing can arouse intense anxiety.

THE FEAR OF COWARDICE AND HUMILIATION.   We may also fear that we will become cowards in the face of death, either because of the accompanying physical pain or because we dread the thought of not existing. Thus the aforementioned sources of death anxiety may well create the "fear of fear itself."

THE FEAR OF FAILING TO ACHIEVE IMPORTANT GOALS.   Some people define the length of their lives in terms of accomplishments, rather than years. If a university professor were asked how long he or she wanted to live, the reply might well be, "Long enough to write two more books." Or an elderly person may express the desire to survive until an important birthday or anniversary, or an offspring's wedding. We may therefore fear death because it will deprive us of cherished goals and experiences.

THE FEAR OF THE IMPACT OF DEATH ON ONE'S SURVIVORS.   Yet another source of death anxiety is the probable impact on one's survivors. Where finances permit, life insurance and trust funds can help parents alleviate the economic impact on their children. But finding some way to relieve the psychological and emotional impact is quite another matter.

THE FEAR OF PUNISHMENT OR OF THE UNKNOWN.   Some religions preach that transgressors are doomed to dire fates, such as consignment to hell. Believers may become profoundly afraid of what they will experience after they die. However, it is also possible that religion will have precisely the opposite effect. That is, those who believe in more supportive religions may find that their faith significantly reduces their fear of death.

THE FEAR OF THE DEATH OF OTHERS.   Death anxiety is not limited to our own demise. We may also fear losing someone close to us and having to experience their physical and psychological suffering. Each of the fears already listed can also be experienced vicariously, in relation to the death of a loved one.

In theory, then, there are numerous reasons why the fear of death might dominate our lives. But does it? To answer this important question, let us now turn to an examination of the relevant research evidence.

Research on Death Anxiety

CONCEPTUAL AND METHODOLOGICAL ISSUES.   Most often, death anxiety has been assessed by written questionnaires. A typical example of these **direct measures** is Templer's (1970) Death Anxiety Scale, which consists of 15 true-false items:

1. I am very much afraid to die.
2. The thought of death seldom enters my mind.
3. It doesn't make me nervous when people talk about death.
4. I dread to think about having to have an operation.
5. I am not at all afraid to die.
6. I am not particularly afraid of getting cancer.
7. The thought of death never bothers me.
8. I am often distressed by the way time flies so very rapidly.
9. I fear dying a painful death.

10. The subject of life after death troubles me greatly.
11. I am really scared of having a heart attack.
12. I often think about how short life really is.
13. I shudder when I hear people talking about a World War III.
14. The sight of a dead body is horrifying to me.
15. I feel that the future holds nothing for me to fear.

The responses to these items are mathematically combined into a single death-anxiety score. Various comparable questionnaires have been devised by other researchers.

How psychometrically sound are these instruments? On the positive side, there is some support for their validity. For example, psychiatric patients who were rated high in anxiety by a clinician scored significantly higher on Templer's scale than did a control group. Subjects who viewed a movie depicting gruesome automobile accidents showed significantly greater death anxiety than did subjects who watched an innocuous movie. Intercorrelations between various death anxiety questionnaires have been found to vary from $+0.41$ to $+0.72$, indicating a fairly high degree of agreement (Handal et al., 1984–1985).

Some researchers have argued that this approach suffers from serious conceptual flaws. First of all, they note that such scales assess only the *public and conscious* aspects of death anxiety. Our *conscious but private* feelings may well be quite different, but too sensitive and intimate to share with other people. If subjects believe such fears are a sign of serious personal weakness or these fears are no one else's business, they may deliberately falsify their answers in order to appear more courageous. Some studies do indicate that when subjects are identified by name, they report less fear of death than when the questionnaires are administered anonymously (Jones & Sigall, 1971; Schulz, Aderman, & Manko, 1976).

Furthermore, the fear of death is typically assumed to be partly or primarily *unconscious*. Because this repressed aspect is hidden even from ourselves, it cannot be assessed by instruments that depend entirely on conscious self-reports, even if subjects are trying their best to be honest and accurate. For this reason, attempts have been made to tap the less conscious aspects of death anxiety by using various **indirect measures**. These include the following:

♦   **The Word Association Test.** The experimenter states a single word, and the subject must reply with the first word that comes to mind (Jung, 1905/1984, 1910). Subjects with greater death anxiety will presumably respond more slowly to death-related words (e.g., *cemetery*), or will give more unusual responses, than is the case with neutral words.

♦   **The Color Word Interference Test.** The subject is asked to state the color in which a word is printed, disregarding its meaning. Here again, subjects with greater death anxiety will presumably respond more slowly to death-related words than to equally common but more neutral words.

♦   **The Death Anxiety Slideshow Measure.** Subjects are shown a series of slides. Some are death oriented, such as a slide of the word *graveyard* followed by a picture of a graveyard; others are neutral, as with the word *greenness* followed by a picture of a backyard lawn scene. During this presentation, a physiological measure of anxiety is obtained by monitoring the subjects' heart rates. Subjects who fear death more will presumably show more pronounced changes in heart rate to the death-oriented slides than to the neutral ones.

In theory, if much of our death anxiety is beyond our awareness, we should show considerably more fear on these indirect measures than on direct questionnaires. Some studies do find this to be the case, indicating that a significant part of death anxiety is covert (e.g., Feifel, 1974; Feifel & Branscomb, 1973; Feifel, Freilich, & Hermann, 1973; Feifel & Nagy, 1980; Hayslip, Servaty, Christman, & Mumy, 1996–1997). However, the evidence in this area is equivocal. Other investigators have reached precisely the opposite conclusion: They report that subjects obtain similar scores on direct overt and indirect covert measures, which implies that we do *not* repress our fear of death (e.g., Littlefield & Fleming, 1984–1985). It has also been argued that the indirect measures of death anxiety are of questionable validity. One study found little or no relationship among these measures, indicating that they do *not* assess the same concept (Handal et al., 1984–1985).

Another problem with most direct questionnaires is that they treat death anxiety as a unidimensional concept. That is, they yield only a single score for each subject. Although this assumption is appealingly simple, it is almost certainly erroneous. We have seen that death anxiety has aspects which are conscious and public, conscious and private, and (very possibly) unconscious. We have also noted various reasons why we may fear death, and it is quite possible to suffer from some of these anxieties but not from others. Thus, an unmarried person may fear the physical suffering associated with dying, but have no survivors to worry about. A devoted parent may be extremely concerned with the impact of his or her death on the children, but much less anxious about the possibility of physical pain. Or dedicated scientists and artists may fear the interruption of their work far more than any other aspect of dying.

Here, the empirical data are more clear cut. Even Templer's straightforward scale has been found to include several distinct factors: the fear of the unknown aspects of death, the fear of suffering, the fear of loneliness at the time of death, and the fear of personal extinction (Conte et al., 1982). Another questionnaire developed by Collett and Lester (1969) distinguishes among four sources of death anxiety, although all are public and conscious: death of self, death of others, dying of self, and dying of others. These investigators obtained low intercorrelations among the four subscales, indicating once again that death anxiety is multidimensional. And still other researchers have drawn a similar conclusion (e.g., Feifel, 1990; Florian & Har-Even, 1983–1984; Kastenbaum & Costa, 1977; Littlefield & Fleming, 1984–1985).

In sum: Research on death anxiety has all too often relied on simple unidimensional scores, based solely on the public and conscious level. It is only recently that investigators have begun to tap the true richness and complexity of this variable, including its multidimensionality and possible unconscious aspects (e.g., Sharma, Monsen, & Gary, 1996–1997).

SUBSTANTIVE FINDINGS.   Death anxiety has been studied in relation to various aspects of adult behavior. As might be expected from the preceding discussion, relatively few clear and consistent patterns have emerged from the available data. In this section, we explore some of the more interesting questions posed by researchers in this area.

Does our fear of death become stronger as we grow older? More recent studies have *not* found pronounced increases in death anxiety during the first half of adulthood, at least at a conscious level. In fact, some studies of young adults have yielded small but statistically significant negative correlations between age and direct measures of death anxiety. This weak, inverse relationship has been observed for junior college students (mean age 27 years) and for members of such death-related professions as funeral personnel and firefighters. However, the same studies also obtained mostly nonsignificant correlations when indirect measures were used to assess death anxiety, and for subjects in such professions as secretarial work and teaching (Handal et al., 1984–1985; Lattaner & Hayslip, 1984–1985). Similar nonsignificant results were reported in an earlier large-scale study, in which the Death Anxiety Scale was administered to more than 2,000 subjects of various ages (Templer, Ruff, & Franks, 1971).

The relationship between aging and the fear of death does appear to be moderated by physical health. Adults who suffer from serious illnesses, especially acute disorders, tend to show greater death anxiety than healthy adults do. These patients are likely to express considerable concern with such fears as physical suffering, nonbeing, and cowardice and humiliation (e.g., "I worry about whether I'll have the strength to die with dignity"). Because ill health is more likely to occur at advanced ages, a corresponding age-related increase in death anxiety may be expected. However, the failure to verbalize such fears does *not* necessarily mean that death anxiety is absent. As we have seen, our conscious and private feelings may differ from those that are conscious and public. Furthermore, the tendency to repress our death anxiety may well increase as we pass middle age and death becomes a more immediate threat. It has been found that adults past the age of 50 are more likely to deny their fears of death, yet their unconscious death anxiety is just as high as that of younger adults (Corey, 1961; Feifel & Branscomb, 1973). As was the case with young adults, however, the evidence does *not* indicate that healthy men and women become more afraid of death (at least at a conscious level) as they grow from middle to old age.

Are such personal characteristics as sex and religious beliefs related to death anxiety? As noted earlier, it is conceivable that religious beliefs might either intensify or alleviate the fear of death. A recent review of 36 studies dealing with this issue found that in 24 of them, or two thirds, increased faith was significantly related to decreased anxiety. That is, those who were more religious were less afraid of death than those who were not as religious. Seven studies failed to detect any significant relationship, and only three studies found that greater faith was related to greater fears of death (Spilka, Hood, & Gorsuch, 1985; see also DaSilva & Schork, 1984–1985; Florian & Har-Even, 1983–1984).

The evidence concerning gender and death anxiety is more inconsistent. Some researchers have found that women show higher anxiety on direct measures and are less likely to repress their fears of death. If this pattern were reliable, it could be argued that men are more reluctant to admit their death anxiety because they regard such fears as unmasculine. However, various other studies have not obtained significant differences in death anxiety between the sexes. (See, for example, DaSilva & Schork, 1984–1985; Pollak, 1979–1980; Lester, 1984–1985.) All too many researchers in this area have based their conclusions solely on unidimensional death anxiety scores, so further research of a multidimensional nature is needed before firm conclusions can be drawn.

Does death anxiety influence the likelihood of participating in life-threatening activities? People who are high in death anxiety might seem less likely to engage in risky, life-threatening professions and avocations. To test this hypothesis, Feifel and Nagy (1980) obtained samples of such risk takers as alcoholics, drug addicts, and inmates serving prison sentences for committing violent crimes. Also included were a sample of deputy sheriffs, who engage in life-threatening behaviors that are socially acceptable; and a control group of federal government employees, who were not involved in such risky behaviors. The results did *not* support the hypothesis; the various risk-taking groups were not significantly lower (or higher) in conscious or unconscious death anxiety than the control group. However, a recent study suggests a possible inverse relation between death anxiety and engaging in dangerous, potentially lethal behaviors such as fast driving, owning a gun, and using drugs. Respondents who were high on death anxiety were less likely to engage in dangerous behaviors (Cotton, 1996–1997).

Do dreams provide any evidence about unconscious fears of death? Most psychologists agree that dreams provide important clues about our unconscious wishes, feelings, beliefs, and motives, although dream interpretation can be a difficult and controversial affair. (See, for example, Foulkes, 1966; Freud, 1900/1965a; Fromm, 1951; Hall, 1966; Jung, 1964.) In one study, subjects who scored either high or low on direct measures of death anxiety had a significantly higher proportion of death-related dreams than did subjects with moderate scores (Handal & Rychlak, 1971). This curvilinear relationship suggests once again that some people who have relatively little death anxiety at the conscious level, public and private, may well be considerably more afraid at an unconscious level.

AFTERWORD.   The evidence reviewed fails to support the existentialist belief as to the overwhelming importance of death anxiety. However, it could be argued that the negative findings are due partly or largely to methodological difficulties. Hypotheses involving the unconscious aspects of death anxiety remain controversial, but a number of studies do suggest that a significant part of these fears is indeed beyond our awareness. More data, and more valid indirect measures, are needed in order to determine the extent to which death anxiety influences human behavior.

With the available evidence, there is no reason to expect that you will become increasingly preoccupied with the prospect of your own death as you grow through adulthood. However, serious physical illnesses represent an important exception. When such disorders make the prospect of death more imminent and real, anxiety is likely to increase markedly; these fears may take various forms because death anxiety is not unidimensional. As a result, helping terminally ill patients deal with their anxieties is far from an easy task—as we see in the following pages.

THE PROCESS OF DYING: THE TERMINAL STAGES OF LIFE

A **terminal illness** is one from which the patient has no reasonable hope of ever recovering, although there may be periods of remission and apparent health. Terminality has been defined in various ways; according to the U.S. Department of Health and Human Services, an illness is terminal if a physician certifies that the individual has a life expectancy of 6 months or less (Schulz & Schlarb, 1987–1988).

The **terminal phase of life** is the last decline in health from which there is *no* major remission and that ends in death. This phase is a time of steady and rapid deterioration, especially of the central nervous system, and it may well be evidenced by sudden sharp declines in scores on mental and psychomotor tests. In most cases, the terminal phase is preceded by acute and chronic illness phases that may facilitate or interfere with an individual's preparation for the terminal phase. Although our focus here is on the terminal phase of life, it is important to acknowledge that the acute and chronic phases of an illness pose significant challenges to the afflicted individual as well as family and friends. Some of the tasks that individuals face in progressing from the acute to the terminal phase of an illness are listed in Table 12–2.

Interest in these terminal stages of life is currently at an all-time high, and for good reason. As we observed at the outset of this chapter, deaths in our society are much more often due to prolonged chronic diseases than to quickly terminating acute illnesses. This is particularly true for the aged, among whom 80% of all deaths occur. Therefore, virtually all of us will eventually have to deal with the *process* of dying—as a patient, as a concerned family member or friend, or perhaps in some professional capacity. Yet there is, at present, relatively little empirical information about such important issues as the typical duration of terminal illnesses; the magnitude of the accompanying disabilities, physical pain, and psychological distress; coping strategies used by terminal patients; or even the number of patients who are aware that their illnesses are terminal.

The Medical Staff and the Dying

For health care professionals, the terminal prognosis implies a dramatic shift in treatment strategy. That is, instead of doing everything possible to bring about a

Myths About Aging

Death and Dying

Myth	Best Available Evidence
You will become more afraid of death as you grow toward old age and your death becomes more imminent.	Serious physical illnesses are related to an increase in death anxiety and are more likely to occur at advanced ages. But the evidence does *not* indicate that healthy men and women become more afraid of death as they grow from adulthood to old age, at least at a conscious level.
Terminal patients go through predictable stages as they approach death.	Most terminal patients experience anxiety and depression before they die but do *not* go through a set series of stages.
A sudden or unexpected death has more adverse effects on the survivors than does a death that is expected.	Research findings do not support this hypothesis. The impact of a death on the survivors is *not* related to its suddenness or predictability.
It is kinder for physicians not to tell elderly patients that they have a terminal illness.	Most people of all ages want to know if they have a terminal illness. Although there are exceptions, the advantages of being a legitimate participant in the treatment process are likely to outweigh the short-term trauma caused by learning the truth.
Older men are likely to die at home, and older women are more likely to die in institutional settings such as hospitals and nursing homes.	The large majority of both men and women die in institutional settings. Men are more likely to die in hospitals than women, and women are more likely to die in nursing homes than men.
Among those adults whose spouses die, elderly widows and widowers are much more likely to die themselves a short time later.	Young adults who lose a spouse to death appear to be at higher risk than older widows and widowers.

TABLE 12–2   Tasks in Life-Threatening Illness

GENERAL	ACUTE PHASE	CHRONIC PHASE	TERMINAL PHASE
1. Responding to the physical fact of disease	1. Understanding the disease	1. Managing symptoms and side effects	1. Dealing with symptoms, discomfort, pain, and incapacitation
2. Taking steps to cope with the reality of disease	2. Maximizing health and lifestyle	2. Carrying out health regimens	2. Managing health procedures and institutional stress
	3. Maximizing one's coping strengths and limiting weaknesses	3. Preventing and managing health crisis	
		4. Managing stress and examining coping	3. Managing stress and examining coping
	4. Developing strategies to deal with the issues created by the disease	5. Maximizing social support and minimizing isolation	4. Dealing effectively with caregivers
		6. Normalizing life in the face of the disease	5. Preparing for death and saying goodbye
		7. Dealing with financial concerns	
3. Preserving self-concept and relationships with others in the face of disease	5. Exploring the effect of the diagnosis on a sense of self and others	8. Preserving self-concept	6. Preserving self-concept
		9. Redefining relationships with others throughout the course of the disease	7. Preserving appropriate relationships with family and friends
4. Dealing with affective and existential spiritual issues created or reactivated by the disease	6. Ventilating feelings and fears	10. Ventilating feeling and fears	8. Ventilating feelings and fears
	7. Incorporating the present reality of diagnosis into one's sense of past and future	11. Finding meaning in suffering, chronicity, uncertainty and decline	9. Finding meaning in life and death

Source: Doka (1995–1996).

recovery, the medical staff must concentrate instead on managing the patient's last days. This can cause significant social, emotional, and psychological problems for all concerned.

ATTITUDES AND BEHAVIORS OF PHYSICIANS AND NURSES.   Numerous studies indicate that physicians and nurses have difficulty dealing with terminal illnesses. To cope with this stressful situation, they may well resort to such psychological defense mechanisms as denial of reality and intellectualization. Thus physicians and nurses may avoid the patient who is in the process of dying, or even fail to make eye contact during those meetings that do take place. They may seek to have minimal contact with the patient's family. Or they may refer to the patient in distant and unemotional terms, for example by using bed location or type of illness rather than the patient's name.

Physicians react more defensively to certain aspects of terminal care than nurses do, possibly because they are more responsible for the patient's treatment. For example, some physicians tend to argue that patients should not participate in decisions about their treatment plans, should not be encouraged to talk about their terminality, and should not be cared for by family members. In contrast, nurses are more concerned with comforting terminal patients and caring for their emotional needs. Further evidence of this difference is provided by nursing journals, which typically concentrate on appropriate emotional responses to the terminal patient. Conversely, nonpsychiatric medical publications on death deal almost exclusively with technical treatment issues.

The defensive behaviors of physicians and nurses have been attributed partly to personality factors and partly to the training they receive. Medical students are taught to focus on saving lives, rather than on helping those who cannot be cured. Student nurses learn to avoid mistakes by concentrating on daily routines, which are designed for nonterminal patients. On a personal level, defeat is distasteful to most people and is likely to be especially painful when it involves such traumatic outcomes as the death of one's patient. Because of their concern and desire to help, physicians and nurses may identify with the patient's fears and death and become anxious themselves. Some investigators also contend that physicians are unusually high in death anxiety, choose this profession as a way of defending against these fears (consciously or unconsciously), and prefer to avoid emotionally threatening cases in which death is inevitable. Or the medical staff members may feel guilty because they cannot effect a cure, an emotion that has been compared to the guilt that often results from remaining alive when a loved one dies. Because feelings of anxiety and guilt tend to be regarded as unprofessional, they are likely targets for such defense mechanisms as repression, denial of reality, and intellectualization (Campbell, 1980; Cassem & Hackett, 1975).

Such defensive behaviors may enable physicians and nurses to avoid excessive stress and to perform more efficiently under admittedly difficult conditions. However, these behaviors may also have unfortunate consequences. In particular, terminal patients are likely to receive less contact and emotional support from the medical staff than they would like. Also, differences in outlook may cause physicians, nurses, and other members of the health care team to clash over how best to care for the dying patient. However, matters may be improving. Physicians who took a course in medical school on dealing with the terminally ill reported better rapport with such patients and less personal discomfort than physicians who did not take such a course (Dickinson & Pearson, 1980–1981). It has also been reported that those physicians with a higher probability of encountering terminally ill patients are more likely to respond openly and to spend more time talking with them (Dickinson & Pearson, 1979;

Rea, Greenspoon, & Spilka, 1975). Hopefully, therefore, health care professionals are learning to deal more effectively with the process of dying.

INFORMING THE PATIENT.   Should physicians tell patients that an illness is terminal? Most people do want to be told, although there are always important exceptions that must be recognized (Blumenthal, Levy, & Kaufman, 1978–1979). Thus some practitioners have argued that it is best to be truthful, but gentle, so patients can be helped to reach a calm acceptance of death. For many patients, the advantages of being a legitimate participant in the treatment process and of taking part in the decisions that will affect the remainder of their lives are likely to outweigh the short-term trauma caused by learning the truth. Nevertheless, it appears that many physicians still prefer *not* to inform patients that their condition is terminal. This is usually justified on emotional grounds: Telling the patient has been likened to the cruelest thing in the world, a torture worse than a Nazi concentration camp. As a result, many terminal patients appear to remain unaware of their condition to the end. In some notable instances, however, researchers have focused on the responses of patients who were told that their days were numbered.

Understanding the Dying Patient

EMOTIONS OF THE TERMINALLY ILL.   According to some theorists, all dying patients proceed through much the same series of emotional stages. For example, Kübler-Ross (1969, 1975) conceptualizes dying as a five-stage process. On learning of the terminal prognosis, the patient's initial reaction is shock and numbness. This is gradually replaced by the first stage, *denial,* wherein patients steadfastly refuse to believe they are doomed. For example, they may argue that their laboratory reports have been confused with someone else's. The following stages consist of *anger* about the terminal prognosis, attempts to *bargain* with God or fate to obtain more time; *depression* about an anticipated or actual turn for the worse, and ultimate *acceptance* and calm about impending death.

Although Kübler-Ross's work is widely known, it has been sharply criticized on the grounds of conceptual ambiguity, sampling problems, investigator bias, and confounding of physical symptoms with psychological responses. Kübler-Ross's conclusions were based on subjective clinical observations of 200 patients, and there is no clear statement of the assessment procedures she used to identify and discriminate among the various stages. This makes it extremely difficult for other health care professionals to determine the stage that a given patient is in, which impairs the predictive and practical value of her theory. (See, for example, Doka, 1995–1996; Kalish, 1981; Schulz, 1978; Schulz & Aderman, 1974; Schulz & Schlarb, 1987–1988; Shneidman, 1973.)

In general, empirical research has failed to support Kübler-Ross's model. For example, on learning that their illnesses were terminal, patients in two studies adopted a pattern of behavior that remained basically unchanged until death. Some withdrew from social relationships and daily activities and stayed inactive until the end. Others continued to pursue their usual activities and even initiated new ones; for them, death came as an interruption in daily living. Another study focused on the facial expressions of terminal patients who were either in the early, middle, or late stages of their illnesses. Contrary to Kübler-Ross's model, sadness increased from the early to the late phase of an illness, and no systematic patterns were found for anger and happiness (Antonoff & Spilka, 1984–1985). Understandably, terminal patients tend to be more depressed than nonterminal patients with similar illnesses, but they may well vacillate between such contrary feelings as hopelessness and contentment or calmness and fear, rather than remaining consistently depressed (Greer & Mor, 1983). *In sum:* The most justified conclusion at present is that dying evokes a variety of predominantly negative emotions, such as fear, anger, sadness, and depression, and these emotions occur in no particular order.

CARING FOR THE TERMINALLY ILL.   Interventions designed to help the terminally ill typically fall into two general categories: easing psychological discomfort and distress, such as the previously discussed painful emotions, and controlling physical pain and discomfort.

With regard to psychological factors, one large-scale study ($N = 1,745$) investigated what terminal patients consider to be important some 2 to 8 weeks prior to their deaths. During this difficult time, supportive friends were most often mentioned as a source of strength, followed by religion and being needed by someone else. When these patients were asked what they wanted during the

Deaths in the United States are much more often caused by prolonged chronic diseases than by quickly terminating acute illnesses. This slow process of dying causes considerable difficulties for the loved ones of the terminally ill patient.
(*Source:* UN/DPI Photo.)

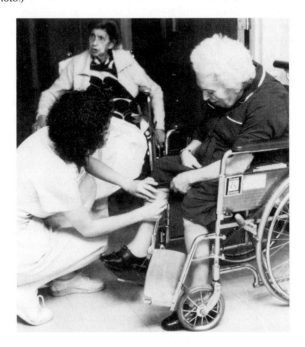

last 3 days of their lives, the most common responses were having certain people present, being physically able to do things, and feeling at peace (Greer & Mor, 1983). Friends and loved ones are thus important sources of emotional support for the terminal patient.

Various forms of psychotherapy have been used to treat the psychological distress of the dying patient, including cognitive therapy and behavior therapy. At present, however, research data are too sparse to permit any firm conclusions regarding the effectiveness of these procedures with the terminally ill (Schulz & Schlarb, 1987–1988).

One fairly new and effective way to help the terminal patient, both physically and psychologically, is the **hospice approach.** The primary goal of hospice care is to help terminally ill patients continue their lives with as little disruption as possible. An interdisciplinary team consisting of a physician, a nurse, a social worker, and a counselor strives to keep the patient alert, involved with family and friends, and as free from pain as possible. The team spends considerable time talking with and listening to patients, comforting and reassuring them, holding their hands, and generally providing a warm emotional atmosphere. Both the family and the patient play an active role in making decisions about the care received. The family may be encouraged to help care for the patient, by providing special meals, and this active involvement may help reduce the feelings of guilt that typically follow the loss of a loved one.

Some studies have not found any significant differences in physical or emotional pain between hospice patients and conventional patients. Others found that hospice patients were more satisfied with their care and less depressed and their families were glad to be actively involved in caring for their loved one, more prepared for the death, and better able to deal with bereavement. An example of the merits of hospice care is provided by the following case history:

A Disfigured 53-Year-Old Terminal Patient

Mr. G. suffered from a particularly unsightly and painful cancer, which was eroding the lower part of his face. He therefore became increasingly depressed, and wished he could die and "get it over with." He and his wife were very close, however, having been married for only six years. Mrs. G. was well aware of her husband's wish for death, but could not accept the thought that she would soon be without him. Her fears, although understandable, added to Mr. G.'s depression and lack of courage.

Drug therapy was used to alleviate Mr. G.'s pain and make his life less intolerable, while those medical staff who were not horrified by his appearance provided close emotional support that helped him to relax. His wife was also given similar support, and began to face up to the situation. Two weeks later, Mr. G.'s general condition was much worse, but both he and his wife were calm and had enjoyed Christmas together. When he then developed pneumonia, his wife agreed that it would be wrong to prolong his life with antibiotics and added, "I'm ready for him to go now." He died, peacefully, the following day. (Parkes, 1981a)

THE RIGHT TO DIE. One aspect of terminal illness has caused considerable controversy in recent years. Modern medical technology can sometimes keep a patient's body alive long after there is no visible sign of life. In some cases, treatment has continued for many years while the patient lay comatose, with virtually no hope of recovery. This can cause severe emotional and financial hardships for the patient's family, who must watch their loved one lie inert and unmoving for year after painful year, breathing only because of the efforts of various machines, while their life savings are drained away.

To prevent this possibility, some people have chosen to execute a living will, stating that life-sustaining procedures should *not* be used for them if the only effect will be to prolong the dying process artificially. An example of such a will, prepared by the Society for the Right to Die, is shown in Figure 12–3.

The **right to die** involves various complicated issues. What constitutes a truly hopeless condition? Must the person be in a vegetative state? Even then,

FIGURE 12–3 **Example of a living will.**
(*Source:* Reprinted by permission of Choice in Dying, formerly Concern for Dying/Society for the Right to Die (250 West 57th Street, New York, NY 10107).)

DISTRICT OF COLUMBIA

DECLARATION

Declaration made this _____ day of _____ (month, year).

I, _____, being of sound mind, willfully and voluntarily make known my desires that my dying shall not be artificially prolonged under the circumstances set forth below, and do declare:

If at any time I should have an incurable injury, disease or illness certified to be a terminal condition by two (2) physicians who have personally examined me, one (1) of whom shall be my attending physician, and the physicians have determined that my death will occur whether or not life-sustaining procedures are utilized and where the application of life-sustaining procedures would serve only to artificially prolong the dying process, I direct that such procedures be withheld or withdrawn, and that I be permitted to die naturally with only the administration of medication or the performance of any medical procedure deemed necessary to provide me with comfort care or to alleviate pain.

Other directions:

In the absence of my ability to give directions regarding the use of such life-sustaining procedures, it is my intention that this declaration shall be honored by my family and physician(s) as the final expression of my legal right to refuse medical or surgical treatment and accept the consequences from such refusal.

I understand the full import of this declaration and I am emotionally and mentally competent to make this declaration.

Signed _____

Address _____

_____

I believe the declarant to be of sound mind. I did not sign the declarant's signature above for or at the direction of the declarant. I am at least eighteen (18) years of age and am not related to the declarant by blood or marriage, entitled to any portion of the estate of the declarant according to the laws of intestate succession of the District of Columbia or under any will of declarant or codicil thereto, or directly financially responsible for declarant's medical care. I am not the declarant's attending physician, an employee of the attending physician, or an employee of the health facility in which the declarant is a patient.

Witness _____

Witness _____

might there not be a miraculous recovery? What about a person in the early stages of Alzheimer's disease, who is currently alert and functioning but does not want to remain alive and suffer the horrifying loss of his or her mind and identity? Doctors, courts, and laypersons are currently grappling with difficult issues like these, ranging from when to remove life support systems to who should make decisions when the patient cannot. (See *Newsweek*, June 18, 1990, pp. 46–49.)

There appears to be increasing sympathy for avoiding the artificial prolongation of life, so long as the patient and family of the loved one is so inclined. Indeed, in some countries such as the Netherlands, policymakers have established specific procedures for implementing physician-assisted death. Patients in the terminal phase of their lives who are suffering may request that a physician perform euthanasia. If the medical staff and patient reach a consensus about terminating life then clearly prescribed humane procedures are followed to achieve this end (Van Der Kloot Meijburg, 1995–1996). To date, several hundred persons have taken advantage of this option. In the United States the debate over hastening the end of life still rages, and it will continue to be an important and controversial issue in the years to come.

AFTERWORD.   As we observed at the outset of this chapter, the majority of people in the United States die at a relatively old age after a fairly lengthy chronic illness. However, much of the existing literature on terminal patients is based on younger adults, under 60 years of age (Schulz & Schlarb, 1987–1988). More data are needed regarding the emotions and behaviors of elderly terminal patients. For example, as one reaches ages 70 and 80 and health problems increase, does the prospect of death arouse the intense emotional reactions previously described? Or does it have much less significance because the patient is older, in poorer health, and more willing to accept that life is nearing an end?

A great deal of research has focused on the emotions of the terminal patient. Although this is an important issue, more data are needed concerning other aspects of dying. How well are pain and other symptoms of terminal illness such as nausea, fatigue, depression, and difficulty breathing (dyspnea) controlled during a terminal illness? To what extent should terminal patients' beliefs and lifestyles be considered when planning their care? How much training should be given to terminal patients in order to involve them in their own care? How open should communications be between the patient, family, and health care staff regarding the prognosis and expected progress of the disease? How can friends and loved ones best provide emotional support during this difficult time? In view of the considerable research interest in the process of dying, answers to these questions may well be forthcoming in the near future.

GRIEF AND BEREAVEMENT

The shattering impact of a terminal illness does not end with the patient's death. The family and friends of the deceased must contend with painful feelings of grief and bereavement, which may last for months or even years.

For most people, **bereavement** is a fact of life. Only those who die young escape the pain of losing someone they love through death. Every year there are more than 1 million new widows and widowers; at least 30,000 Americans commit suicide (and probably many more, because numerous suicides are not reported as such); and approximately 71,000 children under the age of 20 die. Each type of death carries with it a special kind of pain for those who are left behind. As one psychiatrist observed, "When your parent dies, you have lost your past. When your child dies, you have lost your future." (Osterweis et al., 1984, p. 4.)

The anguish of the survivors has always concerned society, and every culture has mourning rituals to deal with this pain. Today, policymakers, educators, and the public are all concerned with the nature of bereavement and its toll on the survivors. Psychologists, gerontologists, and other behavioral and physical scientists have proposed theories to account for the impact of grief and have devised procedures to ease both its acute pain and its longer term effects.

Bereavement and Health Outcomes

Most bereaved individuals successfully overcome their grief without professional assistance. For some, however, bereavement leads to serious health problems. Whether this happens depends on various factors. (See Table 12–3.)

CHARACTERISTICS OF THE BEREAVED INDIVIDUAL.   Some studies have found that men fare more poorly than women after the death of a spouse, especially when the death occurs at an unusually young age, but others reported no significant gender differences. One reason for these conflicting results is that it is difficult to obtain sufficiently large samples of male survivors; as we have seen (Chapter 1), the American population includes significantly more older women than older men.

The research evidence does indicate that bereavement is more intense for younger people, particularly children but also adolescents and young adults. Older adults appear to experience fewer and less intense consequences of bereavement, perhaps because the death of a loved one is temporally normative for them. Also, people with a history of poor mental or physical health, alcohol or drug abuse, or financial problems are more likely to suffer health problems following bereavement.

RELATIONSHIP TO THE DECEASED.   No loving relationship is completely without ambivalence, as Freud has shown; love is always accompanied by some feelings of dislike, or even hate. In a successful relationship, love and positive emotions predominate. But when a relationship is highly ambivalent, involving frequent feelings of both love and hate, the survivor fares more poorly following bereavement. Research evidence also suggests that the same is true for spouses who are unable to function independently.

NATURE OF THE DEATH.   Until recently, it was believed that a sudden death produced more severe psychological consequences than a death that was expected. However, most research findings now indicate that sudden death does

Table 12–3   Variables Associated with Health Outcomes of Bereavement

VARIABLES ASSOCIATED WITH HEALTH OUTCOMES	NATURE OF EFFECT
Characteristics of Bereaved Individuals	
Sex	Evidence is mixed; men appear to do worse when wife dies; men do worse when death is premature
Age	Bereavement reactions more intense for younger people, particularly children, adolescents, and young adults
Prior physical health	Poor health related worse to outcomes
Prior mental health	Poor health related to worse outcomes
Alcohol abuse	At greater risk for health problems after breavement
Socioeconomic status	Financial problems related to poorer outcomes
Relationship to the Deceased	Individuals who had ambivalent relationship with spouse who died do worse; spouses who are unable to function independently do poorly
Nature of Death	
Suddenness	Most research shows that sudden death does *not* result in more negative outcomes
Suicide	Resuts in increased distress, may leave bereaved person vulnerable to suicide
Behavior and Attitudes Appearing Early in the Grieving Process	
Consumption of alcohol, drugs	Consumption tends to increase after death, placing individual at risk of illness
Social support	Has positive effect on health status
Suicidal thoughts	Predicts poorer outcome to bereaved
Morbid grief	Predicts poorer outcome to bereaved

not produce more disturbed survivors. In fact, there is some indication that longer terminal illnesses are more likely to result in health problems for the surviving spouse.

Although expected deaths should allow time to say goodbye and to express love, thereby lessening later feelings of anger and guilt, it may be that the moment of death is always a surprise no matter how much warning there has been. That is, family members may keep telling themselves that there are a few more days before death comes, and miss out on the opportunity to share their feelings with the terminal patient. Or the stress, emotional pain, and physical effort involved in a lengthy terminal illness may complicate the bereavement process.

Suicide is particularly likely to result in psychological problems following bereavement and may leave the survivors vulnerable to suicide as well. Depressed people tend to marry other depressed people, so the surviving spouse is more often someone with a propensity for suicide.

BEHAVIOR APPEARING EARLY IN THE GRIEVING PROCESS. Some individuals begin using alcohol, drugs, or cigarettes after the death of a loved one, whereas those who are already using these substances usually increase their consumption. As a result, they are at greater risk of various illnesses. Suicidal thoughts and morbid grief are also related to health problems following bereavement. Conversely, social support from friends and loved ones helps survivors to overcome their grief successfully—which, as we noted at the outset of this section, is the most common outcome of the bereavement process.

Normal versus Pathological Grief

When **pathological (morbid) grief** does occur, it differs from normal grief in duration and intensity. Acute grief normally lasts for 2 weeks to 2 months after the death of the loved one, and healthy mourning may take from 9 months to 2 years (Arkin, 1981; Margolis et al., 1981, p. xi). Conversely, acute grief would be regarded as pathological if it continued for many months or years after the death. There is no strict timetable for grieving, however, and some bereaved individuals may require more time for the healthy venting of painful emotions than others (Joyce, 1984).

NORMAL GRIEF.   A certain amount of **grief** is beneficial and adaptive. It helps bereaved individuals to detach themselves emotionally from the deceased (Freud, 1917/1963) and to reconcile an internal world filled with memories of the loved one with an external world where that person no longer exists (Parkes, 1972, 1981b). Thus the process of grieving is a process of learning: The bereaved individual gradually and painfully adopts a new view of the world, one in which the loved one is permanently absent.

Normal grieving typically proceeds through several phases. The initial phase begins at the time of death, continues for several weeks thereafter, and is characterized by feelings of confusion, shock, and denial. Thus one widow

After the death of a loved one, painful feelings of grief and bereavement may last for months or even years.

observed that "all during my husband's funeral, I kept wishing the entire process would be over so that he and I could resume our normal life," and her daughter refused to attend the funeral so she could think of her father as still being alive (Vachon, 1981). Emotional numbness may also serve as a barrier against over-whelming pain and suffering:

A 27-Year-Old Widow

Mrs. O. viewed her husband's body shortly after his death from cancer. "I, I didn't want to believe it, and yet I saw it right there, so it was as though I were torn be-tween what I wanted to believe and what was really there. . . . The following few hours was just, I don't know, it was not me or something, I couldn't . . . I just didn't do anything, just, just blank. They gave me his watch and I held it in my hand . . . didn't feel anything, just complete blank." (Parkes, 1981b)

Responses like these normally give way to an all-encompassing sorrow, which is expressed through periods of crying and weeping that may last for days or weeks. The bereaved individual may try to cope by keeping busy with time-consuming activities, or may resort to tranquilizers or sleeping pills. Anger, dis-placement, and projection are common, for example blaming a faultless medical staff or God for the loved one's death. Fears of a nervous breakdown and/or some suicidal wishes are also not unusual during this time.

The Case of Mrs. O. (continued)

Three weeks after her husband's death, Mrs. O's grief was still at its peak, and she was missing him very strongly. "All of a sudden I miss him, then it hurts . . . I try to keep my hands very busy, but I haven't been able to do any reading or anything because my mind just wanders away. . . . I have really simple goals, to make him happy . . . and all of a sudden I felt nothing more to do, feel so lost that I don't know. . . . I tried so hard to have dreams so I can see him, but all I end up is dream-ing that I couldn't find him . . . it's especially hard to realize that he's not there any-more. . . . I wish I [was] not so young so I can join him sooner."

About a month after the funeral, the bereaved individual begins to confront the reality of daily living without the deceased. This intermediate phase may continue for up to a year and is characterized by various forms of behavior. The mourner may engage in obsessional reviews of scenes associated with the loved one's death and express such self-reproaches as "if only I had made him wear his seat belt" or "I should have forced her to go to the doctor sooner." This ver-balization of guilt feelings is primarily beneficial because it allows mourners to expiate their real or imagined transgressions and more readily accept their loss. (See Arkin, 1981; Glick et al., 1974.) The bereaved individual may also express concern as to the meaning of death and wonder why this tragic event had to happen. Some mourners gain relief by attributing the death to the will of God; others are never able to find an answer that satisfies them. Or the bereaved may engage in activities that were formerly shared with the loved one, such as watch-ing television during the evening or going to a favorite restaurant, and experience the illusion that the deceased is present. In fact, the mourner may even call out to the deceased and expect a response. The hallucinations that may occur during bereavement are often therapeutic and usually do not indicate the existence of a severe emotional disturbance (Vachon, 1981).

Ideally, the mourner ultimately realizes that life with the loved one cannot be restored. Because the mourner has not yet been able to replace the old pattern of living with a satisfactory alternative, however, apathy and depression are common. Life is lived from day to day, without much of a plan for the future.

The Case of Mrs. O. (concluded)

One year after her husband's death, Mrs. O. observed, "I'm still rather confused. . . . What action should I take for my future life, and what do I want? I keep on asking myself and I haven't really come up with anything." Mrs. O. kept herself busy in an effort to avoid depression, but was well aware that such activity was futile. She also expressed difficulty adjusting to her new role as an unmarried person. "I'm not exactly married and not exactly single. . . . I'm not waiting to die. I feel I have to live my life." But she had little idea how to achieve this goal. "I feel I'm very depressed, you know."

The final phase of normal bereavement is that of recovery. This phase is often triggered by a conscious decision not to dwell on the past any longer; life must proceed. The first steps in this direction may be small, with relatively minor aspects of life beginning to be enjoyed once again. But eventually a new direction emerges, and periods of depression and pining for the loved one become less frequent. The mourner is now more socially aggressive and actively seeks out new friends and pastimes. (This may not be an easy task, however. Widows and widowers are all too often treated as stigmatized persons, not unlike the handicapped.) The bereaved individual also derives considerable comfort from his or her ability to survive the devastating event and often develops valued new skills as well. Examples include widows who now learn for the first time to balance a checkbook, make minor house repairs, or maintain the automobile. Thus, like a phoenix rising from the ashes, many mourners do emerge from the bereavement process as more capable, self-confident, and emotionally secure people.

PATHOLOGICAL AND TRAUMATIC GRIEF.   Bereavement does not always proceed so favorably. One warning sign that grief may become pathological is a period of apparent calm, well-being, and zeal immediately following the loved one's death. This "calm before the storm" is typically followed by an abrupt and striking change in behavior: irritability or even intense hostility toward relatives and friends, and listlessness so pronounced that the individual does virtually nothing unless compelled by someone else. These bereaved individuals are also more likely to incur such psychosomatic disorders as ulcerative colitis, rheumatoid arthritis, and asthma.

Other forms of pathology that more often occur after bereavement include severe depression, anxiety states, suicide, insomnia, and an extreme degree of identification with the deceased. For example, one woman whose husband was rendered speechless by a stroke became unable to speak for 10 days following his death (Parkes, 1972). Or pathological grief may result in self-destructive behavior, such as giving away all of one's possessions, taking foolish economic risks, or shattering one's professional reputation by behaving stupidly and incompetently (Lindermann, 1944).

Researchers have recently developed measurement tools for identifying individuals who suffer from a variant of pathological grief called **traumatic grief** (Prigerson et al., under review). Persons suffering from this syndrome have an intrusive, distressing preoccupation with the deceased person, feel futile about the future, experience a sense of numbness, detachment or absence of emotional responsiveness, feel stunned, dazed or shocked, have difficulty acknowledging the death, feel that life is empty or meaningless, have difficulty imagining a fulfilling life without the deceased, have lost their sense of security, trust, or control, and are excessively irritable, bitter, or angry in relation to the death. In short, traumatic grief is a trait-like tendency to be devastated by the death.

The long-term prognosis for those suffering from pathological grief is unfavorable. Such individuals are not only more vulnerable to various physical and psychological disorders, but are also more likely to die themselves (Gallagher & Thompson, 1989; Osterweis et al., 1984; Prigerson et al., 1997).

Helping the Bereaved: Professional and Paraprofessional Therapy

It has been estimated that some 25% of the bereaved cannot resolve their grief by themselves. For these mourners, professional or paraprofessional therapy may help to alleviate their emotional pain and suffering.

PROFESSIONAL THERAPY.   During the terminal phase, family members may spend so much time caring for the dying patient that they become overly fatigued, do not follow a proper diet, or have little or no recreation. In such cases, one effective therapeutic measure may simply be to enjoy a good meal, an engrossing movie, or a weekend of respite from the demands of caregiving. However, formal therapy may also be appropriate at this time. Such therapy can forestall the emergence of pathological grief by helping the family release feelings of guilt, anger, and despair and to communicate more openly.

A Case of Terminal Cancer

Mrs. C. was 34 years old, the mother of a two-year-old girl, and a writer by profession. Her terminal cancer required a mastectomy, a prospect that left her distraught, angry, and depressed. "No one can help me now, since I will die anyway. . . . My husband and I are surrounded by physician friends, and sadly enough, I know the implications of [my] cancer. . . . For many years, my husband and I tried to have a child. At long last we conceived, and a beautiful and healthy baby was born. Now both will be robbed of a family." A social worker helped Mrs. C. to understand that her outpouring of feelings, however harsh, was appropriate and needed to be expressed. With the aid of this support, she grew calmer and less angry, and was better able to derive those satisfactions that were available in the time left to her.

Mr. C. was two years older than his wife. Although his appearance clearly reflected his sorrow, he insisted on controlling his emotions. Therapy helped him to realize that expressing his grief was not unmasculine, and that he needed to share these feelings with his wife. "It seems that I'm on a constant seesaw," he observed. "I vacillate between acceptance of my wife's fatal illness and hope for a miracle, especially when she looks fairly well. I walk around with a heavy heart, but it helps so much to talk. We've grown so much closer to each other than ever before . . . I'm so glad there is now."

Only her parents were still alive, and they came from their home in South America to be with her. Because of their grief, and an understandable desire to be helpful, they tended to intrude too much on the dealings between Mrs. C. and her husband. After a family conference with the social worker, they readily agreed to return home, with the understanding that they would be called in case of any emergency. They were present when Mrs. C. died some eight months later, and were of immense comfort to Mr. C. One month after the funeral, Mr. C. decided that he and his daughter would move to South America and live near his in-laws. He had placed his marriage in what appeared to be a healthy perspective. "I will take each day as it comes, and, hopefully, all will turn out fairly well." (Suszycki, 1981)

At the time of death, therapy may take the form of crisis intervention. Some mourners now experience intense grief and require appropriate comforting and emotional support. Yet probably those most in need of therapy are the stoics who remain calm for weeks after the funeral and act as though nothing had happened. This may be due to a misguided belief that outward expressions of anguish are a sign of personal weakness or that they must be strong for the sake of other family members. But experiencing the loss emotionally is necessary for the bereavement process to proceed to a satisfactory conclusion; denying these feelings is likely to be the calm before the storm of pathological grief (as we have seen). These bereaved individuals are therefore encouraged to release their dammed-up emotions and to verbalize their feelings of loss, anger, and sorrow. The therapist may facilitate this catharsis by confronting the mourner with some crucial memento of the deceased, such as a photograph, item of jewelry, or letter. Or the mourner may be asked to talk directly to a fantasized image of the deceased, rather than about the loved one. Or the family may be advised to avoid excessive denial by having a public funeral with an open casket and allowing the children who are old enough to explore the funeral home and hearse openly and freely. Once an emotional catharsis has been achieved, mourners are encouraged to escape the trap of a morbid preoccupation with the past by orienting themselves toward the future. This may involve such activities as acquiring new friends or pastimes, going back to school, or learning how to drive. (See, for example, Gallagher & Thompson, 1989; Horn, 1974; Kalish, 1981; Lindemann, 1944; Nichols, 1981.)

In sum: During the terminal phase, professional bereavement therapy assists the family to function as effectively as possible and to prepare for the coming tragedy. After the patient's death, therapy helps the bereaved adjust to a world without the loved one and find ways to make life meaningful and rewarding. Even mourners who remained grief stricken after several years have been helped to vent their suppressed emotions through appropriate therapy and to bring the bereavement process to a successful conclusion.

PARAPROFESSIONAL THERAPY. Although professional therapy can be effective, it may also be too expensive for some mourners. One increasingly popular alternative is to enlist the aid of formerly bereaved individuals who have been able to resolve their grief. These **paraprofessionals** may serve as group leaders, or the bereaved may meet in leaderless self-help groups.

How effective is this approach? In one study, some 70 widows who responded to a request in a local newspaper participated in a group program for 7 weeks. Some were randomly assigned to self-help groups, and some to groups with paraprofessional leaders. A control group did not experience any form of paraprofessional therapy. Both of the experimental groups subsequently indicated higher self-esteem, greater optimism concerning their future health, and a greater ability to feel and express their grief than did the control group (Barrett, 1978).

Helping the bereaved should not be confused with treating psychopathology; those who suffer from psychological disorders are best advised to consult a trained professional. However, paraprofessional therapy does appear to be an economical way to help alleviate the emotional pain of the bereaved.

FINAL AFTERWORD. Most of us regard the prospect of death with considerable distaste. Yet research dealing with the bereaved indicates that the process of dying is extremely important and need not have only ill effects. If the terminal patient suffers unnecessarily, never comes to terms with this condition, cannot relate well to his or her family, and dies embittered, then death may indeed be seen as a defeat. But when the terminal patient accepts the inevitable, welcomes those pleasures that life still has to offer, enjoys a close and supportive relationship with his or her family, and dies peacefully and free of suffering, this final period of life may well be remembered as a fitting and satisfactory ending.

There are various ways of dying, and the patient and family who rise to the challenge can make something positive out of this otherwise calamitous event. Given the increased prevalence of chronic terminal illnesses, this is a challenge that may well await you in the future.

To die will be an awfully big adventure. (J. M. Barrie, *Peter Pan*)

SUMMARY

The Demography of Death

Chronic illnesses have replaced acute illnesses as the major causes of death in our society. As a result, dying is likely to be a fairly drawn-out process for many of us. The leading causes of death in the United States are heart disease, cancer, and strokes. However, there has been a decline in deaths from heart disease and strokes since 1950. Deaths due to accidents have decreased markedly in the last two decades. Conversely, deaths caused by HIV infections have increased dramatically, particularly among men and blacks. However, recent data indicate that AIDS deaths are beginning to decline.

The Fear of Death

Some theorists contend that the fear of death, conscious and unconscious, is the prime motive underlying all human behavior. Among the reasons for death anxiety are the fear of physical suffering, the fear of loneliness, the fear of nonbeing, the fear that we will become cowards in the face of death, the fear of missing out on cherished experiences and goals, the fear of the emotional and economic impact that death will have on our survivors, and the fear of punishment after death. We may also experience these fears in relation to the death of a loved one. Death anxiety also has aspects that are public and conscious, private and conscious, and (very possibly) unconscious. Thus death anxiety is a multidimensional variable. But all too many researchers have treated death anxiety as unidimensional and have assessed only the public and conscious level.

Perhaps for this reason, relatively few consistent patterns have emerged from the research data. This evidence fails to support the existentialist belief as to the overwhelming importance of death anxiety, but this could be due partly or largely to methodological problems. However, serious physical illnesses do appear to be related to an increase in death anxiety, whereas greater religious faith is related to decreased death anxiety. There is also some indication that a significant part of these fears is beyond our awareness and that some people who claim to have little conscious death anxiety may well be considerably more afraid at an unconscious level.

The Process of Dying:
The Terminal Stages of Life

Numerous studies indicate that physicians and nurses have difficulty dealing with terminal illnesses. They may therefore tend to avoid patients who are in the process of dying, or they may behave in other defensive ways. This may be due partly to the personalities of physicians and nurses and partly to their training, which focuses on helping those who can be cured. Although most people want to know the truth, the majority of physicians prefer not to inform patients that their condition is terminal, and they usually justify this as an act of kindness. However, some data do indicate that health care professionals are becoming more aware of the needs of the terminally ill.

According to some theorists, all dying patients proceed through much the same series of emotional stages. Kübler-Ross's pioneering work posits five such stages, based on her clinical observation: denial, anger, bargaining, depression, and acceptance. However, her theory is not supported by the preponderance of research evidence. Dying evokes a variety of predominantly negative emotions, such as fear, anger, sadness, and depression, which occur in no particular order.

Among the needs of terminal patients are easing of psychological distress, control of physical pain and discomfort, supportive loved ones and friends, and religion. The hospice approach is an effective and increasingly popular way to satisfy the various needs of the terminally ill. The hospice utilizes an interdisciplinary team of physicians, nurses, social workers, and counselors; drug therapy combined with a loving and caring atmosphere; and a treatment plan that includes both terminal patients and their families.

Modern medical technology can sometimes keep a patient's body alive long after there is no visible sign of life. This can cause severe emotional and financial hardships for the patient's family. To prevent this possibility, some people have chosen to execute a living will, which states that life-sustaining procedures should *not* be used for them if the only effect will be to prolong the dying process artificially. Doctors, courts, and laypersons are currently grappling with such difficult issues as when to remove life support systems and who should make such decisions when the patient cannot. The right to die is likely to remain an important and controversial issue in the years to come.

Grief and Bereavement

Bereavement is a fact of life for most people, and every culture has mourning rituals to deal with this pain. Most bereaved individuals successfully overcome their grief without professional assistance. Those most likely to develop serious health problems after bereavement include younger people, particularly children; those with a history of poor mental or physical health or of alcohol or drug abuse; those with financial problems; survivors of a highly ambivalent relationship; spouses who are unable to function independently; survivors of a suicide; those who begin using alcohol, drugs, or cigarettes following bereavement; and those with suicidal thoughts or pathological (traumatic) grief.

Pathological grief reactions differ from normal grief in duration and intensity. A certain amount of grief is beneficial and adaptive. The process of normal grieving is a process of learning: The bereaved individual gradually and painfully adopts a new view of the world, one in which the loved one is permanently absent. Normal grief typically proceeds through several phases, which may include confusion, shock, denial, emotional numbness, sorrow, weeping, self-reproaches, hallucinations of the loved one, and (eventually) the decision that it is time to concentrate on the future because life must proceed. Pathological grief is often preceded by a period of apparent calm and well-being immediately following the loved one's death. It commonly leads to various physical and psychological disorders, and even to death.

It has been estimated that some 25% of the bereaved cannot resolve their grief by themselves. During the terminal phase, professional therapy can help the family function effectively and prepare for the coming tragedy. After the patient's death, such therapy can help mourners to release their dammed-up feelings and bring the bereavement process to a satisfactory conclusion. One effective and increasingly popular alternative is to enlist the aid of paraprofessionals, such as formerly bereaved individuals who have successfully resolved their grief.

The process of dying is extremely important and need not be entirely negative. There are various ways of dying, and the patient and family who rise to this challenge can make something positive out of an otherwise calamitous event. Because of the increased prevalence of chronic terminal illnesses, this is a challenge that awaits many of us in the future.

STUDY QUESTIONS

1. If we were able to extend life substantially (say another 50 years in good health), what would be the likely effects on (a) an individual's personality, attitudes, relations with others? (b) society in general? (c) government policies in this country? (d) insurance companies? (e) family size? Would we be better off?
2. Existentialists contend that the fear of death is the prime motive underlying human behavior. Do you observe any support for this contention in your own behavior or in the behavior of people you know? If the fear of death is repressed, is there any way to determine if (and how) it affects your behavior?
3. Kübler-Ross's five-stage theory of dying has *not* been supported by the preponderance of research evidence. Why, then, has it become so popular with the general public?
4. Should a terminally ill patient ever be helped to end his or her life? Why or why not?
5. In your opinion, in which case is the death of a loved one more traumatic for the survivors: if the death is sudden and unexpected, or if it occurs after a lengthy terminal illness? What would you do and say (or not say) to offer the most comfort to a terminal patient and his or her family? What would you do and say (or not say) to offer the most comfort to the bereaved after the death of their loved one?

TERMS TO REMEMBER

Acute illness
Acquired immunodeficiency syndrome
  (AIDS)
Bereavement
Chronic illness
Death anxiety (fear of death)
Direct measure of death anxiety
Grief

Hospice approach
Indirect measure of death anxiety
Paraprofessional therapy for the bereaved
Pathological grief (morbid grief)
Right to die
Terminal illness
Terminal phase of life
Traumatic grief

GLOSSARY

ACCOMMODATION   Process whereby the eye focuses on objects at different distances. The lens is flattened when viewing an object that is far away and thickened when an object is closer.

ACQUISITION   Occurs when new information enters memory (is learned) and is encoded in some form (e.g., phonemically). The initial process in the act of remembering.

ACTIVITY THEORY   Posits a positive correlation between the social activity of the elderly and their satisfaction with life. That is, reduced social activity is assumed to be dissatisfying to the elderly.

ACUTE ILLNESS   Disorder characterized by a relatively sudden onset and a brief duration.

AGE DISCRIMINATION   Denying an individual a job, a promotion, more pay, or other desired work benefit solely because of his or her chronological age. Although illegal, age discrimination is still a significant problem in the world of work.

AGING   Changes that significantly decrease the probability of survival, caused by processes within the individual that are universal, inevitable, and irreversible.

AGING EFFECT   Occurs when behavior or personality is influenced in some way by growing older.

ALZHEIMER'S DISEASE   Terminal disease associated with physiological changes in the brain. Causes impairments in memory and abstract thought, personality changes, and (ultimately) a total inability to care for oneself.

ANTIDEPRESSANT Drug that relieves depression by producing an elevation in mood.

ANTIOXIDANTS Compounds that block much of the damage to bodily proteins caused by free radicals. Despite claims to the contrary, there is no convincing evidence that dietary supplements of antioxidants extend human life.

ANXIETY Extremely unpleasant emotion similar to intense nervousness.

ANXIETY DISORDER Form of psychopathology characterized by unrealistic or excessive anxiety and worry. Varieties include generalized anxiety, in which severe anxiety occurs without any apparent cause; phobic disorders, which involve an intense but irrational fear of a specific object or situation that is actually not dangerous; and obsessive-compulsive disorders, in which thoughts or actions are repeatedly performed for no apparent reason except to reduce anxiety.

ARMY ALPHA One of the first group-administered intelligence tests for adults, administered to a very large number of adults in World War I. Results from this testing yielded some of the earliest systematic data on the relation between age and mental abilities.

ARTHRITIS Disorder of the joints that is very common after middle age and may take various forms, such as inflammation or degeneration. The resulting pain may consist only of occasional flare-ups, or it may be so severe as to be debilitating.

ASSESSMENT Determining which form(s) of psychopathology afflict a given individual.

ASSISTIVE LISTENING DEVICES (ADLs) Wide array of amplification systems tailored to specific listening environments such as movie theatres, concert halls, or churches. These systems use infrared, FM radio, or other transmission methods to enhance the clarity and volume of an auditory signal.

AUDITORY NERVE Bundle of cells in the cochlea that communicates sound impulses to the brain.

BASAL METABOLISM Rate at which the resting body converts food into energy. Declines by about 3% for every 10 years of life, so older adults need fewer calories per day to maintain the same weight.

BASILAR MEMBRANE Membrane that bisects most of the cochlea, lengthwise. Responsible for most (but not all) sensations of pitch.

BEREAVEMENT State of desolation caused by the death of a loved one. Similar to grief.

BIOLOGICAL TRADITION In stress research the approach associated with Cannon and Selye that emphasizes the role of specific physiological systems in response to a stressor.

BLIND SPOT Point where the optic nerve intersects the retina. Contains no visual receptors and cannot produce any sensations.

B-LOVE In Maslow's theory, love that is unselfish, nonpossessive, giving, honest, and richer and more enjoyable than D-love.

CANCER Uncontrolled growth of abnormal cells that spread to other parts of the body through the blood or lymphatic systems. Varieties include carcinoma, which arises in the surface layer of the skin, glands, or the linings of body organs; melanoma, a specific form of carcinoma that lodges in the cells producing our skin pigment; sarcoma, which emerges in connective or supporting tissues such as bones, cartilage, and fat; lymphoma, which originates in the lymph nodes; and leukemia, which results in transformations of white blood cells.

CARDIOVASCULAR DISEASE   Any problem of the heart or blood circulation. Varieties include heart attacks, which occur when part of the heart muscle dies because of an inadequate flow of blood; chest pains (angina), caused by an inadequate supply of blood and oxygen to the muscles of the heart; and strokes, which occur when a blockage in the flow of blood and oxygen causes brain tissue to be destroyed.

CASE REGISTER METHOD   Determining how often various forms of psychopathology occur by examining hospital or therapist records and tallying the frequency of each disorder.

CATARACTS   Cloudy or opaque areas that may form in part or all of the lens of the eye, inhibiting the passage of light and causing a significant decline in vision. A disorder that can usually be safely resolved through surgery.

CENTRAL AUDITORY IMPAIRMENT   Inability to understand language, even though sound detection is not affected. An incurable but rare disorder that results from damage to nerve centers within the brain, as from a stroke or head injury.

CHEMOTHERAPY   Use of appropriate drugs to treat physical or psychological disorders; usually refers to the treatment of cancer.

CHRONIC ILLNESS   Disorder characterized by a slow onset and a long duration.

CLASSIC AGING PATTERN   Pronounced declines on WAIS performance subtests and smaller declines on the verbal subtests, with increasing age.

COCHLEA   Coiled tube in the inner ear, which contains the basilar membrane and auditory hair cells.

COGNITIVE-BEHAVIOR THERAPY   Form of psychotherapy that is designed to help patients obtain an understanding of the cause and dynamics of their disorders and change self-defeating modes of thought and behavior.

COHORT   Group of individuals that has experienced the same event at the same time; frequently, a group of people born in the same year or in adjacent years.

COHORT EFFECT   Occurs when behavior or personality is influenced in some way by the generation in which the person was born and by the corresponding social and historical forces.

COMPANIONATE LOVE   Form of love highlighted by affection for those who are closely involved in our lives. More common, and more typical of long-term relationships, than passionate love.

COMPENSATION   In life-span development theory, a method for coping with failure and decline.

CONCEPT FORMATION   Type of inductive reasoning test in which the individual attempts to determine the rule (or concept) relating different sets of items to one another.

CONDUCTIVE HEARING LOSS   Decline in the ability to perceive external sounds and speech, caused by blockage in the outer and middle ear. Readily amenable to treatment in most instances.

CONES   Photoreceptor cells in the retina that respond to high levels of illumination and are responsible for daytime vision and sensations of color. Most plentiful in the fovea.

CONFOUNDING   Occurs when two (or more) sources of variation are closely interrelated (e.g., aging and cohort) and when the research design cannot reveal which one is causing the observed changes in the dependent variable.

CONSEQUENCES OF STRESS   Effects of stressors that are further removed in time than responses to stress and are more clearly identifiable as good or bad.

CONTINUITY THEORY   Claims that over time individuals develop a strong sense of who they are, and they attempt to maintain this sense of self over time.

CONTROL   Ability to regulate or influence the outcomes that befall us through the behaviors we choose.

CONTROL GROUP   Group that does not receive the treatment whose effects are being investigated by the researcher; used as a baseline against which to evaluate the performance of the experimental group.

CONVERGENT THINKING   Solving a problem by narrowing down many possibilities and arriving at the one correct answer.

COPING STYLES   Ways in which individuals adapt to and deal with the changing circumstances of life.

COPING WITH STRESS   Using thoughts (conscious or unconscious), actions, or both to eliminate or reduce the demands made by a stressor.

CORRELATIONAL DESIGN   Research wherein two (or more) variables are measured in order to ascertain the relationship between them, without designating any independent or dependent variables or assigning subjects randomly to groups.

CREATIVE PERFORMANCE APPROACH   Measuring creativity (and its relationship to aging) by obtaining data about actual creative achievements (and the ages at which they were made).

CREATIVITY   Solution to a problem of significance to society that is original, unusual, ingenious, and relevant.

CROSS-SECTIONAL RESEARCH   Research wherein all measurements are performed at about the same time.

CRYSTALLIZED INTELLIGENCE   Capacity to use knowledge acquired through education or acculturation.

CUED-RECALL TASK   Experimental procedure wherein subjects must learn lists of items (e.g., common words) and are given clues that will help them retrieve the information from memory, such as the first letter(s), a rhyme, a synonym, or a general description of the correct answer.

DARK ADAPTATION   Process of shifting from cone to rod vision, which enables us to see in a dark room after having been exposed to bright light. Becomes less rapid and less effective as we grow older.

DEATH ANXIETY   Synonym for the fear of death.

DECIBEL   Unit for measuring the relative intensities of sound.

DEFENSE MECHANISM   Method for reducing anxiety, and restoring self-esteem, that is usually (but not always) unconscious. Thus we may flee from stress psychologically (i.e., by concealing the truth from ourselves) as well as physically.

Includes repression, reaction formation, rationalization, projection, displacement, denial of reality, and others.

DEMENTIA   Organic mental disorder that is typified by a gradual and progressive inability to deal with the common activities of everyday life, failures in memory and intellectual functioning, and a disorganization of personality. Presenile dementias occur prior to age 65 (possibly as early as age 40 to 50); senile dementias occur at age 65 or later. Includes Alzheimer's disease and vascular dementia.

DEOXYRIBONUCLEIC ACID (DNA)   Complicated molecule that controls the formation of proteins which cells require to maintain life.

DEPENDENT VARIABLE   Variable presumed to change as a result of changes in one or more independent variables.

DEPRESSION   Emotional state characterized by frequent and powerful feelings of dejection, worthlessness, and hopelessness.

DIABETIC RETINOPATHY   Retinal disorder that occurs when small blood vessels which normally nourish the retina fail to function properly.

DIRECT MEASURE OF DEATH ANXIETY   Measure of death anxiety that taps only the conscious and public level; usually, a written questionnaire.

DISCERNING STYLE OF FRIENDSHIP   Pattern of friendships wherein a clear distinction is drawn between a small number of close, trusted friends and a larger number of casual, impersonal acquaintances.

DISENGAGEMENT THEORY   Posits a process of mutual withdrawal between the aged and society. This decreased interpersonal activity is assumed to be satisfying to the aged, helpful to society, universal, and inevitable.

DIVERGENT THINKING   Solving a problem by producing many different and unusual answers.

DIVERSITY   In life-span development theory, the variety of domains of functioning that individuals are exposed to as they develop.

D-LOVE   In Maslow's theory, the selfish need to receive love and affection from others. A prerequisite to the emergence of B-love.

DRUG THERAPY   Use of appropriate drugs to treat physical or psychological disorders.

DSM-III-R   The 1987 version of the *Diagnostic and Statistical Manual of Mental Disorders*, prepared by the American Psychiatric Association and used to classify the various forms of psychopathology.

DSM-IV   Most current version (published in 1994) of the *Diagnostic and Statistical Manual of Mental Disorders*.

DYNAMIC VISUAL ACUITY   The ability to identify a moving object, or features thereof, by sight.

EARDRUM   Taut membrane that vibrates in response to sound waves entering the outer ear.

EARLY RETIREMENT   Leaving the world of full-time work prior to the age mandated by the company or by law (e.g., 65 or 70). Usually requires the individual to accept lower retirement benefits.

ECHOIC MEMORY   Auditory form of sensory memory.

ECOLOGICAL VALIDITY   Extent to which experimental tasks resemble activities that are common in everyday life.

ELECTROCONVULSIVE THERAPY **(ECT)**   Administering electric shocks to one or both hemispheres of the brain; a method for treating depression.

EMOTION-FOCUSED COPING   Coping with stress by trying to achieve an emotional acceptance of the existing situation.

EMPTY NEST   Years that a married couple spend together after the last child leaves home, up until the death of one spouse.

ENCODING   Process of converting sensory information into a form that is more readily remembered, such as words, imagery, or an abstract representation.

ENVIRONMENTAL CHANGE FACTORS   Changes occurring in the external environment (such as amount of various pollutants, cultural attitudes, etc.) that could be contributing to age-related differences in both cross-sectional and longitudinal comparisons.

ENVIRONMENTAL TRADITION   In stress research the approach that emphasizes the role of variety of life events which cause stress.

EPIDEMIOLOGY   Study of the distribution of illnesses in time and place and of the factors that influence this distribution.

EPISODIC MEMORY   In Tulving's theory, a form of memory that records the time and place of specific personal events.

EXCHANGE THEORY   Posits that we interact with other people to the extent that the rewards we receive, both material and nonmaterial, exceed the costs we incur.

EXPERIMENTAL DESIGN   Research wherein the experimenter manipulates one or more independent variables in order to determine the effects on one or more dependent variables and assigns subjects (usually randomly) to groups.

EXPERIMENTAL GROUP   Group that receives the treatment whose effects are being investigated by the researcher.

EXTERNAL LOCUS OF CONTROL   Consistent belief that obtaining rewards and avoiding punishments depend primarily on mere chance and the actions of other people.

EXTERNAL VALIDITY   Extent to which research findings can be generalized from the specific sample(s) included in the study to the population(s) of interest.

EXTRANEOUS VARIABLE   Variable that may bias the relationship between aging and intelligence (as measured by test scores) by causing scores on an intelligence test to differ from a person's true mental ability.

EXTRAVERSION   Trait characterized by outgoingness, venturing forth with careless confidence into the unknown, and being particularly influenced by other people and events in the external world.

EXTRINSIC BENEFITS OF WORK   Extent to which the income and other benefits obtained from work gratify such nonwork needs and wants as food, housing, clothing, and recreation.

FEAR OF DEATH   Tension and uneasiness caused by the knowledge that our lives will someday end. A multidimensional variable, usually assumed to be partly or primarily unconscious.

FIELD SURVEY   Determining how often various forms of psychopathology occur by assessing the mental health of every person in a specified geographical area, either directly or indirectly.

FIGHT-OR-FLIGHT REACTION   Tendency to resolve a stressful situation by either attacking or escaping. (In actuality, there is also a third alternative: compromise or surrender.)

FLUID INTELLIGENCE   Capacity to use original thinking in order to solve an unfamiliar problem, rather than merely drawing on previously acquired information.

FOVEA   Small circular region located at the center of the retina.

FREQUENCY   (1) Number of times a specified score or range of scores occurs in a particular group of scores. (2) Variable related to the wavelength of a sound, which we perceive as pitch.

GENERAL ADAPTATION SYNDROME   According to Selye, a pattern of responses that occurs whenever an organism faces a threatening or noxious stimulus. Consists of three stages: the alarm reaction, the stage of resistance, and the stage of exhaustion.

GENETIC CELLULAR THEORIES OF AGING   Theories that attribute aging to an innate genetic program, much like a built-in biological clock.

GERIATRICS   Area of specialization within the field of medicine that deals with the scientific study of the diseases, debilities, and care of aged persons.

GERONTOLOGY   Scientific study of aging and the special problems of the aged.

GLAUCOMA   Disease that occurs when the fluid pressure in the eye becomes excessive, causing internal damage and gradually destroying one's vision.

GREGARIOUS STYLE OF FRIENDSHIP   Pattern of friendships that involves psychological closeness with a fairly large number of people, as by having half a dozen special friends and several dozen other people whose company one enjoys, and optimism about making new friends in the future.

GRIEF   Intense sorrow and mental distress caused by the death of a loved one. A certain amount of grief is beneficial and adaptive.

GROWTH HORMONE   Substance secreted by pituitary gland needed for normal growth during childhood and adolescence. Declines in old age and has been linked to physical and psychological declines in old age.

GUSTATION   Sense of taste.

HAIR CELLS OF THE EAR   The auditory receptors, located in the cochlea.

HERTZ   Unit for measuring the frequency of a sound.

HOSPICE APPROACH   Method of caring for terminal patients that is designed to meet such important needs as the alleviation of pain and the desire for attention and love.

HUMAN IMMUNODEFICIENCY VIRUS INFECTION (HIV INFECTION)   Disorder of the immune system that diminishes the body's resistance to infectious organisms and certain cancers. Caused by the HIV virus; transmitted chiefly by sexual contact and contaminated hypodermic needles, and by infected pregnant women to their fetuses. The serious, often fatal illness caused by HIV infection is called AIDS.

HYPERTENSION Consistent pattern of elevated blood pressure that most often occurs after middle age. Causes include excessive weight, stress, and perhaps a high salt intake. Hypertension increases the likelihood of strokes and coronary heart disease.

INCIDENCE RATE Number of new cases of a particular disorder that occur during a specified period.

INDEPENDENT STYLE OF FRIENDSHIP Pattern of friendships that involves personal self-sufficiency, maintaining psychological distance from other people, and a lack of best or close friends.

INDEPENDENT VARIABLE Variable manipulated by the experimenter in order to ascertain its effects on some other (dependent) variables.

INDIRECT MEASURE OF DEATH ANXIETY Measure designed to tap the less conscious aspects of death anxiety. Usually involves relatively complicated experimental procedures.

INDUCTIVE REASONING Reasoning in which relations among elements are determined to allow inferences to be drawn about new elements of the set or extrapolations of a relational series.

INFERENTIAL STATISTICS Mathematical procedures for drawing inferences about what is happening in a population, based on what is observed in a sample from that population.

INFORMATION-PROCESSING MODEL Conception of human learning and memory based on the principles underlying modern electronic computers, such as the ways in which computers perceive, acquire, store, transform, retrieve, and use considerable amounts of information.

INSPECTION INTERVAL Time given a subject to examine each stimulus pair during the study phase of a paired-associate learning task.

INTELLIGENCE Concept that refers to the range of behavior from dull to bright, slow-witted to quick-witted, and so on. There is no universally accepted definition of intelligence, nor is there agreement as to the number of specific abilities involved.

INTELLIGENCE QUOTIENT (IQ) Index of intelligence obtained by dividing an individual's mental age by his or her chronological age, and multiplying the result by 100. Not appropriate for use with adults.

INTENSITY Variable related to the energy or amplitude of a sound, which we perceive as loudness.

INTERFERENCE Forgetting due to prior or subsequent learning.

INTERINDIVIDUAL DIFFERENCES Differences between people or groups of people, as when some individuals show greater age-related declines than do others.

INTERNAL LOCUS OF CONTROL Consistent belief that obtaining rewards and avoiding punishments depend primarily on one's own actions.

INTERNAL VALIDITY Extent to which a study enables us to identify relationships among variables, notably cause-and-effect relationships.

INTRA-INDIVIDUAL CHANGES Changes that occur within a given individual over a period of time.

INTRINSIC BENEFITS OF WORK The extent to which work is gratifying and enjoyable for its own sake.

INTROVERSION   Trait characterized by shyness, inscrutability, and a keen interest in the inner world of one's own psyche.

IRIS   Muscle that surrounds the pupillary opening and controls the amount of light entering the eye.

JOB SATISFACTION   Extent to which one likes or dislikes various aspects of the work situation, including pay and fringe benefits, the work itself (e.g., whether it is interesting or boring), the supervisor, the co-workers, chances for advancement, opportunities for autonomy and control over one's work, job security, and working conditions.

KINESTHESIS   Sense of balance, which arises from sensations of movement or strain in the muscles, tendons, and joints.

LENS   Part of the eye that bends the light rays passing through it in order to produce a sharply focused image on the retina.

LEVELS OF PROCESSING   Idea that effectiveness of memory depends on the depth or level at which the information is encoded, with more elaborate encoding resulting in superior memory.

LIFE EXPECTANCY AT A SPECIFIC AGE   Number of additional years that will probably be lived by the average person who reaches the specified age in a particular year.

LIFE EXPECTANCY AT BIRTH   Number of years that will probably be lived by the average person born in a particular year.

LIPOFUSCIN   Golden brown, insoluble fatty pigment deposited in the cells of various parts of the body, such as the brain, liver, and spleen; the amount increases with increasing age. Sometimes referred to as the "wear-and-tear" pigment or "old-age" pigment.

LOCUS OF CONTROL   Trait characterized by the extent to which one believes that rewards and punishments depend on one's own actions (internal locus of control) as opposed to mere chance and the actions of other people (external locus of control).

LOGICAL MEMORY   Test included in the Wechsler Memory Scale in which the examinee attempts to recall details of a meaningful (i.e., logically interconnected) story.

LONGITUDINAL STUDY   Research wherein subjects are observed over a period of time, often years.

LONG-TERM MEMORY   Synonym for secondary memory.

LOUDNESS   Quantity of sound that is perceived by an individual.

MALE PATTERN BALDNESS   Loss of cranial hair with increasing age, which is caused by hereditary influences. Usually leaves the top of a man's head entirely bare. Also occurs in less severe form among women.

MAXIMUM LIFE SPAN   Extreme upper limit of human life.

MEDIATOR   (1) Verbal or pictorial link between a stimulus and a response. The use of mediators can significantly improve performance on learning and memory tasks. (2) Variable that affects the relationships among stressors, responses, and consequences.

MEDICAID Government health insurance program that pays for health care for certain very poor people: individuals who are pregnant, aged, disabled or blind, and families with dependent children.

MEDICARE Government health insurance program for the elderly that helps pay for basic health care services.

MEMORY SPAN Number of unrelated items (e.g., letters, digits, or words) that can be immediately remembered after a single presentation.

MENTAL HEALTH Ability to deal with the issues of life in an effective way, as by satisfying instinctual drives in ways that are socially acceptable and appropriately flexible.

METHOD OF LOCI Technique for enhancing memory by relying on associations between to-be-remembered items and familiar locations.

MNEMONICS Techniques used to improve or enhance memory, such as the method of loci or the use of interactive images.

MOTOR-SKILL LEARNING Form of learning that involves body movements, such as unlocking a door or buttoning a shirt.

MULTIATTRIBUTE DECISION MAKING Decision making based on several different dimensions or attributes, such as deciding between two jobs that differ in a number of potentially relevant respects.

MULTIDIMENSIONAL VARIABLE In personality theory, the idea that a construct such as personality represents several different dimensions each of which can be measured.

NEURITIC PLAQUES Formed when damaged and dying neurons collect around a core of protein substances in the brain. May be related to Alzheimer's disease and other dementias.

NEUROFIBRILLARY TANGLES Threadlike structures found within the neurons of the brain. May be related to Alzheimer's disease and other dementias.

NEUROTICISM Personality attribute characterized by a lack of self-control, an inability to deal adequately with stress, and unusual proneness to anxiety, anger, depression, and fears of shame and ridicule.

NEUROTRANSMITTERS Chemical substances that facilitate communication among the neurons in the brain and the normal functioning of the body. Examples include dopamine, which is responsible for controlling the motor movements of the body; acetylcholine, involved in memory processes; and norepinephrine, which is linked to memory, learning, and the response of the body to stress.

NONGENETIC CELLULAR THEORIES OF AGING (WEAR-AND-TEAR THEORIES) Theories that attribute aging to progressive cell damage caused by the internal and external environment, rather than to an innate genetic program.

OLFACTION Sense of smell.

OPTIC NERVE Bunch of cells in the retina that communicates visual impulses to the brain.

ORGANIC MENTAL DISORDER   Form of psychopathology caused by physical damage to or pathology of the brain. Includes the dementias, Alzheimer's disease, and organic brain damage caused by a specific substance (e.g., alcohol or drugs).

OSSICLES   Three small bones that communicate incoming sound vibrations from the eardrum to the oval window.

OSTEOPOROSIS   Disease caused by severe bone degeneration and characterized by a loss of bone mass and increased porosity. Makes bone fractures more likely and recovery more difficult.

OVAL WINDOW   Membrane that separates the middle ear from the inner ear and which communicates sound vibrations from the third ossicle to the fluid in the cochlea.

PAIRED-ASSOCIATE LEARNING   Form of learning wherein pairs of items are used (e.g., common words, nonsense syllables); subjects must reply with the second member of each pair when presented with the first member.

PARAMETER   Numerical quantity that summarizes some characteristic of a population.

PARAPROFESSIONAL THERAPY FOR THE BEREAVED   Therapy for the bereaved is conducted by people who are not trained health care professionals but who have lost a spouse and gone through the bereavement process themselves.

PASSIONATE LOVE   Form of love characterized by total absorption in another person, intense physiological arousal, and moments of ecstasy and complete fulfillment.

PATHOLOGICAL GRIEF   Intense sorrow and mental suffering that continues for an unusually long time after the death of a loved one. Often preceded by a period of apparent calm and well-being immediately following the death.

PERSONAL COMPETENCE   Multidimensional variable that includes such characteristics as biological health, ego strength, cognitive skills, and sensorimotor abilities.

PERSONALITY   Organized, distinctive pattern of behavior that characterizes a particular individual. Includes the individual's physical, mental, emotional, and social characteristics.

PHASES OF RETIREMENT   Distinct emotional and psychological periods that are presumably encountered during retirement, such as the honeymoon period, rest and relaxation, disenchantment, reorientation, the daily routine, and termination.

PHYSIOLOGICAL THEORIES OF AGING   Theories that attribute aging to the failure of certain physiological systems to coordinate important bodily functions.

PITCH   Quality of a sound that is perceived by an individual (e.g., different notes on the musical scale).

POPULATION   All of the cases in which a researcher is interested; a (usually very large) group of people, animals, objects, or responses that are alike in at least some respect.

POPULATION AT RISK   All people in a specified geographical area who might conceivably contract the disorder under study.

PRACTICAL INTELLIGENCE   Ability to apply intellectual skills to everyday situations.

PRESBYCUSIS   Progressive loss of hearing in both ears for high-frequency tones; often involves difficulty in understanding speech. Onset is gradual and becomes pronounced after age 50.

PRESBYOPIA   Gradual decline in the ability to focus on nearby objects; normally occurs after age 40.

PREVALENCE RATE   Total number of people in a given community who suffer from a particular disorder, either at a single point in time or during a specified period of time.

PRIMARY CONTROL   Ability to produce behavior-event contingencies; the ability to control the external environment.

PRIMACY EFFECT   In serial learning, the tendency to recall the items at the beginning of the list more easily.

PRIMARY MEMORY   In structural theory, the separate and distinct memory system that has a very small capacity and retains information for periods from 1 or 2 seconds to about half a minute.

PRIMARY MENTAL ABILITIES   Psychometric test of intelligence in which each test is assumed to represent a single pure mental ability.

PROACTIVE INTERFERENCE   Impairments in learning or memory attributable to activities occurring before the presentation of the new material.

PROBLEM-FOCUSED COPING   Coping with stress by taking action intended to resolve or modify the existing situation.

PROPRIOCEPTION   Sensations generated by the body that let us know the location of our limbs in space.

PSYCHOLOGICAL TRADITION   In stress research, the approach that emphasizes the role a person's perception and evaluation of the potential harm posed by a particular environmental event.

PSYCHOMETRIC APPROACH TO CREATIVITY   Measuring creativity by means of written tests, most often of divergent thinking.

PSYCHOMETRIC TESTS   Assessing intelligence and cognition in terms of standardized psychological tests.

PSYCHOPATHOLOGY   Synonym for mental illness (mental disorder).

PSYCHOSIS   Form of psychopathology characterized by gross breakdowns in personality and distortion of reality. Usually requires hospitalization.

PSYCHOTHERAPY   General term that may refer to any established psychological method for treating mental disorders.

PUPILLARY REFLEX   Automatic contraction (dilation) of the pupil of the eye when there is a significant increase (decrease) in illumination.

QUASI-EXPERIMENTAL DESIGN   Research that resembles the experimental design in that independent and dependent variables are clearly specified, but differs in that subjects are not assigned randomly to experimental or control groups.

RADIAL MAZE TESTS   Method of testing memory in rats and other animals in which food is placed in the arms of a spokelike maze and then the animal is examined to determine how frequently it returns to arms where the food had already been consumed.

RANDOM ASSIGNMENT OF STUDY PARTICIPANTS TO GROUPS   Assigning subjects to experimental and control groups in such a way that each subject has an equal chance of winding up in either group.

RANDOM SAMPLE   Selecting a sample in such a way that each person has an equal chance of being selected out of the entire population.

REACTION TIME   A measure of the ability to respond quickly. The time between the onset of a stimulus and a subject's response.

REALITY MONITORING   Ability to distinguish between whether material was actually presented or experienced or merely imagined.

RECALL   Producing a response by searching one's memory for the correct answer, as on an essay examination. One form of retrieval.

RECENCY EFFECT   (1) In serial learning, the tendency to recall the last few items more easily than items in the middle of the list, albeit not as easily as items at the beginning. (2) In free-recall tasks, the tendency to recall the last few items most easily.

RECENCY SEGMENT   The higher level of recall accuracy associated with the last few items presented in a list of words. This is usually the region of the serial position function with the highest accuracy.

RECOGNITION   Identifying an item or event as familiar or previously experienced; multiple-choice examinations test the accuracy of recognition. One form of retrieval.

REFLEX   Automatic reaction to external stimulation such as light or mechanical force.

RESPONSES TO STRESS   Reactions to stressors that are more immediate than consequences, and are not in and of themselves desirable or undesirable. Includes fight, flight, or compromise; cognitions, expectations, and perceptions; physiological changes; and the defense mechanisms.

RETINA   Part of the eye that transforms incoming light energy into impulses that can be communicated to the brain. Includes the cones, rods, and fovea.

RETINAL DETACHMENT   Form of retinal disorder consisting of a separation between the inner and outer layers of the retina.

RETINAL DISORDERS   Most common causes of blindness in the United States. Varieties include diabetic retinopathy, retinal detachment, and senile macular degeneration.

RETIRED PERSON   Individual who is not working full time and who receives at least some income from a pension earned through prior employment.

RETIREMENT   Leaving the world of full-time work and beginning to collect one's pension or related benefits.

RETRIEVAL   Occurs when certain information is distinguished from everything else in memory and is brought back to awareness for current use; the third process in the act of remembering. Material may be retrieved through recognition or recall.

RETROACTIVE INTERFERENCE   Impairments in learning or memory attributable to activities occurring after the presentation of the new material.

RIBONUCLEIC ACID (RNA)   Molecule that transfers genetic information from the DNA molecules to the location in the cell where proteins are assembled.

RIGHT TO DIE   Right to insist that life-sustaining procedures not be used if the only effect will be to artificially prolong the dying process.

RIGIDITY   Trait characterized by an inability to shift from one form of behavior to another, even though such a shift might well be advantageous to the individual.

R**ODS** Photoreceptor cells in the retina that respond to low levels of illumination and are responsible for night vision. Most plentiful in the periphery of the retina, and completely absent from the fovea.

S**AMPLE** Any subgroup of cases drawn from a clearly specified population. In a random sample, each element in the population has an equal chance of being included in the sample.

S**ECONDARY CONTROL** Cognitive processes that help maintain or enhance an individual's ability to exert primary control (e.g., affect the external environment in some way).

S**ECONDARY MEMORY** In structural theory, the separate and distinct memory system that has an enormous capacity and retains information for periods from 1 or 2 minutes to many years.

S**ELECTIVE ATTRITION** Occurs when subjects who drop out during the course of a longitudinal study are not representative of the group as a whole. This results in a sample that is atypical in at least some respects, and may well bias measurements taken during the latter part of the study.

S**ELECTIVITY** In life-span development theory, the idea that individuals must make choices and allocate resources in the pursuit of any kind of developmental path.

S**ELF-DISCLOSURE** Revealing information about oneself that one would normally keep secret. An important aspect of both close friendships and loving relationships.

S**EMANTIC** Pertaining to the meaning of a word.

S**EMANTIC MEMORY** In Tulving's theory, a form of memory that consists of general knowledge, meanings, and abstract relationships.

S**ENILE MACULAR DEGENERATION** Form of retinal disorder wherein a specialized part of the retina that is responsible for sharp central and reading vision loses its ability to function effectively.

S**ENSORY MEMORY** Form of memory that holds incoming visual or auditory information for periods from one quarter of a second to a few seconds after the stimulus is withdrawn.

S**EQUENTIAL RESEARCH** Research strategies designed to eliminate the confounding that occurs in cross-sectional research (between aging effects and cohort effects) and in longitudinal research (between aging effects and time of measurement effects).

S**ERIAL LEARNING** Form of learning wherein the subject must repeat back a list of items (e.g., common words, nonsense syllables) in the exact order in which they were presented.

S**ERIAL POSITION FUNCTION** Plot of recall accuracy of a list of unrelated words as a function of their order of presentation.

S**EX DISCRIMINATION** Denying an individual a job, a promotion, more pay, or other desired work benefit solely because of his or her gender; most often used to refer to the unfair treatment of women at work. Although illegal, sex discrimination is still a significant problem in the world of work.

S**HORT-TERM MEMORY** Synonym for primary memory.

SOCIAL SECURITY   Mandatory federal retirement program that enrolls most of the people in the United States and pays monthly pensions after retirement.

SOMESTHESIS   Sensations that arise from stimulation of the skin, viscera, and kinesthetic receptors.

STAGE   Period in one's life, usually consisting of several years, during which most or all people of the same age supposedly encounter much the same experiences and problems.

STATIC VISUAL ACUITY   Ability to identify a stationary object, or features thereof, by sight. Usually refers to situations where the observer is also stationary.

STATISTIC   Numerical quantity that summarizes some characteristic of a sample.

STATISTICALLY NON-NORMATIVE LIFE EVENT   Major event in one's life that happens to few other people in that culture. In this country, examples include suffering a stroke or winning a state lottery.

STATISTICALLY NORMATIVE LIFE EVENT   Major event in one's life that also happens to the majority of people in that culture. In this country, examples include getting married or retiring from work.

STORAGE   Middle stage in a stage theory of memory responsible for maintaining or preserving the information.

STRESS   Complicated phenomenon that involves the interrelationships among stressors, responses, consequences, and mediators. Typically, there is some threat or demand that affects one's inner stability.

STRESSOR   Stimulus that is likely to impose some demands, or some degree of threat, on an individual.

STROKE   Illness characterized by brain damage and by the often severe physical, cognitive, and social disabilities that result. Most often caused by the occlusion of a cerebral artery, which blocks the flow of blood to the cerebral hemispheres, or by a blood vessel that ruptures and produces a brain hemorrhage.

STRUCTURAL THEORY   Theory that focuses on separate and distinct memory systems which store information in the human brain.

STUDY PHASE   Period during which subjects in an experiment practice and try to learn the material in question.

SYLLOGISM   Type of reasoning problem in which two or more premises are followed by a conclusion and the examinee is instructed to make a decision about the validity of the conclusion.

TEMPORALLY NON-NORMATIVE LIFE EVENT   Major event in one's life that occurs at an age which is atypical for people in that culture. In this country, examples include getting married for the first time at age 45 or becoming a widow at age 25.

TEMPORALLY NORMATIVE LIFE EVENT   Major event in one's life that occurs at an age that is typical for people in that culture. In this country, examples include getting married for the first time in one's 20s or becoming a widow at age 65.

TERMINAL ILLNESS   Illness from which there is no reasonable hope of ever recovering, although there may be periods of remission and apparent health.

TERMINAL PHASE OF LIFE   The last decline in health from which there is no major remission and which ends in death. A time of steady and rapid deterioration, especially of the central nervous system.

TERTIARY MEMORY   Very long-term memory extending for years to decades. Sometimes known as remote memory.

TIME-LAG EFFECTS ON INTELLIGENCE   When performance on tests of intelligence or other cognitive abilities varies according to the time period even among people of the same age.

TIME OF MEASUREMENT EFFECT   Occurs when behavior or personality is influenced in some way by the time periods in which these characteristics are measured.

TRAIT   Specific aspect of personality that initiates and guides consistent forms of behavior, such as shyness, friendliness, ambitiousness, cleanliness, and literally thousands of others.

TRAUMATIC GRIEF   Pathological form of grief in which individuals have an intrusive, distressing preoccupation with the deceased person, feel futile about the future, and experience a sense of numbness, detachment or absence of emotional responsiveness.

TYPE A INDIVIDUAL   Person characterized by intense ambition, competitiveness, aggressiveness, and perfectionism.

TYPE B INDIVIDUAL   Person who is relatively easygoing, seldom impatient, and not compelled by the need to compete or achieve.

VARIABLE   Any characteristic that can take on different values.

VASCULAR DEMENTIA   Stepwise deterioration in intellectual functioning (memory, judgment, abstract thinking) that occurs when localized areas of brain tissue are destroyed because of an inadequate supply of blood. In contrast to Alzheimer's disease, has an abrupt onset, progresses in stages, and is more prevalent among men.

VISUAL ACUITY   Ability to distinguish one object from another by sight.

WAIS PERFORMANCE SCALE   Section of the WAIS consisting of tests in which the examinee is required to assemble, construct, or rearrange physical items. It is thought to be more similar to fluid intelligence than to crystallized intelligence.

WAIS VERBAL SCALE   Section of the WAIS consisting of tests containing verbal material, with the examinee required to define, explain, or interpret the items. It is thought to be more similar to crystallized intelligence than to fluid intelligence.

WECHSLER ADULT INTELLIGENCE SCALE   Most commonly used measure of adult intelligence, consisting of six verbal scales (which require the use of words) and five performance scales (which do not).

WISDOM   Desirable personal characteristic that involves intelligence, good reasoning ability, good judgment, the realization that one may err, the ability to learn from past mistakes, the ability to solve one's own problems and give good advice to others, and an understanding of self and others. More likely to be found among older adults because it is related to experience.

WORK FORCE   All those adults who are currently employed, plus all those who are currently seeking employment.

WORKING MEMORY   Synonym for primary memory, which emphasizes both the limited storage capacity of this memory and the selection or manipulation of the information that it contains.

REFERENCES

Adams, B. (1979). Mate selection in the United States: A theoretical summarization. In W. Burr, R. Hill, I. Nye & R. Reiss (Eds.), *Contemporary theories about the family*: Vol 1. *Research-based theories*. New York: Free Press.

Adams, O., & Lefebvre, L. (1981). Retirement and mortality. *Aging and Work, 4*, 115–120.

Adams, R. G., & Blieszner, R. (Eds.). (1989). *Older adult friendship: Structure and process.* Newbury Park, CA: Sage.

Adams, R. G., & Blieszner, R. (1995). Aging well with friends and family. Special Issue: Aging well in contemporary society. *American Behavioral Scientist, 39*, 209–224.

Adelman, M. (1990). Stigma, gay lifestyles, and adjustment to aging: A Study of later-life gay men and lesbians. *Journal of Homosexuality, 20*, 1–7.

Albert, M. S., Duffy, F. H., & Naeser, M. (1987). Nonlinear changes in cognition with age and their neuropsychologic correlates. *Canadian Journal of Psychology, 41*, 141–157.

Allport, G. W. (1968). *The person in psychology: Selected essays.* Boston: Beacon Press.

Alpaugh, P. K., & Birren, J. E. (1977). Variables affecting creative contributions across the adult life span. *Human Development, 20*, 240–248.

Amato, P. R., & Rogers, S. J. (1997). A longitudinal study of marital problems and subsequent divorce. *Journal of Marriage and the Family, 59*, 612–624.

American Cancer Society. (1997). *Cancer facts and figures.* New York: American Cancer Society.

American Heart Association. (1998). *1998 heart facts.* Dallas: American Heart Association National Center.

American Psychiatric Association. (1987). *Diagnostic and statistical manual of mental disorders* (3rd ed., rev.). Washington, DC: American Psychiatric Association.

American Public Health Association. (1991, January). 1980s saw record U.S. progress in cutting accidental deaths. *The Nation's Health*, p. 1.

Anderson, Y. W., & Rochard, C. (1979). Cold snaps, snowfall, and sudden death from ischemic heart disease. *Canadian Medical Association Journal, 121,* 1580–1583.

Angleitner, A. (1976). Changes in personality observed in questionnaire data from the Riegel questionnaire on rigidity, dogmatism, and attitude toward life. In H. Thomae (Ed.), *Patterns of aging.* Basel-New York: Karger.

Anthony, J. (1974). Children at risk from divorce: A review. In J. Anthony & C. Koupernic (Eds.), *The child in his family: Children at psychiatric risk.* New York: Wiley.

Antonoff, S. R., & Spilka, B. (1984–1985). Patterning of facial expressions among terminal cancer patients. *Omega: Journal of Death and Dying, 15,* 101–108.

Antonucci, T. C. (1984). Personal characteristics, social support, and social behavior. In E. Shanas & R. H. Binstock (Eds.), *Handbook of aging and the social sciences* (2nd ed.). New York: Van Nostrand Reinhold.

Antonucci, T. C., Sherman, A. M., & Akiyama, H. (1996). Social networks, support, and integration. In J. E. Birren (Ed.), *Encyclopedia of gerontology,* Vol. 2 (pp. 505–515). New York: Academic Press.

Arber, S. (1996). Gender roles. In J. E. Birren (Ed.), *Encyclopedia of gerontology,* Vol. 1 (pp. 555–565). New York: Academic Press.

Arbuckle, T.Y., Cooney, R., Milne, J., & Melchior, A. (1994). Memory for spatial layouts in relation to age and schema typicality. *Psychology and Aging, 9,* 467–480.

Arkin, A. M. (1981). Emotional care of the bereaved. In O. S. Margolis, H. C. Raether, A. H. Kutscher, J. B. Powers, I. B. Seeland, R. DeBellis, & D. J. Cherico (Eds.), *Acute grief: Counseling the bereaved.* New York: Columbia University Press.

Arking, G. (1976). The elderly widow and her family, neighbors, and friends. *Journal of Marriage and the Family, 38,* 757–768.

Assmann, G., & Schulte, H. (1986). *PROCAM-trial: Prospective cardiovascular Munster trial.* Zurich: Panscientia Verlag, 8–9, 12.

Atchley, R. C. (1977). *Social forces of later life* (2nd ed.). Belmont, CA: Wadsworth.

Atchley, R. C. (1982). Retirement: Leaving the world of work. *Annals of the American Academy of Political and Social Science, 464,* 120–131.

Atchley, R. C. (1985). *Social forces and aging: An introduction to social gerontology.* Belmont, CA: Wadsworth.

Atchley, R. C. (1989). A continuity theory of normal aging. *The Gerontologist, 99,* 183–190.

Atchley, R. C. (1996). Retirement. In J. E. Birren (Ed.), *Encyclopedia of gerontology,* Vol. 2 (pp. 437–449). New York: Academic Press.

Atchley, R. C., & Miller, S. J. (1980). Older people and their families. In C. Eisdorfer (Ed.), *Annual review of gerontology and geriatrics* (Vol. 1). New York: Springer.

Ausman, L. M., & Russell, R. M. (1990). Nutrition and aging. In E. L. Schneider & J. W. Rowe (Eds.), *Handbook of the biology of aging* (3rd ed.). New York: Academic Press.

Babchuck, N. (1978–1979). Aging and primary relations. *International Journal of Aging and Human Development, 9,* 137–151.

Backman, L., & Dixon, R. A. (1992). Psychological compensation: A theoretical framework. *Psychological Bulletin, 112,* 259–283.

Backman, L., & Molander, B. (1986). Effects of adult age and level of skill on the ability to cope with high stress conditions in a precision sport. *Psychology and Aging, 1,* 334–336.

Baddeley, A. D. (1981). The concept of working memory: A view of its current state and probable future direction. *Cognition, 10,* 17–23.

Bahr, S. J., & Peterson, E. T. (Eds.). (1989). *Aging and the family.* Lexington, MA: Lexington.

Bahrick, H. P., Bahrick, P. O., & Wittlinger, R. P. (1975). Fifty years of memory for names and faces: A cross-sectional approach. *Journal of Experimental Psychology: General*, *104*, 54–75.

Bahrick, H. P., & Hall, L. K. (1991). Lifetime maintenance of high school mathematics content. *Journal of Experimental Psychology: General*, *120*, 20–33.

Balin, A. K., & Vilenchik, M. M. (1996). Oxidative damage. In J. E. Birren (Ed.), *Encyclopedia of gerontology*, Vol. 2 (pp. 233–246). New York: Academic Press.

Ball, K., & Sekuler, R. (1986). Improving visual perception in older observers. *Journal of Gerontology*, *41*, 176–182.

Baltes, P. B., & Baltes, M. M. (1990). Psychological perspectives on successful aging: The model of selective optimization with compensation. In P. B. Baltes & M. M. Baltes (Eds.), *Successful aging: Perspectives from the behavioral sciences*. New York: Cambridge University Press.

Baltes, P. B., Cornelius, S. W., Spiro, A., Nesselroade, J. R., & Willis, S. L. (1980). Integration versus differentiation of fluid/crystallized intelligence in old age. *Developmental Psychology*, *16*, 625–635.

Baltes P. B., & Labouvie, G. V (1973). Adult development of intellectual performance: Description, explanation, and modification. In C. Eisdorfer & M. P. Lawton (Eds.), *The psychology of adult development and aging*. Washington, DC: American Psychological Association.

Baltes, P. B., Reese, H. W., & Nesselroade, J. R. (1977). *Life-span developmental psychology: Introduction to research methods*. Monterey, CA: Brooks/Cole.

Baltes, P. B., Smith, J., & Staudinger, U. M. (1992). Wisdom and successful aging. In T. B. Sonderegger (Ed.), *Nebraska Symposium on Motivation*, Vol. 39 (pp. 123–167). Lincoln: University of Nebraska Press.

Baltes, P. B., & Staudinger, U. M. (1993). The search for a psychology of wisdom. *Current Directions in Psychological Science*, *2*, 75–80.

Barber, C. E. (1989). Transition to the empty nest. In S. J. Bahr & E. T. Peterson (Eds.), *Aging and the family*. Lexington, MA: Lexington.

Barrett, C. J. (1978). Effectiveness of widows' groups in facilitating change. *Journal of Consulting and Clinical Psychology*, *46*, 20–31.

Barton, D., Crowder, M. K., & Flexner, J. M. (1979–1980). Teaching about dying and death in a multidisciplinary student group. *Omega: Journal of Death and Dying*, *10*, 265–270.

Bartoshuk, L. M., Rifkin, L. M., Marks, L. E., & Bars, P. (1986). Taste and aging. *Journal of Gerontology*, *41*, 51–57.

Bartoshuk, L. M., & Weiffenbach, J. M. (1990). Chemical senses and aging. In E. L. Schneider & J. W. Rowe (Eds.), *Handbook of the biology of aging* (3rd ed.). New York: Academic Press.

Baruch, G. K., & Barnett, R. C. (1980). On the well-being of adult women. In L. A. Bond & J. C. Rosen (Eds.), *Competence and coping during adulthood*. Hanover, NH: University Press of New England.

Bashore, T. R. (1989). Age, physical fitness, and mental processing speed. In M. P. Lawton (Ed.), *Annual review of gerontology and geriatrics*, Vol. 9 (pp. 120–144). New York: Springer.

Bass, D. M. (1985). The hospice ideology and success of hospice care. *Research on Aging*, *7*, 307–327.

Beck, S. H. (1982). Adjustment to and satisfaction with retirement. *Journal of Gerontology*, *37*, 616–624.

Beck, S. H. (1984). Retirement preparation programs: Differentials in opportunity and use. *Journal of Gerontology*, *39*, 596–602.

Becker, E. (1973). *The denial of death*. New York: Free Press.

Bee, H. L. (1987). *The journey of adulthood*. New York: Macmillan.

Beisecker, A. E. (1988). Aging and the desire for information and input in medical decisions: Patient consumerism in medical encounters. *Gerontologist, 28*, 330–345.

Bem, D. J., & Allen, A. (1974). On predicting some of the people some of the time: The search for cross-situational consistencies in behavior. *Psychological Review, 81*, 506–520.

Bengtson, V. L., & Robertson, J. F. (Eds.). (1985). *Grandparenthood*. Beverly Hills, CA: Sage.

Bengtson, V., Rosenthal, C., & Burton, L. (1996). Paradoxes of families and aging. In R. H. Binstock & L. K. George (Eds.), *Handbook of aging and the social sciences* (4th ed.) (pp. 253–282).

Bennett, T. S. (1984). Divorce. In R. J. Corsini (Ed.), *Encyclopedia of psychology*. New York: Wiley.

Benoliel, J. Q. (1979). Dying is a family affair. In E. R. Prichard et al. (Eds.), *Home care: Living with dying*. New York: Columbia University Press.

Berglas, S. (1986). *The success syndrome*. New York: Plenum.

Bergman, M. (1980). *Aging and the perception of speech*. Baltimore, MD: University of Baltimore Press.

Bergman, M., Blumenfeld, V. G., Cascardo, D., Dash, B., Levitt, H., & Margulios, M. K. (1976). Age-related decrements in hearing for speech: Sampling and longitudinal studies. *Journal of Gerontology, 31*, 533–538.

Berkman, L. F. (1995). The role of social relations in health promotion. *Psychosomatic Medicine, 57*, 245–254.

Berkman, L. F., Leo-Summers, L., & Horwitz, R. I. (1992). Emotional support and survival following myocardial infarction: A prospective, population-based study of the elderly. *Annals of Internal Medicine, 117*, 1003–1009.

Berkman, L. F., & Syme, S. L. (1979). Social networks, host resistance, and mortality: A nine year follow-up study of Alameda County residents. *American Journal of Epidemiology, 109*, 186–204.

Berscheid, E., & Walster, E. (1974). Physical attractiveness. In L. Berkowitz (Ed.), *Advances in experimental social psychology* (Vol. 7). New York: Academic Press.

Berscheid, E., & Walster, E. (1978). *Interpersonal attraction* (2nd ed.). Reading, MA: Addison-Wesley.

Biegel, D. E., Sales, E., & Schulz, R. (1991). *Family caregiving in chronic illness*. Newbury Park, CA: Sage.

Binet, A., & Simon, T. (1905). Methods nouvelles pour le diagnostic du niveau intellectuel des anormaux. *Année Psychologique, 11*, 191–244.

Binstock, R. H., & George, L. K. (1996) (Eds.). *Handbook of aging and the social sciences* (4th ed.). New York: Academic Press.

Birren, J. E. (1964). *The psychology of aging*. Englewood Cliffs, NJ: Prentice-Hall.

Birren, J. E. (1969). Age and decision strategies. *Interdisciplinary Topics in Gerontology, 4*, 23–36.

Birren, J. E. (1974). Translations in gerontology—from lab to life: Psychophysiology and speed of response. *American Psychologist, 29*, 808–815.

Birren, J. E., & Fisher, L. M. (1990). The elements of wisdom: Overview and integration. In R. J. Sternberg (Ed.), *Wisdom: Its nature, origins, and development* (pp. 317–332). Cambridge: Cambridge University Press.

Birren, J. E., & Renner, J. (1980). Concepts and issues of mental health and aging. In J. E. Birren & R. B. Sloane (Eds.), *Handbook of mental health and aging*. Englewood Cliffs, NJ: Prentice-Hall.

Birren, J. E., & Schaie, K. W. (Eds.). (1996). *Handbook of the psychology of aging* (4th ed.). San Diego: Academic Press.

Blair, S. N., Kohl, H. W., Barlow, C. E., Paffenbarger, R. S., Gibbons, L. W., & Macera, C. A. (1995). Changes in physical fitness and all-cause mortality: A prospective study of healthy and unhealthy men. *Journal of the American Medical Association, 273,* 1093–1098.

Blanchard-Fields, F. (1986). Reasoning on social dilemmas varying in emotional saliency: An adult-developmental study. *Psychology and Aging, 1,* 325–333.

Blau, Z. S. (1981). *Aging in a changing society* (2nd ed.). New York: Franklin Watts.

Blazer, D. (1982). Social support and mortality in an elderly community sample. *American Journal of Epidemiology, 115,* 684–694.

Blazer, D. (1989a). Affective disorders in late life. In E. W. Busse & D. G. Blazer (Eds.), *Geriatric psychiatry.* Washington, DC: American Psychiatric Press.

Blazer, D. (1989b). The epidemiology of psychiatric disorders in late life. In E. W. Busse & D. G. Blazer (Eds.), *Geriatric psychiatry.* Washington, DC: American Psychiatric Press.

Blazer, D. (1989c). The psychiatric interview of the geriatric patient. In E. W. Busse & D. G. Blazer (Eds.), *Geriatric psychiatry.* Washington, DC: American Psychiatric Press.

Blazer, D., Hughes, D. C., & George, L. K. (1989). The epidemiology of depression in an elderly community population. *Gerontologist, 27,* 281–287.

Blieszner, R. (1995). Friendship processes and well-being in the later years of life. Implications for interventions. *Journal of Geriatric Psychiatry, 28,* 165–182.

Boller, F., Goldstein, G., Dorr, C., Kim, Y., Moossy, J., Richey, E., Wagener, D., & Wolfson, S. K., Jr. (1984). Alzheimer and related dementias: A review of current knowledge. In G. Goldstein (Ed.), *Advances in clinical neurophysiology* (Vol. 1). New York: Plenum.

Bondareff, W. (1996). Brain and central nervous system. In J. E. Birren (Ed.), *Encyclopedia of gerontology* (Vol. 1, pp. 217–222). New York: Academic Press.

Booth, A. (1972). Sex and social participation. *American Sociological Review, 37*(2), 183–192.

Booth-Kewley, S., & Friedman, H. S. (1987). Psychological predictors of heart disease: A quantitative review. *Psychological Bulletin, 101,* 343–362.

Botwinick, J., & Birren, J. E. (1963). Cognitive processes: Mental abilities and psycho-motor responses in healthy aged men. In J. E. Birren, R. N. Butler, S. W. Greenhouse, L. Solkoff, & M. R. Yarrow (Eds.), *Human Aging: A Biological and Behavioral Study* (pp. 97–108). Public Health Service Publication No. 896. Washington, DC: U.S. Government Printing Office.

Bowers, I. C. H., & Bahr, J. (1989). Remarriage among the elderly. In S. J. Bahr & E. T. Peterson (Eds.), *Aging and the family.* Lexington, MA: Lexington.

Bradley, R. H., & Webb, R. (1976). Age-related differences in locus of control orientation in three behavioral domains. *Human Development, 19,* 49–56.

Branch, L., & Jette, A. (1983). Elders' use of informal long-term care assistance. *The Gerontologist, 23,* 51–56.

Brandtstadter, J. (1984). Personal and social control over development: Some implications of an action perspective in life-span developmental psychology. In P. B. Baltes & O. G. Brim (Eds.), *Life-span development and behavior,* Vol. 6 (pp. 1–32). Orlando, FL: Academic Press.

Brandstadter, J. (1989). Personal self-regulation of development: Cross-sequential analyses of development-related control beliefs and emotions. *Developmental Psychology, 25,* 96–108.

Brandtstadter, J., & Greve, W. (1994). The aging self: Stabilizing and protective processes. *Developmental Review, 14,* 52–80.

Brandstadter, J., & Renner, G. (1990). Tenacious goal pursuit and flexible goal adjustment: Explication and age-related analysis of assimilative and accommodative strategies of coping. *Psychology and Aging, 5,* 58–67.

Breaugh, J. A., & DiMarco, N. (1979). *Age differences in the rated desirability of job outcomes.* Paper presented at the annual meeting of the American Psychological Association, New York, NY.

Brenton, M. (1974). *Friendship*. New York: Stein & Day.

Breytspraak, L. M. (1984). *The development of self in later life*. Boston: Little, Brown.

Brickman, A. L., & Eisdorfer, C. (1989). Anxiety in the elderly. In E. W. Busse & D. G. Blazer (Eds.), *Geriatric psychiatry*. Washington, DC: American Psychiatric Press.

Brock, D. B., Guralnik, J. M., & Brody, J. A. (1990). Demography and epidemiology of aging in the United States. In E. L. Schneider & J. W. Rowe (Eds.), *Handbook of the biology of aging* (3rd ed.). New York: Academic Press.

Brody, E. (1978). The aging family. *Annals of the American Academy of Political and Social Science, 438,* 13–27.

Brody, E. (1981). Women in the middle and family help to older people. *The Gerontologist, 21,* 471–480.

Brody, E., Johnson, P., Fulcomer, M., & Lang, A. (1983). Women's changing roles and help to elderly parents: Attitudes of three generations of women. *Journal of Gerontology, 38,* 597–607.

Brotman, H. (1980). *Every ninth American*. Washington, DC: Developments in Aging, United States Senate Special Committee on Aging.

Brown, B. B. (1981). A life-span approach to friendship: Age-related dimensions of an ageless relationship. In H. Lopata & D. Maines (Eds.), *Research on the interweave of social roles: Vol. 2. Friendship*. Greenwich, CT: JAI Press.

Buhler, C. (1968). Fulfillment and failure of life. In C. Buhler & F. Massarik (Eds.), *The course of human life*. New York: Springer.

Burnside, I. M. (1975). Sexuality and the older adult: Implications for nursing. In I. M. Burnside (Ed.), *Sexuality and aging*. Los Angeles: University of Southern California Press.

Burt, J. J., & Meeks, L. B. (1985). *Education for sexuality: Concepts and programs for teaching* (3rd ed.). Philadelphia: Saunders College Publishers.

Busse, E. W. (1987). Mental health. In G. L. Maddox (Ed.), *The encyclopedia of aging*. New York: Springer.

Busse, E. W., & Blazer, D. G. (Eds.). (1980). *Handbook of geriatric psychiatry*. New York: Van Nostrand Reinhold.

Cannon, W. G. (1929). *Bodily changes in pain, hunger, fear and rage: An account of recent researches into the function of emotional excitement* (2nd ed.). New York: Appleton.

Cantor, M. H. (1980). The informal support system: Its relevance in the lives of the elderly. In E. Borgatta & N. McCluskey (Eds.), *Aging and society*. Beverly Hills, CA: Sage.

Cantor, M. H. (1983). Strain among caregivers: A study of experience in the United States. *The Gerontologist, 23,* 597–604.

Carstensen, L. L. (1998). The social context of emotional experience. In K. W. Schaie & M. P. Lawton (Eds.), *Annual review of gerontology and geriatrics: Vol. 17. Focus on emotion and adult development* (pp. 325–352). New York: Springer, 1998.

Carstensen, L. L. (in press). A life span approach to social motivation. In J. Heckhausen & C. Dweck (Eds.), *Motivation and self-regulation across the life span*. London: Cambridge University Press.

Carstensen, L. L., Edelstein, B. A., & Dornbrand, L. (Eds.). (1996). *The practical handbook of clinical gerontology*. Thousand Oaks, CA: Sage.

Cash, T. F., & Derlega, V. J. (1978). The matching hypothesis: Physical attractiveness among same-sexed friends. *Personality and Social Psychology Bulletin, 4,* 240–243.

Cassileth, B. R., Lusk, E. J., Strouse, T. B., Miller, D. S., Brown, L. L., Cross, P. A., & Tenaglia, A. N. (1984). Psychosocial status in chronic illness: A comparative analysis of six diagnostic groups. *New England Journal of Medicine, 311,* 506–511.

Cattell, R. B. (1965). *The scientific analysis of personality*. London: Penguin.

Cattell, R. B. (1973). *Personality and mood by questionnaire*. San Francisco: Jossey-Bass.

Cattell, R. B. (1979). *Personality and learning theory: Vol. 1. The structure of personality in its environment*. New York: Springer.

Cattell, R. B. (1980). *Personality and learning theory: Vol. 2. A systems theory of maturation and structured learning*. New York: Springer.

Cattell, R. B. (1987). *Intelligence: Its structure, growth and action*. Amsterdam: North-Holland.

Cattell, R. B., Eber, H. W., & Tatsuoka, M. M. (1970). *Handbook for the Sixteen Personality Factor Questionnaire*. Champaign, IL: Institute for Personality and Ability Testing.

Cavanaugh, J. C. (1990). *Adult development and aging*. New York: Wadsworth.

Cavanaugh, J. C., & Poon, L. W. (1989). Metamemorial predictors of memory performance in young and old adults. *Psychology and Aging, 4*, 365–370.

Cerella, J. (1985). Information processing rates in the elderly. *Psychological Bulletin, 98*, 67–83.

Cerella, J. (1990). Aging and information-processing rate. In J. E. Birren & K. W. Schaie (Eds.), *Handbook of the psychology of aging* (3rd ed.) (pp. 201–221). New York: Academic Press.

Cerella, J. (1995). Reaction time. In G. L. Maddox (Ed.), *The encyclopedia of aging* (2nd ed.) (pp. 792–795). New York: Springer.

Charness, N. (1989). Components of skill in bridge. *Canadian Journal of Psychology, 33*, 1–16.

Cherlin, A., & Furstenberg, F. F. (1985). Styles and strategies of grandparenthood. In V. L. Bengtson & J. F. Robertson (Eds.), *Grandparenthood*. Beverly Hills, CA: Sage.

Chiriboga, D. A. (1979, November). *Marital separation in early and late life: A comparison*. Paper presented at the meeting of the Gerontological Society, Dallas.

Christensen, H., & Hendersen, A. S. (1991). Is age kinder to the initially more able? A study of eminent scientists and academics. *Psychological Medicine, 21*, 935–946.

Christenson, C., & Gagnon, J. (1965). Sexual behavior in a group of older women. *Journal of Gerontology, 20*, 351–356.

Christenson, C., & Johnson, A. B. (1973). Sexual patterns in a group of older never-married women. *Journal of Geriatric Psychiatry, 6*, 80–98.

Cicirelli, V. G. (1981). *Helping elderly parents: The role of adult children*. Boston: Auburn House.

Clarke, R. F., & Goate, A. M. (1993). Molecular genetics of Alzheimer's disease. *Archives of Neurology, 50*, 1164–1167.

Cleek, M. D., & Pearson, T. A. (1985). Perceived causes of divorce: An analysis of interrelationships. *Journal of Marriage and the Family, 47*, 179–191.

Cleveland, J. N., & Shore, L. M. (1996). Work and employment. In J. E. Birren (Ed.), *Encyclopedia of gerontology*, Vol. 2 (pp. 627–639). New York: Academic Press

Cohen, D., & Eisdorfer, C. (1986). *The loss of self: A family resource for the care of Alzheimer's disease and related disorders*. New York: Norton.

Cohen, G., & Faulkner, D. (1989). Age differences in source forgetting: Effects on reality monitoring and on eyewitness testimony. *Psychology and Aging, 4*, 10–17.

Cohen, S., Kessler, R. C., & Gordon, L. U. (1995). Strategies for measuring stress in studies of psychiatric and physical disorders. In S. Cohen & L. U. Gordon (Eds.), *Measuring stress* (pp. 3–26). New York: Oxford University Press.

Comfort, A. (1964). *Aging: The biology of senescence*. New York: Holt, Rinehart and Winston.

Comptroller General of the United States. (1979). *Report to Congress: Hospice care—a growing concept in the United States*. Washington, DC: General Accounting Office.

Conte, H. R., Weiner, M. B., & Plutchik, R. (1982). Measuring death anxiety: Conceptual, psychometric, and factor analytic aspects. *Journal of Personality and Social Psychology, 43*, 775–785.

Cook, T. D., & Campbell, D. T. (1979). *Quasi-experimentation: Design and analysis issues for field settings.* Chicago: Rand McNally.

Corso, J. F. (1987). Sensory-perceptual processes and aging. In K. W. Schaie & C. Eisdorfer (Eds.), Annual review of gerontology and geriatrics, Vol. 7 (pp. 29–55). New York: Springer.

Costa, P. T., Jr., & McCrae, R. R. (1976). Age differences in personality structure: A cluster analytic approach. *Journal of Gerontology, 31,* 564–570.

Costa, P. T., Jr., & McCrae, R. R. (1978). Objective personality assessment. In M. Storandt, I. C. Siegler, & M. F. Elias (Eds.), *The clinical psychology of aging.* New York: Plenum.

Costa, P. T., Jr., & McCrae, R. R. (1980). Still stable after all these years: Personality as a key to some issues in adulthood and old age. In P. B. Baltes & O. G. Brim, Jr. (Eds.), *Life-span development and behavior* (Vol. 3). New York: Academic Press.

Costa, P. T., Jr., & McCrae, R. R. (1995). Primary traits of Eysenck's P-E-N system: Three- and five-factor solutions. *Journal of Personality and Social Psychology, 69,* 308–317.

Costa, P. T., Jr., Somerfield, M. R., & McCrae, R. R. (1996). Personality and coping: A reconceptualization. In M. Zeidner & N. S. Endler (Eds.), *Handbook of coping: Theory, research, applications* (pp. 44–61). New York: Wiley.

Costa, P. T., Jr., Zonderman, A. B., & McCrae, R. R. (1983). *Longitudinal course of social support in the Baltimore Longitudinal Study of Aging.* Paper presented at the NATO Advanced Workshop: Social Support Theory, Research, and Application, Château de Bonas, France.

Cotman, C. W. (1990). Synaptic plasticity, neurotrophic factors, and transplantation in aged brain. In E. L. Schneider & J. W. Rowe (Eds.), *Handbook of the biology of aging* (3rd ed.). New York: Academic Press.

Cotman, C. W., & Neeper, S. (1995). Activity-dependent plasticity and the aging brain. In E. L. Schneider & J. W. Rowe (Eds.), *Handbook of the biology of aging* (4th ed.). New York: Academic Press.

Cotton, A. (1996–1997). Is there a relationship between death anxiety and engagement in lethal behaviors among African-American students? *Omega: Journal of Death and Dying, 34,* 233–246.

Craik, F. I. M., & Salthouse, T. A. (Eds.). (1992). *Handbook of aging and cognition.* Hillsdale, NJ: Erlbaum.

Darley, J. M., Glucksberg, S., Kamin, L. J., & Kinchla, R. A. (1981). *Psychology.* Englewood Cliffs, NJ: Prentice-Hall.

DaSilva, A., & Schork, M. (1984–1985). Gender differences in attitudes to death among a group of public health students. *Omega: Journal of Death and Dying, 15,* 77–84.

Deci, E. L., & Ryan, R. M. (1985). *Intrinsic motivation and self-determination in human behavior.* New York: Plenum.

Delongis, A., Coyne, J. C., Dakof, B., Folkman, S., & Lazarus, R. S. (1982). Relationship of daily hassles, uplifts, and major life events to health status. *Health Psychology, 1,* 119–136.

Desrosiers, J., Hebert, R., Bravo, G., & Dutil, E. (1996). Hand sensibility of healthy older people. *Journal of the American Geriatrics Society, 44,* 974–978.

DeVries, H. M. (1996). Cognitive-behavioral interventions. In J. E. Birren (Ed.), *Encyclopedia of gerontology,* Vol. 1 (pp. 289–297). New York: Academic Press.

Dickinson, G. E., & Pearson, A. A. (1979). Differences in attitudes toward terminal patients among selected medical specialties of physicians. *Medical Care, 17,* 682–685.

Dickinson, G. E., & Pearson, A. A. (1980–1981). Death education and the physicians' attitudes toward dying patients. *Omega: Journal of Death and Dying, 11,* 167–174.

Doering, M., Rhodes, S. R., & Schuster, M. (1983). *The aging worker: Research and recommendations.* Beverly Hills, CA; Sage.

Doka, K. J. (1995–1996). Coping with life-threatening illness: A task model. *Omega: Journal of Death and Dying, 32,* 111–122.

Doty, R. L., Deems, D. A., & Stellar, S. (1988). Olfactory dysfunction in Parkinsonism: A general deficit unrelated to neurologic signs, disease stage, or disease duration. *Neurology, 38*, 1237–1244.

Douvan, E. (1979). Differing views on marriage 1957 to 1976. *Newsletter, Center for Continuing Education of Women (University of Michigan), 12*, 1–2.

Earles, J. L., & Coon, V. E. (1994). Adult age differences in long-term memory for performed activities. *Journal of Gerontology: Psychological Sciences, 49*, P32–P34.

Eisdorfer, C. (1977). Stress, disease, and cognitive change in the aged. In C. Eisdorfer & R. O. Friedel (Eds.), *Cognitive and emotional disturbance in the elderly*. Chicago: Yearbook Medical Publishers.

Ekerdt, D. J., Baden, L., Bossé, R., & Dibbs, E. (1983). The effect of retirement on physical health. *American Journal of Public Health, 73*, 779–783.

Ekerdt, D. J., Bossé, R., & Levkoff, S. (1985). An empirical test for phases of retirement: Findings from the normative aging study. *Journal of Gerontology, 40*, 96–101.

Elliott, G. R., & Eisdorfer, C. (Eds.). (1982). *Stress and human health*. New York: Springer.

Elster, J. (1983). *Sour grapes: Studies in the subversion of rationality*. Cambridge, UK: Cambridge University Press.

Endicott, J., & Spitzer, R. L. (1978). A diagnostic interview: The Schedule for Affective Disorders in Schizophrenia. *Archives of General Psychiatry, 35*, 837–844.

Erikson, E. H. (1963). *Childhood and society* (2nd ed.). New York: Norton.

Erikson, E. H. (1968). *Identity: Youth and crisis*. New York: Norton.

Evans, P. A. L., & Bartolomé, F. (1980). The relationship between professional life and private life. In C. B. Derr (Ed.), *Work, family, and the career: New frontiers in theory and research*. New York: Praeger.

Evans, R. I. (1970). *Gordon Allport: The man and his ideas*. New York: E. P. Dutton.

Ewen, R. B. (1984). Personality theories. In R. J. Corsini (Ed.), *The encyclopedia of psychology*. New York: Wiley.

Ewen, R. B. (1988). *An introduction to theories of personality* (3rd ed.). Hillsdale, NJ: Erlbaum.

Eysenck, H. J. (1967). *The biological basis of personality*. Springfield, IL: Charles C. Thomas.

Eysenck, H. J., & Eysenck, S. B. G. (1969). *Personality structure and measurement*. London: Routledge & Kegan.

Farrell, M. P., & Rosenberg, S. D. (1981). *Men at midlife*. Boston: Auburn House.

Feifel, H. (1974). Religious conviction and fear of death among the healthy and the terminally ill. *Journal for the Scientific Study of Religion, 13*, 353–360.

Feifel, H. (1990). Psychology and death: Meaningful rediscovery. *American Psychologist, 45*, 537–543.

Feifel, H., & Branscomb, A. (1973). Who's afraid of death? *Journal of Abnormal Psychology, 81*, 282–288.

Feifel, H., Freilich, J., & Hermann, L. (1973). Death fear in dying heart and cancer patients. *Journal of Psychosomatic Research, 17*, 161–166.

Feifel, H., Hanson, S., Jones, R., & Edwards, L. (1967). Physicians consider death. *Proceedings of the 75th Annual Convention of the American Psychological Association, 2*, 201–202.

Feifel, H., & Heller, J. (1960). Normalcy, illness, and death. In *Proceedings of the Third World Congress of Psychiatry*. Toronto: University of Toronto Press.

Feifel, H., & Hermann, L. (1973). Fear of death in the mentally ill. *Psychological Reports, 33*, 931–938.

Feifel, H., & Nagy, V. T. (1980). Death orientation and life-threatening behavior. *Journal of Abnormal Psychology, 89*, 38–45.

Felton, B., & Kahana, E. (1974). Adjustment and situationally-bound locus of control among institutionalized aged. *Journal of Gerontology, 29*, 295–301.

Felton, B., & Revenson, T. A. (1987). Age differences in coping with chronic illness. *Psychology and Aging, 2,* 164–170.

Fillenbaum, G. G., George, L. K., & Palmore, E. B. (1985). Determinants and consequences of retirement among men of different races and economic levels. *Journal of Gerontology, 40,* 85–94.

Finch, C. E. (1977). Neuroendocrine and anatomic aspects of aging. In C. E. Finch & L. Hayflick (Eds.), *Handbook of the biology of aging.* New York: Van Nostrand Reinhold.

Finch, C. E., & Landfield, P. W. (1985). Neuroendocrine and autonomic functions in aging mammals. In C. E. Finch & E. L. Schneider (Eds.), *Handbook of the biology of aging* (2nd ed.). New York: Van Nostrand Reinhold.

Fischman, J. (1984). The mystery of Alzheimer's. *Psychology Today, 18*(1), 27.

Fleg, J. L., & Lakatta, E. G. (1988). Role of muscle loss in the age-associated reduction in VO_2 max. *Journal of Applied Psychology, 65,* 1147–1151.

Florian, V., & Har-Even, D. (1983–1984). Fear of personal death: The effects of sex and religious belief. *Omega: Journal of Death and Dying, 14,* 83–91.

Flynn, J. R. (1987). Massive IQ gains in 14 nations: What IQ tests really measure. *Psychological Bulletin, 101,* 171–191.

Fobair, P., & Cortoba, C. (1982). Scope and magnitude of the cancer problem in psychosocial research. In J. Cohen et al. (Eds.), *Psychosocial aspects of cancer* (pp. 9–15). New York: Raven Press.

Folkman, S., & Lazarus, R. S. (1980). An analysis of coping in a middle-aged community sample. *Journal of Health and Social Behavior, 21,* 219–239.

Folkman, S., Lazarus, R. S., Pimley, S., & Novacek, J. (1987). Age differences in stress and coping processes. *Psychology and Aging, 2,* 171–184.

Folstein, M. F., Folstein, S. E., & McHugh, P. R. (1975). "Mini-mental state": A practical method for grading the cognitive state of patients for the clinician. *Journal of Psychiatric Research, 12,* 189–198.

Fozard, J. L. (1990). Vision and hearing. In J. E. Birren & K. W. Schaie (Eds.), *Handbook of the psychology of aging* (3rd ed.) (pp. 150–170). New York: Academic Press.

Freese, A. S. (1980). *Stroke: The new hope and the new help.* New York: Random House.

Freud, S. (1959). *Inhibitions, symptoms, and anxiety.* (Original publication: 1926). Paperback reprint, New York: Norton.

Freud, S. (1963). *Mourning and melancholia.* (Original publication: 1917). Paperback reprint: General psychological theory. New York: Collier.

Freud, S. (1965a). *Three essays on the theory of sexuality.* (Original publication: 1905). Standard edition: London: Hogarth Press, Vol. 7. Paperback reprint: New York: Avon Books.

Freud, S. (1965b). *New introductory lectures on psychoanalysis.* (Original publication: 1933). Standard edition: London, Hogarth Press, Vol. 22. Paperback reprint: New York: Norton.

Freud, S. (1965c). *The interpretation of dreams.* (Original publication: 1900). Paperback reprint: New York: Avon Books.

Freud, S. (1966). *Introductory lectures on psychoanalysis* (rev. ed.). (Original publication: 1916–1917). Standard edition: London: Hogarth Press, Vol. 15–16. Paperback reprint: New York: Norton.

Frick, M. H., Elo, O., Haapa, K., et al. (1987). Helsinki heart study: Primary-prevention trial with gemfibrozil in middle-aged men with dyslipidemia: Safety of treatment, changes in risk factors, and incidence of coronary heart disease. *New England Journal of Medicine, 317,* 1237–1245.

Friedman, H. S., & Booth-Kewley, S. (1988). Validity of Type A construct: A reprise. *Psychological Bulletin, 104,* 318–384.

Friedman, M., & Rosen, R. (1974). *Type A behavior and your heart.* New York: Knopf.

Frisancho, A. R. (1984). New standards of weight and body composition by frame size and height for assessment of nutritional status of adults and the elderly. *American Journal of Clinical Nutrition, 84,* 808–819.

Fristoe, N. M., Salthouse, T. A., & Woodard, J. L. (1997). Examination of age-related deficits on the Wisconsin Card Shorting Test. *Neuropsychology, 11,* 428–436.

Fromm, E. (1951). *The forgotten language: An introduction to the understanding of dreams, fairy tales, and myths.* New York: Holt, Rinehart and Winston.

Frontera, W. R., Meredith, C. N., O'Reilly, K. P., Knuttgen, H. G., & Evans, W. J. (1988). Strength conditioning in older men: Skeletal muscle hypertrophy and improved function. *Journal of Applied Psychology, 64,* 1038–1044.

Gallagher, D., & Thompson, L. W. (1983). Depression. In P. M. Lewinsohn & L. Teri (Eds.), *Clinical geropsychology: New directions in assessment and treatment.* New York: Pergamon Press.

Gallagher, D., & Thompson, L. W. (1989). Bereavement and adjustment disorders. In E. W. Busse & D. G. Blazer (Eds.), *Geriatric psychiatry* (pp. 459–473). Washington, DC: American Psychiatric Press.

Gallagher, M., & Rapp, P. R. (1997). The use of animal models to study the effects of aging on cognition. *Annual Review of Psychology, 48,* 339–370.

Gardner, H. (1983). *Frames of mind.* New York: Basic Books.

Garstecki, D. (1981). Aural rehabilitation for the aging adult. In D. Beasley & G. A. Davis (Eds.), *Aging: Communication processes and disorders.* New York: Grune & Stratton.

Gatz, M., & Siegler, I. C. (1981, August). *Locus of control: A retrospective.* Paper presented at the American Psychological Association Meetings, Los Angeles.

George, L. K. (1989). Social and economic factors. In E. W. Busse & D. G. Blazer (Eds.), *Geriatric psychiatry.* Washington, DC: American Psychiatric Press.

George, L. K. (1995). Social factors and illness. In R. H. Binstock & L. K. George (Eds.), *Handbook of aging and the social sciences* (4th ed.) (pp. 229–252). New York: Academic Press.

Geppert, U., & Heckhausen, H. (1990). Ontogenese der Emotion [Ontogneesis of emotion]. In K. R. Scherer (Ed.), *Ensyklopadie der Psychologie,* Vol. C/IV/3, Psychologie der Emotionen (pp. 115–213). Gottingen: Hogrefe.

Gescheider, G. A., Bolanowski, S. J., Hall, K. L., & Hoffman, K. E. (1994). The effects of aging on information-processing channels in the sense of touch: I. Absolute sensitivity. *Somatosensory and Motor Research, 11,* 345–357.

Gilmore, G. C. (1996). Perception. In J. E. Birren (Ed.), *Encyclopedia of gerontology,* Vol. 2 (pp. 271–279). New York: Academic Press.

Gleitman, H. (1983). *Basic psychology.* New York: Norton.

Glick, I. O., Weiss, R. S., & Parkes, C. M. (1974). *The first year of bereavement.* New York: Wiley.

Goldberg, E. L., & Comstock, G. W. (1980). Epidemiology of life events: Frequency in general populations. *American Journal of Epidemiology, 111,* 736–752.

Gore, S., & Mangione, T. W. (1983). Social roles, sex roles, and psychological distress: Additive and interactive models of sex differences. *Journal of Health and Social Behavior, 24,* 300–312.

Gould, R. (1972). The phases of adult life: A study in developmental psychology. *American Journal of Psychiatry, 129,* 521–531.

Gould, R. (1978). *Transformations: Growth and change in adult life.* New York: Simon & Schuster.

Greer, D., & Mor, V. (1983). *A preliminary final report of the National Hospice Study.* Providence, RI: Brown University.

Gurland, B. J. (1982). The assessment of the mental health status of older adults. In J. E. Birren & R. B. Sloane (Eds.), *Handbook of mental health and aging*. Englewood Cliffs, NJ: Prentice-Hall.

Gurland, B. J., Copeland, J., Kuriansky, J., Kelleger, M., Sharpe, L., & Dean, L. (1983). *The mind and mood of aging*. New York: Haworth Press.

Gurland, B. J., & Toner, J. A. (1982). Depression in the elderly: A review of recently published studies. In C. Eisdorfer (Ed.), *Annual review of gerontology and geriatrics* (Vol. 3). New York: Springer.

Hagestad, G. (1978). *Patterns of communication and influence between grandparents and grandchildren in a changing society*. Paper presented at the World Congress of Sociology, Sweden.

Hagestad, G. (1980). *Role change and socialization in adulthood: The transition to the empty nest*. Unpublished manuscript. State College: Pennsylvania State University.

Hagestad, G. (1985). Continuity and connectedness. In V. L. Bengtson & J. F. Robertson (Eds.), *Grandparenthood*. Beverly Hills, CA: Sage.

Hagnell, O., Lanke, J., Rorsman, B., Ohman, R., & Ojesjio, (1983). Current trends in the incidence of senile and multi-infarct dementia: A prospective study of a total population followed over 25 years. The Lundby study. *ARCHIV für Psychiatrie und Nervenbrankheiten, 233*, 423–438.

Hampson, S. (1995). Personality. In A. S. R. Mansted & M. Hewstone (Eds.), *The Blackwell encyclopedia of social psychology* (pp. 437–442). Oxford, UK: Blackwell.

Handal, P. J., Peal, R. L., Napoli, J. G., & Austrin, H. R. (1984–1985). The relationship between direct and indirect measures of death anxiety. *Omega: Journal of Death and Dying, 15*, 245–262.

Hareven, T. (1996). Life course. In J. E. Birren (Ed.), *Encyclopedia of gerontology*, Vol. 2 (pp. 31–40). New York: Academic Press.

Harkins, S. W., Price, D. D., & Martelli, M. (1986). Effects of age in pain perception: Thermonociception. *Journal of Gerontology, 41*, 58–63.

Harkins, S. W., & Scott, R. B. (1996), Pain and presbyalgos. In J. E. Birren (Ed.), *Encyclopedia of gerontology*, Vol. 2 (pp. 247–279). New York: Academic Press.

Harridge, S. D. R., & Saltin, B. (1996). Neuromuscular system. In J. E. Birren (Ed.), *Encyclopedia of gerontology*, Vol. 2 (pp. 211–220). New York: Academic Press.

Harris, L., & Associates. (1975). *The myth and reality of aging*. Washington, DC: National Council on the Aging.

Harris, L. & Associates. (1981). *Aging in the eighties: America in transition*. Washington, DC: National Council on the Aging.

Hashtroudi, S., Johnson, M. K., & Chrosniak, L. D. (1990). Aging and qualitative characteristics of memories for perceived and imagined complex events. *Psychology and Aging, 5*, 119–126.

Hatfield, E., & Sprecher, S. (1986). *Mirror, mirror: The importance of looks in everyday life*. Albany: State University of New York Press.

Hayflick, L. (1980). Cell aging. In C. Eisdorfer (Ed.), *Annual review of gerontology and geriatrics* (Vol. 1). New York: Springer.

Hayflick, L. (1986). The cell biology of human aging. *Scientific American, 242*, 58–65.

Hayslip, B., Jr., Servaty, H. L., Christman, T., & Mumy, E. (1996–1997). Levels of death anxiety in terminally ill persons: A cross validation and extension. *Omega: Journal of Death and Dying, 34*, 203–219.

Hayslip, B., Jr., & Sterns, H. L. (1979). Age differences in relationships between crystallized and fluid intelligence in problem solving. *Journal of Gerontology, 34*, 404–414.

Hazzard, W. R., & Bierman, E. L. (1978). Old age. In D. W. Smith, E. L. Bierman, & N. M. Robinson (Eds.), *The biologic ages of man*. Philadelphia: W. B. Saunders.

Heckhausen, H. (1984). Emergent achievement behavior: Some early developments. In J. Nicholls (Ed.), *The development of achievement motivation*, Vol. 3 (pp. 1–32). Greenwich, CT: JAI Press.

Heckhausen, J., & Schulz, R. (1995). A life-course theory of control. *Psychological Review*, *102*, 284–304.

Heglin, H. (1956). Problem solving set in different age groups. *Journal of Gerontology*, *11*, 310–317.

Hendricks, J. (Ed.). (1995). *The ties of later life*. Amityville, NY: Baywood.

Hendrie, H., Callahan, C., Levitt, E., Hi, S., Musick, B., Austrom, M., Nurnberger, J., Jr., & Tierney, W. (1995). Prevalence rates of major depressive disorders: The effects of varying the diagnostic criteria in an older primary care population. *American Journal of Geriatric Psychiatry*, *3*, 119–131.

Hertzog, C., Dixon, R. A., & Hultsch, D. F. (1990). Relationship between metamemory, memory predictions, and memory task performance in adults. *Psychology and Aging*, *5*, 215–227.

Hertzog, C., Schaie, K. W., & Gribben, K. (1978). Cardiovascular changes in intellectual functioning from middle to old age. *Journal of Gerontology*, *33*, 872–883.

Hess, B. (1972). Friendship. In M. Riley, M. Johnson, & A. Foner (Eds.), *Aging and society: Vol. 3. A sociology of age stratification*. New York: Russell Sage Foundation.

Hetherington, B. M., Cox, M., & Cox, R. (1977). The aftermath of divorce. In J. H. Stevens, Jr., & M. Mathews (Eds.), *Mother-child, father-child relations*. Washington, DC: National Association for the Education of Young Children.

Hills, B. L. (1980). Vision, visibility, and perception in driving. *Perception*, *9*, 183–216.

Hirsch, B. J. (1981). Social networks and the coping process: Creating personal communities. In B. H. Gottlieb (Ed.), *Social networks and social support*. Beverly Hills, CA: Sage.

Hoerr, S. O. (1963). Thoughts on what to tell the patient with cancer. *Cleveland Clinic Quarterly*, *30*, 11–16.

Hoffman, L. W., & Manis, J. (1978). Influences of children on marital interaction and parental satisfaction and dissatisfaction. In R. Lerner & G. Spanier (Eds.), *Child influences on marital and family interaction*. New York: Academic Press.

Holden, C. (1976). Hospices: For the dying, relief from pain and fear. *Science*, *193*, 389–391.

Holmes, H. H., & Rahe, R. H. (1967). The social readjustment rating scale. *Journal of Psychosomatic Research*, *11*(2), 213–218.

Holt, R. R. (1982). Occupational stress. In L. Goldberger & S. Breznitz (Eds.), *Handbook of stress*. New York: Free Press.

Hooper, F. H., Hooper, J. O., & Colbert, K. C. (1984). *Personality and memory correlates of intellectual functioning*. Basel: Karger.

Horn, J. (1974). Regriefing: A way to end pathological mourning. *Psychology Today*, *1*(2), 184.

Horn, J. L., & Hofer, S. M. (1992). Major abilities and development in the adult period. In R. J. Sternberg & C. A. Berg (Eds.), *Intellectual development* (pp. 44–99). New York: Cambridge University Press.

Horvath, T. B., & Davis, K. L. (1990). Central nervous system disorders in aging. In E. L. Schneider & J. W. Rowe (Eds.), *Handbook of the biology of aging* (3rd ed.) (pp. 306–329). New York: Academic Press.

House, J. S., Robbins, C., & Metzner, H. L. (1982). The association of social relationships and activities with mortality: Prospective evidence from the Tecumseh Community Health Study. *American Journal of Epidemiology*, *116*, 123–140.

Howard, D. V. (1996). The aging of implicit and explicit memory. In F. Blanchard-Fields & T. M. Hess (Eds.), *Perspectives on cognitive change in adulthood and aging* (pp. 221–254). New York: McGraw-Hill.

Hugin, F., Norris, A., & Schock, N. (1960). Skin reflex and voluntary reaction time in young and old males. *Journal of Gerontology, 15,* 388–391.

Hultsch, D. F., & Dixon, R. A. (1990). Learning and memory in aging. In J. E. Birren & K. W. Schaie (Eds.), *Handbook of the psychology of aging* (3rd ed.) (pp. 259–274). New York: Academic Press.

Hunt, E., & Hertzog, C. (1981). *Age-related changes in cognition during the working years.* Arlington, VA: Office of Naval Research.

Hyman, H. H. (1983). *Of time and widowhood.* Durham, NC: Duke University Press Policy Studies.

Idler, E. L., & Angel, R. J. (1990). Self-rated health and mortality in the NHANES-I epidemiologic follow-up study. *American Journal of Public Health, 80,* 446–452.

Idler, E. L., Kasl, S. V., & Lemke, J. H. (1990). Self-evaluated health and mortality among the elderly in New Haven, Connecticut, and Iowa and Washington counties, Iowa, 1982–1986. *American Journal of Epidemiology, 131,* 91–103.

Institute of Medicine. (1992). *Extending life, enhancing life: A national research agenda on aging.* Washington, DC: National Academy Press.

Jenike, M. A. (1989). *Geriatric psychiatry and psychopharmacology.* Chicago: Year Book Medical.

Jenkins, C. D. (1974, June 22). Behavior that triggers heart attacks. *Science News, 105*(25), 402.

Jenkins, C. D. (1975). The coronary-prone personality. In W. D. Gentry & R. B. Williams (Eds.), *Psychological aspects of myocardial infarction and coronary care.* St. Louis: Mosby.

Joyce, C. (1984). A time for grieving. *Psychology Today, 18*(11), 42–46.

Jung, C. G. (1910). *The association method.* (Original publication). Standard edition: Princeton, NJ: Princeton University Press, Vol. 2.

Jung, C. G. (1931). *The aims of psychotherapy.* (Original publication). Standard edition: Princeton, NJ: Princeton University Press, Vol. 16.

Jung, C. G. (1933). *Modern man in search of a soul.* New York: Harcourt, Brace & World.

Jung, C. G. (1964). *Man and his symbols.* London: Aldus Books.

Jung, C. G. (1971). *The stages of life.* (Original publication: 1930–1931). Paperback reprint: *The portable Jung.* New York: Viking.

Jung, C. G. (1972). *Two essays on analytical psychology.* (Original publication: 1917, 1928). Paperback reprint: Princeton, NJ: Princeton University Press.

Jung, C. G. (1976). *Psychological types.* (Original publication: 1921). Paperback reprint: Princeton, NJ: Princeton University Press.

Jung, C. G. (1984). *Psychoanalysis and association experiments.* (Original publication: 1905). Standard edition: Princeton, NJ: Princeton University Press, Vol. 2.

Kahana, B. (1976). Social and psychological aspects of sexual behavior among the aged. In E. S. E. Hafez (Ed.), *Aging and reproductive physiology* (Vol. 2). Ann Arbor, MI: Ann Arbor Science.

Kahn, R. L. (1981). *Work and health.* New York: Wiley.

Kalick, S. M., Zebrowitz, L. A., Langlois, J. H., & Johnson, R. M. (1998). Does human facial attractiveness honestly advertise health? *Psychological Science, 9,* 8–13.

Kalish, R. A. (1981). *Death, grief, and caring relationships.* Monterey, CA: Brooks/Cole.

Kaplan, M. F., & Anderson, N. H. (1973). Information integration theory and reinforcement theory as approaches to interpersonal attraction. *Journal of Personality and Social Psychology, 28,* 301–312.

Kasl, S. (1983). Pursuing the link between stressful life experiences and disease: A time for reappraisal. In C. L. Cooper (Ed.), *Stress research: Issues for the eighties.* New York: Wiley.

Kasl, S., & Berkman, L. F. (1981). Some psychosocial influences on the health status of the elderly: The perspective of social epidemiology. In J. L. McGaugh & S. B. Kiesler (Eds.), *Aging: Biology and behavior*. New York: Academic Press.

Kastenbaum, R. (1995). Suicide. In G. Maddox (Ed.), *Encyclopedia of aging*, 2nd ed. (pp. 915–916). New York: Springer.

Kastenbaum, R., & Aisenberg, R. (1972). *The psychology of death*. New York: Springer.

Kastenbaum, R., & Costa, P. T. (1977). Psychological perspectives on death. *Annual Review of Psychology*, *28*, 225–241.

Kastenbaum, R., & Weisman, A. D. (1972). The psychological autopsy as a research procedure in gerontology. In D. P. Dent, R. Kastenbaum, & S. Sherwood (Eds.), *Research planning and action for the elderly*. New York: Behavioral Publications.

Kausler, D. H. (1982). *Experimental psychology and human aging*. New York: Wiley.

Kay, D. W. K., & Bergmann, K. (1982). Epidemiology of mental disorders among the aged in the community. In J. E. Birren & R. B. Sloane (Eds.), *Handbook of mental health and aging*. Englewood Cliffs, NJ: Prentice-Hall.

Keith, P. M., Schafer, R. B., & Wacker, R. (1992–1993). Outcomes of equity/inequity among older spouses. *International Journal of Aging and Human Development*, *36*, 187–197.

Keller, M. L., Leventhal, H., Prohaska, T. R., & Leventhal, E. A. (1989). Beliefs about aging and illness in a community sample. *Research in Nursing and Health*, *12*, 247–255.

Kelly, J. (1977). The aging male homosexual. *The Gerontologist*, *17*, 328–332.

Kelly, J. B., & Wallerstein, J. S. (1976). The effects of parental divorce: Experiences of child in early latency. *American Journal of Orthopsychiatry*, *46*, 20–32.

Kennedy, G. J., Kelman, J. R., & Thomas, C. (1990). The emergence of depressive symptoms in late life: The importance of declining health and increasing disability. *Journal of Community Health*, *15*, 93–104.

Kenshalo, D. R. (1977). Age changes in touch, vibration, temperature, kinesthesis, and pain sensitivity. In J. E. Birren & K. W. Schaie (Eds.), *Handbook of the psychology of aging*. New York: Van Nostrand Reinhold.

Kerson, T. S. (1985). Heart disease. In T. S. Kerson & W. L. Kerson (Eds.), *Understanding chronic illness: The medical and psychosocial dimension of nine diseases* (pp. 149–186). New York: Free Press.

Kessler, R. C., & McCrae, J. A. (1981). Trends in the relationship between sex and psychological distress. *American Sociological Review*, *46*, 443–452.

Kimbrell, G. McA., & Furchgott, E. (1963). The effect of aging on olfactory threshold. *Journal of Gerontology*, *18*, 364–365.

Kimmel, D. C. (1977). Patterns of aging among gay men. *Christopher Street*, *2*, 28–31.

Kimmel, D. C. (1980). *Adulthood and aging: An interdisciplinary developmental view* (2nd ed.). New York: Wiley.

Kinsey, A. C., Pomeroy, W. B., Martin, C. E., & Gebhard, P. H. (1953). *Sexual behavior in the human female*. Philadelphia: W. B. Saunders.

Kirkwood, T. B. L. (1985). Comparative and evolutionary aspects of longevity. In C. E. Finch & E. L. Schneider (Eds.), *Handbook of the biology of aging* (2nd ed.). New York: Van Nostrand Reinhold.

Kivnick, H. Q. (1982). Grandparenthood: An overview of meaning and mental health. *The Gerontologist*, *22*, 59–66.

Kivnick, H. Q., & Sinclair, H. M. (1996). Grandparenthood. In J. E. Birren (Ed.), *Encyclopedia of gerontology*, Vol. 1 (pp. 611–623). New York: Academic Press.

Kiyak, A., Liang, J., & Kahana, E. (1976, August). *Methodological inquiry into the schedule of recent life events*. Paper presented at an annual meeting of the American Psychological Association, Washington, DC.

Klein, H. A. & Shaffer, K. (1986). Aging and memory in skilled language performance. *Journal of Genetic Psychology, 146,* 389–397.

Klerman, G. L. (1983). Problems in the definition and diagnosis of depression. In L. D. Breslau & M. R. Haug (Eds.), *Depression and aging: Causes, care, and consequences.* New York: Springer.

Kliegl, R., & Baltes, P. B. (1987). Theory-guided analysis of mechanisms of development and aging through testing-the-limits and research on expertise. In C. Schooler & K. W. Schaie (Eds.), *Cognitive functioning and social structure over the life course* (pp. 95–119). Norwood, NJ: Ablex.

Kliegl, R., Smith, J., & Baltes, P. B. (1989). Testing-the-limits and the study of adult age differences in cognitive plasticity of a mnemonic skill. *Developmental Psychology, 25,* 247–256.

Kliegl, R., Smith, J., & Baltes, P. B. (1990). On the locus and process of magnification of age differences during mnemonic training. *Developmental Psychology, 26,* 894–904.

Kligman, A. M., Grove, A. L., & Balin, A. K. (1985). Aging of human skin. In C. E. Finch & E. L. Schneider (Eds.), *Handbook of the biology of aging* (2nd ed.). New York: Van Nostrand Reinhold.

Kline, D. W., & Scialfa, C. T. (1996). Visual and auditory aging. In J. E. Birren & K. W. Schaie (Eds.), *Handbook of the psychology of aging* (4th ed.) (pp. 181–203).

Kline, D. W., & Szafran, J. (1975). Age differences in backward monoptic visual noise making. *Journal of Gerontology, 30,* 307–311.

Kobrin, F. E. (1976). The primary individual and the family: Changes in living arrangements in the U.S. since 1940. *Journal of Marriage and the Family, 38,* 233–239.

Koenig, H. G. (1995). *Research on religion and aging.* Westport, CT: Greenwood Press.

Koenig, H. G., & Blazer, D. G. (1996). Depression. In J. E. Birren (Ed.), *Encyclopedia of gerontology,* Vol. 1 (pp. 415–428). New York: Academic Press.

Koenig, H. G., George, L. K., & Siegler, I. C. (1988). The use of religion and other emotion-regulating coping strategies among older adults. *The Gerontologist, 28,* 303–310.

Kohler, T., & Haimerl, C. (1990). Daily stress as a trigger of migraine attacks: Results of thirteen single subject studies. *Journal of Consulting and Clinical Psychology, 58,* 870–872.

Kolodny, R. C., Masters, W. H., & Johnson, V. E. (1979). *Textbook of sexual medicine.* Boston: Little, Brown.

Kosnik, W., Winslow, L., Kline, D., Rasinski, K., & Sekuler, R. (1988). Visual changes in daily life. *Journal of Gerontology, 43,* 863–870.

Kraus, A. S., & Lilienfeld, A. N. (1959). Some epidemiological aspects of the high mortality rate in the young widowed group. *Journal of Chronic Diseases, 10,* 207–217.

Kryter, K. (1970). *The effects of noise on man.* New York: Academic Press.

Kübler-Ross, E. (1969). *On death and dying.* New York: Macmillan.

Kübler-Ross, E. (1975). *Death: The final stage of growth.* Englewood Cliffs, NJ: Prentice-Hall.

Labby, D. H. (1984). Sexuality. In C. K. Cassel & J. R. Walsh (Eds.), *Geriatric medicine: Vol. 2. Fundamentals of geriatric care.* New York: Springer-Verlag.

Labouvie-Vief, G., DeVoe, M., & Bulka, D. (1989). Speaking about feelings: Conceptions of emotion across the life span. *Psychology and Aging, 4,* 425–437.

Labouvie-Vief, G., Hakim-Larson, J., & Hobart, C. J. (1987). Age, ego level, and the life-span development of coping and defense processes. *Psychology and Aging, 2,* 286–293.

Lachman, M. E. (1983). Perceptions of intellectual aging: Antecedent or consequence of intellectual functioning? *Developmental Psychology, 19,* 482–498.

Lachman, M. E. (1985). Personal efficacy in middle and old age: Differential and normative patterns of change. In G. H. Elder, Jr. (Ed.), *Life-course dynamics: Trajectories and transitions, 1968–1980.* Ithaca, NY: Cornell University Press.

Lachman, M. E. (1986). Locus of control in aging research: A case for multidimensional and domain-specific assessment. *Journal of Psychology and Aging, 1,* 34–40.

Lachman, M. E., & Leff, R. (1989). Perceived control and intellectual functioning in the elderly: A 5-year longitudinal study. *Developmental Psychology, 25,* 722–728.

Lakatta, E. G. (1990). Heart and circulation. In E. L. Schneider & J. W. Rowe (Eds.), *Handbook of the biology of aging* (3rd ed.) (pp. 181–216). New York: Academic Press.

Larson, R. (1978). Thirty years of research on the subjective well-being of older Americans. *Journal of Gerontology, 33,* 109–125.

Larson, T., Sjogren, T., & Jacobson, G. (1963). Senile dementia: A clinical, sociomedical and genetic study. *Acta Psychiatrica Scandinavica, 39* (supplement 167), 1–259.

Last, J. M. (Ed.). (1995). *A dictionary of epidemiology.* New York: Oxford University Press.

Latham, K. R., & Johnson, L. K. (1979). Aging at the cellular level. In I. Rossman (Ed.), *Clinical geriatrics* (2nd ed.). Philadelphia: Lippincott.

Lattaner, B. A., & Hayslip, B., Jr. (1984–1985). Occupation-related differences in levels of death anxiety. *Omega: Journal of Death and Dying, 15,* 53–66.

Lauer, J., & Lauer, R. (1985). Marriages made to last. *Psychology Today, 19,* 22–26.

Lauer, R. H., Lauer, J. C., & Kerr, S. T. (1995). The long-term marriage: Perceptions of stability and satisfaction. In J. Hendricks (Ed.), *The ties of later life* (pp. 35–41). Amityville, NY: Baywood.

Lawton, M. P., Whelihan, W. M., & Belsky, J. K. (1980). Personality tests and their uses with older adults. In J. E. Birren & R. B. Sloane (Eds.), *Handbook of mental health and aging.* Englewood Cliffs, NJ: Prentice-Hall.

Lazarus, R. S. (1966). *Psychological stress and the coping process.* New York: McGraw-Hill.

Lazarus, R. S. (1971). The concepts of stress and disease. In L. Levi (Ed.), *Society, stress, and disease: The psychosocial environment and psychosomatic diseases* (Vol. 1). London: Oxford University Press.

Lee, G. R. (1985). Kinship and social support of the elderly: The case of the United States. *Aging and Society, 5,* 19–38.

Lefcourt, H. M. (1976). *Locus of control: Current trends in theory and research.* Hillsdale, NJ: Erlbaum.

Lehman, H. C. (1953). *Age and achievement.* Princeton, NJ: Princeton University Press.

Lerner, M. (1976). When, why, and where people die. In E. S. Schneidman (Ed.), *Death: Current perspectives.* Palo Alto, CA: Mayfield.

Lester, D. (1984–1985). The fear of death, sex and androgyny: A brief note. *Omega: Journal of Death and Dying, 15,* 271–274.

Levenson, H. (1974). Activism and powerful others: Distinctions within the concept of internal-external control. *Journal of Personality Assessment, 38,* 377–383.

Levinger, G. (1974). A three-level approach to attraction: Toward an understanding of pair relatedness. In T. L. Huston (Ed.), *Foundations of interpersonal attraction.* New York: Academic Press.

Levinger, G. (1978, August). *Models of close relationships: Some new directions.* Invited address presented at the annual meeting of the American Psychological Association, Toronto.

Levinson, D. J. (1978). *The seasons of a man's life.* New York: Knopf.

Levinson, D. J. (1986). A conception of adult development. *American Psychologist, 41,* 3–13.

Levinson, D. J., Darrow, C. M., Klein, E. B., Levinson, M. H., & McKee, B. (1974). The psychosocial development of men in early adulthood and midlife transition. In D. F. Ricks, A. Thomas, & M. Roff (Eds.), *Life history research in psychopathology.* Minneapolis: University of Minnesota Press.

Lieberman, M. A. (1982). The effects of social supports on response to stress. In L. Goldberger & S. Breznitz (Eds.), *Handbook of stress*. New York: Free Press.

Liegner, L. M. (1975). St. Christopher's hospice, 1974: Care of the dying patient. *Journal of the American Medical Association, 234*(10), 1047–1048.

Lindeman, R. D. (1996). Renal and urinary tract function. In J. E. Birren (Ed.), *Encyclopedia of gerontology*, Vol. 2 (pp. 407–418). New York: Academic Press.

Lindemann, E. (1944). Symptomatology and management of acute grief. *American Journal of Psychiatry, 101*, 141–148.

Lindsay, P. H., & Norman, D. A. (1977). *Human information processing* (2nd ed.) New York: Academic Press.

Linn, M. W., Hunter, K., & Harris, R. (1980). Symptoms of depression and recent life events in community elderly. *Journal of Clinical Psychology, 36*, 675–682.

Lipman, P. D., & Caplan, L. J. (1992). Adult age differences in memory for routes: Effects of instruction and spatial diagram. *Psychology and Aging, 7*, 435–442.

Littlefield, C., & Fleming, S. (1984–1985). Measuring fear of death: A multidimensional approach. *Omega: Journal of Death and Dying, 15*, 131–138.

Loevinger, J. (1976). *Ego development*. San Francisco: Jossey-Bass.

Loftus, E. F., Levidow, B., & Duensing, S. (1992). Who remembers best? Individual differences in memory for events that occurred in a science museum. *Applied Cognitive Psychology, 6*, 93–107.

Logan, R. D. (1986). A reconceptualization of Erikson's theory: The repetition of existential and instrumental themes. *Human Development, 29*, 125–136.

Lowenthal, M., Thurnher, M., & Chiriboga, D. (1975). *Four stages of life*. San Francisco: Jossey-Bass.

Lyness, J. M., Bruce, M. L., Koenig, H. G., Parmelee, P. A., Schulz, R., Lawton, P., & Reynolds, C. F., III. (1996). Depression and medical illness in late life: Report of a symposium. *Journal of the American Geriatrics Society, 44*, 198–203.

Makinodan, T. (1974). Cellular basis of immunosenescence. In *Molecular and cellular mechanisms of aging*. Paris: INSERM, Coll. Inst. Nat. Sante Rec. Med., Vol. 27.

Margolis, O. S., Raether, H. C., Kutscher, A. H., Powers, J. B., Seeland, I. B., DeBellis, R., & Cherico, D. J. (1981). *Acute grief: Counseling the bereaved*. New York: Columbia University Press.

Marshall, V. W. (1995). The state of theory in aging and the social sciences. In R. H. Binstock & L. K. George (Eds.), *Handbook of aging and the social sciences* (4th ed.) (pp. 12–30). New York: Academic Press.

Marsiske M., Lang, F. R., Baltes, P. B., & Baltes, M. M. (in press). Selective optimization with compensation: Life-span perspectives on successful human development. In R. A. Dixon & L. Backman (Eds.), *Psychological compensation: Managing losses and promoting gains*. Hillsdale, NJ: Erlbaum.

Martin, G. R., & Baker, G. T. (1993). Aging and the aged: Theories of aging and life extension. *Encyclopedia of Bioethics*. New York: Macmillan.

Martin, L. R. (1982). Overview of the psychosocial aspects of cancer. In J. Cohen et al. (Eds.), *Psychosocial aspects of cancer* (pp. 1–8). New York: Raven.

Maslow, A. H. (1968). *Toward a psychology of being* (2nd ed.). New York: Van Nostrand Reinhold.

Maslow, A. H. (1970). *Motivation and personality* (2nd ed.). New York: Harper & Row.

Mason, S. E., & Smith, A. D. (1977). Imagery in the aged. *Experimental Aging Research, 3*, 17–32.

Masters, W. H., & Johnson, V. E. (1966). *Human sexual response*. Boston: Little, Brown.

Masters, W. H., & Johnson, V. E. (1970). *Human sexual inadequacy*. Boston: Little, Brown.

Matcha, D. A., & Hutchinson, J. (1997). Location and timing of death among the elderly. *Omega: Journal of Death and Dying, 35,* 393–404.

Matlin, M. W. (1984). Perceptual development. In R. J. Corsini (Ed.), *Encyclopedia of psychology.* New York: Wiley.

Matthews, K. A. (1988). Coronary heart disease and Type A behaviors: Update on and alternative to the Booth-Kewley and Friedman (1987) quantitative review. *Psychological Bulletin, 104,* 373–380.

Matthews, S. H. (1986). *Friendships through the life course.* Newbury Park, CA: Sage.

May, R. (1967). Contributions of existential psychotherapy. In R. May, E. Angel, & H. F. Ellenberger (Eds.), *Existence: A new dimension in psychiatry and psychology* (New York: Basic Books, 1958). Paperback reprint: New York: Touchstone Books.

May, R. (1969). *Love and will.* New York: Norton.

Maylor, E. A. (1996a). Age-related impairment in an event-based prospective memory task. *Psychology and Aging, 11,* 74–78.

Maylor, E. A. (1996b). Does prospective memory decline with age? In Brandimonte, M., Einstein, G. O., & McDaniel, M. A. (Eds.), *Prospective memory: Theory and applications* (pp. 173–197). Mahwah, NJ: Erlbaum.

McCall's. (1976, September). Divorcees: The new poor, pp. 103, 120, 122, 124, 152.

McCary, J. L. (1978). *Human sexuality* (3rd ed.). New York: Van Nostrand Reinhold.

McCormick, K. (1982). *An exploration of the functions of friends and best friends.* Unpublished doctoral dissertation, Rutgers University of New Jersey.

McCrae, R. R., & Costa, P. T., Jr. (1984). *Emerging lives, enduring dispositions.* Boston: Little, Brown.

McCrae, R. R., Arenberg, D., & Costa, P. T. (1987). Declines in divergent thinking with age: Cross-sectional, longitudinal and cross-sequential analyses. *Psychology and Aging, 2,* 130–137.

McIntosh, J. L. (1988–1989). Official U.S. elderly suicide data bases: Levels, availability, omissions. *Omega: Journal of Death and Dying, 19,* 337–350.

McIntyre, J. S., & Craik, F. I. M. (1987). Age differences in memory for item and source information. *Canadian Journal of Psychology, 41,* 175–192.

McKinlay, J. B. (1981). Social network influences on morbid episodes and the career of help seeking. In L. Eisenberg & A. Kleinman (Eds.), *The relevance of social science for medicine.* Dordrecht, Holland: D. Reidel.

McLeod, J. D. (1996). Life events. In J. E. Birren (Ed.), *Encyclopedia of gerontology,* Vol. 2 (pp. 41–51). New York: Academic Press.

Meier, D. E. (1988). Skeletal aging. In B. Kent & R. Butler (Eds.), *Human aging research: Concepts and techniques* (pp. 221–244). New York: Raven.

Meinz, E. J., & Salthouse, T. A. (1998). The effects of age and experience on memory for visually presented music. *Journal of Gerontology: Psychological Sciences, 53B,* P60–P69.

Meister, K. A. (1984). The 80s search for the fountain of youth comes up very dry. *American Council on Science and Health News & Views, 9/10,* 8–11.

Miami Herald. (1984, December 14). Sense of smell fades with age, study finds, pp. 1, 16.

Michael, R. T., Fuchs, V. R., & Scott, S. R. (1980). Changes in the propensity to live alone: 1950–1976. *Demography, 17,* 39–56.

Miller, R. A. (1995). Aging and the immune response. In E. L. Schneider, & J. W. Rowe (Eds.), *Handbook of the biology of aging* (4th ed.) (pp. 355–392). New York: Academic Press.

Mischel, W. (1977). The interaction of person and situation. In D. Magnusson & N. S. Endler (Eds.), *Personality at the crossroads: Current issues in interactional psychology.* Hillsdale, NJ: Erlbaum.

Mitchell, R. E., & Trickett, E. J. (1980). Social network research and psychosocial adaptation: Implications for community mental health practice. In P. Insel (Ed.), *Environmental variables and the prevention of mental illness*. Lexington, MA: D. C. Heath.

Mobbs, C. V. (1995). Neuroendocrinology of aging. In E. L. Schneider & J. W. Rowe (Eds.), *Handbook of the biology of aging* (4th ed.) (pp. 234–283). New York: Academic Press.

Moen, P. (1995). Gender, age, and the life course. In R. H. Binstock & L. K. George (Eds.), *Handbook of aging and the social sciences* (4th ed.) (pp. 171–187). New York: Academic Press.

Moon, M. (1983). The role of the family in the economic well-being of the elderly. *The Gerontologist, 23*, 45–50.

Mor, V., & Hiris, J. (1983). Determinants of site of death among hospice cancer patients. *Journal of Health and Social Behavior, 24*, 375–385.

Morgan, D. G., & May, P. C. (1990). Age-related changes in synaptic neurochemistry. In E. L. Schneider & J. W. Rowe (Eds.), *Handbook of the biology of aging* (3rd ed.). New York: Academic Press.

Morgan, L. A. (1976). A re-examination of widowhood and morale. *Journal of Gerontology, 31*, 687–695.

Morrell, R. W., & Park, D. C. (1993). The effects of age, illustrations, and task variables on the performance of procedural assembly tasks. *Psychology and Aging, 48*, 389–399.

Morris, J. N., Mor, V., Hiris, J., & Sherwood, S. (1984). *Satisfaction with the site of death*. Paper presented at the Annual Meeting of the Gerontological Society of America, San Antonio, TX.

Morris, J. N., & Sherwood, S. (1984). Informal support sources for vulnerable elderly persons: Can they be counted on, why do they work? *International Journal of Aging and Human Development, 18*, 81–98.

Mortimer, J. A. (1988). The epidemiology of dementia: International comparisons. In J. A. Brody & G. L. Maddox (Eds.), *Epidemology and aging* (pp. 150–167). New York: Springer.

Murphy, C. (1983). Age-related effects on the threshold, psychophysical function, and pleasantness of menthol. *Journal of Gerontology, 38*, 217–222.

Murphy, C. (1985). Cognitive and chemosensory influences on age-related changes in the ability to identify blended foods. *Journal of Gerontology, 40*, 47–52.

Murstein, B. I., & Christy, P. (1976). Physical attractiveness and marriage adjustment in middle-aged couples. *Journal of Personality and Social Psychology, 34*, 537–542.

Myer, R. J. (1995). Social Security. In G. Maddox (Ed.), *The encyclopedia of aging* (2nd ed.) (pp. 876–884).

Naeim, F., & Walford, R. L. (1985). Aging and cell membrane complexes: The lipid bilayer, integral proteins, and cytoskeleton. In C. E. Finch & E. L. Schneider (Eds.), *Handbook of the biology of aging* (2nd ed.). New York: Van Nostrand Reinhold.

National Center for Health Statistics. (1984). *Health United States*. Washington, DC: U.S. Government Printing Office.

National Center for Health Statistics. (1986). *National Health Interview Survey, advance data from vital and health statistics, No. 125*. DHHS Publ. No. PHS 86-1250.

National Center for Health Statistics. (1990). *Advance report of final mortality statistics, 1988*. Monthly vital statistics report, Vol. 39, No. 7 Suppl. Hyattsville, MD: Public Health Service.

National Institute on Aging. (1989a). *Accidents and the elderly*. Bethesda, MD: U.S. Department of Health and Human Services.

National Institute on Aging. (1989b). *Aging and alcohol abuse*. Bethesda, MD: U.S. Department of Health and Human Services.

National Institute on Aging. (1989c). *Can life be extended?* Bethesda, MD: U.S. Department of Health and Human Services.

National Institute on Aging. (1989d). *Dietary supplements: More is not always better.* Bethesda, MD: U.S. Department of Health and Human Services.

National Institute on Aging. (1989e). *Don't take it easy—exercise!* Bethesda, MD: U.S. Department of Health and Human Services.

National Institute on Aging. (1989f). *High blood pressure: A common but controllable disorder.* Bethesda, MD: U.S. Department of Health and Human Services.

National Institute on Aging. (1989g). *Smoking: It's never too late to stop.* Bethesda, MD: U.S. Department of Health and Human Services.

National Institute on Aging. (1993). *In search of the secrets of aging.* Bethesda, MD: U.S. Department of Health and Human Services.

National Institute on Aging. (1998). *Menopause.* Bethesda, MD: U.S. Department of Health and Human Services. Publication No. 94-3886.

Nesselroade, J. R., & Labouvie, E. W. (1985). Experimental design in research on aging. In J. E. Birren & K. W. Schaie (Eds.), *Handbook of the psychology of aging* (2nd ed.). New York: Van Nostrand Reinhold.

Neugarten, B. L. (1977). Personality and aging. In J. E. Birren & K. W. Schaie (Eds.), *Handbook of the psychology of aging.* New York: Van Nostrand Reinhold.

Neugarten, B. L., & Associates. (Eds.). (1964). *Personality in middle and late life.* New York: Atherton.

Neugarten, B. L., Crotty, J., & Tobin, S. S. (1964). Personality types in an aged population. In B. L. Neugarten & Associates (Eds.), *Personality in middle and later life.* New York: Atherton.

Neugarten, B. L., & Gutmann, D. L. (1958). Age-sex roles and personality in middle age: A thematic apperception study. *Psychological Monographs: General and Applied, 17,* Whole No. 470.

Neugarten, B. L., Havighurst, R. J., & Tobin, S. S. (1968). Personality and pattern of aging. In B. L. Neugarten (Ed.), *Middle age and aging.* Chicago: University of Chicago Press.

Neugarten, B. L., & Weinstein, K. (1964). The changing American grandparent. *Journal of Marriage and the Family, 26,* 199–204.

Newson, J. T., & Schulz, R. (1996). Social support as a mediator in the relation between functional status and quality of life in older adults. *Psychology and Aging, 11,* 34–44.

Newsweek. (1985, April 22). The myths of comparable worth.

Newsweek. (1989, December 18). The brain killer, pp. 54-56.

Newsweek. (1990, June 18). The doctor's suicide van, pp. 46–49.

Newsweek. (1990, July 19). Trading places, pp. 48–54.

Newton, P. A., (1984). Chronic pain. In C. K. Cassel & J. R. Walsh (Eds.), *Geriatric medicine* (Vol. 2). New York: Springer-Verlag.

Nordin, S., Monsch, A., & Murphy, C. (1995). Unawareness of smell loss in normal aging and Alzheimer's disease: Discrepancy between self-reported and diagnosed smell sensitivity. *Journals of Gerontology: Psychological Sciences, 50,* P187–P192.

Northhouse, L. (1988). Social support in patient's and husband's adjustment to breast cancer. *Nursing Research, 2,* 91–95.

O'Brien, A. A. J., & Bulpitt, C. J. (1995). In G. L. Maddox (Ed.), *The encyclopedia of aging* (2nd ed.) (pp. 489–491). New York: Springer.

Okimoto, J. T., Barnes, R. F., Veith, R. C., Raskind, M. A., Inui, T. S., & Carter, W. B. (1982). Screening for depression in geriatric mental patients. *Journal of Psychiatry, 139,* 799–802.

Osterweis, M., Solomon, F., & Green. D. (Eds.). (1984). *Bereavement: Reactions, consequences, and care.* Washington, DC: National Academy Press.

Palmore, E., Fillenbaum, G. G., & George, L. K. (1984). Consequences of retirement. *Journal of Gerontology, 39,* 109–116.

Park, D. C., Morrell, R. W., Frieske, D., & Kincaid, D. (1992). Medication adherence behaviors in older adults: Effect of external cognitive supports. *Psychology and Aging, 7*, 252–256.

Parkes, C. M. (1972). *Bereavement: Studies of grief in adult life*. New York: International Universities Press.

Parkes, C. M. (1981a). Emotional involvement of the family during the period preceding death. In O. S. Margolis et al. (Eds.), *Acute grief: Counseling the bereaved*. New York: Columbia University Press.

Parkes, C. M. (1981b). Psychosocial care of the family after the patient's death. In O. S. Margolis et al. (Eds.), *Acute grief: Counseling the bereaved*. New York: Columbia University Press.

Parkes, C. M., Benjamin, B., & Fitzgerald, R. G. (1969). Broken heart: A statistical study of increased mortality among widowers. *British Medical Journal, 1*, 740–743.

Parmelee, P. A., Katz, I. R., & Lawton, M. P. (1992a). Incidence of depression in long-term care settings. *Journal of Gerontology: Medical Sciences, 46*, M189–196.

Parmelee, P. A., Katz, I. R., & Lawton, M. P. (1992b). Depression and mortality among institutionalized aged. *Journal of Gerontology: Psychological Sciences, 47*, P3–P10.

Parmelee, P. A., Katz, I. R., & Lawton, M. P. (1989). Depression among institutionalized aged: Assessment and prevalence estimation. *Journal of Gerontology: Medical Sciences, 41*, M22–29.

Parnes, H. S., & Nestel, G. (1981). The retirement experience. In H. S. Parnes (Ed.), *Work and retirement: A longitudinal study of men*. Cambridge, MA: MIT Press.

Passamani, E., Frommer, P., & Levy, R. (1984). Coronary heart disease: An overview. In N. Wenger & H. Hellerstein (Eds.), *Rehabilitation of coronary patients* (pp. 1–15). New York: Wiley.

Penninx, B. W. J. H., van Tilburg, T., Kriegsman, D. M. W., Deeg, D. J. H., & van Eijk, J. T. M. (1997). Effects of social support and personal coping resources on mortality in older age: The longitudinal aging study in Amsterdam. *American Journal of Epidemiology, 146*, 510–519.

Perry, E. K., Tomlinson, B. E., Blessed, G., Bergmann, K., Gibson, P. H., & Perry, R. H. (1978). Correlation of cholinergic abnormalities with senile plagues and mental test scores in senile dementia. *British Medical Journal, 2*, 1457–1459.

Pervin, L. A. (1990). *Handbook of personality: Theory and research*. New York: Guilford Press.

Peterson, E. T. (1989). Grandparenting. In S. J. Bahr & E. T. Peterson (Eds.), *Aging and the family* (pp. 157–174). Lexington, MA: Lexington.

Pfeiffer, E. (1974). Sexuality in the aging individual. *Journal of the American Geriatrics Society, 22*, 481–484.

Pfeiffer, E., & Davis, G. C. (1972). Determinants of sexual behavior in middle and old age. *Journal of the American Geriatrics Society, 20*, 151–158.

Pfeiffer, E., Verwoerdt, A., & Davis, G. C. (1972). Sexual behavior in middle life. *American Journal of Psychiatry, 128*, 1262–1267.

Pfieffer, E., Verwoerdt, A., & Davis, G. C. (1974). Sexual behavior in middle life. In P. Erdman (Ed.), *Normal aging II: Reports from the Duke longitudinal studies, 1970–1973*. Durham, NC: Duke University Press.

Pfeiffer, E., Verwoerdt, A., & Wang, H. S. (1968). Sexual behavior in aged men and women. I. Observations on 254 community volunteers. *Archives of General Psychiatry, 19*, 753–758.

Pfeiffer, E., Verwoerdt, A., & Wang, H. S. (1969). The natural history of sexual behavior in a biologically advantaged group of aged individuals. *Journal of Gerontology, 24*, 193–198.

Pichora-Fuller, M. K., Schneider, B. A., & Daneman, M. (1995). How young and old adults listen to and remember speech in noise. *Journal of the Acoustical Society of America, 97*, 593–608.

Pitcher, B. L., & Larson, D. C. (1989). Elderly widowhood. In S. J. Bahr & E. T. Peterson (Eds.), *Aging and the family* (pp. 59–82). Lexington, MA: Lexington.

Plomin, R., Lichtenstein, P., Pederson, N. L., McClearn, G. E., & Nesselroade, J. R. (1990). Genetic influence on life events during the last half of the life span. *Psychology and Aging, 5,* 25–30.

Plude, D. J., & Hoyer, W. J. (1985). Attention and performance: Identifying and localizing age deficits. In N. Charness (Ed.), *Aging and human performance.* London: Wiley.

Plude, D. J., & Hoyer, W. J. (1986). Age and the selectivity of visual information processing. *Journal of Psychology and Aging, 1,* 4–10.

Pocs, O., Godrow, A., Tolone, W. L., & Walsh, R. H. (1977). Is there sex after 40? *Psychology Today, 11*(6).

Pope, M., & Schulz, R. (1990). Sexual attitudes and behavior in midlife and aging males. *Journal of Homosexuality, 20,* 169–179.

Prigerson, H. G., Bierhals, A. J., Kasl, S. V., Reynolds, C. F., Shear, M. K., Day, N., Beery, L. C., Newsom, J. T., & Jacobs, S. (1997). Traumatic grief as a risk factor for mental and physical morbidity. *American Journal of Psychiatry, 154,* 616–623.

Prigerson, H. H., Reynolds, C. F., Jacobs, S. C., Pilkonis, P., Beery, L. C., Shear, M. K., Wortman, C. B., Zisook, S., Williams, J. B. W., Widiger, T. A., Davidson, J., Maciejewsky, P., Weiss, R., Frank, E., & Kupfer, D. J. (under review). Results of a consensus conference to define diagnostic criteria for traumatic grief. *American Journal of Psychiatry.*

Quint, J. C. (1967). *The nurse and the dying patient.* Chicago: Aldine.

Rabbitt, P. (1979). Some experiments and a model of changes in attentional selectivity with old age. In F. Hoffmeister & C. Mueller (Eds.), *Brain functions in old age: Evaluation of changes and disorders.* Berlin: Springer.

Rabinowitz, J. C., Craik, F. I. M., & Ackerman, B. P. (1982). A processing resource account of age differences in recall. *Canadian Journal of Psychology, 36,* 325–344.

Rabkin, J. G., & Struening, E. L. (1976). Life events, stress, and illness. *Science, 194,* 1013–1020.

Radloff, L. S. (1977). The CES-D scale: A self-report depression scale for research in the general population. *Applied Psychological Measurement, 1,* 385–401.

Rappaport, B. Z. (1984). Audiology. In C. K. Cassel & J. R. Walsh (Eds.), *Geriatric medicine: Vol. 1. Medical, psychiatric, and pharmacological topics.* New York: Springer-Verlag.

Raskind, M. A. (1989). Organic mental disorders. In E. W. Busse & D. G. Blazer (Eds.), *Geriatric psychiatry.* Washington, DC: American Psychiatric Press.

Ratner, H. H., Padgett, R. J., & Bushey, N. (1988). Old and young adults' recall of events. *Developmental Psychology, 24,* 664–671.

Raush, H., Barry, W., Hertel, R., & Swain, M. (1974). *Communication, conflict, and marriage.* San Francisco: Jossey-Bass.

Receputo, G., Mazzoleni, G., Di-Fazio, I., Alessandria, I., et al. (1996). Study on the sense of taste in a group of Sicilian centenarians. *Archives of Gerontology and Geriatrics,* Suppl. 5, 411–414.

Rees, T. S., & Duckert, L. G. (1990). Auditory and vestibular dysfunction in aging. In W. R. Hazzard, R. Andres, E. L. Bierman, & J. P. Blass (Eds.), *Principles of geriatric medicine and gerontology* (3rd ed.) (pp. 432–444). New York: McGraw Hill.

Reff, M. E. (1985). RNA and protein metabolism. In C. E. Finch & E. L. Schneider (Eds.), *Handbook of the biology of aging* (2nd ed.). New York: Van Nostrand Reinhold.

Reid, D. W., Haas, G., & Hawkings, D. (1977). Locus of desired control and positive self-concept of the elderly. *Journal of Gerontology, 32,* 441–450.

Reimanis, G., & Green, R. F. (1987). Imminence of death and intellectual decrement in the aging. *Development Psychology, 5,* 270–272.

Reis, H. T. (1995). Love. In A. S. R. Manstead & M. Hewstone (Eds.), *The Blackwell encyclopedia of social psychology* (p. 366). Oxford, UK: Blackwell.

Reynolds III, C. F., Zubenko, G. S., Pollock, B. G., Mulsant, B. H., Schulz, R., Mintun, M. A., Mazumdar, S., & Kupfer, D. J. (1994). Depression in late life. *Current Opinion in Psychiatry, 7,* 18–21.

Rice, R. W. (1984). Organizational work and the overall quality of life. In S. Oskamp (Ed.), *Applied social psychology annual* (Vol. 5). Beverly Hills, CA: Sage.

Robbins, S. (1978). Stroke in the geriatric patient. In W. Reichel (Ed.), *The geriatric patient.* New York: H. P. Publishing.

Roberto, K. A., & Stroes, J. (1995). Grandchildren and grandparents: Roles, influences, and relationships. In J. Hendricks (Ed.), *The ties of later life* (pp. 141–153). Amityville, NY: Baywood.

Robins, M., & Baum, H. M. (1981). The national survey of stroke incidence. *Stroke, 12* (Pt. 2, Suppl. 1), 1-45-1-47.

Rorschach, H. (1942). *Psychodiagnostics: A diagnostic test based on perception.* (Original publication: 1921). Berne: Huber.

Rossi, A., & Rossi, P. (1990). *Of human bonding: Parent-child relations across the life course.* New York: Aldine de Gruyter.

Rotter, J. B. (1966). Generalized expectancies for internal versus external control of reinforcement. *Psychological Monographs, 80* (1, Whole No. 609).

Rowe, J. W., & Kahn, R. L. (1987). Human aging: Usual and successful. *Science, 237* (4811), 143–149.

Rowe, J. W., & Kahn, R. L. (1998). *Successful aging.* New York: Pantheon Books.

Rowlatt, C., & Franks, L. M. (1978). Aging in tissues and cells. In J. C. Brocklehurst (Ed.), *Geriatric medicine and gerontology* (2nd ed.). New York: Churchill Livingstone.

Rubenstein, E., & Federman, D. D. (Eds.). (1982). *Scientific American medicine.* New York: Scientific American, Inc.

Rubin, Z. (1970). Measurement of romantic love. *Journal of Personality and Social Psychology, 16,* 267–268.

Rudman, D., Feller, A. G., Nagraj, H. S., et al. (1990). Effects of human growth hormone in 60 year olds, *New England Journal of Medicine, 323,* 1–6.

Ruth, J-E. (1996a). Personality. In J. E. Birren (Ed.), *Encyclopedia of gerontology,* Vol. 2 (pp. 281–294.). New York: Academic Press.

Ruth, J-E. (1996b). Personality and aging: Coping and management of the self in later life. In J. E. Birren & K. W. Schaie (Eds.), *Handbook of the psychology on aging* (4th ed.) (pp. 308–322.). San Diego, CA: Academic Press.

Ryan, A. S., & Elahi, D. (1996). Body: Composition, weight, height, and build. In J. E. Birren (Ed.), *Encyclopedia of gerontology,* Vol. 1 (pp. 193–201). New York: Academic Press.

Ryff, C. D. (1991). Possible selves in adulthood and old age: A tale of shifting horizons. *Psychology and Aging, 6,* 286–295.

Ryff, C. D.,, & Baltes, P. B. (1976). Value transition and adult development in women: The instrumentality-terminality sequence hypothesis. *Developmental Psychology, 12,* 567–568.

Salthouse, T. A. (1976). Age and tachistoscopic perception. *Experimental Aging Research, 2,* 91–103.

Salthouse, T. A. (1980). Age and memory: Strategies for localizing the loss. In L. W. Poon, L. S. Cermak, D. Arenberg & L. W. Thompson (Eds.), *New directions in memory and aging.* Hillsdale, NJ: Erlbaum.

Salthouse, T. A. (1982). *Adult cognition: An experimental psychology of human aging.* New York: Springer-Verlag.

Salthouse, T. A. (1990). Cognitive competence and expertise in aging. In J. E. Birren & K. W. Schaie (Eds.), *Handbook of the psychology of aging* (3rd ed.) (pp. 311–319). New York: Academic Press.

Salthouse, T. A. (1991a). Cognitive facets of aging well. *Generations, 15,* 35–38.

Salthouse, T. A. (1991b). *Theoretical perspectives on cognitive aging.* Hillsdale, NJ: Erlbaum.

Salthouse, T. A. (1993). Influence of working memory on adult age differences in matrix reasoning. *British Journal of Psychology, 84,* 171–199.

Salthouse, T. A. (1993). Speed mediation of adult age differences in cognition, *Developmental Psychology, 29*, 722–738.

Salthouse, T. A. (1995). Differential age-related influences on memory for verbal-symbolic information and visual-spatial information. *Journal of Gerontology: Psychological Sciences, 50B*, P193–P201.

Salthouse, T. A., & Babcock, R. L. (1991). Decomposing adult age differences in working memory. *Developmental Psychology, 27*, 763–776.

Salthouse, T. A., Babcock, R. L., Skovronek, E., Mitchell, D. R. D., & Palmon, R. (1990). Age and experience effects in spatial visualization. *Developmental Psychology, 26*, 128–136.

Salthouse, T. A., Kausler, D. H., & Saults, J. S. (1988). Investigation of student status, background variables, and the feasibility of standard tasks in cognitive aging research. *Psychology and Aging, 3*, 29–37.

Salthouse, T. A., Mitchell, D. R., Skovronek, E., & Babcock, R. L. (1989). Effects of adult age and working memory on reasoning and spatial abilities. *Journal of Experimental Psychology: Learning, Memory and Cognition, 15*, 507–516.

Sands, L. P., Terry, H., & Meredith, W. (1989). Change and stability in adult intellectual functioning assessed by Wechsler item responses. *Psychology and Aging, 4*, 79–87.

Sayetta, R. B. (1986). Rates of senile dementia-Alzheimer's type in the Baltimore Longitudinal Study. *Journal of Chronic Diseases, 39*, 271–286.

Schacter, D. L., Kaszniak, A. W., Kihlstrom, J. F., & Valdiserri, M. (1991). The relation between source memory and aging. *Psychology and Aging, 6*, 559–568.

Schacter, D. L., Osowiecki, D., Kaszniak, A. W., Kihlstrom, J. F., & Valdiserri, M. (1994). Source memory: Extending the boundaries of age-related deficits. *Psychology and Aging, 9*, 81–89.

Schaefer, C., Coyne, J., & Lazarus, R. (1981). The health-related functions of social support. *Journal of Behavioral Medicine, 4*, 381–406.

Schaie, K. W. (1965). A general model for the study of developmental problems. *Psychological Bulletin, 64*, 92–107.

Schaie, K. W. (1973). Methodological problems in descriptive developmental research on adulthood and aging. In J. R. Nesselroade & H. W. Reese (Eds.), *Life-span developmental psychology: Methodological issues.* New York: Academic Press.

Schaie, K. W. (1977). Quasi-experimental designs in the psychology of aging. In J. E. Birren & K. W. Schaie (Eds.), *Handbook of the psychology of aging.* New York: Van Nostrand Reinhold.

Schaie, K. W. (1978). External validity in the assessment of intellectual development in adulthood. *Journal of Gerontology, 33*, 696–701.

Schaie, K. W. (Ed.). (1983). *Longitudinal studies of adult psychological development.* New York: Guilford Press.

Schaie, K. W. (1988). Ageism in psychological research. *American Psychologist, 43*, 179–183.

Schaie, K. W. (1990). Intellectual development in adulthood. In J. E. Birren & K. W. Schaie (Eds.), *Handbook of the psychology of aging* (3rd ed.) (pp. 291–310). New York: Academic Press.

Schaie, K. W. (1996). *Intellectual development in adulthood: The Seattle Longitudinal Study.* New York: Cambridge University Press.

Schaie, K. W., & Baltes, P. B. (1975). On sequential strategies in developmental research: Description or explanation. *Human Development, 18*, 384–390.

Schaie, K. W., & Hertzog, C. (1983). Fourteen-year cohort-sequential analysis of adult intellectual development. *Developmental Psychology, 19*, 531–543.

Schaie, K. W., Labouvie, G. V., & Buech, B. U. (1973). Generational and cohort-specific differences in adult cognitive functioning. *Developmental Psychology, 9*, 151–166.

Schaie, K. W., & Labouvie-Vief, G. (1974). Generational versus ontogenic components of change in adult cognitive behavior: A fourteen-year cross-sequential study. *Developmental Psychology, 10,* 305–320.

Schaie, K. W., & Parham, I. A. (1976). Stability of adult personality: Fact or fable? *Journal of Personality and Social Psychology, 34,* 146–158.

Schaie, K. W., & Parham, I. A. (1977). Cohort-sequential analyses of adult intellectual development. *Developmental Psychology, 13,* 649–653.

Schiffman, S. (1996). Smell and taste. In J. E. Birren (Ed.), *Encyclopedia of gerontology,* Vol. 2 (pp. 497–504). New York: Academic Press.

Schiffman, S. (1977). Food recognition of the elderly. *Journal of Gerontology, 32,* 586–592.

Schiffman, S., & Pasternak, M. (1979). Decreased discrimination of food odors in the elderly. *Journal of Gerontology, 34,* 73–79.

Schlessinger, B., & Miller, G. A. (1973). Sexuality and the aged. *Medical Aspects of Human Sexuality, 3,* 46–52.

Schludermann, E. H., Schludermann, S. M., Merryman, P. W., & Brown, B. W. (1983). Halstead's studies in the neuropsychology of aging. *Archives of Gerontology and Geriatrics, 2,* 49–172.

Schneider, E. L., & Reed, J. D. (1985). Modulations of aging processes. In C. E. Finch & E. L. Schneider (Eds.), *Handbook of the biology of aging* (2nd ed.). New York: Van Nostrand Reinhold.

Schneider, J. (1984). *Stress, loss, and grief.* Baltimore: University Park Press.

Schneider, W., & Shiffrin, R. M. (1977). Controlled and automatic human information processing: I. Detection, search, and attention. *Psychological Review, 84,* 1–66.

Schoenbach, V. J., Kaplan, B. H., Fredman, L., & Kleinbaum, D. G. (1986). Social ties and mortality in Evans County, Georgia. *American Journal of Epidemiology, 123,* 577–591.

Schulz, J. H. (1995). Economic security policies. In R. H. Binstock & L. K. George (Eds.), *Handbook of aging and the social sciences* (4th ed.) (pp. 410–426). New York: Academic Press.

Schulz, R. (1976). Effects of control and predictability on the physical and psychological well-being of the institutionalized aged. *Journal of Personality and Social Psychology, 33,* 563–573.

Schulz, R. (1978). *The psychology of death, dying, and bereavement.* Reading, MA: Addison-Wesley.

Schulz, R. (1982). Emotionality and aging: A theoretical and empirical integration. *Journal of Gerontology, 37,* 42–52.

Schulz, R. (1985). Emotions and affect. In J. E. Birren & K. W. Schaie (Eds.), *Handbook of the psychology of aging* (2nd ed.). New York: Van Nostrand Reinhold.

Schulz, R., & Aderman, D. (1974). Clinical research and the stages of dying. *Omega: Journal of Death and Dying, 5,* 137–143.

Schulz, R., Aderman, D., & Manko, G. (1976, April). *Attitudes toward death: The effects of different methods of questionnaire administration.* Paper presented at the meeting of the Eastern Psychological Association, New York.

Schulz, R., & Curnow, C. (1988). Peak performance and age among superathletes: Track and field, swimming, baseball, tennis, and golf. *Journal of Gerontology: Psychological Sciences, 43,* 1113–1120.

Schulz, R., & Decker, S. (1983, August). *Long-term adjustment to physical disability: The role of social comparison processes, social support, and perceived control.* Paper presented at the annual meeting of the American Psychological Association, Anaheim, CA.

Schulz, R., & Heckhausen, H. (in press). Emotion and control: A life span perspective. In K. W. Schaie & M. P. Lawton (Eds.), *Annual review of gerontology and geriatrics,* Vol. 17. New York: Springer.

Schulz, R., & Heckhausen, J. (1996). A life-span model of successful aging. *American Psychologist, 51,* 702–714.

Schulz, R., Heckhausen, J., & Locher, J. L. (1991). Adult development, control, and adaptive functioning. *Journal of Social Issues, 47,* 177–196.

Schulz, R., Heckhausen, J., & O'Brien, A. (1994). Control and the disablement process in the elderly. *Journal of Social Behavior and Personality, 9,* 139–152.

Schulz, R., & Kerchis, C. Z. (1996). *Profiling the aged.* Pittsburgh, PA: University Center for Social and Urban Research, Special Report.

Schulz, R. & Manson, S. (1984). Social perspectives on aging. In C. Cassel & J. R. Walsh (Eds.), *Geriatric medicine: Principles and practice* (Vol. 2). New York: Springer.

Schulz, R., Mittelmark, M., Kronmal, R., Polak, J. F., Hirsch, C. H., German, P., Bookwala, J. (1994). Predictors of perceived health status in elderly men and women: The Cardiovascular Health Study. *Journal of Aging and Health, 6,* 419–447.

Schulz, R., Musa, D., Staszewski, J., & Siegler, R. S. (1994). Age and performance of major league baseball players: Implications for development. *Psychology and Aging, 9,* 274–286.

Schulz, R., Newsom, J., Mittelmark, M., Burton, L., Hirsch, C., & Jackson, S. (1997). Health effects of caregiving: The cardiovascular health study. *Annals of Behavioral Medicine.*

Schulz, R., & O'Brien, A. T. (1994). Alzheimer's disease caregiving: An overview. *Seminars in Speech and Language, 15,* 185–194.

Schulz, R., O'Brien, A, T., Bookwala, J., & Fleissner, K. (1995). Psychiatric and physical morbidity effects of Alzheimer's disease caregiving: Prevalence, correlates, and causes. *The Gerontologist, 35,* 771–791.

Schulz, R., & Rau, M. T. (1985). Social support through the life course. In S. Cohen & L. Syme (Eds.), *Social support and health.* New York: Academic Press.

Schulz, R., & Schlarb, J. (1987–1988). Two decades of research on dying: What do we know about the patient? *Omega: Journal of Death and Dying, 18,* 299–317.

Schulz, R., & Tompkins, C. A. (1990). Life events and changes in social relationships: Examples, mechanisms, and measurement. *Journal of Social and Clinical Psychology, 9,* 69–78.

Schulz, R., Tompkins, C. A., & Rau, M. T. (1988). A longitudinal study of the psychosocial impact of stroke on primary support persons. *Psychology and Aging, 3,* 131–141.

Schulz, R., Tompkins, C. A., & Wood, D. (1987). The social psychology of caregiving: Physical and psychological costs of providing support to the disabled. *Journal of Applied Social Psychology, 17,* 401–428.

Schulz, R., Visintainer, P., & Williamson, G. M. (1990). Psychiatric and physical morbidity effects of caregiving. *Journal of Gerontology: Psychological Sciences, 45,* 181–191.

Schulz, R., Williamson, G., Morycz, R., & Biegel, D. (in press). Perspectives on caregiving. In S. Zarit & L. Pearlin (Eds.), *Social structure and caregiving: Family and cross-national perspectives.* Hillsdale, NJ: Erlbaum.

Scialfa, C. T., & Kline, D. W. (1996). Vision. In J. E. Birren (Ed.), *Encyclopedia of gerontology,* Vol. 2 (pp. 605–612). New York: Academic Press.

Scott, R. B., & Mitchell, M. C. (1988). Aging, alcohol, and the liver. *Journal of the American Geriatrics Society, 36,* 255–265.

Sechrest, L. (1976). Personality. *Annual Review of Psychology, 27,* 1–27.

Segerberg, O., Jr. (1974). *The immortality factor.* New York: E. P. Dutton.

Seidler, R., & Stelmach, G. (1996). Motor control. In J. E. Birren (Ed.), *Encyclopedia of gerontology,* Vol. 2 (pp. 177–185). New York: Academic Press.

Seidman, S. N., & Rieder, R. O. (1994). A review of sexual behavior in the United States. *American Journal of Psychiatry, 151,* 330–341.

Sekaran, U. (1983). How husbands and wives in dual-career families perceive their family and work worlds. *Journal of Vocational Behavior, 22,* 288–302.

Selye, H. (1974). *Stress without distress*. Philadelphia: Lippincott.

Selye, H. (1983). The stress concept: Past, present, and future. In C. L. Cooper (Ed.), *Stress research: Issues for the eighties*. New York: Wiley.

Shanan, J., & Jacobowitz, J. (1982). Personality and aging. In C. Eisdorfer (Ed.), *Annual review of gerontology and geriatrics* (Vol. 3). New York: Springer.

Shanas, E. (1979). Social myth as hypothesis: The case of the family relations of old people. *The Gerontologist, 19*, 3–9.

Shanas, E. (1980). Older people and their families: The new pioneers. *Journal of Marriage and the Family, 42*, 9–15.

Shanteau, J., & Nagy, G. F. (1979). Probability of acceptance in dating choice. *Journal of Personality and Social Psychology, 37*, 522–533.

Sharma, S., Monsen, R. B., & Gary B. (1996–1997). Comparison of attitudes toward death and dying among nursing majors and other college students. *Omega: Journal of Death and Dying, 34*, 219–232.

Sheehy, G. (1976). *Passages*. New York: E. P. Dutton.

Shneidman, E. S. (1973). *Deaths of man*. New York: Quadrangle/N.Y. Times.

Shneidman, E. S. (Ed.). (1976). *Death: Current perspectives*. Palo Alto, CA: Mayfield.

Shock, N. W. (1974). Physiological theories of aging. In M. Rockstein, M. L. Sussman, & J. Chesky (Eds.), *Theoretical aspects of aging*. New York: Academic Press.

Shock, N. W. (1985). Longitudinal studies of aging in humans. In C. E. Finch & E. L. Schneider (Eds.), *Handbook of the biology of aging* (2nd ed.). New York: Van Nostrand Reinhold.

Siegel, P. Z., Brackbill, R. M., & Heath G. W. (1995). The epidemiology of walking for exercise: Implications for promoting activity among sedentary groups. *American Journal of Public Health, 85*, 706–709.

Siegler, I. C. (1980). The psychology of adult development and aging. In E. W. Busse & D. G. Blazer (Eds.), *Handbook of geriatric psychiatry*. New York: Van Nostrand Reinhold.

Siegler, I. C. (1983). Psychological aspects of the Duke longitudinal studies. In K. W. Schaie (Ed.), *Longitudinal studies of adult psychological development*. New York: Guilford Press.

Siegler, I. C., & Botwinick, J. (1979). A long-term longitudinal study of intellectual ability of older adults: The matter of selective subject attrition. *Journal of Gerontology, 34*, 242–245.

Siegler, I. C., & Gatz, M. (1985). Age patterns in locus of control. In E. Palmore, E. Busse, G. Maddox, J. Nowlin, & I. E. Siegler (Eds.), *Normal aging III*. Durham, NC: Duke University Press.

Sigall, H., & Landy, D. (1973). Radiating beauty: The effects of having a physically attractive partner on person perception. *Journal of Personality and Social Psychology, 28*, 218–244.

Silverstone, F. A., Brandfonbrener, M., Shock, N. W., & Yiengst, M. J. (1957). Age differences in the intravenous glucose tolerance tests and the response to insulin. *Journal of Clinical Investigation, 36*, 504–514.

Silverstone, G., & Wynter, L. (1975). The effects of introducing a heterosexual living space. *The Gerontologist, 15*, 83–87.

Simonton, D. K. (1988). *Scientific genius: A psychology of science*. Cambridge: Cambridge University Press.

Simonton, D. K. (1990). Creativity and wisdom in aging. In J. E. Birren & K. W. Schaie (Eds.), *Handbook of the psychology of aging* (3rd ed.) (pp. 320–329). New York: Academic Press.

Simonton, D. K. (1991). Creative productivity through the adult years. *Generations, 15*, 13–16.

Simonton, D. K. (1996). Creative expertise: A life-span developmental perspective. In K. A. Ericsson (Ed.), *The Road to Excellence: The Acquisition of Expert Performance in the Arts and Sciences, Sports and Games* (pp. 227–253). Mahwah, N.J.: Erlbaum.

Singh, D. (1970). Preference for bar-pressing to obtain reward over freeloading in rats and children. *Journal of Comparative and Physiological Psychology, 73*, 320–327.

Sivak, M., Olson, P. L., & Pastalan, E. A. (1981). Effect of driver's age on nighttime legibility of highway signs. *Human Factors, 23*, 59–64.

Skinner, E. A., & Connell, J. P. (1986). Control understanding: Suggestions for a developmental framework. In M. M. Baltes & P. B. Baltes (Eds.), *The psychology of control and aging* (pp. 35–71). Hillsdale, NJ: Erlbaum.

Slawinski, E., B., Hartel, D. M., & Kline, D. W. (1993). Self-reported hearing problems in daily life throughout adulthood. *Psychology and Aging, 8*, 552–561.

Smith, D. W. E. (1993). *Human longevity*. New York: Oxford University Press.

Smith, D. W., Bierman, E. L., & Robinson, N. M. (Eds.). (1978). *The biologic ages of man*. Philadelphia: W. B. Saunders.

Smith, R. P., Woodward, N. J., Wallston, B. S., Wallston, K. A., et al. (1988). Health care implications of desire and expectancy for control in elderly adults. *Journal of Gerontology, 43*, 1–7.

Soldo, B., & Hill, M. C. (1995). Family structure and transfer measures in the health and retirement study. *Journal of Human Resources* (Suppl), S108–137.

Soldo, B. J. (1979). *The housing and characteristics of independent elderly: A demographic overview*. Occasional Papers in Housing and Urban Development, No. 1. Washington, DC: U.S. Department of Housing and Urban Development.

Soldo, B. J., Sharma, M., & Campbell, R. T. (1984). Determinants of the community living arrangements of older unmarried women. *Journal of Gerontology, 39*.

Solnick, R. E., & Corby, N. (1983). Human sexuality and aging. In D. S. Woodruff & J. E. Birren (Eds.), *Aging: Scientific perspectives and social issues* (2nd ed.). Monterey, CA: Brooks/Cole.

Solomon, S., & Saxe, L. (1977). What is intelligent, as well as attractive, is good. *Personality and Social Psychology Bulletin, 3*, 670–673.

Spearman, C. E. (1904). "General intelligence," objectively determined and measured. *American Journal of Psychology, 15*, 201–292.

Spilka, B., Hood, R., & Gorsuch, R. (1985). *The psychology of religion: An empirical approach*. Englewood Cliffs, NJ: Prentice Hall.

Spirduso, W. W. (1995). *Physical dimensions of aging*. Champaign, IL: Human Kinetics.

Spitzer, R. L., Williams, J. B., Gibbon, M., & First, M. B. (1992). The Structured Clinical Interview for DSM-III-R (SCID). I: History, rationale, and description. *Archives of General Psychiatry, 49*, 624–629.

Sprott, R. L., & Austad, S. N. (1995). Animal models for aging research. In E. L. Schneider & J. W. Rowe (Eds.), *Handbook of the biology of aging* (4th ed.) (pp. 3–23). New York: Academic Press.

Spirduso, T., & MacRae, C. (1990). Cognitive and motor performance. In J. E. Birren & K. W. Schaie (Eds.), *Handbook of the psychology of aging* (3rd ed.). New York: Academic Press.

Staines, G. L., & Pleck. J. H. (1983). *The impact of work schedules of the family*. Ann Arbor: University of Michigan.

Starratt, C., & Peterson, L. (1997). Personality and normal aging. In P. D. Nussbaum (Ed.), *Handbook of neuropsychology and aging*. New York: Plenum Press.

Staudinger, U. M., Marsiske, M., & Baltes, P. B. (1993). Resilience and levels of reserve capacity in later adulthood: Perspectives from life-span theory. *Developmental and Psychopathology, 5*, 542–566.

Stefansson, E. (1990). The eye. In W. R. Hazzard, R. Andres, E. L. Bierman, & J. P. Blass (Eds.), *Principles of geriatric medicine and gerontology* (3rd ed.) (pp. 422–431). New York: McGraw Hill.

Stephens, M. A. P., Crowther, J. H., Hofoll, S. E., & Tennenbaum, D. L. (1990). *Stress and coping in later-life families*. New York: Hemisphere.

Sterns, H. L., Barrett, G. V., & Alexander, R. A. (1985). Accidents and the aging individual. In J. E. Birren & K. W. Schaie (Eds.), *Handbook of the psychology of aging* (2nd ed.). New York: Van Nostrand Reinhold.

Stevens, J. E., & Patterson, M. Q. (1995). Dimensions of spatial acuity in the touch sense: Changes over the life span. *Somatosensory and Motor Research, 12,* 29–47.

Stewart, A. L., Greenfield, M. D., Hays, R. D., Wells, K., Rogers, W. H., Berry, S. D., McGlynn, E. A., & Ware, J. E., Sr. (1989). Functional status and well-being of patients with chronic conditions. *Journal of the American Medical Association, 262,* 907–913.

Stine, E. A. L., Wingfield, A., & Myers, S. D. (1990). Age differences in processing information from television news: The effects of bisensory augmentation. *Journal of Gerontology: Psychological Sciences, 45,* P9–P16.

Stotland, E. (1984). Stress. In R. J. Corsini (Ed.), *Encyclopedia of psychology.* New York: Wiley.

Stroebe, W., & Stroebe, M. S. (1987). *Bereavement and health.* Cambridge: Cambridge University Press.

Stroebe, W., Stroebe, M. S., Gergen, K. J., & Gergen, M. (1982). The effects of bereavement on mortality: A social psychological analysis. In J. R. Eiser (Ed.), *Social psychology and behavioral medicine.* New York: Wiley.

Stueve, C. A., & Fischer C. (1978, September). *Social networks and older women.* Paper presented at the Workshop on Older Women, Washington, DC.

Stueve, C. A., & Gerson, K. (1977). Personal relations across the life cycle. In C. S. Fischer et al. (Eds.), *Networks and places: Social relations in the urban setting.* New York: Free Press.

Suinn, R. M. (1977). Type A behavior pattern. In R. B. Williams, Jr., & W. D. Gentry (Eds.), *Behavioral approaches to medical treatment.* Cambridge, MA: Ballinger.

Suls, J., & Mullen B. (1982). From the cradle to the grave: Comparison and self-evaluation across the life-span. In J. Suls (Ed.), *Psychological perspectives on the self,* Vol. 1 (pp. 97–125). Hillsdale, NJ: Erlbaum.

Suszycki, L. (1981). Intervention with the bereaved. In O. S. Margolis et al. (Eds.), *Acute grief: Counseling the bereaved.* New York: Columbia University Press.

Suzman, R. M., Willis, D. P., & Manton, K. G. (1992). *The oldest old.* New York: Oxford University Press.

Szinovacz, M. E. (1998). Grandparents today: A demographic profile. *The Gerontologist, 38,* 37–52.

Tamir, L. M. (1989). Modern myths about men at midlife: An assessment. In S. Hunter & M. Sundel (Eds.), *Midlife myths: Issues, findings, and practical implications* (pp. 157–180). Newbury Park: Sage.

Templer, D. (1970). The construction and validation of a death anxiety scale. *Journal of General Psychology, 82,* 165–177.

Templer, D. (1971). Death anxiety as related to depression and health of retired persons. *Journal of Gerontology, 26,* 521–523.

Templer, D., & Ruff, C. (1971). Death anxiety scale means, standard deviations, and embedding. *Psychological Reports, 29,* 173–174.

Templer, D., Ruff, C., & Franks, C. (1971). Death anxiety: Age, sex, and parental resemblance in diverse populations. *Developmental Psychology, 4,* 108.

Thomae, H. (1980). Personality and adjustment to aging. In J. E. Birren & R. B. Sloane (Eds.), *Handbook of mental health and aging.* Englewood Cliffs, NJ: Prentice-Hall.

Thomas, J. L. (1995). Gender and perceptions of grandparenthood. In J. Hendricks (Ed.), *The ties of later life* (pp. 181–193).

Thurstone, L. L., & Thurstone, T. G. (1941). Factorial studies of intelligence. *Psychometric Monographs, 2.*

Tice, R. R., & Setlow, R. B. (1985). DNA repair and replication in aging organisms and cells. In C. E. Finch & E. L. Schneider (Eds.), *Handbook of the biology of aging* (2nd ed.). New York: Van Nostrand Reinhold.

Time. (1986, March 17). Extra years for extra effort, p. 66.

Time. (1986, November 24). Men have rights too, pp. 87–88.

Troll, L. E. (1980). Grandparenting. In L. W. Poon (Ed.), *Aging in the 1980s: Psychological issues.* Washington, DC: American Psychological Association.

Troll, L. E., & Bengtson, V. (1979). Generations in the family. In W. Burr, R. Hill, F. I. Nye, & I. Reiss (Eds.), *Contemporary theories about the family.* New York: Free Press.

Troll, L. E., & Smith, J. (1976). Attachment through the life span: Some questions about dyadic bonds among adults. *Human Development, 19,* 156–170.

Tulving, E. (1985). How many memory systems are there? *American Psychologist, 40,* 385–398.

Turner, R. J., & Wheaton, B. (1995). Checklist measurement of stressful life events. In S. Cohen, R.C. Kessler, & L. U. Gordon (Eds.), *Measuring stress* (pp. 29–53). New York: Oxford University Press.

United States Bureau of the Census. (1976). *Current population reports: Some characteristics of the population.* Washington, DC: U.S. Government Printing Office.

United States Bureau of the Census. (1980). *Social indicators III.* Washington, DC: U.S. Government Printing Office.

United States Bureau of the Census. (1981). *Statistical abstract of the United States.* Washington, DC: U.S. Government Printing Office.

United States Bureau of the Census. (1987, September). *Current population reports: State population and household estimates with age, sex, and components of change: 1981 to 1986.* Washington, DC: U.S. Government Printing Office.

United States Bureau of the Census. (1989). *Statistical abstract of the United States: 1989* (109th ed.). Washington, DC: U.S. Government Printing Office.

United States Bureau of the Census. (1997). *Statistical abstract of the United States: 1997* (117th ed.). Washington, DC: U.S. Government Printing Office.

United States Senate Special Committee on Aging. (1983). *Aging America.* Washington, DC: U.S. Government Printing Office.

United States Senate Special Committee on Aging. (1985). *America in transition: An aging society* (1984–1985 ed.). Washington, DC: U.S. Government Printing Office.

Vachon, M. L. S. (1981). Type of death as a determinant in acute grief. In O. S. Margolis et al. (Eds.), *Acute grief: Counseling the bereaved.* New York: Columbia University Press.

Vachon, M. L. S., Freedman, K., Formo, A., Rodgers, J., Lyall, W. A. L., & Freeman, S. J. J. (1977). The final illness in cancer: The widow's perspective. *Canadian Medical Association Journal, 177,* 1151–1154.

Van Der Kloot Meijburg, H. H. (1995–1996). How health care institutions in the Netherlands approach physician assisted death. *Omega: Journal of Death and Dying, 32,* 179–196.

van Geert, P. (1987). The structure of Erikson's model of eight stages: A generative approach. *Human Development, 30,* 236–254.

Vaupel, J. W., & Gowan, A. E. (1986). Passage to Methuselah: Some demographic consequences of continued progress against mortality. *American Journal of Public Health, 76,* 430–433.

Verhaeghen, P., Marcoen, A., & Goossens, L. (1993). Facts and fiction about memory aging: A quantitative integration of research findings. *Journal of Gerontology: Psychological Sciences, 48,* P157–P171.

Verhaeghen, P., & Salthouse, T. A. (1997). Meta-analyses of age-cognition relations in adulthood: Estimates of linear and nonlinear age effects and structural models. *Psychological Bulletin, 122,* 231–249.

Vijg, J. (1996). DNA and gene expression. In J. E. Birren (Ed.), *Encyclopedia of gerontology*, Vol. 1 (pp. 441–453). New York: Academic Press.

Viney, L. L. (1984–1985). Loss of life and loss of bodily integrity: Two different sources of threat for people who are ill. *Omega: Journal of Death and Dying, 15*, 207–222.

Viney, L. L. (1987). A sociophenomenological approach to life-span development complementing Erikson's sociodynamic approach. *Human Development, 30*, 125–136.

Vital and Health Statistics. (1989). *Remarriages and subsequent divorces: United States* Series 21, No. 45.

Wachtel, P. L. (1980). Investigation and its discontents: Some constraints on progress in psychological research. *American Psychologist, 35*, 399–408.

Walford, R. L. (1974). The immunologic theory of aging. *Federal Proceedings, 33*, 2020–2027.

Wallerstein, J. S., & Kelly, J. B. (1976). The effects of parental divorce: Experiences of the child in later latency. *American Journal of Orthopsychiatry, 46*, 256–269.

Wall Street Journal. (1983, March 10). Older Americans: Actress and ex-senator believe in conquering age by staying active, pp. 1, 10.

Wall Street Journal. (1992, March 2). Older Americans: In a retirement town, the main business is keeping yourself busy, pp. 1, 17.

Walsh, D. A. (1983). Age differences in learning and memory. In D. S. Woodruff & J. E. Birren (Eds.), *Aging: Scientific perspectives and social issues* (2nd ed.), Monterey, CA: Brooks/Cole.

Walster, E., & Walster, G. W. (1978). *Love*. Reading, MA: Addison-Wesley.

Washington Post. (1985, July 18). Health frauds: Quackery thriving among elderly, ill.

Wasow, M. (1977). Sexuality in homes for the aged. *Concern in the Care of Aging, 3*(6), 20–21.

Waugh, N., & Barr, R. (1980). Memory and mental tempo. In L. W. Poon, J. L. Fozard, L. S. Cermak, D. Arenberg, & L. W. Thompson (Eds.), *New directions in memory and aging: Proceedings of the George A. Talland Memorial Conference*. Hillsdale, NJ: Erlbaum.

Weale, R. (1985). What is normal aging? Part XI. The eyes of the elderly. *Geriatric Medicine Today, 4*(3), 29–37.

Wechsler, D. (1958). *The measurement and appraisal of adult intelligence* (4th ed.). Baltimore: Williams & Wilkins.

Wechsler, D. (1997). *WAIS-III/Wechsler Memory Scale—Third Edition*. San Antonio, TX: The Psychological Corporation.

Weinstein, B. E., & Ventry, L. M. (1982). Hearing impairment and social isolation in the elderly. *Journal of Speech and Hearing Research, 25*, 593–599.

Weisenberger, J. M. (1996). Touch and proprioception. In J. E. Birren (Ed.), *Encyclopedia of gerontology*, Vol. 2 (pp. 591–603).

Welford, A. T. (1984). Psychomotor performance. In C. Eisdorfer (Ed.), *Annual review of gerontology and geriatrics* (Vol. 4). New York: Springer.

Welkowitz, J., Ewen, R. B., & Cohen, J. (1991). *Introductory statistics for the behavioral sciences* (4th ed.). San Diego: Harcourt Brace Jovanovich.

Whitbourne, S. K. (1987). Personality development in adulthood and old age: Relationships among identity style, health, and well-being. In K. W. Schaie & C. Eisdorfer (Eds.), *Annual review of gerontology and geriatrics* (Vol. 7). New York: Springer.

White, R. W. (1959). Motivation reconsidered: The concept of competence. *Psychological Review, 66*, 297–333.

Wiener, J. M., & Illston, L. H. (1996). The financing and organization of health care for older Americans. In R. H. Binstock & L. K. George (Eds.), *Handbook of aging and the social sciences*, 4th ed. (pp. 427–445).

Williams, M. E. (1995). *Complete guide to aging and health*. New York: Harmony Books.

Williamson, G. M., & Schulz, R. (1990). Relationship orientation, quality of prior relationship, and distress among caregivers of Alzheimer's patients. *Psychology and Aging, 5*, 502–510.

Williamson, G. M., & Schulz, R. (1992). The relationship between physical illness and depression. *Psychology and Aging, 7,* 343–351.

Williamson, G. M., & Schulz, R. (1995). Caring for a family member with cancer: Past communal behavior and affective reactions. *Journal of Applied Social Psychology, 25,* 93–116.

Wilson, K., & DeShane, M. R. (1982). The legal rights of grandparents: A preliminary discussion. *The Gerontologist, 22,* 67–71.

Wilson, K., & Schulz, R. (1983). Criteria for effective crisis intervention. In M. A. Smyer & M. Gatz (Eds.), *Mental health and aging.* Beverly Hills, CA: Sage.

Wolfe, J. (1998). Growth hormone: A physiological fountain of youth? *Journal of Anti-aging Medicine, 1,* 9–25.

Wood, J. V. (1989). Theory and research concerning social comparison of personal attributes. *Psychological Bulletin, 106,* 231–248.

Wood, V., & Robertson, J. F. (1978). Friendship and kinship interaction: Differential effects on the morale of the elderly. *Journal of Marriage and the Family, 40,* 367–375.

Wright, L. (1988). The Type A behavior pattern and coronary artery disease. *American Psychologist, 43,* 2–14.

Wrightsman, L. S., & Deaux, K. (1981). *Social psychology in the 80s* (3rd ed.). Monterey, CA: Brooks/Cole.

Yarmey, A. D., & Kent, J. (1980). Eyewitness identification by elderly and young adults. *Law and Human Behavior, 4,* 359–371.

Yates, F. E. (1996). Theories of aging: Biological. In J. E. Birren (Ed.), *Encyclopedia of gerontology,* Vol. 2 (pp. 545–555). New York: Academic Press.

Young, A. J. (1991). Effects of aging on human cold tolerance. *Journal of Experimental Aging Research, 17,* 205–213.

Youngjohn, J. R., & Crook, T. H. II (1996). Dementia. In L. L. Carstensen, B. A. Edelstein, & L. Dornbrand (Eds.), *The practical handbook of clinical gerontology* (pp. 239–273). Thousand Oaks, CA: Sage.

Yurick, A. G., Spier, B. E., Robb, S. S., Ebert, N. J., & Magnussen, M. H. (1984). *The aged person and the nursing process* (2nd ed.). Norwalk, CT: Appleton-Century-Crofts.

Zelinski, E. M., & Burnight, K. P. (1997). Sixteen-year longitudinal and time lag changes in memory and cognition in older adults. *Psychology and Aging, 12,* 503–513.

Zelinski, E. M., Gilewski, M. J., & Anthony-Bergstone, C. R. (1990). Memory functioning questionnaire: Concurrent validity with memory performance and self-reported memory failures. *Psychology and Aging, 5,* 388–399.

Zung, W. (1965). A self-rating depression scale. *Archives of General Psychiatry, 12,* 63–70.

Zung, W. (1967). Depression in the normal aged. *Psychosomatics, 8,* 287–292.

CREDITS

Chapter 1: Page 1, Blair Seitz/Photo Researchers, Inc.; **p. 4,** Day Williams/Photo Researchers, Inc.; **p. 8,** John Eastcott/Yva Momatiuk/Photo Researchers, Inc.

Chapter 2: Page 17, Stock Boston; **p. 24, left,** UPI/Corbiss-Bettman, **center,** Voran Kahana/Shooting Star International Photo Agency, **right,** Ron Davis/ Shooting Star International Photo Agency; **p. 29,** Barbara Alper/Stock Boston; **p. 32,** Sam C. Pierson, Jr./Photo Researchers, Inc.

Chapter 3: Page 43, Pam Francis/Liaison Agency, Inc.; **p. 45,** Bobby Neel Adams; **p. 47,** Virginia Blaisdell/Stock Boston.

Chapter 4: Page 80, Jack Star/PhotoDisc, Inc.; **p. 86,** Michael Newman/PhotoEdit; **p. 89,** Dan Chidester/The Image Works; **p. 93,** Ezio Peterson/UPI/Corbis-Bettmann.

Chapter 5: Page 108, Russell D. Curtis/Photo Researchers, Inc.; **p. 115,** Joel Gordon Photography; **p. 131,** PhotoDisc, Inc.

Chapter 6: Page 134, Jeff Greenberg/Omni-Photo Communications, Inc.; **p. 139, top,** copyright © 1981 from The Psychological Corporation. All rights reserved.; **p. 147,** Corbis-Bettmann; **p. 149,** John Eastcott/Yva Momatiuk/The Image Works.

Chapter 7: Page 160, Dinodia/Omni-Photo Communications, Inc.; **p. 162,** David Young-Wolff/PhotoEdit; **p. 171,** from Eibel-Eibesfeldt, Irenaus. Human Ethology (New York: Aldine de Gruyter). © 1989 Eibel-Eibesfeldt. Reprinted with permission.

Chapter 8: Page 190, Silver Burdett Ginn; **p. 193,** Michal Heron/Simon & Schuster/PH College; **p. 216,** Frank Siteman/Picture Cube, Inc.; **p. 222,** David Wells/The Image Works; **p. 226,** UN/DPI Photo.

Chapter 9: **Page 236,** Tony Freeman/PhotoEdit; **p. 242,** Mark Richards/PhotoEdit; **p. 248,** AP/Wide World Photos; **p. 259,** John Maher/Stock Boston.

Chapter 10: **Page 270,** K. Preuss/The Image Works; **p. 278,** Nancy Bates/Picture Cube, Inc.; **p. 286,** Rhoda Sidney/PhotoEdit; **p. 290,** Guy Gillette/Photo Researchers, Inc.

Chapter 11: **Page 296,** Billy E. Barnes/PhotoEdit; **p. 299,** Kathy Sloane/Photo Researchers, Inc.; **p. 312,** Jack Kightlinger/The White House Photo Office; **p. 318,** Will McIntyre/Photo Researchers, Inc.

Chapter 12: **Page 327,** John Eastcott/Yva Momatiuk/Photo Researchers, Inc. **p. 343,** UN/DPI Photo; **p. 349,** Lawrence Migdale/PIX.

INDEX